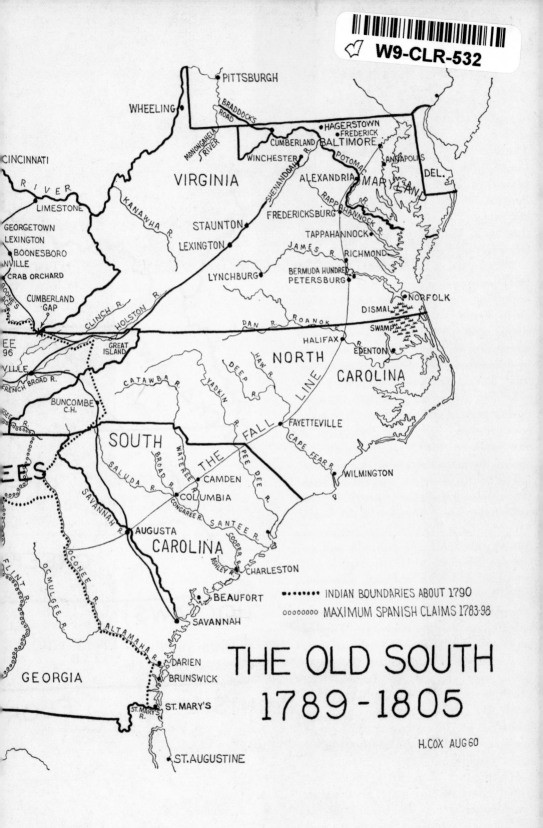

•••••• INDIAN BOUNDARIES ABOUT 1790
ooooooo MAXIMUM SPANISH CLAIMS 1783-98

# THE OLD SOUTH
# 1789-1805

H. COX   AUG 60

# A HISTORY OF THE SOUTH

## VOLUMES IN THE SERIES

*Volume IV*

THE SOUTH IN THE NEW NATION

1789–1819

# A HISTORY

# OF

# THE SOUTH

*Volume IV*

*EDITORS*

WENDELL HOLMES STEPHENSON

PROFESSOR OF HISTORY

AT THE UNIVERSITY OF OREGON

E. MERTON COULTER

REGENTS' PROFESSOR OF HISTORY AT THE

UNIVERSITY OF GEORGIA

# The South in the New Nation

## 1789-1819

BY THOMAS P. ABERNETHY

LOUISIANA STATE UNIVERSITY PRESS

THE LITTLEFIELD FUND FOR SOUTHERN
HISTORY OF THE UNIVERSITY OF TEXAS

1961

# PUBLISHERS' PREFACE

A HISTORY OF THE SOUTH is sponsored by Louisiana State University and the Trustees of the Littlefield Fund for Southern History at the University of Texas. More remotely, it is the outgrowth of the vision of Major George W. Littlefield, C.S.A., who established a fund at the University of Texas in 1914 for the collection of materials on Southern history and the publication of a "full and impartial study of the South and its part in American history." Trustees of the Littlefield Fund began preparations in 1937 for the writing of the history that Major Littlefield contemplated. Meanwhile, a plan had been conceived at Louisiana State University for a history of the South as a part of that institution's comprehensive program to promote interest, research, and writing in the field of Southern history.

As the two undertakings harmonized in essentials, the planning groups united to become joint sponsors of *A History of the South*. Wendell Holmes Stephenson, then professor of American history at Louisiana State University, and the late Charles W. Ramsdell, professor of American history at the University of Texas, were chosen to edit the series. They had been primarily interested in initiating the plans, and it was appropriate that they should be selected to edit the work. Upon the death of Professor Ramsdell in 1943, E. Merton Coulter, professor of history at the University of Georgia, was named his successor.

Volumes of the series are being published as the manuscripts are received. This is the eighth published volume; it follows Volume III. When completed, the ten-volume set will represent about twenty-five years of historical planning and research.

vii

# AUTHOR'S PREFACE

THOUGH this is the fourth volume of the series, it is the first to deal with the South as a section, for there could be no sectionalism until there was a spirit of nationalism, and such a spirit could not have been produced immediately—not even by the adoption of a document known as the Constitution. It takes a long time to weld a strong social and political unit. Indeed, the majority of citizens during the early period thought they had a right to leave the Union as easily as they had entered it. In signing the compact, Virginia reserved the right to withdraw, and for several decades the young nation was faced with one separatist movement after another, both in New England and the early West. It was, in fact, the bitter contest with Great Britain over the right of our ships to sail the high seas unmolested that first engendered a spirit of nationalism in the states so recently united; and it was in the region south of the Mason and Dixon line that this sentiment first took definite shape. It is true that Hamilton's financial measures were aimed at producing a strong central government, but it was to be a government dominated by a class in the interest of that class, not a government representing a united nation. And it was the Hamiltonian Federalists of the East who most vociferously resented the patriotic nationalism of the South and West.

These developments tend to demonstrate that sectionalism was not a product of the slavery issue, but that this issue was a product of sectionalism. Even under the Confederation there had been sectional controversies over control of the Western lands, most of which were claimed, on the basis of colonial charters, by Virginia, North Carolina, and Georgia; but deep cleavages are more often produced by ideological than by economic differences. In this country such cleavages were due mainly to the fact that the North inherited, not Puritanism, but a puritanical attitude toward life, while the South maintained the traditions of the Mother Country, with her liberal Anglicanism and her stratified society. This at least was the attitude of the older South, and this older South extended its influence to the fertile stretches of the Bluegrass sections of Kentucky and Tennessee, as well as to the Black Belt of Alabama and to the Mississippi Delta.

Important as these considerations are for the history of the period, sectionalism takes a secondary place in this volume. In 1789 the Southern frontier, both in Florida and Louisiana, was beset by the Spaniards, who constantly tried to enlist the Southern Indians and Western settlers as their allies. Then, too, the British were often able to use Florida as a base for their operations against the most vulnerable link in the defenses of the United States. For this reason it has been necessary to devote much space to the international and interracial contest which, sometimes as a hot and sometimes as a cold war, was waged for possession of the old Southwest during the thirty turbulent years from 1789 to 1819.

With five new Southern states added to the original five during the first three decades under the Constitution, the westward movement of the population is an important phase of the history of the period. The pattern of migration was complicated by the presence of slaveowners who usually occupied the richest and most valuable lands; by the proximity of active or potential enemies, both red and white; by the disparity of soils and transportation facilities; and finally, by the activities of hordes of land speculators. Another peculiarity of this migration was that it did not move from east to west in a steady succession of waves, according to the Turnerian pattern. Men of means and speculators first bypassed the mountainous and barren regions to occupy the rich Bluegrass lands of Kentucky and Tennessee, while Tories and other adventurers took the long journey down the Mississippi or the more hazardous route through the Creek country to settle on the Lower Mississippi and the Gulf Coast, whether on Spanish or American soil. The trail having been broken by these more hardy and prosperous elements of the population, the poorer people, with little enterprise and less means, then followed and occupied the piney woods, the "pennyroyal" and wiregrass country, as well as the good grazing and farming tracts in the coves of the hilly and mountainous regions. Thus a democracy and a landed gentry grew up side by side, and this has always been, to strangers, a puzzling characteristic of Southern society. The one is no more a myth than the other, and it is hoped that this study of the period, largely from firsthand sources, will help to set straight a record which has been largely—and often—distorted and misrepresented. The author regrets that the necessity of devoting so much space to the problems connected with the conquest and settlement of the Southern and Western frontiers has made it impossible for him to trace the social and economic development of the region. The deficiency is largely compensated for by Charles S. Sydnor's careful analysis of these factors in the following volume.

During the years that have been devoted to the preparation of this work, numerous librarians and curators throughout the states of the older South and at the Library of Congress have rendered generous assistance. Particular acknowledgment is due to those, here at the University of Virginia, who have always given abundantly of both time and assistance. This would include almost the entire staff of the Alderman Library, but especially John Wyllie, the librarian; Francis Berkeley and Louise Savage, the associate librarians; William Runge, curator of the McGregor Library; and Katherine Beville of the circulation division. I am also indebted to Harold E. Cox, who drew the maps, and to Hamilton M. Hutton, who except as otherwise indicated made the vote charts. Equally essential has been the financial assistance received from the local Social Science Research Council, of which the late Professor Wilson Gee was director, and whose secretary, Ruth Ritchie, expertly typed the manuscript. In addition, I gratefully acknowledge a small grant obtained from the national Social Science Research Council.

Finally, I am deeply indebted to Dean James Southall Wilson for sustaining aid and encouragement and to Professors Merton Coulter and Wendell H. Stephenson for their arduous and painstaking editing of the manuscript. My wife, Ida Robertson Abernethy, should have been credited with joint authorship of the book, for she collaborated in all stages of its preparation and contributed an equal share to its production. Unfortunately, there were technical reasons why her name could not appear on the title page, and I hope that I may be absolved of the charge of ingratitude.

T. P. A.

University of Virginia

# CONTENTS

# MAPS AND CHARTS

CHAPTER I

# THE SOUTHERN SCENE, 1789

I T IS difficult to people the past, for the favored few pre-empt the scene and the voice of the average man is all but lost in the wastes of time. It is especially hard to envisage the South as it was in the early days of the Republic, for images of determined men in gray and charming ladies in crinoline arise in our minds to obscure an earlier time when the South was largely a sprawling wilderness, inhabited by elusive Indians and hard-bitten pioneers.

Although the Southern states were radically different in topography and resources, they nevertheless formed an entity, a cohesive culture. This was due to the fact that they inherited a system of values from the English landed gentry, to which they clung tenaciously through the decades, and to the further fact that the Southern population was almost wholly homogenous. There was a sprinkling of French and other nationalities among the people, but the white population was overwhelmingly Anglo-Saxon. Thus the ties of blood and kinship were remarkably strong and the ramifications of social and family bonds were extraordinary. Cousin Tom or Cousin Mary, four times removed, might migrate from the Seaboard to the "Western Waters," but they never wholly cut family ties to the eastward.

When on April 30, 1789, Washington, on the balcony of the Federal Building in Wall Street, New York, took the oath of office as President of the United States, the Constitution was merely a document and the Union was a patriotic ideal in the minds of hopeful people. As Plato so truly said, there could be no ideal republic without a lot of ideal republicans. Now it remained

1

to be seen how many ideal republicans the bantling nation could produce. There could be no sectionalism until nationalism developed; but the Mason-Dixon line and the Ohio River divided the slave states from those which were already free, or were soon to become so, and there had always been a marked social difference between the two regions. The states in the South contained slightly more than half the total population of about four million, but three out of eight of the Southerners were Negroes.[1]

The South was half again as large as the North in area, but its Southern boundary was still disputed with Spain. According to the peace treaty signed with Britain in 1783, the line between Spanish Florida and the United States was to run from the Mississippi River along the thirty-first parallel to the Chattahoochee River, thence south to its junction with the Flint, then in a direct line eastward to the source of the St. Marys River, and down that stream to the sea. But Spain did not admit that Britain could grant all this territory. She was still in possession of Natchez on the Mississippi, and she claimed all the land lying south of the Tennessee River and west of the Appalachian Mountains. Thus the jurisdiction of the United States fell considerably short of her claims.

The South that was actually possessed by Americans was a vast and sparsely settled country. It was divided into East and West by the Appalachian chain of mountains, which runs southwestward from the Maryland border to what is now central Alabama, and it is rarely less than a hundred miles in width. The area west of the great mountain barrier is again divided into two regions, with the larger northern part, including the present states of Kentucky and Tennessee and the northern third of Alabama, drained by rivers flowing into the Ohio. The southern area is drained by streams which flow into the Gulf of Mexico.

The mountains are intersected by many valleys, but the most important of these is the great Valley of Virginia, lying between the Blue Ridge and the Allegheny Mountains. This extends southwestward into the Valley of the Tennessee, and it has always been an important route for travel and trade.

[1] John A. Krout and Dixon R. Fox, *The Completion of Independence, 1790–1830* (New York, 1944), 7, 122; United States *Census of 1790* (Philadelphia, 1791), 3.

The Piedmont Region, lying between the mountains and the fall lines of the eastward-flowing rivers, is a country of fertile rolling hills and red clay soils located not too far from the Atlantic ports to carry on trade with them. Hardwood forests covered most of the area, and many of the swift, clear streams were navigable for small boats.

Between the fall line and the coast lies the Tidewater region. That section with rivers which could be navigated by ocean-going vessels carried on its trade and kept up intellectual contacts with Britain and the rest of Europe. Its soils were of sand, loam, and yellow clay, and though they were fertile when first cleared, they soon wore out under cultivation. Much of the land was covered with pine forests, and overland communication was frequently obstructed by wide streams and extensive swamps. The rivers were therefore the main arteries of trade and travel.

Though the early South never developed important fisheries, the rivers and coastal waters teemed with fish; sturgeon especially were plentiful in the James and other rivers. Game was abundant in the forests, with elk and several other species of deer affording the best hunting. Herds of buffalo fed on the cane which grew in the low grounds west of the mountains, but they rarely ventured east of the Blue Ridge where the winter forage was scanty. Cattle, however, did manage to subsist through the winter even on the Atlantic Seaboard, and large herds roamed the woods in the more thinly settled parts of the Carolinas and in the Old Southwest. Next to deer, wild turkey was the favorite game; parakeets were still common, and passenger pigeons—now extinct—were often so numerous that they darkened the sky and broke the limbs of trees on which they roosted. It was a region teeming with life before the white man wrought his devastation.

Indians inhabited most of the country west of the mountains, with the Choctaw nation occupying what is now southern Mississippi, the Chickasaw northern Mississippi and Alabama, the Creek eastern Alabama and southern and western Georgia, and the Cherokee the western Carolinas, northern Georgia, and eastern Tennessee. In all, they probably did not number more than sixty thousand,[2] but they were still capable of making serious trouble

[2] R. S. Cotterill, *The Old South* (Glendale, Calif., 1936), map, 55.

for the men who formed the spearhead of the westward-thrusting frontier.

Of the nearly two million whites and Negroes who inhabited the South in 1790, the overwhelming majority lived east of the mountains. Parts of the Tidewater region had been settled for nearly two hundred years and its predominant population had come from England in the seventeenth century. Although there was a small admixture of French Huguenots and other nationalities, they had been absorbed into the British stock, and life was modeled after the pattern of the Old Country.

Agriculture was the occupation of almost everybody; the great majority were small farmers, owning less than five hundred acres of land. About a third of them owned one or two families of slaves, but they were all "grass-root" farmers who lived close to the soil. Most of them lived in log cabins, wore homespun clothes, and subsisted largely on "hog and hominy."[3] Some, however, had comfortable weatherboarded houses, characterized by a wide hall running through the center and a front porch extending the entire width of the house. There was a kitchen and a porch attached at the rear, with a well or spring to furnish water, and at a little distance there would be an enclosed barnyard with a stable, smokehouse, and other dependencies. If there were slaves, their quarters would be still farther from the main house.[4] The pioneer had his own type of architecture. It grew naturally from the one-room log cabin, could be expanded to suit his needs, and was in accord with his substantial taste.

Though the owner of such a place might be a man of some local importance—perhaps an officer of the militia or even a justice of the peace—his life was quite simple. He usually owned a few books and read an occasional newspaper at the tavern where he liked to spend his idle hours, but his spoken English was provincial and his writing was crude. There was little place for either reading or writing in his home, but he had dogs and guns for hunting and horses for riding. These were his main diversions.

[3] Bureau of the Census, *A Century of Population Growth, 1790–1900* (Washington, 1909), 296–98.

[4] Lewis C. Gray, *History of Agriculture in the Southern United States to 1860* (Washington, 1933), I, 540.

Isolated as he was on his farm, he was by nature strikingly gregarious and he loved company. Guests were received with hearty cordiality and fed from a bountiful larder. The mistress of such an establishment was a busy person and rarely got away from home except to visit neighbors within a radius of a few miles. Her dress was a blousy "Mother Hubbard" and a poke bonnet made of homespun material. Her husband, also dressed in homespun, enjoyed drinking at the nearest tavern where he joked with other rustics and placed bets on cockfights and "quarter races." Now and then, being well fortified with "spirits," he himself indulged in a bit of fighting.[5] In addition to the frolicking at the taverns, there were militia musters and court days, which also furnished occasions for merrymaking. On the whole, the life of the farmer was not as drab as it sometimes appeared to be, and according to common report, he did not spend as much time at the tail of the plow as might have been desirable.[6]

Below the landowning farmers was a smaller group of landless whites. This element was made up of unmarried sons of farmers, the mechanics and clerks in the towns, the tenant farmers (who were more numerous than is commonly supposed), and men who farmed as "squatters" on land which they did not own. In this last group were the "poor whites" who lived on the fringes of the settlements and ordinarily seemed to have no ambition above living in listless ease and sometimes pilfering or begging from their more industrious neighbors. But not all of the landless people were shiftless. There was a vast difference in caliber among them, and often the tenant farmers and the laborers in town and country were able to rise in a world which offered so many opportunities to the ambitious and industrious. The habits of the more intelligent laborers did not differ much from those of the small

[5] Eugene P. Link, "The Democratic Societies of the Carolinas," in *North Carolina Historical Review* (Raleigh), XVIII (1941), 267; Annapolis *Maryland Gazette*, November 20, 1800; Isaac Weld, *Travels through the States of North America . . . during the years 1795, 1796, and 1797* (London, 1807), I, 156–57; John Bernard, *Retrospections of America, 1797–1811* (New York, 1887), 202–209; Gray, *History of Agriculture in the Southern United States*, I, 499; Krout and Fox, *Completion of Independence*, 109, 128.

[6] Richmond *Virginia Gazette, and General Advertiser*, July 2, 1789; John Davis, *Travels of Four Years and a Half in the United States of America; during 1798, 1799, 1800, 1801, and 1802* (London, 1803), 49–54.

farmers with whom they mingled in public places and with whom they enjoyed the cockfights and the races.[7]

At the other end of the social scale were the larger landowners, whose estates, with slight feudal overtones, might consist of several thousand acres and who occasionally owned more than a hundred slaves. This was indeed a small section of the population. In Maryland, for instance, out of 12,226 slave-owning families in 1790—this being 36 per cent of the total population—only 829 owned more than 20 slaves, and in the Carolinas the proportion was even smaller.[8] But these were the people who dominated Southern life. They had their faults and, like most capitalists, they were engaged in exploitation, yet they were also builders. Without their leadership there would have been little progress.

In the period under discussion a member of the upper classes could be recognized anywhere in the Western World by his dress. Americans followed the European fashion, and it was changing during the period of the French Revolution. The small clothes and cocked hats of our late colonial period were being replaced with tight-fitting pantaloons of white doeskin and fair-top boots. Scarlet coats were cut like modern "tails" and worn with ruffled shirts, voluminous stocks, and high silk or beaver hats. Women were abandoning stays for low-cut and simply draped gowns of light materials and were turning from elaborate, powdered coiffures to hair cut relatively short and worn in ringlets about the face.[9] Straw bonnets were fashionable, and some lines taken from a London newspaper asked: "Who but must mourn Maria's lot that sees her head thus 'gone to pot'?" [10]

The upper classes followed a daily routine very different from that of the laboring people. A gentleman arose fairly early and occupied himself until breakfast by riding, walking, or reading. It was not unusual in the South for him to fortify himself for the day with a mint julep (made of sugar, water, rum, and mint) or other stimulating beverage such as eggnog or toddy. Break-

[7] Weld, *Travels through the States of North America*, I, 190–93.

[8] Bureau of the Census, *Century of Population Growth*, 296–98.

[9] Halifax *North-Carolina Journal*, July 3, 1793; Samuel Mordecai, *Richmond in By-gone Days* (Richmond, 1946), 184–89; Krout and Fox, *Completion of Independence*, 32–36, 151.

[10] Norfolk *Herald, August* 17, 1799.

fast, between seven and eight o'clock, commonly consisted of ham, eggs, coffee, tea, and a hot bread of some kind; on the coast fish was often served at this first meal of the day. The dinner hour was usually around three o'clock and the main meal, consisting largely of various kinds of meats, was put on the table at one time. Light wines, but more frequently peach brandy or rum mixed with water, were served with the meal. Next, the "sweets," consisting of cakes, pies, and jellies, were served. After this, the ladies withdrew, the cloth removed, and the gentlemen drank Madeira with their fruit and nuts. Meanwhile, tea was served to the ladies in the "withdrawing" room. Supper was often a cold collation served about eight o'clock. Since lighting was mostly by candle, one usually went to bed by nine o'clock, and it seems fairly certain that little work was done by the gentry after the three-o'clock dinner.[11]

Though the gentleman was known by his dress, this was merely a symbol of more important considerations. These were not the same in all societies, but the South still tended to follow the rural English pattern, while the commercial cities of the North, with strong Puritan or Quaker traditions and much new wealth, were developing a pattern peculiar to themselves.

Among the qualifications of the Southern gentleman, manners were important. And it was not only the gentleman who had good manners, for it was generally conceded by various outside observers that good manners in the South permeated lower down than in other regions of the country. Even the plain people who enjoyed few advantages displayed an unkempt though genuine politeness not found in their peers elsewhere. For the gentleman, Lord Chesterfield was the social arbiter of his day, but one did not usually get his deportment from books. Despite the cynicism of Chesterfield, good manners then, as always, involved consideration for others, particularly on the social level. This was a fine art and was not easily acquired. The habit of paying especial attention to strangers—of putting one's guest at ease, en-

[11] Savannah *Georgia Gazette*, May 26, 1791; William Attmore, *Journal of a Tour to North Carolina, 1787* (Chapel Hill, 1922), 46; Harry Toulmin, *The Western Country in 1793; Reports on Kentucky and Virginia,* edited by Marion Tinling and Godfrey Davies (San Marino, Calif., 1948), 25.

couraging him to talk about the things which interested him most, and of paying subtle compliments—these accomplishments were as desirable as being a good conversationalist and a connoisseur of food and drink.[12]

A gentleman was expected to be "a man of honor." This term, often associated with the code duello and gambling debts, has been much abused, but it was not meaningless. Fundamentally, it meant that a man must live up to his social and economic obligations and that his word could be trusted. He did not insult others gratuitously, and he would not tolerate an insult, either by word or deed. This was where the duel came in, and association during the Revolution with British and French officers—devotees of the code duello—had increased its vogue. Although the most famous American duel was that between Alexander Hamilton and Aaron Burr, both colonels in the late war, the code did not appeal to the Northern society of merchants and small farmers. The rural aristocracy of the South was closer to the European tradition and the duel was a part of it.[13] The Southern gentleman assumed the yoke of government as a matter of course, for he also followed the English tradition in taking it for granted that he belonged to "the governing class" and that he should take that responsibility seriously. He commonly served without pay as a justice of the peace or as a member of the legislature, but if he were merely a planter and slaveowner, he took the care of his people as a private trust. A newcomer from England remarked in 1793 that "those European prejudices are not known which insulate the man of rank and property and make him solitary in the midst of society. The man who made such pretensions to superiority would be despised." It was no accident that the South furnished such excellent leadership during the Revolution and the early days of the Republic.[14]

It is more difficult to say what the intellectual requirements of the gentleman were. He might be merely literate, as was Washington, although the eighteenth century put a premium

[12] Bernard, *Retrospections of America*, 148; Hugh A. Garland, *The Life of John Randolph of Roanoke* (New York, 1866), 174.

[13] Lexington *Kentucky Gazette*, August 2, 1791; Davis, *Travels . . . in the United States*, 67–101.

[14] Toulmin, *The Western Country in 1793*, p. 40.

8

upon the liberal arts, with especial emphasis on a knowledge of the classics. Science also was in vogue, it being then an amateur avocation, and there were many Southern planters who, like Jefferson, dabbled in the sciences and had at least a smattering of Latin and Greek. These were looked on as social accomplishments. More important still was a good English style in writing, and the better letter writers of that day were far more accomplished than are most of those of our own time. Above all, because he lived in rural isolation and carried a heavy responsibility, both public and private, the Southern planter was an individualist, preferring to follow traditional customs, keeping himself currently informed, but scorning to wear the mental habiliments of other men. His originality and sincerity tended to make him an agreeable companion.[15]

During the earlier colonial period, the Southern gentry accepted the Anglican faith as a part of its British heritage, but as the eighteenth century progressed, rationalism gained vogue and the Revolution did much to discredit the Church and to popularize the views of Thomas Paine. Many of the Revolutionary leaders were deists and Paine's *Age of Reason* was widely read during the period which followed. Chesterfield's cynicism had its influence, and orthodox religion was at a low ebb among men of the upper classes. Franklin and Jefferson were typical of their day in this respect.[16] Soon, however, rationalism and skepticism were displaced by a new order which circuit riders, plodding their weary way through the forests, spread throughout the length and breadth of the frontier. The Great Revival erupted around eighteen hundred. It was essentially mob psychology practiced with telling effect, some of it leading to genuine religious faith, most of it to a crude, effervescent emotionalism wholly removed from spiritual concepts. So far-reaching was the influence of the Great Revival that in time a man who was merely wellborn and well-educated was no longer an authentic gentleman—he had to be a Christian gentleman.

The rationalism and cynicism before the Great Revival partly

[15] Mrs. St. Julien Ravenel, *Charleston, The Place and The People* (New York, 1925), 389.

[16] Savannah *Georgia Gazette*, June 11, 1789; October 20, 1796; Thomas P. Abernethy, *From Frontier to Plantation in Tennessee* (Chapel Hill, 1932), 210–20.

explains the lax moral tone which pervaded society; the South merely followed the prevailing trend. Not much of Victorianism survives in the world today, but the status of the modern woman is largely a product of the Victorian attitude. It is therefore startling to realize that in earlier generations women enjoyed no more —often even less—consideration than did men.[17] Southern newspapers carried much ribaldry concerning women, though the South was not peculiar in this respect. Even ladies of the gentry were not exempt from such scurrility.[18]

This does not mean that the moral standard was notably low among the upper classes or that there was no respect for women; the cynical tone of European society was merely imitated. Women were occasionally criticized in the newspapers for using profane language and indulging in loose talk. They were also chided for playing cards to excess, thereby discouraging the fine art of conversation.[19] A more accurate appraisal of this situation was made in 1799 by John Bernard, the actor: "Of the planters' ladies I must speak in terms of unqualified praise; they had an easy kindliness of manner, as far removed from rudeness as from reserve, which being natural to them . . . was the more admirable." He said that they married and faded early, but "to the influence of their society I chiefly attribute their husbands' refinement." [20]

The most popular diversions among the upper classes were dancing, cardplaying and horse racing. All the more important towns had jockey clubs and racecourses, and men and women of every degree attended the meets. Blooded horses had been imported from England during the colonial period and gentlemen took much pride in their steeds. Races were then run, as in England, from right to left and distances of three and four miles were commonly covered. The victory went to the horse which

[17] Edenton *State Gazette of North-Carolina*, January 16, 1790; May 28, 1795; Halifax *North-Carolina Journal*, January 30, June 26, 1793; Annapolis *Maryland Gazette*, March 5, 1795; March 2, 1797.

[18] Richmond *Virginia Gazette, and General Advertiser*, October 27, 1790; March 9, 1791; April 4, 1792.

[19] Halifax *North-Carolina Journal*, January 9, 1793; Richmond *Virginia Gazette, and General Advertiser*, June 27, 1792; Carl Bridenbaugh, *Myths and Realities, Societies of the Colonial South* (Baton Rouge, 1952), 19–20; Krout and Fox, *Completion of Independence*, 33.

[20] Bernard, *Retrospections of America*, 149–50.

won two out of three heats. Purses were sometimes considerable and betting was widely practiced. In Lexington, Kentucky, the interest was so great that racing horses in the streets or showing studhorses there had to be prohibited by law.[21]

Whist was the usual card game and it was generally played for money. In Virginia, reels and jigs were the most popular dances even among the gentry, and there were dancing masters in the towns and sometimes on the plantations. In Charleston, where the French influence was strong, the waltz and the minuet were favored, but country dances prevailed throughout the rural areas, with all classes of society enjoying them.[22]

While gentlemen were addicted to horse racing, cockfighting appears to have appealed principally to those less genteel, but mixed crowds were attracted by both sports. Charleston as well as Norfolk had exhibitions of bearbaiting and bullbaiting. Strangely enough, neither prize fighting nor wrestling seems to have developed a following, and there were no ball games of any kind except in Savannah which had a golf club dating from colonial times.[23]

Except for the three R's, education was practically limited to the upper classes. Private tutors were often employed by the wealthier planters, and most of the towns and some rural areas had "academies" where boys received instruction in the classical languages, mathematics, geography, rhetoric, and a few other subjects. Academies for girls taught a variety of the more "polite" subjects, such as music, drawing, fancy needlework, and dancing, as well as French, geography, cyphering, letter writing, and elocution. Occasionally the public contributed to the support of these schools, but they were nearly always privately conducted and sometimes were run by men and women of real ability.[24]

---

[21] *Ibid.*, 154–58; Bridenbaugh, *Myths and Realities*, 22; Weld, *Travels through the States of North America*, I, 185; Lexington *Kentucky Gazette*, February 8, October 11, 1794.

[22] Norfolk *Herald*, February 4, 1800; Mordecai, *Richmond in By-gone Days*, 246–48.

[23] Savannah *Georgia Gazette*, September 22, 1796; September 25, 1799; Norfolk *Herald*, September 18, 1798; Davis, *Travels . . . in the United States*, 139–40; Winslow C. Watson (ed.), *Men and Times of the Revolution; or Memoirs of Elkanah Watson* (New York, 1856), 161–62.

[24] Annapolis *Maryland Gazette*, April 10, August 14, 1794; May 30, 1799; New Bern *North-Carolina Gazette*, October 19, 1793; Raleigh *Register*, July 15, 1800.

Before the Revolution the College of William and Mary was the only institution of its kind in the South, but during the last decades of the eighteenth century, Washington College (now Washington and Lee University) and Hampden-Sydney College were chartered in Virginia; the foundations of the College of Charleston were laid; the universities of North Carolina and Georgia were chartered; Washington and St. John's colleges were established in Maryland; and beyond the mountains, Blount College in Knoxville, Tusculum College also in East Tennessee, and Transylvania College in Lexington, Kentucky, were founded. Though the opportunities for higher learning were meager, the upper classes in the South as elsewhere were committed to the proposition that a gentleman should be well-informed and should, if possible, have a classical education.[25]

But it did not occur to men of that day that an education could be acquired only in college. One who was ambitious usually started with a few years in an academy or under a tutor and then devoted himself to serious reading. Plenty of books were available. Charleston and Richmond had library societies, and most towns had a bookshop, often run by the local printer. Few novels were carried on their shelves, but most of the well-known English authors were there, and occasionally there was an American book,[26] though the public as a rule did not care for the works of American authors, much preferring the European classics.

It was natural for a man who did his reading independently to do his thinking in the same way. The relative isolation of his existence and the responsibility which he necessarily assumed for those, both white and black, who lived about him and carried out his instructions made it inevitable that he would be a self-reliant person, proud of his independence, both material and intellectual. The small voice within him was not drowned out by the din of modern civilization. Above all else, he was an individualist.

[25] Bernard, *Retrospections of America*, 149; Charles F. Thwing, *A History of Higher Education in America* (New York, 1906), *passim.*

[26] Richmond *Virginia Gazette, and General Advertiser*, January 25, 1793; November 4, December 30, 1795; Norfolk *Herald*, January 24, 1795; November 9, 1797; Fayetteville *North-Carolina Chronicle*, September 27, 1790; Edenton *State Gazette of North-Carolina*, January 31, 1794; Raleigh *Register*, May 27, 1800.

Towns in the South were few, small, and far between, but they were important. Charleston was the largest with 16,359 people in 1790, of whom 7,684 were slaves. Even so, it was the fourth city of the nation, ranking just below Boston in size. Fast-growing Baltimore came next, with a population of 13,503, of whom 1,255 were slaves. Richmond, with its classical new capitol which Jefferson had designed, was populated by only 3,761 in 1790; the busy port of Norfolk had about 7,000; Savannah's population was 2,300; Lexington, the largest town in Western America, had 834 inhabitants; and Nashville numbered no more than 500. North Carolina had no town with a population of more than 2,000.[27]

With all its rurality, the South was still not the most thinly populated section of the country. Maryland had a population density in 1790 of twenty-three per square mile, Virginia had nearly eleven, South Carolina ten, and North Carolina eight, while New York had seven and a half and Pennsylvania nine.[28] The South was, by tradition and because of its commercial connections, the most British of the sections, and unless New York's landed families were really rural, it had the only agricultural aristocracy which ever flourished in the United States.[29]

While the South maintained its traditional ruralism, the Middle Atlantic and the New England states were rapidly developing their commerce and manufactures. Economic rivalry, Puritan influences, as well as antislavery sentiment and egalitarian doctrine, were producing a sectional antagonism which became

[27] Bureau of the Census, *Century of Population Growth*, 78; Adam Seybert, *Statistical Annals . . . of the United States of America* (Philadelphia, 1818), 47; Krout and Fox, *Completion of Independence*, 19, 131.

[28] Seybert, *Statistical Annals . . . of the United States*, 45.

[29] Bridenbaugh, *Myths and Realities*, 27, 45–46. Speaking of the Chesapeake Society in this volume, the author states: "Among this busy people who, by force and by preference, favored conversation to reading and scribbling, there developed significant qualities of speech, which immediately caught the ear of Englishmen accustomed to a 'peculiar dialect' in each county of the mother country. With William Eddis, they seldom failed to notice 'that a striking similarity of speech universally prevails; and it is strictly true, that the pronunciation of the generality of people has an accuracy and elegance, that cannot fail of gratifying the most judicious ear.'" Still speaking of the same region, Bridenbaugh quotes another Englishman as saying: "Being early introduced into company . . . they are of a livelier, readier wit than we in England . . . may boast of."

13

stronger with the passage of time. Some indications of this feeling showed themselves during the early years of the Republic. Even during the Revolution, Robert Morris had said to the French Minister, Conrad Alexandre Gérard, that the strength of the Union must always lie in the North and that this section should be kept in the ascendancy by curtailing the territory on the Southwest.[30]

Although the South was essentially rural, agricultural products required a market, and markets required towns. Such communities grew up in accord with local conditions, yet all served the same purposes and they had many features in common. The smaller ones usually straggled along a single thoroughfare or clustered about some county courthouse. Williamsburg and Savannah, like Philadelphia, were planned before they were settled, and so were Charlottesville, Nashville, and some other Southern towns. Despite the abundance of cheap land, the dwellings in the larger towns were often three-story row houses built flush with the sidewalk. So usual was the habit of crowding buildings together in Europe for lack of room that, even in the wide open spaces of the early South, farmhouses usually had no windows at the lateral ends. Thus did custom cast its long shadow down the path of history.

Next to their commercial functions, the main contributions of the towns were social and intellectual. Their taverns were centers of community life. Here the Fourth of July and Washington's birthday were celebrated, and a formal dinner often given for the distinguished visitor; here the local tipsters met the traveling public, which frequently included foreigners, and discussed the news of the world. Here the flowing bowl was always at hand; and around the glowing hearth chess and whist could be played, politics discussed, and in good weather the guests could go outside to witness a cockfight, a quarter race, or a friendly fisticuff.[31]

Many of the towns had their uniformed companies of volunteers which furnished the color for patriotic occasions. Such

[30] Thomas P. Abernethy, *Western Lands and the American Revolution* (New York, 1937), 203–204.

[31] Raleigh *Register*, October 29, 1799.

were the Monticello Guards, the Richmond Blues, and others which still maintain their organizations and their colonial costumes. In 1799 Charleston had a regiment of artillery, two of infantry, and a squadron of cavalry, and their musters, parades, and reviews added greatly to the festivity of public gatherings.[32]

In addition to their jockey clubs and racecourses, the larger towns usually maintained a theater or a "long room," and in the smaller ones plays were given at the tavern or the courthouse. In small towns such as Nashville when the theater or courthouse was inadequate for the audience, occasionally riders would rein their horses under the windows and, for a greatly reduced price, from that vantage point watch the performance on the stage—or so much of it as they could see. Amateur theatricals and acrobatic performances were popular, but migratory companies of professional players came from England and furnished amusement for the "season" in such places as Charleston, Baltimore, Norfolk, and Richmond. Neither Shakespeare nor Sheridan appeared often on their bills, but ephemeral contemporary plays, then as now, were most popular. After the drama there was usually a "short, laughable farce," which was more often tipped with vulgarity than with wit. During intermission the actors sang, and a small orchestra accompanied the troupe. The performance normally began at about six in the evening, and those who had engaged seats were advised to send their slaves to hold them until the family arrived. Theaters were constructed as in Europe, with the pit for unattached men, the boxes for the more affluent families, and the gallery for the nondescript. On one occasion the Charleston theater was urged to close the gallery because of the disturbance commonly made by its occupants, some of whom were prostitutes.[33]

---

[32] Charleston *City Gazette*, April 23, 1789; April 8, May 29, 1799.

[33] Martin S. Shockley, "First American Performances of English Plays in Richmond before 1819," in *Journal of Southern History* (Baton Rouge, Nashville, Lexington, Houston), XIII (1947), 91–105; Thomas J. Wertenbaker, *Norfolk, Historic Southern Port* (Durham, 1931), 130; Charleston *City Gazette*, August 14, 1792; March 25, 1793; Charleston *Times, City Gazette and Merchants' Evening Advertiser*, March 4, 1801; Norfolk *Herald*, January 21, 1800; Norfolk *Herald, and Norfolk and Portsmouth Advertiser*, June 24, July 4, 11, 1795; *Virginia Gazette, and Richmond Daily Advertiser*, October 1, 1792.

In addition to its theater Charleston had its circus and its Vauxhall Gardens. Richmond, Nashville, and other towns had similar outdoor places of entertainment, consisting of a garden with illuminated walks, benches, an orchestra, and both liquid and solid refreshments. Sometimes fireworks or other exhibitions were presented, and the new delicacy, ice cream, was served in Charleston as early as 1798.[34]

The larger towns had an "Exchange" or a "Coffee House" where the merchants could read the newspapers, talk with their friends over a pot of porter, or transact business.[35] The public market, which existed in even the smaller towns, was still more popular. It was usually built in a central location, either occupying the middle of a wide street or a public square. The town appointed officials to supervise its operation, and only here could country produce be sold. To its stalls the nearby farmers brought their eggs, butter, vegetables, and meats, and the local populace came during the early hours of the morning to procure their supplies. It was necessary for the municipality to regulate this trade because of the perishability of most of the produce. But, as usual, public control produced infractions of the law, and forestalling became a common abuse. Slaves and free Negroes would descend upon the farmers as soon as they reached the market or even before and buy up all of their eggs or other edibles. Then, contrary to law, they would hawk these about the streets and sell them at a higher price than would have been charged at the market. The municipal corporations passed special legislation to outlaw this practice, but they found it difficult to control.[36]

Free Negroes created a problem in the towns, for they were accused of engaging in various forms of illicit traffic and of congregating in public places on Sundays and holidays and disturbing the peace. To curb this nuisance, numerous municipal reg-

[34] Norfolk *Herald and Public Advertiser*, August 28, September 4, October 5, 1797; Norfolk *Herald*, September 1, 1798; Charleston *City Gazette and General Advertiser*, May 11, 1798; Charleston *City Gazette, and Daily Advertiser*, January 14, February 8, June 20, 1799.

[35] Savannah *Georgia Gazette*, June 4, 1795.

[36] Mordecai, *Richmond in By-gone Days*, 23; Raleigh *Register and North-Carolina Weekly Advertiser*, October 22, 1799; Charleston *City Gazette*, September 11, 1793; August 27, 1797; February 4, 1799.

ulations were made; slaves were not allowed to sell anything without a license from their masters, and in Savannah free Negroes had to obtain a license before they could sell cakes and beer on the streets.[37] But it was not the Negroes alone who gave trouble. There were complaints that groups of ruffians would assemble on Sundays and disturb divine worship; a Lexington, Kentucky, merchant complained that his shop was infested with loungers who annoyed his customers and drove them away.[38]

Society in the larger towns was rather highly organized. In addition to the jockey clubs, the thespian societies, the voluntary military companies, the night watches, and the fire companies with their hand pumps and leather buckets, there were various social and charitable groups. The most famous of these was the St. Cecilia Society of Charleston. In the early period it was a musical organization which sponsored periodic concerts and employed professional performers to collaborate with the amateurs.[39] Some of the larger towns had dancing assemblies which were open to anyone who wished to subscribe. In Charleston the most numerous groups were the nationalistic organizations, such as the St. George Society for the English, the St. Andrews Society for the Scots, and the St. Patrick Society for the Irish. In addition, there was the *Freundschaftsbund* for the Germans and the Huguenot Society for the French.[40]

But in the smaller towns life was simpler. The commercial side of town life usually eclipsed its amenities, and its conveniences were few. The streets were unpaved and muddy or dusty according to the weather. The sidewalks were sometimes bricked and sometimes shaded, but they were likely to be obstructed by the goods which merchants displayed in front of their shops. Garbage was rarely collected, and sewerage and running water were nonexistent. Most towns, even the largest of them, had public

[37] Charleston *City Gazette*, September 27, 1792; Savannah *Georgia Gazette*, February 5, 1795.

[38] Charleston *City Gazette*, June 19, 1790; Lexington *Kentucky Gazette*, December 17, 1791.

[39] Savannah *Georgia Gazette*, May 7, 1789; May 1, 1794; June 23, 1796; Charleston *City Gazette*, January 6, 1790; January 7, 1796; Bridenbaugh, *Myths and Realities*, 65.

[40] Savannah *Georgia Gazette*, November 13, 1794; Norfolk *Herald*, December 13, 1798.

wells at intervals along the main streets, and there the citizens who did not have their own wells got water for drinking, laundering, and personal ablutions. Cattle and hogs often wandered about the thoroughfares, and mudholes frequently obstructed passage.[41] "Necessary houses" furnished the only sanitary facilities, and flies and mosquitoes were common pests. Miscellaneous odors must have permeated the more thickly settled areas. John Randolph of Roanoke could not understand why any gentleman wished to live in a town. The Charleston gentry felt differently about it, but they were exceptional in the South.

To this point, reference has been made chiefly to descendants of the people, mostly English, who first came to America in the early seventeenth century, established themselves in the Tidewater regions of the South Atlantic states, and penetrated as far inland as the northern and central Piedmont areas of Virginia. But the interior of the South was settled by other peoples. The Scotch-Irish and Palatine Germans coming down from Pennsylvania penetrated the Shenandoah Valley in the 1730's. The Germans, bringing with them the best agriculture that was known to the colonies, settled on the good lands that they found in the lower Shenandoah Valley, while some continued on into the Catawba River Valley of North Carolina. The Scotch-Irish, a more venturesome people, moved on down the Valley and, crossing the Blue Ridge where the Roanoke River breaks through to the east, settled the Carolina Piedmont Region. Others continued on down the Great Valley and settled the area that is now East Tennessee. Some of the more intrepid of these pioneers set off from the Long Island of the Holston River near present-day Kingsport, Tennessee, and following the trail that Daniel Boone had blazed, passed through Cumberland Gap in 1775 and planted some of the first settlements in Kentucky. Four years later Nashville on the Cumberland River was settled by pioneers from the same locality. Thus, the frontier bred a new and hardy race—our first backwoodsmen who were reared in the shadow of the ancient forests—and it was they who extended civilization farther west than any English-speaking people had ever gone before.

[41] Charleston *City Gazette*, June 19, 1790; Savannah *Georgia Gazette*, July 31, 1794; Rosa F. Yancey, *Lynchburg and Its Neighbors* (Richmond, 1935), 32–33.

In 1789 the vast stretches of the West were practically unknown and hence presented alluring vistas for their possibilities of yielding home and fortune. The Kentucky and Tennessee settlements were growing in number and strength, the former being still a part of Virginia and the latter of North Carolina. At the same time, the Carolina Piedmont and contiguous parts of Virginia and Georgia possessed a fairly well-developed society. Though there were other elements in these regions, the Scotch-Irish predominated spiritually if not numerically, and the Presbyterian Church was the most influential denomination. It was not seriously affected by the prevailing rationalistic philosophies and was staunch in defense of the rigid faith and strict morality of John Calvin. These people had come to America to escape hard conditions imposed on them in their homeland by the English, and having lived in interior America at some distance from Seaboard influences, they were not only religious but more peculiarly American than were the dwellers near the coast. Where these Covenanters settled in considerable numbers and could establish churches and schools, they maintained a well-ordered society. But where their more restless spirits wandered into the mountains and vacant spaces of the West, some of them became a rugged lot indeed.[42]

Thus, while Englishmen predominated in settling the coastal regions of the South, the typical American frontiersman was likely to be of Scotch-Irish extraction. These men were not impoverished drifters; they were fighting for empire and they knew it. Of Celtic blood, they were a sturdy breed: they blazed trails, fought Indians, established governments, founded churches and schools, speculated in lands, and dabbled in politics. They were bold, aggressive, and imaginative, possessing every quality for planting civilization in the wilderness.

Such were the people of the South; such was their environment and such their manner of life when the Nation was very young.

[42] Bridenbaugh, *Myths and Realities,* 128, 132, 181; Thomas J. Wertenbaker, *The Old South; The Founding of American Civilization* (New York, 1942), 218–19.

CHAPTER II

# THE SOUTH AND THE NEW NATION

IN CONSIDERING the South, one naturally thinks of sectionalism, but of course there could be no sectionalism in the national sense until there was a Union. It is true that during the period of the Confederation there had been a nascent sectionalism which grew out of conflicting views as to ownership of the Western lands. In the Constitutional Convention the principal conflict of interests was between the large and the small states, but this was satisfactorily settled by the compromise concerning representation in the two houses of Congress and apparently had no effect on the vote by which the new instrument of government was adopted.

The sectionalism which showed up in that vote did not reveal a cleavage between the Northern and Southern states but one between the eastern and western areas of the individual states. Charles Beard and others have ably analyzed this intrastate rift, but certain factors have commonly been overlooked. In the first place, the alignment was by no means clear-cut as between a Seaboard region, where most of the wealth was concentrated and where a stronger government was needed to protect and promote economic interests, and on the other hand, an interior area where small farmers demanded that the states issue increasing amounts of paper money and where the people feared a central government strong enough to enforce the prompt payment of overdue obligations.[1]

[1] Charles A. Beard's conclusions have been attacked in two meticulous studies: Forrest McDonald, *We the People; The Economic Origins of the Constitution* (Chicago, 1958); and Robert E. Brown, *Charles Beard and the Constitution* (Prince-

The poor, of course, outnumbered the wealthy in both regions, but only a small minority of the adult males—probably not more than one in fifteen—actually voted on the adoption of the Constitution.[2] Since wealth has always brought influence and power, it seems safe to assume that a few leaders of that minority determined the votes of the majority. Thus a small number of influential individuals could control a constituency, and it was only in backward areas, where men of wealth were almost non-existent or where they became tribunes of the poor, that the debtor interest could win. If this were not so, the comparatively poor would always have ruled.

Among those who were moderately wealthy at the time of the adoption of the Constitution, there were two principal elements: those whose property was in landed estates, and those who gained wealth by engaging in trade. In the Eastern states the mercantile interest predominated, while landowners were generally dominant in the South. This situation naturally resulted in conflicting economic interests. But in the vote on the adoption of the Constitution it was the sectionalism within the individual states that was the more pronounced, and in the South there was not only the difference between large and small landowners but between those who grew the staple agricultural crops, principally tobacco and rice, and those whose chief reliance was on wheat or other small grain.

It was the clause in the Constitution giving the Federal government control over commerce between the several states and with foreign countries which had the most telling influence on the vote. Tobacco growers generally had adequate transportation to the ports of Virginia and Maryland, and most of their product found its market in England, where heavy duties had to be paid on it. A strong central government would not greatly change this situation, and therefore the tobacco planters were, in general, not inclined toward federalism.

---

ton, 1956). For the geographical distribution of the vote on the adoption of the Constitution, see insert map in Orin G. Libby, *The Geographical Distribution of the Vote of the Thirteen States on the Federal Constitution, 1787–8* (Madison, 1894).

[2] Charles A. Beard, *An Economic Interpretation of the Constitution of the United States* (New York, 1913), 324–25.

Though the rice growers of South Carolina and Georgia sold some of their product in the countries of southern Europe, their best market was in the West Indies, all of those islands being owned by European powers which tried to monopolize their trade and exclude American products. Only by the negotiation of trade treaties could this situation be ameliorated, and only an effective central government could accomplish this negotiation. Therefore the rice planters were in favor of the proposed Constitution. The market of the wheat growers was similar to that of the producers of rice except that much wheat was shipped from one American state to another. Hence the wheat men were also usually Federalists. Other factors were involved, but these were apparently the most important in determining the vote of the Southern states on adoption of the Constitution.

Though Maryland was geographically the smallest of the Southern states, her agricultural and commercial situation produced a rather complex political picture. Tobacco was grown extensively on her Western Shore, but grain was the principal product of the Eastern Shore as well as of the transmontane region. Trade came down the Susquehanna from Pennsylvania to Baltimore, and down the Potomac to the Chesapeake. The Potomac was entirely subject to the jurisdiction of Maryland, but the capes giving access to the Chesapeake were both in Virginia, and it was problems arising from this situation which led to the calling of the Annapolis Convention of 1786, which in turn brought about the move for the Philadelphia Convention of 1787. The Eastern Shore was closer to Virginia and Delaware than it was to the rest of Maryland, and therefore practically all trade of the peninsula had to cross state lines. Thus with her commerce inextricably tied up with that of the neighboring states, Maryland was overwhelmingly Federalist.

Yet there was one relatively small but significant area which cast its vote against adoption. The cities of Baltimore and Annapolis, like practically all cities, went Federalist, but the Western Shore counties surrounding them were opposed, and this opposition was led by some of the ablest lawyers in the state— notably Luther Martin, William Pinkney, William Paca (the only non-Anglo-Saxon signer of the Declaration of Independence), and Samuel Chase.[3] This is difficult to account for with any degree of certainty, but it may have been due to the fact that the tobacco growers there did not feel the need of a strong central government, or as has been suggested, it may have been because the political leaders, especially Martin, Chase, Paca, and John Francis Mercer, were heavy investors in Tory property which had been confiscated by the state during the Revolution and which new Federal courts might restore to the original owners under the terms of the treaty of 1783. This group also favored the printing of paper money by the state as an aid to speculation.[4] Another possibility is that the wealthy merchants of Baltimore, who usually lived outside the city, did not wish to create a government which might take a hand in developing the navigation of the Potomac and thus divert the trade of western Maryland down that stream to Georgetown or Alexandria, thereby undercutting the overland route to Baltimore.[5]

The people of the Eastern Shore of Virginia, like those of the contiguous area of Maryland, ate Philadelphia scrapple and shipped wheat to the West Indies. Consequently, a majority of their votes were cast for adoption. Across the Bay, the Tidewater region of Virginia was also overwhelmingly for adoption, but here the situation was more complicated. During colonial times the lands had been exhausted by the continual cultivation of tobacco, and wheat was now the major crop. Furthermore, the fortunes of war had hit this area hard and most of the great colonial estates were in an impoverished condition. The only hope of economic rehabilitation seemed to lie in the improvement of the grain trade, and therefore a strong central government was desirable. In spite of this situation, many of the old established Virginian leaders were opposed to adoption. Among

[3] Philip A. Crowl, *Maryland During and After the Revolution* (Baltimore, 1943), 118; Matthew P. Andrews, *History of Maryland, Province and State* (Garden City, 1929), 390–92.

[4] Crowl, *Maryland During and After the Revolution*, 63, 127; Beard, *Economic Interpretation of the Constitution*, 281; John F. Mercer, "An Introductory Discourse to an Argument in Support of the Payments made of British debts into the Treasury of Maryland in the late War," in Annapolis *Maryland Gazette*, August 6, 1789.

[5] Irving Brant, *James Madison, The Virginia Revolutionist* (Indianapolis, 1941), 336.

them were such important personages as Richard Henry Lee, George Mason, Patrick Henry, James Monroe and his uncle Joseph Jones, John Tyler, Sr., and Benjamin Harrison.

The attitude of these leaders is not easy to explain. All of them were landowners, but probably only Henry could be classified as a speculator in lands. Certainly state rights feeling was strong among them, and this largely accounts for their stand. Eight Northern states could be expected to out-vote five Southern states in the new Congress, and thus the commercial interest would outweigh the agricultural. The great landowners of New York were anti-Federal, and it was perhaps natural that those of Virginia should take the same stand. But the needs of the grain trade outweighed local considerations and Tidewater Virginia followed Washington and Madison into the Federalist camp. This has been accounted for on the ground that most of the capital and the trade of the state were concentrated in this area, but actually, it was poverty rather than wealth that produced the result. It is also significant that most of the Virginia planters who owed pre-Revolutionary debts to British merchants lived in Tidewater rather than in the more western regions of the state. The adoption of the Constitution would create machinery by which these debts might be collected, and this fact may have influenced the anti-Federalist leaders, but the section actually voted against its economic interests in this matter.[6]

In the Piedmont Region—that area lying between the Blue Ridge Mountains and the fall lines of the rivers—the situation was quite different. Tobacco was the principal crop here, and the bulky hogsheads were boated, carted, or rolled down to the navigable rivers and thence shipped to British or Continental ports. No commercially dominated central government was likely to improve the transportation or the market, and hence the Piedmont people voted overwhelmingly against adoption.

More revealing was the situation in the Great Valley. The northern half of this valley is drained by the Shenandoah River,

<hr>

[6] Libby, *Geographical Distribution of the Vote . . . on the Federal Constitution,* 18–26, 66–67; Beard, *Economic Interpretation of the Constitution,* 282–91, 318; Harry Ammon, "The Republican Party in Virginia, 1789–1824" (Ph.D. dissertation, University of Virginia, 1948), 75–82.

which flows into the Potomac at Harpers Ferry. Grain and other country produce were boated down these rivers to Georgetown, Alexandria, or even Baltimore, and when the shipments reached the Potomac they were within the jurisdiction of Maryland. A government to regulate this interstate commerce and to improve the navigation of the Potomac was thus desirable. Consequently the people who were dependent upon this river to take their produce to market favored adoption.

Westward, between the Shenandoah Valley and the Great Kanawha River, which bisects the present state of West Virginia and flows into the Ohio at Point Pleasant, the mountainous country was sparsely settled by self-sustaining farmers. Such tenuous contact as they had with the outside world was by way of the upper Ohio and its tributaries or the upper Potomac. These were also interstate routes, and the vote of the region was for adoption.

South of the Shenandoah, the Great Valley is drained by the upper reaches of the James and Roanoke rivers, and by the New River which, farther west, helps to form the Great Kanawha. This region is known as Southwest Virginia, and its trade routes were almost as difficult as were those of the Kanawha Valley, but they led by way of Lynchburg to Richmond and thus lay altogether within the state. Virginia alone was interested in the improvement of the navigation of the James, and there was no demand here for a strong central government. It may be true also that the few self-sustaining farmers of the region had an interest in the issuance of paper money by the state and state relief laws for the benefit of debtors. Certainly they were not interested in the creation of new courts for the collection of debts nor in the imposition of new Federal taxes.[7] Isolationism is normal to the backwoodsman, and so was antifederalism at that time.

Much of this same spirit pervaded the region which was presently to become the state of Kentucky, but here other factors were involved. Such trade as there was had to go down the Ohio and Mississippi rivers to Spanish New Orleans, a port normally closed to Americans. In 1786 John Jay proposed to the Continental Congress that the United States enter into a treaty with

[7] Beard, *Economic Interpretation of the Constitution,* 296–99.

Spain whereby our claim to the navigation of the Mississippi should be abandoned for a period of twenty years. This angered the Kentuckians and made them feel that the Eastern states were opposed to their interests. They also felt that neither Congress nor the state of Virginia had ever afforded them adequate protection against the Indians. They believed, too, that taxes collected in the West were mostly spent in the East, and Eastern land policies were not usually in line with Western interests. The political, commercial, and diplomatic maneuvers of the rascally James Wilkinson (to be discussed later) also weighed in the anti-Federalist scale and were more than sufficient to outweigh the influence of Thomas Marshall, father of John, and his Federalist friends in the Louisville neighborhood. Therefore, out of fourteen Kentucky members in the Virginia convention of 1788, eleven voted against adoption.[8]

It is generally admitted that if a majority of the adult males in Virginia had voted, the decision would have been against adoption, but as it was, the Federalists won by a narrow margin. This approval was accompanied by a recommendation for amendments constituting a Bill of Rights and with a proviso that the people of Virginia should have the right to rescind ratification whenever the powers granted the Union "should be perverted to their injury or oppression." [9] Thus the result was qualified by concessions, and if it had been different, it is hard to imagine what direction our history would have taken.

In 1788 North Carolina was, economically and politically, a comparatively undeveloped state. She lacked the strong planter-class leadership which existed in Virginia, and her trade passed largely through the ports of Virginia and South Carolina. She therefore tended to follow the lead of her neighbors to the north and south. The oldest settlements were in the Albemarle-Pamlico Sound region, and the principal exports were timber and naval stores. These were usually sent in small coasting vessels to the ports of other states or overland to Petersburg or Norfolk in Virginia. Such interstate trade called for a stronger central gov-

[8] Arthur P. Whitaker, *The Spanish-American Frontier: 1783–1795* (Boston, 1927), 124–25.

[9] Clement Eaton, *A History of the Old South* (New York, 1949), 148.

ernment, and the leaders here were conservative lawyers and educated men who favored repealing the laws penalizing former Tories. At the same time, they opposed laws postponing the collection of debts and those providing for new issues of paper money. Here the vote was strongly in favor of the Constitution.[10]

Practically all the rest of the state voted in the negative, but this did not amount to a clear-cut rejection of the Constitution. William Blount, merchant, politician, and unscrupulous land speculator, was the Federalist leader in North Carolina, but he and most of his followers were defeated when the ratifying convention of 1788 was elected. The leader of the anti-Federalists was Willie (pronounced Wyllie) Jones, a wealthy planter of Halifax, an interior county, and a devoted follower of Thomas Jefferson. Strongly opposed to adoption, he was aided in his stand by Mason and Henry of Virginia. He was also supported by radicals who favored maintaining the laws against former Tories, issuing new paper money, and postponing collection of debts. Then, too, he had the support of such orators as a certain Baptist preacher, a candidate for the convention, who explained to a large and enthusiastic audience that, if the Constitution were adopted, the Federal government would establish its capital in a walled city ten miles square. Here, he said, it would maintain an army of fifty thousand or one hundred thousand men and send them forth to enslave the people.[11]

When the convention assembled, Virginia and nine other states had already ratified and North Carolina was likely to be put in an embarassing position, both economically and politically. As a result of this situation, Jones arose on the floor of the convention and quoted a letter from Jefferson advocating postponement of ratification until such amendments as had been sponsored by Virginia had been adopted.[12] With this policy he carried practically all of the state except the Albemarle Sound area and the commercial towns, the vote being 188 to 84.[13]

[10] Henry M. Wagstaff, *Federalism in North Carolina* (Chapel Hill, 1910), 5–44.

[11] Watson (ed.), *Memoirs of Elkanah Watson*, 262–64.

[12] Gilbert L. Lycan, "Alexander Hamilton and the North Carolina Federalists," in *North Carolina Historical Review* (Raleigh), XXV (1948), 448.

[13] Delbert H. Gilpatrick, *Jeffersonian Democracy in North Carolina, 1789–1816* (New York, 1931), 22–36; William K. Boyd, *History of North Carolina: The Federal Period, 1783–1860* (Chicago, 1919), 41–42.

In South Carolina the vote was strongly in favor of adoption because the coastal region, or Low Country as it is called locally, had an advantage in the matter of representation. With one-fifth of the population of the state and three-fourths of the wealth, it held preponderance of power in the legislature. The Low Country rice planters had their best market in the West Indies, and a strong central government could help them obtain more favorable treatment. It would also protect them against the inflationist policies of the radicals. Consequently, they voted almost solidly for adoption, with Charles Pinckney leading them.

Since short-staple cotton was not yet a commercial product, the upcountry settlers carried on a self-sustaining economy, based primarily upon the growing of corn and livestock. They helped to supply the Charleston market with country produce, but no navigable rivers connected them with that port, and their contacts with the outside world were quite limited. Rawlins Lowndes, a Low Country planter, was their leader. Like their counterparts in other states, they favored inflationary measures; hence they followed the usual trend of backwoodsmen and voted, with few exceptions, against adoption. The Federalists won by a vote of 149 to 73, but if numbers had counted, the upcountry would have defeated them.[14]

Georgia was the youngest, weakest, and most exposed of the Southern states. The settled area along the Savannah River and the Atlantic Coast was threatened by the Creek and Cherokee Indians, who occupied most of Georgia's western lands, and by the Spaniards, who controlled Florida on the south. Furthermore, rice was the state's principal export crop and her West Indian trade was important. Thus needing both military and economic protection, she voted unanimously for the Constitution.[15]

After eleven states ratified the Constitution and the new government was inaugurated in New York City, North Carolina

[14] John H. Wolfe, *Jeffersonian Democracy in South Carolina* (Chapel Hill, 1940), 28–32; David D. Wallace, *The History of South Carolina* (New York, 1934), II, 343–45; Ulrich B. Phillips, "The South Carolina Federalists," in *American Historical Review* (New York), XIV (1908–1909), 529–43; Beard, *Economic Interpretation of the Constitution*, 288–89.

[15] Beard, *Economic Interpretation of the Constitution*, 290; Libby, *Geographical Distribution of the Vote . . . on the Federal Constitution*, 44–45.

found herself, along with Rhode Island, in an isolated position. She faced the possibility of having to pay tariff and tonnage duties in her trade with the other states, and she did not like the company she was keeping. Furthermore, the submission to the states of Madison's Bill of Rights, in the form of amendments to the Constitution, promised to remove North Carolina's main objection to that instrument. Consequently, a second convention met at Fayetteville on November 16, 1789, and proceeded to ratify by a vote of 195 to 77. With scattered exceptions, it was only in the Piedmont Region, where the influence of Willie Jones remained powerful, that the anti-Federalists were able to hold their own.[16]

All the Southern states had now accepted the new order, but it had not been an overwhelming victory. If the discrimination against the upcountry and the disfranchisement of the landless class had not prevented the majority of adult white males from throwing their full weight into the balance, the Constitution would almost certainly have been defeated in Virginia and South Carolina; and in that case it is not likely that a second convention would have been called in North Carolina. An isolated Georgia could hardly have functioned as an effective member of the Union. Thus the Potomac would have been the Southern boundary of the new government. Certainly in the Southern states most of the leaders of the popular cause were opposed to the adoption of the Constitution.

However, the spirit of change was in the air, and while Maryland, Virginia, and North Carolina continued for many years to function under their constitutions of 1776, Georgia adopted a new one in 1789 and South Carolina did the same the next year. The Georgia instrument was by no means radical, but it clearly reflected the influence of the new Federal Constitution and marked a modest advance in the direction of liberalism. A unicameral legislature had been set up in 1777, but now provision was made for a Senate and House of Representatives, and

---

[16] Richmond *Virginia Gazette*, December 3, 1789; Charleston *City Gazette*, February 16, 1789; Samuel A. Ashe, *History of North Carolina* (Greensboro, 1908–1925), II, 111; Lycan, "Alexander Hamilton and the North Carolina Federalists," *loc. cit.*, 449; Boyd, *History of North Carolina*, 43–44.

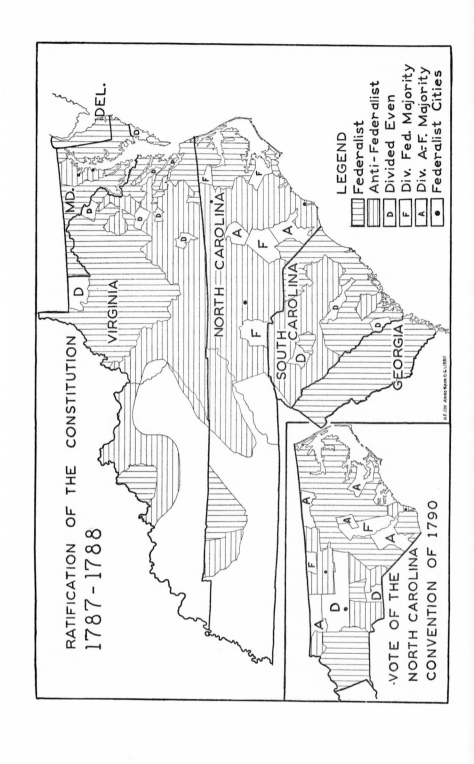

RATIFICATION OF THE CONSTITUTION
1787-1788

VOTE OF THE
NORTH CAROLINA
CONVENTION OF 1790

LEGEND
Federalist
Anti-Federalist
D    Divided Even
F    Div. Fed. Majority
A    Div. A-F. Majority
•    Federalist Cities

DEL.
MD.
VIRGINIA
NORTH-CAROLINA
SOUTH CAROLINA
GEORGIA

H.E.COX JR'60 ⓒ FROM D.G.LIBBY

the governor was to be elected by the Senate from a list of three names submitted by the House. High property qualifications were required of both legislators and governor, and the power of the executive was increased. He would serve two years instead of one as formerly allowed, and for the first time he was given the veto and the pardoning power. All religious qualifications for officeholding were dropped, and no clergyman of any denomination could be a member of the General Assembly. All elections would be by ballot, and the new instrument provided that "electors of the members of both branches of the general assembly shall be citizens and inhabitants of this State, and shall have attained to the age of twenty-one years, and have paid tax for the year preceding the election, and shall have resided six months within the county." [17] This was more liberal than the property qualification required for voting in the other Southern states, and there was nothing in the letter of the law to prevent women from voting if they so desired, but the changes were opposed by some radical politicians as being more conservative than the constitution of 1777.[18] There was the usual conflict of interests between the older settlements and the rapidly growing back country, and this manifested itself principally in a struggle over the apportionment of representation. Though this constitution of 1789 set up a rigid apportionment as between the counties, it anticipated future difficulties by providing for another convention to meet five years later.

On the other hand, the constitution which South Carolina adopted in 1790 was to remain in effect, with few changes, until 1865. Since the upcountry was grossly underrepresented under the old government, its demand for a redistribution of seats in the legislature and for the permanent location of the capital at Columbia was primarily responsible for the calling of this convention. Columbia was designated as the location of the capital in 1786; the legislature first met there in an unfinished wooden statehouse in January, 1790. The convention met there in May, and the permanent location of the seat of government was one

[17] William W. Abbot, "The Structure of Politics in Georgia, 1782–1789," in *William and Mary Quarterly* (Williamsburg), 3d ser., XIV (1957), 47–65.
[18] Savannah *Georgia Gazette*, January 1, 1789.

of its major problems. After a bitter fight between the upcountry and Low Country factions, Columbia won by a vote of 109 to 105. Nevertheless, important state offices were still to be maintained in Charleston, and the legislature was given the right to change the location of the capital by a two-thirds vote—a power which it never exercised.

The question of representation was even more important. Up to this time the Low Country districts had undisputed control of state politics. The upcountry was insistent in its demand for a change in this situation, but members of the convention were elected according to the old distribution and with the old property qualifications for voting. The natural result was that the conservatives were still in control and, though the upcountry was given a 67 per cent increase in the House and some increase in the Senate, the Low Country aristocracy retained control of both houses, a control maintained until 1807.[19] This was neither democratic nor politically just, but the traditions of private honor and public responsibility maintained by the landed gentry furnished a leadership well above the American average.[20] The Charlestonians apparently were in full accord with Thomas Carlyle's dictum that one cannot secure wisdom in government through the collective ignorance and folly of swarms of men.

Like the framers of the constitutions of the Revolutionary years, these also distrusted executive authority and placed practically all powers in the hands of the legislature. It elected the governor, who was not given the veto, and chose practically all other state and local officials. The fact that democracy was not a potent force at the time is demonstrated by the lack of opposition to the retention of high property qualifications for members of the legislature. Voters were required to possess a fifty-acre freehold or to pay a three-shilling tax in the district where they lived. If the convention was not democratic, it was liberal according to eighteenth-century standards, for it ordered the aboli-

[19] Wolfe, *Jeffersonian Democracy in South Carolina*, 5–6, 44–47; Benjamin Perley Poore (ed.), *The Federal and State Constitutions, Colonial Charters, and Other Organic Laws of the United States* (Washington, 1878), II, 1628–34; Wallace, *History of South Carolina*, II, 343–51.

[20] Wallace, *History of South Carolina*, II, 351.

tion of primogeniture and, for the first time, established complete religious freedom in the state. But it did not submit its handiwork for ratification by a vote of the people.[21]

Though political conservatism was in the ascendant in all Southern states, the outbreak of the French Revolution in the summer of 1789 aroused a wave of enthusiasm throughout the entire region. In the beginning it was not a radical movement, and Lafayette's participation seemed to link the old allies in a bond of common sympathy. Thomas Paine, in his *Rights of Man* in 1791, was loud in praise of the American system of government. It was widely read and approved in this country, and Thomas Jefferson gave it his benediction. But there were partisans of Britain who, like John Randolph of Roanoke, condemned it, and a lively controversy was carried on in the Richmond press.[22] In Norfolk two French officers who came ashore with women passengers were requested to return to their ship when they refused to remove their cockades.[23]

When news of the French victory at Valmy reached this country, there was widespread rejoicing. Governor William Moultrie of South Carolina ordered an elaborate military parade in Charleston to celebrate the event.[24] There was jubilation also at Halifax, North Carolina, where "a number of gentlemen, friends of the French Revolution," assembled to celebrate the success of the French armies over their enemies. They drank patriotic and sentimental toasts, each accompanied by a discharge of cannon. In Richmond a member of the Society of the Cincinnati proposed a meeting to express satisfaction over the French victory and to consider disbanding the Society, "as artificial distinctions are unrepublican." Little, however, was heard of the "September massacres" resulting from the French victory.[25]

[21] *Ibid.*, 350–51; Poore (ed.), *Federal and State Constitutions*, II, 1628–34.

[22] Richmond *Virginia Gazette*, June 1, July 13, August 3, 10, 24, 31, 1791; Henry B. Fearon, *Sketches of America* (London, 1818), 359; William P. Cresson, *James Monroe* (Chapel Hill, 1946), 116; Garland, *John Randolph of Roanoke*, 54–58, 76; William E. Dodd, *The Life of Nathaniel Macon* (Raleigh, 1903), 71–72.

[23] Annapolis *Maryland Gazette*, August 18, 1791.

[24] Charleston *City Gazette*, January 13, 1793.

[25] Halifax *North-Carolina Journal*, January 23, 1793; Lexington *Kentucky Gazette*, March 23, 1793.

The scene changed when, in 1793, the execution of the King and Queen, the Reign of Terror, and Britain's entry into the war against France strengthened the friends of England and promoted the development of the first political parties in America.

In domestic matters there was a deceptive calm as the new government got under way. The popularity of Washington tended to reconcile the late anti-Federalists, and the return of prosperity created a favorable atmosphere. All the Southern states sent Federalist majorities to Congress; but Virginia's two Senators, Richard Henry Lee and William Grayson, were anti-Federalists. They were succeeded before the end of the first Congress by John Taylor of Caroline and James Monroe, who were of the same political creed. North Carolina's delegation in the House was made up of three Federalists and two anti-Federalists, and in the Virginia delegation the Federalists outnumbered their opponents seven to three, with James Madison taking the lead in support of Administration measures.[26]

Washington's first year in office saw the government set up in New York City, and the measures necessary for its organization met no serious opposition; not even Alexander Hamilton's tariff bill which levied import duties averaging 8 per cent aroused any appreciable hostility. It is true that there was some conflict of interest, for the South imported most of its manufactured goods, whereas the industrial towns of the North were suffering from British competition. Southern leaders, however, recognized the justice of the demand of the craftsmen and shopkeepers for a moderate degree of protection, and no sectional quarrel developed over this issue.[27]

The situation was similar in regard to tonnage duties and excise taxes. At this time the Southern states were more dependent than the Northern on foreign shipping, and to levy tonnage duties on foreign vessels would result in increased freight rates.

[26] *Annals of Congress*, 1 Cong., 1 Sess., 381.

[27] *American State Papers. Documents, Legislative and Executive, of the Congress of the United States* (Washington, 1832–1861), VII, 5; *The Journal of William Maclay, United States Senator from Pennsylvania, 1789–1791* (New York, 1929), 57–58.

However, Madison supported this measure, and so did most of his Southern colleagues.[28]

There was more serious opposition to the excise tax on spirituous liquors which, after bitter debate, became law in 1791. The making of whisky was rapidly becoming a widespread domestic industry in the western parts of the Southern states, where it was difficult to ship grain to market and where the hardy farmer had developed a taste for the contents of the little brown jug. Indeed, many frontiersmen felt whisky to be as much the staff of life as bread. In North Carolina, especially, was the feeling against the excise strongly pronounced, and the legislature of the state expressed that feeling by instructing its delegation in Congress to vote against the tax. Her two Federalist Senators, Samuel Johnston and Benjamin Hawkins, refused to obey, but the delegation in the House voted solidly against the measure. So strong was the opposition in this and other Southern states that the law was amended the next year by reducing the tax and exempting small distilleries altogether.[29] Thus a serious situation in the back country, where tax collectors were unpopular, was averted.

Even more widespread was the opposition to Hamilton's plans for funding the national debt and assuming those of the states. There was no question as to the obligation of the new government to discharge the financial obligations, both foreign and domestic, of the old, but there was a wide difference of opinion as to how this should be accomplished. Hamilton's proposal was to pay off the old Continental currency at the rate of one dollar for one hundred. This amounted almost to repudiation, but the loan certificates which had been issued by the Continental Congress would be redeemed at face value plus accrued interest. These certificates had sold as low as three shillings eight pence in the pound as late as 1786, but the expectation that the new

[28] *Annals of Congress*, 1 Cong., 1 Sess., 643; *Journal of William Maclay*, 94; Garland, *John Randolph of Roanoke*, 41; Krout and Fox, *Completion of Independence*, 152–53.

[29] Edenton *State Gazette of North-Carolina*, August 27, 1790; Richmond *Virginia Gazette, and General Advertiser*, February 22, July 13, September 14, 1791; Wagstaff, *Federalism in North Carolina*, 19; Gilpatrick, *Jeffersonian Democracy in North Carolina*, 53–54; Henry M. Wagstaff, *State Rights and Political Parties in North Carolina, 1776–1861* (Baltimore, 1906), 34–35.

government would redeem them at some figure caused them to rise to a value of eight shillings in the pound—40 per cent of par value—in 1789.[30] If they had been redeemed at the current rate there would have been no speculation and no problem, but both Hamilton and Madison thought that the national credit would be compromised if less than face value were paid. Yet the two differed on one important point. Hamilton wished to pay the full value to the actual holder, whereas Madison urged in the House that the original holders who had disposed of their certificates should share the profit with those who then possessed them.[31] This was the parting of the way between these two men, both of whom had worked for a more powerful Union than that actually created by the Constitution.

Hamilton, by a vote of thirty-six to fifteen, won his case for the actual holders of certificates and thereby set off a holocaust of speculation. He was not personally involved, but his Assistant Secretary, William Duer, plunged heavily and so did Robert Morris and a number of Congressmen. Swift couriers and fast-sailing ships were dispatched to the South to buy up certificates of unsuspecting holders, and many fortunes were made in Philadelphia, New York, and Boston. Though the boom ended in a financial panic in Philadelphia in 1792, and Duer took refuge in prison to escape an angry mob, a belief became widespread in the South that a "paper aristocracy" was being created in the North by the new government; this was one of the factors which was soon to bring about the creation of a new political party under Jefferson's leadership.[32]

Thus opposition to the funding of the national debt was more pronounced after the fact than it had been before. This was hardly the case in regard to assumption of state debts, and in

[30] Richmond *Virginia Gazette, and General Advertiser*, September 29, 1790; Edward Channing, *A History of the United States* (New York, 1905–1925), IV, 69.

[31] Claude G. Bowers, *Jefferson and Hamilton; The Struggle for Democracy in America* (Boston, 1944), 53.

[32] *Annals of Congress*, 2 Cong., 1 Sess., 1685; *Journal of William Maclay*, 173–75, 231; Richmond *Virginia Gazette, and General Advertiser*, April 25, 1792; Charleston *City Gazette*, May 17, 1792; Beard, *Economic Interpretation of the Constitution*, 287; Charles A. Beard, "Some Economic Origins of Jeffersonian Democracy," in *American Historical Review*, XIX (1913–1914), 282–98; Bowers, *Jefferson and Hamilton*, 49; Channing, *History of the United States*, IV, 102.

the House of Representatives Maryland voted four to two against it. The legislature of Virginia passed resolutions condemning the measure by a vote of eighty-eight to forty-seven, and in Congress her representatives all opposed it except Richard Bland Lee and Alexander White. Theodoric Bland did not vote.[33] Lee and Bland represented the impoverished Tidewater section which felt the need of Federal assistance and White spoke for the nationalistic Shenandoah Valley. The North Carolina representatives cast a solid vote against it, for both she and Virginia had paid off a considerable part of their Revolutionary debts and did not wish to be taxed to help pay those of other states.[34] South Carolina favored assumption and her delegation in Congress voted solidly for it. This was because she had taken over the debts which Congress owed her citizens, and thus a large balance would be due her under Hamilton's plan.[35] On the other hand, Georgia would come in for a very small proportion of the payments to be made to the states, far less than her rightful share, as she claimed, and thus was bitterly opposed to assumption.[36] The opposition was sufficiently strong to defeat the move until Jefferson made his famous deal with Hamilton whereby the Secretary of State lined up enough Virginia votes to assure the passage of the Assumption Bill on condition that Hamilton would use his influence to have the permanent national capital located on the Potomac.[37]

Hamilton's move to charter a Bank of the United States ran into similar opposition. The commercial states favored it, but the agricultural interests were opposed. Since four-fifths of the ten million dollars of stock would be sold to private investors, agrarians feared that too much financial and political power

[33] Irving Brant, *James Madison, Father of the Constitution, 1787–1800* (Indianapolis, 1950), 325; Charles H. Ambler, *Sectionalism in Virginia from 1776 to 1861* (Chicago, 1910), 61–63.

[34] Edenton *State Gazette of North-Carolina*, May 1, 1790; Richmond *Virginia Gazette, and General Advertiser*, January 12, 1791; Lycan, "Alexander Hamilton and the North Carolina Federalists," *loc. cit.*, 450–52; Gilpatrick, *Jeffersonian Democracy in North Carolina*, 42–52.

[35] Charleston *City Gazette*, March 27, 1789; January 22, 1792; Wolfe, *Jeffersonian Democracy in South Carolina*, 56; *Journal of William Maclay*, 281.

[36] Savannah *Georgia Gazette*, May 14, 1789; May 9, 1793.

[37] *Annals of Congress*, 2 Cong., 1 Sess., 1755.

would be placed in the hands of capitalists who would be concentrated in the Eastern cities, or even in foreign countries. The opposition stressed the fact that the Constitution had not stated that the Federal government had the right to establish such an institution, and they argued that no powers other than those specifically delegated to it should be assumed by the central authority.[38] Thus the issue of state rights was clearly drawn, but Hamilton won and the bank was established. Of the twenty votes cast against it in the House, nineteen were those of Southern members and no Southern state had a majority in its favor.[39]

Another important measure which provoked considerable debate was the Judiciary Act. No one denied the fact that Congress had to establish a system of Federal courts, but when it was provided that the Supreme Court could entertain appeals from the highest state courts when the interpretation of the Federal Constitution was involved and rights claimed under it were denied, the state rights element was disturbed. State laws would thereby come under Federal scrutiny and stand the chance of being held invalid. This was in accord with the clause in the Constitution making Federal laws and treaties the supreme law of the land, yet it threatened the power of the individual states. Therefore it was opposed by some Southern members of Congress, but without success.[40]

It was not long before this question became a practical one. In 1790 the North Carolina Superior Court refused to honor a certiorari from the Federal Circuit Court in the case of a suit by a British creditor. The state court referred the matter to the legislature which approved the Superior Court's action and, furthermore, declined to require state officials to take an oath to support the Federal Constitution.[41] British merchants sued for a recovery of their debts in Richmond, and with Patrick

[38] Henry H. Simms, *Life of John Taylor* (Richmond, 1932), 56–57; Ashe, *History of North Carolina*, II, 126; Lycan, "Alexander Hamilton and the North Carolina Federalists," *loc. cit.*, 454.

[39] Lycan, "Alexander Hamilton and the North Carolina Federalists," *loc. cit.*, 453; Savannah *Georgia Gazette*, May 9, 1793; *Annals of Congress*, 1 Cong., 3 Sess., 2012; Bowers, *Jefferson and Hamilton*, 75–76; Simms, *John Taylor*, 50.

[40] *Annals of Congress*, 1 Cong., 1 Sess., 928–29.

[41] Ashe, *History of North Carolina*, II, 122–23.

Henry and Richard Henry Lee pleading the cause of the defendants, the merchants lost their case. The old established merchants in Charleston circularized those in the other states with a view to petitioning Congress for relief.[42]

In 1792 Georgia became the defendant in two cases before the Supreme Court, and in both of them she was defeated. In Georgia v. Brailsford the high tribunal held that pre-Revolutionary debts owed the British merchants would have to be paid despite the fact that the state had confiscated them. In the more famous case of Chisholm v. Georgia, the state refused to defend herself, but the court ruled, in a decision handed down in 1793, that a state could be sued by citizens of other states and of foreign countries. Thus the sovereignty of the states was denied and a furor was aroused which had financial as well as constitutional implications. By 1798 the Eleventh Amendment reversed this nationalistic decision, but in the meantime Georgia, largely because of this and the trouble she had with the Federal government over the Indian question, was converted from a strongly Federalist to a strongly Republican point of view.[43]

Thus political factions developed, and the leaders of the country were drifting apart. Though Jefferson and Hamilton collaborated in bringing about the passage of the Assumption Bill, the contrasting personalities and conflicting opinions of the two Secretaries were certain to result in a severing of relationship before long. Madison split with Hamilton on the question of funding the national debt, and at about the same time he made a move which was fraught with important political consequences. John Fenno, an editor of "great vituperative gifts," began printing the Gazette of the United States in New York in 1789 and presently followed the government to Philadelphia. He did the printing for the Treasury and the Senate; his columns set forth the opinions of Adams and Hamilton on political matters. When Madison split with Hamilton, he was anxious to combat the influence of Fenno's Gazette and approached Jefferson about setting

[42] Charleston City Gazette, February 27, 1792.
[43] Halifax North-Carolina Journal, March 20, 1793; Savannah Georgia Gazette, March 4, 1792; May 9, 1793; Ulrich B. Phillips, Georgia and State Rights (Washington, 1902), 15–28.

up a paper under the editorship of Philip Freneau, Revolutionary poet and hack writer of acknowledged ability. It was finally arranged that Freneau would become a part-time translation clerk in Jefferson's Department of State, thereby having access to official papers, and would set up an anti-Hamilton paper at the seat of government. The first issue of the *National Gazette* came off the press on October 31, 1791, with Madison, Jefferson, and Henry Lee—Federalist governor of Virginia—all turning in lists of subscribers.[44] The newspaper war was now on between the rival leaders, and political parties were in the making.

By the end of Washington's first administration parties were definitely forming, but the lines were not yet clearly drawn. In 1792 Henry Lee was re-elected governor of Virginia. Washington's birthday was celebrated by this Federalist with a dinner at the Eagle Tavern in Richmond. Toasts were drunk to the French King, to the legislature, and to the people of France; to the King, diet, and people of Poland; and to Madison, "the Congressional defender of the rights and happiness of the people." Some apprehension was expressed by a toast which urged that "the government of the United States obey and not pervert the principles of the Constitution," and another which demanded that Congress hold no secret debates.[45]

The popularity of the President was not always shared by his Secretary of the Treasury; as the first term of the first President drew to a close, Hamilton's enemies tried to discredit him. Leaders of the opposition in the House of Representatives were Madison and William Branch Giles of Virginia, along with Nathaniel Macon of North Carolina. On February 27, 1793, Giles, an able, voluble, and aggressive young man, brought in nine resolutions —generally attributed to the suggestion of Jefferson and the pen of Madison—criticizing the administration of the Secretary of the Treasury. These resolutions received much notice in the Southern press and the *Virginia Gazette* of Richmond published

[44] Stephen Decatur, Jr., *Private Affairs of George Washington, From the Records and Accounts of Tobias Lear, Esquire, His Secretary* (Boston, 1933), 284; Brant, *James Madison, Father of the Constitution*, 336.

[45] Richmond *Virginia Gazette, and General Advertiser*, February 15, October 27, 1792.

at length the debates which they produced. The most serious charge made against Hamilton was that he borrowed $400,000 from the Bank of the United States at 5 per cent interest when the Treasury already had more than that sum on hand subject to his disposal.[46] When this resolution was put to vote, only eight members supported it, namely: John B. Ashe, Federalist of North Carolina; Abraham Baldwin, Federalist of Georgia; William Findley, Irish democrat of Westmoreland County, Pennsylvania, later involved in the Whisky Rebellion; John Francis Mercer of Maryland; Nathaniel Macon of North Carolina; and Giles Madison, and Josiah Parker of Virginia.[47] The term "Federalist" at this time referred to one who had supported the adoption of the Constitution, and this vote shows that a new alignment was taking place. It shows also that Hamilton's star was in the ascendant, and that Madison, Jefferson, and Freneau had made little headway against him.

Though the opposition was worsted, it was not dead, and within a few years it was to win a resounding victory. Its strength lay in its support of the agrarian cause, its adherence to the liberal principles of the American Revolution, and its sympathetic attitude toward the revolution which was going on in France.

There were three important economic groups in the South: the small farmers who operated a self-sufficing agricultural system and depended mostly on their own labor, the large landowners who produced the staple crops by means of slave labor, and the merchants who furnished credit to the planters. Of these groups, the farmers were never inclined to favor strong-handed governments and were, therefore, predominantly opposed to the adoption of the Constitution and to the measures which Hamilton brought forward to implement it. The planters were divided in their views, but as stated, those who devoted their attention to the production of small grain and rice needed a strong central government to promote interstate and West Indian trade and

[46] *Ibid.*, May 23–June 3, 1793; Lexington *Kentucky Gazette*, August 3, September 7, 1793; *Annals of Congress*, 2 Cong., 2 Sess., 899 ff.; Dice R. Anderson, *William Branch Giles; A Study in the Politics of Virginia and the Nation from 1790 to 1830* (Menasha, Wis., 1914), 21–25.

[47] *Annals of Congress*, 2 Cong., 2 Sess., 959–60; Lexington *Kentucky Gazette*, September 7, 1793.

therefore favored the adoption of the Constitution and a strong central authority. The tobacco planters needed no such support and they were normally anti-Federalists. The merchants were overwhelmingly Federalist, but Hamilton's measures alienated some whose interests were largely local; the Albemarle Sound region, along with Georgia, transferred its allegiance to the Jeffersonian party. Thus in the Southern states federalism was left as a decidedly minority element except in South Carolina.

The political differences of these years were not sectional in nature, and both the Southern and Northern states divided their allegiance between Hamilton and Jefferson. Yet the agrarian interest predominated below the Mason and Dixon line, as did the mercantile interest north of it. "The South" as we know it had not come into existence, for the term always carries Confederate connotations; the usual reference was to "the Southern States," but sectional differences did exist. These were based as much upon differences in culture as upon those arising from diverse economic interests, but they were no less strong for that reason. Northern papers frequently spoke slightingly of the South as a land of slavery and loose living, while the Charleston *City Gazette* published an article in April, 1792, lamenting the hostile tone which Southern papers took toward the North. "The enemies of our union take care to fan the flame," it declared and reminded its readers that not all Northerners were speculators.[48]

[48] Knoxville *Gazette*, November 17, 1792; Halifax *North-Carolina Journal*, October 30, 1793; Edenton *State Gazette of North-Carolina*, February 13, April 10, 1790; Charleston *City Gazette*, April 20, 1792.

# CHAPTER III

# CONTEST FOR THE WEST

WHILE George Washington was organizing the government of the United States and the people who lived along the Atlantic Seaboard were taking advantage of their newly acquired opportunities in political and economic affairs, the country west of the Appalachian Mountains was in turmoil. In 1783 Britain recognized our right to the land as far west as the Mississippi River and as far south as the thirty-first parallel, but in Louisiana and Florida Spain controlled the country to the south and west and also claimed all that region lying south of the Tennessee River and west of the Appalachians. In New Orleans she had the only port through which the Kentucky and Tennessee settlements could send their bulky exports to market; and Natchez, though in territory claimed by the United States, was in Spanish possession.

This, moreover, was not the only hold which Spain had on the Southwest. Except for a few isolated white settlements, the whole region was Indian country, and the Spanish governors at New Orleans and Pensacola undertook to control the native tribes. The strongest of these were the Creeks, who lived on the headwaters of the Alabama and the lower reaches of the Chattahoochee River in southern and western Georgia. Their chief was the famous half-breed, Alexander McGillivray, whose Scottish father had been a Charleston merchant. During the Revolution he had taken the British side and as a consequence had lost an estate valued at thirty thousand pounds. Alexander had been educated in Charleston and New York and was intelligent and shrewd, but his knowledge of the white man's civilization did nothing to soften his bitterness against the Americans. He now owned Negro

43

slaves and lived in primitive opulence on a plantation at the Indian village of Little Tallassee near the present town of Wetumpka, Alabama.[1]

The Indians were dependent on the whites for guns and ammunition as well as for many other necessary articles. Spain was not a manufacturing nation, and when she received Florida from the British in 1783, it was for this reason that she permitted the Scottish firm of Panton, Leslie and Company of Pensacola to continue its trade under Spanish auspices. It was from this firm that the Creeks normally got their supplies. In order to promote trade as well as to guarantee the influence of the Spanish government among the natives, Panton made McGillivray a partner in the business. At about the same time the Indian chief signed a treaty of alliance with the governor of Louisiana, who made him a Spanish agent with the rank and pay of colonel.[2]

Another reason for hostility between the Creeks and the Americans was the quarrel with Georgia over lands. Until 1785 the Georgia settlements were confined to a narrow strip of territory along the Savannah River and the Atlantic Coast, but as a result of brief wars during that and the next year the Creeks were forced to agree to the treaties of Galphinton and Shoulder-Bone, which ceded territory extending all the way to the Florida line. But McGillivray was determined that there should be no peace with Georgia as long as she lay claim to any land beyond the Ogeechee River. The Spaniards thus had a powerful ally, but he was not habitually tractable.[3]

[1] Fayetteville *North-Carolina Chronicle*, October 11, 1790; Samuel C. Williams, "French and Other Intrigues in the Southwest Territory, 1790–96," in East Tennesee Historical Society *Publications* (Knoxville), No. 13 (1941), 21; Arthur P. Whitaker, "Spain and the Cherokee Indians, 1783–98," in *North Carolina Historical Review*, IV (1927), 253; George White, *Historical Collections of Georgia* (New York, 1854), 154.

[2] Henry Knox to George Washington, July 6, 1789, in *American State Papers, Indian Affairs*, I, 15–16; Stephen Catterell to W. W. Grenville, April 17, 1790, in *American Historical Review*, VIII (1902–1903), 78–86; Albert J. Pickett, *History of Alabama* (reprint, Birmingham, 1900), 395–96; Louise F. Hays, *Hero of Hornet's Nest; A Biography of Elijah Clarke* (New York, 1946), 181–82.

[3] Bonds, Bills of Sale, Deeds of Gifts, Powers of Attorney (Georgia Department of Archives and History, Atlanta), D (1792–1813), 260; Alexander McGillivray to Esteban Miró, February 1, 1789, in East Tennessee Historical Society *Publications*, No. 19 (1947), 82–85.

In 1786 Spain was represented in Philadelphia by Don Diego de Gardoqui, who was trying to negotiate a commercial treaty with John Jay on behalf of the old Congress. He proposed to make certain concessions to the states in their trade with Spain, though not with her West Indian possessions, in case Congress relinquished for a period of twenty or thirty years the American claim to free trade down the Mississippi River.[4] The Eastern states favored this proposal and Jay, who represented their interests, recommended its adoption by Congress, but the Southern states, and especially their western settlers, were incensed. Development of the West depended upon the navigation of the river, and if this should remain closed, it seemed certain that the country beyond the Appalachians would eventually break its connection with the Atlantic states and come to terms with the power which could open to them the port of New Orleans. Gardoqui well understood this situation, and it is clear that he was much more interested in the separation of the West than in the trade of the East.[5]

Though the Western settlements were few and isolated, immigrants poured in by the thousands during the years following the Revolution, and they were rugged men. They could float down the rivers to New Orleans without hindrance and that city was almost defenseless. Esteban Miró, governor of both Louisiana and Florida, was keenly aware of the vulnerability of his capital, and his main reliance was upon his Indian allies. But if the West could be separated from the East, the danger would be removed.

In order to separate the West from the East, it was necessary that the leading settlers in the Tennessee and Kentucky country should favor the scheme, but as long as the Indians were attacking the settlements, presumably with Spanish support, there was no chance of an agreement. McGillivray and his Creeks were not only attacking the Georgia frontiers; they were making common

[4] Whitaker, *Spanish-American Frontier*, 74–77.
[5] James Wilkinson to Miró, February 12, 14, 1789, in Charles Gayarré, *History of Louisiana* (New Orleans, 1885), III, 231, 240–47; excerpt from New York *Gazette*, inclosed in Diego Gardoqui to Floridablanca, March 4, 1789, in East Tennessee Historical Society *Publications*, No. 19 (1947), 92–93.

cause with the Chickamauga branch of the Cherokee nation, whose villages were near the present city of Chattanooga, to attack the Kentucky settlements and those about Nashville on the Cumberland River. Though Miró made treaties with the Chickasaw and Choctaw nations, as well as with the Creeks, Spain did not claim the territory of the Cherokee and Miró did not try to bring them under his control, but they received their arms from Spanish Florida and their attacks were credited to Spanish influence.[6]

Gardoqui, who represented the views of the Spanish court, was anxious to make friends of the Western settlers. In 1786 he approached John Brown, a member of Congress who represented the Kentucky District of Virginia, and suggested that, if the Westerners would separate themselves from the East and enter into an alliance with Spain, they would be allowed political and religious freedom and granted free use of the port of New Orleans. Brown relayed this information to his Kentucky friends, George Muter, Samuel McDowell, and Christopher Greenup. The "Spanish Conspiracy" was thus under way.[7]

John Brown, however, was not to be the leading actor in this drama. James Wilkinson, a native Marylander, had married Anne Biddle, daughter to John Biddle and sister to Owen and Clement Biddle of a prominent Quaker family of Philadelphia. He had served as Clothier General in the Revolution with considerable discredit and later was a Brigadier General of Pennsylvania militia. Finding himself at loose ends after the war, he migrated to Kentucky in 1784 and set himself up in the mercantile business.[8] Here his ambition was not confined to the prosaic pursuits of trade and he began to look about for more exciting enterprises. He thought he saw an opportunity when George Rogers Clark made a raid on some Spanish trading boats at Vin-

---

[6] Whitaker, "Spain and the Cherokee Indians," *loc. cit.*, 254; John Sevier to Governor George Mathews, August 3, 1787, in *American Museum*, II (Philadelphia, 1788), 580.

[7] Lexington *Kentucky Gazette*, July 12, 1806; Joseph H. Daveiss, *A View of the President's Conduct Concerning the Conspiracy of 1806* (Frankfort, 1807), reprinted in *Quarterly Publications of the Historical and Philosophical Society of Ohio* (Cincinnati), XII (1917), 61–62.

[8] Allen Johnson *et al.* (eds.), *Dictionary of American Biography* (New York, 1928–), XX, 222–26; James R. Jacobs, *Tarnished Warrior; Major-General James Wilkinson* (New York, 1938), 59–61.

cennes toward the end of the year 1786. Wilkinson wrote to the Spanish commandant at St. Louis, giving an account of this affair and warning that Clark and Colonel Thomas Green were planning an attack on Natchez for the spring of 1787.[9]

In 1784 the Spaniards closed the trade of the Mississippi to Americans and were seizing boats of the Westerners when they arrived at Natchez. Wilkinson evidently heard of the conversations between Brown and Gardoqui and took this occasion to apply to the Spaniard for a passport to New Orleans. He made the same request of Governor Edmund Randolph of Virginia, but in neither case did he receive a favorable response.[10] Being a man of resource and determination, he did not allow these refusals to deter him but decided to gamble on the event. Collecting a cargo of tobacco, pork, and flour, he loaded a large flatboat and headed down the Ohio to New Orleans. On June 16, 1787, he reached Natchez and Governor Don Carlos de Grand Pré permitted him to proceed without a passport. On arrival at his destination, he made contact with Daniel Clark, an Irish merchant who had migrated to New Orleans by way of Philadelphia and who now had considerable influence with Governor Miró. The result was that Miró bought Wilkinson's tobacco at a high price on behalf of the government monopoly and gave him the sole right to grant licenses to Kentuckians who wished to engage in the New Orleans trade. Wilkinson, on his part, took an oath of allegiance as a subject of the King of Spain. He gave Miró to understand that the attack by the Kentuckians had been postponed only because of his negotiations and that this monopoly of the tobacco trade would induce them to seek similar privileges by setting up a separate government, subordinate to Spain. Finally, he boarded a ship for Charleston in September.[11]

[9] *Hispanic American Historical Review* (Baltimore, Durham), VII (1927), 42–48; James A. James, *The Life of George Rogers Clark* (Chicago, 1928), 372–78.

[10] Louis Pelzer, "Economic Factors in the Acquisition of Louisiana," in Mississippi Valley Historical Association *Proceedings* (Cedar Rapids), VI (1912–1913), 114; Arthur P. Whitaker, "James Wilkinson's First Descent to New Orleans in 1787," in *Hispanic American Historical Review*, VIII (1928), 83–97.

[11] Whitaker, "James Wilkinson's First Descent to New Orleans in 1787," *loc. cit.*, 83–97; Pelzer, "Economic Factors in the Acquisition of Louisiana," *loc. cit.*, 117; William H. Safford (ed.), *The Blennerhassett Papers* (Cincinnati, 1861), 68–69;

Proceeding overland to Kentucky, he collected a large supply of tobacco and provisions, and in May, 1788, his agent, Major Isaac B. Dunn, set out for New Orleans with twenty-five armed flatboats and one hundred fifty men. He carried a letter from Wilkinson to Miró saying that Kentucky was to separate from Virginia and that a constitutional convention had been called. He thought that Congress would accept the new state, but because of the apparent willingness of that body to surrender the navigation of the Mississippi, the people preferred a connection with Spain on condition that the port of New Orleans be opened to their trade.[12] However, if the Westerners were to be conciliated, McGillivray's attacks against the frontier would have to be stopped. The Spanish government decided to undertake this difficult task, and toward the end of 1787 Miró was ordered to stop the supply of arms to the Creeks and to open the navigation of the Mississippi to the Americans upon payment of a 15 per cent duty.[13]

So fierce were McGillivray's attacks that on January 4, 1788, James Robertson and Anthony Bledsoe of the Cumberland settlements wrote to Governor Samuel Johnston of North Carolina urging him to appeal to Gardoqui to put a stop to Creek hostilities. John Sevier of the Watauga settlements wrote to the same effect, and the governor sent their letters to Dr. James White, member of Congress from North Carolina and Superintendent of Indian Affairs for the Southern Department. White showed these letters to Gardoqui, who, on April 18, wrote to Johnston, Robertson, and Sevier, expressing the good will of Spain.[14]

---

deposition of Richard Thomas, n.d., in Harry Innes Papers (Division of Manuscripts, Library of Congress), Bk. 22, Pt. II; statement of Daniel Clark, *American State Papers*, XX, 704–705.

[12] Extract of a letter dated Louisville, January 16, 1789, in East Tennessee Historical Society *Publications*, No. 19 (1947), 96; Safford (ed.), *Blennerhassett Papers*, 13–14; Jacobs, *Tarnished Warrior*, 83; Joseph C. Robert, *The Story of Tobacco in America* (New York, 1949), 53.

[13] John W. Caughey, *McGillivray of the Creeks* (Norman, Okla., 1938), 34–35.

[14] Archibald Henderson, "The Spanish Conspiracy in Tennessee," in *Tennessee Historical Magazine* (Nashville), III (1917), 232–33.

Letters which Robertson and Bledsoe wrote directly to Mc-Gillivray received a less favorable response,[15] but Gardoqui decided to take advantage of the distress of the Westerners to forward his plan to separate them from the Eastern states. During 1788 the state of affairs both in North Carolina and Virginia clearly seemed to favor his operations. In 1784 the settlements in what is now East Tennessee declared their independence from North Carolina and set up the "State of Franklin," with Sevier as governor.[16] By 1788 this wilderness republic had run its course, but North Carolina now voted against the adoption of the new Federal Constitution, and Sevier saw a fresh opportunity in this situation. If, by making terms with Spain, he could acquire the right to establish settlements along the southern bank of the Tennessee as far west as the headwaters of the Tombigbee and Yazoo rivers, his people could trade with both New Orleans and Mobile and establish an inland empire of importance. Gardoqui now sent Dr. White to negotiate with him, and Sevier was in proper mood to accept the offer of a Spanish alliance. On September 12 he wrote Gardoqui that the inhabitants of "Frankland" were unanimous in their "vehement desire" to form an alliance and make a treaty of commerce with Spain, putting themselves under her protection. In aid of his plan, Sevier was soon negotiating with the Cherokee Indians for a cession of land on the Tombigbee River.[17]

White next visited the Cumberland settlements where he owned property. He talked with Robertson and other local leaders and found they had no such ambitions as did Sevier. Nevertheless, seeing no other chance of freeing themselves from the merciless attacks of the Indians or of obtaining an outlet for their trade down the Mississippi, they expressed readiness to listen to the Spanish overtures and then proceeded to name their district for the Louisiana Governor.[18] White then went to New

---

[15] *Ibid.*, 238–39; Caughey, *McGillivray of the Creeks*, 34–35.

[16] Abernethy, *From Frontier to Plantation in Tennessee*, 57, 67–72.

[17] Henderson, "Spanish Conspiracy in Tennessee," *loc. cit.*, 231; Gayarré, *History of Louisiana*, III, 257.

[18] Abernethy, *From Frontier to Plantation in Tennessee*, 96, 99; Abernethy, *Western Lands*, 342.

York to report his success to Gardoqui, who next sent him, accompanied by Sevier's son James, to New Orleans to discuss the project of the separation of the West with Governor Miró.[19] Gardoqui was pleased with what he had accomplished and on October 24 wrote to the Conde de Floridablanca, the Spanish Secretary of State, as follows: "I think I have done all possible to make it possible for the Government of New Orleans to reap benefit from the present situation of the United States. . . . Those people intend to live on friendly terms with Spain and we no longer hear the threats we formerly heard." He went on to say that it was difficult to tell what the Kentucky convention, scheduled to meet in November, would decide, because the Indian menace was more serious than it was supposed to be. He thought the Kentuckians would consider well before deciding, both because of their close ties with the United States and because of the Indian threats. If they did turn to Spain for help against the Indians, Gardoqui continued, "we must not neglect them. I think time will bring them to the King." Gardoqui further said that, by the last letter from Jay and by what he had found out about Jay's secret conference, it was clear that the extreme fear of some of the states that Spain would exclude them from the Mississippi had furnished the Spaniards "with what H.M. had planned." Yet, Gardoqui continued, "I have complained about the delay and threatened them with the exclusion of their goods or increased duties. . . . I believe the New Government will not dare to accept the arrangment that I agreed on with Mr. Jay until . . . [the government] becomes firmly established, in spite of the fact that the Atlantic states want it—people here are beginning to see the disadvantages of westward migration. I have postponed my voyage home until I see the result of the Kentucky Convention of Nov. 3, though I do not expect anything favorable from it immediately. It is important to cut off all communications from here to our possessions—this hint is significant." [20] Thus the Spanish Court was playing off the East against the West

[19] Gardoqui to Miró, October 3, 1788, in East Tennessee Historical Society *Publications*, No. 18 (1946), 132–33; Gayarré, *History of Louisiana*, III, 257–60; Henderson, "Spanish Conspiracy in Tennessee," *loc. cit.*, 232, 236.

[20] Gardoqui to Floridablanca, October 24, 1788, in East Tennessee Historical Society *Publications*, No. 18 (1946), 133–37.

with the object of bringing about the separation of the two regions.

Gardoqui sized up the situation in Kentucky quite accurately. The pioneers of the Bluegrass region were anxious to set up a separate state, and Virginia authorized this division of her territory. A Kentucky convention had voted in favor of applying to Congress for admission as a member of the Confederation, and on February 29, 1788, John Brown presented this petition to Congress. On July 28 the sixth Kentucky convention assembled to frame a constitution for the new state, but Congress took no action on the question of admission. Since Virginia made membership in the Confederation a condition of statehood, nothing could be done until Congress acted, and thus the convention was unable to proceed with its assignment. On July 3 the Congress, under the influence of certain members opposed to Western interests, finally came to the conclusion that, since the new Constitution would soon go into effect, the question of the admission of Kentucky should be referred to the government of the new Union.[21]

Brown looked upon this decision as another victory of the East over the West and thought that Kentucky could expect as little consideration from the new as from the old Congress so long as it was dominated by the seven states north of Maryland. He at once got in touch with Gardoqui, who told him that the Kentuckians could remove the difficulty by setting themselves up as a separate and sovereign state and negotiating with Spain for the free use of the port of New Orleans. Brown replied that he thought there was not the slightest doubt that the Kentucky convention would accept this proposal. At about the same time Wilkinson's agent, Major Dunn, called on Gardoqui, who reported to Miró that Dunn "went away apparently convinced by my reasoning—and those two are not the only ones who have gone away with similar instructions. In this way I hope they will produce the effect that is suitable to His Majesty's service." Brown informed Gardoqui that he was returning to Kentucky

[21] J. Dawson to Governor Beverley Randolph, January 29, 1789, in *Calendar of Virginia State Papers* (Richmond, 1875–1893), IV, 554–56; Lewis Collins, *History of Kentucky* (Covington, 1878), I, 21.

to work for the separation of that country from the Union and for an alliance with Spain, and Gardoqui sent an agent to New Orleans to inform Miró of this development.[22]

Meanwhile, on July 10 Brown wrote to his friend, Judge George Muter, about the action of Congress regarding separation of Kentucky and added: "The eastern states would not, nor do I think they ever will—assent to the admission of this district into the Union as an independent State unless the province of Vermont or Maine is brought forward at the same time. The change in the General Government is made the ostensible reason for this rejection—and jealousy of the growing importance of the Western country and unwillingness to add an extra vote to the Southern interest are the real causes of opposition." The Senator said that they now had to decide whether to remain a part of Virginia or declare their independence, and it was generally expected that Kentucky would declare her independence. He noted that Gardoqui assured him "in most explicit terms that if Kentucky will declare her independence and empower some proper person to negotiate with him, that he has authority and will engage to open the Mississippi to navigation on terms of mutual advantage, but that this privilege can never be extended to Kentucky while part of the United States by reason of commercial treaties existing between Spain and other powers of Europe." [23]

When news reached the Kentucky convention that Congress had postponed the question of statehood, indignation was hotly expressed by many of its members, but Wilkinson must have been jubilant, for the event made his problems much simpler. When Major Dunn set out for New Orleans in May, he carried a letter from Wilkinson to Miró saying that he thought Congress would admit Kentucky but that he planned to carry out his program for separation regardless of any such development. He assured his correspondent that, as soon as the new state government should be established, he would send agents to New Orleans

[22] Gardoqui to Miró, October 2, 1788, in East Tennessee Historical Society *Publications*, No. 18 (1946), 131–32; Charleston *City Gazette*, February 27, 1789.

[23] George Muter to Editor of the Frankfort *Kentucky Palladium*, August 20, 1806, quoted in Lexington *Kentucky Gazette*, September 1, 1806; *ibid.*, August 21, 1806; Frankfort *Kentucky Palladium*, August 20, 1806, quoted in Washington *National Intelligencer*, September 26, 1806; Richmond *Enquirer*, September 26, 1806.

to treat for a Spanish alliance. He was supported in Kentucky by most of the lawyers, land speculators, and politicians, including Harry Innes, Caleb Wallace, and Benjamin Sebastian, who now, for the first time, came out for prompt separation from the Union, but the Spanish connection was discreetly kept in the background. The opposition was led by Thomas Marshall, father of the future Chief Justice, and a few of his friends.[24]

In order to carry their point without revealing their real objectives, the Wilkinson clique succeeded in inducing the convention to pass resolutions calling for the election of a seventh convention "with full power to take such measures for obtaining admission of the district as a separate and independent State of the Union, and the navigation of the Mississippi, as may appear proper, and to form a constitutional Government in the District—or to do and accomplish whatever on a consideration of the state of the district may in their opinion promote its interests." [25] Plenary powers were thus bestowed upon a body which could have no legal existence unless the authority of Virginia were first obtained.

During September and October Kentucky waged an acrimonious contest over the election of members to this convention, with all factions airing their views in successive issues of the *Kentucky Gazette*. Opponents of the Wilkinson group urged that no election should be held because there was no authority for holding a convention and because the wide powers which were proposed for it would make it a dangerous conclave. Marshall's friends led the opposition, but the militia officers of the district proposed a compromise. According to their plan, elections would be held and the convention would meet, but the voters were to instruct the delegates as to their stand on the question of separation.[26]

On November 4 the seventh Kentucky convention assembled. John Brown returned from Congress for a seat in the body, and Wilkinson and most of his friends were delegates. The campaign

[24] Wilkinson to Miró, February 12, 1789, in Gayarré, *History of Louisiana*, III, 223–40.
[25] Abernethy, *Western Lands*, 348–49.
[26] Lexington *Kentucky Gazette*, January 3, 1789.

probably opened the eyes of the separatists to the fact that, though most of the Kentucky politicians were on their side, the people were not inclined to follow them. Nevertheless, they made an attempt to carry through their plans. Samuel McDowell was once again chosen president, and from the Chair he called on Wilkinson to tell of his negotiations of the previous year with the Spanish governor in New Orleans. Wilkinson responded by reading the memorial which he presented to Miró on that occasion. Then Brown related his experiences in Congress. Having sensed the local opposition to the Spanish intrigue, he spoke in a guarded manner but stressed the hostility of Congress to the idea of a new state and the benefits held out by Spain in case Kentucky should set up a government independent of the Confederation.[27]

But the people had instructed the delegates, and it soon became clear that a majority favored continued co-operation with Virginia. Wilkinson's friends realized their defeat and acquiesced. After some controversy a resolution was adopted which called once more on Virginia to extend the time allowed for the admission of Kentucky into the Union and to provide for the election of still another convention.[28] Brown drafted this resolution, and on November 23 he wrote to Madison that he had abandoned his plan for setting up a government independent of Congress.[29] Wilkinson also became discouraged and sent Major Dunn to petition Gardoqui for a grant of six hundred thousand acres on the Yazoo River to which he might retire in case of necessity.[30] Because of the Southern and Western agitation against it, Congress now suspended negotiation with Gardoqui regarding the surrender of the navigation of the Father of Waters, and the first phase of the Spanish Conspiracy thus came to an end.[31] But the idea

[27] Wilkinson to Miró, February 12, 1789, in Gayarré, *History of Louisiana*, III, 227–29; Thomas Marshall to Washington, February 12, 1789, in S. M. Hamilton (ed.), *Letters to George Washington* (Boston, 1901), IV, 245–51.

[28] Lexington *Kentucky Gazette*, April 20, 1827.

[29] Abernethy, *Western Lands*, 350.

[30] Major Isaac E. Dunn to Gardoqui, December 17, 1789, in East Tennessee Historical Society *Publications*, No. 19 (1947), 93; Gardoqui to Floridablanca, March 4, 1789, *ibid.*, 86–92; Wilkinson to Gardoqui, January 1, 1789, in Gayarré, *History of Louisiana*, III, 247; Wilkinson to Miró, February 14, 1789, *ibid.*, 240–47.

[31] Wilkinson to Miró, February 12, 1789, in Gayarré, *History of Louisiana*, III, 224–27; Whitaker, *Spanish-American Frontier*, 119–20.

was not dead, and it might well have succeeded had not the East surrendered in the matter of the navigation of the Mississippi and had not the new Constitution provided for a stronger central government to go into operation early in 1789.

Before the question of separation reached a culmination in Kentucky, the British made a feeble attempt to recapture the American West. Though the treaty of 1783 granted the United States all the territory east of the Mississippi River which lay between Florida and the Great Lakes, the British still held Detroit and a few other Northwestern posts, from which they carried on trade with neighboring tribes of Indians and exercised considerable influence over them. In the South they had no similar foothold, but they were still not reconciled to the loss of Florida to Spain and were anticipating renewal of hostilities with that power. If Spain could connive with the Kentuckians for a separation from the United States, so could Britain; and Lord Dorchester, Governor General of Canada, knew that there were leading characters, both in the East and the West, who favored such a separation and who preferred that it should be carried out under British rather than Spanish auspices. He accordingly opened correspondence with certain Eastern leaders and sent agents to Detroit and to Pittsburgh to investigate the situation in those places.[32] He also had correspondents in Kentucky and was furnished with a paper purporting to be that of a "Committee of Private Correspondence" there—probably drafted by Wilkinson himself—which advocated the creation of an independent West under British auspices.[33]

On October 25, 1788, Dr. John Connolly, who had been a British agent at Fort Pitt during the Revolutionary struggle, appeared in Louisville. He called on his old friend, John Campbell, who introduced him to Wilkinson and Thomas Marshall, the leaders respectively of the anti-Federalist and Federalist factions in Kentucky. Lord Dorchester reported to his government

---

[32] Schuyler D. Haslett, "Some Notes on British Intrigue in Kentucky," in *Register of the Kentucky State Historical Society* (Frankfort), XXXVIII (1940), 54–56; Lord Dorchester to Viscount Sydney, June 7, 1789, Colonial Office Papers (Public Record Office, London), Ser. XLII, No. 65; Abernethy, *Western Lands,* 357.

[33] Dorchester to Sydney, April 11, 1789, Colonial Office Papers, Ser. XLII, No. 64.

that private councils in Kentucky favored the establishment of
an independent government, of seizing New Orleans, and looking
to England for assistance. He submitted a memorial by a gentleman of Kentucky—presumably Wilkinson—declaring that the
West must be independent and must look to that power which
controlled the navigation of the Mississippi, whether it be Spain
or Great Britain. Actually Marshall refused to have any dealings
with the British agent, and Wilkinson presently informed Miró
that he had employed a hunter to feign an attack upon Connolly,
who fled in great fright. It was true that a burly backwoodsman
threatened Connolly in a tavern and caused his hasty departure,
an incident which tended to confirm Wilkinson's claim that he
was responsible for the affair. However, this archintriguer gave
Miró to understand that he could turn to the British in case
Spain did not meet his terms.[34]

While this intrigue was going on, another one was taking
shape in the South. In January, 1788, Miró informed McGillivray
that Spain would no longer furnish him with arms for his war
with the Georgians. This greatly disturbed the Creek chief, but
he had friends that he knew not of. Lord Dunmore, the last
colonial governor of Virginia, was now governor of the Bahama
Islands, and the Pensacola firm of Panton, Leslie and Company
carried on its Creek trade largely through Nassau, his capital
on New Providence Island. Dunmore had a connection with the
rival Nassau firm of Miller and Bonnamy, and together they

[34] Lexington *Kentucky Gazette*, July 12, 1806; Isaac J. Cox, "The Louisiana-Texas
Frontier," Pt. I, in *Southwestern Historical Quarterly* (Austin), XVII (1913–1914),
40–41; Frederick J. Turner, "The Diplomatic Contest for the Mississippi Valley,"
in *Atlantic Monthly* (Boston), XCIII (1904), 676–91, 807–17; Collin McCleod to
John Connolly, January 25, 1789, in George Morgan Papers (Illinois Historical
Survey, University of Illinois, Urbana); Gardoqui to Thomas Hutchins, February 25,
1789, *ibid.;* Dawson to Governor Randolph, January 29, 1789, in *Calendar of Virginia State Papers*, IV, 554–56; Thomas Marshall to Washington, February 12, 1789,
in Hamilton (ed.), *Letters to George Washington*, IV, 245–51; Madison to Washington, March 8, 1789, *ibid.*, 251–52; Gayarré, *History of Louisiana*, III, 236–37;
Thomas M. Green, *The Spanish Conspiracy* (Cincinnati, 1891), 250–53; Abernethy,
*Western Lands*, 358; Arthur Campbell to Washington, May 10, 1789, in Papers
of the Continental Congress (Division of Manuscripts, Library of Congress), Ser.
LXXVIII, Vol. VI, 369; Antonio Valdés to Miró, June 3, 1789, in Lawrence Kinnaird (ed.), *Spain in the Mississippi Valley, 1765–1794*, in American Historical Association *Annual Report*, 1945, II–IV (Washington, 1946–1949), Pt. II, 275.

hatched a scheme to undermine Panton and his Spanish patrons.

William Augustus Bowles was a native Marylander who had espoused the Tory cause and served with the British forces in Florida during the revolution. After being drummed out of the garrison at Pensacola, he resided in the Lower Creek towns, married the daughter of a chief, learned the native language, and become acquainted with McGillivray. In the summer of 1788 he reappeared in these towns with a supply of powder and lead for the Creeks, and McGillivray came down to meet him and accept the gift. Bowles promised that he would return in the fall with additional presents.[35]

In November Bowles arrived with two ships and some thirty-odd men, making his landing on the Indian River. He expected to be joined by the Creeks, to capture Panton's stores on the St. Johns River and at St. Marks on Apalachee Bay, and then to set up an Indian state with an Atlantic port through which to carry on the trade with Nassau. But these ambitious plans soon miscarried. Twenty-six of his men deserted and fled to the Spanish post at St. Augustine, where they made the following deposition: "That in September last they were enlisted in New Providence for an expedition fitting out there in two vessels for the coast of East Florida, by and at the expense of John Miller, a member of the Council, and his partner, Mr. Bromfield Bonnamy, which expedition they were given to understand was promoted and aided by the Earl of Dunmore, Governor of the Bahamas, and was to be commanded by Mr. W. A. Bowles, a half-pay officer in the British service and formerly of the Corps of Maryland Loyalists." Provided with horses and aided by Indians, they were promised goods and Negroes seized in Georgia and Florida. The deserting recruits further deposed that various criminals and undesirables were enlisted for the enterprise, the first object of which was to crush Panton, Leslie and Company and to establish Miller, Bonnamy and Company in trade, a feat which Bowles

[35] Elisha P. Douglass, "The Adventurer Bowles," in *William and Mary Quarterly*, 3d ser., VI (1949), 7–9; Duvon C. Corbitt and John T. Lanning (eds.), "A Letter of Marque Issued by William Augustus Bowles as Director General of the State of Muskogee," in *Journal of Southern History*, XI (1945), 246–49; Caughey, *McGillivray of the Creeks*, 35–36; Whitaker, *Spanish-American Frontier*, 135–37; Pickett, *History of Alabama*, 411–13.

declared would be easy, since McGillivray had ceded to him all the authority and influence he possessed in the Creek Nation. The deposition stated that Bonnamy returned to Nassau to go aboard a a schooner, hired from one George Johnson of that town, for the purpose of going to St. Marks to reduce the Spanish government and burn Panton's stores.[36] The Creeks were disappointed in the small amount of supplies which Bowles brought and failed to join him in the projected attack on Panton's establishment. Without their help the freebooter was able to accomplish nothing; however, he remained in the Creek country until April, 1789, and then returned to Nassau.[37]

With only a little help from Bowles and with the supply of arms from Pensacola cut off, McGillivray was reduced to a state of despondency. In September, 1788, he informed William Panton that Philip Nolan had visited him and, at Miró's request, he had sent him on to the Cumberland settlements with proposals for a peace treaty; but nothing came of his peace mission at this time. The Creek chief further informed Panton that Georgia had proclaimed a truce with him on July 31, but that he regretted he had not been allowed to follow up his blows against that state, and that his work would now have to be done all over again. The Cherokee, he said, were still engaged in hostilities, and he was helping them.[38]

Seeing that his Indian ally was irreconcilable and fearing the loss of his support, Miró gave in to him and, early in 1789, agreed to renew the supply of arms, urging McGillivray, however, not to use them for attacks on the Americans. The half-breed chief thanked his sponsor and proceeded to ignore his advice. On May 29 General Elijah Clarke of the Georgia militia notified

[36] Valdés to Captain General of Florida, April 21, 1789, in Kinnaird (ed.), *Spain in the Mississippi Valley*, Pt. II, 271; *Florida Historical Quarterly* (Tallahassee), X (1931–1932), 79–85.

[37] Richmond *Virginia Gazette, and General Advertiser*, February 19, 1789; Caughey, *McGillivray of the Creeks*, 37; Douglass, "Adventurer Bowles," *loc. cit.*, 9–10; Corbitt and Lanning (eds.), "Letter of Marque Issued by William Augustus Bowles," *loc. cit.*, 250; R. Faulder, *Memoirs of William Augustus Bowles* (London, 1791), reprinted in *Magazine of History* (New York), XII (1916), 103–27.

[38] Richmond *Virginia Gazette, and General Advertiser*, February 19, 1789; McGillivray to William Panton, September ?, 1788, in Pickett, *History of Alabama*, 385–88.

the governor that the Creeks were attacking the frontiers and that he had called out the militia and was making all possible efforts to repel them.[39]

On January 12, 1789, John Sevier reported to the Council of the revived State of Franklin that he had won a signal victory over a band of hostile Creeks and Cherokee.[40] But his relations with the Chickasaw were still friendly and his agent, Bennett Ballew, was continuing to work with them for a cession of land on the upper waters of the Tombigbee and Yazoo rivers. Sevier still hoped that the Spanish authorities would agree to the establishment of settlements in this region, with a separate government and access to the ports of Mobile and New Orleans.[41]

The Cumberland settlements also were still interested in the establishment of a separate state with a Spanish connection. North Carolina had failed to ratify the new Federal Constitution, the Indians were constantly attacking, and the Western inhabitants were convinced that they could expect no assistance from the people who lived east of the mountains. Early in 1789 Robertson and Daniel Smith wrote to Miró about a plan of separation, and on April 16 Dr. James White arrived in New Orleans by way of Havana, where he had presented José de Ezpeleta a memorial in which he urged the importance of a separation of the Western settlements from the United States.[42] In New Orleans he assured Miró that both Sevier and his Franklinites as well as the settlers on the Cumberland River wished to set up an independent state in alliance with Spain. Within a few days Miró wrote to Robertson and Smith, covertly encouraging the movement to set up an independent government; then he wrote to Wilkinson giving a

---

[39] McGillivray to Miró, February 1, 1789, in East Tennessee Historical Society *Publications*, No. 19 (1947), 82–85; Savannah *Georgia Gazette*, June 4, 1789; Richmond *Virginia Gazette, and General Advertiser*, June 25, 1789.

[40] Lexington *Kentucky Gazette*, May 16, 1789, giving extract of letter dated Green County, N.C., January 10, 1789; Richmond *Virginia Gazette, and General Advertiser*, April 9, 1789; Savannah *Georgia Gazette*, April 24, 1789.

[41] Abernethy, *From Frontier to Plantation in Tennessee*, 116; Abernethy, *Western Lands*, 341.

[42] Daniel Smith to Miró, March 11, 1789, in East Tennessee Historical Society *Publications*, No. 19 (1947), 97; Dr. James White to Captain General José de Ezpeleta, December 24, 1788, *ibid.*, No. 18 (1946), 143–46; Ezpeleta to Valdés, December 29, 1788, *ibid.*, 139–43; James Robertson to Miró, January 29, 1789, *ibid.*, No. 19 (1947), 81.

full account of the affair and solicited his advice concerning it.[43]
On September 2 Robertson wrote to Miró saying that a Cumberland convention had instructed the local delegates in the legislature to insist on separation from North Carolina and that the Indians were daily attacking the settlements. "Unprotected," he declared, "we are to be obedient to the New Congress of the United States, but we cannot but wish for a more interesting connection." [44]

That this was a remedy of desperation is proved by the sequel. After the requisite number of states ratified the Federal Constitution, North Carolina reconsidered her act of rejection. In November, 1789, a new convention was assembled and, by a vote of 195 to 77, it decided to enter the Union. During the next month the legislature met and made a new offer to cede the Western lands to the United States. On April 2, 1790, the Federal Congress accepted this offer, and on May 26 the "Territory South of the River Ohio" was created with essentially the same form of government as that already adopted for the Northwest Territory.[45] William Blount was appointed governor; he in turn appointed Sevier to command the militia of the East Tennessee settlements and Robertson to command in the Cumberland region. All along, these men had desired the support of their fellow citizens east of the mountains, and now that they had it, no more was heard of the Spanish Conspiracy in the country which was soon to become the State of Tennessee.[46]

[43] Henderson, "Spanish Conspiracy in Tennessee," *loc. cit.*, 239–40; Whitaker, *Spanish-American Frontier*, 111–14; Miró to Wilkinson, April 22, 1789, in Gayarré, *History of Louisiana*, III, 260; White to Miró, April 18, 1789, in Kinnaird (ed.), *Spain in the Mississippi Valley*, Pt. II, 267–68, also in East Tennessee Historical Society *Publications*, No. 20 (1948), 103–104; Miró to White, April 20, 1789, in L.H.S. Translations, Filson Club Manuscripts (Louisville), also in Kinnaird (ed.), *Spain in the Mississippi Valley*, Pt. II, 169–70, and in East Tennessee Historical Society *Publications*, No. 20 (1948), 104–105; Miró to Smith, April 24, 1789, *ibid.*, 107–108; Miró to Wilkinson, April 23, 1789, *ibid.*, 105–107; Miró to Valdés, April 30, 1789, *ibid.*, 108–10; Miró to Robertson, April 20, 1789, in Kinnaird (ed.), *Spain in the Mississippi Valley*, Pt, II, 268–69.

[44] Robertson to Miró, September 2, 1789, in Kinnaird (ed.), *Spain in the Mississippi Valley*, Pt. II, 279–80.

[45] Abernethy, *From Frontier to Plantation in Tennessee*, 110–13.

[46] William Blount to John Steele, July 10, 1790, in John Steele Papers (North Carolina Historical Commission, Raleigh), I (1777–1802).

In Kentucky the situation was quite different. When the convention of November, 1788, turned down Wilkinson's plan for setting up a separate state without the consent of Congress, it petitioned Virginia to authorize the calling of still another convention.[47] On December 29 the Virginia Assembly complied and provided that July 20, 1789, should be the date for the convening of that body. But the terms now offered were not so liberal as were those previously granted. According to the new act, Virginia veterans were allowed unlimited time in which to perfect their titles to bounty lands lying within the confines of the new state, and Kentucky was asked to pay her proportionate part of Virginia's public debt.[48]

Kentucky sentiment was divided over accepting the new conditions and Wilkinson and his friends now changed front and opposed separation. Wilkinson explained to Miró that he feared the new Congress would agree to the admission of Kentucky as a state, and he wished to postpone the issue until he could be sure that no such danger existed.[49] A sufficient number of the people agreed with the conspirators to defeat the move for separation in the eighth convention, which met as scheduled in July and forthwith appealed to Virginia for more liberal terms and authority to call still another convention. On December 18 the General Assembly of Virginia complied with both requests.[50]

On February 12, 1789, Wilkinson again wrote to Miró that he now favored postponing the separation of Kentucky from Virginia and that he composed the memorials which the November convention sent to Richmond and Philadelphia. He thought that

[47] Abernethy, *Western Lands*, 350.

[48] Lexington *Kentucky Gazette*, February 14, 1789; April 20, 1827; Mann Butler, *A History of the Commonwealth of Kentucky* (Louisville, 1834), 181.

[49] Thomas Marshall to George Nicholas, April 26, 1789, in Innes Papers, Bk. 22, Pt. I; George Nicholas to Madison, May 8, 1789, in James Madison Papers (Division of Manuscripts, Library of Congress), XVI; Lexington *Kentucky Gazette*, May 23, 24, 1789.

[50] Levi Todd to Governor Randolph, May 27, 1789, in *Calendar of Virginia State Papers*, IV, 630; George Nicholas to Madison, November 2, 1789, in Madison Papers, XVII; Virginia House of Delegates *Journal*, October 20, November 3, December 2, 14, 1789; Temple Bodley (ed.), *Littell's Political Transactions* (reprint, Louisville, 1926), appendix, 109–10; Lexington *Kentucky Gazette*, August 15, 29, 1789; April 20, 27, 1827.

the new Congress would turn down Kentucky's application for admission to the Union and that the Westerners would then turn to Spain for protection from the Indians and the opening of the Mississippi River to their trade. He still disapproved of the policy of opening the river trade to Americans at a 15 per cent duty and the encouragement offered them to settle in Louisiana. Finally, he asked for the repayment of five thousand dollars which he claimed to have spent in order to win friends in Kentucky for Spain.[51]

On April 11 Miró wrote to Antonio Valdés, secretary for colonial affairs in the Spanish ministry, that he had informed Wilkinson, whom he credited with the defeat of Connolly's project, that the King had approved his appointment as the principal Spanish agent in the American West. He said he had bought 235,000 pounds of tobacco from him and recommended payment of the five thousand dollars which the general requested.[52] On the twenty-third he notified Wilkinson of Dr. James White's arrival in New Orleans and of the letters which he was sending by him to Robertson and Smith. He suggested that his correspondent co-operate with these leaders of the Separatist movement in the Cumberland settlements and added that he had asked permission to buy eight million pounds of American tobacco.[53]

After the July convention postponed the question of separation, Wilkinson made a second journey to New Orleans. On September 17 he addressed a note to Miró in which he reiterated his opposition to opening the river to Americans upon payment of a 15 per cent duty but changed his attitude on the question of immigration.[54] As a reinsurance policy the Spaniards had been encouraging American migration to Louisiana, and Gardoqui had made some large grants of territory for this purpose. The most impor-

[51] Wilkinson to Miró, February 12, 1789, in Gayarré, *History of Louisiana*, III, 223–40.

[52] Miró to Valdés, April 11, 1789, *ibid.*, 255; also in L.H.S. Translations from the Pontalba Papers, Filson Club Manuscripts.

[53] Miró to Wilkinson, April 23, 1789, *ibid.*; also in East Tennessee Historical Society *Publications*, No. 20 (1948), 105–107.

[54] Daniel Clark, *Proofs of the Corruption of Gen. James Wilkinson* (Philadelphia, 1809), 15–16.

tant of these was one assigned to George Morgan, a Philadelphia merchant who, during the late colonial period, had bargained with the Indians for enormous grants north of the Ohio River. His claims had been turned down by Congress, and he now arranged with Gardoqui for an extensive grant on the west bank of the Mississippi where he undertook to establish a settlement at New Madrid.[55] Gardoqui made other large grants, such as one to an Irishman, Colonel Peter Bryan Bruin, who settled just north of Natchez, but Miró did not approve of this procedure— nor did Wilkinson. Miró refused to validate the Morgan grant but, as an alternative plan, proposed to grant 320 acres each to actual settlers. Wilkinson now gave his approval to this proposal but suggested that three thousand acres be granted to the more important immigrants who planned to establish plantations. He also admitted to Miró that he had applied to Gardoqui for a grant of six hundred thousand acres on the Yazoo in order to undermine Morgan's scheme, the tract to be used as a refuge in case his position in Kentucky should become untenable. That he was sincere in this stand is indicated by the fact that on December 26 the *Kentucky Gazette* published Miró's proclamation of September 2, inviting immigration to Louisiana.[56]

Never unmindful of the loaves and the fishes, Wilkinson took this opportunity to tell Miró that, in order to encourage trade between Kentucky and Louisiana, he had shipped seventy-four thousand pesos worth of goods from New Orleans to the Falls of the Ohio and that he had lost money in the transaction. As compensation he asked that Miró purchase two hundred hogsheads of tobacco on his account. He also sent a list of twenty-two persons

[55] Gardoqui to Floridablanca, March 4, 1789, in East Tennessee Historical Society *Publications*, No. 19 (1947), 86–92; Hutchins to Gardoqui, January 25, 1789, *ibid.*, 93–95; Dawson to Governor Randolph, January 29, 1789, in *Calendar of Virginia State Papers*, IV, 554–55; Gardoqui to Hutchins, February 25, 1789, in Morgan Papers, No. 142.

[56] Wilkinson to Miró, September 17, 1789, in *American Historical Review*, IX (1903–1904), 751–59; Miró to Morgan, May 23, 1789, in Morgan Papers, No. 100; Morgan to Miró, May 24, 1789, in L.H.S. Translations from the Pontalba Papers; Miró to Valdés, June 18, 1789, in East Tennessee Historical Society *Publications*, No. 20 (1948), 113–14; Lexington *Kentucky Gazette*, December 26, 1789; Gayarré, *History of Louisiana*, III, 264–66.

in Kentucky whose good will should be enlisted by the granting of Spanish pensions.[57] On December 31 Miró wrote to Valdés that he had advanced seven thousand dollars to Wilkinson and advised that he be granted an annual pension of two thousand dollars. He also proposed to grant pensions to those whom Wilkinson recommended and advocated the annual purchase of ten million pounds of American tobacco.[58]

Returning to Kentucky with Philip Nolan, Wilkinson was beset by creditors, but he busied himself with a project that he had started before his departure: the establishment of the town of Frankfort on the Kentucky River. Here he laid out streets, sold lots, and set up a mercantile business in partnership with Peyton Short, brother-in-law of William Henry Harrison. Short furnished most of the money for the venture, but Wilkinson, being a man of extravagant tastes, built a pretentious mansion on "Wilkinson Street" and, according to his custom, entertained lavishly.[59] However, business did not prosper. Wilkinson quarreled with his original agent, Major Dunn, who presently committed suicide. Dunn was succeeded by Thomas Power, a young Irishman who had become a Spanish citizen and taken up residence at Natchez.[60]

The partnership of Wilkinson and Short lost money on the goods brought up from New Orleans, and since the Spanish authorities had opened this port early in 1789 to all comers at a duty of 15 per cent, Wilkinson no longer had a monopoly. However, he set up his own inspection warehouse and charged high transportation and handling fees. In 1790 over twenty-five thousand pounds of American tobacco were received at New Orleans, but in 1791 the Spanish authorities reduced their pur-

---

[57] Wilkinson to Miró, September 17, 1789, and inclosure No. 3, in *American Historical Review*, IX (1903–1904), 759; Jacobs, *Tarnished Warrior*, 97.

[58] Miró to Valdés, December 31, 1789, in L.H.S. Translations from the Pontalba Papers; Abernethy, *Western Lands*, 353–54.

[59] Lexington *Kentucky Gazette*, August 8, December 19, 1789; Jacobs, *Tarnished Warrior*, 98; Clark, *Proofs of the Corruption of Gen. James Wilkinson*, 10; Royal O. Shreve, *The Finished Scoundrel, General James Wilkinson* (Indianapolis, 1933), 82–83.

[60] William Short to Wilkinson, December 20, 1791; January 3, 1792, in Innes Papers, Bk. 23, Pt. I; Richmond *Virginia Gazette, and General Advertiser*, August 13, 1789; James Wilkinson, *Memoirs of My Own Times* (Philadelphia, 1816), II, 240.

chases from two million to forty thousand pounds, and Governor Miró was no longer able to purchase all that was sent down from Kentucky. Finally, on March 17, 1791, Wilkinson shipped his last large consignment, consisting of 5 boats with 120 hogsheads, in charge of a Lexington merchant named Hugh McIlvain. That the general's trading monopoly was at an end was demonstrated by the instructions which he gave his agent. McIlvain was to assume an air of authority and bluff his way past the Spanish post at New Madrid. When he arrived at Natchez he was to request the Spanish commandant there to administer an oath of allegiance to Spain and get a certificate showing that he was a subject of the King. This would enable him to proceed to New Orleans without paying the 15 per cent duty. Having arrived at the Louisiana capital, he was to tell Miró that the leading men of Kentucky, with Wilkinson at their head, were friendly to Spain, and he was to pay the general "any other compliments you may think I deserve." After his conference with the governor, McIlvain was to seek out Philip Nolan, show him letters from Wilkinson, get his advice, and offer four thousand dollars to get the tobacco into the royal warehouses. McIlvain was to keep his connection with Wilkinson secret, and all business concerning the shipment was to be transacted in McIlvain's name, but at the sole risk and profit of Wilkinson.[61]

Meanwhile, debts had eaten up all possible profits, and Wilkinson was financially on the rocks. He had failed as a merchant, but he was a man of resource and had never ceased to plan for a more glamorous career. His pecuniary embarrassment was somewhat relieved when, on October 26, 1791, the Spanish government authorized Governor Miró to recompense the general for his services and continue his pension of two thousand dollars per year from January 1, 1789.[62] Presently a man by the name of

---

[61] Peyton Short to Wilkinson, January 4, 1790, in Innes Papers, Bk. 23, Pt. I; Wilkinson to Hugh McIlvain, March 17, 1791, *ibid.*; Philip Nolan to Wilkinson, April 6, 1791, in Wilkinson, *Memoirs of My Own Times*, II, Appendix 2; Thomas R. Hay and M. R. Werner, *The Admirable Trumpeter; A Biography of General James Wilkinson* (Garden City, 1941), 105–106; Robert, *Story of Tobacco in America*, 53–54.

[62] Wilkinson to _____, January 20, 1790, in Reuben T. Durrett Manuscripts (University of Chicago Library); royal order to Miró, October 26, 1791, in Archivo Histórico Nacional (Madrid), *expediente* 15, pp. 557–59; Lexington *Kentucky Gazette*,

John Ballenger arrived in Frankfort with two pack mules laden with six thousand Spanish dollars for Wilkinson. This shipment was shortly followed by another. The general explained that the money came from the profits of his tobacco trade, but his creditors knew that there had been no profits.[63]

These Spanish dollars enabled Wilkinson to keep up appearances, but they were not sufficient to pay off the heavy debts that he had incurred in the tobacco trade and in his extensive land speculations. He needed an additional, and a more obvious, source of income, and his teeming mind began casting about for a solution to his problem. The title of "General," which he had acquired during the Revolution, was his proudest possession; the glamor of the military uniform still appealed to him, though he had never demonstrated any keen enthusiasm for the smell of gunpowder. With the British still in possession of Detroit and the Indians still attacking from across the Ohio, Kentucky had need of soldiers.

When George Washington organized the Federal government in New York, the defense of the frontier was one of the first problems which presented itself to his attention, and he soon took steps to meet it. General Arthur St. Clair was appointed governor of the Northwest Territory and Fort Washington was built on the site of Cincinnati. Here General Josiah Harmar was put in command of a force of regulars and militia, numbering about fifteen hundred men, and ordered to attack the Miami villages. The result was that in the fall of 1790 Harmar suffered a humiliating defeat, with the loss of 180 of his men. General St. Clair was now put in command and ordered to organize another expedition, but meanwhile, the Kentucky frontier was bleeding.[64]

Since the governor of Virginia had discharged the scouts entrusted with protection of this frontier, the Kentuckians decided in the spring of 1791 that they would have to depend on themselves. Accordingly, they organized an expedition of eight hundred men under Brigadier General Charles Scott, who com-

---

January 16, 1790; James, *George Rogers Clark*, 402; Jacobs, *Tarnished Warrior*, 128, 134; Clark, *Proofs of the Corruption of Gen. James Wilkinson*, 36.
    [63] Shreve, *Finished Scoundrel*, 82–83.          [64] Jacobs, *Tarnished Warrior*, 111.

manded the Kentucky militia. Wilkinson, chosen as second in command, styled himself "Colonel Commandant." On June 1 this force made a surprise attack on the Indian villages on the Wabash, where they destroyed crops and took prisoners in addition to killing a number of the enemy. According to all accounts, Wilkinson had a prominent part in this skirmish, and he particularly boasted that no scalpings or other barbarities were permitted. Naturally he and his companions returned as heroes, and soon he organized another expedition which he himself commanded.[65]

It was hardly without the "Colonel Commandant's" knowledge that George Nicholas recommended to Madison on September 16, 1791, the appointment of Wilkinson to a military command in the regular United States Army. On the twenty-ninth of the same month Secretary of War Henry Knox wrote in the name of Washington to thank Wilkinson for his services, but the Secretary was soon saddened by the news that, on November 4, St. Clair had suffered a crushing defeat at the hands of the Miami Indians.[66]

Wilkinson's plans, however, turned out as he had hoped, for on October 22 he was commissioned a lieutenant colonel in the Army of the United States and put in command of the garrison at Fort Washington.[67] In view of Wilkinson's well-known connection with the Spanish Conspiracy and the suspicion that he was receiving a Spanish pension, it is surprising that Washington should have taken him into the army, but friends in Philadelphia and New York, including Alexander Hamilton, recommended him. Even his Kentucky enemy, Thomas Marshall, spoke in his favor, but he explained this by saying: "I considered Wilkinson well qualified for a commission—I considered him dangerous

[65] *Ibid.*, 112–14; Humphrey Marshall, *The History of Kentucky* (Frankfort, 1824), I, 352–53, 373–75. Lexington *Kentucky Gazette*, May 21, June 18, 25, July 9, 1791; Savannah *Georgia Gazette*, September 8, 1791.

[66] Innes to Jefferson, August 27, 1791, in Thomas Jefferson Papers (Division of Manuscripts, Library of Congress); Nicholas to Madison, September 16, 1791, in Madison Papers; Knox to Wilkinson, September 29, 1791, in Lexington *Kentucky Gazette*, November 19, 1791; *ibid.*, July 16, November 12, December 10, 1791; January 26, February 4, March 3, 10, 1792; Annapolis *Maryland Gazette*, December 8, 1791; Channing, *History of the United States*, IV, 125.

[67] Marshall, *History of Kentucky*, I, 290–91.

to the quiet of Kentucky, perhaps to her safety. If the commission does not secure his fidelity, it will at least place him under control, in the midst of faithful officers, whose vigilance will render him harmless, if not honest." [68] Washington apparently took the same view, for he wrote to Hamilton that he found it expedient to appoint Wilkinson and that a responsible situation would "feed his ambition, soothe his vanity and by arresting discontent produce a good effect." [69]

In January, 1792, Lieutenant Colonel Wilkinson went from his home in Frankfort to his station at Fort Washington. He wrote to his friends that, disgusted by disappointment and misfortunes and because of an ignorance of commerce, he was glad to resume the sword of his country. "My views in entering the Military Line," he was frank to acknowledge, "are 'Bread & Fame'—uncertain of either, I shall deserve both." [70] He was indeed in a position to show his mettle, for the situation at Fort Washington was appalling. The remnants of St. Clair's defeated army and the motley recruits sent across the mountains formed a disorderly garrison. Lax discipline and drunkenness led to frequent clashes between the soldiers and the citizens of the village of Cincinnati, and the situation called for an efficient drill master and disciplinarian. Wilkinson proved adequate to this emergency and, appointing a young ensign by the name of William Henry Harrison to act as a military policeman, he soon restored order.[71]

On March 5 Wilkinson was promoted to the rank of brigadier general, but he did not achieve his ambition to command the Western forces. When General Anthony Wayne was selected for this post, Wilkinson forthwith proceeded to plot against him, and in December he wrote Governor Francisco de Carondelet, who had succeeded Miró at New Orleans, to make use of the opportunity offered by "an incompetent Secretary of War, an ignorant Commander-in-Chief, and a contemptible Union." [72]

---

[68] Shreve, *Finished Scoundrel*, 86.
[69] Hay and Werner, *Admirable Trumpeter*, 109.　　　[70] *Ibid.*
[71] Shreve, *Finished Scoundrel*, 86–87; Jacobs, *Tarnished Warrior*, 116–17.
[72] Wilkinson to Innes, May 10, 1792, in Innes Papers, Bk. 23, Pt. I; Jacobs, *Tarnished Warrior*, 115.

In spite of military preferment Wilkinson's debts were pressing, and creditors were threatening to make trouble. In this emergency he placed his financial affairs in the hands of his close friend and loyal supporter, Harry Innes, with instructions to sell lands in order to meet obligations, especially those due to his former partner, Peyton Short, and to his associate in the Spanish Conspiracy, Benjamin Sebastian.[73] Then there befell a sudden stroke of good fortune. Kentucky was admitted to the Union as the fifteenth state and Wilkinson's town, Frankfort, was selected as the capital of the new commonwealth.[74]

This event could not have been entirely unexpected. After the convention of November, 1788, rejected the effort of Wilkinson and Brown to bring about the complete independence of Kentucky, they gave up hope of forming an immediate connection with the Spanish authorities in Louisiana and offered no further opposition to her incorporation as a state of the Federal Union.[75] The act of separation which the Virginia Assembly passed on December 18, 1789, provided that another convention should assemble on July 26, 1790, and finally decide on the question of separation, making it a condition that the new state should immediately become a member of the Federal Union. On the appointed day the ninth Kentucky convention met at Danville and proceeded to accept the terms of separation proposed by the Virginia Assembly, fixing June 1, 1792, as the date when the new state should be established. It provided that elections should be held in December, 1791, to choose delegates to a constitutional convention which would meet in Danville on the first Monday in April, 1792. Since Congress would have to act on the admission of the new state, a memorial was sent to President Washington, praying that he and Congress sanction these proceedings.[76]

The Eastern states were so hostile to Western development that the District of Kentucky took no part in the election of the

[73] Wilkinson to Michel Lacassagne, January 4, 1791, in Innes Papers, Bk. 23, Pt. I; Wilkinson to Innes, January 4, 1791; April 3, 10, May 31, June 22, 1792, *ibid.*
[74] Wilkinson to Innes, December 22, 1792, *ibid.*
[75] Abernethy, *Western Lands*, 350.
[76] Lexington *Kentucky Gazette*, April 27, 1827; Collins, *History of Kentucky*, I, 21; Butler, *History of the Commonwealth of Kentucky*, 170.

first President; but by an agreement to admit Vermont along with Kentucky, this opposition was silenced and in February, 1791, Congress passed an act for the admission of Kentucky.[77]

On April 3 the constitutional convention met in Danville. For some time there was heated argument over the form of government to be adopted, and John Bradford, editor of the *Kentucky Gazette,* admirably practiced the doctrine of freedom of the press by publishing communications from all factions. Correspondents used fictitious names and it is impossible to identify most of them, but it is clear that there were two strongly opposing points of view. The conservatives wished to follow the aristocratic traditions of Virginia, while the radicals, taking their cue from Thomas Paine and the radicals of the American Revolution as well as from the egalitarianism of the French Revolution, desired a really popular democracy. They were dedicated believers in the class struggle and condemned all lawyers, planters, capitalists, and the upper classes in general. To guard against the domination of such people, they proposed the selection of county committees to nominate and instruct delegates to the convention. They evidently distrusted the usual election machinery, but their opponents pointed out that the proceedings of their committees might well be carried out behind closed doors.[78]

It is uncertain what elements made up this radical group, but it is clear that David Rice, the leading Presbyterian clergyman in Kentucky, along with a group of Baptist and other evangelistic ecclesiastics, were among the leaders. Their followers seem to have consisted largely of landless Virginia backwoodsmen and immigrants from Pennsylvania and New Jersey.[79]

These people elected a considerable number of their spokesmen to the convention, but the conservative Virginians dominated that body. Samuel McDowell was elected to preside, as he had presided over most of the eight previous Kentucky conventions. George Nicholas, a newcomer to Kentucky, member of a distinguished Virginia family, and a close friend of Thomas Jeffer-

[77] Z. F. Smith, *The History of Kentucky* (Louisville, 1901), 300.

[78] Thomas P. Abernethy, *Three Virginia Frontiers* (Baton Rouge, 1940), 69–78; John D. Barnhart, *Valley of Democracy; The Frontier Versus the Plantation in the Ohio Valley, 1775–1818* (Bloomington, Ind., 1953), 80.

[79] Barnhart, *Valley of Democracy,* 77–78.

son, was the author of, and leading spokesman for, the constitution adopted here.[80]

Except for that of Vermont, this was the first state constitution to provide for manhood suffrage, and it has therefore been heralded as a signal example of frontier democracy. It is certainly true that frontier conditions did play their part in shaping it, for it would have been unrealistic in a new community where land titles were so much in dispute to require a freehold as a prerequisite for voting. But the conservative leaders had no intention of turning the government—lock, stock, and barrel—over to the unrestrained will of the majority, and they accordingly provided that the governor and the senate should be chosen by an electoral college which would be selected by the voters every fourth year.[81]

The radicals proposed that the use of the English common law be prohibited in Kentucky courts and even suggested that a bill of rights—which might serve to protect property in slaves whose liberation they desired—be omitted.[82] The conservatives rejected such proposals. Influenced not only by the spirit of the frontier but by the provisions of the Federal Constitution and those of the new instrument of government which was adopted in Pennsylvania in 1790, they approved several articles which were definitely more liberal than those of the Virginia constitution of 1776. Representation would be apportioned according to the number of free male inhabitants; the counties would be divided into precincts for purposes of election; and voting would be by ballot. Furthermore, sheriffs, coroners, and the officers of militia companies would be elected, but judges of both superior and inferior courts, as well as most other state officers, would be appointed by the governor. Perhaps the strangest, and certainly the most controversial, provision of this constitution was that which declared: "The [state] supreme court shall have original and final jurisdiction in all cases respecting the titles to land under the present land-laws of Virginia." [83] This clause was insisted on by

---

[80] *Ibid.*, 91, 95–104; Abernethy, *Three Virginia Frontiers*, 75.
[81] Smith, *History of Kentucky*, 303.     [82] Abernethy, *Three Virginia Frontiers*, 71.
[83] Poore (ed.), *Federal and State Constitutions*, I, 651; Barnhart, *Valley of Democracy*, 101–103.

Nicholas, and it was obviously intended to protect vested interests against the action of landless juries. Naturally, it raised a storm of protest. Yet, on the whole, this was a liberal, but by no means a radical, constitution. After only seven years it would be supplanted by a new and more democratic one.[84]

Thus, after a struggle which had lasted for eight years and after the calling of ten conventions, Kentucky was admitted to the Union on June 1, 1792. Not only was Wilkinson gratified by the selection of Frankfort as the capital of the state, his friend Harry Innes was made judge of the Federal District Court and John Brown went to the United States Senate. In making his appointments President Washington inexplicably overlooked the friends of the staunch Federalist, Thomas Marshall, and appeared to favor the group which had been involved with Wilkinson in the Spanish Conspiracy. However, Isaac Shelby, who was elected the first governor, was not one of them.[85]

It was a game for high stakes that Gardoqui had played with John Jay and the Congress. His proposal was to open the trade of the Spanish peninsula to the United States in return for their giving up all claim to the navigation of the Mississippi River for a period of twenty or thirty years. The Northern states, with a bare majority in Congress, were anxious to accept these terms, though Gardoqui made no concession as to the West Indian trade, which was vastly more important than that of Continental Spain. The Southern states, led by the Virginia delegation in Congress, bitterly opposed any such arrangement, for the development of the West was dependent on the right to trade down the Mississippi to New Orleans. Since a two-thirds vote of Congress was necessary to the ratification of a treaty, the South was able to defeat the Spanish proposal and thus save the West for the United States, as it seems certain that, if Congress had agreed to give up the navigation of the Great River, the Tennessee and Kentucky settlers, with Wilkinson at their head, would have set up an independent republic and made their own terms with the power

[84] Samuel McDowell to Campbell, May 21, 1792, in Kings Mountain Manuscripts, Lyman Draper Collection (Wisconsin State Historical Society, Madison), 9DD69.
[85] Thomas Marshall to Washington, September 7, 1792, in James A. Green, *William Henry Harrison; His Life and Times* (Richmond, 1941), 278–79, 288.

which controlled the trade of New Orleans.[86] That was what Gardoqui had tried to accomplish, but now Kentucky was a member of the Union and the region which was soon to become the State of Tennessee was a territory of the United States.

[86] Whitaker, *Spanish-American Frontier,* 74–77.

CHAPTER IV

# THE YAZOO LAND COMPANIES
# OF 1789

IN 1789 the country lying west of the mountains, north of
the thirty-first parallel, and south of the territory which was
soon to become the State of Tennessee, was practically a no
man's land. Though the treaty of 1783 granted everything north
of the thirty-first parallel to the United States, Spain still held
Natchez and claimed all the land south of the Tennessee River.
Congress, of course, claimed the whole area, but so did the state
of Georgia, maintaining that it was a part of her colonial possessions. Actually, except for the settlements in the neighborhood
of Natchez and a small number of white people and half-breeds
who lived on the lower Tombigbee River just above Mobile Bay,
Indians were the only inhabitants.

Of these, the Creeks claimed most of what is now Alabama and
southern and western Georgia. The Choctaw claimed the southern two-thirds of present Mississippi, while the Chickasaw claimed
the rest of it and contested with the Cherokee the right to the
Tennessee River valley in present northern Alabama.[1] In all
this country there was then, besides Natchez, only one good site
for a settlement, the Walnut Hills where the Yazoo River flows
into the Mississippi—the location of modern Vicksburg. The
Spanish settlements around Natchez extended northward only
eighteen miles to Coles Creek, where a large land grant had recently been made to an Irishman named Peter Bryan Bruin. The
Walnut Hills site was not occupied even by Indians, and since it

[1] Charles C. Royce (comp.), *Indian Land Cessions in the United States*, in Bureau
of American Ethnology, *Eighteenth Annual Report . . . 1896–97*, Pt. II (Washington, 1899), plates 1, 2, 36.

had obvious possibilities for both Indian and river trade, it offered a tempting prize to bold adventurers.

One other site afforded considerable possibilities for the Indian trade—the Muscle Shoals of the Tennessee River. Not only was it the head of navigation on that river, the headwaters of both the Yazoo and the Tombigbee lay within a few miles of it. Boats coming down the Tennessee could not navigate the Shoals except when the water was high, but by a short portage they could be transferred to the Tombigbee and floated down to the Spanish port of Mobile. This route would afford much the most direct outlet to the Gulf for all that region which now constitutes East Tennessee and North Alabama, and there were forward-looking men who had already noted the possibility.

The State of Georgia was aware of the value of these undeveloped lands and was keen to take advantage of it. In 1783 William Blount obtained a grant from the Cherokee Indians to the land in the Great Bend of the Tennessee—that is, the area lying between the river and the present southern boundary of Tennessee. To exploit his prize, he organized a company which included such important persons as Richard Caswell, Revolutionary governor of North Carolina; John Sevier, future governor of Tennessee; Wade Hampton of South Carolina; Patrick Henry of Virginia; and Henry's land agent, Joseph Martin. In 1784 Georgia accommodated Blount by providing for the organization of a county government for the Bend tract and the company proceeded to carry out some explorations, but the plan fell through. Times were too unstable and Indians too hostile to permit the establishment of settlements in the region at this time, but neither Blount nor his associates lost sight of their objective, nor did a certain Zachariah Cox, whom they employed as an explorer.[2]

The next year, 1785, Georgia became even bolder and set up, on paper, the county of Bourbon, which was to include the territory on the Mississippi between the thirty-first parallel and the

[2] Thomas Napier to the Governor and Council of Georgia, August 24, 1785, with inclosures, in Telamon Cuyler Manuscripts (University of Georgia Library); Georgia House of Representatives Journal, December 2, 1789 (Georgia Department of Archives and History, Atlanta); Hays, *Hero of Hornet's Nest*, 190–92; Whitaker, *Spanish-American Frontier*, 55; Abernethy, *Western Lands*, 260–61.

Yazoo River. Four commissioners were sent to Natchez to organize the government, but the Spanish authorities rather naturally objected and the commissioners departed. But this was the beginning rather than the end of an important venture.[3]

In 1786 a trader named John Wood secured from the Choctaw Indians a grant of between two and three million acres which included the Walnut Hills. The Bourbon County Act provided that lands would be sold to such persons as undertook to acquire the Indian claim, and thus Wood's grant appeared to have some actual value.[4] He presently disposed of it to a Georgian named Thomas Washington, and in 1789 Washington associated himself with three South Carolina partners, William Clay Snipes, Isaac Huger, and Alexander Moultrie, the last a brother to Governor William Moultrie. In August of the same year this group purchased two thousand pounds worth of goods and dispatched Captain John Holder, a Revolutionary veteran, to Kentucky to recruit four hundred families and conduct them to the Walnut Hills before the end of 1789. Holder was to use a part of the supplies to conciliate the Choctaw Indians, and he was also to make terms with the Spaniards.[5]

Three months later the speculators decided to extend their operations by taking in additional partners to the total number of twenty. Articles of association were adopted and the organization now styled itself the South Carolina Yazoo Company. On November 20 it presented a petition to the Georgia legislature, setting forth that the company, having already begun a settlement under the Bourbon County Act, desired a confirmation of its interest.[6] But by this time other groups of speculators had become aroused, and the legislature was presented with petitions from

[3] Abernethy, *Western Lands,* 312–13.
[4] Charles H. Haskins, "The Yazoo Land Companies," in American Historical Association Papers (Washington), V (1891), 64; George White, *An Accurate Account of the Yazoo Fraud, Compiled from Official Documents* (Marietta, Ga., 1852), 7–8.
[5] White, *Accurate Account of the Yazoo Fraud,* 10–11; [Robert Goodloe Harper], *An Extract from the Minutes of the South Carolina Yazoo Company, Containing an Account of its Views, Transactions and Present State* (The Company, 1791), 3–38; James O'Fallon to the Editor, Lexington *Kentucky Gazette,* March 31, April 7, 1792; John C. Parish, "The Intrigues of Dr. James O'Fallon," in *Mississippi Valley Historical Review,* XVII (1930–1931), 238–39; Gayarré, *History of Louisiana,* III, 272.
[6] Haskins, "Yazoo Land Companies," *loc. cit.,* 65.

the Virginia Yazoo Company headed by Patrick Henry and Joseph Martin, as well as from the Tennessee Yazoo Company, whose leading spirits were Zachariah Cox and John Sevier, with William Blount an interested party.[7]

Despite bitter opposition, the legislature passed, and on December 21 the governor signed, an act providing for enormous grants to all three companies. The South Carolina group would receive a tract containing more than ten million acres, bounded on the west by the Mississippi River, on the east by the Tombig-

bee, on the north by the thirty-third parallel, and on the south by a line extending directly eastward from the point where Coles Creek runs into the Mississippi and where Peter Bryan Bruin occupied the northernmost Spanish grant. This included the Walnut Hills location, where the company planned to establish a town and carry on extensive trading operations.[8]

The Virginia Company received 11,400,000 acres—all the land

[7] W. B. Stevens, *History of Georgia* (New York, 1859), II, 461–66.

[8] Savannah *Georgia Gazette*, January 7, 28, 1790; *American State Papers, Documents Legislative and Executive*, I, 114.

claimed by Georgia west of Bear Creek and the headwaters of the Tombigbee and north of the thirty-third parallel. On the east, this tract extended almost, but not quite, to the Muscle Shoals and included no obvious site for a settlement, nor did the company make any immediate plans for colonization. The four million acres allotted the Tennessee Company extended eastward from Bear Creek and included all the rest of the Great Bend of the Tennessee. Even before the grant was made, this group planned a settlement at the Muscle Shoals. The South Carolina Company was, within two years, to pay $66,964, the Virginia Company $93,741, and the Tennessee Company $46,875 for their territory.[9] Thus the average price was less than one cent per acre, but there was no suggestion of bribery in connection with this deal. Georgia was merely trying to capitalize on a doubtful asset and one which she was not capable of developing single-handed.

The state made no provision for the establishment of civil government within the ceded territory and left it to the companies to extinguish the Indian claims. Furthermore, there was no specification that the new governments should become members of the Federal Union. Without consent of the Spanish authorities in Mobile, New Orleans, and Natchez, they would not be able to engage in foreign trade, and in view of the Spanish influence with the neighboring Indians, it was not certain that they could even exist.[10]

Important land speculators must have maintained an efficient system of communication, for on January 4, 1790, just two weeks after the Yazoo Act was passed by the Georgia legislature, Wilkinson applied to the South Carolina Company for appointment as its Western agent. The next day he notified Governor Miró that he had done so.[11] But in February the company chose as its representative in Kentucky Dr. James O'Fallon—a man who appeared to be well qualified for his assignment. A native of

[9] King's Mountain Manuscripts, Draper Collection, 11DD85a; Haskins, "Yazoo Land Companies," *loc. cit.*, 66.

[10] Arthur P. Whitaker (ed.), "The South Carolina Yazoo Company," in *Mississippi Valley Historical Review*, XVI (1929–1930), 383–94.

[11] Gayarré, *History of Louisiana*, III, 275–81.

Ireland and a Roman Catholic, he had been sent to Rome to enter the Church, but changed his mind and went to Edinburgh, where he studied medicine at the University. At the age of twenty-six he migrated to America on the eve of the Revolution and served as a surgeon in the Continental Army. At the end of the war he settled in Charleston and became involved in municipal politics as a member of the popular party. Not succeeding in this, in 1788 he applied to Governor Vincente Manuel de Zéspedes of East Florida for permission to settle five thousand Catholic families south of the border. Neither Zéspedes nor Gardoqui was favorably impressed with this scheme, but they prolonged the correspondence with O'Fallon in order to keep him quiet. Since nothing came of the idea, the versatile doctor was now ready to join the Yazoo group in a new venture, and on February 27 he set out for Kentucky.[12]

In Kentucky John Holder, having squandered the goods with which he had been provided, accomplished nothing. O'Fallon, who had been made a full member of the company, was to replace him and carry out the assignment of conducting four hundred families to the Walnut Hills. Since both Sevier and Wilkinson had applied for membership in the company, Moultrie invited them to become subagents for their respective localities. O'Fallon was instructed to visit Sevier in Jonesborough on his journey westward, and on reaching his destination he was to deliver the message to Wilkinson. On February 19 Moultrie also wrote to Alexander McGillivray and invited him to join the company as a full partner.[13]

It was thus with high hopes that O'Fallon, endowed with an uninhibited tongue and a vivid imagination, set out to found a new empire on the Lower Mississippi. He found Sevier, an old

---

[12] Louise P. Kellogg, "Dr. James O'Fallon," in *American Historical Review*, XIX (1923–1924), 501–504; Parish, "Intrigues of Doctor James O'Fallon," *loc. cit.*, 230–31, 235–37; James, *George Rogers Clark*, 403.

[13] Arthur P. Whitaker, "Alexander McGillivray, 1789–1793," in *North Carolina Historical Review*, V (1928), 295; White, *Accurate Account of the Yazoo Fraud*, 10–11; [Harper], *Extract from the Minutes of the South Carolina Yazoo Company*, 3–38; Alexander Moultrie to McGillivray, February 19, 1790, in Whitaker (ed.), "South Carolina Yazoo Company," *loc. cit.*, 391–94; O'Fallon to Sevier, April 7, 1790, in Tennessee Manuscripts, Draper Collection, 5XX23.

hand at land speculation, eager to participate in this new venture, and having reached Kentucky on April 27, he unfolded his designs to Wilkinson, who was ready to collaborate.[14] Next, on May 13 O'Fallon wrote confidently to Miró that he was planning to visit New Orleans to concert measures with him,[15] and he wrote again on May 24 that he would be in New Orleans in June. He said that the government which he planned to establish would be independent of the United States and thus free to form an alliance with Spain. Because of the advantageous position which it would occupy for carrying on both river and export trade, he thought all the Western country would finally join it in setting up an independent Western empire.[16]

Miró had recently thwarted George Morgan's scheme for setting up such a regime at New Madrid on the western bank of the Mississippi, and no wise man would have expected him to favor this one. Individual settlers were still welcomed in Spanish territory, but governments set up by Americans were hardly to be trusted. Nor would the merchants of New Orleans and Natchez care to have their trade intercepted at the Walnut Hills. Yet Wilkinson, who had previously made an unsuccessful application to Gardoqui for a large grant in the Yazoo country, was fascinated with this new scheme and on June 20 wrote Miró that he was in full sympathy with O'Fallon's plans.[17] But he reckoned without his host. He had evidently not yet received Miró's letter of April 30, saying that a settlement at the Walnut Hills would be resisted by force if this became imperative. With some lack of sincerity, Miró wrote on May 22 to Antonio Valdés, Colonial Secretary in the Spanish cabinet, that Wilkinson discouraged

[14] Parish, "Intrigues of Doctor James O'Fallon," *loc. cit.*, 240; Williams, "French and Other Intrigues in the Southwest Territory," *loc. cit.*, 22–23; Gayarré, *History of Louisiana*, III, 272.

[15] Whitaker, *Spanish-American Frontier*, 126–27; O'Fallon to Miró, May 13, 1790, in Kinnaird (ed.), *Spain in the Mississippi Valley*, Pt. II, 341–42; O'Fallon to Peter Bryan Bruin, May 13, 1790, *ibid.*, 338–41; Bruin to Miró and Manuel Gayosa de Lemos, June 27, 1790, *ibid.*, 354–55.

[16] Parish, "Intrigues of Doctor James O'Fallon," *loc. cit.*, 241; Gayarré, *History of Louisiana*, III, 288.

[17] Gayarré, *History of Louisiana*, III, 293; Jacobs, *Tarnished Warrior*, 103; Haskins, "Yazoo Land Companies," *loc. cit.*, 67–70.

the Yazoo project and that the Walnut Hills would be fortified if necessary.[18]

Meanwhile, O'Fallon was having his troubles in Kentucky, where he found that the spendthrift Holder still made no progress toward recruiting settlers to go to the Walnut Hills, and his company was running into difficulties with the Georgia authorities. After the state treasurer received partial payment for the land, the legislature in June, 1790, resolved that only specie or Georgia currency should be accepted. The act granting these lands did not state what kind of money was receivable in payment, but the companies had assumed that accredited certificates representing the state's Revolutionary debt would be accepted, though these were currently worth only about one-eighth of their face value in specie.[19] The companies were not able to meet the stated terms, and soon "poor Tom" Washington, a charter member of the South Carolina group, was caught forging Georgia notes. Much embarrassed, the company offered to buy him out, but he declined the offer and retained his interest. Two years later he was hanged for his crime.[20]

Apparently sensing that Miró was not as co-operative as he should be, O'Fallon decided to take a bolder stand with him. In 1790 Spain was on the verge of war with England over the Nootka Sound affair, and France was in the throes of revolution and unable to come to the assistance of her old ally. Therefore O'Fallon thought he was on safe ground when he wrote a long

[18] Parish, "Intrigues of Doctor James O'Fallon," loc. cit., 240; Gayarré, History of Louisiana, III, 281, 287, 293.

[19] John Neal, treasurer, to Governor Edward Telfair, January 25, 1790, in Yazoo Papers (Division of Manuscripts, Library of Congress); certificates of same, December 17, 19, 1791, in Bonds, Bills of Sale, Deeds of Gifts, Powers of Attorney, D (1792–1813); "Report of Committee on the memorials of Alexander McGillivray and the Virginia Yazoo Company, January 7, 1804," in [Harper], Extract from the Minutes of the South Carolina Yazoo Company, 3–38; John E. Anderson and William J. Hobby, The Contract for the Purchase of Western Territory made with the Legislature of Georgia in the year 1795 (Augusta, 1799), 38 ff.; White, Accurate Account of the Yazoo Fraud, 10–11; Savannah Georgia Gazette, January 7, 1790.

[20] Jacob Weed to Thomas Carr, January 30, 1790, in Thomas Carr Manuscripts (University of Georgia Library); [Harper], Extract from the Minutes of the South Carolina Yazoo Company, 41–44.

letter to Miró on July 16 protesting his loyalty to Spain and his desire to see all the Western country separated from the Federal Union and brought into close alliance with His Catholic Majesty. He also stressed the military strength which his prospective colony would possess and threatened to use force if Miró should try to prevent the establishment of the Walnut Hills settlement.[21] He doubtless expected British aid, and Miró was sufficiently disturbed to assure O'Fallon in a conciliatory manner that he would be cordially received in case he visited New Orleans. But Wilkinson now realized that he could no longer be in both camps, and accordingly in August he severed his connection with the South Carolina Company.[22]

Realizing that without Wilkinson there was little chance of Spanish support, O'Fallon now made an about-face. Obviously without knowledge of Washington's proclamation condemning settlement on lands reserved by treaty to the Indians, he wrote the President on September 25 indirectly soliciting consent to his project.[23] In spite of these difficulties, O'Fallon was still optimistic. Wilkinson tried to conceal his opposition; Miró continued to write friendly letters; and Philip Nolan, Wilkinson's agent in New Orleans, said that the Spanish authorities would not oppose the settlement. Thus encouraged, the doctor wrote for the *Kentucky Gazette* a glowing misrepresentation of his accomplishments and prospects and informed the company that within a few days he would send down, from the Falls of the Ohio, the first group of settlers, consisting of three hundred men in seven boats.[24] But O'Fallon soon became convinced that

[21] O'Fallon to Miró, July 16, 1790, in Kinnaird (ed.), *Spain in the Mississippi Valley*, Pt. II, 357–64; Parish, "Intrigues of Doctor James O'Fallon," *loc. cit.*, 241–42.

[22] Parish, "Intrigues of Doctor James O'Fallon," *loc. cit.*, 243, 246; Whitaker, *Spanish-American Frontier*, 140; Miró to O'Fallon, September 30, 1790, in Kinnaird (ed.), *Spain in the Mississippi Valley*, Pt. II, 379.

[23] Clarence E. Carter (ed.), *Territorial Papers of the United States* (Washington), IV, *The Territory South of the River Ohio, 1790–1796* (1936), 34; *American State Papers, Indian Affairs*, I, 115; Parish, "Intrigues of Doctor James O'Fallon," *loc. cit.*, 247–48.

[24] Parish, "Intrigues of Doctor James O'Fallon," *loc. cit.*, 245; [Harper], *Extract from the Minutes of the South Carolina Yazoo Company*, 38–39; "Extract of a letter from a Gentleman in Lexington to his friend in Philadelphia," October 20, 1790, in

Wilkinson was no longer his friend, and George Rogers Clark was appointed to succeed him as deputy agent of the company.[25]

As the situation grew worse, the Irish physician grew bolder. On December 17, 1790, he wrote Miró that Colonel Thomas Marshall had been informed (correctly, it appears) that the Spanish authorities were inciting the Indians against the company; that Wilkinson and Benjamin Sebastian were involved; and that they, as well as Harry Innes and John Brown, held Spanish commissions. O'Fallon also informed the governor that Clark would command the troops sent down by the company and that they would fight if resisted.[26] On the same day letters went to Edward Phelan and Peter Bryan Bruin saying that the company would soon send about 19,000 settlers from Georgia, the Carolinas, Tennessee, and Kentucky, of whom about 10,000 would be enrolled in the militia. In addition, there would be the regiment of 750 privates, exclusive of officers, "now raised & inlisted for 2 years." [27]

On his return from a journey to the settlements in East Tennessee and those on the Cumberland River, O'Fallon wrote again to Miró on February 18, 1791. He had been informed that the Spanish governor had stirred up the Choctaw and Chickasaw Indians to oppose any settlement in the Yazoo country and that Edward Phelan, because his name sounded like Fallon, had been arrested while at the Bruin plantation on Coles Creek. He expressed his continued hope for the co-operation of the Spanish authorities, because his settlement would be independent of the United States, but threatened to use force in case his project were opposed.[28] A month later Wilkinson informed Miró that

---

Lexington *Kentucky Gazette*, February 26, 1791; Haskins, "Yazoo Land Companies," *loc. cit.*, 72.

[25] Parish, "Intrigues of Doctor James O'Fallon," *loc. cit.*, 248–49, 252; James, *George Rogers Clark*, 404–405; Williams, "French and Other Intrigues in the Southwest Territory," *loc. cit.*, 25.

[26] Parish, "Intrigues of Doctor James O'Fallon," *loc. cit.*, 249–50; Carlos de Grand Pré to Miró, October 2, 1790, in Kinnaird (ed.), *Spain in the Mississippi Valley*, Pt. II, 380–81.

[27] Kinnaird (ed.), *Spain in the Mississippi Valley*, Pt. II, 393–95; Haskins, "Yazoo Land Companies," *loc. cit.*, 72.

[28] Parish, "Intrigues of Doctor James O'Fallon," *loc. cit.*, 25; Williams, "French and Other Intrigues in the Southwest Territory," *loc. cit.*, 25.

O'Fallon thought he could take the Walnut Hills without a fight because of the trouble between Britain and Spain over the Nootka affair.[29]

By this time the doctor was experiencing difficulties from another quarter. On January 24, 1791, there was read in the United States Senate a letter which O'Fallon wrote during the previous September discussing the plans of the South Carolina Company and also charging Wilkinson with complicity in the earlier Spanish Conspiracy.[30] It is probable that President Washington received additional information before issuing a proclamation on March 19 reciting reports that O'Fallon was "levying an armed force in . . . Kentucky . . . [defying] the treaties of the United States with the Indian tribes," the Congressional acts regulating trade with them, and Presidential proclamations of the preceding August 14 and 15. He therefore warned "those who have incautiously associated themselves with the said James O'Fallon . . . of their danger," and declared "that all persons violating the treaties and act aforesaid shall be prosecuted with the utmost rigor of the law." [31]

Still worried about the possibility of trouble on the Yazoo, Miró wrote another temporizing letter to O'Fallon on March 26, denying the allegation that he had incited the Indians and urging the Irishman to visit New Orleans.[32] But as soon as Wilkinson heard of the President's proclamation, he knew that O'Fallon's race was run. Accordingly, on March 30 he wrote an anonymous letter informing him of the move which the Administration had made and suggesting flight in the face of this threat.[33] But O'Fallon did not flee, nor were any charges brought against him by George Nicholas, the district attorney for Kentucky. However, the proclamation put an end to his efforts on behalf of the South Carolina Yazoo Company. Just how zealous these efforts had been, it is impossible to say. He wrote many letters

[29] O'Fallon to Miró, February 18, 1791, in Kinnaird (ed.), *Spain in the Mississippi Valley*, Pt. II, 401–404; Parish, "Intrigues of Doctor James O'Fallon," *loc. cit.*, 246–47.
[30] Parish, "Intrigues of Doctor James O'Fallon," *loc. cit.*, 253; Jacobs, *Tarnished Warrior*, 103; *Journal of William Maclay*, 367.
[31] James D. Richardson (ed.), *A Compilation of the Messages and Papers of the Presidents* (Washington, 1903), I, 93–94; Lexington *Kentucky Gazette*, May 7, 1791.
[32] Parish, "Intrigues of Doctor James O'Fallon," *loc. cit.*, 251.      [33] *Ibid.*, 254.

and did much talking, but there is no evidence that he enlisted any appreciable number of the thousands of settlers that he proposed to recruit. On April 15 he was ordered by the company to disband his battalion and discontinue operations in Kentucky.[34] At about the same time the Spanish authorities decided to allow no new settlements between the Tennessee and the Mississippi rivers, and Gayoso de Lemos, Commandant at Natchez, built Fort Nogales at the Walnut Hills.[35]

While Sevier was a prominent member of the South Carolina Company, he was also closely associated with the Tennessee Company. The proprietors in this group were Zachariah Cox, Thomas Gilbert, and John Strother, with Cox serving as the actual head of the company. He was a Georgian who in 1786 had explored land near the Muscle Shoals in connection with the Houston County project, of which William Blount was the moving spirit. Blount, as well as Sevier, was also interested in this new scheme to establish a settlement at the Muscle Shoals.[36]

These speculators were obviously co-operating with the South Carolina group, and on December 12, 1789, nine days before the Georgia legislature made the Yazoo grants, their agent, Bernard Gaines, advertised in the *Kentucky Gazette* that a party would start for the Shoals in March and that two hundred acres would be granted to each settler.[37] The company was formally organized at Augusta in February, 1790; officers were chosen and plans for settlement drawn up. Sevier busied himself in the interest of both companies and sent his agent, Bennett Ballew, who styled himself "Agent and Plenipo for the United Nations of Indians," to hold a conference with the Cherokee, Choctaw, and Chickasaw at the mouth of the Tennessee River in June, 1790.

[34] *Ibid.*, 255; O'Fallon to Captain Philip Buckner, n.d., Kentucky Manuscripts, Draper Collection, 4CC170; *American State Papers, Indian Affairs*, I, 115–17; [Harper], *Extract from the Minutes of the South Carolina Yazoo Company*, iii, 15.

[35] Parish, "Intrigues of Doctor James O'Fallon," *loc. cit.*, 256–57; Whitaker, *Spanish-American Frontier*, 148, 214.

[36] Georgia House of Representatives Journal, December 2, 1789; Isaac J. Cox (ed.), "Documents Relating to Zachariah Cox," in *Quarterly Publications of the Historical and Philosophical Society of Ohio*, VIII (1913), Nos. 2–3, pp. 31 ff.; Carter (ed.), *Territory South of the River Ohio*, 55 n.; Lexington *Kentucky Gazette*, January 15, 1790; Abernethy, *Western Lands*, 313–14.

[37] Lexington *Kentucky Gazette*, December 12, 19, 1789.

Ballew reported that not only these nations but also McGillivray expressed a desire for peace.[38]

On September 2, 1790, the Tennessee Company announced that on January 10 a party would start from the confluence of the French Broad and Holston rivers to establish the settlement at the Shoals and that five hundred acres of land would be granted to each family taking part in the project.[39] But already this group, like the South Carolina Company, had run into difficulties with the State of Georgia. The treasurer, John Neal, acting on the advice of Governor Edward Telfair, refused to accept payment in state certificates. To remedy this situation Thomas Carr of Augusta, a member of the Tennessee Company, wrote on December 11, 1790, to Alexander Moultrie of the South Carolina Company that the legislature had adjourned without making any provision for receiving the certificates but that a plan was now on foot for obtaining the grants immediately. "The Treasurer," he said, "has agreed to resign on conditions [sic] of being paid one thousand pounds for his office. . . . a friend of ours will be appointed who will receive the papers and receipt for them as Dollars which will be sufficient for our purpose." He said the Tennessee Company was prepared to pay its proportion of the stated amount, and he hoped that the South Carolina and Virginia companies would pay theirs. He felt sure that they would not be able to secure their grants in any other way, "for Yazoo will be held up as a scare crow to the people of Georgia. Profound secrecy must be observed, as a discovery may destroy the measure." [40]

Undeterred by such developments, on January 1, 1791, the Tennessee proprietors, Cox, Gilbert, and Strother, drew up detailed plans for their settlement and announced that on March 10 a party would leave Danville, Kentucky, for the Shoals under the leadership of John Gordon and Bernard Gaines, assistant agents for the company. Five hundred acres in fee simple would

[38] Carr to Weed, February 13, 1790, in Carr Papers; Bennett Ballew to Sevier, n.d., in Edenton *State Gazette of North-Carolina*, May 8, 1790.

[39] Cox (ed.), "Documents Relating to Zachariah Cox," *loc. cit.*, 31 ff.; *American State Papers, Indian Affairs*, I, 115.

[40] Neal to Governor Telfair, January 25, 1790, in Yazoo Papers (Library of Congress); Carr to Alexander Moultrie, December 11, 1790, in Carr Manuscripts.

be granted to each male over sixteen years of age provided he carried his own arms, ammunition, and provisions for one year and remained until he had harvested a crop of Indian corn.[41] There is no record of the departure of an expedition from Danville, but on March 26 Cox with his partners and twenty-nine others set out from the mouth of the French Broad, where before the end of the year William Blount would establish the town of Knoxville.[42] Blount had long been interested in the settlement of the Muscle Shoals area and had some connection with the Tennessee Company, but he was now governor of the Southwest Territory, and as a Federal official he had to obey Washington's instructions to prevent settlement of the Yazoo grants. Accordingly, he warned Cox to give up his project, and when this was refused, he notified McGillivray and the Cherokee and recommended that they remove the intruders. The Creek chief hardly needed any urging in this matter and on June 1 wrote to Secretary of War Knox that he had sent a party of warriors to carry out Blount's instructions.[43]

Apparently the Creek warriors did not make contact with Cox, who obtained the consent of the Chickasaw to establish a trading post and build a blockhouse on an island at the Shoals. By the end of the summer he was back in the Holston settlements, and Blount had him brought before a grand jury, which, however, refused to indict him. Thus encouraged, the speculator now advertised that he would lead another expedition from the mouth of the French Broad in November.[44] In Blount's absence the Territorial Secretary, Daniel Smith, issued a proclamation forbidding the adventurers to proceed through the Territory and warning all citizens not to associate with them. On December 9 Smith wrote to Secretary of State Jefferson that the Muscle Shoals party was making no noise at the moment, and he hoped

[41] Proposed Settlement at Muscle Shoals by the Tennessee Company, January 1, 1791, in Kinnaird (ed.), *Spain in the Mississippi Valley*, Pt. II, 400–401; Lexington *Kentucky Gazette*, February 12, 1791.

[42] Blount to Steele, July 22, 1791, in Steele Papers; Carter (ed.), *Territory South of the River Ohio*, 55 and n.; Lexington *Kentucky Gazette*, May 19, 1792.

[43] McGillivray to Knox, June 1, 1791, in Charleston *City Gazette*, August 16, 1791.

[44] Blount to Robertson, September 3, 1791, in Carter (ed.), *Territory South of the River Ohio*, 79; Daniel Smith to Secretary of State, October 4, 1791, *ibid.*, 83–84.

they had abandoned their project.[45] On January 17, 1792, Secretary Knox reported to Washington that the Cherokee had requested that the settlement of the Tennessee Company at the Muscle Shoals be prevented, and he was informed that the President had prohibited the project and that the Indian agent (Blount) had been instructed to carry out the order. This was soon done by the Cherokee, who forced the withdrawal of Cox's small party from the Shoals.[46]

Meanwhile, the Virginia Company was much less active than the other two groups. Early in 1789 Patrick Henry inquired of William Grayson and Richard Henry Lee, Virginia's two Senators in Congress, as to the validity of Georgia's claim and also as to the attitude of Spain toward the navigation of the Mississippi and emigration from the United States. Assured that the territory unquestionably belonged to Georgia, Henry organized a group of Virginia speculators and applied to the legislature of Georgia, along with the South Carolina and Tennessee companies, for a grant which, as previously stated, was consummated on December 21, 1789.[47] On January 19 following, Henry met with his partners, Francis Watkins, John B. Scott, John Watts, David Ross, William C. Ellis, and Abram B. Venable at Prince Edward Courthouse and formally organized the Virginia Yazoo Company. The partners then resolved to accept the terms of the Georgia legislature and appointed Scott their agent to make the required payment and receive the grant.[48]

None of these men except Ross knew much about Western lands, but Henry had a friend, Colonel Joseph Martin of Albemarle County, who was well informed on the subject. In 1788 Martin was appointed by Congress to act as deputy agent for the

[45] Daniel Smith to Jefferson, December 9, 1791, ibid., 105.

[46] Report of the Secretary of War to the President, January 17, 1792, ibid., 112; Cox (ed.), "Documents Relating to Zachariah Cox," loc. cit., 31 ff.; Pickett, History of Alabama, 408–10.

[47] William Cowan, Memorial of the Virginia Yazoo Company to the Congress of the United States (Washington, 1803), 3–5; Bonds, Bills of Sale, Deeds of Gifts, Powers of Attorney, D (1792–1813), 286; Haskins, "Yazoo Land Companies," loc. cit., 76.

[48] Memorandum dated January 19, 1790, in Yazoo Manuscripts (University of Georgia Library).

Cherokee and Chickasaw, but on November 8 of the same year he wrote McGillivray that he wished to settle five hundred families on the Tombigbee and declared: "I am determined to leave the United States for reasons that I can assign you when we meet, but durst not trust to paper." [49] This letter was intercepted and turned over to Governor George Mathews of Georgia, who submitted it to the legislature, and a committee of the House made a scathing report on it.[50] The incident caused both Martin and Patrick Henry much embarrassment. On January 29, 1790, Henry wrote Richard Henry Lee an explanation and then added: "No doubt you will hear of me or my Doings in the Georgia purchase. All the companys together get 15,000,000 acres it is said. I am a partner in one. And I own to you that some late occurrences in politics first suggested the thought, for if your present system grows into Tyranny is not a Frontier position most eligible? And a central one most to be dreaded?" [51]

Henry was obviously well informed as to the plans of Sevier and the Tennessee Yazoo Company, whose lands were contiguous to those of the Virginia Company. North Carolina had voted against ratification of the new Federal Constitution, and her western settlements, conscious of their exposed position on the Spanish and Indian frontiers, were concerned about their future. Sevier and his former Franklinites, Robertson, and the Cumberland settlers favored a separation of the Tennessee country from the parent state. Both these leaders had been in correspondence with Governor Miró of Louisiana with the idea of making terms which would protect them from the Indians and admit their trade to the port of New Orleans. On September 2, 1789, Robertson notified the Spanish governor that the Cumberland people had held a convention and petitioned for a separation from North

[49] Patrick Henry to R. H. Lee (?), January 29, 1790, in Miscellaneous Papers, John Brown Mason Collection (Yale University Library, New Haven); Joseph Martin to Henry, January 18, 1790, in Southern History Association *Publications* (Washington), VI (1902), 28–32; Henderson, "Spanish Conspiracy in Tennessee," *loc. cit.*, 240; Abernethy, *Western Lands*, 190, 338.

[50] Georgia House of Representatives Journal, January 24, 1789.

[51] Henry to Lee, January 29, 1790, in William Wirt Henry, *Patrick Henry, Life, Correspondence and Speeches* (New York, 1891), III, 412–15.

Carolina.[52] Sevier was working toward the same end, and it was hoped that McGillivray might be brought into the movement and the Muscle Shoals country incorporated in the new government. Whether this government should apply for admission to the Union or remain independent and seek an alliance with Spain was, for the time being, an open question, its decision depending on future developments.

It seems clear that Henry and the Virginia Yazoo Company, with Martin as their Western agent, were planning to make common cause not only with the Tennessee Yazoo Company, in which Henry proposed to buy a share, but with the Tennessee settlements on the Holston and Cumberland rivers. As soon as these settlements should obtain their independence from North Carolina, he expected them to put their public lands on the market, thus making it possible for the Virginia speculators to buy up the unoccupied tract bordering the Mississippi and adjoining their Georgia grant. The Chickasaw Bluffs, where Memphis now stands, lay within this area, and here a flourishing trade and extensive settlement might be established.[53]

The Chickasaw Indians occupied this region, and it would have been dangerous to attempt a settlement without coming to terms with them. This was where Martin came into the picture, but he declined to venture into the Chickasaw country. In December, 1788, Sevier had tried through Ballew to open negotiation with McGillivray in regard to a proposed settlement on the Tombigbee, and at the same time he wrote letters to the leading Chickasaw chiefs which Ballew undertook to deliver. The object was to secure cession of a part of the lands of that nation, but Ballew was intercepted by a band of Cherokee who took possession of his letters, which were later published. Sevier and Ballew, however, kept up their efforts among the Chickasaw as well as the Cherokee, and since these nations claimed the lands now sought by both the Virginia and the Tennessee companies, Martin looked on Ballew as his enemy. Yet Patrick Henry was anxious

---

[52] Robertson to Miró, September 2, 1789, in Kinnaird (ed.), *Spain in the Mississippi Valley*, Pt. II, 279.

[53] *Ibid.*, 317–21; Henry to Lee, January 29, 1790, in Henry, *Patrick Henry*, III, 412–15; Abernethy, *Western Lands*, 341.

to collaborate with Sevier and the Tennessee group and there is no other evidence that Sevier was unfriendly, although the situation was rapidly changing.[54]

In 1789 North Carolina elected a second convention which proceeded to ratify the Federal Constitution. The first legislature which met under the new government took up the question of the disposition of the Western lands. Some years previously Blount and a number of his friends staked out large claims to tracts in this area, and now he and his supporters proposed to cede to Congress, on condition that all existing land claims be made good, the region which was presently to become the state of Tennessee. The opposing faction in the legislature countered with a proposal to grant independence to the transmontane people, leaving them free to draw up their own constitution and dispose of their public lands. Thus the Blount group might have lost its claims and the Henry group might have been able to acquire them. But the Blount group won, and the lands were ceded to Congress with all previous claims guaranteed.[55]

The North Carolina cession was made in December, 1789, and during the following month Henry received the news, but he apparently was not informed as to the terms. When these finally reached him, he wrote to Martin on March 10: "I still think great things may be done in the Tennessee Country and below. For surely the people of Franklin will never submit to be given away with the Lands like slaves, without holding a Convention of their own as the Kentucky people have done under our Laws. . . . I am apprehensive Sevier may be hushed by preferment so as to make no opposition. But really it is a

<hr />

[54] Sevier to McGillivray, December 29, 1788, in *Georgia Historical Quarterly* (Savannah), XXI (1937), 288; Ballew to McGillivray, January 17, 1789, *ibid.*, 289–90; Sevier to Ballew, March 10, 1789, in Savannah *Georgia Gazette*, September 24, 1789; Martin to Henry, July 23, 1789; January 1, 1790, in Southern History Association *Publications*, VI (1902), 28–32; Martin to Henry, July 2, 1789, in Tennessee Manuscripts, Draper Papers, 2XX30; Panton to McGillivray, June 7, 1789, in *Georgia Historical Quarterly*, XXI (1937), 375–76; Panton to McGillivray (?), September 1, 1792, *ibid.*, 373; Richmond *Virginia Gazette, and General Advertiser*, July 30, 1789; Abernethy, *Western Lands*, 341.

[55] David Ross to Sevier, February 20, 1790, in Tennessee and King's Mountain Manuscripts, Draper Collection, 11DD86a; Abernethy, *From Frontier to Plantation in Tennessee*, 112.

pity some other person would not, as the Law is destructive of the people's Liberty and right to chuse [their] form of government, which belongs to every free man. . . . If you were to live there you might be the means of procuring proper terms for the people. . . . If Sevier has not turned tail on his former professions of zeal for the rights of the Franklin people and means to support their just pretensions, it will be well to join heart and hand with him or any other person so as to bring about a union of the District in supporting their just claims. . . . I really do think the act [of cession] shows more of Injustice and Tyranny than any public act since the Revolution . . . Franklin only wants some good person to lead them in a just and temperate manner to secure this and other rights." [56] Thus spoke the Voice of Liberty! Already David Ross, Henry's most active partner in the company, had written to Sevier on February 20, expressing similar sentiments. "The property of the unappropriated lands," he said, "is given up to Congress so that nothing is left the District but to labor and pay taxes." [57]

These protests, of course, came to nothing. Though Blount was closely associated with Sevier in organizing the Tennessee Company, his interest in North Carolina's Western lands was more important, and it was largely for this reason that he accepted the governorship of the Southwest Territory. Sevier and Robertson were appointed brigadier generals of militia in the new jurisdiction, and all three of them were now obligated to carry out President Washington's policy of preventing encroachments on Indian lands. This turn of events naturally blighted the prospects of both the Tennessee and the Virginia Yazoo companies.[58] They did not lose hope, however, and on April 10, 1791, David Ross wrote to Governor Beverley Randolph of Virginia in behalf of himself and other members of the Virginia Company.[59]

There is, in fact, no evidence that either the Tennessee or the

[56] Henry to Martin, March 10, 1790, in Tennessee and King's Mountain Manuscripts, Draper Collection, 11DD87a.

[57] Ross to Sevier, February 20, 1790, *ibid.*, 11DD86a.

[58] Blount to Steele, July 10, 1790, in Steele Papers, I; Abernethy, *From Frontier to Plantation in Tennessee*, 116.

[59] Ross to Governor Randolph, April 10, 1791, in *Calendar of Virginia State Papers*, V, 287–88.

Virginia Company ever planned to set up governments separate from the United States, and when O'Fallon first stated that the South Carolina Company contemplated such a move, he said that the other groups were not involved. There are reasons to believe, however, that they did at first consider such a possibility in case Congress, as seemed likely, should oppose the creation of new Western states.

When Washington took Blount and Sevier into his camp, he struck a heavy blow against the Yazoo companies, but it was not his only one. Alexander McGillivray was a crucial figure in the situation. His estates in Georgia were confiscated during the Revolution, and certain Creek chiefs who did not accept his leadership had, in 1785, concluded with Georgia the Treaty of Galphinton whereby they surrendered the Indian claim to all lands lying east of the Oconee River and a line from the north of the Oconee to the headwaters of the St. Marys River. McGillivray was determined that these lands should not be surrendered and that Georgia should have no peace so long as she claimed them.[60]

Having made up his mind to subdue the Northern Indians and wishing to avoid war on two fronts at the same time, the President was anxious to make peace with the Creeks. Accordingly, he appointed commissioners to treat with McGillivray. It is perhaps significant that no Georgian was selected, but the three appointees—General Benjamin Lincoln, Cyrus Griffin, and David Humphreys—were men of considerable distinction. They at once proceeded to Savannah and thence hastened to meet McGillivray at the Rock Landing on the Oconee.[61] When they arrived at their destination on September 30, 1789, they found McGillivray already there with some nine hundred of his followers. The Creek chief was induced to come partly by a hope of regaining his estates and partly by the desire of Spanish authorities that he make peace with the United States. They were not willing, it is true, that he should make any concessions as to sovereignty or trade, but they wished him to come to an agreement concerning

[60] Hays, *Hero of Hornet's Nest*, 182–85, 194–95; R. S. Cotterill, *The Southern Indians* (Norman, Okla., 1954), 66.
[61] Caughey, *McGillivray of the Creeks*, 39.

friendship and boundaries. In 1788 they had cut off his supplies in order to bring him to terms, but just before the meeting at the Rock Landing they had weakened and, through Panton, furnished him again with arms, thus considerably strengthening his diplomatic position.[62]

The fate of the Rock Landing meeting was foredoomed, for the commissioners were instructed to insist upon cession of the lands which Georgia claimed under her earlier treaties with the Creeks. They also insisted that the Nation recognize the suzerainty of the United States and its exclusive right to the Indian trade. It seems that the negotiations were left largely to Humphreys, who has been accused of arrogance in his dealings with the natives, but it is hardly just to blame him for failure of the mission. To have accepted the terms offered him would have meant for Mc-Gillivray a complete break with Spain and an unconditional commitment of his cause to the mercies of the American government. Naturally he did not consider such a move, and without taking leave of the commissioners, he broke camp and departed with his followers.[63]

This turn of events disturbed Governor Miró, for he feared a renewal of war on the American frontier and did not know where it might end. President Washington was also disappointed, but he was not inclined to accept the outcome as final. Not only did he fear a renewal of the Creek war, but in December Georgia posed a new threat to peace on the frontier by her grants to the Yazoo companies. The situation was critical and the President, engaged in a war with the Indians north of the Ohio, felt that he must exert every effort to preserve peace in the Southwest.

In this emergency he turned to Colonel Marinus Willett. With a message from the President and a letter from Senator Benjamin Hawkins of North Carolina, Willett made his way through the back country of the Carolinas and then through the Indian country to McGillivray's plantation, the "Apple Grove," at Little Tallassee on the Coosa River. He found this to be a commodious,

[62] McGillivray to Panton, August 10, 1789, in Pickett, *History of Alabama*, 389; White, *Historical Collections of Georgia*, 154; Cotterill, *Southern Indians*, 82–83.
[63] Cotterill, *Southern Indians*, 82; Caughey, *McGillivray of the Creeks*, 39; Lucia B. Kinnaird, "The Rock Landing Conference of 1789," in *North Carolina Historical Review*, IX (1932), 349–65; Whitaker, "Alexander McGillivray," *loc. cit.*, 290.

slave-operated estate where the half-breed chief lived comfortably in the tradition of the Southern squire, except for his plural wives.[64]

In view of the urging by his Spanish sponsors for him to make peace with the United States and taking into consideration the probability that the dons were on the verge of war with Britain because of the Nootka Sound controversy, the Creek chief decided to accept the invitation to visit New York. He accordingly agreed to accompany Willett and, having notified Panton and Miró of his intentions, set off on the long journey.[65] On arrival in New York foreign agents vied with American officials in doing honor to the native chief in the best traditions of Rousseauan primitivism and diplomatic intrigue. Washington was represented as motivated by justice and humanity and as the true friend of the Indian, but it was also made clear that he was interested in asserting the right of the United States to the Western territory and in defeating the claims of Georgia and the Yazoo companies. In these circumstances McGillivray was able to negotiate under favorable conditions.[66]

The treaty to which he agreed amounted to a compromise. The Creeks were to cede to Georgia the lands east of the Oconee, which had already been occupied by white settlers, but were to retain those south and west of that river and of the Altamaha, thus invalidating claims which Georgia had set up under her earlier treaties. The United States was recognized as sovereign over such Creek lands as lay within the national limits, but since Spain still claimed much of the transmontane area, the significance of this provision was not immediately apparent. True to his connection with Panton, McGillivray refused to agree to open Creek trade to the United States unless a war between Spain and Britain should make it necessary. Since it was not possible to induce Georgia to restore McGillivray's confiscated property, the United States agreed to pay him an annual salary of twelve hundred dollars and commission him a brigadier general in the

[64] Caughey, *McGillivray of the Creeks*, 40–41.
[65] Blount to Steele, July 10, 1790, in Steele Papers, I; Gayarré, *History of Louisiana,* III, 300.
[66] Weed to Carr, August 19, 1790, in Carr Papers; Whitaker, "Alexander McGillivray," *loc. cit.,* 296–300; Caughey, *McGillivray of the Creeks,* 42.

United States Army. In addition, several other chiefs received small annuities, and fifteen hundred dollars was allotted to the Nation as a whole. The treaty was concluded on August 7, 1790, and soon afterward the chief departed from New York in triumph and returned to his native land.[67]

This negotiation established an important precedent in American history. It not only indicated the manner in which many future Indian treaties would be negotiated; it asserted the right of the United States to determine the boundaries of Indian lands and to deal exclusively with the natives who inhabited them. This necessarily involved the development of a system of control and Congress provided for this by passage of an "Act for Regulating Trade and Intercourse with the Indian Tribes." This was approved by Washington the day McGillivray arrived in New York. It provided that the Indian trade be limited to traders licensed by a superintendent or other Presidential appointee. In the case of the Southern tribes, this appointee was William Blount, who was made Indian agent at the same time that he became governor of the Southwest Territory.[68]

In order to put teeth into his policy, Washington authorized the Creeks to expel by force any intruders on the lands guaranteed them by the treaty, and McGillivray alleged that he was repeatedly urged during the negotiations to break up the settlements of the Yazoo companies. However, the Chickamauga villages of the Cherokee Nation relieved him of this responsibility and expelled the settlers who had been conducted to the Muscle Shoals by Zachariah Cox. In this case the Chickamaugas showed unwonted restraint and did not resort to murder.[69] The final blow was struck against the companies when, in December, 1791, Georgia refused to receive payment in depreciated state certificates. However, when Hamilton arranged for assumption by the Federal government of the Revolutionary debts of the states, these securities at once rose to par value and Patrick Henry and

[67] Randolph C. Downes, "Creek-American Relations, 1790–1795," in *Journal of Southern History*, VIII (1942), 350–54; Whitaker, *Spanish-American Frontier*, 135–37; Cotterill, *Southern Indians*, 86.
[68] Cotterill, *Southern Indians*, 87.
[69] Whitaker, *Spanish-American Frontier*, 137.

his fellow Yazoo speculators stood to reap a handsome reward in an entirely unexpected manner.[70]

From the point of view of the Washington administration, the Treaty of New York was a distinct triumph, but neither the Georgians nor the Spaniards were inclined to accept it with equanimity. It has been customary to condemn the Georgians for their desire to acquire Indian lands, but they did not monopolize this ambition. The difference was that, except for a few small reservations, the Indian title had already been extinguished in all the other cismontane territory of the Southern states by 1789. The Treaty of New York increased by about one-third the area in Georgia which was open to white settlers, but much the largest part of the state was now guaranteed to the Creeks and placed under Federal control. Since Georgia then claimed most of present-day Alabama and Mississippi, she actually had possession of less than one-tenth of the land within her boundaries.[71] This denial of state jurisdiction by the Federal government was certainly as drastic as any modern movements in that direction. Naturally, the Georgians were incensed. Their General Assembly adopted resolutions condemning the treaty, and Senator James Jackson declared that Washington had disregarded the report of the three Federal commissioners of 1789 and had ceded away three million acres of land guaranteed to Georgia by the Constitution.[72]

The Spaniards had less reason to complain than did the Georgians, but they too were displeased. Though McGillivray had sworn allegiance to the United States, he had recognized American sovereignty only within the national boundaries and had refused to surrender his trade relations with Panton, Leslie and Company. Both Panton and Miró suspected that he had made greater concessions than he had actually made, and they

---

[70] Cowan, *Memorial of the Virginia Yazoo Company to the Congress of the United States,* 5–20; Jefferson to Washington, April 24, 1791, in A. A. Lipscomb and A. E. Bergh (eds.), *The Writings of Thomas Jefferson* (Washington, 1903–1904), VIII, 185.

[71] Extract of a letter from Wilkes County, Georgia, to a gentleman in Kentucky, October 17, 1790, in Lexington *Kentucky Gazette,* January 15, 1791; McGillivray to Secretary of War, June 1, 1791, in Charleston *City Gazette,* August 16, 1791.

[72] Hays, *Hero of Hornet's Nest,* 213–16; Caughey, *McGillivray of the Creeks,* 45.

proceeded to try to nullify the treaty and to undermine McGillivray's influence with the Creeks. However, taking the view that
discretion was the better part of valor, the Spanish authorities
raised the pension of the Creek chief to $2,000, and a little
later this was increased to $3,500. The Washington adminis-
tration also profited, for an imminent resumption of the Georgia-
Creek war was averted, and McGillivray's aid was enlisted against
the Georgia land companies.[73] When the chief returned from
New York to his home on the Coosa, he appeared for a time to
be at the zenith of his power and popularity. But throughout the
winter his health was poor and in January, 1791, he was confined
to his fireside by his old enemies, fever and rheumatism. The
coming of spring brought improved health and vigor and the
following months were really the happiest days of his life.[74]

In the autumn this calm was shattered by the return of that
remarkable adventurer, William Augustus Bowles. After ex-
pulsion from the Creek Nation in 1789, he went to the Florida
keys, then to Nova Scotia and Quebec, and thence to London,
where he was granted an audience with the Ministers and feted
by the public. This cordial reception was due to the fact that
Britain was expecting war with Spain and Bowles could be used
in gaining the favor of the Creeks in this emergency. But the
war did not materialize and the Ministry at once lost interest in
him.[75]

Returning empty-handed to Nassau, Bowles was again able to
interest Governor Dunmore and the firm of Miller and Bonnamy

[73] Miró to McGillivray, July 6, 1791, in Kinnaird (ed.), *Spain in the Mississippi Valley*, Pt. II, 412–13; Whitaker, *Spanish-American Frontier*, 138–39; Whitaker, "Alexander McGillivray," *loc. cit.*, 300–301.

[74] Caughey, *McGillivray of the Creeks*, 46–47.

[75] David Craig to Blount, March 15, 1792, in *American State Papers, Indian Affairs*, I, 264–65; Grenville to George Hammond, January 3, 1792, in Bernard Mayo (ed.), *Instructions to the British Ministers to the United States, 1791–1812*, in American Historical Association, *Annual Report*, 1936, III (Washington, 1941), 20–21; Turner, "Diplomatic Contest for the Mississippi Valley," *loc. cit.*, 681; Frederick J. Turner, "English Policy Toward America in 1790–1791," in *American Historical Review*, VII (1901–1902), 726–34; Cox, "Louisiana-Texas Frontier," *loc. cit.*, 41–42; Whitaker, *Spanish-American Frontier*, 140, 166–67; Anon., *The Life of General W. A. Bowles* (London, reprinted New York, 1803), 18–21; [Captain Bryan], *Authentic Memoirs of William Augustus Bowles, Esquire, Ambassador from the United Nations of Creeks and Cherokees to the Court of London* (University of Georgia Library), 1–75.

in trying to wean the Creeks away from their commercial alliance with Panton, Leslie and Company. Provided by them with a ship and presents for the Indians, he landed late in September, 1791, near the mouth of the Apalachicola River and made his way to the lower towns of the Creeks on the Chattahoochee. Here, by distributing presents and promises, he gained support of the villagers, who listened with apparent approval to his denunciation of the Treaty of New York and presently proclaimed him "General and Director of the Affairs of the Nation." In this capacity he wrote a letter to Governor Arturo O'Neill at Pensacola announcing friendship for Spain, offering a Creek and Cherokee alliance, and demanding free navigation privileges for the commerce of the Indians.[76]

Meanwhile, McGillivray was at home entertaining Ensign John Heth, who came to Little Tallassee with $2,900 in gold to pay the annuities promised at New York. At Rock Landing on the Oconee, Andrew Ellicott with his surveying party awaited the Creek delegation which was to help run the boundary line. On October 26 Bowles wrote them a letter from the Ufachees' village, saying that his followers had repudiated the treaty and the line would not be surveyed. On hearing of the presence of Bowles in the Lower Towns, McGillivray dismissed Heth, left the surveyors to return home, and hurried down to the villages on the Chattahoochee. Unable to capture his enemy there, he put a price on his head and then set off on a prearranged visit to New Orleans.[77] The thwarted chief appeared to be losing his

[76] Jared Irwin and John Watts to Governor Telfair, October 20, 1791, in Indian Letters, 1782–1839 (Georgia Department of Archives and History), 18; Timothy Bernard to James Seagrove, May 10, 1792, in *American State Papers, Indian Affairs,* I, 297; Whitaker, "Alexander McGillivray," *loc. cit.,* 301; Lawrence Kinnaird, "The Significance of William Augustus Bowles' Seizure of Panton's Apalachee Store in 1792," in *Florida Historical Society Quarterly,* IX (1931), 156 ff.; Mayo (ed.), *Instructions to the British Ministers,* 20 n.; Downes, "Creek-American Relations," *loc. cit.,* 354–55; Caughey, *McGillivray of the Creeks,* 49.

[77] Turner, "English Policy Toward America in 1790–1791," *loc. cit.,* 734–35; Kinnaird, "William Augustus Bowles' Seizure of Panton's Apalachee Store in 1792," *loc. cit.,* 156–66; War Department to Arthur St. Clair, December 2, 1791, in *American State Papers, Indian Affairs,* I, 183–84; *ibid.,* 126; Pickett, *History of Alabama,* 410–11; Richmond *Virginia Gazette, and General Advertiser,* December 21, 1791; January 11, 1792; Lexington *Kentucky Gazette,* January 21, May 19, 1792; Savannah *Georgia Gazette,* December 1, 1791.

grip, but Bowles did not profit by the opportunity. When his supplies ran low, he seized Panton's store at St. Marks on January 16, 1792, and soon thereafter accepted an invitation to visit the new Spanish governor at New Orleans, the Baron de Carondelet. Violating his safe-conduct, this forceful Castilian arrested his visitor and shipped him off by way of Havana to Spain, whence he was committed to a long captivity in the Philippine Islands.[78]

As far as McGillivray was concerned, Bowles had done nothing more than prevent him from carrying out the terms of the Treaty of New York, but the ailing chief did not live to regain his once formidable power. On his way home from New Orleans he contracted a violent fever at Mobile and when he got back to Little Tallassee early in October he was still a sick man. Partially recovering his strength during the winter months he journeyed to Pensacola to visit his friend William Panton, but here he was

---

[78] Blount to Secretary Robert Smith, April 27, 1792, in Carter (ed.), *Territory South of the River Ohio*, 144; Secretary of War to Washington, January 17, 1792, *ibid.*, 114; Knox to McGillivray, February 17, 1792, *American State Papers, Indian Affairs*, I, 246; Robert Leslie to Patton, March 9, 10, 1792, in *Georgia Historical Quarterly*, XXII (1938), 184–89; Patton to Baron de Carondelet, April 12, 1792, *ibid.*, 289–90; Whitaker, "Alexander McGillivray," *loc. cit.*, 302; Downes, "Creek-American Relations," *loc. cit.*, 355; Whitaker, *Spanish-American Frontier*, 166–67; Cotterill, *Southern Indians*, 90–91; Caughey, *McGillivray of the Creeks*, 49–50; Anon., *Life of General W. A. Bowles*, 21 ff.; Douglass, "Adventurer Bowles," *loc. cit.*, 16–23.

William Cunningham accompanied his chief to New Orleans and, on April 2, 1792, made a deposition stating that Bowles's project was the result of a plot engineered by Lord Dunmore and the three Yazoo companies to seize the territory claimed by them, as well as Pensacola and New Orleans. They would then erect a separate state, independent of both Britain and the United States, but their trade would be carried on with the Bahama merchants, who supported the enterprise and to whom the companies bound themselves, "by the double oath of secrecy and performance, having raised about 18 thousand men for the purpose." Cunningham said he had seen the different plans of the Yazoo companies, as well as some of the troops they were raising. He also said that Dr. James White, concerned in earlier separatist movements, was "one of the principal undertakers of the three different companies." There is some evidence that the Yazoo companies did approach Bowles, and since both McGillivray and the Spanish authorities had opposed them, they might have done so. But some of Cunningham's statements are highly fanciful, and they are certainly not entitled to full credence. Kinnaird, "William Augustus Bowles' Seizure of Panton's Apalachee Store in 1792," *loc. cit.*, 177. Furthermore, in his letter to Ellicott's surveying party at the Rock Landing, Bowles condemned the Yazoo grants. Lexington *Kentucky Gazette*, May 19, 1792; Savannah *Georgia Gazette*, December 1, 1791; Anon., *Life of General W. A. Bowles*, 9–10.

once again stricken. On the night of February 16, 1793, the great chief died, at the age of thirty-four, and because he was not a Roman Catholic, he was buried with full Masonic honors in Panton's garden.[79]

[79] Caughey, *McGillivray of the Creeks*, 53.

# CHAPTER V

# BURGEONING DEMOCRACY

I T WAS not until the last year of Washington's first administration that foreign affairs began to assume a major role in
our national history. The French Revolution had erupted
only a few months after the first President took office, and most
Americans were aroused by this stroke for freedom in the land
of their late ally. They were still more jubilant when, on September
21, 1792, France was declared a republic, but when the King
was executed four months later, they experienced mixed emo-
tions.[1] And so did a young man of thirty who waited anxiously
in Paris for news of that fateful event.

His name was Edmond Charles Genêt, commissioned the first
minister of the Republic of France to the government of the
United States. He was wellborn and well educated and was a
friend of some of the most powerful leaders of his nation at that
moment, including Brissot de Warville and Madame Roland.
Both he and his father served Louis XVI in important posts
and his eldest sister was first lady-in-waiting to Queen Marie
Antoinette, but he became an ardent revolutionist as a member of
the moderate Girondist Party. Both he and the party wished to
save the life of the King and Genêt waited in Paris hoping that
he might accompany the deposed ruler to America, but the guillotine ended his hopes, and the next day the youthful Minister
set out on his journey alone.

His appointment had been arranged three months previously
by his friend Brissot and the Minister of Foreign Affairs, Charles-
François Lebrun; his instructions, which he wrote himself, were
the subject of considerable debate. The United States had, in the

[1] Annapolis *Maryland Gazette,* July 11, 1793.

days of their peril, entered into a military alliance with France which obligated them to defend the French West Indies and to bar the privateers of hostile powers from their ports. France was already at war with Austria and Prussia and she expected Britain and Spain soon to be added to the number of her enemies. In these circumstances the United States would be more valuable as a source of supplies for herself and her West Indian possessions, especially in the categories of foodstuffs and timber, than as an active belligerent. Consequently, Genêt was not to ask for military assistance but to undertake the negotiation of a new commercial treaty. He was also to fit out privateers and authorize French consuls to take jurisdiction over the prizes which they would bring to port.[2]

Since war with Spain was expected, the Spanish-American colonies came in for careful consideration, and in this matter Brissot and his associates received ample advice from interested parties. Among the most important of these was Francisco de Miranda, the Venezuelan patriot who made the liberation of Spanish-America his life's work. At first his advice was apparently accepted, for on November 9, 1792, Colonel William S. Smith, son-in-law of Vice-President John Adams, left Paris with a message for Secretary of State Thomas Jefferson, informing him that a French fleet of forty-five ships of the line under command of Miranda would be sent to the mouth of the Mississippi and thence sweep southward in a movement to liberate Mexico and other Spanish dominions. Louisiana would be organized as a separate government, but the United States might be allowed to annex the Floridas and have the right to navigate the Mississippi. This was a large order, and before Genêt sailed, more modest counsel prevailed.[3]

[2] Grenville to George Hammond, March 12, 1793, in Mayo (ed.), *Instructions to the British Ministers*, 37; Halifax *North-Carolina Journal*, January 29, 1794; Frederick J. Turner, "The Origin of Genêt's Projected Attack on Louisiana and the Floridas," in *American Historical Review*, III (1897–1898), 654; Turner, "Diplomatic Contest for the Mississippi Valley," *loc. cit.*, 685; E. Wilson Lyon, *Louisiana in French Diplomacy, 1759–1804* (Norman, Okla., 1934), 69.

[3] Turner, "Origins of Genêt's Projected Attack on Louisiana and the Floridas," *loc. cit.*, 655; Frederick J. Turner, "The Policy of France toward the Mississippi Valley in the Period of Washington and Adams," in *American Historical Review*,

Brissot visited the United States in 1788, and in 1791 he published a three-volume work entitled *Nouveau Voyage dans les États-Unis*. Here he explained how the Western Americans hated Spain because she would not permit them to export their produce by way of the Mississippi River. This theme was enlarged upon by Captain Gilbert Imlay, who spent a year in Kentucky and who, in 1792, published in London a volume entitled *A Topographical Description of the Western Territory of North America*. Shortly afterward he made his way to Paris, became associated with Brissot, and presented the Executive Council of the National Convention with a document entitled *Mémoire sur la Louisiane*. Here he argued that France should organize an expedition in the American West to take possession of Louisiana.[4]

Of even greater import is the fact that a similar project was advanced by that hero of all Western heroes, General George Rogers Clark. Washington thwarted the project which Clark and his brother-in-law, Dr. James O'Fallon, sponsored under the aegis of the South Carolina Yazoo Company for setting up an independent government on the Lower Mississippi. Now their plan was in abeyance, but hope was revived when they received news that France had become a republic. O'Fallon knew Thomas Paine during the hectic days of our own Revolution, and that zealous and articulate Irishman was now a member of the French National Convention. To him O'Fallon and Clark sent a memorial urging that an expedition against Louisiana be organized in Kentucky with France as the sponsor and Clark as the leader.[5]

This reached Paris before Genêt's departure and Paine laid it

---

X (1904–1905), 259–60; Frederick W. Keller, "American Politics and the Genêt Mission, 1793–1794" (M.A. thesis, University of Pittsburgh, 1951), 52, 92.

[4] Keller, "Amercan Politics and the Genêt Mission," 91, 575–77; Turner, "Origin of Genêt's Projected Attack on Louisiana and the Floridas," *loc. cit.*, 658; Turner, "Diplomatic Contest for the Mississippi Valley," *loc. cit.*, 684; Lyon, *Louisiana in French Diplomacy*, 68–69; sketch of Gilbert Imlay in *Dictionary of American Biography*, IX, 461–62.

[5] Paine to O'Fallon, February 17, 1793, in *American Historical Review*, XXIX (1923–1924), 504–505; Williams, "French and Other Intrigues in the Southwest Territory," *loc. cit.*, 25; Eugene P. Link, *Democratic-Republican Societies, 1790–1800* (New York, 1942), 134–35; Richard Lowitt, "Activities of Citizen Genêt in Kentucky, 1793–1794," in *Filson Club History Quarterly* (Louisville), XXII (1948), 253; Turner, "Origin of Genêt's Projected Attack on Louisiana and the Floridas," *loc. cit.*, 650; Keller, "American Politics and the Genêt Mission," 93, 431, 584–86.

before the Executive Council. It doubtless had some weight in the formulation of Genêt's instructions, which provided for the organization of expeditions against both Louisiana and the Floridas. In aid of these projects revolutionary movements would be fomented, not only in these Spanish possessions, but in British Canada. The Minister was supplied with blank commissions for the Americans who would be chosen to lead the Louisiana and Florida expeditions under the French flag, and he also had three hundred letters of marque which, by a stroke of the pen, would convert American merchantmen into French privateers.[6]

Genêt set sail for the United States during the last week in February, 1793, but instead of making port at Philadelphia and presenting his credentials to President Washington and Secretary of State Jefferson, he landed at Charleston where he was met by the French consul, Michel Ange Bernard de Mangourit. Whether this change of destination was a result of chance or design is not certain, but Mangourit's well-laid plans indicate that it was according to preconceived arrangement.[7]

France had already declared war on Britain and hostilities with Spain soon followed. This rendered her largely dependent on neutral shipping, and consequently she opened all her ports, both at home and in the West Indies, to American ships.[8] She was dependent on the United States for supplies of foodstuffs and timber, and American merchants, especially those of the Middle and Southern states, were carrying on a brisk trade with her. Genêt was, therefore, to negotiate a new commercial treaty barring enemy vessels from our ports but not requiring us to defend the French West Indies in accord with the treaty of 1778. Naturally the British government objected to having its enemy supplied by our ships, and an order in council declared foodstuffs a contraband of war and therefore subject to seizure. Britain also declared that ports which were not open to neutrals in time of peace could not be considered open in time of war, and this,

[6] Keller, "American Politics and the Genêt Mission," 94–99, 567–68, 584–86; Turner, "Origin of Genêt's Projected Attack on Louisiana and the Floridas," *loc. cit.*, 657–58, 660; Richard K. Murdoch, "Citizen Mangourit and the Projected Attack on East Florida in 1794," in *Journal of Southern History*, XIV (1948), 524.

[7] Channing, *History of the United States*, IV, 127.

[8] Halifax *North-Carolina Journal*, May 8, 1793; Link, *Democratic-Republican Societies*, 125–26; Whitaker, *Spanish-American Frontier*, 174.

of course, applied to the French West Indies. In accordance with these regulations British warships began capturing American merchantmen in large numbers and having them condemned by her admiralty courts.[9]

American merchants usually carried on their business by means of British capital and most of their imports came from Britain. Then, too, Britain's war with France made it necessary for her to open her West Indies ports to a limited trade with the United States. For these reasons most of our citizens engaged in commerce were pro-British in their sympathies, but the French trade was lucrative and some of the leading Charleston merchants favored the French cause.[10] The old Huguenot population of this city was enthusiastic for Genêt and organized its own patriotic society to support the French cause, but the refugees who were arriving in large numbers from Santo Domingo were no friends of the Revolution. Though in the South generally the townspeople were pro-British, many of the planters sympathized with the French. However, the main support of the Democratic Societies came from the ranks of the average citizen. The small farmer, the craftsman, the Revolutionary veteran who believed in democracy had an affection for our old ally and espoused the cause of the French Revolution with all his heart. Except for the veterans, the Francophiles were mostly young men, and the dandies among them affected the sartorial style of the *sans culotte,* wore unpowdered cropped hair, short-waisted, high-collared coats, "pudding bag" cravats, and "those slovenly things called pantaloons flapping about their ankles." The aristocratic pro-British element adhered to the traditional long hair which was powdered and tied back, to knee-length breeches (*culotte*), silk stockings, slippers with silver buckles, and long coats with laced cuffs.[11]

[9] Charleston *City Gazette,* March 25, 1794; Halifax *North-Carolina Journal,* September 4, 1793; Turner, "Policy of France toward the Mississippi Valley," *loc. cit.,* 261; Bernard Mayo, *Henry Clay* (Boston, 1937), 36; Channing, *History of the United States,* IV, 127.

[10] Lexington *Kentucky Gazette,* April 5, 1799; Halifax *North-Carolina Journal,* August 28, 1793; Edenton *State Gazette of North-Carolina,* February 7, 1794; Link, *Democratic-Republican Societies,* 49 n., 74–75.

[11] Link, *Democratic-Republican Societies,* 87, 93, 98–99; Link, "Democratic Societies of the Carolinas," *loc. cit.,* 262, 268; Savannah *Georgia Gazette,* January 29, 1795; Bernard Mayo, *Jefferson Himself* (Boston, 1942), 198–99.

Even before the arrival of Genêt, Mangourit had been active. On January 9 he gave a banquet at which Governor Moultrie, the presiding officers of the South Carolina House and Senate, as well as the important merchant and citizen, Christopher Gadsden, were present. At least two other similar celebrations were held during the month and presently the Republican Society of Charleston was organized. Alexander Moultrie, brother to the governor and head of the South Carolina Yazoo Company, was a leader of this group, which chose Stephen Drayton president and William Tate secretary. Robert Goodloe Harper and other leading citizens were prominent members. Drayton belonged to one of the most important Charleston families and was secretary to Governor Moultrie. William Tate was a wealthy landowner and industrialist of the Pendleton district, which presently organized its own Democratic Society. Speculators in Western lands—notably the members of the South Carolina Yazoo Company—were interested in opening the navigation of the Mississippi and consistently supported Genêt with enthusiasm. Intellectuals, especially members of the American Philosophical Society, also supported the French cause, but it attracted few of the clergy.[12] Despite such aristocratic leadership, both here and elsewhere, these organizations were popular in nature and were, even in the case of the Charleston group, often formed around a militia company as a nucleus.[13] Such societies came into being in most of the states south of New England, with twelve in the Middle states and seventeen in the Southern. The most important of them was organized in Philadelphia on May 30, with such prominent men as A. J. Dallas, David Rittenhouse, Charles Biddle, and Dr. Charles Logan taking an active part in the movement.[14] Early in 1794 this group published an address to the French population of Louisiana, saying that a French naval force would soon appear on their coast and that a Western army would shortly come down

---

[12] Wolfe, *Jeffersonian Democracy in South Carolina*, 72; Link, *Democratic-Republican Societies*, 65–66, 78–83, 134–35; Link, "Democratic Societies of the Carolinas," *loc. cit.*, 267; Wallace, *History of South Carolina*, I, 353; Turner, "Origin of Genêt's Projected Attack on Louisiana and the Floridas," *loc. cit.*, 663; Hays, *Hero of Hornet's Nest*, 241; Bowers, *Jefferson and Hamilton*, 223.

[13] Link, *Democratic-Republican Societies*, 76–77, 181–82.

[14] *Ibid.*, 6–15, 63; Lexington *Kentucky Gazette*, August 24, 1793.

the Mississippi to assist them in throwing off the yoke of Spain. With this aid they were to establish their independence and enter into alliance with France or the United States. The appeal was circulated in Louisiana by secret agents.[15]

Such societies were not new to the political scene. Similar organizations existed during the American Revolution; the Jacobin Clubs of France furnished a more recent example, and Democratic Clubs were formed in London before they were introduced in America.[16] Though a few opposition groups were organized in the United States, the great majority, usually calling themselves either Democratic or Republican Societies, were vociferously pro-French. They accepted the philosophy of Rousseau and Thomas Paine and declared themselves in favor of liberty and equality. On a more concrete level they advocated manhood suffrage, proportional representation, and the right of the people to assemble, to discuss, and to instruct their representatives. Some of the more radical even advocated rotation in office and objected to the appointment, or indirect election, of public officials. What the more doctrinaire Rousseauans were aiming at was majority rule unhampered by constitutional restraints, but they formed only a small minority of the membership of the Democratic Societies. It is worthy of note that, at the other extreme, members of the South Carolina Yazoo Company were among the leaders of the Charleston group.[17]

Having had the ground well prepared for him, Genêt was royally received in Charleston. Mangourit introduced him to the more important citizens, including Governor Moultrie. He was lavishly entertained, and the "Marseillaise" and "Ça Ira" were sung with fervor on all occasions.[18] Encouraged by the overtures which he received, Genêt went about his work with characteristic energy. Not only did he purchase large quantities

---

[15] Safford (ed.), *Blennerhassett Papers*, 99; Gayarré, *History of Louisiana*, III, 337.

[16] Link, "Democratic Societies of the Carolinas," *loc. cit.*, 259; Lexington *Kentucky Gazette*, April 14, 1792, quoting London item, July 30, 1791.

[17] Link, *Democratic-Republican Societies*, 9–13, 103 ff., 163; Link, "Democratic Societies of the Carolinas," *loc. cit.*, 269–73; Charleston *City Gazette*, July 25, 1794; Savannah *Georgia Gazette*, October 2, 1794.

[18] Williams, "French and Other Intrigues in the Southwest Territory," *loc. cit.*, 26; Keller, "American Politics and the Genêt Mission," 569.

of supplies for France, he fitted out four privateers and sent them to cruise against British shipping. Soon they were bringing prizes into port, some of them captured within the three-mile limit, and these were condemned by French consular courts and sold. Not only in Charleston, but at other Atlantic ports, letters of marque were issued to owners of American vessels, which proceeded to cruise as French privateers. Baltimore alone furnished forty or fifty of them.[19]

Genêt's other major activity consisted in starting preparations for the expeditions to be sent against Florida and Louisiana. To lead one of these he selected the redoubtable Elijah Clarke, Major General of Georgia militia and the mainstay of that state in its continuing war with the Creek Indians. In the fall of 1793 Clarke resigned his Georgia post to accept a commission as major general in the French service.[20] To act as his chief lieutenants, William Tate and Samuel Hammond were made brigadiers. The latter, with his brother Abner, who was made a colonel of cavalry, operated a mercantile establishment in Savannah which engaged extensively in the Indian trade. He was to rally the Georgia frontiersmen and make a treaty with the Creeks, and it is not unlikely that he had an eye on the business which William Panton was doing with this Nation at Pensacola. Though he thus had ulterior motives, Samuel Hammond was an able man who, during the Revolution, had fought at the Battle of King's Mountain, then later served in Congress and succeeded Wilkinson as governor of Upper Louisiana. He was at this time Surveyor General of Georgia.[21]

[19] Grenville to Hammond, January (?), 1794, March 7, 1795, in Mayo (ed.), *Instructions to the British Ministers*, 45, 78–80; Charleston *City Gazette*, April 29, 1793; Halifax *North-Carolina Journal*, May 8, 1793; Edenton *State Gazette of North-Carolina*, October 12, 1793; Savannah *Georgia Gazette*, December 25, 1794; Annapolis *Maryland Gazette*, April 10, 1795; John T. Scharf, *History of Maryland, from the Earliest Period to the Present Day* (Baltimore, 1879), II, 581–82.

[20] E. Merton Coulter, "Elijah Clarke's Foreign Intrigues and the 'Trans-Oconee Republic,'" in Mississippi Valley Historical Association *Proceedings* (Cedar Rapids), X, Pt. II (1919–1921), 261–62, 267; Keller, "American Politics and the Genêt Mission," 581–82.

[21] Keller, "American Politics and the Genêt Mission," 577–79; Turner, "Policy of France toward the Mississippi Valley," *loc. cit.*, 262; Turner, "Diplomatic Contest for the Mississippi Valley," *loc. cit.*, 686; Hays, *Hero of Hornet's Nest*, 244–48; Link, *Democratic-Republican Societies*, 68–69, 137.

The generals were furnished with blank commissions to fill out for their field and company officers, and soon the Hammonds recruited sixteen hundred men and marched them to Camden County, where they were stationed at posts on the St. Marys River. To give this operation the color of legality, the men would be taken into the Indian country before being sworn into the French service. Three French frigates with a thousand men were stationed at Beaufort, South Carolina, and the plan was for Hammond to be met by a French fleet at Savannah in order to make a sea-borne attack on St. Augustine. Clarke was to collect his forces from upper Georgia and South Carolina, rendezvous at St. Marys, and co-operate with Hammond and the French fleet in the attack on St. Augustine, after which he was to march against Pensacola. East Florida was to be established as an independent republic and eventually form a union with West Florida and Louisiana, should they also be liberated.[22] In the meanwhile, Tate was to negotiate with the Cherokee and Choctaw, collect a force in the upper Carolinas, and conduct it down the Tennessee River to join another force which George Rogers Clark was to lead from Kentucky against New Orleans.[23] Having set this elaborate scheme on foot, Genêt left Mangourit to carry it out and, on April 17, set out by way of Richmond and Baltimore for Philadelphia.[24]

In order that the people might be rallied to his cause, he sent couriers ahead to announce his coming, and he was greeted by eager crowds in the towns through which he passed. But his reception in Philadelphia was not quite so overwhelming. Even before he reached this city, Washington, on April 22, issued his proclamation of neutrality, and the President greeted Genêt

[22] Genêt to Jefferson, February 1, 1793, in Halifax *North-Carolina Journal*, February 19, 1793; Instructions and Authorization of Citizen Consul Mangourit, 1793, in East and West Florida Papers (Georgia Department of Archives and History), 45–48; Murdoch, "Citizen Mangourit," *loc. cit.*, 527, 533–34; Hays, *Hero of Hornet's Nest*, 244–48.

[23] Lexington *Kentucky Gazette*, April 25, 1794; Turner, "Origin of Genêt's Projected Attack on Louisiana and the Floridas," *loc. cit.*, 667–68; Turner, "French Policy toward the Mississippi Valley," *loc. cit.*, 202; Keller, "American Politics and the Genêt Mission," 578; Link, "Democratic Societies of the Carolinas," *loc. cit.*, 274; Hays, *Hero of Hornet's Nest*, 241 ff.

[24] Halifax *North-Carolina Journal*, May 8, 1795.

with cold formality. However, in the Secretary of State the Frenchman had an ardent Francophile and a sympathetic friend to whom, on July 5, he revealed his plans to occupy Louisiana with the assistance of George Rogers Clark and to establish it as an independent government with close commercial ties with the United States. Jefferson warned Genêt that Americans could not legally engage in such an enterprise, but he was willing that Louisiana should be revolutionized, and Genêt thought he was sympathetic to his project.[25]

André Michaux was a French naturalist with whom Jefferson had become acquainted and with whom he had discussed an exploring expedition up the Missouri River and across the continent to the Pacific. Now Michaux was commissioned to go to Kentucky and make preliminary plans for the organization of a military force for an attack on New Orleans under the French flag. Jefferson gave him a letter of introduction to Governor Isaac Shelby and sent him, with two aides, on his way. Four additional agents were sent to assist him in Kentucky.[26] Michaux carried with him Paine's answer to O'Fallon's letter, which Genêt brought with him from Paris, and he delivered a commission as major general to George Rogers Clark, who was to lead the expedition against New Orleans. This appointment is not surprising, for as soon as Clark heard of Genêt's appointment, he offered his services in a letter delivered to the Minister on his arrival in the Quaker City.[27]

It should not be assumed that Clark was acting from any

[25] Keller, "American Politics and the Genêt Mission," 486–87, 570; Turner, "Origin of Genêt's Projected Attack on Louisiana and the Floridas," *loc. cit.*, 666–68; Turner, "French Policy toward the Mississippi Valley," *loc. cit.*, 263; Turner, "Diplomatic Contest for the Mississippi Valley," *loc. cit.*, 687; R. W. Griswold, *Republican Court* (Philadelphia, 1855), 350.

[26] Keller, "American Politics and the Genêt Mission," 584–86; Turner, "Diplomatic Contest for the Mississippi Valley," *loc. cit.*, 686–88; Lowitt, "Genêt in Kentucky," *loc. cit.*, 256–58, 260; Whitaker, *Spanish-American Frontier*, 187.

[27] Keller, "American Politics and the Genêt Mission," 431; Turner, "Origin of Genêt's Projected Attack on Louisiana and the Floridas," *loc. cit.*, 653, 655; Turner, "Diplomatic Contest for the Mississippi Valley," *loc. cit.*, 685; Lowitt, "Genêt in Kentucky," *loc. cit.*, 259; Paine to O'Fallon, February 17, 1793, in *American Historical Review*, XXIX (1923–1924), 504–505; Link, *Democratic-Republican Societies*, 134–35.

motives which he considered unworthy. The cause of the French Revolution was even more popular in the West than it was east of the mountains. This spirit was demonstrated on February 8 when a supper and ball were held in Lexington to celebrate French victories. The ladies' dresses and the hall were decorated in the colors of the Republic, and toasts were drunk to the patriots of France and to "The Republican Interest in the United States." Moreover, Kentuckians hated Spaniards who would not permit free navigation of the great river and who were suspected of stirring up the Indians. If France would help them drive Spain out of Louisiana and open the navigation of the Mississippi, they had no qualms about co-operating with the new Republic.[28]

In order to foster this spirit, John Bradford suggested the organization of a Democratic Society in Lexington.[29] Just as in the case of the Charleston and Philadelphia societies, the Lexington group, organized in August, 1793, was to serve as a central body for the state and encourage the organization of affiliated societies in the counties, several of which were established. On August 28 John Breckinridge—perhaps the most influential citizen of Kentucky and later to serve as President Jefferson's Attorney General—was elected president, and Thomas Bodley and Thomas Todd were chosen clerks. Among the members were most of the leading men of the community, with the exception of Wilkinson and his friends Benjamin Sebastian and Harry Innes, Judge of the Federal District Court.[30] Only these two had completely committed themselves to Wilkinson during the Spanish Conspiracy of 1788, and their attitude now showed that they still felt themselves bound to the Spanish interest,

[28] Lexington *Kentucky Gazette*, February 16, 1793; May 17, 1794.

[29] E. Merton Coulter, "Efforts of the Democratic Societies of the West to Open the Navigation of the Mississippi," in *Mississippi Valley Historical Review* (Cedar Rapids), XI (1924–1925), 377–78; Link, *Democratic-Republican Societies*, 13; Niels H. Sonne, *Liberal Kentucky, 1780–1828* (New York, 1939), 28–29.

[30] Lexington *Kentucky Gazette*, August 31, November 2, 1793; Safford (ed.), *Blennerhassett Papers*, 163; Archibald Henderson, "Isaac Shelby and the Genêt Mission," in *Mississippi Valley Historical Review* (Cedar Rapids), VI (1919–1920), 452; Lowitt, "Genêt in Kentucky," *loc. cit.*, 255; Keller, "American Politics and the Genêt Mission," 572; Link, *Democratic-Republican Societies*, 138–39; Savannah *Georgia Republican*, January 30, 1807; Daveiss, *View of the President's Conduct Concerning the Conspiracy of 1806*, 64.

though Innes kept in close touch with the work of the society and with the French agent, Auguste Lachaise. His correspondence is the best source of information as to the society's activities. Others, such as Senator John Brown and George Muter, Chief Justice of the Kentucky Court of Appeals, were interested only in opening the navigation of the Mississippi and were prepared to resort to any available means for accomplishing that object. For this purpose France was a much more congenial partner than Spain.[31]

The Democratic Society of Lexington was interested in reform of the criminal code, abolishment of imprisonment for debt, and adoption of a more democratic constitution for Kentucky; but the Mississippi question overshadowed all other considerations. General Lachaise, a Louisianian who was acting as one of Genêt's agents in Kentucky, appeared before the society in support of Clark's projected expedition against New Orleans and urged that an address be sent to the National Convention or to the Executive Council of France. The second suggestion was not approved, but the Clark expedition was heartily endorsed, and Lachaise was declared to be entitled to "the respect of this Society and the particular attention of the Nation of which he is a citizen." In October, 1793, the society resolved "That the right of the people on the western waters of the Mississippi, to the navigation, was *undoubted,* and . . . ought to be *peremptorily* demanded of Spain by the Government of the United States." [32] On December 13 it adopted an "Address to the Inhabitants of the United States west of the Alleghany Mountains" which declared that repeated memorials on this subject had been presented to Congress and that they had been treated with neglect and contempt. Money had been taken from the Westerners by means of "an

[31] Humphrey Marshall's amended statement to complaint of Innes in case of Innes *v.* Marshall, in Innes Papers; Testimony of Joseph Crockett, *ibid.*; Testimony of Isaac Shelby, *ibid.*; Thomas C. Cherry, "Robert Craddock and Peter Tardiveau, Two Revolutionary Soldiers of Warren County, Kentucky," in *Filson Club History Quarterly,* IV (1930), 78 ff.

[32] Communication to Innes, n.d., in Lexington *Kentucky Gazette,* November 16, 1793; Innes Papers, Bk. 19; Deposition of John Bradford, n.d., *ibid.,* Bk. 22, Pt. I; Lexington *Kentucky Gazette,* October 12, 1793; April 12, 1794; Henderson, "Isaac Shelby and the Genêt Mission," *loc. cit.,* 453; Link, *Democratic-Republican Societies,* 139–42, 152–53.

odious and offensive excise, but means of procuring money by exercise of our rights denied us. A local policy appears to have undue weight in the councils of the Nation. It seems to be the object of that policy to prevent the population of this Country, which would draw from the Eastern states their industrious citizens. This conclusion inevitably follows from a consideration of the measures taken to prevent the purchase and settlement of lands [by the Yazoo companies] bordering on the Mississippi. Among those measures the unconstitutional interference which rescinded sales, by one of the States to private individuals, makes a striking object." All must join, it said, in firm remonstrance to the President and Congress, and added that "the present opportunity is favorable to gain the navigation of the river as Spain is engaged in war." The address ended with a proposal that Democratic Societies should be formed in every county of the state.[33]

On the last day of 1793 the Lexington Society proceeded to publish its remonstrance to the President and the Congress. After proposing that a ship be fitted out and sent down the Mississippi to the Gulf to prove whether or not the river was open to navigation, it framed the following protest: "Your remonstrants yield not in patriotism to any of their fellow citizens, but patriotism, like every other thing, has its bounds. We love those states from which we all congregated and no event (not even an attempt to barter away our best rights) shall alien our affections from the individual members which compose them. But attachment to government sease [sic] to be natural when they cease to be mutual. To be subject to all the burthens and enjoy none of the benefits arising from government is what we shall never submit to. Our situation compels us to speak plainly. . . . From the General Government of America therefore your Remonstrants now ask protection in the free enjoyment of the river Mississippi, which is withheld from them by the Spaniards. . . . We declare it to be a right which must be obtained, and do also declare if

[33] Address to the Inhabitants of the United States West of the Allegheny Mountains by the Democratic Society of Kentucky, December 13, 1793, in Innes Papers, Bk. 19; Henderson, "Isaac Shelby and the Genêt Mission," *loc. cit.*, 459; Coulter, "Efforts of the Democratic Societies of the West to Open the Navigation of the Mississippi," *loc. cit.*, 379–80; Lycan, "Alexander Hamilton and the North Carolina Federalists," *loc. cit.*, 451–53.

the General Government will not procure it for us, we shall hold ourselves not answerable for any consequences that may result from our procurement of it." [34] A copy of this protest was sent to Andrew Jackson for circulation in Tennessee.[35]

This being the spirit of Kentucky, it is not surprising that George Rogers Clark was able to find recruits for his expeditionary force; John Breckinridge, John Bradford, Levi and Thomas Todd, Robert Patterson, and other prominent men contributed to his ammunition fund. He was hampered by the failure of Genêt to remit funds; but a dollar a day, a thousand acres of land in the conquered territory for one year's service, and such plunder as should fall into their hands were offered to all who would enlist. By means of these inducements a force of several hundred men was collected at Louisville and an advance party sent down the Ohio to within fifty miles of the nearest Spanish post on the west bank of the Mississippi.[36]

When, in November, 1793, Michaux returned from Kentucky to the East, he traveled by way of the Cumberland Gap and the Long Island of the Holston, but he made no attempt to contact Sevier, Governor Blount, or any of the political leaders of the Southwest Territory. This is not surprising, for he knew that Blount was an avowed supporter of the Federal Administration and opposed to all the works of Citizen Genêt.[37]

Colonel John Montgomery, who served under George Rogers Clark during the Revolution and afterward participated in the settlement of Clarksville on the Cumberland River, naming the town for his old commander, wrote to Clark on October 26, 1793, applying for a commission and saying he could raise several hundred men. Clark accepted the offer and on January 12, 1794,

[34] Remonstrance of the Citizens West of the Allegheny Mountains to the President and Congress, December 3, 1793, in Innes Papers, Bk. 19; Coulter, "Efforts of the Democratic Societies to Open the Navigation of the Mississippi," *loc. cit.,* 380.

[35] Letters of James Brown, in *Louisiana Historical Quarterly,* XX (1937), 58–68.

[36] Lexington *Kentucky Gazette,* January 4, February 8, 1794; Lowitt, "Genêt in Kentucky," *loc. cit.,* 264; Link, *Democratic-Republican Societies,* 137; Keller, "American Politics and the Genêt Mission," 458–59, 590–92; Halifax *North-Carolina Journal,* January 22, 1794; Hays, *Hero of Hornet's Nest,* 244.

[37] Blount to Robertson, January 18, 1794, in Carter (ed.), *Territory South of the River Ohio,* 325; Blount to Sevier, February 9, 1794, *ibid.,* 327; Whitaker, *Spanish-American Frontier,* 187; Williams, "French and Other Intrigues in the Southwest Territory," *loc. cit.,* 26, 28–29.

Montgomery reported that he had bought on credit 30 pounds of powder, 177 pounds of lead, about 19,000 pounds of beef, 1,000 pounds of bear meat, 70 pairs of venison hams, 500 bushels of corn, and 10,000 pounds of pork; also that he had built a large flatboat and four pirogues. Proceeding with about two hundred men to the mouth of the Cumberland River, he built a rude fort and stopped all boats descending to New Orleans with provisions. When General Wayne heard of this development, he sent an expedition which destroyed the fort and released the captured boats. Then, in order to stop any of Clark's boats which might try to pass, he put up a fortification on the site of an old French fort near the mouth of the Tennessee River and, using the ancient name, called it Fort Massac.[38]

Meanwhile, Genêt was having his troubles in Philadelphia. Washington's neutrality proclamation met with an unfavorable reaction from the public. The Democratic Societies denounced it, as did Madison and Jefferson. The Secretary of State, crediting its terms to Hamilton, called it pusillanimous.[39] The French Minister naturally believed that the American people were sympathetic to his cause, and he was angered by the cold reception which Washington had accorded him. But there were even greater disappointments in store. Genêt expected to finance his operations by funds derived from the sale of prizes and from payments which he expected the Federal government to make against the balance it still owed France on account of loans made during the American Revolution. Washington, with Jefferson's concurrence, declined to make such advance payments, and he also ordered that no more privateers be commissioned nor should French consular courts have jurisdiction over prizes.[40]

Believing that the government was in these matters acting in opposition to the wishes of its citizens, Genêt threatened, so it

[38] Williams, "French and Other Intrigues in the Southwest Territory," loc. cit., 26–28; Henderson, "Isaac Shelby and the Genêt Mission," loc. cit., 466; Safford (ed.), Blennerhassett Papers, 104.

[39] Turner, "Diplomatic Contest for the Mississippi Valley," loc. cit., 686; Turner, "Origin of Genêt's Projected Attack on Louisiana and the Floridas," loc. cit., 664; Keller, "American Politics and the Genêt Mission," 191; Link, Democratic-Republican Societies, 129–30.

[40] Link, Democratic-Republican Societies, 127; Halifax North-Carolina Journal, October 30, 1793; Annapolis Maryland Gazette, October-November, 1793.

was reported, to appeal directly to the people. He denied this and said that he proposed instead to appeal to Congress, through the medium of the Executive of the United States, to ask for an examination of his proceedings. The President accepted the original account of the matter and was highly indignant.[41] By this time popular sentiment was beginning to turn against Genêt, but it was the affair of the *Little Democrat* which led immediately to his recall. This vessel was a brigantine which he fitted out with fourteen guns and was preparing to dispatch to the mouth of the Mississippi to blockade the river in aid of Clark's expedition against New Orleans. He was ordered by Washington and Jefferson not to let the vessel sail until given specific authority to do so, but in defiance of their demands, he sent his brigantine to sea on July 12. Washington at once took up with the Cabinet the matter of Genêt's recall and the formal order requesting it was issued on September 15, 1793.[42]

Genêt's Girondist Party fell from power more than three months before Washington requested his recall. The radical Jacobins, who took over direction of the French Revolution, complied with alacrity and appointed Citizen Antoine Joseph Fauchet to represent them in Philadelphia. However, it was not until February 22, 1794, that the new Minister presented his credentials and not until March 6 that he issued a proclamation declaring: "Every Frenchman is forbidden to violate the neutrality of the United States. All commissions or authorizations tending to impugn that neutrality are revoked and are to be returned to the agents of the French Republic." [43] Disregarding

[41] Governor Moultrie to Genêt, September 5, 1793, Genêt to Moultrie, October 15, 1793, in Halifax *North-Carolina Journal*, November 6, 1793; A. J. Dallas to the Public, December 7, 1793, in Savannah *Georgia Gazette*, January 9, 1794; Turner, "Policy of France toward the Mississippi Valley," *loc. cit.*, 263; Keller, "American Politics and the Genêt Mission," 530–32.

[42] Halifax *North-Carolina Journal*, August 28, 1793, quoting letter from Philadelphia, August 16; Annapolis *Maryland Gazette*, August 29, 1793; Keller, "American Politics and the Genêt Mission," 275, 479–80; Turner, "Diplomatic Contest for the Mississippi Valley," *loc. cit.*, 688; Turner, "Policy of France toward the Mississippi Valley," *loc. cit.*, 263; Turner, "Origin of Genêt's Projected Attack on Louisiana and the Floridas," *loc. cit.*, 675.

[43] Charleston *City Gazette*, March 28, 1794; Keller, "American Politics and the Genêt Mission," 595; Lexington *Kentucky Gazette*, April 26, 1794; Murdoch, "Citizen Mangourit," *loc. cit.*, 536–37.

this order, Mangourit wrote Fauchet on March 31 that preparations for the East Florida expedition were practically completed and that he was certain of success. Four days later he sent Hammond a proclamation to be published to the Floridians as soon as the frontier had been crossed. This was his last dispatch to Georgia, for the new vice-consul appointed by Fauchet reached Charleston in April and put a stop to the hostile preparations.[44]

It proved harder to discourage Genêt's followers. By January, 1794, Tate had reported that he had two thousand men under arms, and in April Hammond collected his forces on the St. Marys with the intention of starting the campaign against St. Augustine on April 10. But these militant plans met with strong opposition.[45] Though Governor Moultrie favored Genêt, the South Carolina legislature held opposite views and, on December 2, 1793, instructed the governor to issue a proclamation prohibiting enlistments for the French service. Also a committee was appointed to investigate recruiting activities. A week later Moultrie issued the proclamation but made no attempt to enforce it.[46] On the other hand, the legislative committee went about its business with enthusiasm and ordered Drayton, Tate, John Hamilton, and others taken into custody and their papers searched. Colonel Wade Hampton, in the capacity of sheriff, was ordered to carry out the search and seizure, and he proceeded to do so. Drayton then brought suit against Hampton and the committee on the ground that there was no law against filibustering and the President could not, by proclamation, make an act a crime when there was no law to make it so. He employed Colonel William Moultrie to handle his case, but the legislature retaliated by passing a resolution to the effect that "any attorney bringing suit against a member of the legislature for any action in official capacity is unworthy of his office and ought not to be permitted to practice law in this state." A few days later a grand jury pre-

[44] Murdoch, "Citizen Mangourit," loc. cit., 538–40; Charleston City Gazette, April 12, 1794; Keller, "American Politics and the Genêt Mission," 582–83.

[45] Keller, "American Politics and the Genêt Mission," 582.

[46] Murdoch, "Citizen Mangourit," loc. cit., 531–32; Coulter, "Elijah Clarke's Foreign Intrigues and the 'Trans-Oconee Republic,'" loc. cit., 265; Wolfe, Jeffersonian Democracy in South Carolina, 74; Phillips, "South Carolina Federalists," loc. cit., 731–33; Halifax North-Carolina Journal, May 8, 1793.

sented the United States Circuit Court sitting at Columbia with a true bill against Drayton.[47]

This did not mean, however, that the friends of France were routed in South Carolina. Recruiting continued actively in the western counties, and about the middle of February the Republican Society of Charleston celebrated with a feast at which pro-French toasts were drunk: to the French Republic, to Citizen Genêt, to the damnation of the enemies of the French Republic "in whatever clime they may be found," to Citizen Madison and the Republican Party in Congress, to the hope of a speedy revolution in Great Britain and Ireland "upon *sans culotte* principles," and to the guillotine for "all tyrants, plunderers and funding Speculators." When the last toast was drunk, the cap of liberty was placed on the head of the president and then on each member of the society. Stephen Drayton made the speech of the occasion and the society sang the "Marseillaise," after which the company marched back to the hotel with drums beating and fifes playing "Ça Ira." And it had recently been reported from Greenville County that a spirit "of recruiting prevails here to a great degree for an expedition, under French authority, against West Florida, New Orleans and St. Augustine." [48]

Of course, South Carolina was not the only state in which there was conflict of opinion. In September, 1793, the *North-Carolina Journal* published an article headed "Aristocracy and Democracy" which stated that the world was engaged in a contest to determine whether the people shall rule or be slaves and that the success or failure of the French Republic would decide the question. The article went on to say: "Were the people proof against the corruption of wealth, they would soon convince these tyrants, *that the right is originally and at all times in them,* and that power and competency would follow." [49] A more conservative attitude was expressed three days later when the merchants of New Bern resolved that the President's declaration of neutrality

---

[47] Alexander Moultrie, *An Appeal to the People on the Conduct of a Certain Public Body in South Carolina, Respecting Col. Drayton and Col. Moultrie* (Charleston, 1794), Appendix, 22; Halifax *North-Carolina Journal,* January 15, 1794, from Charleston *City Gazette,* December 10, 1793; *ibid.,* January 21, 31, May 15, 17, 1794.

[48] Charleston *City Gazette,* January 3, February 13, 15, April 12, 1794.

[49] Halifax *North-Carolina Journal,* September 11, 1793.

was dictated by wisdom and was for the true interests of the people and should have their hearty approbation.[50]

A similar attitude was expressed on January 11, 1794, in the General Assembly of North Carolina. A committee, to whom was referred a message from the governor, together with the resolutions of the South Carolina legislature regarding Genêt's activities and the enlistment of American citizens to fight for the French Republic, moved that the North Carolina governor issue a similar proclamation.[51] The Virginia House of Delegates expressed like views when, on November 1, 1793, it approved the President's proclamation of neutrality by a vote of seventy-seven to forty-eight; and the Maryland House of Delegates took the same stand by a unanimous vote.[52] But the Francophiles were still active, and news of the success of French armies over the combined forces before Dunkirk "gave such unusual joy to every republican" that in Richmond on November 18 three barrels of gunpowder were delivered to the militia of the city to celebrate the event. This celebration took place in Capitol Square with great éclat.[53]

On December 12, 1793, the Georgia legislature ordered a procession and dinner in honor of the French Revolution. General Elijah Clarke attended, and the president of the Senate made an address to which the governor replied. But the French cause had its opponents also. On January 8 a public meeting held at the "Filature" in Savannah adopted resolutions condemning Genêt's attempt to raise an armed force within the United States and endorsing Washington's policy of neutrality. Yet an article in the same newspaper which published the proceedings carried a communication saying that the majority has an absolute right to govern the minority but that the "Filature" resolutions were the work of a few men and not the real voice of Chatham County.[54]

Governor Mathews of Georgia gave ample evidence of his

[50] *Ibid.*, October 16, 1793; New Bern *North-Carolina Gazette*, September 21, 1793.
[51] Halifax *North-Carolina Journal*, February 5, 1794.
[52] *Ibid.*, November 13, December 25, 1793.
[53] New Bern *North-Carolina Gazette*, November 27, 1793.
[54] Savannah *Georgia Gazette*, January 16, 1794; Hays, *Hero of Hornet's Nest*, 244–48.

pro-French attitude, but his official position made it necessary for him, like Governor Moultrie, to take action which did not accord with his sympathies. "Generals" Samuel Hammond and Elijah Clarke were moving men and supplies down to the St. Marys River, just across from Spanish territory, and they even sent Abner Hammond down into Florida to recruit among the Georgians who had moved across the line. The Spaniards arrested him and his most important recruit, Colonel John McIntosh; then by way of precaution they began evacuating the territory between the St. Marys and the St. Johns rivers. On January 3 Colonel Howard, who commanded the Spanish forces on that frontier, protested to Governor Mathews about the threatened invasion, and soon Governor Juan N. Quesada of East Florida made a similar protest.[55] On February 21 Mathews replied to Quesada that he regretted to hear that citizens of Georgia were engaged in the French service with views hostile to Spain and that he would prevent trouble by every legal means. He promised to try to discover the guilty parties but regretted that Quesada had not sent proof of his charges, for citizens could not be arrested without evidence. At about the same time he notified the Georgia delegation in Congress of this development, asked General Jared Irvin to submit any evidence that he could collect, and wrote Judges Fort W. Stith, George Walton, and John Y. Noel, as well as Attorney General George Walker that the report, if true, would inevitably draw the Union into a war which would in turn involve Georgia. He requested them, in their official capacities, to use all means to bring offenders to justice. Finally, on March 5 he issued a proclamation prohibiting the arming of Georgia citizens under foreign commissions as likely to involve the United States in war with a country at peace with us.[56]

[55] Governor Mathews to Colonel Howard, February 21, 1794, Mathews to John Wallace, February 21, 1794, in Governor's Letter Book, 1793–1794 (Georgia Department of Archives and History); Lexington *Kentucky Gazette*, April 6, May 22, 1794; Charleston *City Gazette*, February 18, 27, 1794; Savannah *Georgia Gazette*, March 13, 1794.

[56] Proclamation by Governor Mathews, March 5, 1794, East and West Florida Papers; Coulter, "Elijah Clarke's Foreign Intrigues and the 'Trans-Oconee Republic,'" *loc. cit.*, 265; Governor Mathews to Governor Juan Nepomuceno de Quesada, February 21, 1794, Governor's Letter Book, 1793–1794; Governor Mathews to Georgia delegation in Congress, February 14, 1794, Mathews to Jared Irvin, Feb-

On August 27, 1793, more than four months before Quesada's protest to Governor Mathews, the Spanish agents in Philadelphia, Josef de Jáudenes and Josef de Viar, protested to Jefferson about the expedition which George Rogers Clark was preparing in Kentucky. Two days later the Secretary of State transmitted this address to Governor Shelby and instructed him to take legal measures to prevent such a move.[57] On October 5 Shelby replied that he was persuaded no such enterprise was contemplated in Kentucky. Five weeks later Jefferson sent him the names of Genêt's four agents in Kentucky, urging the governor to use the militia if necessary. Henry Knox, Secretary of War, wrote simultaneously to the same effect. Two days earlier General Arthur St. Clair, governor of the Northwest Territory, informed Shelby that a number of French officers had arrived at the Falls of the Ohio and that boats for the expedition were being prepared there. On December 7 Shelby issued a proclamation against the project. Though the Kentucky legislature was in session at this time, the governor made no mention of these events in his communications to that body.[58]

As early as October, 1793, the Democratic Society of Lexington demanded the opening of the navigation of the Mississippi, and on November 15 George Nicholas wrote Madison: "The French may be induced to join us in procuring what we are now satisfied our government wants inclination and spirit to obtain for us. . . . We can have no reason to suppose that a people who make money their God will enter into a war to procure a just right for a particular part of America when the greater part, besides the expenses of the war, suppose that this right will be prejudicial to them. . . . You [Congress] must determine whether America shall continue united or whether a division shall take

---

ruary 17, and to Judges Stith, Walton, and Noel, February 24, 1794, *ibid.*; Hays, *Hero of Hornet's Nest,* 250–55; *Georgia Historical Quarterly,* XXIV (1940), 259–60.

[57] Henderson, "Isaac Shelby and the Genêt Mission," *loc. cit.*, 453; Lowitt, "Genêt in Kentucky," *loc. cit.*, 260–61; Turner, "Diplomatic Contest for the Mississippi Valley," *loc. cit.*, 676–91, 807–17; Keller, "American Politics and the Genêt Mission," 589, 592.

[58] Keller, "American Politics and the Genêt Mission," 592–93; Lowitt, "Genêt in Kentucky," *loc. cit.*, 262–66; Henderson, "Isaac Shelby and the Genêt Mission," *loc. cit.*, 453–56.

place, which will necessarily be attended with applications to foreign powers for support. We must, we will have what we are entitled to. . . . The Western Country united can bid defiance to the rest of America and to the Spaniards too." [59] Somewhat later John Breckinridge expressed sentiments of a very similar nature, declaring: "The Mississippi we will have. If government will not procure it, we will procure it for ourselves—either by the sword or by negotiations. This is my opinion respecting the temper and sentiments of the people here." [60]

On November 25 Genêt's agents, Auguste Lachaise and Charles Depeau, wrote Shelby that they had heard he had been ordered to arrest them and anyone who assisted them. They asked his advice and requested him to distribute some handbills to "that noble society of democrats." Shelby answered by merely repeating the instructions he had received from the Secretary of State.[61] On January 13 he wrote Jefferson that he would carry out any "constitutional" orders sent him by the President but that he doubted his own legal authority to take action, declaring that he would not wish to assume power against his friends in favor of "an enemy and tyrant who openly withholds from us an invaluble right and instigates the Indians against us."[62]

In these circumstances it is not surprising that, on January 25, 1794, there appeared in the *Centinel of the Northwest Territory*, a newspaper published in Cincinnati, "Proposals by George R. Clark, Major-General in the armies of France and Commander-in-Chief of the French Revolutionary Legions on the Mississippi River, for raising volunteers for the reduction of the Spanish posts on the Mississippi River, for opening the trade of said River and freeing its inhabitants." A little later this notice was published

[59] George Nicholas to Madison, November 15, 1793, in Huntley Dupree, "The Political Ideas of George Nicholas," in *Register of the Kentucky State Historical Society*, XXXVIII (1941), 214.

[60] Coulter, "Efforts of the Democratic Societies to Open the Navigation of the Mississippi," *loc. cit.*, 387–88.

[61] Keller, "American Politics and the Genêt Mission," 593; Lowitt, "Genêt in Kentucky," *loc. cit.*, 263; Henderson, "Isaac Shelby and the Genêt Mission," *loc. cit.*, 457.

[62] Henderson, "Isaac Shelby and the Genêt Mission," *loc. cit.*, 461–62; Lowitt, "Genêt in Kentucky," *loc. cit.*, 265; Keller, "American Politics and the Genêt Mission," 593.

in the *Kentucky Gazette,* but time was running out for Clark.[63] On January 6 General Wayne urged Shelby to suppress the expedition and placed at his disposal a squadron of horse, which was stationed near Lexington. Shelby replied on February 10 that there "is not the smallest probability that such an enterprise will be attempted; if it should be, the militia of this state, I am fully persuaded, are able and willing to suppress every attempt that can be made here to violate the laws of the Union." This was an equivocal letter; Shelby still failed to make any move.[64]

Finally, on March 24 President Washington issued a proclamation "solemnly warning every person, not authorized by laws, against enlisting any citizen or citizens of the United States, or levying troops, or assembling any persons within the United States for the purposes aforesaid, or proceeding in any manner to the execution thereof, as they will answer for the same at their paril [*sic*]." [65] This amounted to creating an offense by executive fiat, but at last on June 5 Congress passed an act making filibustering illegal. Naturally, Governor Shelby considered this as a justification of his former stand in the matter.[66]

Even in these most discouraging circumstances Clark did not lose hope, and on April 28 he wrote a last letter to Genêt: "On receipt of your letter by Michaux we agreed to set about the intended business on the Mississippi immediately. Emissaries in Louisiana assure that the appearance of a small force in that country would cause a general revolt, and upwards of 2,000 men are impatiently waiting to penetrate into that country and declare themselves citizens of France and give freedom to their neighbors on the Mississippi. We have actually had a small camp fortified within 50 miles of the enemy lines and 400 [in] advance of this place [Louisville] for four months past. The people of the back country are universally for the enterprise except the aristocratical party. The Democratic Society of Kentucky have made some advances in ammunition and given all encourage-

---

[63] Lexington *Kentucky Gazette,* February 8, 1794; Charleston *City Gazette,* March 14, 1794; Halifax *North-Carolina Journal,* March 26, 1794; Henderson, "Isaac Shelby and the Genêt Mission," *loc. cit.,* 463.

[64] Henderson, "Isaac Shelby and the Genêt Mission," *loc. cit.,* 458, 563–64.

[65] Richardson (ed.), *Messages and Papers of the Presidents,* I, 149–50.

[66] Henderson, "Isaac Shelby and the Genêt Mission," *loc. cit.,* 466.

ment in their power—all expecting Michaux with supplies of money. Business has gone on rapidly and the interest of the [French] Republic continually in our view until the declaration by M. Fauchet of March 6, which has damped the whole." [67]

The next month Lachaise addressed the Democratic Society of Lexington. He said that unforeseen events had stopped the march of the Kentuckians toward their rendezvous, that the Louisianians waited only for orders to act and by their concerted efforts hoist up the flag of the French Republic and "lay the foundation of the prosperity and happiness of two nations situated so and destined by nature to be one." Lachaise remarked that, after fourteen years of absence from France, three years of proscription, there was now no course left him except to return and express to the French people the general wish of Louisianians to become a part of the French Republic and of the Kentuckians to engage in any enterprise which would open to them the navigation of the Mississippi. He was as good as his word. He returned to France to take service in the army of the Republic,[68] and William Tate of South Carolina also joined the French Army.[69]

The collapse of the expedition which Genêt planned was not due to any lack of enthusiasm on the part of the American backwoodsmen nor to lack of effort on the part of men chosen to lead them against the hated Spaniard. George Rogers Clark advanced $4,680 of his own funds, and various other individuals, as well as the Democratic Societies, contributed either money or supplies. Though Genêt promised financial support, he was never able to furnish it.[70] Even so, Kentucky did not give up her fight for the navigation of the Mississippi. On May 24 a public meeting, held in Lexington, adopted a remonstrance to the President and Congress denouncing the appointment of John Jay, "the enemy of the West," to negotiate with England

[67] Clark to Genêt, April 28, 1794, in *American Historical Review*, XVIII (1912–1913), 780–83; New Bern *North-Carolina Gazette*, March 29, 1794.

[68] Auguste Lachaise to the Democratic Society of Lexington, May 29, 1794, in Innes Papers, Bk. 19; Gayarré, *History of Louisiana*, III, 343–44.

[69] Link, "Democratic Societies of the Carolinas," *loc. cit.*, 264.

[70] Keller, "American Politics and the Genêt Mission," 594–95; Lowitt, "Genêt in Kentucky," *loc. cit.*, 264; James, *George Rogers Clark*, 425.

and demanding that the grievances of the West be given consideration. All Kentucky counties were urged to organize committees
of correspondence and to arrange for the election of a convention
to consider means of securing Western rights.[71]

The eclipse of Genêt left General Elijah Clarke in the lurch.
When, in May, 1794, he found himself stranded on the St. Marys
with 150 to 300 men and nobody to fight, he marched them onto
the Indian lands west of the Oconee and established a settlement
in defiance of the Creeks and the government of the United
States. The Creeks made no hostile moves, and the Secretary of
War instructed Governor Mathews to clear the ground. The
governor sent troops to blockade the river, and not wishing to
fight his fellow citizens, the embittered Clarke gave up without
a struggle and his "Trans-Oconee Republic" came to an un-
timely end.[72]

It should not be assumed that the Genêt project was a complete
fiasco, for the forces which were collected by George Rogers
Clark and Elijah Clarke had a wholesome effect on Governor
Carondelet of Louisiana. When he succeeded Miró in 1792, he
exerted strenuous efforts to bring all the Southern Indians under
his control, including even the Cherokee, whose lands lay outside the area claimed by Spain, and he would have brought on
hostilities at once had he not been restrained by his government.[73]
Now he took quite a different tone and induced the Creeks,
who had been committing constant depredations on the Georgia
frontier, to make a peace treaty in November, 1793, with James
Seagrove, the American Indian agent. He also removed some
restrictions on American trade.[74]

[71] Lexington *Kentucky Gazette*, May 31, July 16, 1794; Coulter, "Elijah Clarke's
Foreign Intrigues and the 'Trans-Oconee Republic,'" *loc. cit.*, 384–85.

[72] Governor Mathews to the Head Men and Warriors of the Creek Nation, August
14, 1794, in Governor's Letter Book, 1793–1794; Mathews to Generals John Twiggs,
Morrison, and John Clark, August 24, 1794, *ibid.*; Savannah *Georgia Gazette*, August
7, September 25, October 16, November 20, 1794; Absalom H. Chappell, *Miscellanies
of Georgia* (Atlanta, 1874), Pt. I, 41–55; *Florida Historical Society Quarterly*, IX
(1930–1931), 185.

[73] Communication from Savannah, March 28, 1793, in Halifax *North-Carolina
Journal*, April 17, 1793; Fayetteville *Gazette*, May 21, 1793; Halifax *North-Carolina
Journal*, June 12, November 13, 1793; Lexington *Kentucky Gazette*, Nov. 9, 1793.

[74] Seagrove to Governor Telfair, September 22, 1793, in Halifax, *North-Carolina
Journal*, November 6, 1793; Lexington *Kentucky Gazette*, November 9, 1793; April

Realizing that New Orleans was practically defenseless and that the Louisianians would probably go over to the enemy in case Clark came down the river under the flag of France, Carondelet called on his government to furnish him with additional troops and, expecting New Madrid to be the first point of attack, he hurriedly reinforced it by a garrison of 150 regulars and 5 galleys, each carrying a force of 60 men. For the protection of New Orleans he began the construction of a wooden stockade around the city with a fort at each corner and a battery in the *Place d'Armes;* he later reported that $300,000 were spent on these defensive efforts. Lastly, he reopened negotiations with Wilkinson, reviving Miró's earlier plan to bring about a separation of the western United States.[75]

Even more important than the effect on our Spanish neighbors was the effect which Genêt's mission had on the American political scene. After his recall and the collapse of his military program, most of the Democratic Societies ceased to function, though a few continued for a while to hold meetings. There were several reasons for their decline. The Reign of Terror dampened the enthusiasm of many Americans for the French Revolution, but the connection of Brissot and Genêt with the Parisian group known as the *Amis des Noirs* had an even more telling effect among Southerners. It was this organization which first stirred up the revolt of the Mulattoes and Negroes of Santo Domingo, culminating in the wholesale massacres of the white population of that French colony in 1793.[76] In July a fleet of 137 French vessels sailed into Hampton Roads under escort of two ships of the line and three frigates. Their decks were crowded with refugees from the stricken island. Some of them landed at Norfolk, while others proceeded to other ports. In the same month fifty-three ships brought one thousand white

5, May 22, 1794; Halifax *North-Carolina Journal,* October 24, 1793; Annapolis *Maryland Gazette,* February 6, 1794; Pickett, *History of Alabama,* 433; Gayarré, *History of Louisiana,* III, 337.

[75] Keller, "American Politics and the Genêt Mission," 588–89; Turner, "Origin of Genêt's Projected Attack on Louisiana and the Floridas," *loc. cit.,* 667–68.

[76] Isaac J. Cox, *The Louisiana-Texas Frontier* (Austin, 1906–1913), I, 50; Isaac J. Cox, *West Florida Controversy, 1798–1813* (Baltimore, 1918), 24-25; James, *George Rogers Clark,* 422–27; Gayarré, *History of Louisiana,* III, 337.

and five hundred colored refugees to Baltimore, and large numbers poured into all the Southern, as well as some Northern, ports.[77] These dispossessed people were royalists and they hated the Revolution which was responsible for their misery. Naturally they were no friends of Genêt, and they advertised his connection with the *Amis des Noirs*. His popularity in the South declined accordingly.[78] Fearing the wrath of the Jacobins because of the failure of his mission, Genêt remained in America, married the daughter of Governor Clinton of New York, and settled on Long Island as a farmer.

Only the first half of the Revolutionary doctrine of "liberty and equality" was acceptable to most Southerners. At first it was only a slogan representing a popular cause, but on sober second thought it represented something which the South did not generally accept—not even the plainer sort of people who made up the rank and file of the Democratic Societies. But the leadership of the societies came largely from the upper classes and this leadership, though pro-French and anti-Administration in its views, was not enthusiastic about the more radical pronouncements of some of the societies, such as advocacy of majority rule.[79]

While most of the societies ceased to exist by the end of 1795, the movement which they inaugurated did not die. Despite the presence of a radical fringe, their domestic program consisted principally of opposition to Hamilton's financial measures and, in the West, a demand for the opening of the navigation of the Mississippi. They were strong supporters of the opposition in Congress, of which Madison, William B. Giles of Virginia, and Nathaniel Macon of North Carolina were the outstanding leaders. When the societies disappeared these were the men who assumed command of the cause they had done so much to promote. In other words, the post-Revolutionary democratic movement in America received its initial impetus from the Democratic So-

[77] Link, *Democratic-Republican Societies,* 184–86; Keller, "American Politics and the Genêt Mission," 582–83.

[78] Halifax *North-Carolina Journal,* August 7, November 13, 1793; Andrews, *History of Maryland,* 404; Wertenbaker, *Norfolk, Historic Southern Port,* 97.

[79] Murdoch, "Citizen Mangourit," *loc. cit.,* 530; Wolfe, *Jeffersonian Democracy in South Carolina,* 75 n.; Phillips, "South Carolina Federalists," *loc. cit.,* 134; Link, "Democratic Societies of the Carolinas," *loc. cit.,* 276.

cieties, but when Jay's Treaty with England was negotiated and Jefferson emerged as the leader of the anti-Administration forces, the Republican Party took over where the Democratic Societies left off.[80]

By the spring of 1794 relations with Britain became strained to the point where war seemed almost inevitable. During March word was received in Philadelphia that some three hundred American ships had been seized in the West Indies as a result of the British orders in council and that the Governor General of Canada had delivered an address to hostile Indians of the Northwest, against whom General Wayne was preparing to march.[81] Since most Americans were still pro-French in sympathy, these developments gave rise to an outburst of hostility against England, and a resolution proposing to prohibit trade with that country was introduced in Congress. It was opposed by Hamilton and the Eastern commercial interests. A small minority of Southern Congressmen, including William Barry Grove of North Carolina and William Smith of South Carolina, took the same side, the latter pointing out that Britain accounted for half of our national trade, furnished half the Federal revenue, and supplied most of the capital on which our merchants depended.[82] Nevertheless, the House passed the resolution on April 21 by a vote of fifty-eight to thirty-eight, with only four Southern members opposing: one from the Charleston district in South Carolina, one from Washington's home district in Virginia, and two from Maryland. But the Senate killed the measure and left the Administration free to carry on the Hamiltonian policy of conciliation with the British.[83]

In May John Jay, then Chief Justice of the United States, was appointed to succeed Thomas Pinckney as our Minister to the

[80] Link, "Democratic Societies of the Carolinas," *loc. cit.*, 273–76.

[81] *Ibid.*, 133, 202, 204–205; Testimony of Major Thomas Bodley, in Innes Papers, Bk. 22, Pt. II; Phillips, "South Carolina Federalists," *loc. cit.*, 735; Wolfe, *Jeffersonian Democracy in South Carolina*, 79–81; Lexington *Kentucky Gazette*, July 5, 1794; Charleston *City Gazette*, August 14, 1794; New Bern *North-Carolina Gazette*, July 9, 1796.

[82] Edenton *State Gazette of North-Carolina*, May 2, 1794; May 14, 1795; Mayo, *Henry Clay*, 36.

[83] Lycan, "Alexander Hamilton and the North Carolina Federalists," *loc. cit.*, 458; Savannah *Georgia Gazette*, April 17, 1794; Anderson, *William Branch Giles*, 30–31.

Court of St. James, while Pinckney was sent to Madrid with the object of settling our differences with Spain. From all parts of the country there came protests over this mingling of judicial and executive functions in the hands of the same persons, and in the South there was indignation because of Jay's close relations with Hamilton and because in 1786 he had proposed that the United States surrender to Spain the exclusive right to navigate

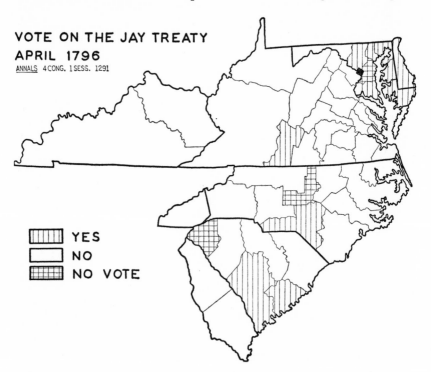

**VOTE ON THE JAY TREATY
APRIL 1796**
ANNALS 4 CONG. 1 SESS. 1291

YES
NO
NO VOTE

the lower waters of the Mississippi River. Washington, however, refused to be moved and Jay went to London.[84] With England anxious to avoid adding the United States to the number of her enemies, Jay might have secured a better treaty had not Hamilton weakened his hand by furnishing Lord Grenville with secret information.[85] As it was, nobody thought the treaty

[84] *Annals of Congress*, 3 Cong., 1 Sess., 90.

[85] Resolutions of the Democratic Society of Prince William County, Virginia, June 7, 1794, in Innes Papers, Bk. 19; John Brown to Innes, April 10, 1794, *ibid.*; Lexington *Kentucky Gazette*, May 31, 1794; Charleston *City Gazette*, May 15, 1794; Link, *Democratic-Republican Societies*, 130.

which Jay negotiated was a good one from the American point of view, but Washington, after much hesitation, decided that it was better than no treaty at all.

On June 24, 1795, the Senate ratified the agreement by a vote of twenty to ten, barely the two-thirds majority necessary for favorable action. Voting with the majority were Senators Humphrey Marshall of Kentucky, James Gunn of Georgia, Jacob Read of South Carolina, and the two Maryland Senators.[86] Though the Senate resolved to keep the text of the document secret, Senator Stevens Thomson Mason of Virginia immediately had it published in the Philadelphia *Aurora*. Of course, it was republished in papers throughout the country and then the storm broke.[87]

The opposition was not confined to the South, but the most vociferous objections came from the Southern states.[88] Norfolk, Virginia, passed up July 4 and celebrated Bastille Day on the 14th.[89] On August 5 George Wythe presided over a meeting in Richmond which condemned the treaty; a week later a similar meeting was held in Petersburg, and the Virginia legislature passed resolutions opposing it. On August 1 a public meeting in Savannah condemned the treaty and petitioned Washington not to sign it. Jay and Gunn—the Georgia Senator who had voted for ratification—were then burned in effigy.[90] On July 20 a public meeting in Charleston denounced the treaty, and Christopher Gadsden, John and Edward Rutledge, John Rutledge, Jr., J. J. Pringle, and David Ramsay participated in the proceedings. Charles Pinckney also opposed it.[91] The citizens of the Orangeburg

[86] Brown to Innes, January 31, 1795, in Innes Papers, Bk. 19; Lexington *Kentucky Gazette*, August 22, 1795; Wolfe, *Jeffersonian Democracy in South Carolina*, 20; Link, *Democratic-Republican Societies*, 229–32.

[87] *Annals of Congress*, 3 Cong., 2 Sess., 862–63; Lexington *Kentucky Gazette*, August 8, 1795.

[88] Savannah *Georgia Gazette*, September 10, 1795; Charleston *City Gazette*, November 3, 1795; New Orleans *Louisiana Gazette*, September 24, 1814; Richmond *Virginia Gazette, and General Advertiser*, July 22, 29, 1795; Edenton *State Gazette of North-Carolina*, July 30, 1795.

[89] Norfolk *Herald*, July 11, 1795.

[90] Richmond *Virginia Gazette, and General Advertiser*, August 5, 12, 26, 1795; Savannah *Georgia Gazette*, August 6, 1795; Mayo, *Henry Clay*, 37; David K. McCarrell, "The Formation of the Jeffersonian Party in Virginia" (Ph.D. dissertation, Duke University, 1937), 185.

[91] Wolfe, *Jeffersonian Democracy in South Carolina*, 83–85; Savannah *Georgia Gazette*, July 30, 1795.

and Camden districts of South Carolina held a meeting at Columbia to express their disapproval, and a popular assembly in the Edgefield district adopted a resolution declaring that the treaty was "highly derogatory to the national character of America as free, sovereign, and independent, an air of superiority being manifested through the whole of the treaty in favor of Britain, indicating a mean submission and acquiescence on the part of John Jay." On December 11 the lower house of the South Carolina legislature denounced the treaty by a vote of sixty-nine to nine.[92]

On the other hand, Robert Goodloe Harper, who had taken an active part in the proceedings of the Republican Society of Charleston, came out for the treaty, and when the Federal House of Representatives requested Washington to submit the documents pertaining to it, the President declined to send them and was supported in this stand by Harper and William Smith, while the other four South Carolina Representatives were opposed.[93] When Washington nominated John Rutledge to the Supreme Court, the Senate turned him down because of his stand on the treaty.[94]

Feeling in North Carolina was especially bitter because Article IX of the treaty gave British nationals the right to hold land in the United States. This threatened to annul the Revolutionary confiscation of the Grenville Tract and would thus jeopardize about a third of the land titles in the state. In September a meeting in Warren County sent a memorial to the President stating that those present "were desirous of showing hearty concurrence with the almost unanimous sense of our fellow citizens, who deem many parts of it [the treaty] inimical to the constitution and most of it disadvantageous to the interests and derogatory to the honor and dignity of the United States." It urged Washington not to sign the document and commended the ten members of the Senate who voted against ratification.

[92] Charleston *City Gazette*, October 20, November 3, December 21, 22, 1795; Halifax *North-Carolina Journal*, November 16, 1795.

[93] Richmond *Virginia Gazette, and General Advertiser*, March 9, 1796; Wolfe, *Jeffersonian Democracy in South Carolina*, 90.

[94] Wolfe, *Jeffersonian Democracy in South Carolina*, 90; Dodd, *Nathaniel Macon*, 157.

Both North Carolina Senators, Timothy Bloodworth and Alexander Martin, opposed ratification, and William B. Grove was the only member of the House from the Old North State who voted to accept it.[95] In Kentucky it was thought that the treaty put the Indians and the Mississippi trade under British control, and feeling against it was very strong. On September 8 a meeting of the "free citizens" of Clark County addressed a petition and remonstrance to Washington declaring that if he approved the treaty "we prophesy Western America is gone forever, lost to the Union," though "the bosom congealed by schemes of private pecuniary speculation may prefer a union with Great Britain." [96] A little later the *Kentucky Gazette* published a communication stating that Jay's treaty was the offspring "of a vile aristocratical few who have too long governed America and who are enemies to the equality of man. . . . I believe the time is at hand when Americans will cease to approve the conduct of the Federal Executive because they esteem the man who fills the Chair of state. . . . I sincerely believe that the Senator from Kentucky who voted for the treaty was actuated by most dishonorable motives and that he would sell his country for a price easily to be told." [97] It is interesting to note that this agitation was carried on by means of public meetings, not by meetings of the Democratic Societies, and so completely had Genêt been discredited that Jefferson had come to look on him as a liability to the nascent Republican Party.[98]

But even in the South not all of the agitation was hostile to the Administration. There were favorable demonstrations in Norfolk and in Savannah in the spring of 1795. In October a grand jury of the New Bern district of North Carolina condemned the antitreaty meetings as disorderly gatherings. In Virginia, Washington's home county, Westmoreland, held a public meeting which adopted resolutions praising both him and the treaty. Patrick Henry was quoted as having said that, if anything could make

[95] Halifax *North-Carolina Journal*, September 7, 1795; Lycan, "Alexander Hamilton and the North Carolina Federalists," *loc. cit.*, 459–60.
[96] Lexington *Kentucky Gazette*, September 19, 1795; Mayo, *Henry Clay*, 53–54.
[97] Lexington *Kentucky Gazette*, September 26, 1795.
[98] Norfolk *Herald*, February 2, 25, 1795; McCarrell, "Formation of the Jeffersonian Party in Virginia," 114 ff.

him execrate and damn a Republican government, it would be the abuse of and ingratitude toward Washington, and if he should outlive the great and good old man, he would once more come into the Assembly of Virginia on purpose to have a monument erected at Mount Vernon inscribed with a summary of the virtuous deeds of that pure patriot. In November Governor Henry Lee issued a proclamation forbidding the circulation of antitreaty petitions.[99]

It was after much hesitation that Washington signed Jay's Treaty on August 18, but this did not finally dispose of the matter. It was necessary for the Federal House of Representatives to appropriate money to carry out some of its provisions, and the final vote on this measure did not come up until April, 1796. It passed by the narrow margin of fifty-one to forty-eight, but only four members from the states south of Maryland voted in the affirmative. One of these was from the Lynchburg district of Virginia and one from the Fayetteville district of North Carolina, upcountry commercial centers in these states; the other two were from the South Carolina districts which carried on their trade through Charleston. Of Maryland's eight districts, only the one which was made up of the transmontane area went against the treaty.[100]

The result of this bitter controversy was that Georgia, the Carolinas, and Virginia, already disgruntled because of Hamilton's financial measures, were permanently lost to the Federalist Party. In the South Carolina Low Country there was a powerful element which had strong commercial and sentimental ties with England, but for the time being the anti-Administration forces had the upper hand. Among the Southern states only Maryland

---

[99] Norfolk *Herald*, March 1, 1795; Lexington *Kentucky Gazette*, December 12, 1795; Halifax *North-Carolina Journal*, October 26, 1795; August 29, 1796; Richmond *Virginia Gazette, and General Advertiser*, June 3, October 7, November 18, 25, 1795; Gilpatrick, *Jeffersonian Democracy in North Carolina*, 67–74.

[100] Savannah *Georgia Gazette*, March 10, 1796; Hamilton Hutton, "Southern Nationalism, 1790–1817" (M.A. thesis, University of Virginia, 1940), 17–18, map; Garland, *John Randolph of Roanoke*, 79; Ashe, *History of North Carolina*, II, 142–45; Dodd, *Nathaniel Macon*, 86–88; Charles H. Ambler, *Thomas Ritchie; A Study in Virginia Politics* (Richmond, 1913), 44–50.

was still staunchly Federalist, and her legislature unanimously passed a resolution which praised the President in the highest terms.[101]

[101] Presentment of the grand jury of the United States Circuit Court for the Georgia district, April, 1793, in Halifax *North-Carolina Journal*, June 12, 1793; Ulrich B. Phillips, *Georgia and State Rights* (Washington, 1902), 90–91; Phillips, "South Carolina Federalists," *loc. cit.*, 435–36; Gilpatrick, *Jeffersonian Democracy in North Carolina*, 67–74; Anderson, *William Branch Giles*, 41–43; Dodd, *Nathaniel Macon*, 68, 73, 157; McCarrell, "Formation of the Jeffersonian Party in Virginia," 164; Ashe, *History of North Carolina*, II, 146–47.

# CHAPTER VI

# THE YAZOO LAND COMPANIES
# OF 1795

THOUGH the Yazoo speculation of 1795 involved the same lands, with some additions, as those which were included in the grants to the earlier companies, there was an important difference between the two ventures. The companies of 1789 were organized by Southern speculators who, in every case, planned to establish settlements. But with the exception of the Tennessee Company which Zachariah Cox revived in 1795, these later companies were largely financed by Northern, and even European, speculators who planned to resell their holdings for a quick profit. As to acreage, their operations were the most stupendous that have ever been undertaken in this country, but their methods were quite typical of those employed by other speculators of their day.

During the late colonial period there had been some ambitious projects involving huge tracts of land, but there had never been much floating capital with which to finance such schemes. The creation of the Federal government and Hamilton's funding operations produced a spirit of optimism and furnished the fluid assets which enabled the new nation to begin its career with a flourish of speculation. Large numbers of refugees were already arriving from war-torn Europe and ravaged Santo Domingo. When England and France locked horns in 1793, a boom period for America was the result. Commerce flourished as never before, and as usual, lands—lands for the refugees and for a restless native population—were the main object of speculation. Wishing to conduct their operations on a large scale, the speculators were especially interested in unoccupied lands, and since they expected to sell to innocent purchasers, they were not overly scrupulous as to the quality of the tracts they acquired. Most of the states contained areas which met their requirements. No opportunity was neglected, but Georgia, most of whose land was uninhabited except by Indians, offered unusual advantages.

In 1790 this state acquired from the Creeks undisputed possession of the area between the Ogeechee and the Oconee rivers and Washington County was organized to take jurisdiction here. Settlers flocked into the fertile upper reaches of this area, but its lower lands contained nothing but pine barrens, "sad with perpetual verdure, with streaming, ever-gray long moss and the aerial moaning of the lordly pines over those vast and lonely wilds. Here the sandy barrens salute us—the land of the gopher and salamander, of fish and game, of wiregrass and wild cattle and of herdsmen and hunters almost as wild, who love their rough lives of desultory labor and leisure, never fearful of want, however scanty their store in hand, for the woods and streams hold always stores for them, which their pleasure in capturing is scarcely less than their zest in enjoying." [1]

However delightful this country may have been for the isolated hunter and herdsman, it was not good for the farmer. In 1793 Georgia cut it off from Washington County and created a new jurisdiction called Montgomery County. In 1789 a law was passed giving justices of the peace authority to issue warrants for unappropriated lands. All that was required of claimants was a survey of the land at their expense. Thus the floodgates were open for a raid on a region that was "so barren as not only to have attracted no immigration but no attention." Justices of the peace certified fictitious surveys which stated that corners were marked by blazes on hickory, oak, and walnut trees—indicating fertile land—which did not grow in the pine barrens. Four early governors signed and affixed the great seal of the state to grants "without the slightest authority under the law, and contrary to all laws on the subject of 'head right' grants." Between November 3, 1794, and January 3, 1795, Governor Mathews awarded to thirty-five individuals such grants totaling nearly 3,000,000 acres. So shamelessly and carelessly was this

[1] Chappell, *Miscellanies of Georgia*, Pt. II, 43.

fraud carried out that in Montgomery County alone more than 7,000,000 acres were granted where less than 500,000 actually existed. By 1796 over 29,000,000 acres were granted in the twenty-four existing counties where there were actually less than 9,000,000 acres in all.[2]

The chief promoters of this "Pine Barren" speculation were Senator James Gunn of Georgia; Nathaniel Pendleton, Judge of the United States District Court of Georgia; and James Wilson, Associate Justice of the Supreme Court of the United States,

who from time to time sat with Pendleton on the Circuit Court bench. One of the principal purchasers of these claims was Robert Morris, who in 1795 pooled his holdings with those of John Nicholson and James Greenleaf to form the North American Land Company, with total assets of 6,000,000 acres of undeveloped lands, 2,314,796 of which consisted of these Georgia holdings.[3]

[2] Hays, *Hero of Hornet's Nest*, 237–38, 362 n.; A. M. Sakolski, *The Great American Land Bubble* (New York, 1932), 142; Chappell, *Miscellanies of Georgia*, Pt. II, 45–47; S. G. McLendon, *History of the Public Domain of Georgia* (Atlanta, 1924), *passim*.

[3] Sakolski, *Great American Land Bubble*, 143; Anon., *Plan of Association of the North American Land Company* (Philadelphia, 1795), 3–22; "Schedule of Lands of the Company, 1795," in De Renne Collection (University of Georgia Library), 22–24.

Nicholson, Receiver General of Pennsylvania during the Revolution, had dictatorial power to enforce tax payments. On charges of dishonesty, he was impeached in 1789 but was not convicted.[4] Greenleaf, born in Boston in 1765 in a family of which the poet Whittier was a later scion, eventually settled in New York, where he formed the importing firm of Watson and Greenleaf. Soon thereafter he left for Holland to interest Dutch capital in the purchase of United States securities and to serve as consul in Amsterdam from 1789 to 1793.[5]

The North American Land Company has been called the "largest land trust ever known in America," and its sole purpose was to dispose of the vast and widely dispersed tracts of land which its three sponsors acquired. It issued 30,000 shares of stock with a par value of one hundred dollars, and the sponsors guaranteed interest at the rate of 6 per cent per annum. Though each share was supposed to represent two hundred acres of land, it was stock and not land which was offered for sale, for no surveys had been made, at least not in the Pine Barrens.[6]

The company made strenuous efforts to sell its securities, publishing letters which gave false pictures of the agricultural advantages of the barrens [7] and issuing pamphlets for distribution in Europe. One of these was written by Robert Goodloe Harper, who was associated with Morris in this venture. Another pamphlet, entitled *Topographical Description of the Western Territory of North America,* was published in London in 1797 by Gilbert Imlay. So persistent were the attempts to sell such land claims in France that Joseph Fauchet, the Minister from that country to the United States, published two letters in Paris attacking Morris, especially because of the poor quality of his pine barren lands.[8]

[4] Richmond *Enquirer,* August 20, 27, 1805, quoting Philadelphia *Aurora.*
[5] Shaw Livermore, *Early American Land Companies* (New York, 1939), 164–65 n.
[6] *Ibid.,* 162–71.
[7] Observations of George Willing by request of Dr. John Hall, May 1, 1793, in Anon., *Observations on the North-American Land-Company, lately instituted in Philadelphia, containing an Illustration of the Object of the Company's Plan, the Articles of Association, with a Succinct Account of the States where their Lands lie* (London, 1796), 62; Robert Hoops of Virginia, late of New Jersey, to Robert Morris, February 5, 1795, in De Renne Collection, 72–73; Robert G. Harper to a gentleman in Philadelphia, September 16, 1795, *ibid.,* 105–10.
[8] Sakolski, *Great American Land Bubble,* 48–52.

While Morris, Greenleaf, and Nicholson were trying to market their North American Land Company stock, they joined in another equally spectacular speculation. At the same time that Andrew Ellicott was surveying the streets and lots of the new Federal City, which Major Pierre Charles L'Enfant had planned, building sites were offered for sale, but they proved to be a drug on the market. Thinking that they saw a chance for a good speculation, the promoters of the North American Land Company purchased 6,000 lots—more than half the total number— at eighty dollars per lot. This came to nearly $500,000 and over $100,000 was actually paid, but still the lots did not sell, nor did the holdings of the North American Land Company. Europeans, instead of coming to America, were dying on the battlefields of the Napoleonic wars and, consequently, land speculators found themselves unable to meet their obligations. In 1798 Morris joined Greenleaf and Nicholson in the Philadelphia debtors' prison on Pine Street.[9]

The handwriting on the wall was not yet obvious in the fall of 1794. In November the Georgia legislature met in the little Savannah River town of Augusta. The place was already swarming with land speculators. During the previous year Eli Whitney had invented the cotton gin, and the western empire of the state took on a new significance. The former Yazoo speculation was not forgotten, and it now seemed that it might be revived with brighter financial prospects and better chances for success. Though by this time Genêt's threat against Spanish Florida and Louisiana had collapsed, the Kentuckians were still determined to open the navigation of the Mississippi to American trade, and during this November Washington sent Thomas Pinckney to Madrid to negotiate for this concession and for a recognition of the thirty-first parallel as our southern boundary from the Mississippi to the Chattahoochee River. The speculators obviously counted on his success or on the use of force to accomplish his objectives.[10]

The most conspicuous figure in Augusta on this occasion was Senator James Gunn, who had absented himself from his post

[9] Charles R. King, *The Life and Correspondence of Rufus King* (New York, 1894–1900), II, 213; Channing, *History of the United States*, IV, 108–12.

[10] Chappell, *Miscellanies of Georgia*, Pt. II, 81–82.

in Philadelphia to promote the new Yazoo venture, and he pre-pared the ground by assuring his associates that Spain had no choice but to accept the terms which Pinckney would propose. The rise of Senator Gunn in Georgia politics was remarkable. He had served without distinction as a captain during the Revolution and had acquired the Senatorial toga by making use of the arts of the demagogue. He was now in Augusta to secure his re-elec-tion and then to carry through the new Yazoo speculation.[11] But another group of speculators anticipated his plans and presented the legislature with the first bid.

On November 12, 1794, John Wareat, a former president of the Executive Council of Georgia who had recently visited Phil-adelphia, made an offer on behalf of Albert Gallatin, Alexander J. Dallas, and Jared Ingersoll—all prominent Philadelphians, two of whom would become Secretaries of the Treasury—for the lands previously granted to the South Carolina Yazoo Com-pany. He offered the same price—approximately $67,000, which the earlier company had agreed to pay—but no arrangement appears to have been made with the former grantees, nor was anything heard from them at the time.[12]

Unlike the South Carolina Company, the old Virginia Com-pany maintained its interest in its original grant and sent one of its members, John B. Scott, to renew its claim before the Georgia leg-islature. His petition, presented in November, 1794, was successful and a bill renewing the original grant to Patrick Henry's old com-pany passed the House. It was only after this bill had been en-grossed that the name and the sponsors of the company were changed, so that in its final form the act granted these lands to John B. Scott, Wade Hampton, and John C. Nightingale, now calling their group the Upper Mississippi Company.[13] Hampton had recently bought from David Ross a 5 per cent interest in the

[11] Stevens, *History of Georgia*, II, 473, 479; Chappell, *Miscellanies of Georgia*, Pt. II, 71–72; *American State Papers, Public Lands*, I, 147.

[12] Anon., *State of Facts Showing the Right of Certain Companies to the Lands lately Purchased by them from the State of Georgia* (n.p., 1795), 30–32, Appendix 7, p. 5; William C. Snipes to Governor John Milledge, January 24, 1806, in Cuyler Manuscripts; Haskins, "Yazoo Land Companies," *loc. cit.*, 81.

[13] Anon., *State of Facts Showing the Right of Certain Companies to the Lands*, 30, Appendix 9, p. 53; *Remarks occasioned by the View taken of the Claims of 1789 in a Memorial to Congress of the Agents of the New England Mississippi Land Company, with a Vindication of their Title at Law*, annexed (Washington, 1805), 3–14.

old company, but it is not known how Nightingale became involved. Scott later reported to Henry and his partners that he organized the new company only when it became clear that he could accomplish nothing for the old one, but this statement does not stand up in view of the fact that the grant to the original company was on the point of final passage when its claims were dropped and the new company took its place. Hampton later testified that he believed Scott was still acting for the old Virginia Company, but on December 31, 1794, Scott petitioned Governor Mathews for the repayment of the deposit he had made for his company in 1790. This would have invalidated any claims that the original company still had, and the fact that Scott hastened within ten days to sell out his interest in the new company for $10,000 indicates that he acted in a most unscrupulous manner.[14]

The only one of the old companies to be revived was the Tennessee Company. On January 12, 1793, with most of the original members present, it held a meeting at Washington, Georgia, and voted not to withdraw the down payment made on the purchase of 1789. Then, on December 3, 1794, Zachariah Cox, with William Maher as his only active partner, petitioned for a renewal of the grant. This was presently agreed to, the price being $60,000 as against only $35,000 paid by the Upper Mississippi Company. In this transaction Maher appears as a mysterious character. He was a Charleston merchant who was shortly to leave for a three-year sojourn in Europe. He apparently put up most of the purchase money, but there is no information as to the means whereby he supplanted Cox's partners in the earlier venture. However this may be, the new partners proceeded to issue 420 shares of stock, of which they retained 134 each. Among those who became financially and otherwise interested, the names of William Blount and John Sevier are notable.[15]

---

[14] Charleston *City Gazette*, May 5, 1810; John B. Scott to Governor of Georgia, December 31, 1794, in Yazoo Papers (Library of Congress); William Cowan, *Memorial of the Virginia Yazoo Company to the Congress of the United States* (Washington, 1803); Livermore, *Early American Land Companies*, 155.

[15] Minutes of the meeting of January 12, 1793, in Yazoo Papers (Library of Congress); Stevens, *History of Georgia*, 173 ff.; *American State Papers, Public Lands*, I, 141–43, 243–44; *Sundry Papers in relation to Claims commonly called the Yazoo Claims* (Washington, 1809), 113–18.

While the legislature was concerning itself with these matters, Senator Gunn was not idle. He waited until his re-election to the Senate was assured before coming out into the open as a land speculator. His election accomplished, he and his associates petitioned for a grant of approximately 17,000,000 acres, including most of the old South Carolina grant but adding to it an enormous tract containing all the land bounded on the north by the thirty-fourth parallel, on the west by the Tombigbee River, and on the east by the Alabama and Coosa rivers. For this area, which included about half the present states of Alabama and Mississippi, they proposed to pay $250,000, or about one and a half cents an acre.[16]

The last of the four companies of 1795 was known as the Georgia Mississippi Company. Its backers were Georgians of little prominence, but they were closely associated with Senator Gunn and they received the most strategically located grant. This tract ran east and west from the Mississippi to the Tombigbee River, and north and south from parallel 31°18′ to 32°40′. It is not clear why it did not start at 31°, which was the southern limit of the territory claimed by Georgia, but the extension above the mouth of the Yazoo River at 32°28′ was made in order to include Fort Nogales which the Spanish authorities had built at the Walnut Hills. Of course, the grant included all the Natchez district, to which the Indian claim had long been extinguished and which was, therefore, the only tract open to immediate settlement in the whole domain sought by the speculators; but Spain had conflicting claims here.[17] It is thus obvious that the speculators were expecting an early extinction of Spanish claims, but they could hardly have hoped for much sympathy from the landowners of the Natchez district, who were, in fact, later warned of the predicament in which the grant placed them.[18] The company was to pay $155,000 for its tract, making

[16] Chappell, *Miscellanies of Georgia*, Pt. II, 81–82; Hays, *Hero of Hornet's Nest*, 280 ff.

[17] *Grant to the Georgia Mississippi Company, the Constitution Thereof . . .* (Augusta, 1795), 7–16, 23–24; Anon., *State of Facts Showing the Right of Certain Companies to the Lands*, Appendix 10, pp. 53–55.

[18] Augustus C. George Elholm, Augusta, to Isaac Gailliard, Natchez, June 14, 1795, in Cuyler Manuscripts.

a total of $500,000 offered by the four companies for grants containing not less than 35,000,000 acres. In each case about one-fifth of the purchase money was to be deposited before the passage of the act, and payment of the balance was due before November 1, 1795.[19]

When, on December 8, the proposals of the four companies were presented in a single bill to the legislature, they ran into stubborn opposition, for John Wareat was not prepared to surrender without a fight. Enlisting the support of William Gibbons, Jr., former president of the Georgia Constitutional Convention of 1787 who now spoke for the old South Carolina Company; of Gibbons' brother-in-law, former Governor Edward Telfair; of John Twiggs, a general of Georgia militia; and of William Few, a Georgia delegate to the Constitutional Convention of 1787, Wareat organized the Georgia Union Company and on December 11 presented a counterproposal to the legislature. Making no opposition to the proposals of the old Tennessee and Virginia companies, this group offered to pay $500,000 for all the lands which the Georgia Mississippi companies were seeking. They estimated this region to contain 23,000,000 acres, 5,000,000 of which they proposed to set aside and sell at the original price to citizens of Georgia in tracts of five to ten thousand acres. The remaining 18,000,000 acres were to be divided into 720 shares of 25,000 acres each and sold for one hundred dollars per share. The company was able to raise only $5,000 for a down payment, but the balance was to be paid in full by December 1, 1795. An exemption from taxation for twenty years was requested as compensation for extinguishing the Indian claim to the land.[20]

On the very day that these proposals were presented by the Union Company, a joint committee reported in favor of grants to the other four companies, and the bill came up in the House on December 13. An amendment providing that the state should lose none of its jurisdiction or sovereignty in parting with the

[19] Haskins, "Yazoo Land Companies," *loc. cit.*, 81–82.

[20] Proposals of the Georgia Union Company, December 11, 1794, in Yazoo Papers (Georgia Department of Archives and History); *Remarks occasioned by the View taken of the Claims of 1789 in a Memorial to Congress of the Agents of the New England Mississippi Land Company,* 31–34; Savannah *Georgia Gazette,* May 26, 1796; Hays, *Hero of Hornet's Nest,* 280 ff.

lands in question was defeated by a vote of fifteen to ten. The original bill was then passed, with seventeen ayes and eight noes. Two days later the Union Company offered to increase its down payment from $5,000 to $15,000, and on the twentieth the offer was again increased to $21,355, which was all the money the partners could raise at the moment.[21] Rejecting these offers, the legislature proceeded to pass the grants to the other four companies, but the friends of the Union Company complained that it had proposed the most liberal terms and should have been successful in its bid for the lands. Fearing that such protests would induce Governor Mathews to veto the bill which favored them, Senator Gunn and the land speculators associated with him drew up a petition urging the governor to sign the measure then before him.[22] But charges of bribery were now being made against Scott, Cox, and Maher; and Senator Gunn strode about town in broadcloth, top boots, and beaver hat, carrying a loaded whip with which he threatened opposing members of the legislature. On December 28 the governor vetoed the bill, objecting especially that no lands were to be reserved for purchase by Georgia citizens.[23] Encouraged by this turn of events, the Union Company came forward on January 1, 1795, with a new proposal. It now offered $800,000, with a $40,000 deposit for all the lands sought by the other four companies, but their bill was defeated in the House by a vote of fourteen to twelve.[24]

On the same day the Georgia Company, having framed a new petition to meet the governor's objections, signed formal articles of agreement according to which it divided its stock into ten

[21] The Union Company to the Georgia Senate, December 15, 20, 1794, in Yazoo Papers (Georgia Department of Archives and History); Anon., State of Facts Showing the Right of Certain Companies to the Lands, 31, 56–60; Savannah Georgia Gazette, March 19, 1795.

[22] James Gunn et al. to Governor Mathews, December 25, 1794, in Yazoo Papers (Georgia Department of Archives and History).

[23] Albert J. Beveridge, The Life of John Marshall (New York, 1916–1919), III, 550; Claude G. Bowers, Jefferson in Power (Boston, 1936), 299–300; Anon., State of Facts Showing the Right of Certain Companies to the Lands, 61.

[24] Savannah Georgia Gazette, March 24, April 7, 1796; John Twiggs to the Georgia legislature, January 1, 1795, in Yazoo Papers (Georgia Department of Archives and History); Twiggs and John Wareat to Governor Mathews, January 3, 1795, ibid.; Sundry Papers in relation to Claims, 103.

shares, assigning one to Zachariah Cox, one to William Long-
street who was Gunn's spokesman and manager in the legislature,
two to Gunn himself, and three to Wade Hampton.[25] But these
were not the only important participants. Associate Justice James
Wilson and District Judge Nathaniel Pendleton had recently
been holding sessions of the United States Circuit Court in Savannah. These two jurists, it will be recalled, had participated in
the "Pine Barren" speculation, and now they came to Augusta
to take part in the new venture, Wilson purchasing 750,000 acres
of the Georgia Company's grant for $25,000. In addition, tracts
of 50,000 acres each were distributed to members of the legislature who voted for the grants, all but one of them having been
thus bribed.[26]

On January 2 the revised proposal of the four companies
passed the House by a vote of nineteen to nine, and the next
day the Senate passed it with ten voting in the affirmative and
eight against. Governor Mathews signed it on the seventh and
thereby became party to a controversy that would spread into
every section of the nation and agitate the Federal government
for nearly two decades.[27]

In order to meet the objections of Governor Mathews to their
original bill, the four companies modified their proposals in only
one important respect. The act as finally passed and signed provided that each company should reserve a certain portion of its
lands, making a total of 2,000,000 acres, which would be offered
for sale to citizens of Georgia at the original price, a stipulation
similar to one originally proposed by the Union Company. Certain other terms of the Yazoo grant are peculiar. Whereas Georgia

[25] *American State Papers, Public Lands,* I, 147; Articles of Agreement of the Georgia
Company, January 1, 1795, in Yazoo Manuscripts (University of Georgia Library);
*Sundry Papers in relation to Claims,* 103.

[26] Savannah *Georgia Gazette,* November 20, 1794; Deposition of Clement Lanier,
*ibid.,* March 5, 1795; Beveridge, *John Marshall,* III, 546–48; Chappell, *Miscellanies
of Georgia,* Pt. II, 93–97; M. C. Klingelsmith, "James Wilson and the So-Called
Yazoo Frauds," in *University of Pennsylvania Law Review and American Law
Register* (Philadelphia), LVI (1908), 1–27; *Sundry Papers in relation to Claims,* 103–12.

[27] White, *Accurate Account of the Yazoo Fraud,* 19; Yazoo Fraud, in East and
West Florida Papers, 70 ff.; *Sundry Papers in relation to Claims,* 119–22; Edenton
*State Gazette of North-Carolina,* February 26, 1795, quoting letter from Augusta
dated December 29, 1794.

did not previously permit the sale of lands to foreign citizens, the four companies were denied only the right to sell to foreign governments. That they planned to sell to foreigners is indicated by the fact that Zachariah Cox's partner, William Matthias Maher, departed for Europe shortly after the purchase was made and remained abroad for three years.[28]

Even more peculiar were the provisions that the companies would be responsible for liquidating the Indian claims to their lands and that no taxes would be levied until counties with representation in the state legislature were formed within the boundaries of the grants. It would be hard to make a case for the legality of the first of these provisions, for the Constitution gave the Federal government exclusive jurisdiction over the Indians and it had already adopted a British precedent to the effect that only the central authority could extinguish the Indian rights. As to the provision regarding counties, it is impossible to tell how it might have worked out, but it seems that local jurisdictions might have been set up which could have avoided Georgia taxes merely by neglecting to send representatives to the Georgia legislature. The rejection of an amendment to the Yazoo bill which was intended to guarantee Georgia sovereignty in the area would seem to indicate that independent jurisdictions were looked upon as a possibility, but this point was not stressed at the time. The situation in the Southwest was decidedly fluid and the companies obviously wished to have as free a hand as possible.[29]

No sooner was the Yazoo Act passed than reaction set in. Having previous notice of the sale, Senator James Jackson wrote on January 6 from Philadelphia to a friend that if the Yazoo Act had been passed, as he had been informed, "I consider Georgia as having passed a confiscation act of the rights of your children and mine and [of] unborn generations, to supply the rapacious grasp of a few sharks; . . . and two thirds of Georgia will

[28] Chappell, *Miscellanies of Georgia*, Pt. II, 89.

[29] Richmond *Enquirer*, July 5, 9, 1800; [James Jackson], *The Letters of Sicilius to the Citizens of the State of Georgia, on the Constitutionality, the Policy, and Legality of the Late Sales of Western Lands in the State of Georgia* . . . (Augusta, 1795).

be held and owned by residents of Philadelphia in six months.
. . . [Robert] Morris, Nicholson, Ketters [?], Wilson the Judge
and one or two others here are those principally concerned, although in Georgia the application appears from Georgians—
they all have agents in Georgia and the others will sell to those
persons in six months from this day." [30]

One of the first to protest was a young schoolteacher by the
name of William H. Crawford. Soon grand juries in all but two
Georgia counties made presentments against the sale. One member of the legislature who had voted for it fled the state, and
another narrowly escaped hanging. General James Jackson, the
newly elected Senator, was urged to return to Georgia and head
the fight for repeal of the grants.[31] On February 17 President
Washington sent a copy of the act to Congress and on the twenty-
third that body adopted a resolution condemning it.[32] On March
4 Governor Carondelet of Louisiana wrote to Josef de Jáudenes, a
member of the Spanish legation in Philadelphia, complaining
that the Georgia grants encroached on the lands of the Choctaw
Indians who were under the protection of Spain; and Jáudenes
protested to Edmund Randolph, who had succeeded Jefferson
as Secretary of State, that this act of Georgia might lead to serious
international complications.[33] Certainly it would not help Thomas
Pinckney in his negotiations at Madrid. More direct action was
taken by the Spanish governor of the Natchez district, Gayoso
de Lemos, who, on hearing of the Yazoo grants, hastily sent a
detachment up the Mississippi to hold the Chickasaw Bluffs—
where Memphis was to rise—until his arrival with reinforcements. On May 30, 1795, he began construction of Fort San
Fernando de las Barrancas. Governor Carondelet approved this
move and at once dispatched instructions, reinforcements, and
supplies. He also persuaded Panton, Leslie and Company to

[30] Thomas U. P. Charlton, *The Life of Major General James Jackson* (Augusta, Ga.,
1809), 206–208.

[31] Savannah *Georgia Gazette*, March 5, 19, August 27, September 10, October 1,
1795; Charleston *City Gazette*, March 30, 1795; Beveridge, *John Marshall*, III, 552;
Haskins, "Yazoo Land Companies," *loc. cit.*, 84.

[32] *Sundry Papers in relation to Claims*, 48.

[33] Carondelet to Josef de Jáudenes, March 4, 1795, in Yazoo Fraud, East and
West Florida Papers, 61; Jáudenes to Edmund Randolph, July 8, 1795, *ibid.*, 87.

send one of their partners, John Forbes, with a boatload of goods to open a store at the new fort.[34]

Meanwhile, the Yazoo grantees hastened to pay the full amount due on their contracts, and some of the more provident among them proceeded to sell for a quick profit. On January 16 and 17, 1795, Wade Hampton bought out his partners in the Upper Mississippi Company, and on March 6 he sold out to Adam Tunno, James Miller, and James Warrington for $120,000. Since Georgia received only $35,000 for this tract, the South Carolina magnate cleared a handsome profit. Warrington departed immediately for Europe to resell the land,[35] and Hampton was elected to Congress.

Even more spectacular were the operations of James Greenleaf, who on August 22, 1795, purchased 13,500,000 acres of the Georgia Company's grant and on November 13 deeded 9,000,000 acres of it to Boston and New York speculators. On February 3, 1796, a similar group agreed to pay him $1,138,000 for the whole of the grant to the Georgia Mississippi Company. So important was the tract and so unimportant were the original grantees, that one is led to the conclusion that Greenleaf had, in collaboration with Gunn, sponsored the deal from the beginning, which, if true, would make them the most important figures in the whole Yazoo speculation. And this, in addition to his connection with the North American Land Company and his speculation in Washington City real estate, would render him the most important land speculator that the United States has produced. The men—mostly fellow New Englanders—to whom Greenleaf sold his Yazoo holdings proceeded to open offices in Boston where they sold their stock to eager purchasers at an average price of fourteen cents an acre.[36] Early the next year the

[34] Whitaker, *Spanish-American Frontier*, 214–15.

[35] Statement by James Warrington, in Charleston *City Gazette*, June 15, 1797; *The Claims of the Upper Mississippi Company, presented to the Commissioners of the United States in January, 1803* (n.p., n.d.), 100–103; *Sundry Papers in relation to Claims*, 147; John Willson [sic] to Governor of Georgia, October 26, 1795, in Yazoo Manuscripts (University of Georgia Library); George Walker to Governor Mathews, October 27, 1795, in Yazoo Papers (Library of Congress).

[36] *Articles of Association and Agreement constituting the New-England Mississippi Land Company* (n.p., *circa* 1797); Savannah *Georgia Gazette*, April 20, June 15, 1798.

proprietors of the Georgia Mississippi Company transferred their claims to a related group of Boston speculators, who in February, 1797, organized the New England Mississippi Land Company, which made elaborate plans for issuing stock and selling lands, including those already settled in the Natchez district, thirty-three cents an acre being the usual price.[37]

The convention which drafted the Georgia constitution of 1789 provided that its work should be submitted for amendment to a new convention to be elected in 1794. This body met in the little town of Louisville on May 16, 1795, and to it were submitted the various protests by grand juries and individuals against the Yazoo grants. But since the convention had been elected at the same time as the legislature which made the grants, it was not inclined to take drastic action. Instead, it deferred the meeting of the next General Assembly from November to January and passed the protests along to that body. Yazoo opponents maintained that the meeting of the legislature was postponed in order to give the grantees more time in which to dispose of their claims. The convention made no significant changes in the constitution but fixed upon Louisville as the permanent capital of the state and provided for the election of still another amending convention in 1797.[38]

Fortune was again kind to the speculators when Thomas Pinckney brought his negotiations with the Spanish government to a successful conclusion, and the Treaty of San Lorenzo was signed on October 27, 1795. This document, in addition to allowing American boats coming down the Mississippi to land their goods at New Orleans and transship them on ocean-going

[37] Livermore, *Early American Land Companies*, 153–54; *Remarks occasioned by the View taken of the Claims of 1789 in a Memorial to Congress of the Agents of the New England Mississippi Land Company; American State Papers, Public Lands,* I, 147; Bowers, *Jefferson in Power*, 299–306; Sakolski, *Great American Land Bubble*, 135; Beveridge, *John Marshall*, III, 567–68; Haskins, "Yazoo Land Companies," *loc. cit.*, 81–88.

[38] Poore (ed.), *Federal and State Constitutions*, I, 387; Chappell, *Miscellanies of Georgia*, Pt. II, 121–22; *Protest of Richmond County to President and Members of the Convention of Georgia* (n.p., 1795), broadside in Yazoo Manuscripts (University of Georgia Library); Savannah *Georgia Gazette*, May 21, 28, 1795; Charleston *City Gazette*, May 28, 1795; *Sundry Papers in relation to Claims*, 122–45; Anderson and Hobby, *Contract for the Purchase of Western Territory*, 43–45.

vessels, fixed the thirty-first parallel as the southern boundary of the United States west of the Chattahoochee River and thus surrendered all Spanish claims to the lands granted to the Yazoo companies.

In spite of these favorable developments, the speculators were running into difficulties, for the Georgia people were aroused. On July 7 Senator Jackson returned to Savannah from Philadelphia and in his "Letters of Sicilius" made a scathing attack on the validity of the Yazoo grants. On October 30 a Chatham County committee urged him to resign from the Senate and lead the anti-Yazoo fight in the legislature. He was offered half a million acres to hold his tongue, but he scorned the bribe and accepted the challenge. On November 2 he was elected to the Georgia House of Representatives. Of English birth, Jackson had migrated to Georgia at an early age, joined the American army during the Revolution, distinguished himself on the field of battle, and rose to the rank of colonel. When peace was restored he took an active part in politics, and his election to the United States Senate was a natural consequence. He was never involved in land speculations, and in stepping down from his senatorship to a seat in the lower house of the legislature, he appears to have been actuated by no motive except a desire to perform a public service.[39]

When the legislature met in Louisville in January, 1796, Jackson was elected chairman of a committee set up to consider the Yazoo Act. On the twenty-fifth it brought in a report declaring that the grants were obtained by the use of bribery and that they were unconstitutional because the lands in question were confirmed to the Choctaw and Chickasaw Indians by the treaties of Hopewell, negotiated by the Continental Congress in 1786. These treaties were still valid under the new government, which alone had the right to negotiate with the natives for cessions of land. For these and some less important reasons, on February 13 the legislature declared the Yazoo Act invalid. The lawmakers

[39] Savannah *Georgia Gazette*, July 9, November 5, 1795; Charlton, *Life of Major General James Jackson, passim;* Savannah *Georgia Republican and State Intelligencer,* April 8, 1806; Everett S. Brown (ed.), *William Plumer's Memorandum of Proceedings in the United States Senate, 1803–1807* (New York, 1923), 133–34.

went still further and proceeded to tear the offending pages from the journal and, forming a procession, burned them before the capitol by means of "fire brought down from Heaven"—with a magnifying glass. Six days later the House passed a resolution to the effect that Senator Gunn had forfeited its confidence.[40]

It was on the very day the Rescinding Act was passed that Greenleaf sold the claims of the Georgia Mississippi Company to New York and Boston speculators. The purchasers, realizing the damage the investment might suffer as a result of the turn of events, secured an opinion from Hamilton that Georgia had violated the obligation of a contract and that her Rescinding Act was therefore illegal under the Federal Constitution. Hamilton's brother-in-law, Robert Goodloe Harper, who at the time was a Federalist Congressman from South Carolina, was employed by the speculators as their attorney and he defended their claim in a pamphlet entitled "The Case of the Georgia Sales." This document was signed on August 3, 1796, but was not published until 1799, after the organization of the New England Mississippi Land Company.[41]

As a result of Jackson's leadership of the anti-Yazoo faction, he was assaulted on the streets of Augusta and was forced to fight at least four duels with advocates of the Yazoo cause. Colonel Robert Watkins was his opponent in three of these, and in the last, which occurred in June, 1802, Jackson received a ball in the spine on the fifth exchange of shots. On March 19, 1806, Senator William Plumer of New Hampshire recorded in his journal: "This morning in this city died my friend James Jackson, one of the Senators from Georgia. . . . I never knew him quibble or evade a question. Being a man of honor, he had fought several duels. I do not recollect he ever killed a man, but

[40] White, *Accurate Account of the Yazoo Fraud*, 23–24; Lexington *Kentucky Gazette*, February 4, April 9, 1796; Manuscript copy of the Yazoo Act of February 13, 1796, in Abraham Baldwin Papers, 1790–1796 (University of Georgia Library); Committee Report, January 22, 1795, *ibid.*

[41] [Robert Goodloe Harper], *The Case of the Georgia Sales on the Mississippi, Considered with a Reference to Law Authorities and Public Acts* (Philadelphia, 1799); Livermore, *Early American Land Companies*, 157–58 n.; Sakolski, *Great American Land Bubble*, 135.

suffered from wounds he received. Ardent spirits shortened his life." He was fifty years of age when he died.[42]

When, on February 17, 1795, Washington sent Congress a copy of the Yazoo Act, the Senate reacted six days later by adopting resolutions condemning the grants. It then called on the Administration for pertinent documents and appointed a committee, headed by Aaron Burr, to investigate the matter. On May 20, 1796, this committee recommended that the President be authorized to treat with Georgia for a cession of her lands lying west of the Chattahoochee River and, as soon as Pinckney's Treaty should be ratified, to establish a temporary government for the area between the latitudes 31° and 32°28′, but this act was not to infringe upon any adverse claims to either the land or the jurisdiction involved.[43]

Congress took no immediate action, but on January 29, 1798, the Georgia House of Representatives adopted, by a vote of thirty-two to two, a recommendation to the coming convention that it make provision for cession to the United States lands lying west of the Chattahoochee River on condition that the Federal government pay Georgia $1,500,000 and remove the Indians from all the territory remaining to the state.[44]

When the constitutional convention of 1798 met at Louisville on May 8, it carried out the intent of this resolution. Stating that the boundaries of the state extended to the Mississippi River, it authorized sale to the Federal government of the area west of the Chattahoochee and the establishment of one or more states therein. To this it added a proviso that "monopolies of land by individuals being contrary to the spirit of our free government, no sale of territory of this State, or any part thereof,

[42] Annapolis *Maryland Gazette*, July 15, 1802; Charleston *City Gazette*, April 12, 1799; Savannah *Georgia Gazette*, March 3, 1796; Brown (ed.), *William Plumer's Memorandum*, 429; Judge George Walton's Charge to the Grand Jury of Jefferson County, Louisville, April 11, 1799 (Governor Jackson's typed copy in Georgia Department of Archives and History); Charlton, *Life of Major General James Jackson*, 159–63.

[43] Printed copy of committee report, May 20, 1796 (Georgia Department of Archives and History); Beveridge, *John Marshall*, III, 569–70.

[44] Savannah *Georgia Gazette*, February 23, 1798; J. F. H. Claiborne, *Mississippi, as a Province, Territory and State* (Jackson, 1880), 202.

shall take place to individuals or private companies, unless a county or counties shall have been first laid off, including such territory, and the Indian rights shall have been extinguished thereto." The Rescinding Act was also confirmed and the next legislature required to provide for the return of all monies paid in by the Yazoo companies.[45]

Up to this point the Spanish government had refused to carry out the provisions of Pinckney's Treaty, but on March 29, 1798, it finally evacuated Natchez and agreed to the survey of the boundary line.[46] On April 7 Congress passed an act authorizing the President to appoint three commissioners to negotiate with Georgia commissioners to settle conflicting land claims between the two jurisdictions. He was also instructed to establish a government for the Mississippi Territory, which should be bounded on the north by the parallel intersecting the mouth of the Yazoo River at 32°28′ and on the east by the Chattahoochee River. But since Georgia's claims were still to be adjusted, this act was not to prejudice the pretensions of either party in respect to land or jurisdiction.[47]

By this time all the original grantees under the Yazoo Act, with the exception of Cox and his Tennessee Company, had disposed of their claims. Ever since the abortive attempt of Georgia in 1784 to establish Houston County and thereby aid John Sevier and William Blount, with Cox among their associates, to make a settlement in the "Bend of the Tennessee," these three had maintained their interest in the project. They visualized the digging of a short canal to connect the waters of the Tennessee at some point above the Muscle Shoals with those of the Tombigbee River and thus make it possible to ship produce to Mobile by a much shorter route than that down the Mississippi to New Orleans. As governor of the Southwest Territory, Blount had to co-operate with President Washington in thwarting the attempt

[45] Governor Jackson to Secretary of State, June 17, 1798, in Governor's Letter Book, 1795–1796, 1798; Chappell, *Miscellanies of Georgia*, Pt. II, 127–28; Poore (ed.), *Federal and State Constitutions*, I, 390–91.

[46] Claiborne, *Mississippi, as a Province, Territory and State*, 206.

[47] Poore (ed.), *Federal and State Constitutions*, II, 1049–50; *Sundry Papers in relation to Claims*, 49–52; Claiborne, *Mississippi, as a Province, Territory and State*, 202.

of Cox and the Tennessee Company of 1789 to carry out this project, but Tennessee became a state in 1796 and Blount was chosen to represent it as one of its first Senators. In this position he no longer had to take orders from the President and was free to co-operate with Cox and the Tennessee Company of 1795. Since he was more interested in Tennessee lands than in those lying to the southward, he never became a large investor in the Tennessee Yazoo Company, but he did invest in it and gave it his support.[48]

As early as 1796 Cox began planning for the establishment of the Mississippi-Mobile Commercial Company as an offshoot of the Tennessee Yazoo Company. The plan was to establish a settlement on the Ohio River near the mouth of the Tennessee and another at the Muscle Shoals, thus developing a line of communications which would shorten the distance to the Gulf of Mexico by several hundred miles. With the approbation of Governors James Garrard of Kentucky and Sevier of Tennessee, Cox employed a Captain John Smith to find a suitable site on the Ohio between the mouths of the Tennessee and Cumberland rivers. In February, 1797, he arrived on the scene and named the place Smithland. Having obtained the approval of Captain Zebulon Pike at nearby Fort Massac, Cox visited the Cumberland settlements and returned to Smithland on March 10 with thirty-five men. Soon there were 225 settlers, and the number continued to increase. Under Kentucky law and with the co-operation of Colonel Moses Shelby of Christian County, six companies of militia were organized and a fort was planned. Each settler was granted a lot in the town and a thousand-acre tract at the Muscle Shoals.[49]

Having been informed of Cox's plans to establish a settlement at the Muscle Shoals, the Chickasaw and Cherokee complained;

[48] Zachariah Cox to General Assembly of Georgia, n.d., Yazoo Manuscripts (University of Georgia Library); Lexington *Kentucky Gazette*, September 13, 1797; *American State Papers, Public Lands*, I, 243–44; Haskins, "Yazoo Land Companies," *loc. cit.*, 79; Cox, *West Florida Controversy*, 140.

[49] R. Buntin to Wilkinson, August 1, 1798, in *American State Papers, Miscellaneous*, I, 359; Major Thomas Gist to Commanding Officer of New Madrid, May 20, 1798, *ibid.*, 359; Order by Lieutenant Colonel Moses Shelby, June 5, 1798, *ibid.*, 360; Warrant dated June 1, 1798, *ibid.*

and Benjamin Hawkins, Federal Superintendent of the Southern Indians, denied his right to trade there. Cox was also ordered not to traverse the Indian country by way of the Tennessee, but he proceeded with his plans. To transplant settlers from East Tennessee to the Shoals, he built a remarkable boat at the mouth of the Nolichucky River where it flows into the French Broad near the present Sevierville. The boat was so large that it was called a ship and the sides were so heavily reinforced that it was impregnable to small arms. Well provided with howitzers and small ordnance, it constituted a good floating battery. To prevent the descent of this boat Colonel Thomas Butler of the regular Army placed a battery at Southwest Point where the Clinch River flows into the Tennessee; and on November 2, 1797, he issued orders to the officers in charge to fire on any boat of Cox's party that might attempt to pass. Governor Sevier was called on to assist the Federal Administration in thwarting Cox, but the Tennessee governor merely asked him to state his intentions. We have no copy of the reply, but on September 23 Sevier submitted the correspondence to the legislature, a committee of which presently reported that "no expedition of a hostile nature, or plan inimical to the Government is intended or contemplated." [50]

Smithland in the meantime received settlers and supplies from Kentucky and the Cumberland settlements and was flourishing in spite of Federal opposition. In the *Kentucky Gazette* of May 17, 1797, Benjamin S. Cox advertised that he would leave Lexington on the twentieth with a party to establish a settlement in the Great Bend of the Tennessee. On August 6 Hawkins, then at the Tennessee capital of Knoxville, received a communication from Cox, avowing his intention of establishing an armed settlement at the Bend. Hawkins again peremptorily forbade it and sent Cox's printed proclamation to the Secretary of War. Despite this, on September 13 Cox advertised in the *Kentucky Gazette*

[50] Hawkins to Chickasaw Nation, May 21, 1797, in *Letters of Benjamin Hawkins, 1796–1806*, in *Collections of the Georgia Historical Society* (Savannah), IX (1916), 176–77; Hawkins to David Henley, November 9, 1797, *ibid.*, 223; Hawkins to Secretary of War, July 5, 1797, *ibid.*, 181; Hawkins to Colonel Thomas Butler, November 9, 1797, *ibid.*, 221; Cherokee Indians to President Washington, April 28, 1797, *ibid.*, 163–64.

that on June 1, 1798, he would open an office in Knoxville for the disposal of lands in the Bend. As late as November Hawkins understood that Cox was planning to descend the Tennessee from Knoxville in full force, "having a large boat, 60 x 23 ft., and armed with cannon." [51]

But by the following summer Cox had radically changed his plan of campaign. In early July of 1798 he left Smithland with more than a hundred men and floated down the Ohio rather than proceeding up the Tennessee, but he was stopped at Fort Massac by Major Jacob Kingsbury. Through the intercession of Colonel Moses Shelby, his boats were allowed to pass with thirty-five men, but seventy-five others made their way around the fort by land and joined Cox's boats below it. On August 1 General Wilkinson arrived at Fort Massac on his way to Natchez to take command of the troops who were to occupy that town as soon as the Spanish forces should evacuate it. He now sent a message to Natchez to warn the governor that Cox was engaged in a conspiracy which extended from Georgia to the Monongahela and which would come to a head in the following December.[52]

On August 11, 1798, Cox arrived at Natchez and there confronted a highly confusing situation. Though Spain had not yet ratified Pinckney's Treaty of 1795, the United States was making preparations to occupy the east bank of the Mississippi as far south as the thirty-first parallel. Andrew Ellicott was appointed to act for the United States in surveying the boundary line, and General Wilkinson was ordered to take possession of the territory. On May 20, 1797, he instructed Major Isaac Guion to occupy the Spanish posts in the area, and this officer proceeded to displace the garrison at the Chickasaw Bluffs and to build Fort Pickering at that point.[53]

---

[51] Notice of Benjamin S. Cox, Lexington, April 19, 1797, in Lexington *Kentucky Gazette*, May 17, 1797; Hawkins to Zachariah Cox, August 6, 1797, *Letters of Benjamin Hawkins*, in *Collections of the Georgia Historical Society*, IX (1916), 189–90; Hawkins to Colonel Henry Gaither, November 13, 1797, *ibid.*, 232; Lexington *Kentucky Gazette*, September 13, 1797.

[52] Wilkinson to Winthrop Sargent, August 2, 1798, in *American State Papers, Miscellaneous*, I, 558–59; Buntin to Wilkinson, August 1, 1798, *ibid.*, 359.

[53] Cox (ed.), "Documents Relating to Zachariah Cox," *loc. cit.*, 550 ff.; Catherine Van Cortlandt Mathews, *Andrew Ellicott, His Life and Letters* (New York, 1908), 150; Claiborne, *Mississippi, as a Province, Territory and State*, 178–82.

In December Guion's troops reached Natchez. Expecting annexation to the United States, the citizens of the area had risen in revolt against Don Gayoso de Lemos, commandant of the district, and under the leadership of Ellicott forced him to agree to submit to the dictates of a popular assembly. But in July Gayoso had the good fortune to be relieved of this embarrassing situation and was appointed governor of the Province of Louisiana. His place in Natchez was taken by Stephen Minor, an Irishman who had once been a merchant in Philadelphia. Finally on March 29, 1798, the Spanish garrison evacuated the town and left the American authorities in control.[54]

On April 18, 1798, President John Adams nominated General George Mathews governor of Mississippi Territory and Judge Asher Miller secretary. This was done at the instance of the Secretary of State, Timothy Pickering, and both men, who were in Natchez when Cox arrived, were agents of the New England Mississippi Company with which Pickering was connected and which now claimed the land on which Natchez stood, as well as millions of acres in the Territory. With Pickering's influence and Cox's armed men, they were prepared to take over the local government in the interest of the speculators, but their plans miscarried. James McHenry, then Secretary of War, complained of Mathews' connection with the Yazoo speculation, and Adams withdrew his name and appointed instead Winthrop Sargent, a native of Massachusetts then serving as Secretary of the Northwest Territory, and named as secretary of the new jurisdiction John Steele, a North Carolina friend of William Blount. At the same time Daniel Clark, who had been nominated for a Territorial judgeship, was also dropped.[55]

[54] Ellicott to Anthony Hutchins, October 17, 1797, in Halifax *North-Carolina Journal*, February 12, 1798; Clarence E. Carter (ed.), *The Territory of Mississippi, 1798–1817* (Washington, 1937), V, 3–8, 9–12, 13–14, 15; Claiborne, *Mississippi, as a Province, Territory and State*, 172–77, 195; Mathews, *Andrew Ellicott*, 154–56.

[55] Isaac J. Cox, "The Border Missions of General George Mathews," in *Mississippi Valley Historical Review*, XII (1925–1926), 309–10; Sargent to Mathews, October 13, 1798, in Dunbar Rowland (ed.), *Mississippi Territorial Archives, 1798–1803* (Nashville, 1905), I, 61; Mathews to Timothy Pickering, October 14, 1798, in Carter (ed.), *Territory of Mississippi*, V, 27–28 n., 48–50; Franklin L. Riley, "Transition from Spanish to American Rule in Mississippi," in Mississippi Historical Society *Publications* (Oxford), III (1900), 261–311.

When he arrived in Natchez, Sargent found the situation quite discouraging. Since a majority of the settlers were of American origin, they were pleased to be put, at last, under jurisdiction of the United States, but this was not an unmixed blessing. Most of them held their lands under Spanish grants, which were usually hard to verify by documentary evidence. Few of the old settlers could be sure that the Federal government would recognize their claims, and no provision had been made for selling lands to newcomers. In fact, until the Yazoo claims were disposed of, no land titles were secure. Such a situation was more conducive to emigration than to immigration, and the new governor had reason to be worried.[56]

Dr. James White, a French-speaking Catholic who migrated to North Carolina from Philadelphia, became a political ally of William Blount shortly after the Revolution. Doubtless as a result of this connection he was elected in December, 1785, to represent his adopted state in the Continental Congress.[57] Presently he became involved with Wilkinson and other Kentucky and Tennessee leaders in their intrigues with the Spanish *chargé*, Don Diego de Gardoqui, in their plan to create a separate government west of the Appalachian Mountains which would be free to enter into an alliance with Spain and thus open the navigation of the Mississippi.[58] When this plan failed, White continued to serve his Spanish masters by urging Americans to migrate to Spanish territory, where they would be granted free lands and allowed to bring in their property, including slaves, duty free. Furthermore, there would be no taxes except import and export duties and no interference in the matter of religion except that public worship was not permitted otherwise than according to the rites of the Catholic Church.[59]

White and Mathews were in Natchez when Cox arrived, and Governor Sargent got the impression that the three of them were intriguing against him. On August 18, 1798, he therefore had

[56] Proclamation by Governor Sargent, October 4, 1798, in Rowland (ed.), *Mississippi Territorial Archives*, I, 59–60.

[57] Abernethy, *Western Lands*, 332.　　　　　[58] *Ibid.*, 340.

[59] Sargent to Pickering, December 11, 1798, in Rowland (ed.), *Mississippi Territorial Archives*, I, 93–94; Abernethy, *Western Lands*, 354.

Cox arrested and confined to jail, but the bars were not strong enough and on the twenty-sixth the prisoner escaped and fled to New Orleans.[60] The next day Wilkinson arrived at Natchez, and on the twenty-eighth Sargent called on Governor Gayoso to return the fugitive. Refusing this request, Gayoso treated Cox with consideration and allowed him to return to Tennessee by way of Mobile and the Tombigbee settlements.[61] On reaching Nashville he was arrested by Federal authorities and detained for nearly three months. No formal charges were ever brought against him, and he was released when it was proved that his Smithland settlement did not encroach on Indian lands. This adventure behind him, Cox returned to Georgia and gave up the struggle for lands in the Great Bend of the Tennessee.[62]

Meanwhile, in August of 1798 Ellicott began the survey of the boundary line along the thirty-first parallel, and Wilkinson moved some of his troops to Loftus Heights, just above the boundary, and began the construction of Fort Adams. American jurisdiction was thus definitely established, but the local situation was still precarious. Lacking the spirit of adventure, Governor Sargent found his position distinctly distasteful and wrote to Wilkinson that "Natchez, from the perverseness of some of the people, the inebriety of the Indians and Negroes on Sundays, has become

[60] Later Sargent ordered the arrest of James White and several others. Warrant issued by Sargent on November 7, 1798, in Rowland (ed.), *Mississippi Territorial Archives*, I, 77–79; Cox to Congress, November 1, 1803, in *American State Papers, Miscellaneous*, I, 361–62; Sargent to Senator James Ross, October 17, 1798, in Rowland (ed.), *Mississippi Territorial Archives*, I, 65–68; Sargent to Pickering, August 20, 1798, *ibid.*, 30–33; Sargent to Captain Isaac Guion, August 18, 1798, *ibid.*, 29; Jacobs, *Tarnished Warrior*, 174.

[61] Sargent to Gayoso, September 18, 1798, in Rowland (ed.), *Mississippi Territorial Archives*, I, 51–53; Sargent to M. Filhue, December 1, 1798, *ibid.*, 84–85; Sargent to Wilkinson, October 20, 1798, *ibid.*, 72–75.

[62] Zachariah Cox to General Assembly of Georgia, n.d., Yazoo Manuscripts (University of Georgia Library); Pickering to Sargent, December 10, 1798; May 20, 1799, in Carter (ed.), *Territory of Mississippi*, V, 53, 58–59; Sargent to Wilkinson, January 8, 1799, in Rowland (ed.), *Mississippi Territorial Archives*, I, 100–102; Sargent to Thomas Butler, January 15, 1799, *ibid.*, 102; Sargent to Judge McNairy, March 2, 1799, *ibid.*, 109; Sargent to Wilkinson, March 22, 1799, *ibid.*, 118–19; Cox to Governor Jackson, June 14, 1800, in Yazoo Manuscripts (University of Georgia Library); Remonstrance and Memorial of Zachariah Cox to Congress, November 2, 1803, in *American State Papers, Miscellaneous*, I, 361 ff.

a most abominable place." [63] To Pickering he complained that the country was infested with Spanish brigands and that the Choctaw were very numerous and almost always in the settlements, living upon the people. No mail route was established, Colonel Peter Bryan Bruin was the only one of the three Territorial judges who was on the scene, and the counties had only temporary justices of the peace and no jails. Furthermore, the militia was without arms and the people were defenseless. Sargent recommended that conflicting land claims be settled and a land office for the sale of the public domain be opened so that migration to Spanish territory could be checked. He also thought that provision should be made for giving annual presents to the Choctaw to wean them away from their former Spanish connection. [64]

Georgia's constitution of 1798 made provision for the cession of the lands west of the Chattahoochee to the Federal government, and the legislature of 1799, under the influence of General James Jackson, who had been elected governor, expressed its willingness to make such a cession under certain conditions. [65] During the next year Congress provided for the creation of a legislature for the Mississippi Territory according to the terms of the Northwest Ordinance and also authorized the Federal commissioners to inquire into and report on the claims of individuals—including the Yazoo companies—to the territory south of Tennessee. [66] The commissioners whom President Adams had appointed to treat with Georgia were Pickering, Oliver Wolcott, and Samuel Sitgreaves; but Jefferson, having succeeded Adams as President, appointed three members of his cabinet, Madison, Gallatin, and Levi Lincoln, to constitute the commission. [67] In doing this, he was probably unaware that Gallatin

[63] Sargent to Wilkinson, November 14, 1798, in Rowland (ed.), *Mississippi Territorial Archives*, I, 82–83; Claiborne, *Mississippi, as a Province, Territory and State*, 179, 208.

[64] Sargent to Pickering, September 29, December 20, 1798, in Rowland (ed.), *Mississippi Territorial Archives*, I, 53–56, 89–92.

[65] Chappell, *Miscellanies of Georgia*, Pt. II, 127–28.

[66] Poore (ed.), *Federal and State Constitutions*, II, 1051–52; Chappell, *Miscellanies of Georgia*, Pt. II, 129; *Sundry Papers in relation to Claims*, 52–55, 179–85.

[67] Haskins, "Yazoo Land Companies," *loc. cit.*, 89.

had been one of the group which had bid unsuccessfully against the Yazoo companies for Georgia's western lands, but the other two were not connected with either group.

The commissioners entered into negotiations with Jackson, Abraham Baldwin, and John Milledge, who had been appointed by the state, and in April, 1802, Congress ratified their proposal that Georgia would cede to the Federal government all lands lying west of her present boundary in return for a payment of $1,250,000 and a pledge to extinguish all Indian claims to the territory remaining to the state. The ceded territory would in due time be admitted as a state or states, and all land claims deriving from British or Spanish grants, as well as from the Bourbon County Act of 1785, would be confirmed in the case of settlers actually in residence prior to the Spanish evacuation. It was also stipulated that 5,000,000 acres be reserved for the settlement of other (Yazoo) claims. The boundary of the Mississippi Territory was now extended northward from latitude 32°28′ to the southern boundary of Tennessee.[68]

The report of the commission respecting private land claims reached the House of Representatives on February 16, 1803, and a bill to carry out its terms was introduced. John Randolph immediately opened an attack on the measure by offering a resolution excluding the Yazoo claimants from any share in the settlement. This was the beginning of a famous and protracted controversy, and it must have shocked the members of the House to hear the Administration floor leader make such an assault on an Administration measure.[69] Randolph's ire was doubtless whetted by the fact that the New England Mississippi Company employed Gideon Granger, Jefferson's Postmaster General, to represent its interests before Congress, and to see this gentleman openly lobbying on behalf of the Yazoo claimants confirmed all Randolph's suspicions of executive influence in the matter.[70] Despite this opposition, the act was passed on March 3, and though it denied the validity of the Yazoo claims, it stipu-

[68] *Ibid.*, 89–90; *Sundry Papers in relation to Claims*, 56–79.

[69] Norman K. Risjord, "The Old Republicans: Southern Conservatives in Congress, 1806–1824" (Ph.D. dissertation, University of Virginia, 1960), 30–32.

[70] *Ibid.*, 35–38.

lated that the 5,000,000 acres reserved according to the agreement with Georgia should be appropriated to the quieting of so much of them as Congress might later provide for. Thus the question was left open and absolutely subject to the future determination of the Federal legislature.[71]

Early in 1804 a bill was introduced in the House authorizing the commissioners to settle the Yazoo claims according to what they should deem to be the best interests of the United States. This report favored the appropriation of the five million acres for this purpose and it set off a debate which was carried on intermittently for ten years, in which Randolph and a solid phalanx of Southern Republicans took issue with Madison and the Jefferson administration, while all the Federalists and some Northern Republicans favored the implementation of the committee report. This was the first rift in the ranks of the Jeffersonian Party. It created strange bed fellows and had important political repercussions,[72] but the merits of the immediate question are difficult to assess.

When the Georgia legislature passed the Rescinding Act, it provided that the half million dollars which were paid in by the four Yazoo companies should be refunded. Shortly after his return from Natchez, Zachariah Cox, through his brother William, applied to Governor Jackson for the return to him of half the money paid by the Tennessee Company. Senator Gunn of the Georgia Company, as well as others, took advantage of this proposal, and by August, 1803, nearly two-thirds of the purchase money had been returned to the original buyers.[73] It was ap-

---

[71] Senator Jackson to Governor Milledge, February 18, 1803, in Charlton, *Life of Major General James Jackson*, 193–97; *American State Papers, Public Lands*, I, 132, 159; Report of the Commissioners, in Savannah *Georgia Republican*, May 25, 1803; Garland, *John Randolph of Roanoke*, 200 ff.

[72] Richmond *Enquirer*, January 1, November 5, 1805; Savannah *Georgia Republican and State Intelligencer*, April 11, 1805; *Sundry Papers in relation to Claims*, 185–95; Haskins, "Yazoo Land Companies," *loc. cit.*, 92; Bowers, *Jefferson in Power*, 344–46; Beveridge, *John Marshall*, III, 576.

[73] Dr. John Hall to Governor Jackson, November 10, 1800, in Cuyler Manuscripts; "George Sibbald on the Yazoo Purchase, 1802," in *Bulletin of the New York Public Library* (New York), VIII (1904), 151–52; Peter Allen to Governor Jackson, August 22, 1800, in Personal File (Georgia Department of Archives and History); John Holland to Governor Milledge, March 8, 1803, in Yazoo Papers (Library of Congress); White,

parently assumed that the original purchasers would reimburse those to whom they sold their claims, but certainly in most cases no such reimbursement was made, and thus those who purchased from the original grantees were left holding the bag. Of these unfortunates, the New England Mississippi Company was the most important and it now prepared to press its case before Congress, as did Matthias Maher and the investors in the Tennessee Company who had not shared in the reimbursement made to Cox. Adam Tunno and his associates who represented the purchases they made from Wade Hampton as well as from the old Virginia and South Carolina companies of 1789 also filed claims.[74] The proponents of the Yazoo claims had powerful backers, including all the Federalist members of the House of Representatives, as well as Postmaster General Gideon Granger and Secretary of War Samuel Dexter, both of whom were financially interested.[75]

While Randolph was blocking every move made in Congress to grant compensation to the claimants, the reorganized Tennessee Company resorted to direct action. In 1806 the United States acquired from the Cherokee Indians the western two-thirds of their claims lying in the Great Bend of the Tennessee River in Mississippi Territory.[76] This was fertile soil and settlers began

---

*Accurate Account of the Yazoo Fraud,* 47; order for payment signed by Governor Jackson, January 3, 1798 (Georgia Department of Archives and History); William Cox to Governor Jackson, August 3, 1799; March 6, April 16, 1800, *ibid.*

[74] Writ of attachment against Zachariah Cox, June 1, 1797, in Yazoo Papers (Library of Congress); Arthur Harper to Governor Jackson, January 13, 1800, *ibid.*; Percy Martin *et al.* to Governor Jackson, May 3, 1800, *ibid.*; George R. Clayton to Gallatin, August 12, 1802, *ibid.*; Sheriff of Jefferson County to James Meriweather, September 8, 1789, in Cuyler Manuscripts; George Sibbald to Governor Jackson, December 9, 1799, *ibid.*; Thomas Williams, Jr., to Shaler Hillyer, October 24, 1799, in Linton R. Massy Collection (privately owned, Keswick, Va.); Savannah *Georgia Gazette,* June 17, 1802; *Sundry Papers in relation to Claims,* 148–53; *Report of the Committee to whom was referred . . . the Memorials of Alexander Moultrie . . . and of the Virginia Yazoo Company by William Cowan, their agent* (Washington, 1804).

[75] Deed of Trust, June 20, 1800, in De Renne Collection; Memorial to Congress from Percy Martin and Gideon Granger, November 30, 1804, in *American State Papers, Public Lands,* I, 209–10; Richmond *Enquirer,* April 4, 1806; Philadelphia *Aurora,* February 25, 1807, from the Petersburg (Va.) *Intelligencer;* Garland, *John Randolph of Roanoke,* 244–45; Sakolski, *Great American Land Bubble,* 135–36.

[76] Bureau of American Ethnology, *Eighteenth Annual Report,* Pt. II, plate 1.

to move down from the older communities in the Cumberland basin. Most of them were merely individuals looking for new homes, but some were Yazoo claimants. On September 30, 1808, the Nashville *Clarion* announced that the Tennessee Company had made a settlement of about four hundred families near the Muscle Shoals, had set up a government, and was selling land for four dollars an acre.[77] During the previous year Congress had allowed pre-emption rights to settlers already on the land, and accordingly on November 5, 1808, the President directed the governor of Mississippi Territory to allow settlers in the Bend of the Tennessee to remain as tenants at will, as elsewhere in the Territory, but to eject Yazoo claimants by force if necessary.[78] At the same time Madison County was created from a part of the ceded territory and civil officials were appointed, Yazoo men being specifically declared ineligible. The county seat was fixed at a large spring where a primitive settlement grew into the town of Huntsville. In 1809 a group of substantial planters from Petersburg, Georgia, came in search of new lands on which to plant cotton, and soon the forest was giving way to the plowed field.[79]

By this time the Federal government had surveyed much of the land in the county and offered it for sale at auction on the usual terms, a minimum price of two dollars an acre. On October 29, 1809, the Secretary of the Treasury reported to the President that Yazoo claims had not affected sales and that within three weeks 24,000 acres had been sold for more than $60,000.[80] However, the Yazoo men had not surrendered. On January 17 the *Kentucky Gazette* reported that they had located a thousand families on their claims, and in September, 1809, it was stated that Colonel Nicholas Harrison, a Yazoo claimant, headed a set-

[77] Richmond *Enquirer*, September 30, 1808, quoting Nashville *Clarion;* Carter (ed.), *Territory of Mississippi* (Washington, 1938), VI, 25 ff.

[78] Gallatin to John Milledge and William H. Crawford, February 23, 1808, in Yazoo Papers (Georgia Department of Archives and History); Secretary of Treasury to Governor Robert Williams, November 5, 1808, in Carter (ed.), *Territory of Mississippi*, V, 660.

[79] Thomas P. Abernethy, *The Formative Period in Alabama, 1815–1828* (Montgomery, 1922), 10–11; Carter (ed.), *Territory of Mississippi*, VI, 17–18.

[80] Carter (ed.), *Territory of Mississippi*, VI, 25–26.

tlement of about three hundred families in Madison County and that they were prepared to repel by force any who claimed the same land by purchase from the government.[81] No such controversies disturbed the settlers on the Tombigbee River, and on July 4, 1809, they drank toasts to John Randolph of Roanoke—he who had fought against Yazoo.[82]

But presently the Supreme Court of the United States came to the assistance of the speculators. In 1809 the claims of the New England Mississippi Company came before this tribunal in the case of Fletcher v. Peck, with Chief Justice John Marshall presiding and with Luther Martin, John Quincy Adams, and Robert Goodloe Harper representing the appellants.[83] Marshall had been considerably involved in land speculations on his brother's account and, therefore, had an understanding heart where other speculators were concerned. His principal biographer, Albert Beveridge, thinks that the Supreme Court should not have entertained this case, since it was a collusive one, but it nevertheless proceeded to do so and, on March 16, 1810, handed down an opinion favorable to the speculators.[84]

This case is one of the landmarks of American constitutional history, for Marshall now declared that a land grant constituted a contract and that the Constitution prohibited a state from invalidating the obligation of a contract. Thus the Georgia Rescinding Act of 1796 was void and the Yazoo grants of 1795 were still valid. But more important, the case of Fletcher v. Peck endowed vested interests with perpetuity and limited the states in the exercise of their right of eminent domain. It was thus a notable turning point in the history of Federal consolidation.[85]

Although the Supreme Court has the final word as to the status of the law, it is subject to human error and its decisions can, and

---

[81] Lexington Kentucky Gazette, January 17, 1809; Carter (ed.), Territory of Mississippi, VI, 20–21, 61–62; Notice by Jack Peck, Boston, in New Orleans Louisiana Gazette, September 6, 1810.

[82] Raleigh Register, November 9, 1809.

[83] Haskins, "Yazoo Land Companies," loc. cit., 99.

[84] Raleigh Register, March 29, 1810; New Orleans Louisiana Gazette, June 19, 1810; Richmond Enquirer, July 27, August 3, 1810; Beveridge, John Marshall, III, 581–82.

[85] Haskins, "Yazoo Land Companies," loc. cit., 100–101; Beveridge, John Marshall, III, 594–95.

should, be questioned as to their logic and propriety. It is distinctly ironical that the great champion of the Federal prerogative should, in this instance, have ruled against the validity of that prerogative. Under the Constitution the Federal government alone had jurisdiction over the Indians and the sole right to acquire lands from them. Yet the Georgia legislature granted the Yazoo companies the right to extinguish the Indian claims to the lands in question, and it also provided that the state should have no jurisdiction over the ceded lands until counties should be formed and representatives be sent to the legislature. Governor Jackson thought that this permitted the Yazoo companies to set up independent governments if they chose to do so, and it does seem that the possibility existed. Marshall rather slyly ignored the question as to whether the Georgia legislature originally had the right to make the grants and confined himself to the question as to whether, once made, they could be revoked. Thus limiting his approach, he was able to make a plausible case, and he has received the praise from his beneficiaries that his efforts have deserved.[86]

As important as was this decision from the constitutional point of view, it did not greatly strengthen the position of the Yazoo claimants. During the long struggle since the Rescinding Act of 1796 most of them had given up hope and sold their claims at a sacrifice to speculators, for whom the New England Mississippi Company was still the principal spokesman. But only Congress could grant compensation, and as long as the doughty John Randolph held his seat in the House of Representatives, there was little chance that a compromise of the claims could be effected. Finally, however, in the elections of 1813 Randolph was defeated by Jefferson's son-in-law, John Wales Eppes, and in March, 1814, the House, by a vote of 84 to 76, adopted the compromise which the Yazoo commissioners had originally recommended in 1804. Signed on March 31, 1814, this act provided that $5,000,000 from the proceeds of land sales in the Mississippi Territory be shared among the original companies in the following proportions:

---

[86] [Jackson], *Letters of Sicilius*, No. 3, pp. 18–19; No. 4, pp. 29–33, 44; No. 9, pp. 51–57; No. 10, 58–66; Citizens of Screven County, *To the Honorable the President and the Honorable the Members of the Convention of the State of Georgia* (n.p., 1795), a broadside bearing signatures; Chappell, *Miscellanies of Georgia*, Pt. II, 135.

Upper Mississippi Company, $350,000; Tennessee Company, $600,000; Georgia Mississippi Company, $1,550,000; Georgia Company, $2,250,000; and citizens' rights under the several companies, $250,000. Commissioners would be appointed to decide all cases finally, and nothing would be paid to those who had voluntarily surrendered the evidences of their claims or received back any of the purchase money.[87] Francis Scott Key, John L. Law, and Thomas Swann were appointed to make the settlement, and they began their arduous task during the next year. In 1818 the Treasury reported a final settlement which involved the payment of $4,282,151.12. But because of its failure to complete payment for its holdings, the New England Mississippi Company was not allowed the full amount of its claims under the compromise.[88]

Thus ended the greatest land speculation in American history. It had involved, on one side or the other, many of the leading figures of the day. A significant sidelight is furnished by the stand taken by William Lattimore, delegate to Congress from the Mississippi Territory who favored a settlement of the Yazoo, as well as British and Spanish claims, to validate land titles and thus promote immigration. A similar stand was taken by Representative Matthew Lyon of Kentucky, who got favorable mail contracts from Granger.[89] On the other hand, Governor Jackson opposed any compromise, not only because of the corruption involved in the original Yazoo grants, but because the settlement of lands which they claimed would tend to depopulate the Seaboard states. It is noteworthy that Presidents Jefferson and Madison took a different view and favored the development of the Southwest.

[87] Lexington Kentucky Gazette, April 4, 1814; Charleston Courier, April 5, 1814; Sakolski, Great American Land Bubble, 141; Haskins, "Yazoo Land Companies," loc. cit., 101–102.

[88] Proof Sheets of Senate Bill 93, Report 42, 1838, Thomas L. Winthrop et al., the New England Mississippi Land Company, in De Renne Collection; American State Papers, Public Lands, III, 549; White, Accurate Account of the Yazoo Fraud, 61.

[89] Matthew Lyon to his Constituents, March 4, 1805, in Charleston Courier, May 3, 1805; Philadelphia Aurora, April 27, 1807; Washington Republican, April 6, May 4, 1814; Speech of William Letterman in House of Representatives, in New Orleans Louisiana Gazette, June 9, 1814.

# CHAPTER VII

# THE "BLOUNT" CONSPIRACY

W HEN William Blount was appointed governor of the Southwest Territory in 1790, he was also made superintendent of Indian Affairs for the Southern Department. Already the white and Negro population of the Territory amounted to 35,691, and it was increasing rapidly. During the first stage of Territorial government all authority, including legislative, executive, and judicial functions, was concentrated in the hands of the governor, the secretary, and the three Territorial judges. But when the population should amount to five thousand adult males, a Territorial legislature could be organized. Since this number was already exceeded, the people were anxious to organize a representative assembly.[1]

At first Blount, wishing to retain as much power as possible, opposed this step, but by 1793 he realized that he would have to give way and accordingly authorized the election of a house of representatives. When it assembled on February 26, 1794, it chose Dr. James White of Spanish Conspiracy fame as Territorial delegate to Congress and nominated Sevier and several other active land speculators to make up the five-member council, the upper chamber of the legislature.[2]

This second phase of Territorial government, however, was hardly a logical stopping place for restless pioneers. General Wayne's victory over the Northern Indians at the Battle of Fallen Timbers in 1794 removed a formidable obstacle to the development of the West and settlers from the Southern states were

[1] First Census of the United States (Washington, 1908), 8.
[2] Abernethy, From Frontier to Plantation in Tennessee, 133–34.

crossing the mountains in ever increasing numbers. In this year a post office was established at Knoxville, the town which Blount and his friend, Colonel James White—not to be confused with the doctor of the same name—established to serve as the Territorial capital, and by 1795 this frontier metropolis could boast of two or three hundred houses. By this time the old horse trail to Nashville was widened into a wagon road, and two years later the mail service was extended to this center of the Cumberland River settlements.[3]

Having made up his mind that statehood was desirable, Governor Blount called the second session of the Territorial legislature to meet in June instead of October, 1795. This body provided that a new census should be taken and that the people should vote on the question of statehood. The returns showed a larger population than was required and revealed a majority in favor of statehood. Governor Blount accordingly ordered the election of a convention by manhood suffrage, and this body met in Knoxville on January 11, 1796. As could have been expected, Blount was chosen to preside, and a young frontier lawyer, Andrew Jackson, was appointed to represent Davidson County on the drafting committee.[4]

The frame of government here produced was based on that of North Carolina, but there were some interesting modifications. Representation would be apportioned according to taxable population instead of by territorial units, the governor would be elected by the people instead of by the Assembly, and the property qualification for voters was abolished in case a residence qualification could be met. These features represent an advance in democracy, but as usual, the advance was more apparent than real. Although North Carolina had, since 1784, been accustomed to tax all acreage at the same rate regardless of value, there was no provision to this effect in the constitution, but such a principle was written into the instrument for Tennessee. It was also provided that the justices of the peace should be elected for life by the Assembly and that they in turn should choose

[3] *Ibid.*, 156–58; New Bern *North-Carolina Gazette*, May 30, 1795.
[4] Abernethy, *From Frontier to Plantation in Tennessee*, 135–36.

most of the other county officials, thus rendering local government completely undemocratic.[5]

It was assumed by Blount and the people generally that as soon as the population amounted to sixty thousand and a constitution was framed, the Territory would have the right of statehood without question. Accordingly, Blount's friend, Joseph McMinn, was selected by the convention to present the Tennessee constitution to Congress and to apply for admission to the Union. President Washington, in a message acknowledging the prescriptive right of the Territory to statehood, recommended admission. The House committee reported favorably, but the Senate committee through Rufus King dissented, holding that the state should be laid out and the census taken under Congressional authority before the question of admission could be considered. The high Federalists, taking their usual stand, were attempting to obstruct the development of the West.[6]

Without waiting for Congressional authority or submitting their work to the people for ratification, the Tennessee convention ordered elections to be held under the new instrument. The choice for governor fell upon the old Indian fighter, John Sevier, and the legislature of the new state convened at Knoxville on March 28, 1796. This body proceeded forthwith to elect Blount and William Cocke to the United States Senate, to choose Presidential electors pledged to vote for Jefferson, and to provide for the election of two representatives to Congress.[7] On June 1, 1796, despite the opposition of the Federalists who knew that the new state would favor Jefferson if admitted in time to vote in the forthcoming election, Congress provided for admission but allowed Tennessee only one member in the Federal House of Representatives. Andrew Jackson was presently chosen by the people to occupy the single seat.[8]

Blount had entered upon his duties as governor of the Southwest Territory as an appointee of President Washington and he con-

[5] John D. Barnhart, "The Tennessee Constitution of 1796: A Product of the Old West," in *Journal of Southern History*, IX (1943), 532–48; Abernethy, *From Frontier to Plantation in Tennessee*, 136.

[6] Abernethy, *From Frontier to Plantation in Tennessee*, 138.

[7] *Ibid.*                [8] *Ibid.*, 138–40.

sistently tried to support the policies of his chief. When England
and France went to war in 1793, he favored the English and was
intensely hostile in his attitude toward Citizen Genêt. On June
4, 1793, toasts were drunk in Jonesborough condemning "the
murderers of Louis XVI." [9] This is not what one would expect
of the frontier, and it was not the brand of sentiment to which
the West usually gave birth. A communication appeared in the
Knoxville *Gazette* censuring the Jonesborough toasts, and those
drunk the next year and in 1795 at similar celebrations were
sufficient to develop the other side of the picture. These condemned aristocracy in a vehement manner and were loud in
praise of the French Republic and the "Democratic party." [10]
Public opinion was on this side and contrary expressions became
less and less frequent. In fact, the apparent willingness of Congress to sacrifice the Southwest for the sake of other interests
went far toward cooling the Federalism of the governor himself.
When Secretary of State Pickering wrote him on March 23, 1795,
and remarked, "Upon the whole, Sir, I cannot refrain from saying
that the complexion of some of the Transactions in the Southwest territory appears unfavorable to the public interest," Blount's
enthusiasm for the party to which that gentleman belonged
probably died a natural death. If this were not enough, the Federalist opposition to the admission of Tennessee as a state filled
the cup, and the governor came out against Jay's Treaty and for
Jefferson's election. On the same side in these matters was
Blount's friend and Tennessee's representative in Congress,
Andrew Jackson.[11]

Of course Blount, whose brothers were engaged in extensive
mercantile operations in North Carolina, did not forget his own
economic interests. He owned enormous tracts of Tennessee
lands; and in July, 1795, Dr. Nicholas Romayne of New York
sailed for England to sell some of this acreage for himself and
Blount, while James C. Montflourence, attaché at the American
legation in Paris, would act as Blount's land agent in France.
To keep up communication with his distant partner in this
business, the governor employed the services of his personal
Indian agent, Captain John Chisholm, an aggressive and enter-

[9] *Ibid.,* 142.     [10] *Ibid.,* 142–43.     [11] *Ibid.*

prising but illiterate native of Scotland who came to America with the British Army during the Revolution. He changed sides with the advent of peace and became an early Indian trader and a justice of the peace in Knoxville.[12]

While Romayne was still on the high seas, Britain suffered a severe blow in her war against revolutionary France. On July 22 her Spanish ally withdrew from the struggle, a settlement having been negotiated on the part of Spain by her principal Minister, Manuel de Godoy. England naturally feared a *rapprochement* between the two Latin nations, and accordingly, on October 24 the Duke of Portland sent secret instructions to Lieutenant-Governor John G. Simcoe of Upper Canada to promote friendly relations with the leading settlers of Kentucky and the Western country in the hope that they might be used in case of trouble with Spain. Simcoe was also to cultivate the good will of the Southern and Western Indians and to investigate the route between Lake Michigan and the Mississippi. On both sides of the Atlantic there was a suspicion that Louisiana might be retroceded to France, and the seriousness of this danger was demonstrated when in March of 1796 the French Minister to the United States, M. Pierre Adet, sent General Victor Collot to make a military reconnaissance of the Ohio and Mississippi rivers. The clouds became thicker when on August 19 France and Spain entered into a defensive alliance and thus closed the Mediterranean to English ships. In October war was declared between England and Spain.[13]

[12] Arthur P. Whitaker, *The Mississippi Question, 1795–1803* (New York, 1934), 106; Statement of John Chisholm to Rufus King, November 29, 1797, in Frederick J. Turner (ed.), "Documents on the Blount Conspiracy, 1795–1797," in *American Historical Review*, X (1904–1905), 595; Clarence E. Carter (ed.), *The Territory of Orleans, 1803–1812* (Washington, 1940), 67 n.; Deposition of Dr. Nicholas Romayne, in Marcus J. Wright, *Some Account of the Life and Services of William Blount* (Washington, 1884), 40–42; Charleston *City Gazette*, January 6, 1798; Walter B. Posey, "The Blount Conspiracy," in *Birmingham-Southern College Bulletin* (Birmingham), XXI, No. 6 (December, 1929), 12; William Masterson, *William Blount* (Baton Rouge, 1954), 277–78; King, *Life and Correspondence of Rufus King*, II, 254–56.

[13] Duke of Portland to John G. Simcoe, October 24, 1795, in Turner (ed.), "Documents on the Blount Conspiracy," *loc. cit.*, 575–76; Posey, "Blount Conspiracy," *loc. cit.*, 13; Isabel Thompson, "The Blount Conspiracy," in East Tennessee Historical Society *Publications*, No. 2 (1930), 3–21.

Land values declined sharply in 1796 and Romayne did not make any sales in England, but having received part of his education there, he made some friends in government circles, prominent among whom were Sir William Pulteney and Henry Dundas. Before returning home the doctor made plans for renewing the speculation after Blount should have secured the passage of an act enabling foreigners to own land in Tennessee, and Romayne and Pulteney kept in touch by correspondence for some time thereafter.[14]

It is impossible to tell with certainty who started the affair known as the Blount Conspiracy, but it was not William Blount. Robert Liston, the British Minister in Philadelphia, was the kingpin in the plot, but he was careful to give the impression that Blount's former Indian agent, John Chisholm, was the author. This seems doubtful, though the Senator's protégé was certainly the most active participant in the scheme.

According to his own egotistical account of the affair, Chisholm traveled widely in the Indian country during the summer and fall of 1796 and got in touch with the former Tories, numbering one thousand to fifteen hundred, who were now carrying on trade with the Southern tribes or living among them in some capacity. Journeying to Philadelphia in November as a guide to a party of sight-seeing natives, Chisholm presented James Mc-Henry, Washington's Secretary of War, with a petition from about twenty-five of his Tory friends who now wished to become citizens of the United States. When the Secretary received this petition without enthusiasm, Blount's erstwhile Indian agent, with the approval of his principal, went forthwith to Liston and proposed himself as the leader of an expedition to be made up chiefly of his Tory and Indian friends and supported by an English naval force, to conquer West Florida and Louisiana for Britain.[15] Liston wrote up the plan and Chisholm revealed it to Blount as well as to James Carey, interpreter for the Cherokee

[14] G. Ragsdale to J. G. Blount, October 20, 1796, in J. G. Blount Papers (North Carolina Historical Commission, Raleigh); Deposition of Dr. Nicholas Romayne, in Wright, *Life and Services of William Blount*, 40–42, 45.

[15] Robert Liston to Grenville, January 25, 1797, in Turner (ed.), "Documents on the Blount Conspiracy," *loc. cit.*, 576–77; Statement of Chisholm to King, November 29, 1797, *ibid.*, 595–600, 601; Posey, "Blount Conspiracy," *loc. cit.*, 15.

and assistant storekeeper at Tellico, and to John Rogers, a former captain in the British Army now residing among the Indians. These two friends accompanied Chisholm to Philadelphia; he then told them that he was to go to England to discuss the affair with the Ministry, while they were to inform his friends in the Indian country of the project.

On January 25, 1797, Liston sent a dispatch to Lord Grenville, British Foreign Secretary, submitting Chisholm's plan to raise a force of Loyalists living among the Creek and Cherokee Indians and lead them in attacks on Mobile and Pensacola.[16] Chisholm now went to New York, accompanied by Carey and Rogers and also by four Creek and four Cherokee chiefs. There he visited Dr. Romayne, with whom he had done business for Blount as early as 1792. There, too, he met several land speculators, as well as members of the Parliament of Lower Canada and a number of Northern Indian chiefs, including the powerful Iroquois, Joseph Brant, who was later reported to have agreed to participate in the expedition against Florida. Another new acquaintance was a New England surveyor named John Mitchell, who had visited New Orleans and had considerable knowledge of the Spanish posts on the Upper Mississippi River. When Chisholm returned to Philadelphia, Mitchell followed and introduced a Major Craig, formerly of the American Army and then living in Pennsylvania. Thereafter these three were often together.[17]

During February Blount also visited New York to discuss with Romayne their old plan for selling Tennessee lands in England. The doctor now informed Blount that France was about to take Louisiana from Spain, free the slaves, close the navigation of the Mississippi, and thus ruin the value of Western lands. He said that lands bordering on Canada were more valuable than those near the Spanish possessions and expressed a wish that Florida and Louisiana were in British hands. Blount then in-

[16] Deposition of John Franklin, December, 1796, in Wright, *Life and Services of William Blount*, 59–62; Halifax *North-Carolina Journal*, December 25, 1797; Posey, "Blount Conspiracy," *loc. cit.*, 15.

[17] Turner, "Documents on the Blount Conspiracy," *loc. cit.*, 595–600, 604; Statement of Chisholm to King, November 29, 1797, in King, *Life and Correspondence of Rufus King*, II, 254–56. This could have been the same Mitchell who served as a Spanish spy in 1794. Whitaker, *Spanish-American Frontier*, 196–97.

formed Romayne that Chisholm, with the aid of an important person in Philadelphia (Liston), had concocted a filibustering scheme against Florida, but neither of these two men considered the illiterate Chisholm a proper person to lead such an expedition. They now decided to take over the project and enlarge it. Blount was to consult friends in Philadelphia and on the frontier, paying especial attention to those who had been associated with Genêt. Then in May he was to sail for England. Romayne offered to furnish letters of introduction to his British friends, but the object of the visit was to be kept secret. William Duer, Robert Morris' old associate in land speculation, was charged with having helped to formulate the plot. Thus the "conspiracy" was really a two-pronged affair, with Blount and Romayne competing with Chisholm and Liston.[18]

During March the situation became tense. General Collot had returned in January from his military reconnaissance, and he later asserted that while at Natchez he discovered a British plot to attack Louisiana from Canada. A mixed force of whites and Indians would descend the Mississippi and capture St. Louis. From that point one expedition would march against Santa Fé while another descended the river to attack New Orleans.[19]

It is not surprising that Collot should have heard such rumors at Natchez. Ellicott, who had been sent there to survey the Spanish-American boundary line, recorded in his diary that a gentleman who left Philadelphia in December and journeyed to Natchez at government expense had been loud in his praise of Senator Blount and had conferred with Anthony Hutchins, one of the wealthiest planters of the neighborhood and a former Tory who, according to Ellicott, was still a major in the British military establishment. Having failed to strike a responsive chord in the surveyor, the stranger only informed him that the Spanish authorities would use the British threat as an excuse to delay

<hr/>

[18] Chisholm's statement, in Turner, "Documents on the Blount Conspiracy," *loc. cit.*, 599; Charleston *City Gazette*, January 16, 1798; Posey, "Blount Conspiracy," *loc. cit.*, 13–14; Wright, *Life and Services of William Blount*, 31–32, 40–50; Thompson, "Blount Conspiracy," *loc. cit.*, 17.

[19] Victor Collot, *A Journey in North America* (Paris, 1826), II, 64–68.

the boundary survey, and he then went on to Mobile and Pensacola, where he visited the connections of the British firm of Panton, Leslie and Company and remained until the "Blount conspiracy" exploded.[20]

Ellicott gave no further hint as to the identity of the mysterious stranger, but his description would seem to fit none other than General Mathews of Georgia, who as governor had signed the infamous Yazoo Act of 1795. It will be recalled that, at the instance of Pickering, he was appointed governor of the newly created Mississippi Territory but that the appointment was withdrawn when McHenry revealed the fact that Mathews was acting as agent for the New England Mississippi Yazoo Company. Naturally the Yazoo claimants had the same interest in preventing a French occupation of Louisiana as did land speculators in Tennessee, and Blount's connection with Zachariah Cox and the Tennessee Yazoo Company has already been mentioned.[21]

While rumors were circulating at Natchez, they were also spreading in Kentucky. On March 2 George Rogers Clark wrote to Colonel Samuel Fulton that "we have here English agents from Canada to enroll volunteers destined to march against Louisiana. Some days ago I received propositions from the Government of Canada to march at the head of 2,000 men against the Spanish establishments in New Mexico." He described a two-pronged expedition from St. Louis against Santa Fé and New Orleans identical to that of which Collot was warning Don Carlos Yrujo in Philadelphia. Clark said that the British offered him a colonelcy but that he declined the proposal.[22] It was hardly a fortuitous coincidence that in May a similar proposal was made to General Elijah Clarke by a Captain William Carrick, who represented himself as a British officer living in Charleston. This veteran Indian fighter would retain his rank as a general in the Georgia militia and receive a salary of ten thousand dollars

[20] *Journal of Andrew Ellicott*, 64–65; Cox, *West Florida Controversy*, 52–53; Ellicott to Pickering, September 24, 1797, in Carter (ed.), *Territory of Mississippi*, V, 7.

[21] Cox, "Border Missions of General George Mathews," *loc. cit.*, 109–10; Whitaker, *Mississippi Question*, 104, 109.

[22] Turner, "Documents on the Blount Conspiracy," *loc. cit.*, 576 n.; Posey, "Blount Conspiracy," *loc. cit.*, 13; Thompson, "Blount Conspiracy," *loc. cit.*, 16–17.

while operating against the Spanish possessions, but he curtly declined the offer to serve a government which he hated.[23] Still more mysterious were the activities of William Tatham, an English-born resident of East Tennessee and a former supporter of John Sevier when he was governor of the State of Franklin. Now Tatham, who made a trip to Europe in this connection, was collecting information for Lieutenant-Governor Simcoe of Canada. On February 16 Lieutenant-Governor Sir Robert Prescott of Quebec wrote Liston of the difficulty of sending supplies for the proposed expedition against the Floridas unless the United States favored the enterprise. These scattered facts furnish sufficient evidence to prove that Simcoe and Liston were collaborating in an effort to organize an expedition against Spanish territory, and this could not have been done except on orders from the British Secretary of State, Lord Grenville. William Blount could hardly have been the author of the plot.[24]

On the last day of February, 1797, Yrujo notified Pickering that the British were preparing an expedition on the Lakes for a descent on St. Louis and New Madrid. Being a pro-British Federalist, Pickering ignored this warning, but three days later Yrujo renewed the charge. Somewhat irritated, the American Secretary of State now attempted a counterattack by charging that the Spaniards were trumping up an excuse to delay the survey of the Florida boundary, but he notified Liston of Yrujo's allegation, and the British Minister denied it categorically.[25]

The sincerity of this denial may be judged by a letter Liston wrote to Secretary Grenville on March 16, 1797, in which he in-

[23] Pickering to Yrujo, August 8, 1797, in *American State Papers, Foreign Relations*, II, 93; Deposition of General Elijah Clarke, April 27, 1798, in Wright, *Life and Services of William Blount*, 78–79, 80–81; Franklin L. Riley, "Spanish Policy in Mississippi," in Mississippi Historical Society *Publications*, I (1898), 50–72; Coulter, "Elijah Clarke's Intrigues and the 'Trans-Oconee Republic,'" *loc. cit.*, 277–78; Halifax *North-Carolina Journal*, December 25, 1797.

[24] Yrujo to Pickering, April 21, 1797, in *American State Papers, Foreign Relations*, II, 68; William Tatham to [Simcoe], November 23, 1796, in Turner (ed.), "Documents on the Blount Conspiracy," *loc. cit.*, 576 n., 577 n.

[25] Liston to Grenville, May 10, 1797, in Turner (ed.), "Documents on the Blount Conspiracy," *loc. cit.*, 588–89; Yrujo to Pickering, March 2, 1797, in *American State Papers, Foreign Relations*, II, 68; Charleston *City Gazette*, January 15, 1798; Collot, *Journey in North America*, II, 64–68.

formed his superior that "the Bearer of this letter is Mr. Chisholm the Gentleman mentioned in my Letters No 2 and 3 as having been charged by certain Persons inhabiting near the South West Frontiers of the United States, to propose a Plan for the Conquest of the Floridas. He has lately received Letters from some of the Adventurers who wish the most ardently to engage in the Enterprise and urging an early decision regarding it. Mr. Chisholm's Correspondents appear to have given him an account of the Dispositions of the Inhabitants of the Spanish Territories adjoining the United States that has persuaded him of the possibility of joining to the Acquisition of Florida the Reduction of the Forts on the Mississippi, the conquest of New Mexico, and a Diversion that might ultimately contribute to the Independence of South America,—The Certainty . . . of the farther Continuance of the War, the Probability of the Cession of Louisiana to the French by the Spaniards and the advantages of his scheme led me to consent to his proposals and to pay his passage to England, giving him hope of Gov't paying his expenses in London and return home. Infractions of the Neutrality of the United States might be avoided by the Proposal of Captain Chisholm that the Adventurers (who have become citizens of America) should all pass over to the Spanish Territory, before they begin their Military Preparations." But, Liston warned, the treaty between the United States and Spain bound each to prevent Indian hostilities against the other.[26] On the same day the British Minister wrote to his Dutch friend, J. H. Goverts, introducing Chisholm and stating: "He goes to Europe to dispose of certain Lands situated in different parts of America, but particularly in the South." Liston cautioned the Dutchman to consider the long letter he had written him on the thirteenth before taking any definite steps or promising Chisholm any money. He said that he thought it possible that Chisholm would push on to London if he were not completely successful in Hamburg, and he ended his communication by asking Goverts not to refuse Chisholm if he applied to him for letters of introduction to Goverts' friends in London, for "I do not intend he shall re-

[26] Liston to Grenville, March 16, 1797, in Turner (ed.), "Documents on the Blount Conspiracy," *loc. cit.,* 582 ff.

turn *re infecta.*" It is thus obvious that Liston had private as well as public business in mind.[27]

The day after these letters were penned, Chisholm wrote to his friends Mitchell and Craig that they must be in Tennessee by the first of May in order to carry out their plan. At the same time he wrote to Blount and Colonel John McKee, informing them that he was leaving the next day for England; actually, however, it was not until the twenty-first that his ship made sail. Liston paid the expenses of the voyage.[28]

These developments seemed to leave Blount—who had never had any direct dealings with Liston—and Romayne out in the cold, but they were not inactive. On March 15 Romayne wrote to his friend that the political leaders in New York, including Hamilton, had decided that the war in Europe would go on, and they dreaded the transfer of Louisiana to France. Romayne urged Blount to play up this danger in Tennessee and Kentucky and instructed him to "burn or destroy my letters." Two days later Blount answered that decisive action would have to be taken by May 1 and warned, "Keep yourself prepared to go [to England] and I will do the same." On March 21, just as Chisholm set sail, Romayne notified Blount that he was ready to start for Europe if his correspondent agreed.[29] Their object was apparently to circumvent Chisholm and to make their own contacts with Pulteney and Grenville, but the British Secretary of State saved them the trouble, writing Liston on April 8 that Chisholm's project for the conquest of the two Floridas was disapproved by the Ministry on the grounds that the means to the end proposed were inadequate and that it was undesirable to employ the Indians or to originate an expedition within the United States.[30]

[27] Liston to J. H. Goverts, March 16, 1797, in King, *Life and Correspondence of Rufus King,* II, 198.

[28] Timothy Pickering to Committee of the House of Representatives, July 26, 1797, in Charleston *City Gazette,* January 15, 1798; Halifax *North-Carolina Journal,* December 18, 1797; Wright, *Life and Services of William Blount,* 35, 54, 115.

[29] Turner (ed.), "Documents on the Blount Conspiracy," *loc. cit.,* 602; Wright, *Life and Services of William Blount,* 32–35.

[30] King to Pickering, August 28, 1797, in King, *Life and Correspondence of Rufus King,* II, 217–18; Liston to Grenville, August 30, 1797, in Mayo (ed.), *Instructions to the British Ministers,* 141 n.; Turner (ed.), "Documents on the Blount Conspiracy," *loc. cit.,* 595–600, 602; Grenville to Liston, April 7, 1797, in Mayo (ed.), *Instructions to the British Ministers,* 132.

It was not long before another blow was struck against the plot. When General Collot returned from his Western travels in January, he dutifully reported to the French Minister at Philadelphia, M. Pierre Adet. Since France and Spain were now allies, the general in a letter of March 1 warned Yrujo of the danger threatening Louisiana, but he gave no details.[31] Two weeks later this deficiency was remedied when John Mitchell made a deposition which Adet took down in French and Collot transmitted to Yrujo. According to this statement, Chisholm had enlisted a thousand Tennesseans to attack the Spanish posts on the Lower Mississippi; then the Creek and Cherokee Indians would be sent to invade Florida and Louisiana. Mitchell further declared that he had a list of fifteen hundred British Loyalists residing in the Natchez district whom Chisholm had enlisted to attack Lower Louisiana and then undertake a campaign against Santa Fé. In addition, fifteen hundred British regulars in Upper Canada, reinforced by seven hundred Canadian militiamen and two thousand Indians under Chief Brant, would descend the Illinois River and proceed to St. Louis, New Madrid, and Santa Fé. According to Mitchell, Chisholm made these plans and, after conferring with Liston, set out on March 28 (actually March 21) for London to inform the British government of the project and demand the necessary funds and ships for its execution. To prove that he knew what he was talking about, the informer turned over to his patrons the letter which Chisholm had written to him and to Craig on March 17, telling them that the American contingent would rendezvous at Knoxville on May 1 and that they should be there at that time.[32]

Collot commented that Mitchell combined two enterprises that had no connection, for he thought the Western Americans, interested only in capturing the posts which they claimed on the Lower Mississippi, would refuse to help the British capture Louisiana and Florida and that the Indians and British Loyalists would be unwilling to help the Americans. For these reasons, and because of the early warning given the Spanish governors, Collot

[31] Collot to Yrujo, March 1, 9, 1797, in Turner (ed.), "Documents on the Blount Conspiracy," *loc. cit.,* 577–82.

[32] Collot, *Journey in North America,* II, 64–68; Collot to Yrujo, April 15, 1797, in Turner (ed.), "Documents on the Blount Conspiracy," *loc. cit.,* 585–87.

thought that the danger was not great. It is worthy of note that Mitchell, who in December, 1793, gave information concerning Genêt to the Spanish authorities at Natchez, named Chisholm as the sole source of his information and made no mention whatever of Blount, though he said that certain Federalist Senators were involved and that Governor Sevier of Tennessee was definitely committed to the plot.[33] With admirable restraint Yrujo waited almost a week and then wrote to Pickering: "I have new reasons for believing the British plan to attack Upper Louisiana." [34]

Actually, Mitchell's account of the plot differed in important details from that which Chisholm later divulged. According to the latter, Chief Brant and his Iroquois Indians were to be joined on the Ohio by Mitchell and Craig with reinforcements recruited on the frontiers of New York and Pennsylvania; this force, after capturing and garrisoning New Madrid would proceed to the source of the Red River and take possession of the silver mines there. The Tennessee and Kentucky volunteers, along with the Choctaw Indians and the Natchez Tories, presumably under command of William Blount, would take New Orleans, while Chisholm, leading the Cherokee and Creek contingents along with white recruits from Florida, would take Pensacola. British commissions would be given the leaders of these expeditions, and six British frigates would blockade Pensacola and the mouth of the Mississippi. Louisiana and the Floridas would become British colonies, while New Orleans and Pensacola would be declared free ports, and the navigation of the Mississippi would be opened to the nationals of both countries. The attacks on New Madrid, New Orleans, and Pensacola were to be made on the same day, but the Spanish posts on the east bank of the Mississippi above the thirty-first parallel, claimed by the United States, would not be molested.[35] Chisholm made no mention of the use of Canadian regulars and militia in these expeditions, nor of an attack on Santa Fé, and therefore Mitchell claimed to

[33] Turner (ed.), "Documents on the Blount Conspiracy," *loc. cit.*, 586–87.
[34] Yrujo to Pickering, April 21, 1797, in *American State Papers, Foreign Relations*, II, 68.
[35] Statement of Chisholm to Rufus King, November 29, 1797, in Turner (ed.), "Documents on the Blount Conspiracy," *loc. cit.*, 595–600, 603.

know more of Simcoe's operations that did Chisholm. Pending further investigation, it is impossible to tell whether Mitchell actually did have secret Canadian contacts or whether he was making liberal use of his imagination.

Blissfully ignorant of both Grenville's veto and Mitchell's treachery, Senator Blount left Philadelphia in mid-March for a leisurely journey to his home in Knoxville. At King's ironworks, near the Long Island of the Holston, he received word that President Adams had called a special session of Congress to meet on May 15. The Senator at once decided to return to Philadelphia without visiting Knoxville, but an attack of rheumatism detained him for some time at the ironworks and he devoted his enforced leisure to the writing of letters to associates with whom he had hoped to discuss his plans. In messages to Sevier and Robertson he urged that Andrew Jackson, who had resigned his seat in the House, be sent to the Senate and that William C. C. Claiborne be elected to the vacant seat in the House, while Sevier should be retained as governor. Other letters dealt with financial affairs, but the most important ones related to the anti-Spanish plot, and these were addressed to Colonel John McClellan, Major James Grant, John Rogers, and James Carey.[36]

In the letter to Carey, dated April 21, Blount said he was not entirely certain that the projected attack on the Spanish possessions would be carried out, but if Romayne's mission to England were successful, the writer would probably be at the head of the business on the part of the British. Meanwhile, Carey was urged to keep up the Senator's "consequence" with the Creeks and Cherokee and to do everything possible to discredit Benjamin Hawkins, who had succeeded Blount as superintendent of Indian Affairs for the Southern Department. Furthermore, if the Cherokee should criticize Blount in connection with the Holston Treaty which he had negotiated with them in 1791, "it may be said by my friends, at proper times and places,—that, though I made the treaty, that I made it by the instructions of the President, and, in fact, it may with truth be said, that I was by the President instructed to purchase much more land than the In-

<hr>

[36] Deposition of John Rogers, in Wright, *Life and Services of William Blount,* 65–73, 75–76; Masterson, *William Blount,* 312–13.

dians would agree to sell. This sort of talk will be throwing all the blame off me upon the late President, and as he is now out of office, it will be of no consequence how much the Indians blame him. . . . Can't Rogers contrive to get the Creeks to desire the President to take Hawkins out of the nation? for, if he stays in the Creek nation, and gets the good will of the nation, he can and will do great injury to our plan. When you have read this letter over three times, then burn it. I shall be in Knoxville in July or August." [37]

This communication was delivered to Carey by his friend James Grant, and Carey forthwith showed it to his employer James Byers, who managed the government trading post at Tellico Blockhouse and against whom Blount had warned him. Recognizing the importance of the document, Byers, anxious to play the part of hero, mounted his horse and rode hard for Philadelphia. Arriving on June 20, he delivered the incriminating document into the eager hands of McHenry and Pickering.[38]

Grenville's letter of April 8 notifying Liston that the British Ministry did not sanction Chisholm's projected campaign against the Floridas did not reach its destination until late in June, and it was still another week before Blount's letter to Carey reached Philadelphia. Meanwhile, Dr. Romayne had a friendly but non-committal communication from Sir William Pulteney, and on April 14 he forwarded this to Liston with some vague hints as to the projected expeditions against the Spanish posts in the West. On the twenty-eighth Liston replied with equal ambiguity: "Taking it for granted that I understand to what business you allude, I could wish to have a full explanation of your sentiments on the subject; it may be done, I think, in writing, you may depend on secrecy and discretion on my part. The general sketch of what has taken place here is, that a person came to me to make certain important propositions of enterprise, to which I listened,

[37] Halifax *North-Carolina Journal*, July 17, 1797; Lexington *Kentucky Gazette*, July 26, 1797; Masterson, *William Blount*, 312–13; Wright, *Life and Services of William Blount*, 14–16, 35.

[38] Deposition of James Grant, in Wright, *Life and Services of William Blount*, 69–72; Lexington *Kentucky Gazette*, August 16, 1797; Masterson, *William Blount*, 316; Posey, "Blount Conspiracy," *loc. cit.*, 17–18; Wright, *Life and Services of William Blount*, 36–37, 69–72.

but said I had no power to act. He [Chisholm] appeared determined and active, though illiterate and unfit to assume command. He urged to have my consent to go to Europe, to tell his own story, to which I consented. . . . It strikes me that if a person of confidence, with proper authority from home, were to accompany him to the scene of action, something might possibly be effected. Information of every sort will be faithfully received." [39] It is clear from this letter that Blount and Romayne were trying to supplant Chisholm and that Liston was still keeping all avenues open. Furthermore, it may have been a knowledge of Blount's attitude toward Chisholm that prompted Carey to turn against the Senator.

On May 12 Romayne wrote to Blount that he had two letters from Pulteney on the subject of their business but that there was nothing decisive. The next day he wrote again that he expected to sail for Europe the middle of the following week and he wished to see his friend before he left.[40]

By this time Blount had completed the long journey from Tennessee to Philadelphia and had taken a room with his brother Thomas. Land values had been falling sharply since the early part of the previous year, and the Senator, like all other land speculators, was experiencing financial trouble. However, he forestalled many of his creditors by a nominal deed to his half brother Willie (pronounced Wyllie) of much of his land, all of his twenty-six slaves, his household furnishings, and his farm stock and equipment. Soon his old Yazoo confederate, Lachlan McIntosh, arrived from Georgia in an effort to extricate Zachariah Cox from the bankruptcy which had swamped Robert Morris and John Nicholson of the North American Land Company. This incident demonstrates the close relation that existed between Morris' company, the Yazoo speculation, and Blount's latest project.[41]

On his return McIntosh carried orders from Blount to his Western confederates, but Romayne's letters remained unanswered. Both plotters appear to have become discouraged by the

[39] *Annals of Congress,* 5 Cong., 3 Sess., 2351–52; Wright, *Life and Services of William Blount,* 35–36.
[40] Charleston *City Gazette,* January 16, 1798; Wright, *Life and Services of William Blount,* 36, 44.
[41] Whitaker, *Mississippi Question,* 105, 109; Masterson, *William Blount,* 314–15.

continued success of the French armies and the financial difficulties which England was experiencing. On May 13 Romayne
notified Blount that the vessel on which he planned to leave for
England sailed without him, and on the twenty-ninth Blount
apologized for not having answered his previous letters. Finally,
on July 2 the doctor sent a last message to the Senator in which
he renounced their project entirely.[42]

By June 24 Liston received Grenville's letter of April 8 and
he hastened to write his superior that he regretted it had not
come in time to prevent Chisholm's departure for England.
Meanwhile, Blount's letter to Carey was turned over to McHenry
and Pickering, and the Secretary of State rushed to the British
Minister with the startling news. After Blount deserted the Federalist Party, Pickering was his bitter enemy and he relished this
opportunity to expose him. Because Liston had, to some extent,
involved his government in the Chisholm plot, the Minister was
not anxious to have the business brought to the attention of Congress and the public. He explained to Grenville that Pickering
thought the French were to get Louisiana and that they would
incite rebellion on the Southwestern frontiers. The attributing
of these plans to Britain was, according to Pickering, a mere
pretext to cover French designs. His hatred of France, as well as his
anxiety to expose Blount, led him to communicate to Congress all
he had discovered. Liston thought he had persuaded the eager Secretary that the exposure would only give Spain a pretext to retain
the posts on the Lower Mississippi and throw odium on Britain,
while the American citizens involved might escape on the plea that
they were merely trying to get possession of rich lands soon to fall
to France.[43]

At first Pickering weakened, but Adams could not resist the opportunity to strike a blow at his enemies. Accordingly, on July 1
the Secretary sent a formal note to Liston saying that his name had
been mentioned in connection with the Blount plot and asking for

[42] Charleston *City Gazette*, January 16, 1798; Masterson, *William Blount*, 315;
Posey, "Blount Conspiracy," *loc. cit.*, 17; Wright, *Life and Services of William Blount*,
36–39, 44–50, 115.
[43] Liston to Grenville, June 24, 1797, in Turner (ed.), "Documents on the Blount
Conspiracy," in *loc. cit.*, 589–92.

information! The next day Liston answered that a scheme for attacking the Spanish provinces was mentioned to him but that he declined to participate in it and so informed his superiors. Then without loss of time a Presidential message was dispatched to the Senate on the third, and the horrified Blount heard his letter of April 21 to Carey read to his colleagues.[44]

This startling disclosure set off an explosion among the exultant but somewhat frightened Federalists. Pickering undertook a campaign to get Blount indefinitely imprisoned and to demonstrate to the world the purity and innocence of the British government, and especially of Minister Liston. Even the elder statesman, George Washington, seethed with rage and expressed hope for drastic punishment, while the benign Abigail Adams joined the rabid "Porcupine," William Cobbett, in lamenting the absence of a guillotine in Philadelphia.[45] The whole affair convinced Spain's Minister Godoy of the necessity of complying at last with Pinckney's Treaty of 1795, but it also gave renewed arguments to the Spanish agents in the United States for the continued retention of the Mississippi posts.

The British Minister found his situation somewhat embarrassing and, in order to put himself in the best light, wrote to Grenville on July 8 that he was acquainted with neither Blount nor Romayne, nor did he know anything of plans for a British expedition from Canada or the offer alleged to have been made to General Elijah Clarke of Georgia. Despite this seeming innocence, he advised that the project "must now be renounced unless the United States becomes embroiled with Spain." [46]

When the Carey letter was first read before the Senate, Blount declined either to admit or deny that he had written it. The next day, July 4, he asked for further time to prepare his defense, but the Senate responded by naming a committee, headed by James Ross, which it empowered to send for persons and records and to

[44] McHenry to Adams, June 30, 1797, in *American State Papers, Foreign Relations,* II, 72; Pickering to Liston, June 1, 1797, *ibid.,* 70–71; Liston to Pickering, July 2, 1797, *ibid.,* 71; *Annals of Congress,* 5 Cong., 1 Sess., 34; Lexington *Kentucky Gazette,* June 29, 1797; Masterson, *William Blount,* 315–17.

[45] Masterson, *William Blount,* 317–18.

[46] Liston to [Grenville], July 8, 1797, in Turner (ed.), "Documents on the Blount Conspiracy," *loc. cit.,* 592–94.

report on the proper procedure. Panic then seized the Senator and, denying that he had any recollection of having written the Carey letter, he tried to escape by boat from Philadelphia, but the Ross committee thwarted this attempt. Deciding now to face his accusers, Blount employed Alexander J. Dallas and Jared Ingersoll —Philadelphia lawyers who had participated in the Yazoo speculation of 1795—to serve as his counsel, and on July 6 he returned to his seat in the Senate.[47] That body agreed to hear him the next day, but in the interim the Ross committee had his quarters searched and his luggage and papers seized. There was much heated argument over this incident, but on the eighth the Senate, by a vote of twenty-five to one, adopted the adverse report of the Ross committee and Blount became the first United States Senator to be expelled by his colleagues. He was accused of high misdemeanor and abuse of public trust, but actually since he had committed no overt act, it is doubtful whether a court of law could have taken action against him.[48]

On the day before the Senate voted to expel Blount, Samuel Sitgreaves in the House of Representatives brought a bill of impeachment against him and, having been released from his bond to attend the Senate hearings, he was placed under a new one of a thousand dollars to appear for the impeachment trial. Congress adjourned on July 10, and on that day a messenger reported that Blount had filed his bond and been released, but he did not put in a personal appearance. While the legislators angrily ordered the recording of his nonappearance and sent transcripts of their proceedings to the governor of Tennessee, the fallen statesman was spurring his horse urgently down the Valley road to safety.[49]

Pickering hastily sent out instructions for the arrest of the fugitive Senator, but by avoiding main roads and the larger towns

[47] *Annals of Congress*, 5 Cong., 1 Sess., 34; Halifax *North-Carolina Journal*, July 17, 1797; Masterson, *William Blount*, 314–20; Wright, *Life and Services of William Blount*, 18.

[48] Pickering to King, July 8, 1797, in King, *Life and Correspondence of Rufus King*, II, 196–98; *Annals of Congress*, 5 Cong., 1 Sess., 39–44; Masterson, *William Blount*, 320–22; Wright, *Life and Services of William Blount*, 18–20; Posey, "Blount Conspiracy," *loc. cit.*, 19.

[49] *Annals of Congress*, 5 Cong., 1 Sess., 44–45; Halifax *North-Carolina Journal*, July 17, 24, 31, August 7, 1797; Masterson, *William Blount*, 320–23.

Blount made his way past Staunton, Virginia, to Abingdon and then, turning eastward, rode to Raleigh, where his wife was recovering from an injury caused by a fall from her carriage. Here he remained through the hot months of August and September, 1797, while Andrew Jackson and other friends worked for his rehabilitation in Tennessee.[50] Before leaving Philadelphia Blount wrote to some of these friends to acknowledge and defend the writing of the Carey letter. For distribution on a wider scale he had a circular printed which, while not specifically acknowledging authorship, reproduced the letter and put the question: "I ask you to examine it with attention and determine for yourself, if the contemplated plan . . . had gone into effect, what would have been the result to the citizens of Tennessee, whose good it has ever been, and ever will be, my happiness to promote. . . . I repeat, read and judge regardless of popular clamor. Shortly I will be in Tennessee." [51]

Finally, in early autumn Blount decided to leave his still ailing wife in Raleigh and return to Knoxville. When he approached the town, he was met by an honorary escort of volunteer cavalry and a large group of citizens headed by his long-time friend, Colonel James White. So unmoved were Blount's fellow Republicans in Tennessee by any plots against the Spaniards or by any Federalist accusations against the former governor that they proposed to defy the Administration by re-electing him to the Senate. No one offered to oppose him, but not wishing to return to Philadelphia, Blount declined to run. Joseph Anderson was chosen to complete his unexpired term, while Andrew Jackson, who had first represented Tennessee in the House, was elected for the six-year term in the Senate, with William C. C. Claiborne replacing him in the House. These men were all fast friends of the "disgraced" Senator, who was presently sent to the state Senate, James White having resigned to make a place for him, and he was forthwith chosen to preside over that body. In view of these developments, it is not surprising that when James Matthews, the Sergeant-at-Arms of the

[50] Lexington *Kentucky Gazette*, August 5, 1797; Halifax *North-Carolina Journal*, August 17, 1797; Masterson, *William Blount*, 324.

[51] Lexington *Kentucky Gazette*, August 16, 1797; Halifax *North-Carolina Journal*, August 7, 1797; Wright, *Life and Services of William Blount*, 38–39.

United States Senate, appeared in Knoxville with a warrant for Blount's arrest, he was treated with marked courtesy by the citizens of the town but failed to find a single person who would assist him to perform his duty. He departed without his prisoner.[52]

Meanwhile, the House of Representatives pursued its impeachment policy. After adjournment, the Sitgreaves committee continued its hearings and employed Captain William Eaton to collect evidence that has been a boon to the few historians who have concerned themselves with *l'affaire Blount*. Dr. Romayne was brought from New York to testify, and he complained bitterly that Federal agents had attacked his house in the dead of night and forced him to make the journey to Philadelphia under humiliating circumstances. According to his account, he requested a private conference with Pickering and talked freely with him, but the Secretary of State proved to be no gentleman and misrepresented his disclosures.[53]

The session of Congress which lasted from November, 1797, into July, 1798, made little progress in the impeachment proceedings. Sitgreaves' committee continued to gather evidence, drew up formal charges, and dispatched a summons to Blount, but the Senate defeated any effort to start proceedings before the next session. At the same time Republicans under Jefferson began to plan a defense of the former Senator. Finally, on December 17, 1798, the first impeachment trial in the history of the United States got under way, but it was not until January 11, 1799, that a decision was reached. By a vote of fourteen to eleven it was then ruled that Senators were not impeachable civil officers, and the case was dismissed for lack of jurisdiction.[54]

With his fortune imperiled and his career wrecked, Blount's health was seriously affected and he died at his home in Knoxville

[52] Blount to J. G. Blount, November 28, 1797, in J. G. Blount Papers; Lexington *Kentucky Gazette*, October 21, November 1, 1797; Charleston *City Gazette*, October 21, 1797; Masterson, *William Blount*, 324; J. G. M. Ramsey, *The Annals of Tennessee* (Kingsport, 1926), 698–99.

[53] Halifax *North-Carolina Journal*, August 17, 1797, quoting New York *Daily Advertiser*; Wright, *Life and Services of William Blount*, 25.

[54] Halifax *North-Carolina Journal*, December 25, 1797; Masterson, *William Blount*, 331, 341–42.

on March 21, 1800.[55] Thus passed, in his fifty-first year, one of the notable figures of the early Southwest. He had been a leader—and an unscrupulous one—both in land speculation and in politics, but he was expelled from the Senate for writing a letter which involved neither crimes nor any disloyalty to the government of the United States.

[55] Lexington *Kentucky Gazette*, April 24, 1800; Masterson, *William Blount*, 345–46.

CHAPTER VIII

# WILKINSON'S LATER MANEUVERS

HAVING devoted some space to developments affecting the region to the southward, the discussion must now return to Kentucky and the revival of the intrigue which James Wilkinson and his friends began with the Spanish authorities in Louisiana as early as 1787. The adoption of the Federal Constitution put a quietus on this first Spanish Conspiracy and the cauldron of intrigue only simmered during the next few years. Early in 1792 Wilkinson was promoted to the rank of brigadier general in the Army of the United States but remained in command of Fort Washington, overlooking the Ohio at Cincinnati. Despite this official position, he did not lose interest in the Spanish pension which Governor Miró of Louisiana recommended for him back in 1789 and which was approved and made retroactive by the home government in 1791. On February 1, 1792, Miró's successor, the Baron Francisco de Carondelet, confirmed this arrangement.[1]

While old friends were thus keeping up their acquaintance, the next year brought increased tension on the Southern frontier. Though the Province of Louisiana embraced an enormous extent of territory, New Orleans was its only considerable settlement and the defense as well as the government of the whole colony depended upon this city, which Carondelet well knew was indefensible. The neighboring Indian tribes could muster about 13,000 fighting men, the American army numbered between three and

[1] Jacobs, *Tarnished Warrior*, 128; *American State Papers, Miscellaneous*, I, 704–705; Clark, *Proofs of the Corruption of Gen. James Wilkinson*, 6–9; Arthur P. Whitaker (ed.), "Harry Innes and the Spanish Intrigue: 1794–1795," in *Mississippi Valley Historical Review*, XV (1928–1929), 246.

four thousand, and Carondelet could muster no more than 1,620 regular troops.[2] But the "long rifles" of Kentucky and Tennessee were more effective than any of these forces; they could have conquered Louisiana without serious difficulty had they ever attempted it, provided the Indians did not intervene.

Carondelet recognized that his safety depended on the Indians and, abandoning Miró's pacific policy, he determined to make full use of their military potential. In fact, he would have undertaken an open war against the American frontier had he not been restrained by the government at Madrid. Ordered to remain on the defensive, he chafed at the restriction and did what he could to promote hostilities.[3] In pursuance of this objective, he commissioned the able commandant of the Natchez district, Manuel Gayoso de Lemos, to hold a conference at Fort Nogales on October 28, 1793, with all the principal Southern tribes. The governor instructed his agent to assert Spanish jurisdiction over all the Southern Indians, including the Cherokee, who were not previously considered as within the Spanish sphere of influence and who were not represented at the conference. Furthermore, Indian boundaries would be restored, by the use of Spanish arms if necessary, to the status of 1784, thus challenging the American treaties of New York and Holston. This would certainly have meant war between the two countries and Gayoso wisely failed to carry out the instruction, probably influenced in his decision by the activities of Citizen Genêt. Later, in 1795, Gayoso did build and occupy Fort San Fernando de las Barrancas at Chickasaw Bluffs.[4]

But the red men did not require much encouragement to raise the bloody tomahawk. The Creeks and Cherokee attacked all along

[2] Turner, "Diplomatic Contest for the Mississippi Valley," *loc. cit.*, 688; George W. Kyte, "A Spy on the Western Waters: The Military Intelligence Mission of General Collot in 1796," in *Mississippi Valley Historical Review*, XXXIV (1947–1948), 427–42; E. Wilson Lyon (ed.), "Milfort's Plan for a Franco-Creek Alliance and the Retrocession of Louisiana," in *Journal of Southern History*, IV (1938), 77.

[3] Whitaker, *Spanish-American Frontier*, 209; Williams, "French and Other Intrigues in the Southwest Territory," *loc. cit.*, 33.

[4] Carondelet to the Cherokees, July 4, 1794, in East and West Florida Papers; Carondelet to Jáudenes, March 4, 1795, *ibid.*; Whitaker, *Spanish-American Frontier*, 178–81, 215; Arthur P. Whitaker, "Spain and the Cherokee Indians, 1783–98," in *North Carolina Historical Review*, IV (1927), 252–69; Gayarré, *History of Louisiana*, III, 328–29.

the frontier, not by any means confining their warfare to areas where the white man encroached on their lands. The people built and manned forts wherever that was possible, but even so, many a frontier family was tomahawked as it tried to flee from its burning cabin.[5] For four weeks the following notice appeared in the Knoxville *Gazette*: "The Creek Nation must be destroyed or the south western frontier from the mouth of the St. Mary's to the western extremities of Kentucky and Virginia will be incessantly harrassed [*sic*] by them—and now is the time. *Delenda est Carthago!*" [6] Driven to desperation by their losses, the frontiersmen could not understand why the Washington administration prohibited offensive operations against the enemy. They believed that they were quite able to take care of themselves if given the opportunity, and on more than one occasion did take things into their own hands.[7]

The Indian menace was more deadly along the Georgia and Tennessee frontiers than in Kentucky, for in that state natives from across the Ohio caused the most trouble. Now the Federal government was waging an offensive, but so far unsuccessful, war against them and Kentucky was receiving considerable economic advantage from the funds expended in this enterprise. The Kentuckians were convinced that Congress, dominated by the East, consistently pursued policies which were intended to discourage the settlement and development of the West and that the frontier would therefore have to rely on its own resources, which they believed to be amply adequate to the emergency.[8] In these circumstances they had a choice of two possible courses: they could either conquer Louisiana or separate from the Union and come to terms

[5] New Bern *North-Carolina Gazette*, November 9, 1793; April 12, 1794; James White to Governor Blount, January 30, 1793, in Charleston *City Gazette*, April 11, 1793; Richmond *Virginia Gazette*, June 27, 1793, quoting dispatch from Knoxville, June 1; Lexington *Kentucky Gazette*, April 20, 1793, quoting letter from Nashville, April 8.

[6] Halifax *North-Carolina Journal*, August 14, 1793.

[7] Memorial and Petition of the Convention of Miró District to President Washington, *ibid.*, October 16, 1793; New Bern *North-Carolina Gazette*, September 14, 1793, quoting Knoxville dispatch of July 13; Halifax *North-Carolina Journal*, July 10, 1793, quoting letter from Nashville, May 18.

[8] "Aristides," in Lexington *Kentucky Gazette*, January 11, 15, February 1, 8, 15, 1794; Richmond *Enquirer*, January 10, 1807.

with the Spanish authorities as to the navigation of the Father of Waters.[9]

Despite the lowering storm and the trouble caused by his constantly tangled financial affairs, General Wilkinson found life at Fort Washington at this time comparatively tranquil. Still, there was ever present the problem of money, and in the autumn Michel Lacassagne went again to New Orleans to collect the general's pension from Governor Carondelet.[10] He returned in December with $4,000 and an oral message for Wilkinson. The Frenchman had had a confidential conversation with Carondelet in which he doubtless described the situation in Kentucky as the general wished the governor to see it; that is, Louisiana would be invaded unless Kentucky—presumably followed by the other transmontane communities—could be separated from the Union. Carondelet replied vaguely that the court of Spain was disposed to grant the people on the "Western Waters" certain privileges on certain conditions.[11]

Not satisfied with this noncommittal response, Wilkinson and his friends, knowing that they must act while Genêt's agents were still busy in Kentucky, undertook to put pressure on the Louisiana governor. During the first two months of 1794 the general assured Carondelet that the time had come when Spain must take a decisive stand in its relations with the Kentuckians, for they were determined to open the river, either by secession or conquest. Wilkinson also consulted his principal associates, Harry Innes, Benjamin Sebastian, and William Murray, a group known to Carondelet as the "Secret Committee of Correspondence of the West." Both Innes and Sebastian undertook to convince Gayoso that Louisiana was in grave danger, but the Natchez commandant thought that he could stop any invading force at Fort Nogales.[12] Carondelet, however, was more easily impressed and from April to July, 1794, he warned Godoy that the Western Americans could send 60,000 men against New Orleans. It would be difficult, he thought,

[9] Thomas Cooper, *Some Information Respecting America* (London, 1795), I, 27.
[10] Hay and Werner, *James Wilkinson*, 138–39.
[11] Whitaker, *Spanish-American Frontier*, 189.
[12] *Ibid.*, 196–97; Gayoso to Daniel Clark, January 31, 1794 (Louisiana Historical Museum, New Orleans).

to defend Louisiana against such a force, but if Kentucky could be separated from the Union, the rest of the West would follow and the danger would be averted. He thought this could be brought about by increasing Wilkinson's pension, granting generous stipends to his friends, and furnishing arms and munitions to support the revolution. Then, once independence had been achieved, Spain should open to the Kentuckians the navigation of the Mississippi as far south as New Orleans.[13]

On February 14 Innes wrote to Gayoso: "I have been informed that Baron Carondelet in a confidential conversation with a gentleman of this state [Lacassagne] declared that the court of Spain was disposed to grant to the people on the western waters certain *privileges* on certain *conditions,* but they cannot long be amused with hints of this kind. If your Court hath any *serious* intention of making propositions to the people of Kentucky, this is the critical moment to do so, which, if liberal, will no doubt be supported by every influential character in the state. In case you are inclined to correspond with me, a cypher would guard against mischief." [14]

No word assuring protection of Western communities came from Philadelphia, and in February, 1794, Lord Dorchester, Governor General of Canada, told the Indians that the British were about to go to war with the Americans. During April Governor Simcoe, who commanded on the Canadian frontier, challenged General Wayne to attack by establishing a fort at the rapids of the Maumee River, more than sixty miles south of the important base at Detroit, which England still held despite the treaty of 1783.[15]

While the British were assuming a threatening attitude north of the Ohio, Jáudenes and Viar, Spanish agents at Philadelphia, were sending a young man named Mitchell to Kentucky to consult with Wilkinson, Innes, Sebastian, and Murray. These gentlemen informed Mitchell that during the coming year there would be either a pro-Spanish revolution in Kentucky or an invasion of

---

[13] Whitaker, *Spanish-American Frontier,* 191–92, 209–13; Pelzer, "Economic Factors in the Acquisition of Louisiana," *loc. cit.,* 118.

[14] Whitaker, *Spanish-American Frontier,* 194; *Mississippi Valley Historical Review,* XV (1928–1929), 245–47.

[15] Turner, "Diplomatic Contest for the Mississippi Valley," *loc. cit.,* 689; Jacobs, *Tarnished Warrior,* 138; Channing, *History of the United States,* IV, 140–41.

Louisiana by the Kentuckians, for they were determined to have the Mississippi opened to their traffic. If Spain wished to avert an invasion, she must aid the revolution by sending arms and ammunition and permit duty-free navigation of the river. Definite assurances of Spain's agreement to these terms must be returned to Kentucky by April 1, 1795; otherwise Louisiana would be invaded without delay. On the other hand, if the terms were met, Spain might retain all the territory south of the Tennessee River and north and west of the Illinois.[16]

On the very day, June 20, 1794, that Mitchell reported these terms to Gayoso, Wilkinson sent a message to Carondelet. Five days earlier he wrote to Innes: "I invited Owen . . . to meet me here on the 12th Inst. I had in view for him an enterprise which might have proved important to him—if he does not arrive by Tuesday, he will be too late and the occasion to serve him will be beyond my reach. . . . I have a magic wand at the touch of which . . . difficulties are to vanish." [17] Now, on the twentieth, the letter to Carondelet stated that the author had succeeded in preventing the projected invasion under George Rogers Clark but that he needed $200,000 to secure the assistance and support of certain prominent Kentuckians. Wilkinson said that he was sending Henry Owen and Joseph Collins to New Orleans to transmit letters and verbal information concerning the situation in Kentucky. Owen, an educated Irishman who saw seven years of military service in Europe and who, for some time, was on intimate terms with Judge Innes, was said to "have full knowledge of all my secrets." Collins, a rough backwoodsman but a man of great courage, resource, and intelligence, lacked this information. Wilkinson asked that he be reimbursed for his expenditure of $8,640, as supported by "satisfactory documents," and that he receive $12,000 in addition, *"por mi pension."* He furthermore insisted that Carondelet should always write him without address or salutation so that in case of loss or capture of the letters, his identity would not be revealed.[18]

Collins, disguised as a trader and accompanied by Owen, set

[16] Whitaker, *Spanish-American Frontier*, 196–97.

[17] Wilkinson to Innes, June 15, 1794, in Innes Papers, Bk. 23, Pt. II.

[18] Manuel Serrano ȳ Sanz, *El Brigadier Jaime Wilkinson* (Madrid, 1915), 60 n.; Humphrey Marshall's arguments, in Innes Papers, Bk. 22, Pt. II; Hay and Werner, *James Wilkinson*, 140–41.

out late in June for New Orleans. To avert suspicion they gave it out that Kaskaskia was their destination, but in early August the two travelers completed their journey southward.[19]

The Spanish governor decided to meet Wilkinson halfway and sent him $12,000. He suggested that $4,000 of this amount be considered as payment on account of the pension and the other $8,000 taken as compensation for alleged expenditures incidental to the thwarting of Clark's projected expedition. This money was to be divided into two equal shipments, Owen being charged with the delivery of the first half, while Collins was to follow at a later date with the balance. At the same time that he made these arrangements, Carondelet urged Wilkinson that either he or some of his confidential associates come to New Madrid to concert their plans.[20]

Toward the end of August Owen boarded a keelboat at New Orleans and began his journey up the river with three small barrels containing 6,000 silver dollars for General Wilkinson. At the mouth of the Ohio he and his precious cargo were transferred to a pirogue and provided by Thomas Portell, commandant at New Madrid, with a pilot and crew of six oarsmen. As they neared the present site of Evansville, the crew murdered Owen and absconded with the three barrels of silver. Presently three of the culprits were captured in Kentucky, taken to Frankfort, and arraigned before Judge Innes. To the amazement of everybody, this Federal judge declined to try the case on the ground that the accused were Spanish subjects, but instead of sending them to New Madrid, as had been requested by Portell, he turned them over to a guard commanded by his brother-in-law and paid by himself, and sent them to Wilkinson at Fort Washington. This strange procedure was probably occasioned by the fact that Owen was also carrying dispatches from Carondelet to Wilkinson, which had been sewed in the collar of his coat.[21]

Whether the general extracted any information from his prison-

[19] Hay and Werner, *James Wilkinson*, 142.

[20] *American State Papers, Miscellaneous*, I, 104–105; Hay and Werner, *James Wilkinson*, 142.

[21] Wilkinson to [Innes], December 25, 1794, in Innes Papers, Bk. 23, Pt. II; Whitaker (ed.), "Harry Innes and the Spanish Intrigue," *loc. cit.*, 243; O. Thurston to Innes, December 28, 1810, in Innes Papers, Bk. 22, Pt. I; Jacobs, *Tarnished Warrior*, 137–38.

198

ers is not known, but not wishing to attract publicity, he hurried them off to Portell at New Madrid under the same guard that had brought them from Frankfort. The guard tried to slip past Fort Massac at night, but Major Thomas Doyle, who commanded there, had been ordered by General Wayne to be on the alert against intercourse between Wilkinson and the Spaniards and he intercepted them. Since no one at Massac understood Spanish, Captain Zebulon Pike applied to Portell to send an interpreter, and it was none other than Wilkinson's henchman Thomas Power who appeared to act in this capacity. As was expected of him, he found no guilt in the prisoners, and they were forthwith returned to New Madrid. Wilkinson was so relieved to be free of the murderers that he guaranteed to pay them $200 if they should not be compensated by the Spanish government, and at the same time he suggested to Portell certain measures which he considered to be "proper and necessary." [22]

At about the time Owen was leaving New Orleans, Wilkinson was moving north to make war on the Indians, and as second in command under General Wayne, he took part in the Battle of Fallen Timbers on August 20. The redmen were defeated, but the British commander, Major William Campbell, refused to surrender the fort at the rapids of the Maumee River. Yet the Northern Indians never again posed a serious threat to the settlement of Kentucky.[23] The situation in the West was still further improved when Jay's controversial treaty was signed during the following November and the British thereby agreed to evacuate Detroit and the other post which they still held south of the Great Lakes.

While these momentous events were transpiring, Wilkinson's other agent, Joseph Collins, was busy in New Orleans. According to his own account, he sold flour to Gilbert Leonard, the Spanish treasurer there, and received $6,330 to deliver to his employer. Returning by way of Charleston and Pittsburgh, he lost $2,500 of Wilkinson's money in a land speculation; and by the time Collins finally arrived at Fort Washington in April, there remained but

[22] Wilkinson to Innes, July 6, 1795, in Innes Papers, Bk. 23, Pt. II; Shreve, *Finished Scoundrel*, 88–89; Hay and Werner, *James Wilkinson*, 142–43.

[23] Wilkinson to Innes, November 10, 1794, in Innes Papers, Bk. 23, Pt. II; Lexington *Kentucky Gazette*, July 19, 1794; Hay and Werner, *James Wilkinson*, 120–24; Jacobs, *Tarnished Warrior*, 138–42.

$1,740 for the general. This, according to Wilkinson, was all that he received out of the more than $12,000 which Carondelet had sent by Owen and Collins.[24]

Wars and financial worries might intervene, but the conspiracy was not interrupted; nor were the people of Kentucky convinced that their troubles were over on account of the favorable developments north of the Ohio. The Southern Indians were as ferocious as ever. In defiance of Washington's orders to the contrary, a force of mounted infantry and volunteers from Kentucky and others from the Holston and the Cumberland settlements assembled at Nashville with the sanction of General Robertson and attacked and destroyed the Cherokee towns of Nickajack and Running Water on September 13, 1794. In this engagement at least fifty warriors were killed and a number of women and children made prisoners. Since the attack was a complete surprise, only one lieutenant and two privates from the Holston volunteers were wounded. The frontiersmen found at Nickajack and Running Water two fresh scalps, a quantity of ammunition, powder and lead lately sent the Indians by the Spanish government, a Spanish commission for the "Breath"—the head man of the town who was killed—a number of horses, and various other articles which the soldiers recognized as having been the property of settlers who had been killed by Indians in the course of the last year.[25]

While President Washington was thus being defied on the Southern frontier, Kentucky was contemplating the next move relative to the navigation of the Mississippi. On July 20, 1794, a large public meeting at Harrodsburg adopted a remonstrance to the President and Congress on this subject. Meetings of the Democratic Societies now became frequent, and on August 11 one was held in Lexington, with John Breckinridge in the Chair, which appointed a committee of three to discover the real intentions of Congress on the subject of negotiations with Spain concerning the Mississippi question.[26] In September Breckinridge issued a state-

[24] Jacobs, *Tarnished Warrior*, 148; James Sterrett to Daniel Clark, in New Orleans *Louisiana Gazette*, September 20, 1808; Clark, *Proofs of the Corruption of Gen. James Wilkinson*, 19–20, Appendix 189.

[25] Major James Ore to Governor Blount, September 24, 1794, in Ramsey, *Annals of Tennessee*, 616–17; Lexington *Kentucky Gazette*, October 4, 1794.

[26] Lexington *Kentucky Gazette*, July 12, 26, 1794; Coulter, "Efforts of the Democratic Societies of the West to Open the Navigation of the Mississippi," *loc. cit.*, 386.

ment in answer to his Eastern critics. He declared that he was shocked at John Jay's appointment, said that Westerners considered themselves deluded by the general government and sacrificed to the local policy of the Eastern states, and asserted that Virginia was wrong in thinking that Kentucky wished to separate from the Union or negotiate with Britain or Spain. Then he concluded: "I wish the rulers of Am[eric]a revered the British as little as we do . . . even the name of the former is odious here as it was with you in '76. . . . let Government take care they do not drive us to . . . [a foreign connection]. The Miss[issippi] we *will* have! If Government will not procure it for us, we must procure it for ourselves. Whether that will be done by the sword or by negotiation is yet to scan. . . . This is my opinion respecting the temper & sentiments of the people here." [27] On December 20 the Kentucky legislature instructed its Senators to demand that the Federal administration furnish information as to negotiations with Spain regarding the question of navigation; and a few days later James Innes, Attorney General of Virginia and brother to Wilkinson's friend Harry, arrived at Frankfort, having been sent by President Washington to furnish Governor Shelby with the desired information and thus attempt to calm the frayed nerves of the Kentuckians.[28] Innes's conversations with Shelby appear to have smoothed the troubled waters for a time, but actually he could report little except the appointment of a special envoy to Madrid. The post was offered to Jefferson, but not wishing to undertake what seemed a hopeless assignment, he declined and Thomas Pinckney, our Minister in London, was then given the difficult task.[29]

Meanwhile, Wilkinson was still working on his old project, but Judge Innes began to grow wary. On July 27, 1794, Gayoso, having received instructions from Carondelet, wrote Innes suggesting that

[27] Coulter, "Efforts of the Democratic Societies of the West to Open the Navigation of the Mississippi," *loc. cit.*, 387–88.

[28] Innes to W. C. Nicholas, June 10, 1807, in Innes Papers, Bk. 19; Wilkinson to Innes, December 16, 25, 1794, *ibid.*, Bk. 23, Pt. II; James Brown to Monroe, December 5, 1794, in *Louisiana Historical Quarterly*, XX (1937), 71–72; Henderson, "Isaac Shelby and the Genêt Mission," *loc. cit.*, 468; Savannah *Georgia Republican*, January 30, 1807, quoting Frankfort *Palladium* (extra), December 6, 1806; Whitaker (ed.), "Harry Innes and the Spanish Intrigue," *loc. cit.*, 242.

[29] Bradford notes, in Lexington *Kentucky Gazette*, January 2, 1839; Whitaker, *Spanish-American Frontier*, 186, 202–203.

Kentucky should first establish her independence and then negotiate with Spain in regard to the use of the Mississippi. In early
December Innes replied, "Your ideas are so different from mine
that I have communicated them only to one friend, who coincides
with me in opinion." Before entering into any further negotiations Innes insisted on being advised by the Spanish government
"what benefits are we to derive from the measure?" He added: "No
change can ever be expected unless real & substantial advantages
are to be acquired thereby, & before any attempt is made pointed
& unequivocal assurances of Indemnity to those characters who
may be active in bringing about so important an object." [30] Thus
Carondelet was trying to get the Kentuckians to take responsibility
for the proposed revolution in their state, and Innes was insisting
that it should be assumed by the Spanish authorities. From this
time forward Innes tended to lose interest in the conspiracy.

Not so with General Wilkinson. On August 6, 1794, Carondelet
wrote him suggesting that Innes, Sebastian, and possibly others
be sent to New Madrid to confer with certain Spanish officials on
matters of mutual interest. "You can assure them, from me," he
said, "that their services, when performed, will be rewarded by
suitable pensions." [31] This proposal was not taken up immediately,
probably because of the visit of James Innes to Kentucky, but in
the interim the Spanish Court was slowly making up its mind. It
finally decided to accept Wilkinson's suggestion in principle but
ordered that the intrigue with the "Secret Committee of Correspondence of the West" be continued only for defensive purposes
and in such manner as not to interfere with the pending negotiations with the United States.[32]

On receipt of these instructions Carondelet wrote Wilkinson
that he was authorized "to treat privately with the agents chosen
and sent by the state of Kentucky to New Madrid for that purpose." He proposed to send Gayoso to conduct the negotiations,
with power to agree privately with the Kentucky representatives
on the plan of separation. He agreed with Wilkinson that pensions

[30] Whitaker (ed.), "Harry Innes and the Spanish Intrigue," *loc. cit.,* 136–39; Hay
and Werner, *James Wilkinson,* 145.

[31] Hay and Werner, *James Wilkinson,* 145; Jacobs, *Tarnished Warrior,* 149.

[32] Hay and Werner, *James Wilkinson,* 147.

of $2,000 a year should be offered to Innes, Sebastian, George Nicholas, and the famous Breckinridge, "whose talents and writings will be useful to bind the minds of the western People in favor of our Plan." Carondelet then suggested that Wilkinson might acquire in the West the same dignity which Washington enjoyed in the East.[33]

Gayoso brought the governor's communications up the Mississippi as far as the mouth of the Ohio and from there forwarded them to Wilkinson by Thomas Power, who delivered them early in October. The general received the messenger warmly, but a month later he treated him rudely under his own roof. When Power protested, Wilkinson replied: "The commanding officer of the American legion [Wayne] has declared publicly at his table, that you were a spy for the British, a spy for the Spanish and a spy for somebody else. . . . imputations like these from such a high authority, however founded, render you an improper companion for a public officer, who, whatever his own opinions, owes respect to those of his superior." To this Power replied: "I mean not to apply the epithet 'contemptible puling villain' to Mr. A. Wayne . . . but to such as have availed themselves of his weakness and imposed on his credulity."[34] Here the "Trumpeter" was only throwing up a smoke screen, for his relations with Power remained unchanged. This incident may explain why Wilkinson wrote to Sebastian and later informed Gayoso: "The more effectively to conceal my agency & to mask my intervention in this transaction it has been agreed after deliberate discussions, between Sebastian & myself, that the Baron's letter to me of 16 July should be addressed to himself (Sebastian) & in that form be submitted to our friends of Spain in Kentucky."[35]

This suggestion was accepted, and accordingly a meeting was

[33] Carondelet to Wilkinson, July 16, 1793, in *Mississippi Valley Historical Review*, XV (1928–1929), 247–48; Wilkinson, *Memoirs of My Own Times*, II, 170–74; Whitaker (ed.), "Harry Innes and the Spanish Intrigue," *loc. cit.*, 244–45; Jacobs, *Tarnished Warrior*, 149.

[34] Wilkinson to Thomas Power, November 11, 1795, in E. Bacon, Chairman, *Report of the Committee Appointed to Inquire into the Conduct of General Wilkinson, February 26, 1811* (Washington, 1811), 72; Power to Wilkinson, November 10, 12, 1795, *ibid.*, 70–71, 73–76.

[35] Carondelet to Benjamin Sebastian, July 16, 1795, in Richmond *Enquirer*, January 8, 1807; Wilkinson, *Memoirs of My Own Times*, II, Appendix 45.

presently held between Innes, Murray, and Sebastian at the residence of Judge Nicholas in Mercer County. Here it was agreed that Sebastian should go alone to New Madrid to treat with Gayoso, Innes having declined to accompany him. In addition, this group approved a letter written by Sebastian to Gayoso on November 19, 1795. It spoke of the opportunity of attaching the Western people to the Spanish cause by opening the navigation of the Mississippi, "which they no longer hope to obtain by the aid of their own government." An attack was threatened in case this were not done, but the group did not assert that it was authorized to speak for Kentucky.[36] Wilkinson, now turning his back on his friends, wrote a cipher letter to Gayoso and sent a verbal message by Power, urging that Spain make no concession but strengthen her defenses on the Mississippi and increase her efforts to subvert Kentucky.[37]

In December Sebastian went to New Madrid, joining Power en route, and Gayoso came to meet them. The two agents drew up a commercial agreement for the transportation of Kentucky products down the river to New Orleans, but as they could not agree on details, they went together to the Louisiana capital to confer with Carondelet, reaching their destination about the first of the year. During February, 1796, the governor received the text of the Treaty of San Lorenzo, by which Spain permitted American shipping to make free use of the navigation of the Mississippi. After this development, the Kentucky conspiracy seemed less important to all concerned. Sebastian was paid $4,000 and embarked for Philadelphia, still accompanied by Power. From Philadelphia these two took the road for Cincinnati and reached that place on May 19.[38]

When Power arrived at Fort Washington, Wilkinson was not

[36] Manuscript 29CC52, Draper Collection; Documents translated from the Pontalba Collection of the Louisiana Historical Society, Filson Club, *Publications*, No. 31, LXXXI–II; H. Marshall's amended statement in case of Innes v. Marshall, n.d., Innes Papers, Bk. 22, Pt. I; Washington *National Intelligencer*, January 7, 1807; Richmond *Enquirer*, January 5, 1807; Smith, *History of Kentucky*, 335–36; Answers to charges against the late Colonel George Nicholas, n.d., in Samuel Smith Papers (University of Virginia Library).

[37] Wilkinson, *Memoirs of My Own Times*, II, Appendix 45.

[38] *American State Papers, Miscellaneous*, I, 704–705; Gayarré, *History of Louisiana*, III, 358; Filson Club, *Publications*, No. 31, LXXXIII–V; Wilkinson, *Memoirs of My Own Times*, II, Appendix 45; Richmond *Enquirer*, January 8, 1807; Savannah *Georgia Republican*, January 28, 1807.

there, having been called to Fort Greenville to take command of the army in the absence of General Wayne. Since he had dispatches from Carondelet and a present of two boxes of Havana "segars" from Gayoso and Don Andrés Armesto, the governor's secretary and interpreter, Power wrote the general and asked permission to visit Greenville. Knowing of Wayne's suspicions, Wilkinson did not reply until the request was repeated several times, but he finally gave in and consented to the visit. He hardly repented this step when Power informed him that Carondelet was sending $9,640 to Portell for the general's use. Immediately the messenger was dispatched to fetch the money.[39]

This transaction is partially explained by a statement of Wilkinson's account with the governors of Louisiana since 1790. Dated January 6, 1796, it was transmitted by the general's friend and protégé, Philip Nolan, whose accompanying letter, written at New Orleans, stated that he had arrived from his third trip to the *"unknown land,"* bringing 250 horses which he left in a rush brake at Natchez; that he had examined Wilkinson's account with Miró, who was reported dead; and that he had demanded the balance due but could only get $9,000, which he was forwarding by the Mississippi to avoid the cost of shipment by sea. He enclosed a copy of the account "rendered by Gilberto [Leonard] to me, which leaves a balance of $2,095 due you." Nolan warned Wilkinson that the Intendant, Don Juan Ventura Morales, was his enemy, and added: "If you have any future commercial views to this place, you should endeavor to do away with his prejudice."[40]

The $9,640 which Nolan obtained for Wilkinson was hidden in barrels of sugar and coffee and shipped up the Mississippi to Portell at New Madrid. Power called for it there in June and, after some hesitation because Wilkinson had not given him a written order, the money was turned over to him. However, this transaction was reported to General Wayne, and as a result, Power's

---

[39] Power to Wilkinson, May 20, 26, 1796, in Bacon, *Report of the Committee Appointed to Inquire into the Conduct of General Wilkinson,* 72, 78–81; Wilkinson to Power, May 25, June 8, 1796, *ibid.,* 78–82.

[40] Nolan to Wilkinson, July 21, 1797, *ibid.,* 56–57, 60; Nolan to Wilkinson, January 6, 1796, in Wilkinson Papers (Chicago Historical Society), I; Cox, "Louisiana–Texas Frontier," Pt. II, *loc. cit.,* XVII (1913–1914), 51–59; Clark, *Proofs of the Corruption of Gen. James Wilkinson,* 56–57.

barrels were searched at Fort Massac, but the Spanish dollars escaped detection. Power plied his men with whisky to give zest to their rowing and reached Louisville in safety, from whence he hastened to Cincinnati to inform the general of his good fortune. By this time Nolan had reached Kentucky and Wilkinson directed Power to turn the money over to him. Accordingly, the sugar and coffee barrels were opened in the store of Montgomery Brown at Frankfort. The sugar was sold in Cincinnati and this time Wilkinson received his valuable cargo intact.[41]

Though arrangements for this payment were made in January, 1796, the money was not finally delivered to Power at New Madrid until June. Carondelet had known since February that the Treaty of San Lorenzo had been signed and that he could no longer bargain with the Kentuckians as to the navigation of the Mississippi. Why did he then consider it worthwhile to continue Wilkinson's pension? This question is at least partially answered by a letter which Gayoso wrote Daniel Clark on June 17, 1796. He thought the provision of the treaty which stipulated that the thirty-first parallel between the Mississippi and the Chattahoochee rivers should be recognized as the boundary between Spanish and American territory would never be carried out. If Spain surrendered her suzerainty over the Southern Indians, Louisiana and Florida would be deprived of their last defensive barrier, and Gayoso thought that the forts at the Walnut Hills (Nogales), the Chickasaw Bluffs (San Fernando) and on the Tombigbee (Confederation) should be held by Spain notwithstanding the treaty and that the Western states would still find it necessary to declare their independence and make terms with the power controlling the rivers.[42]

Godoy decided to negotiate the Treaty of San Lorenzo with Pinckney and surrender to the United States on both the boundary and the navigation disputes because he was changing sides in the European war. In 1793 Spain joined England in the war against revolutionary France, but in July, 1795, Godoy deserted his ally and made peace with France by the Treaty of Basle. Because Jay's

[41] *James Wilkinson-John Randolph Correspondence* (Washington, 1807); Carondelet to Thomas Portell, January 20, 1796, Power to Portell, June 27, 1796, Portell to Power, June 27, 1796, in *American State Papers, Miscellaneous*, I, 937–38.

[42] Gayoso to Daniel Clark, June 17, 1796, in *American State Papers, Miscellaneous*, I, 707.

Treaty brought about a *rapprochement* between Britain and the United States, he now feared that these two naval powers would unite in an assault against Spanish America. This fear became even more realistic when, on August 19, France and Spain entered into an alliance, which led to a declaration of war between Spain and England on October 7, 1796.[43]

But as Carondelet became aware of the unpopularity of Jay's Treaty, he agreed with Gayoso that Pinckney's Treaty should not be carried out. Once the Spanish forts were surrendered, the West, he said, would have no recourse against its Eastern masters, and he thought Kentucky and her neighbors would not relish this eventuality. He accordingly intended to delay the day of evacuation.[44] In fact, larger stakes were probably involved. An intercepted letter written by Gayoso in 1798 indicated that Spanish officials were so loathe to see Louisiana pass into the hands of France that they wished to revolutionize the American West as a preliminary to revolutionizing Latin America. Gayoso's letter said: "General Wilkinson is to proceed from Kentucky with a body of troops . . . by the way of the Illinois into New Mexico, which will be a central position—the route has been already explored [by Nolan], nine tenths of the officers of the Louisiana regiment are at this time corrupted and the officers of the Mexican regiment which is now in this country are but little better." It appears that Carondelet's professed zeal for the dignity of the Crown was merely intended to cover his designs until the great plan, which was the establishment of a new empire, was brought to maturity.[45]

In the meantime Wilkinson, who continued to dabble clandestinely in trade, sold 12,000 acres of land to a Cincinnati firm for $2,000 worth of merchandise, to be delivered to Philip Nolan. Nolan was to go by water to New Madrid and deliver a letter to Gayoso.[46] Traveling in the opposite direction, the general, ac-

---

[43] Turner, "Diplomatic Contest for the Mississippi Valley," *loc. cit.*, 691.

[44] Thompson, "Blount Conspiracy," *loc. cit.*, 5; Carondelet to Spanish Officers of Louisiana, July 10, 1796, in *American State Papers, Miscellaneous*, I, 712.

[45] Ellicott to Pickering, November 14, 1796, in Mathews, *Andrew Ellicott*, 160–63.

[46] John Hollingsworth to Wilkinson, March 30, 1795, in Wilkinson Papers (Chicago Historical Society), I; Wilkinson to Abijah Hunt, September 22, 1796, in Mississippi Historical Society *Publications*, IV (1901), 283; Wilkinson, *Memoirs of My Own Times*, II, Appendix 31; Ellicott to Pickering, November 8, 1798, in *American State Papers, Miscellaneous*, I, 710–12.

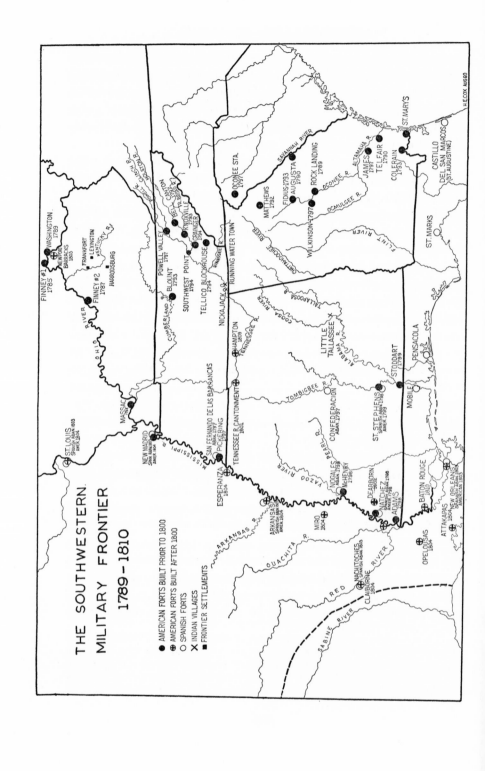

THE SOUTHWESTERN
MILITARY FRONTIER
1789–1810

● AMERICAN FORTS BUILT PRIOR TO 1800
⊕ AMERICAN FORTS BUILT AFTER 1800
○ SPANISH FORTS
✕ INDIAN VILLAGES
■ FRONTIER SETTLEMENTS

H.E.COX AUG60

companied by his wife and a military escort, set out early in October for Philadelphia in General Wayne's barge, "fitted up in style, convenience, and even magnificence." On reaching Pittsburgh he generously offered the boat to Andrew Ellicott, who was going down to Natchez to mark the boundary line agreed on by the Treaty of San Lorenzo.[47]

Now that Spain and France had become allies, the latter took a renewed interest in the American West. The Directory decided that Spain should retrocede Louisiana to France and thus make possible the development of a Franco-American empire on the ruins of the decadent Spanish power, but Godoy was not ready to make so humiliating a concession.[48] Nevertheless, General Victor Collot was sent to make a military reconnaissance of the Ohio and Mississippi rivers and to report his findings to the French government.[49] With letters from the French Minister Adet to Carondelet, Collot set out on his journey in March, 1796, mapping the rivers in detail and making drawings of all important fortifications. On reaching New Orleans he was arrested and finally deported by the governor.[50] His expedition is interesting primarily because it shows that France was seriously interested in the acquisition of Louisiana before Napoleon came to power and also because Collot's writings furnish some interesting information concerning the West at that time.

Collot interpreted Jay's Treaty as the adoption of a hostile attitude toward France. Since the population of Louisiana was almost entirely French, he was convinced that it would welcome the return of the province to French control, but he thought that even his own government would have difficulty in defending it unless the American West could be separated from the Union and combined with Louisiana to form a new sovereignty. Though he looked upon the Spanish forts on the Mississippi and even New Orleans itself as indefensible, he thought that the American West south of the Ohio could easily be defended by a modest force

[47] Hay and Werner, *James Wilkinson*, 156; Jacobs, *Tarnished Warrior*, 159.
[48] Channing, *History of the United States*, IV, 303–304.
[49] Cox, "Louisiana-Texas Frontier," I, *loc. cit.*, 62–67.
[50] Turner, "Policy of France toward the Mississippi Valley," *loc. cit.*, 272–73; Collot, *Journey in North America*, I, frontispiece, 114–23, 274–76; Channing, *History of the United States*, IV, 303–304.

posted at the Long Island of the Holston, where all the roads from the Northeast and Southeast converged.[51] It was Collot's opinion that access to the Gulf by way of four great rivers would "forever prevent these [transmontane] states from becoming tributary of those of the Atlantic. . . . From thence I conclude that the Western states of the North American republic must unite themselves with Louisiana and form in the future a single compact nation; else that colony to whatever power it shall belong will be conquered or devoured. I have now shown what Nature has done for the independence, peace and safety of the Western states." Taking a broader view of the American scene, he gave a description of the process of frontier settlement which closely paralleled that later formulated by Frederick Jackson Turner.[52]

As Collot was making his way down the Ohio, he met Power at Louisville and the two traveled in company for some distance. Though the Frenchman carried a letter of introduction from Burr to Wilkinson, Power suspected his motives and on reaching New Orleans communicated his fears to Carondelet. This warning, along with a similiar message from Jáudenes, accounts for Collot's arrest.[53] Power was sent by Carondelet to initiate another intrigue with Wilkinson in the summer of the following year, but in the interim Philip Nolan, with Wilkinson's merchandise and his letter of September 22 to Gayoso, set out for Natchez in January, 1797, and at the mouth of the Ohio happened to fall in with Ellicott's party. The surveyor carried instructions from President Washington to keep a careful watch on Wilkinson's activities, while the general's letter to Gayoso warned his correspondent: "For the love of God and friendship, enjoin great secrecy and caution in all our concerns. Never suffer my name to be written or spoken. The suspicion of Washington is wide awake—there are spies every where." [54]

Ellicott, a not-so-pious Quaker and a member of the American Philosophical Society, reached Natchez on February 24 and found

---

[51] Collot, *Journey in North America*, II, 61, 237, 247–48, 264–66, 271–72.
[52] *Ibid.*, 258–59 n., 272.      [53] *Ibid.*, 1–2, 114–20.
[54] Wilkinson to Gayoso, September 22, 1796, in *James Wilkinson-John Randolph Correspondence*, 3; Deposition of Andrew Ellicott, in Wilkinson, *Memoirs of My Own Times*, II, Appendix 28; Charleston *Courier*, January 16, 1808; Mathews, *Andrew Ellicott*, 144–45; Clark, *Proofs of the Corruption of Gen. James Wilkinson*, 69–72.

Gayoso quite unprepared to surrender the town and proceed with the survey. His excuse was that the Indians had ceded the Chickasaw Bluffs, the Walnut Hills, and the site of Fort Confederation on the Tombigbee River to Spain, and they would resent their surrender to the United States. He further complained that the Americans had no right, according to the terms of Jay's Treaty, to give the British the privilege of navigating the Mississippi River.[55]

Most of the inhabitants of Natchez were Americans who had recently come to take advantage of new opportunities offered in the production of upland cotton, and they naturally hoped that the United States would soon establish its jurisdiction in the region above the thirty-first parallel. But Gayoso, while promising protection to American citizens, had manned the fort and forbidden Lieutenant Pope of the United States Army to enter the town. Accordingly, Pope halted his detachment at the Walnut Hills, but Ellicott urged him to proceed and he reached Natchez on April 24. This was none too early, for the situation there was explosive.[56]

Two prominent planters of the neighborhood, Thomas Green, a native of Virginia, and Anthony Hutchins, still a British officer, offered to raise forces and help Ellicott and Pope take Gayoso and the Spanish fort. These offers were declined and Gayoso had Green arrested, but he escaped to Tennessee.[57] Hutchins made his proposal shortly after he talked with a visitor who had come from Philadelphia and was there in the interest of the Blount Conspiracy—possibly this was the former governor of Georgia, General George Mathews.[58] On April 24 Nolan wrote Wilkinson from New Orleans that Governor Carondelet had heard that the British were preparing to bring a force down from Canada to attack Upper Louisiana and that he was using this as an excuse for not evacuating the Spanish posts or marking the boundary line.[59]

On May 1 Gayoso notified Ellicott that Yrujo had informed him of a proposed attack against the Spanish part of Illinois—

[55] Gayarré, *History of Louisiana*, III, 366: *Journal of Andrew Ellicott*, 101–103; *Dictionary of American Biography*, VI, 89–90.

[56] Proclamation by Gayoso, March 29, 1797, in *Journal of Andrew Ellicott*, 65–67; Ellicott to Gayoso, March 31, 1797, *ibid.*, 68–69, 74–77.

[57] *Journal of Andrew Ellicott*, 73.     [58] *Ibid.*, 147, 173.

[59] Nolan to Wilkinson, April 24, 1797, in Bacon, *Report of the Committee Appointed to Inquire into the Conduct of General Wilkinson*, 60.

Upper Louisiana—by the British from Canada. He added that, since such an expedition would have to pass through United States territory, Yrujo had sent this information also to Pickering. Furthermore, said Gayoso, the Spanish commanding general found it necessary to put several points on the river in a state of defense, particularly Nogales (Walnut Hills), and the governor announced his decision to suspend evacuation of the fort and to halt the running of the boundary line.[60] On May 20 Wilkinson issued orders to Captain Guion to take possession of the Spanish forts on the Lower Mississippi. Nine days later Carondelet wrote Wilkinson that the forts would not be surrendered, and two days later he issued a proclamation to that effect.[61]

During May Ellicott was told that for the past eight months Spanish authorities had been stirring up the Chickasaw and Choctaw Indians to oppose running of the boundary line,[62] but Carondelet had still another string to his bow. He would send Power for another conference with Wilkinson, the object of which was to renew the effort to separate the West from the Union. Power's instructions were drawn up on May 26, and Carondelet stated that they were to be known only to himself, his secretary Don Andrés Armesto, and the courier. After explaining to Wilkinson why the posts could not now be surrendered, Power would proceed to the main object and tell the people of the West that the delivery of the posts was contrary to their interests, as they "must one day separate from the Atlantic States and would find themselves without any communication with lower Louisiana, . . . from whence they will receive military stores as soon as they separate. . . . If $100,000 distributed in Kentucky, could cause it to rise in insurrection, I am very certain that the minister [Godoy], . . . would sacrifice them with pleasure, and you may, without exposing yourselves too much, promise them to those who enjoy the confidence

[60] Gayoso to Ellicott, May 1, 1797, in *Journal of Andrew Ellicott*, 80–82; *American State Papers, Foreign Relations*, II, 67.

[61] Carondelet to Wilkinson, May 29, 1797, in Bacon, *Report of the Committee Appointed to Inquire into the Conduct of General Wilkinson*, 93–95; *Journal of Andrew Ellicott*, 94–95, 101–103; Hay and Werner, *James Wilkinson*, 158–59.

[62] Wilkinson to Gayoso, December 10, 1797, in Wilkinson, *Memoirs of My Own Times*, II, Appendix 46; *Journal of Andrew Ellicott*, 85.

of the people, with another equal sum, to arm them, in case of necessity, and twenty pieces of field artillery. . . . On taking fort Massac, we will send him [Wilkinson] instantly arms and artillery, and Spain, limiting herself to the possession of the forts of Natchez and Walnut Hills, as far as fort Confederation, will cede to the Western States all the Eastern bank of the Ohio, which will form a very extensive and powerful republic." This, with Spain, he said, would control the Indians. Carondelet concluded: "The threats of Congress authorise me to succor on the spot, and openly, the Western States." [63] Power was to start on his journey at once, and after trying to persuade Ellicott to visit New Orleans for a conference with the governor, he was to make an effort to prevent Guion's detachment from coming down the river until new orders could be received from Wilkinson. On June 4 Power reached Natchez, and the next day Ellicott, having been informed by Daniel Clark, wrote to Pickering that the Spanish agent was going north to visit Wilkinson and renew the effort to revolutionize Kentucky.[64]

Meanwhile, the situation in Natchez was reaching the boiling point. The trouble started on June 9 when Gayoso arrested a Baptist preacher, Hannah by name, because of some trouble between himself and some Irish Catholics. Ellicott determined to use this minor incident to force a showdown with the Spanish authorities. He and Lieutenant Pope began organizing militia companies and encouraging the people to declare themselves American citizens. This activity was accompanied by some disturbances and Gayoso found it necessary to take refuge in the fort. Thus put on the defensive, the commandant asked Ellicott for a conference and the two met on June 18 at Stephen Minor's house. Here a compromise was worked out: a state of neutrality was declared for the time being and authority was placed in the hands of a committee to be elected by the people. Though there was considerable rivalry as to the personnel of this committee and a second election had to be held early in July, no violence occurred during the period of dis-

[63] Power to Sebastian, July 19, 1797, in Richmond *Enquirer*, January 6, 10, 1807.
[64] Ellicott to Secretary of State, June 5, 1797, in *American State Papers, Miscellaneous*, I, 710; Ellicott to Wilkinson, January 21, 1808, in Clark, *Proofs of the Corruption of Gen. James Wilkinson*, 69–72; Wilkinson, *Memoirs of My Own Times*, II, 164–65, 184; *Journal of Andrew Ellicott*, 97–98; Jacobs, *Tarnished Warrior*, 176–78.

order and both Gayoso and Carondelet had no choice but to accept the results of Ellicott's bloodless little revolution.[65]

While these events were transpiring on the Lower Mississippi, life had not stood still for General Wilkinson. He and Mrs. Wilkinson left Cincinnati early in October for a visit in Philadelphia. Reaching his destination early in November, the general set about doing what he could to discredit his chief, General Wayne, for the army was soon to be reduced and one of them would have to go. Fortunately for Wilkinson, Wayne died on December 15 and President Washington appointed the Spanish pensioner Commanding General of the United States Army. On March 3 Wilkinson and other officials attended a brilliant ball given for the retiring President by the merchants of Philadelphia. Next day John Adams was inaugurated and Wilkinson was presently confirmed in his appointment. However, in reducing the army Congress abolished the rank of major general, and Wilkinson had to be content to remain a brigadier.[66]

The commanding general returned to Fort Washington in April, 1797, and the next month, as previously stated, he issued orders to Captain Guion to take possession of the Spanish posts on the Lower Mississippi. On the same day he wrote to Winthrop Sargent, acting governor of the Northwest Territory, that he had received "satisfactory evidence" of the refusal of the Spaniards in Louisiana to execute the treaty. The event, he said, "may be considered the precursor of serious consequences." [67] Shortly after writing this letter he set out to make an inspection of the garrisons at Fort Wayne and Detroit.

Not long after Wilkinson left Cincinnati, Power left Natchez with his instructions from Carondelet regarding the revival of the Spanish Conspiracy. On July 19 he met Sebastian in Louisville and gave him in writing the substance of Carondelet's plans and offers, but he had to agree that the new state would extend as far south as the mouth of the Yazoo River. Sebastian called on Judge Innes and presented Power's proposals. Innes thought the plan

[65] *Journal of Andrew Ellicott*, 99–104, 107–17, 138–43; Cox, *West Florida Controversy*, 40, 42, 50–52; Isaac J. Cox, "The New Invasion of the Goths and Vandals," in Mississippi Valley Historical Association *Proceedings*, VIII (1914–1915), 176–200.
[66] Hay and Werner, *James Wilkinson*, 156–57.        [67] *Ibid.*, 158–59.

dangerous and one that "ought not to be countenanced, as the Western people had now obtained the navigation of the Mississippi, by which all wishes were gratified." Nicholas agreed with Innes, as did Sebastian, and they gave Power an answer in writing, as he had requested. At the same time they took a copy of Power's proposals for the separation of Kentucky.[68]

Leaving Louisville to seek Wilkinson in Detroit, Power was pursued, overtaken, and searched, but was allowed to proceed when no incriminating evidence was found. When he reached Detroit on August 16 he found the general absent on his tour of inspection and he was arrested under orders from General Wayne. He was thus forced to send Carondelet's proposals to Wilkinson by messenger, and the general received them just as he was entering the St. Clair River from Lake Huron. Setting out on September 2, he hastened back to Detroit, meanwhile sending orders ahead that Power should be kept under surveillance. Arriving late in the evening of September 3, the general sent for Power, who gave him the details of Carondelet's proposals. Receiving his visitor coolly, Wilkinson exclaimed: "We are both lost, without having been able to derive advantage from your journey." After rejecting Carondelet's proposals as "chimerical" because Pinckney's Treaty satisfied all the demands of the Western people, the general said Spain had no choice but to comply fully with the treaty, which had overturned all his plans and rendered useless the labors of more than ten years. He said he had destroyed his cipher and torn up all his correspondence with the Spanish government. Wilkinson then informed Power that he had been instructed to place him under arrest preparatory to a trial in Philadelphia; but as this would be extremely hazardous for both of them, and as General Wayne was now dead, Wilkinson offered to provide a military escort to take the Spanish agent back to New Orleans by way of New Madrid. Power protested that he wished to return by way of Louisville for further conferences with Sebastian and his friends,

[68] Narrative of Thomas Power, in Wilkinson, *Memoirs of My Own Times*, II, Appendix 54; Power to [Sebastian], July 19, 1799, in Innes Papers, Bk. 19; Answer to Charges against the late Colonel George Nicholas, n.d., in Smith Papers; Savannah *Georgia Republican*, January 28, 1807; Washington *National Intelligencer*, January 7, 9, 1807; Smith, *History of Kentucky*, 337–38; Yrujo to Pedro de Cevallos, January 17, 1807, in Archivo Histórico Nacional, 5545, *expediente* 15, pp. 485–91.

but since he had no real choice in the matter, he gave in and left Detroit with an escort commanded by Captain Benjamin Shaumberg.[69]

While Power was meeting with rebuffs in Kentucky and at Detroit, the Spanish effort to hold on to the posts on the Lower Mississippi neared an end. On July 26, 1797, Gayoso was rescued from his humiliating situation in Natchez by promotion to the governorship of Louisiana and West Florida. His place in Natchez was taken by Stephen Minor as acting commandant, but outside the fort he had no real authority, and soon even the semblance of Spanish rule would disappear. On September 22 Godoy finally ordered the evacuation of the posts that remained to Spain on the east bank of the Mississippi above the thirty-first parallel. By the end of March, 1798, the garrisons at Natchez and the Walnut Hills dismantled the forts and took passage down the river. Ellicott was now free to begin the survey of the boundary between Spanish Florida and the United States.[70]

[69] Sterrett to Daniel Clark, June 25, 1805, in *American State Papers, Miscellaneous,* I, 704–705; Wilkinson to Carondelet, September 4, 1797, in Wilkinson, *Memoirs of My Own Times,* II, Appendices 48 and 54; New Orleans *Louisiana Gazette,* January 7, 1807; September 20, 1808; Gayarré, *History of Louisiana,* III, 395–96; Bacon, *Report of the Committee Appointed to Inquire into the Conduct of General Wilkinson,* 19–22; Letter to General Wilkinson, in Charleston *Courier,* April 18, 1807.

[70] Gayoso to Wilkinson, January 10, March 30, 1798, in Wilkinson, *Memoirs of My Own Times,* II, Appendices 49 and 51; Gayoso to Ellicott, January 10, 1798, in *Journal of Andrew Ellicott,* 140; Whitaker, *Mississippi Question,* 64–67.

# CHAPTER IX

# TRIUMPHANT DEMOCRACY

URING Washington's administration, while the Southern states were struggling with problems involving Western lands, unfriendly neighbors, and foreign relations, they also faced difficulties resulting from the domestic policies of the new Federal government. Conspicuous among these was the opposition that developed to the excise tax which, at the instance of Alexander Hamilton, Congress imposed in 1791 on the production of distilled spirits.

In the colonial period tipplers who desired something stronger and more economical than wine relied mostly on New England or West Indian rum, which mixed with water was known as grog. But in Maryland and Virginia the farmers preferred brandy made from the yield of the peach and apple orchards, and for a long time there were a few sentimental souls who were fond of applejack. Such distilled spirits were widely used in the South because, for various reasons, neither wine, beer, nor cider could be satisfactorily produced locally.

Whisky was hardly known before the Revolution, but on the eve of independence, the Scotch-Irish began to distill rye in western Pennsylvania, and in 1789 the process of making bourbon from corn was evolved in Kentucky. Made cheaply from corn or rye, whisky sold at forty or fifty cents a gallon and quickly became the standard Western bracer. Gradually its use spread eastward and tippling became, more and more, a between-meals habit.[1]

---

[1] Solon J. and Elizabeth H. Buck, *The Planting of Civilization in Western Pennsylvania* (Pittsburgh, 1939), 466–67; Leland D. Baldwin, *Whiskey Rebels; The Story of a Frontier Uprising* (Pittsburgh, 1939), 24–28; Channing, *History of the United States,* IV, 138–40.

When the excise tax was levied in 1791, the invasion of the seaboard market had hardly begun. Whisky was still a frontier product and only Western communities were seriously concerned about it. Rum was produced in the East in far larger quantities than was whisky in the West, and distillers of molasses (treacle) paid most of the tax. The act provided that a duty of twenty to forty cents a gallon be paid on imported spirits, mostly French brandy, according to proof; on domestic spirits distilled from molasses, sugar, or other foreign material, a duty of from eleven to thirty cents; and on spirits distilled from domestic produce in any city, town, or village, a duty of nine to twenty-five cents, according to proof. Private stills set up in rural areas would pay a yearly tax of sixty cents a gallon on their capacity.[2] In the fiscal year 1791–1792 these rates produced a revenue of $260,997 from Massachusetts, $76,236 from Rhode Island, $23,000 from Pennsylvania, $22,000 from Virginia, $7,000 from South Carolina, $2,000 from North Carolina, and $307 from Georgia.[3]

It is thus obvious that the rum distillers of Massachusetts bore the brunt of the tax; that the states south of Virginia imported nearly all of their spirits; and that the excise paid in Pennsylvania and Virginia did not, in any appreciable degree, come from the distillers of whisky. These facts would appear to illustrate, as well as any facts could, the regionalism which existed during the early years of the Republic. Commercial New England was prepared to accept Federal supervision; the Southern states differed among themselves as to their commercial interests and political attitudes, but the West was resentful of any outside interference with its way of life.[4]

Accordingly, while western Pennsylvania organized for resistance and Kentucky expressed its disapproval of the excise, Daniel Stevens, supervisor of revenue for the District of South Carolina, defended the measure in an article published in the Charleston *City Gazette* of August 5, 1791. He said reports had reached him of opposition in the interior of the state, but he thought this was

[2] *The Laws of the United States of America* (Philadelphia, 1796), I, 301–37.
[3] *American State Papers*, VII, Finance, I, 250–51.
[4] Wolfe, *Jeffersonian Democracy in South Carolina*, 67; Ammon, "Republican Party in Virginia," Chap. III, 116; Lexington *Kentucky Gazette*, October 1, 1791.

due to a misconception. "The duty in question," he explained, "had been the consequence of a measure from which you derive more benefit and relief in proportion than any other part of the United States. I mean the assumption of the State debt." Stevens then pointed out that the amount of South Carolina's debt assumed by Congress was $4,000,000, which was nearly one-fifth of the entire state debts assumed. South Carolina's payment of interest on that amount, he asserted, would not be more than one-fifteenth, assuming the state's consumption of distilled spirits to be in proportion to that of other states; and, said he, since South Carolina's distillation of spirits was only a fortieth of that in the entire union, no tax could be more favorable to her interest. "Would you," Stevens asked, "prefer a general increase of duties on imported articles?" Clearly the answer would be no; for, as he reminded the Carolinians, they had scarcely any manufactures of their own and would pay a very high proportion of all import duties. Congress believed it had no alternative to the excise tax except a tax on land, Stevens continued. "Would your burden," he queried, "have been lightened by laying, under a proportional contribution, your valuable plantations? Should the United States assume your debts and make no provision for the paying of them?" [5] Early federalism favored foreign commerce over domestic manufacture, and the above statement fully explains the position of the Palmetto State at that time.

Georgia's economic interests were similar to those of South Carolina, but because of her opposition to the Administration in the matter of Indian claims and Western lands, she was already developing a point of view which stressed the reserved rights of the states. Accordingly, in the autumn of 1791 a grand jury impaneled by the Federal Court for the District of Georgia presented the excise law as a grievance, saying that it was "partial and unjust . . . it ought to have been general and cyder and malt liquors should be included." Of more fundamental importance was the statement: "We present as a grievance that Congress has laid heavy duties on many of the essential necessaries in the Southern States, which duties operate merely as a bounty and encouragement in the most opulent Northern states. We present as a griev-

[5] Charleston *City Gazette*, August 5, 1791.

ance every measure of the general government by which the territorial rights of this state are or may be infringed." [6] Thus Georgia came out for state rights while South Carolina took a nationalistic stand.

The popularity of President Washington was still sufficient to incline Virginia to a Federalist point of view, which was exemplified by her governor, Henry "Light Horse Harry" Lee. Thus, a Virginian wrote to one of his friends in Kentucky early in the spring of 1792 that the conduct of Kentucky in regard to the whisky tax was highly reprehensible, especially since the impost on whisky was lower than that on imported spirits or New England rum.[7] But this factor did not simplify the problem of Thomas Marshall, father of the future Chief Justice, who was Inspector of Revenue for the District of Kentucky. In March, 1792, he warned the local distillers that the tax would be collected. On April 28 he asked them to meet him in Lexington to discuss means of carrying the law into effect, and on November 17 he warned the collectors that unless they proceeded to levy the sums due for the preceding and the current year, their bonds would be forfeited.[8]

This effort to collect the tax seems to have given offense and on March 16, 1793, the *Kentucky Gazette* published a letter from a Kentuckian: "I am told the Federal excise officers in many parts have been very ill treated, and some severely beaten. . . . Although the Herald omitted to advertise the excise man, yet nevertheless, the enraged people have found out that innocent officer and as his office most affects their present feelings, they have vented their spite on him." [9] There is no other indication of violence at this time and the Kentucky distillers adopted a policy of peaceful resistance, calling for a meeting in Lexington on July 8 to organize and petition Congress for "reasonable" changes in the excise law.[10]

This meeting was held as scheduled and Richard Steele was chosen to preside. An address to the people and legislature of Kentucky, as well as to Congress, was forthwith adopted. This protest maintained that the collection of a tax of seven cents a

[6] *Ibid.*, November 1, 1791; Baldwin, *Whiskey Rebels,* 105.
[7] Lexington *Kentucky Gazette,* September 21, 1791; March 17, 1792.
[8] *Ibid.*, March 24, April 28, November 17, 1792.
[9] *Ibid.*, March 16, 1793; Baldwin, *Whiskey Rebels,* 105.
[10] Lexington *Kentucky Gazette,* June 1, 1793.

gallon on distilled spirits, payable in specie, was oppressive since the Mississippi River was closed to American trade and hence Western grain could not be sent to market. The protest also pointed out that a former petition to Congress had been laid on the table and stated that the West could not, like the East, produce cider and beer as a substitute for stronger drink.[11]

Despite this plea the people of Kentucky were not greatly impressed by the plight of the distillers and on August 10 the *Kentucky Gazette* published, for the second time, a full page of information regarding the excise law, which had been furnished by Edward Carrington, the supervisor for the District of Virginia.[12] Then, on the last day of the same month, this Lexington newspaper carried a communication condemning the eight distillers who had met in that town on the eighth to protest against the whisky tax. The writer said that they had done all in their power to resist a just law but that they had not even been supported by their own profession. He charged that they had raised the price of their product because of the tax and kept the money instead of paying it to the government. He also declared that the citizens of Kentucky were not suffering because they could not sell their grain in New Orleans. The campaign against the Indians north of the Ohio brought more specie than ever before into the state and also furnished a market for her surplus products. In answer to the malcontents, he replied, "You say we serve as a barrier against the Indians, but we experience the most pleasant warfare that the most timid or interested could desire. For instead of depredations committed on us in time of peace, we now enjoy the treasures of the Union almost without the loss of a citizen." [13]

Yet there were others in Kentucky who were more critical of the Federal administration. On September 14 the *Gazette* published a letter from "Aristides" to the Democratic Society of Kentucky which lauded its efforts "to preserve free government." The author stated that if the Revolutionary heroes who died in the cause of liberty could arise and witness "the ceremonial farce exhibited by their chief," they would think themselves in a country nurtured by corruption. "The day may perhaps arrive," he said, "when the children of the West . . . may stretch forth an

[11] *Ibid.*, August 10, 1793.　　　[12] *Ibid.*　　　[13] *Ibid.*, August 31, 1793.

arresting hand to the support of their Atlantic brethren enfeebled by that corruption, the progress of which they now wish to check." [14]

Opposition to the excise tax finally came to a head in western Pennsylvania in 1794, the lead taken by the three Democratic Societies which were organized in the area at this time. On the last day of the previous year Lexington's Democratic Society adopted a remonstrance to the President and Congress which complained of the excise and demanded the opening of the navigation of the Mississippi River. Copies of this memorial were sent to other Western communities, and on March 24, 1794, it was laid before the Democratic Society of Washington County, Pennsylvania. After some debate this society adopted the Kentucky memorial and sent copies to their representatives in Congress and to President Washington.[15]

Opposition to the excise law resulted in violence in July, 1794, when warrants were served on distillers in western Pennsylvania who had not paid the tax. The defendants were required to appear before the United States district court in Philadelphia rather than before local state courts, and this was an additional cause for resentment. Thirty-nine of the warrants were served without resistance, but when the United States marshal, accompanied by General John Neville, inspector for the Western District of Pennsylvania, attempted to serve the fortieth, shots were fired by a group of drunken harvest hands and the marshal and Neville were forced to flee. Two days later a mob of four or five hundred men attacked Neville's house, "Bower Hill," and burned the place, after their leader, James McFarlane, was killed.[16]

The four counties of southwestern Pennsylvania—Westmore-

---

[14] *Ibid.*, September 14, 1793.

[15] William F. Keller, *The Nation's Advocate: Henry Marie Brackenridge and Young America* (Pittsburgh, 1952), 43–45; Link, "Democratic Societies of the Carolinas," *loc. cit.*, 259–77; Baldwin, *Whiskey Rebels*, 96–97; Democratic Societies of Washington County, Pennsylvania, to Citizen Brackenridge, April 8, 1794; June 23, 1794, in Innes Papers, Bk. 19.

[16] Buck, *Western Pennsylvania*, 469–70; John A. Carroll and Mary W. Ashworth, *George Washington, First in Peace* (New York, 1957), 184; Baldwin, *Whiskey Rebels*, 113–14; Henry M. Brackenridge, *History of the Western Insurrection in Western Pennsylvania, Commonly Called the Whiskey Rebellion, 1794* (Pittsburgh, 1859), 40–41; Savannah *Georgia Gazette*, August 21, 1794.

land, Washington, Fayette, and Allegheny—along with the contiguous county of Virginia named Ohio, now organized for resistance, and the disaffection spread eastward across the Allegheny Mountains as far as Cumberland, Maryland.[17] The climax of the insurrection was a muster of the militia of the western counties, held at Braddock's Field near Pittsburgh on August 1 with a view to seizing Fort Fayette and possibly burning Pittsburgh, but the Pittsburgh militia fraternized with their country cousins and thwarted the attempt.[18] On the fourteenth 226 delegates elected by the western townships held a meeting at Parkinson's Ferry, now Monongahela City, and a standing committee of one delegate from each township was elected to take further measures. During the meeting word was received that commissioners had been appointed by President Washington to treat with the insurgents at the mouth of the Youghiogheny, and a committee, including Hermon Husband of "Regulator" fame, Albert Gallatin, and H. M. Brackenridge, was appointed to confer with them.[19] The conference was held on August 20, and after a popular referendum in the disaffected counties, the United States commissioners reported on September 24 that although the majority of western Pennsylvania inhabitants favored submission, a determined minority was ruling by terror and would have to be dealt with by force.[20]

Determined to see that the law was enforced, Washington had already, on September 9, approved the orders Hamilton prepared for a general rendezvous of some 12,000 troops consisting of militia, volunteers, paid substitutes, and drafted men from New Jersey, Pennsylvania, Maryland, and Virginia; and Governor Henry Lee of Virginia was appointed to command them. After receiving the report of the commissioners, the President issued marching orders to the troops.[21] Washington blamed the disorders on the "self-constituted" Democratic Societies, whose activities he attributed to

[17] Scharf, *History of Maryland*, II, 584–85; Link, "Democratic Societies of the Carolinas," *loc. cit.*, 145–49.

[18] Buck, *Western Pennsylvania*, 470; Baldwin, *Whiskey Rebels*, 141 ff.; Brackenridge, *History of the Western Insurrection*, 99–117; Halifax *North-Carolina Journal*, August 20, 1794.

[19] Lexington *Kentucky Gazette*, September 20, 1794; Halifax *North-Carolina Journal*, September 17, 1794.

[20] Buck, *Western Pennsylvania*, 471.

[21] Carroll and Ashworth, *George Washington*, 198.

the influence of Citizen Genêt, and he bitterly denounced them. As was certainly expected, no armed resistance was met when the troops reached their destination, but the might of the new Federal government had been amply demonstrated.[22]

This authoritative action was heartily approved by James Iredell of Edenton, North Carolina, who, by Washington's appointment, was now an Associate Justice of the Supreme Court. He wrote to Governor Lee to congratulate him on putting down the "Whisky Rebellion," and commented that the disposition of North Carolina toward the Administration was favorable and that the same would be true of her representation in Congress but for influence of the Virginia delegation.[23] That he was right as to the attitude of Virginia is indicated by a letter of December 28 in which Jefferson stated to Madison: "The information of our militia returned from the westward is uniform that though the people here let them pass quietly they were objects of their laughter, not of their fear; that one thousand men could have cut off their whole force in a thousand places of the Allegheny; that their detestation of the Excise Law is universal, and has now associated to it a detestation of the government; and that a separation [of the Western people], which was perhaps a very distant and problematical event, is now near and certain, and determined in the mind of every man." [24] A similar attitude was expressed by the Virginia House of Delegates when, on November 19, it requested Governor Lee to submit all the information he possessed concerning his appointment to command the force which Washington had sent into western Pennsylvania. Two days later it adopted by a vote of seventy-three to fifty-two a resolution declaring that, according to an act of 1788, the governor automatically vacated his office on the day that he accepted a lucrative office under the authority of the Federal government.[25]

Feelings elsewhere in the South were mixed. Early in 1795 the Kentucky legislature passed resolutions instructing members of Congress from that state to work for the repeal of the whisky tax,

[22] Buck, *Western Pennsylvania*, 471–73; Lexington *Kentucky Gazette*, February 7, 1795.

[23] Gilpatrick, *Jeffersonian Democracy in North Carolina*, 65.

[24] Mayo, *Jefferson Himself*, 197.

[25] Virginia House of Delegates Journal, November 19, 21, 1794.

but a grand jury of the Hamilton district in the Southwest Territory protested against the excise only because the Territory was not represented in Congress, declaring that the levy was otherwise wise and just. Even in western Pennsylvania the Presbyterian clergy of Pittsburgh took measures to purge the church of "those corrupt members who have been active in the late insurrection." [26]

Except for the domestic manufacture of applejack and peach brandy, an old custom in Virginia and Maryland, and the birth of King Bourbon in Kentucky, the Southern states produced little in the way of distilled spirits and were not greatly disturbed by Hamilton's tax on intoxicating liquors. His funding measures and the consequent creation of a "paper aristocracy" were far more unpopular in the states devoted to the production of the staple crops; but Jay's Treaty, which offended all those who sympathized with the democratic aspirations of our Revolutionary ally, was, south of the Potomac, the most hated measure of the Washington administration.

The sectionalism which had already developed in American politics was demonstrated in the election of 1796. Maryland, a commercial state, cast a majority of her votes for Adams, and he got one each from Virginia and North Carolina. All the rest of the Southern votes were cast for Jefferson, who lost by a vote of seventy-one to sixty-eight. If Virginia and North Carolina had voted solidly for Jefferson, he would have been elected. As it was, he became Vice-President.[27]

It was fortunate for Jefferson that he was not elected at this time, because the next four years proved extremely trying ones for the President. Before retiring to Mount Vernon, Washington yielded to the promptings of Hamilton and Pickering and replaced the strongly pro-French Monroe with the strongly pro-British Charles Cotesworth Pinckney as our Minister in Paris.[28] Already irritated by the negotiation of Jay's Treaty, which she naturally looked upon as a desertion by the country whose independence she

[26] Lexington *Kentucky Gazette*, February 7, 1795; New Bern *North-Carolina Gazette*, May 30, 1795; Halifax *North-Carolina Journal*, June 1, 1795.

[27] See Chapter V, n. 91; Scharf, *History of Maryland*, II, 597–98; Savannah *Georgia Gazette*, November 10, 1796; Charleston *City Gazette*, December 10, 1796; Edenton *State Gazette of North-Carolina*, December 22, 1796.

[28] Channing, *History of the United States*, IV, 178.

helped to establish, France tried to put pressure on the United States by ordering the seizure and confiscation of American vessels bound to or from British ports or having British goods on board. Consequently, French privateers swarmed in the Mediterranean and to the West Indies and many American ships were being captured and confiscated along with their cargoes. In the same spirit, the Directory refused to receive Pinckney.[29]

Adams thought of sending the pro-French Vice-President to Paris, but this was opposed by both Pickering and Jefferson, and following the advice of the Cabinet, he decided to send a three-man commission, including Pinckney, to represent the United States before the French Directory. John Marshall of Virginia and Francis Dana of Massachusetts were named as the other two members of the delegation, but Dana refused to serve and Elbridge Gerry, a Massachusetts Republican, was appointed in his place.[30]

President Adams continued to acquiesce, as Washington had done, in the British orders in council which declared foodstuffs contraband of war. American provision ships were captured in the West Indies in large numbers, and the British admiralty courts enforced with the utmost rigor Jay's Treaty as to contraband, but the captured provisions were paid for.[31] It is therefore not surprising that the French Directory did not receive the American commissioners. Instead, our envoys were visited by mysterious agents who suggested that the United States lend money to the French government and also pay a *doceur* to the Directors and their Minister of Foreign Affairs, M. Talleyrand.[32]

The Americans did not abhor the thought of buying the Directors and Talleyrand any more than our government had previously objected to bribing the native Indians or the Algerine pirates to make treaties with us, but they refused to involve the United States in any breach of neutrality such as a loan to France. As our commissioners would make no concessions and the French were equally firm, the negotiations came to an abrupt end in March, 1798.[33]

[29] *Ibid.*, 184; Garland, *John Randolph of Roanoke*, 98–102.
[30] Channing, *History of the United States*, IV, 182.     [31] *Ibid.*, 183.
[32] *Ibid.*, 187; Samuel F. Bemis, *A Diplomatic History of the United States* (New York, 1950), 116; Garland, *John Randolph of Roanoke*, 145–55.
[33] Channing, *History of the United States*, IV, 187–88.

When the dispatches from our envoys were received in Philadelphia and the American people got news of this rebuff, a wave of indignation against France spread throughout the country. President Adams himself was deeply stirred and in successive communications to Congress he enlarged on the perfidy of the French and advocated preparations for war. He also submitted the correspondence of our commissioners with the agents of Talleyrand, designated as Messrs. X, Y, and Z. As a result of these developments, the pro-French Jeffersonian majority in Congress melted away, the members either going home or voting with the Federalists.[34]

The XYZ affair was followed by Congressional revocation of all treaties with France and prohibition of commercial intercourse with her. Congress also hastened to put the country in a state of defense by creating a Navy Department and organizing an army of ten thousand men. Washington accepted nominal command of the new army, and the effective efforts of insistence by Pickering and Washington placed Hamilton second in command in commissioning major generals. Hamilton's design, indicated in letters to Rufus King and to Francisco de Miranda, called for the liberation of Latin America. To Miranda he wrote that the plan called for a fleet from Great Britain, an army from the United States, and "a government for the liberated territory agreeable to both the co-operators, about which there will be no difficulty." [35]

Thus the stage was set for the liberation of Latin America in case Napoleon should try to take over Spanish possessions in that quarter. The British Ministry, hoping to acquire Santo Domingo for England, was prepared to acquiesce in the conquest of Louisiana and Florida by the United States; but Hamilton apparently planned for the establishment of independent governments in all the areas liberated from Spanish rule, with the United States profit-

[34] *Ibid.*, 189; Pickering to Ellicott, in Carter (ed.), *Territorial Papers*, V, 142–44; *Maryland Gazette*, April 12, June 7, July 12, 1798; Bemis, *A Diplomatic History of the United States*, 117; J. E. D. Shipp, *Giant Days, or the Life and Times of William H. Crawford* (Americus, Ga., 1909), 117–18.

[35] Channing, *History of the United States*, IV, 183–96; Garland, *John Randolph of Roanoke*, 117–20, 145–55; Annapolis *Maryland Gazette*, April 12, June 7, July 12, 1798; John C. Hamilton (ed.), *The Works of Alexander Hamilton* (New York, 1851), VI, 347–50; King, *Life and Correspondence of Rufus King*, II, 283–84.

ing by the opening of navigation of the Mississippi and the rivers flowing through Florida to the Gulf.[36] On June 13, 1798, the *Kentucky Gazette* quoted the Philadelphia *Aurora* to the effect that it had been only a year since the same party which expelled William Blount from the United States Senate for co-operating with the British to wrest Louisiana from Spain and attach it to England now armed the citizens to effect objects much greater and more favorable to the British government.[37]

Neither Washington nor Adams was aware of this intrigue with Miranda, but the President was anxious to take revenge for French spoliations at sea. Benjamin Stoddert was appointed Secretary of the Navy, and three splendid frigates, the *United States*, the *Constitution*, and the *Constellation* that had been on the stocks for years, were launched. Soon fourteen men-of-war and eight converted merchantmen were at sea and the French privateers were driven from our coast and followed to the West Indies. Since neither side had declared war, unarmed ships were not molested, but the *Constellation* won a decisive victory over *L'Insurgent* and before the shooting stopped about eighty-five armed French vessels had been captured.[38]

Despite these favorable developments, not all Americans were happy about the status of our foreign affairs, and especially was this the case in the Southern states. Here France had more friends than England, and though the XYZ affair had alienated many and temporarily put North Carolina along with South Carolina and Maryland in the Federalist camp, Virginia, Georgia, Kentucky, and Tennessee were still staunchly Republican.[39] The native Fran-

---

[36] Grenville to Liston, June 8, 1798, in Mayo (ed.), *Instructions to the British Ministers*, 158; Whitaker, *Mississippi Question*, 116, 124–25; Bowers, *Jefferson and Hamilton*, 427–28; S. H. Wandell and Meade Minnigerode, *Aaron Burr* (New York, 1925), II, 13.

[37] Lexington *Kentucky Gazette*, June 13, 1798.

[38] Norfolk *Herald*, September 13, 1798; Channing, *History of the United States*, IV, 200.

[39] Annapolis *Maryland Gazette*, August 16, 1798; Halifax *North-Carolina Journal*, September 13, 1798; Gilpatrick, *Jeffersonian Democracy in North Carolina*, 82–84; Ambler, *Sectionalism in Virginia*, 65. In August of 1797, in Henry Crist's ballroom in Baltimore, there was an exhibit of three hundred portraits of French Revolutionary leaders and also an "optican machine" showing the interior of the Bastille and views of its capture. Annapolis *Maryland Gazette*, August 10, 1797.

cophiles got vociferous support from a considerable number of French refugees and liberal Englishmen who had sought asylum on our shores. To put a quietus on these meddling foreigners, several of whom edited newspapers, Congress passed in June and July, 1798, the Alien and Sedition acts. It is probably not too much to say that the Sedition measure was the most pernicious act ever passed by the Congress of the United States, and it was a palpable violation of the First Amendment to the Federal Constitution.

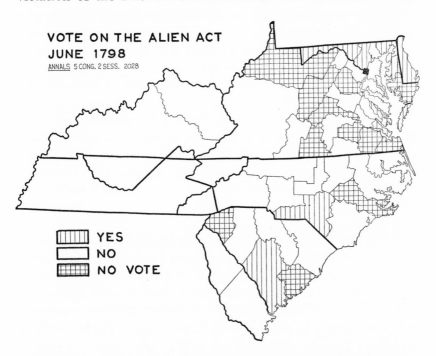

VOTE ON THE ALIEN ACT
JUNE 1798
ANNALS 5 CONG. 2 SESS. 2028

YES
NO
NO VOTE

In passing the act the Federalists went too far and Southern Republicans reacted strongly, while even many Federalists disapproved. This did not include Washington, who definitely favored the measure, but President Adams was lukewarm and Hamilton warned, "Let us not be cruel or violent." [40] In the South such strong Federalists as John Marshall, who was a candidate for Congress at the time, and Governor William R. Davie of North Caro-

[40] Marshall Smelser, "George Washington and the Alien and Sedition Acts," in *American Historical Review*, LIX (1953–1954), 422–34; Norfolk *Herald*, December 20, 1798; Channing, *History of the United States*, IV, 223.

lina disapproved of the legislation, which in fact received in the House of Representatives only one affirmative vote from South Carolina, one from North Carolina, three out of nine from Virginia, and two out of six from Maryland. Kentucky, Tennessee, and Georgia cast one negative vote each, with none in the affirmative.[41]

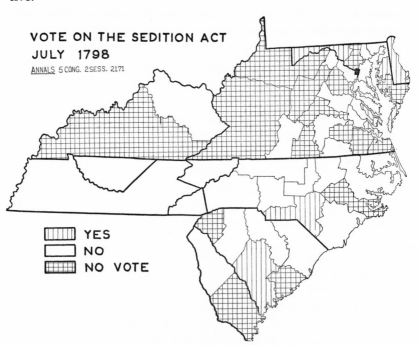

**VOTE ON THE SEDITION ACT
JULY 1798**
ANNALS 5 CONG. 2 SESS. 2171

YES
NO
NO VOTE

Southern opposition to the legislation did not stop here. Public meetings were held in various places to condemn it, Kentucky easily taking the lead in this form of activity. With many Revolutionary veterans settled among them, the citizens of this state had never lost their love for France nor forgotten their hatred of England. Naturally, there were few Federalists among them, their support going overwhelmingly to Jefferson.[42] On July 4, 1798, "a Re-

[41] Ambler, *Sectionalism in Virginia*, 75; Dodd, *Nathaniel Macon*, 130. Wolfe, in *Jeffersonian Democracy in South Carolina*, 118–19, says that both Rutledge and Harper supported it.

[42] Marshall, *History of Kentucky*, II, 251, 284; "A Citizen," in Lexington *Kentucky Gazette*, September 17, October 17, 1798.

publican" published a statement in the *Kentucky Gazette* to the effect that the present danger to the liberty and happiness of America was more serious than any since the Revolution and that the interests of the Western country would be deeply affected by measures which might be pursued by the Federal government. The silence of Kentuckians, he said, might be construed as unpatriotic indifference to the welfare of their country and an abandonment of their right to direct the councils of their representatives. The writer then called for an assembly at the Presbyterian meeting-house in Lexington on the next court day in August. On August 1 George Nicholas published a communication in which he stated his belief that the Sedition Act violated the First Amendment.[43]

These protests were supported by public meetings in many parts of the state, the first held in Clark County on July 24. Here the following resolutions were adopted with only one dissenting vote: "That every officer of the Federal Government, whether legislative, executive or judicial, is the servant of the people and amenable and accountable to them; that being true; it becomes people to watch over their conduct and to censure and remove them when they think expedient—the higher the office, the closer it should be scrutinized." The resolutions then stated that war with France was impolitic and would be ruinous to America in her present condition; that the people would, at the hazard of their lives, support the Union and the Constitution; that an alliance with Great Britain would be dangerous, and should defensive measures be found necessary, they would rather support the burden of them alone. The power given the President to raise armies when he thought necessary, without restriction as to numbers, and the power to borrow money to support them, without limitation as to the sum, were viewed as dangerous and unconstitutional. In conclusion the resolutions stated that the Alien Act was "impolitic, unjust and disgraceful to the American character"; that the privilege of speaking and publishing their sentiments on all public questions was inestimable and that "it is unequivocally acknowledged and secured to us by the Constitution of the United States; that all laws made to destroy or impair it are void, and that we will assert our just right to this privilege in opposition to any law that

[43] Lexington *Kentucky Gazette,* July 4, August 1, 1798.

may be passed to deprive us of it." A copy of these resolutions was sent to the President and to Congress.[44] On August 13 a similar meeting of about a thousand people was held in Lexington. George Nicholas was the principal speaker on this occasion, and here the young Henry Clay made his political debut.[45]

A meeting held in Montgomery County gave voice to the usual anti-Administration views and, in addition, resolved that France, by capturing our vessels, had greatly injured and provoked us but that we were accessory to this depredation by our late treaty with Great Britain, which was much to our disadvantage. A war with France, the resolutions said, would be wicked and especially dangerous for the Western country. If hostilities should become necessary, the Kentuckians declared, "we should rely on ourselves and repudiate the very thought of alliance with Great Britain." After stating that the Alien Law was an infringement on guaranteed rights, the resolutions went on to declare "that all indirect taxation is unjust and dangerous, as it tends to favor monopolizing and is hardest on the common man, it keeps the expenses of government out of sight for a time and hidden from the ordinary citizen, it is dangerous in the end." Meetings in Bourbon and Mercer counties adopted resolutions to much the same effect.[46]

At this time the outstanding leaders in Kentucky politics were John Breckinridge and George Nicholas, both native Virginians and both close friends of Jefferson. An even closer friend was George's brother, Wilson Cary Nicholas, a near neighbor and a frequent visitor at Monticello. While the agitation over the Alien and Sedition acts was at its height, John Taylor of Caroline County, Virginia, suggested to Jefferson that Virginia and North Carolina secede from the Union and form a new confederation. Jefferson disapproved of this idea and suggested that only a protest against the hated law be made by the states. He accordingly drew up a series of resolutions in the expectation that they would be put forth by the legislature of North Carolina. This plan was foiled by the Federalist victory there in the 1798 elections. In October Breckinridge was in Virginia visiting relatives, and he promptly

[44] *Ibid.*

[45] Charleston *City Gazette,* September 25, 1798; Lexington *Kentucky Gazette,* November 28, 1798; Mayo, *Henry Clay,* 73–75.

[46] Lexington *Kentucky Gazette,* August 15, 29, September 3, 1798.

stepped into the breach, proposing that he present Jefferson's resolutions to his own legislature for adoption.[47]

Meanwhile, the Federalist press in the North was bitter in its denunciation of the proceedings in Kentucky. Nettled by this criticism, Governor Garrard appeared before the legislature on November 7 and stated that reports had been circulated in the East highly unfavorable to the political character of the people of Kentucky, who were represented as being, if not in a state of insurrection, yet utterly disaffected to the Federal government and determined to afford it no support, waiting only for an opportunity to withdraw from the Union. As for himself, the Governor doubted the truth of these assertions but suggested the expediency of demonstrating their falsity by making a specific declaration of attachment to the Union.[48] On the tenth the House adopted the following resolution:

"*1*. That the several states composing the United States of America, are not united on the principle of unlimited submission to the general government; but that by compact under the style and title of a Constitution of the United States and of amendments thereto, they constituted a general government for special purposes, delegated to that government certain definite powers, reserving each state to itself, the residuary mass of right to their own self-government, and that whensoever the general government assumes undelegated powers, its acts are unauthoritative, void, and of no force: That to this compact each State acceded as a State, and is an integral party, its co-States forming, as to itself, the other party: That the government created by this compact was not made the exclusive or final judge of the extent of the powers delegated to itself; since that would have made its discretion, and not the Constitution, the measure of its powers; but that as in all other cases of compact among parties having no common Judge, *each party has an equal right to judge for itself, as well of infractions as of the mode and measure of redress*." [49]

[47] John Brown to Jefferson, September 15, 1798, in Jefferson Papers (Library of Congress); Ambler, *Sectionalism in Virginia*, 65–66, 70; Ashe, *History of North Carolina*, II, 158; Channing, *History of the United States*, IV, 225.

[48] Lexington *Kentucky Gazette*, November 14, 28, 1798.

[49] *Ibid.*, November 14, 1798; Henry S. Commager (ed.), *Documents of American History* (New York, 1948), 177–78.

On December 14 John Adair wrote from Frankfort to his friend General Wilkinson in Natchez that "the Kentuckians very Generally reprobate the Alien and Sedition Bills as unconstitutional. I send you a copy of the resolution of the Legislature on that subject." [50] Jefferson was the author of these resolutions, which constitute a clear and concise exposition of the doctrine of government by compact. The Federalists denied this interpretation of the origin and nature of the Constitution of the United States and maintained that the central government rested directly upon the consent of the people. In so doing, they denied the validity of the reasoning which the same author used in the Declaration of Independence! [51]

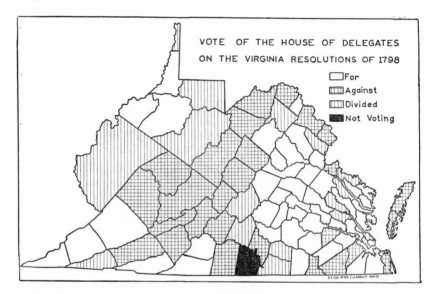

Madison wrote the similar, but milder, resolutions adopted by the General Assembly of Virginia on December 24. They were introduced by John Taylor of Caroline and strongly supported by W. C. Nicholas, William B. Giles, and James Barbour. As originally written they included a statement that the Alien and Sedition acts were "not law, but utterly null, void, and of no force or

[50] John Adair to Wilkinson, December 14, 1798, in Durrett Collection, Miscellaneous Manuscripts, 44608.
[51] Anderson, *William Branch Giles,* 69–70.

effect," but General Henry Lee moved that this expression be deleted, and it was so ordered. Then the resolutions as amended passed by a vote of 100 to 63. The opposition came mainly from the Great Valley, only two counties which lay between the Blue Ridge and the Allegheny Mountains casting both their votes for the resolutions. Also opposed were those southcentral counties which were settled largely by the Scotch-Irish who came down the Valley and then turned eastward through the water gap of the Roanoke River. The two counties of the Eastern Shore voted solidly against the resolutions, as did a few Tidewater and Potomac counties. On the other hand, the strength of the state rights men was in the central Piedmont Region—the tobacco country—which voted solidly for the resolutions. On the same side were most of the trans-Allegheny counties.[52]

The legislature of Maryland condemned the Kentucky resolutions by a vote of forty-eight to fourteen and the merchants of Baltimore raised $40,300 to build two sloops of war, the *Chesapeake* and the *Maryland,* for the Federal navy.[53] Among the Northern states, New Jersey, Pennsylvania, Delaware, Rhode Island, Massachusetts, New York, Connecticut, New Hampshire, and Vermont adopted hostile resolutions,[54] but more surprisingly, no official support came from any of the states to the South. None could have been expected from Federalist South Carolina, where the citizens of Charleston raised $100,000 for the construction of a sloop of war of 550 tons and twenty-four guns. She was to be christened *The Adams* and donated to the United States Navy. The Palmetto State had five Federalists to only one Republican

[52] Richmond *Virginia Gazette, and General Advertiser,* February 19, April 30, 1799; Charleston *City Gazette,* May 1, 1799; Lexington *Kentucky Gazette,* October 10, 1798; Elinor J. Weeder, "Wilson Cary Nicholas, Jefferson's Lieutenant" (M.A. thesis, University of Virginia, 1946), 30–35; McCarrell, "Formation of the Jeffersonian Party in Virginia," 239; Ambler, *Sectionalism in Virginia,* 70–75; *The Virginia Report of 1799–1800, Touching the Alien and Sedition Laws, together with the Virginia Resolutions of December 21, 1798, the Debates and Proceedings thereon in the House of Delegates of Virginia, and Several Other Documents Illustrative of the Report and Resolutions* (Richmond, 1850), 148–50, 157–61.

[53] Halifax *North-Carolina Journal,* January 14, 1799; Richmond *Virginia Gazette,* January 8, 1799; Scharf, *History of Maryland,* II, 599–600.

[54] Richmond *Virginia Gazette, and General Advertiser,* January 29, February 15, March 9, April 2, 1799; *Virginia Report of 1799–1800,* 168–77.

in the Federal House of Representatives, and the state Senate by a vote of fourteen to eleven declined to consider the resolutions.[55]

In the North Carolina elections of 1798 the resentment against France as a result of the XYZ affair resulted in a victory for the Federalists, who won a majority in the state Senate and increased strength, though not a majority, in the House. Seven out of the ten members elected to the lower house of Congress ran on the Federalist ticket, but only four of them remained true to the party. Davie, a staunch Federalist, was elected governor by the legislature and when, on December 21, he submitted the Kentucky resolutions to this body, the action taken was described by the venerable Samuel Johnston in acid terms. When these resolutions, he said, "with a most indecent and violent Philippic on the measures of the General Government," were laid before the Commons, which heard them impatiently, they were ordered to lie on the table, and several persons near him, Johnston declared, proposed that they be thrown in the fire! When Davie resigned as governor to accept appointment to the French commission, he was succeeded by Benjamin Williams, a mild Federalist.[56]

But not for long were the Federalists to enjoy their triumph. Up to this point they had the advantage in the Southern press. They enjoyed the active support of such important papers as the *Georgia Gazette,* the *North-Carolina Journal,* the New Bern *Gazette,* the Charleston *City Gazette,* the *South Carolina Gazette,* the Richmond *Virginia Gazette, and General Advertiser,* the Norfolk *Herald,* and the *Maryland Gazette.*[57] Judging by the newspaper press, one would have come to the conclusion that the Southern states favored the Federalist cause, but the Republicans were improving their publicity. The Richmond *Examiner,* edited by Meriwether James, with James Thomson Callender, the Scottish renegade, furnishing the fireworks, was hardly a credit to the cause, and

[55] Charleston *City Gazette,* August 11, October 11, 1798; April 29, June 11, 1799; Wolfe, *Jeffersonian Democracy in South Carolina,* 120–23, 128.

[56] Halifax *North-Carolina Journal,* July 23, 1798; Lycan, "Alexander Hamilton and the North Carolina Federalists," *loc. cit.,* 461–62; Blackwell P. Robinson, *William R. Davie* (Chapel Hill, 1957), 300, 303; Gilpatrick, *Jeffersonian Democracy in North Carolina,* 93–102, 107, 110–16; Ashe, *History of North Carolina,* II, 153–54.

[57] Richmond *Virginia Gazette, and General Advertiser,* January 29, February 5, 12, March 29, November 12, 1799; Charleston *South Carolina Gazette and Timothy's Daily Advertiser,* February 6, March 3, 1800; New Bern *Gazette,* February 23, 1799.

threats of violence were made against both Callender and the *Examiner*,[58] but the founding of the Raleigh *Register* in 1799 by Joseph Gales was another matter. An English liberal, Gales published the Sheffield *Register* until forced to flee his native land in 1794. Coming to this country, he settled in Philadelphia and undertook the publication of the *Independent Gazette* until Thomas Blount and Willie Jones backed him in the establishment of a Republican paper in the new capital of North Carolina.[59] Though at first his friends did not succeed in having the legislature elect him to the remunerative post of public printer, his paper flourished and he also profited from his business of selling books. Even in this capacity his interest in politics is indicated by the titles of the pamphlets which he advertised for sale in December, 1799. They included: *Proceedings on the Impeachment of William Blount; Letter from George Nicholas to his Friend in Virginia Justifying the Conduct of Kentucky; An Account of Tennessee, with its Constitution; Thoughts on Emigration; Report of the Minority of the Virginia Legislature Favoring the Alien and Sedition Acts; The American Remembrancer;* three volumes of tracts on Jay's Treaty, and similar works.[60]

In Virginia the Federalists could muster no more than a vigorous minority whose strength lay mainly in the Shenandoah Valley, the counties bordering the Potomac River and Chesapeake Bay, and in the commercial towns of which Richmond and Norfolk were the most important.[61] In 1799 they elected eight out of nineteen Congressmen, six of whom represented old Federalist districts; and they scored an important psychological victory when Washington persuaded Patrick Henry to become a candidate for the House of Delegates in the hope that he could there checkmate the activities of Madison, who also was a candidate. Although only sixty-three years of age, Henry had already retired to his "Red

---

[58] Richmond *Virginia Gazette, and General Advertiser*, May 21, July 30, August 2, 6, 9, 13, October 11, 29, 1799; Annapolis *Maryland Gazette*, June 19, 1800; James M. Smith, "Sedition in the Old Dominion: James T. Callender and *The Prospect Before Us*," in *Journal of Southern History*, XX (1954), 157–82.

[59] Gilpatrick, *Jeffersonian Democracy in North Carolina*, 75, 104–107.

[60] Raleigh *Register*, December 17, 1799.

[61] Ambler, *Sectionalism in Virginia*, 71; Ammon, "Republican Party in Virginia," 198–99; Link, *Democratic-Republican Societies*, 165, 203–204.

Hill" farm on the Staunton River and was now an old and broken man. Nevertheless, Washington tried for some time to wean him away from his old political allies. When, in 1795, Edmund Randolph quit the Cabinet, Henry was given the opportunity to succeed him as Secretary of State, but though he resented the partisan abuse to which the President was subjected, he felt that he was not equal to the task and declined the offer. Within three months Washington proposed to make him Chief Justice of the United States but this honor he also declined, though he was now definitely classified as a Federalist. Finally, in the same year, President Adams appointed him, along with William Vans Murray and Oliver Ellsworth, to the French mission which was to try to pull the XYZ chestnuts out of the fire. Henry declined this offer, too, and Davie was sent in his stead.[62]

At last the Orator of the Revolution yielded to Washington's entreaty to offer himself as a candidate for the House of Delegates. Thus on a cold and blustering March day at Charlotte Courthouse he made his last political speech. His opponent was a gaunt young man of flaxen hair and high-pitched voice who was making his debut in politics as a candidate for Congress. Both John Randolph and Patrick Henry won their elections, but within three months Henry was dead and in December Washington followed him to the grave.[63] Though this was a severe blow to the Virginia Federalists, the shock was cushioned by the election of John Marshall and seven other Federalists to the House of Representatives, while the Republicans, in addition to Randolph, elected nine. The Republican majority which was returned to the legislature elected Wilson Cary Nicholas to the United States Senate and James Monroe governor of the state. The final result showed that the Federalists had gained strength in Tidewater and in the trans-Allegheny regions but lost votes in the Valley.[64]

[62] *Dictionary of American Biography*, VIII, 559; Richmond *Virginia Gazette, and General Advertiser*, September 7, 1796; Halifax *North-Carolina Journal*, August 29, 1796; Ammon, "Republican Party in Virginia," 208–209.

[63] Richmond *Virginia Gazette, and General Advertiser*, April 19, 23, May 10, June 14, 1799; Norfolk *Herald*, December 19, 28, 1799; Annapolis *Maryland Gazette*, December 20, 1799; Garland, *John Randolph of Roanoke*, 121; Davis, *Travels . . . in the United States*, 144–45.

[64] Charleston *City Gazette*, May 29, 1799; Raleigh *Register*, December 17, 1799; Ambler, *Sectionalism in Virginia*, 75–76.

The stage was now set for one of the great events in American history—the Presidential election of 1800. The Virginia and Kentucky resolutions were undoubtedly intended to serve as campaign material, and they appear to have had some effect on the elections in Virginia. In 1799 the Federalists sent fifty members to the legislature, but in 1800 only half that number were elected and the Republicans did not fail to take advantage of their victory. Remembering that they had lost one electoral vote to Adams in 1796, the legislature now provided by a vote of seventy-eight to seventy-three that the Presidential electors should be chosen by general ticket; that the voting should, for the first time, be by secret ballot; and that the governor should appoint the election supervisors. This foresight paid off, for though the Republicans carried the November election by a vote of 21,311 to 6,024, the Federalists had a majority in Loudoun, Berkeley, Hampshire, Hardy, Pendleton, Bath, and Augusta counties, all in the valleys of the Shenandoah and the south branch of the Potomac. In addition, there were large minorities for Adams in several counties of the lower Tidewater, and the vote in the eastern towns and cities was almost evenly divided, but because the election was by general ticket, Jefferson received all of Virginia's electoral vote.[65]

In Maryland, as in Virginia, the Alien and Sedition acts hurt the Federalist cause; the Republicans won five out of nine seats in the lower House of Congress. When a new legislature was elected in October, 1800, the Republicans won forty-four seats to thirty-two for the Federalists, whose strength was concentrated in the lower Potomac and Eastern Shore counties. In the Presidential election Maryland voted by districts and Adams and Jefferson came out even, with five votes each. Thus the Federalist lost two of the electoral votes which had been cast for him in 1796.[66]

In 1800 North Carolina turned from the Federalist Party, which

---

[65] Ammon, "Republican Party in Virginia," 242–43; Ambler, *Sectionalism in Virginia*, 79–80, giving 13,363 to 7,434; Simms, *John Taylor*, 93, 96–97; McCarrell, "Formation of the Jeffersonian Party in Virginia," 272; Charleston *South Carolina Gazette*, November 29, 1800.

[66] Annapolis *Maryland Gazette*, April 24, June 26, July 3, 10, 24, August 14, September 4, 11, 1800; Raleigh *Register*, October 21, 1800; Charleston *South Carolina Gazette*, November 12, 29, 1800; Andrews, *History of Maryland*, 408–409; Scharf, *History of Maryland*, II, 602.

the state had embraced in 1798 as a result of the XYZ affair, and elected a strongly Republican legislature which promptly chose Joseph Gales as public printer. This change appears to have been due largely to the Alien and Sedition acts, but Jefferson did not profit thereby, for Presidential electors were chosen by district and the Federalists won four to eight for the Republicans. Thus Adams received three more votes than the North Carolina electors had cast for him four years previously. His support came from the Fayetteville, Wilmington, New Bern, and Salisbury districts, located in the southcentral and southeastern sections, and the four Federalists who represented the state in Congress came from these same districts.[67]

It is notable that South Carolina, a Federalist stronghold in the South, should have cast her entire electoral vote for Jefferson both in 1796 and 1800. This was due to the fact that the legislature chose the electors by majority vote and the strongly Republican back country was able, under the astute political management of Charles Pinckney, to outvote the Federalists who dominated Charleston and the Low Country. Not only was the Republican majority in the legislature able to throw all eight of South Carolina's electoral votes to Jefferson, it also elected John Drayton governor and sent John Ewing Calhoun to join Charles Pinckney in the Senate.[68] But the Federalists were more successful in the Congressional elections and were able to send Benjamin Huger, John Rutledge, and Thomas Lowndes to the House of Representatives. The Republicans elected Thomas Moore, Thomas Sumter, and William Butler, who replaced the Federalist Robert Goodloe Harper, these representing a gain of two members by the party.[69] Like South Carolina, Georgia cast all her electoral votes for Jefferson, as she had done in the previous election, and she sent General James Jackson, the hero of the fight against the Yazoo speculators,

---

[67] Gilpatrick, *Jeffersonian Democracy in North Carolina*, 110–16, 122–27; Raleigh *Register*, June 8, August 12, October 21, November 25, 1800; New Bern *Gazette*, August 15, 1800; Henry M. Wagstaff, *State Rights and Political Parties in North Carolina—1776–1861* (Baltimore, 1906), 38.

[68] Wolfe, *Jeffersonian Democracy in South Carolina*, 141, 151–52; Charleston *South Carolina Gazette*, April 12, October 3, 8, 11, 13, December 9, 1800.

[69] Charleston *South Carolina Gazette*, July 9, October 21, November 4, 18, 20, December 15, 1800; Annapolis *Maryland Gazette*, November 13, 1800.

to the Senate. Tennessee and Kentucky also went solidly Republican.[70]

After all the storm and fury of the election and the strong opposition to the Alien and Sedition acts, it is not a little surprising to find that Adams received exactly the same number—nine—of electoral votes from the Southern states which he received in 1796. According to Edward Channing, Jefferson's election was due entirely to the political maneuvers by which Aaron Burr captured the New York City vote and thus won the entire electoral vote of New York State for the Republican ticket. It was not Burr's fault that one of the South Carolina electors failed to cast his vote for George Clinton as expected and thus produced a tie between himself and Jefferson which had to be fought out so painfully in the House of Representatives.[71]

[70] Charleston *South Carolina Gazette,* November 28, 1800; Raleigh *Register,* December 2, 1800.

[71] Channing, *History of the United States,* IV, 234-37; Gilpatrick, *Jeffersonian Democracy in North Carolina,* 123.

# CHAPTER X

# GULF COAST PROBLEMS

WHEN on March 4, 1801, Thomas Jefferson, with Aaron Burr on his right hand and John Marshall on his left, stood in the little Senate chamber of the new capitol building in Washington and took the oath of office as third President of the United States, he could hardly have imagined that the Gulf Coast would occupy so much of his attention during the next four years. Pinckney's Treaty of 1795 presumably settled all the major problems that vexed that distant region. By its terms our Spanish neighbors agreed to recognize the thirty-first parallel as the international boundary from the Mississippi to the Chattahoochee River, and they promised not to tamper with the Indians on our side of the line. Furthermore, they agreed to permit our river boatmen to unload their produce in New Orleans in order that it might be transshipped, duty free, on ocean-going vessels. It was a part of the agreement, however, that nothing should be sold locally, for Spain like other European powers still tried to monopolize the trade of her colonies. Yet in spite of this amicable arrangement, trouble was already brewing on the Southern border before Jefferson came into office.

The situation could hardly have been otherwise, for West Florida included all the coast from the Mississippi to the Apalachicola River, with the exception of the "island" of New Orleans, and the Indians, both north and south of the line, were largely under the influence of the Spanish authorities. Furthermore, Spain did not agree to evacuate Natchez and permit the survey of the boundary until three years after the treaty was signed. Finally, in 1798 Andrew Ellicott, principal surveyor on the part of the United States, commenced the running of the line, and by September, 1799, he reached the Chattahoochee River.[1]

Though the marking of this boundary did not deprive the Indians of any lands, the natives had an understandable suspicion of the white man's shiny instruments, which never seemed to work to the redman's advantage. From the Escambia to the Chattahoochee the Creeks and Seminoles carried on pilfering and other marauding forays; then at the Chattahoochee they assembled in such large numbers as to indicate that they meant to halt the survey. Benjamin Hawkins, the Indian agent who came down to consult with Ellicott, thought that the work could continue without further trouble, and the Creek escort declared itself willing to go on, but Ellicott, confronted by still greater hostility on the part of the natives, abandoned the task, dismissed his escort, and started in his patched-up boat down the Apalachicola to go by sea to the St. Marys, at the headwaters of which the line was to terminate.[2] Even today the dark forest crowds the banks of the Apalachicola, and in this solitude a ship had recently gone aground on St. George's Island just east of the mouth of the river. The crew was still aboard and Ellicott's curiosity was aroused. However, before he could make an investigation, he was astonished when a messenger arrived announcing the presence of the well-known adventurer and freebooter, William Augustus Bowles.[3]

On his last trip to Florida, Bowles, having failed to detach the Creeks from their famous chief, Alexander McGillivray, had accepted an invitation from Governor Carondelet to visit New Orleans. Seized while under this safe-conduct, he was sent to Havana, Cadiz, Madrid, and then to the Philippines. While being returned to Cadiz in 1797 he escaped and made his way to London. By the summer of 1799 he was back in the West Indies and on August 10 he and his party left Jamaica for Nassau in His Majesty's schooner Fox. Then, setting sail in the same vessel, they steered for the mouth of the Ochlockonee River but, having sailed too far west,

[1] Whitaker, Mississippi Question, 66–67.    [2] Cotterill, Southern Indians, 126–27.
[3] Ibid.; Merritt B. Pound, "Colonel Benjamin Hawkins—North Carolinian—Benefactor of the Southern Indians," in North Carolina Historical Review, XIX (1942), 168–86.

ran aground on the eastern end of St. George's Island, where Ellicott so unexpectedly came upon them.[4]

In a note to the surveyor, dated September 22, Bowles invited him to come aboard: "I wish much to see you. Although we may differ in politics, yet as gentlemen we may associate." Not only did Ellicott visit the grounded vessel, but a rough spell of weather forced him to remain for eight days.[5] Bowles told him that the Spaniards had not imprisoned him until he refused to accept a commission to fight against the United States, and he then asked his guest to transport him to the mainland.[6] Ellicott refused this request but left some needed supplies and then sailed to the Spanish fort of St. Marks at the junction of the St. Marks and Wakulla rivers. Here he informed the commandant of his encounter with Bowles, and later he notified the Spanish garrisons at Pensacola and St. Augustine, as well as Colonel Hawkins and the Secretary of State.[7]

Bowles came to Florida with the intention of setting up an independent state among the natives who would aid the British in their war with Spain. He constructed a post at Wekiwa, where the Flint and Chattahoochee rivers unite to form the Apalachicola. Here he assembled as many Creeks and Seminoles as would come and, on October 26, 1799, with their consent and approval, proclaimed the founding of the state of Muskogee, with himself as Director General. He then announced that no more Indian lands would be ceded to the whites, that no dividing line would be run, and that no persons holding commissions under the United States would be permitted within Muskogee boundaries. Though it is clear that Bowles meant to include all of the Creeks and Seminoles in his Muskogee state, for the time being he limited his operations to the Florida Seminoles because he could not expect British support in a war waged against the United States. However, he had many friends among the Lower Creek towns on the Chattahoochee River. Among the Upper Creeks on the headwaters of the Alabama River he did not fare so well, for Colonel Hawkins was able to dominate the situation there. Forays, skir-

[4] Whitaker, *Mississippi Question*, 165–67.　　[5] Mathews, *Andrew Ellicott*, 73.
[6] Whitaker, *Mississippi Question*, 167; Mathews, *Andrew Ellicott*, 174.
[7] Mathews, *Andrew Ellicott*, 176–79.

mishes, and intrigues continued on the Indian frontier until 1803, involving both East and West Florida as well as the United States, with English governors in the West Indies lending support to the adventurer's activities.[8]

Despite the trouble with Bowles, Colonel Hawkins achieved some success in inducing the Creeks, whose fighting force he estimated at 3,500 warriors, to adopt the ways of civilization. In the spring of 1803 he reported that they had four hundred farms which were fenced and plowed and that two hundred spinning wheels were in use among them. And he was now about to achieve an even greater triumph.[9]

In May, 1803, the Upper Creeks met delegations of the Cherokee, Chickasaw, and Choctaw at their council town of Tuckabatchee. John Forbes of the Pensacola firm of Panton, Leslie and Company was there to seek a cession of land in payment of debts to the merchants, and Colonel Hawkins was also present. On May 26 Bowles and a band of his Seminole followers put in their appearance, though the renegade knew that his enemies were setting a trap for him. He thought he had sufficient friends among the natives to bid defiance to those who sought to take him, but in this he was mistaken. On the twenty-seventh he was first separated from his Seminole warriors, then arrested by order of Colonel Hawkins, and finally secured with handcuffs made to order by the American blacksmith maintained among the Creeks.[10] Though thus arrested on American soil and under the authority of the United States, the prisoner was immediately turned over to a party of Indians who took him to Pensacola, delivered him into the hands of Governor Vizente Folch, and collected the reward. This was plain kidnapping, yet it was accomplished with the full co-operation of Colonel Hawkins and his deputy. From Pensacola Bowles was sent under guard to New Orleans and thence to Havana, where he passed the short remainder of his life as a prisoner in Morro

[8] Cotterill, *Southern Indians*, 126–30, 135–38; Whitaker, *Mississippi Question*, 168, 171, 172; Merritt B. Pound, *Benjamin Hawkins, Indian Agent* (Athens, 1951), 107, 138, 172, 191.

[9] "Journal of John Forbes, May, 1803," in *Florida Historical Society Quarterly*, IX (1930–1931), 279–89.

[10] Raleigh *Register*, July 4, 1803; Pickett, *History of Alabama*, 470–71; Cotterill, *Southern Indians*, 12; Pound, *Benjamin Hawkins*, 194.

Castle. Thus ended a career as fantastic as any in the annals of the American frontier.[11]

While Bowles was muddying the waters in East Florida, a major crisis developed in Louisiana. After Spain, in 1798, agreed to the survey of the boundary line along the thirty-first parallel, the international situation seemed to be developing satisfactorily. Not only was Natchez finally occupied by American troops, but Fort Adams was built on the east bank of the Mississippi River just above the boundary.[12] In May of the next year Spanish forces evacuated Fort St. Stephens on the Tombigbee River and in July Fort Stoddert was built near the point where the line crossed the river just above Mobile Bay, and two companies of American troops were garrisoned there.[13] Then, to provide a political organization for the settlers who were beginning to flock into this latter region, the Mississippi Territory in June, 1800, created Washington County and assigned to it the vast area between the Pearl and the Chattahoochee rivers, most of which was still Indian country.[14]

American citizens were now at last beginning to feel secure in this southwestern corner of the United States when, on October 1, 1800, a momentous treaty was signed at the Spanish village of San Ildefonso. By the terms of this document Spain agreed to retrocede to France, now dominated by Napoleon Bonaparte as First Consul, the whole of the province of Louisiana, but for the time being this transaction was kept secret.[15] Secrets have a way of leaking, however, and on March 29, 1801, Rufus King, our Minister in London, warned the Administration that he feared Louisiana would be returned to France. President Jefferson received his first hint of it in May, but it was not until November 20 that King was able to get a copy of the treaty and forward it to Madison, who had succeeded Pickering as Secretary of State.[16]

It is difficult now for us to realize the cataclysmic nature of this

[11] Whitaker, *Mississippi Question*, 173–74.

[12] Claiborne, *Mississippi, as a Province, Territory and State*, 198.

[13] Pickett, *History of Alabama*, 461.          [14] *Ibid.*

[15] M. L. Fletcher, "Louisiana as a Factor in French Diplomacy," in *Mississippi Valley Historical Review*, XVII (1930–1931), 376–77.

[16] Gayarré, *History of Louisiana*, III, 448; Lyon, *Louisiana in French Diplomacy*, 148; Channing, *History of the United States*, IV, 307; Cresson, *James Monroe*, 184.

turn of events. Nothing more than nagging irritation was to be feared from the weak hand of Spain, which controlled our access to the Gulf of Mexico. To have Napoleon in control of New Orleans and all of Louisiana was a very different matter. President Jefferson was by no means overstating the case when he wrote to Robert R. Livingston, our Minister in Paris, the famous letter which contained the solemn warning: "The day that France takes possession of New Orleans, fixes the sentence which is to retain her forever within her low-water mark. It seals the union of two nations, who, in conjunction, can maintain exclusive possession of the ocean. From that moment, we must marry ourselves to the British fleet and nation." [17]

The situation was indeed critical, for Napoleon no less than Jefferson was fixed in his purpose. Having, on March 25, 1802, concluded the Peace of Amiens with Britain, he meant to take advantage of the cessation of hostilities to build in America an empire that would be strong enough to defend itself in case of a renewal of hostilities in Europe. The crux of this adventure lay in the island of Santo Domingo, which for a decade had been in the throes of a revolution, now led by the famous Negro partisan, Toussaint L'Overture. Though this holocaust was, in the beginning, inspired by the French doctrines of liberty, equality, and fraternity, Napoleon sent General Charles Victor Emmanuel Leclerc to suppress it. With French authority restored there, Louisiana would be garrisoned and developed to supply the French West Indian islands with foodstuffs and timber. And since New Orleans controlled the navigation of the entire Mississippi basin, it did not seem unreasonable to hope that that entire region might finally fall into the orbit of the nation which could grant or deny it access to the outside world.[18] William Cobbett's *Political Register* realistically declared: "The regicide peace is made and Louisiana is ceded to France. They have calculated the means of severing Tennessee and Kentucky from the Union. Remember that I, whose voice you refused to listen to in 1796, now tell you that unless you give up to them a great portion of your commerce with England, those states will, in less than two years, be attached to the Repub-

[17] Lipscomb and Bergh (eds.), *Writings of Thomas Jefferson*, X, 311–16.
[18] Lyon, *Louisiana in French Diplomacy*, 196–97.

lic of France." The navigation of the Great River, Cobbett said, was vital to the West, and the Federal Union must buy it for the Western states or they would join France. That nation, he said, wanted for her West Indian trade the supply of provisions and timber which could be had cheaply and in abundance in Kentucky and Tennessee, and France would rather take possession of settlements already established than establish new ones herself.[19]

To carry out his ambitious project, Napoleon appointed a full complement of officials, headed by General Victor Collot as Captain General of Louisiana, with a salary of 70,000 francs, and Pierre-Clément Laussat as Colonial Prefect, with a salary of 50,000 francs. The Prefect was unknown in America, but General Collot had made the military survey of the Ohio and Mississippi rivers in 1796 and had, therefore, unusual qualifications for his new post. Three thousand troops would go with the general to take possession of Louisiana, and Dunkirk would be the port of embarkation. The expedition would carry adequate presents for all the Indians in the territories along the Mississippi, and two hundred medals were struck for the chiefs. Denis Decrès, Minister of the Navy and Colonies, forwarded them to General Collot in February, 1803.[20]

The royal order from Spain for the delivery of Louisiana, having been signed on October 15, arrived in Paris on October 25, 1802, but the Dunkirk project was now abandoned and General Collot was informed that the troops would sail from Helvöet Slury, a small port about thirty kilometers southwest of Rotterdam. When the general arrived at the newly designated port of embarkation, he did not find the expedition ready to sail, for the steady drain of troops for Santo Domingo had required all available transports. Because of this delay it was decided to send Prefect Laussat on in advance, and he accordingly sailed for New Orleans on January 10, 1803.[21]

Already, on December 19, 1802, Collot had received orders from Napoleon to depart immediately, but at the same time he

---

[19] Richmond *Virginia Gazette, and General Advertiser*, May 19, 1802.

[20] Lyon, *Louisiana in French Diplomacy*, 133–36.

[21] *Ibid.*, 125, 134, 137; Daniel Clark to Madison, April 27, 1803, in *American Historical Review*, XXXIII (1927–1928), 335–42.

was instructed to leave one of his regiments to reinforce Leclerc at Santo Domingo. However, despite the apparent haste, the Captain General found the necessary preparations far from complete, and on December 22, 1802, he estimated that two or three weeks would be required to assemble his supplies and complete the repairs on his ships. This delay proved fatal, for during part of January and all of February Collot's force was icebound, and thus the weather came to the rescue of the United States.[22] In April a violent storm damaged several of the French transports and necessitated a further delay of two weeks. The troops were on the point of departure when a courier arrived at full speed and announced the sale of Louisiana to the United States, a transaction consummated on April 30, 1803. On May 15 Great Britain renewed hostilities by declaring war on France.[23]

Thus narrowly was Louisiana spared an occupation by the troops of Napoleon Bonaparte, but even without the defeat of Leclerc in Santo Domingo, the aid of an unusually cold winter, and the renewal of war in Europe, it is not certain that France could have made good her bid for an American empire. President Jefferson confidently expected a renewal of the war in Europe and felt certain that Britain would be prepared to use force to prevent French occupation of Louisiana. He was taken completely by surprise when on October 16, 1802, the Intendant of Louisiana, Juan Ventura Morales, withdrew the American right of deposit at New Orleans, in violation of Pinckney's Treaty of 1795. Americans naturally jumped to the incorrect conclusion that this was really the work of Napoleon, and they were now sure that he was planning to build up a hostile empire on their Western border. The whole American West would then be threatened unless effective countermeasures were taken without delay.[24]

In Natchez General Wilkinson, Governor Claiborne, and the wealthy and ambitious New Orleans merchant, Daniel Clark, hatched a scheme to seize control of the port city before the arrival of General Collot's troops and such a move had wide support in

---

[22] Lyon, *Louisiana in French Diplomacy*, 138–40.     [23] *Ibid.*, 142.

[24] W. E. Hulings to Madison, January 20, 1803, in *American Historical Review*, XXXII (1926–1927), 822–24; Lexington *Kentucky Gazette*, May 15, 1800; February 1, 1803; Gayarré, *History of Louisiana*, III, 398–99.

the Southern press. In Congress the moribund Federalists, led by Senator James Ross of Pennsylvania, with the unofficial support of Hamilton, sought to make political capital by proposing a similar move, to be accomplished by sending Kentucky militia down the Mississippi. But the Kentuckians were mostly Republicans and they naturally looked to the President, rather than to the Federalists, for leadership. A considerable section of the Southern press took a similar stand, and despite the common impression to the contrary, that leadership was not wanting.[25]

By the end of November, 1802, Jefferson was informed of the closure of the port of New Orleans and his reaction was prompt and positive. Visualizing a war between England and France which might result in the violation of American territory, he concentrated first on strengthening our frontier posts, especially those guarding the Spanish border on the south and those along the Canadian line. Next he planned to purchase extensive tracts of land along the eastern shore of the Mississippi River and settle them with a population which would furnish a ready and self-perpetuating force for the defense of our Western outposts.[26] Finally, in order to open up new opportunities for the fur traders who would be displaced from the lands lying east of the Mississippi, the President projected an exploration of the Missouri Valley and a transcontinental route to the Pacific Ocean. The history of the Lewis and Clark expedition is well known, but it is not always realized that it was planned before the purchase of Louisiana was anticipated. Jefferson publicly stressed the scientific objectives of this incursion into Spanish territory in order to cloak the economic and military motives which lay behind it. If England and France were destined to stage a struggle for possession of the trans-Mis-

[25] Yrujo to Cevallos, February 21, 1803, in Archivo Histórico Nacional, *Estado, Legajo,* 5630, p. 341; Daniel Clark to Madison, March 8, 1803, in *American Historical Review,* XXXIII (1927–1928), 331–35, also in *American State Papers, Miscellaneous,* I, 713; Charleston *Courier,* January 11, 14, 20, March 12, April 2, May 11, 1803; Richmond *Virginia Gazette,* December 18, 1802; March 5, 19, April 12, May 14, 1803; Annapolis *Maryland Gazette,* December 2, 1802; Savannah *Georgia Republican,* April 28, 1803; Cox, "New Invasion of the Goths and Vandals," *loc. cit.,* 188–89; Claiborne, *Mississippi, as a Province, Territory and State,* 238, 240–41; Whitaker, *Mississippi Question,* 201, 218; Buck, *Western Pennsylvania,* 480.

[26] Gayarré, *History of Louisiana,* III, 500, 527–58; Lyon, *Louisiana in French Diplomacy,* 224.

sissippi West, our government would need to have authentic information as to the arena of a contest in which we might well become involved.[27]

Still another of Jefferson's objects was the possibility of diplomatic maneuvers. On May 1, 1802, Madison suggested to Livingston that he negotiate for the purchase of New Orleans and the Floridas. At about the same time Pierre du Pont de Nemours, a French businessman and government official who, with his family, migrated to the United States in 1800, was planning to return temporarily to his native country. To him Jefferson entrusted letters for Livingston which were left unsealed for du Pont to read. In his reply, dated May 12, 1802, the Frenchman made precisely the same suggestion which Madison had made just previously.[28]

On December 31, 1802, Jefferson received a letter from du Pont in Paris, saying he thought Napoleon was ready to come to terms and outlining a treaty for the purchase of New Orleans and both Floridas for $6,000,000 dollars. Accepting this advice, the President asked Congress for an appropriation of $2,000,000 for diplomatic purposes and immediately nominated James Monroe as Minister Extraordinary to join Livingston in Paris and assist him in an effort to make the desired purchase.[29] The unexpected culmination of this project in the purchase of all Louisiana is too well known to require elaboration here.

This acquisition nearly doubled the territory of the United States; and Eastern Federalists, seeing their section dwarfed by this enlargement of the West, generally took a dim view of the purchase. Senator Plumer, in fact, went so far as to declare that he was confident "the ratification of that treaty and the possession of that immense territory will hasten the dissolution of our present

[27] Ralph B. Guinness, "The Purpose of the Lewis and Clark Expedition," in *Mississippi Valley Historical Review*, XX (1933–1934), 90–100; Mary Adams, "Jefferson's Reaction to the Treaty of San Ildefonso," in *Journal of Southern History*, XXI (1954), 173–88.

[28] Pierre du Pont de Nemours to Jefferson, May 12, October 4, 1802, in Gilbert Chinard (ed.), *The Correspondence of Jefferson and du Pont de Nemours* (Baltimore, 1931), II, 55–58, 63–65; Lyon, *Louisiana in French Diplomacy*, 163, 183–87.

[29] Jefferson to Governor Garrard, January 18, 1803, in Lexington *Kentucky Gazette*, February 9, 1803; John Breckinridge to his "friend near Frankfort," January 20, 1803, *ibid.*; Brown (ed.), *William Plumer's Memorandum*, 17–18; Gayarré, *History of Louisiana*, III, 475–77; Lyon, *Louisiana in French Diplomacy*, 177.

government." Admit this Western world into the Union, he said, "and you destroy with a single operation the whole weight and importance of the eastern states in the scale of politics." On the other hand, the Charleston *Courier* was convinced that the value of all Western lands would be increased and that the Union would have a monopoly of supplying the West Indies with provisions. The treaty had the support of all Jeffersonian Republicans in the Senate and on October 19, 1803, it was ratified by a vote of twenty-four to seven.[30]

This accomplished, the question at once arose as to the extent of the acquisition. The treaty said that we should have Louisiana "with the same extent it now has in the hands of Spain, and that it had when France possessed it." These were ambiguous terms, but it is clear that the territory which Spain surrendered to France and France to us included only the "island" of New Orleans east of the Mississippi River, while on the west it stretched across Texas to the Rio Grande.[31] Yet so anxious was the Administration to control the Gulf Coast east of the Mississippi and so little value did it attach to lands west of that river that it made no attempt to occupy Texas but insisted on a specious claim to the land France had originally occupied as far east as the Perdido River.[32]

Not even President Jefferson knew much about the empire that he had purchased. He had already sent Lewis and Clark to explore it, and he began collecting information from such men as Daniel Clark in New Orleans, William Dunbar in Natchez, and Dr. John Sibley in Natchitoches.[33] Aside from the last-named settlement on

[30] Charleston *Courier*, June 23, 1803; Savannah *Georgia Republican*, August 16, 1803; Savannah *Georgia Republican and State Intelligencer*, October 25, 1803; Brown (ed.), *William Plumer's Memorandum*, 6–9, 13–14; Lyon, *Louisiana in French Diplomacy*, 243.

[31] Daniel Clark to Madison, May 13, December 13, 1803, in *American Historical Review*, XXXIII (1927–1928), 343, 355–58; Richard Stenberg, "The Western Boundary of Louisiana, 1762–1803," in *Southwestern Historical Quarterly*, XXXV (1931–1932), 95–108; Lyon, *Louisiana in French Diplomacy*, 225; Chadwick, *Relations of the United States and Spain*, 67–69.

[32] Chadwick, *Relations of the United States and Spain*, 68–69; Gayarré, *History of Louisiana*, III, 529; Brown (ed.), *William Plumer's Memorandum*, 400–405.

[33] Daniel Clark to Jefferson, August 18, 1803, in Jefferson Papers; John Sibley to Governor Claiborne, October 10, 1803, in Carter (ed.), *Territory South of the Ohio*, 72–78; Daniel Clark to Secretary of State, September 2, 1803, *ibid.*, 28–47; Description of Louisiana communicated to Congress, November 14, 1803, in *American State Papers, Miscellaneous*, I, 344–56; Cox (ed.), *Louisiana-Texas Frontier*, II, 6 ff.

the Red River in what is now western Louisiana, the only upriver
villages of any importance were St. Louis and New Madrid; but
all these outposts were tributary to and overshadowed by New
Orleans, which was the capital of the province.[34] The total population of this vast area in 1803 was only 42,375, of whom 21,244
were free white, 1,768 free colored, and 12,920 slaves, in addition
to an estimated Indian population of 25,000 or 30,000.[35] The great
majority of the white population was of French descent, though
New Orleans with about 10,000 inhabitants was more cosmopoli-
tan.[36] The old French inhabitants, known as Creoles, dominated
the business and social life of the city, but they were elbowed by
two new and more aggressive elements: namely, refugees from
Napoleonic France and Americans seeking opportunities for profits.[37] In addition, there were numerous Negroes and Mulattoes,
who furnished the city with most of its craftsmen and made up
two companies of the local militia. The Catholic faith was established by law, but there was in the city only one state-supported
school for boys and one good private school for girls—the Ursuline
Convent, which is still functioning. Approximately half the people were supposed to be able to read and write, but only about
two hundred could do it well, and very few possessed more than
an elementary education. Moral standards were, according to all
accounts, definitely lax, with concubinage looked upon as an established institution.[38]

Physically, New Orleans had many peculiarities. Ever since its
founding in 1718, its existence was made possible only by the
building of levees to hold back the waters of the Mississippi River.
And since it was below water level, it was not possible to dig base-
ments or graves in the city. Only river water, which then bore a
milky complexion, was available for drinking, but it was considered quite healthful and an antidote for rheumatic complaints.
Most of the people lived within the area now known as the *Vieux
Carré*, which Governor Carondelet in 1793 surrounded with an

[34] Gayarré, *History of Louisiana*, III, 622.
[35] Raleigh *Register*, December 5, 1803; Lyon, *Louisiana in French Diplomacy*, 116.
[36] Raleigh *Register*, December 5, 1803; Gayarré, *History of Louisiana*, III, 622.
[37] Raleigh *Register*, December 5, 1803.
[38] *Ibid.*, December 19, 1803; Claiborne to Jefferson, August 24, 1803, in Carter (ed.),
*Territory of Orleans*, 16–25, 28; Gayarré, *History of Louisiana*, III, 595.

American-style stockade—already in ruins at the time of the purchase—with forts at the four corners and a battery in the *Place d'Armes,* now Jackson Square. Here the Cathedral of St. Louis and the Cabildo were erected near the end of the Spanish regime, and since devastating fires had recently destroyed a large proportion of the old wooden houses in the center of the town, these were replaced by the low brick and plaster structures built around terraced patios such as one sees there today.[39]

After the treaty of 1795 granted the United States a place of deposit in New Orleans, the trade of the city increased enormously, but it involved some difficult problems. The flour, salt meat, corn, and tobacco which were floated down from the Ohio and Cumberland valleys in keel and flatboats were unloaded and stored anywhere in the city until reloaded on ocean-going vessels. No duties were paid, and nothing was supposed to be sold in the city, American property being, officially, merely goods in transit. But such a system was naturally unenforceable, and no serious attempt was made to enforce it. In fact, while Spain was at war with England, trade with the Americans was an absolute necessity, but during the interval of peace provided by the Treaty of Amiens, Louisiana could trade with any European country with which Spain was at peace, a 6 per cent duty being levied on imports and exports, but all such trade had to be carried on under the Spanish flag. It was only because this source of supply was available that King Charles IV now found it possible to forbid all commerce between Spanish and American citizens. He also prohibited the granting of Louisiana lands to Americans and authorized the Intendant, Morales, to withdraw the right of deposit in New Orleans.[40]

These moves were no doubt inspired by the fact that Americans were accused by Morales of extensive smuggling operations in New Orleans. Also, they were the beneficiaries of most of the land grants made in recent years, and they owned and operated one-third of the mercantile houses in the city. In fact, in 1802, 170 American

[39] Raleigh *Register,* December 5, 1803.

[40] Panton to John Forbes, April 26, 1800, in *Florida Historical Society Quarterly,* XIV (1935–1936), 275–78; Daniel Clark to Madison, June 22, 1802, in *American Historical Review,* XXXII (1926–1927), 821–22; Lexington *Kentucky Gazette,* February 1, 15, 1803; Richmond *Virginia Gazette,* April 6, 1803; Whitaker, *Mississippi Question,* 189–94; Gayarré, *History of Louisiana,* III, 456, 483.

and 97 Spanish vessels—and only one French ship—totaling 33,725 tons, entered the port of New Orleans; while 158 American, 104 Spanish, and three French ships, totaling 31,241 tons were cleared there.[41] The total value of exports from New Orleans at this time was $2,158,000, and it was estimated that this included 20,000 bales of cotton weighing 300 pounds each, valued at $1,200,000; 45,000 casks of sugar of 1,000 pounds each, $260,000; 800 casks of molasses of 100 gallons each, $32,000; indigo decreasing rapidly, but the remains of former crops valued at $100,000; peltries worth $200,000; lumber exports declining, but valued at $80,000. The exports of lead and corn were not reported, and no horses nor cattle were exported by sea.[42] In 1802, while England and France were still at war, three-fourths of the cotton and half the peltries and indigo shipped through New Orleans were sent to the United States, the payment of duties thus being avoided under the pretext that they were received as American goods in the "place of deposit in New Orleans." The remainder of the exports, except lumber, pitch, tar, and provisions, was freighted on American ships and dispatched impartially to England and France, the principal European belligerents. Luxury goods, which were not the product of American soil, were usually listed as contraband, for smuggling was a lucrative and officially recognized business, and among its more skillful practitioners were the brothers Laffite of Barataria Bay.[43] It was largely because of the illegal trade that duties, which were the only taxes levied, failed to meet the cost of administration and consequently Spain had to face an annual deficit of about $337,000 incurred by the Province of Louisiana, which thus served no useful purpose for the mother country except as a barrier against the United States.[44]

New Orleans was approximately a hundred miles by water from the mouth of the Mississippi, and her communication with the

---

[41] Raleigh *Register*, January 2, 1804; *American Historical Review*, XXXVII (1931–1932), 280–83; Lyon, *Louisiana in French Diplomacy*, 114, 117, 169–75.

[42] *American State Papers, Miscellaneous*, I, 354; Raleigh *Register*, December 19, 1803; Gayarré, *History of Louisiana*, III, 622–23.

[43] Evan Jones to Madison, May 15, 1801, in *American Historical Review*, XXXII (1926–1927), 814; Carter (ed.), *Territory of Orleans*, 28 ff.; Lyon, *Louisiana in French Diplomacy*, 116–17.

[44] Lyon, *Louisiana in French Diplomacy*, 109.

outside world was not good. Sailing ships could go downstream without difficulty, but it sometimes took as long to make the passage between the Balize—the pilot station at the Main Pass into the river—and New Orleans as was required for the voyage from New York to the Balize. This was principally due to the sharp bend at the English Turn, which was only a short distance below the city. Sometimes ships were delayed two or three weeks at this point, and for this reason New Orleans was not vulnerable to attack from the sea until steamships under Admiral Farragut replaced sailing vessels. Below the English Turn there was little solid ground on the banks of the wide and sluggish stream, but Fort Plaquemines, a substantial structure having bastions faced with brick, frowned over the waters about ten miles from the river's mouth. Then finally, at the Balize was a stark wooden tower about forty feet high. It had no light but furnished crude shelter for twenty-four pilots, mostly lazy Spaniards, who were maintained by the government. Vessels bound for New Orleans paid a pilotage fee of twenty dollars and took on a customs officer "who is much disappointed if he is not bribed to permit smuggling as the vessel ascends the river." [45]

Though the Great River was the main outlet for the commerce of New Orleans, it was not the only one. Governor Carondelet constructed a canal from the ramparts of the city to Bayou St. John, which connects with Lake Pontchartrain. Small vessels could navigate this route from Lake Pontchartrain to Lake Borgne and thence sail eastward along the Gulf Coast. Also, during the high water season from February through June, such vessels could leave the Mississippi at Manchac, follow the Iberville River to its junction with the Amite, and thence cross lakes Maurepas, Pontchartrain, and Borgne to reach the Gulf. By this route, as well as that by the Bayou St. John, commerce was carried on with Mobile and Pensacola. From these ports the Louisiana metropolis imported ship timbers, pitch, tar, lime, charcoal, and some cattle; and during 1802 some five hundred sloops and schooners of from eight to forty tons were engaged in this trade. As for overland communications, except for a road along the river from New Orleans by

[45] John Pintard to Madison, September 14, 1803, in Carter (ed.), *Territory of Orleans*, 49–54.

way of Baton Rouge to Natchez, there was nothing available but mere paths through the forests.[46]

Outside of New Orleans the only well-established settlements in Louisiana stretched along the Mississippi from Chalmette, some fifteen miles below the city, to the Iberville River which, just below Baton Rouge, marked the boundary between West Florida and Louisiana. Here sugar cane was grown after Etienne Boré, the San Domingan refugee, had in 1796 proved it to be practicable.[47] But here the river, contained by the levees, was above the level of the surrounding country, and its borders, built up by alluvial deposits, were above the level of the lands beyond. Thus there existed an alluvial strip of fertile land varying from one-half to a full mile beyond the levee which furnished excellent soil for the growth of sugar cane. Beyond this the swamp was all but impenetrable. Similar conditions existed along the sluggish bayous which wound through the half-drowned land lying south and west of the lower reaches of the Mississippi. But farther westward along the Gulf the land in the parishes of Attakapas and Opelousas was largely open meadow with forested areas interspersed. This was good grazing country and many American drovers had recently established themselves in the region. From Natchitoches Dr. Sibley reported in 1803 that cattle and horses abounded and that in 1802 over 3,000 bales of cotton were shipped down the Red River, along with equally valuable amounts of perique tobacco and peltry. He said there were twenty-four or twenty-five cotton gins on the river and more were being built. Furthermore, he estimated that there were already a hundred sugar plantations west of the Mississippi and this number could be increased tenfold.[48]

Agriculture and cattle raising thus held considerable promise, but of manufactures there were almost none. In this same year, 1803, Daniel Clark reported that there were two machines for spinning cotton in Louisiana, one in Iberville parish and one in Opelousas, but they did practically no business. However, in the

[46] Raleigh *Register*, December 5, 1803; January 2, 1804; Collot, *Journey in North America*, II, 75; Gayarré, *History of Louisiana*, III, 351–53.

[47] Carter (ed.), *Territory of Orleans*, 28; Raleigh *Register*, December 12, 1803.

[48] Daniel Clark to Madison, October 20, 1803, in *American Historical Review*, XXXIII (1927–1928), 346–50; Carter (ed.), *Territory of Orleans*, 13–14, 72–78.

back country a number of the poorer farmers spun and wove some "negro" cloth of mixed wool and cotton. In New Orleans, he reported, there was a little cordage, shot, and hair powder made, and in the city or nearby were a dozen distilleries which produced annually 4,000 casks, each containing fifty gallons of tafia (a cheap rum). There was also one sugar refinery making about 200,000 pounds of loaf sugar annually.[49]

Such was the province, containing one small city and millions of acres of unexplored territory, that the United States almost accidentally acquired by purchase in 1803. The next problem was to take possession of the promised land. For this purpose President Jefferson appointed Wilkinson, the ranking General of the Army, and Governor William C. C. Claiborne of the Mississippi Territory. However, because Spain stipulated that Napoleon was not to transfer Louisiana to any other country, Jefferson feared that the Dons might oppose the transfer of the province. For this reason he issued a call for five hundred mounted volunteers from the Mississippi Territory to join the regular troops at Fort Adams and proceed immediately to New Orleans to take possession of Louisiana. Meanwhile, Tennessee was to hold in readiness to march at a moment's notice, 2,000 volunteers; Kentucky was to furnish 4,000, and Ohio, 5,000.[50]

Meanwhile, five hundred Tennessee militiamen assembled at Natchez and, on December 10, Governor Claiborne marched southward with only a volunteer company of mounted Mississippi militia to meet General Wilkinson at Fort Adams. By this time it was clear that no resistance would be met, and accordingly the two commissioners set out for New Orleans with only the volunteers and the garrison of the fort.[51] On December 17, 1803, they made camp within two miles of the city. On the thirtieth of the previous month Spain had surrendered the province to Laussat, whom

---

[49] Carter (ed.), *Territory of Orleans*, 28 ff.; Raleigh *Register*, December 19, 1803.

[50] Madison to Daniel Clark, October 31, 1803, in Carter (ed.), *Territory of Orleans*, 95–96; Daniel Clark to Governor Claiborne, November 7, 1803, in *American Historical Review*, XXXIII (1927–1928), 351–52; Lexington *Kentucky Gazette*, November 22, 1803; Gayarré, *History of Louisiana*, III, 334–36, 544, 618; Bowers, *Jefferson in Power*, 209–10; Whitaker, *Mississippi Question*, 241.

[51] Daniel Clark to Madison, November 28, 1803, in *American Historical Review*, XXXIII (1927–1928), 352–53.

Napoleon had originally appointed to serve as Prefect under General Collot and who came to Louisiana to prepare the way for his superior. The First Consul designated him as the agent to receive and to surrender the Province and he consequently ruled in New Orleans without a staff, but without incident, for three weeks. To him on the eighteenth the American commissioners sent a messenger inquiring whether he was ready to receive them. Laussat assented and the next day was given over to the exchange of civilities.[52]

Finally, on the twentieth the Prefect ordered all the militia companies of the city drawn up under arms at the *Place d'Armes* in front of the recently completed Cabildo, and a large crowd gathered to witness the ceremonies. The commissioners of the United States arrived at the gates of the city with their troops and, on entering, were greeted with a salute of twenty-one guns from the forts. When the American troops reached the public square they were drawn up on one side, facing the local militia on the other, with the French flag flying from its pole between them. After carrying out the formalities of the transfer within the Cabildo, the commissioners made their appearance on one of the balconies. As soon as they were seen, the French flag was lowered and the American standard went up. When the two ensigns met half way, a gun was fired as a signal, and immediately the land batteries and the guns on the armed ships in the river set up a rolling cannonade. A group of American citizens who stood at a corner of the square greeted this stirring scene by waving their hats, and a few of them shouted, but no emotion was manifested by any of the French and Spanish spectators. Thus Louisiana became a part of the United States.[53]

Latin gallantry could not let so important an occasion pass without a fitting celebration, and accordingly the Marquis de Casa Calvo, one of the Spanish commissioners, honored his "archenemy" Laussat with a splendid ball which was said to have cost 15,000 francs. Not to be outdone, Laussat returned the Spaniard's hospi-

[52] Daniel Clark to Madison, November 29, 1803, *ibid.*, 353-55; André Lafargue, "A Reign of Twenty Days, Pierre Clément de Laussat," in *Louisiana Historical Quarterly*, VIII (1925), 398-410; Gayarré, *History of Louisiana*, III, 594, 618.
[53] Gayarré, *History of Louisiana*, III, 619-20.

tality with a ball at which four or five hundred people spent the whole night in eating, drinking, gambling, and dancing.[54] The Americans were hardly expected to equal such elegance, but General Wilkinson was not to be denied. In the liberal spirit of modern diplomacy, he inaugurated a celebration which lasted from December 20, 1803, until April 24, 1804, and cost his government $6,619.72. Among the refreshments served the guests were 844 bottles of claret, 196½ gallons plus one quarter-cask of Madeira, four gallons of sherry, 144 bottles of champagne, 60 bottles of white wine, 100 bottles of "hermitage" wine, 588 bottles of red wine, six bottles of cordials, 67 gallons of brandy, 81 bottles of porter, one case of gin, 258 bottles of ale, five gallons of rum, 2⅛ gallons of whisky, three barrels of cider, and 11,360 "Spanish Segars." Along with the liquid refreshments went a like quantity of food, and the Federal government was also called on to pay for six dozen knives and forks, three pairs of plated candlesticks, two pairs of snuffers, twelve barrels of charcoal, thirty pounds of bar iron, one pair of andirons, one looking glass, and other accessories. On this occasion the general fully earned his reputation as a *bon vivant*. But he also had more important business—! [55]

---

[54] Mary P. Adams, "Jefferson's Military Policy, with Special Reference to the Frontier, 1805–1809" (Ph.D. dissertation, University of Virginia, 1958), 53.

[55] *Ibid.*, 53–60.

# CHAPTER XI

# THE BURR CONSPIRACY

W HILE General Wilkinson was dispensing his lavish hospitality, he was not permitting himself to forget some of the sterner aspects of life.[1] The Spanish pension which had been granted him in 1788 had not been paid since 1793, and the present seemed a favorable time to agitate for its renewal. Accordingly, he arranged an interview with the Marquis de Casa Calvo and the governor of West Florida, Don Vizente Folch, both of whom were conveniently in the city, and proposed that their government renew the stipend, while making up back pay in the sum of $20,000. In return, the general proposed to furnish all present and future information which might be useful for the defense of Florida and Mexico.

For the present he advised that the West Florida and Texas frontiers be fortified against possible attack by the United States, that the Lewis and Clark expedition be arrested, that all neighboring Indian tribes be kept under control, and that Spain work for the retrocession of all Louisiana territory west of the Mississippi River. For the future he proposed that correspondence be carried on in cipher, with himself referred to only as No. 13.

The Spanish officials were sufficiently impressed with these proposals to agree to a renewal of the pension and a grant of 12,000 pesos in lieu of back pay. In March of 1804 Casa Calvo forwarded Wilkinson's propositions to Don Pedro Cevallos, the Spanish Foreign Minister, and advocated their adoption, but suggested in addition that his government try to regain title to all of Louisiana,

[1] This chapter is based primarily upon the author's study, *The Burr Conspiracy* (New York, 1954). Footnotes are supplied only where additional material has been used.

including the "island" of New Orleans, as well as the territory west of the Mississippi. Cevallos approved the pension renewal terms, and thus the Commanding General of the United States Army again entered the service of the power with which his own country was most likely to go to war.

Spain could not hope to regain Louisiana without making some real sacrifice, and the terms suggested by Casa Calvo involved the transfer of East and West Florida to the United States, along with the granting of commercial facilities in New Orleans and an unspecified monetary consideration. Such an exchange of territory, suggested by several influential Americans, did not appear to be an unreasonable proposition. Vast areas of undeveloped land were not considered especially valuable at the time, but Spain needed Louisiana for the protection of Texas and all Mexico, while the United States needed Florida to safeguard her southern frontier. The Americans claimed West Florida as far east as the Perdido River, and there was considerable sentiment in favor of taking it by force if it could not be acquired otherwise.

Indeed, the prospect of the transfer of West Florida furnishes the only obvious explanation of an international land speculation which took place in New Orleans during the early months of 1804. Juan Ventura Morales, it will be recalled, had been Intendant of Louisiana under the Spanish regime, and he now held the same office in West Florida, but he had never left New Orleans. He was a very wealthy man and had acquired, even among Spanish officials, the reputation of adeptness at intrigue. The Irish-American merchant, Daniel Clark, was reputed to be equally wealthy and equally gifted as a schemer. He and Morales were close friends, and they were now joined in many of their endeavors by a newcomer, Edward Livingston. Member of a prominent New York family and brother of Robert Livingston, this gentleman came to New Orleans to recoup a large fortune which he had lost, and success at once attended his efforts, for he was soon recognized as leader of the legal profession in his new home.

Under the Spanish system of colonial administration, the Intendant had charge of the public lands, and therefore Morales was in position to serve any friends who wished to speculate in West Florida real estate, the value of which was expected to soar upon annexation to the United States. Clark and Livingston were keenly interested in such a venture, and they and their patron took up many thousands of acres. General Wilkinson was invited to participate, but he declared that his official position prohibited such a speculation. Indeed, he seems generally to have adhered to this rule, though he did, somewhat later, acquire a claim to Dauphin Island at the entrance to Mobile Bay.[2]

While adventurers were taking advantage of unsettled conditions in the neighborhood of New Orleans, Congress debated and passed a bill to provide a civil government for Louisiana. The act of March 26, 1804, divided Louisiana by the line which is now the northern boundary of the state. The part south of the thirty-third parallel would constitute Orleans Territory with New Orleans as its capital, while all the vast and little-known area north of that line would be the District of Louisiana with St. Louis as the capital. This sprawling district was, for the time being, to be administered by the governor of Indiana Territory.

Appointment as governor of Orleans Territory was first offered to James Monroe, who declined it. Jefferson then wished to tender it to Lafayette, but since the Frenchman was in prison at Olmutz, he was not available.[3] William C. C. Claiborne's availability was the obvious reason for his selection. A native of Virginia and an alumnus of the College of William and Mary, he had studied law and, after moving to Tennessee, was appointed by Governor Sevier to the Supreme Court of that new state. At the age of twenty-two he was sent to Congress to succeed Andrew Jackson and served for five years. In the critical election of 1800 he held Tennessee for Jefferson, and at the age of twenty-six was appointed governor of Mississippi Territory. He was only twenty-eight when he became governor of Orleans Territory, a position which would have tried the soul of any man.[4]

The old French population of Louisiana—the Creoles—was accustomed to rule by foreigners and consequently was inclined to take the new regime philosophically, but the refugees from Napoleonic France were a troublesome lot, and so were some of those

---

[2] Carter (ed.), *Territory of Orleans*, 150–51.

[3] *Ibid.*, 281–84; Bowers, *Jefferson in Power*, 226.

[4] *Dictionary of American Biography*, IV, 115–16.

from Santo Domingo. Equally troublesome were the newly arrived fortune-seeking Americans, headed by Livingston and ably seconded by Evan Jones, an old resident who had served as American consul in New Orleans under the Spanish regime, and by Daniel Clark, who had become a naturalized citizen when Natchez was occupied in 1798.[5]

The government of Orleans Territory would consist of the usual governor, secretary, three judges to constitute a Territorial superior court, and in addition, a Legislative Council of thirteen. This body would have plenary legislative powers, and its members would be appointed by the President, who, quite naturally, looked to the governor to make nominations.[6]

These provisions were based on those made earlier for the Northwest, Mississippi, and Indiana territories, but they were somewhat more liberal in providing for a genuine legislative body, albeit an appointive one. As the great majority of the people of Louisiana were French and knew no other language, and had no experience with democratic institutions, the government which was provided for them would appear to have been well adapted to the situation, but a great hue and cry was immediately raised against the absence of elective offices and lack of participation by the people in legislation as well as other phases of the new regime. Land titles had to be proved, and there were often no written documents to prove them; direct taxes had to be paid, whereas only tariff duties had been levied by the Spaniards; and English became the official language among a people who understood only French.

Left to themselves, the Creoles would have accepted American institutions as no worse than the Spanish, but Livingston and his friends would not have it so. They masterminded a public meeting which assembled on July 1, 1804, and adopted a memorial to Congress, which Livingston had drafted, demanding immediate statehood and the continuation of the slave trade, which Congress had prohibited. A later meeting elected delegates—Jean Noël Destréhan, Pierre Sauvé, and Peter Derbigny—to present this petition to Congress. All three were natives of France, and while Derbigny

---

[5] Sargent to Pickering, October 12, 1799, in Rowland (ed.), *Mississippi Territorial Archives*, I, 150–51, 177–78; Carter (ed.), *Territory of Orleans*, 86, 371–75, 385.
[6] Poore (ed.), *Federal and State Constitutions*, I, 691–95.

and Sauvé were friendly toward the United States, Destréhan was an apostle of Napoleon, a tool of Laussat, and deeply mortified over the cession of Louisiana to the United States. He spoke no English, but his wealth gave him influence, and he tried to dominate the delegation.[7] General Wilkinson at first favored a strong military regime for Louisiana, but before leaving New Orleans he, like his friends, came out for immediate statehood. On the other hand, Thomas Paine, the great apostle of freedom, denounced the Louisianians for demanding as rights, privileges which they had not earned and were hardly qualified as yet to assume.[8]

It was thus among a people, the great majority of whom did not understand his language and the minority of whom were Americans who hated him, that Governor Claiborne undertook to establish his administration. The appointment of the Legislative Council was most pressing, and it was here that he met the opposition head on. Having been led to believe that Clark, Boré, and Jones would serve, he trustingly appointed them, and they made capital of his credulity by declining the proffered trust. But other and more dependable Creoles and Americans were found to take their places, and the Legislative Council met for the first time on November 7, 1804.[9] It had to make up for lost time in providing for the administration of justice and proper functioning of the executive department, but it also protested against the continued presence of Spanish troops in New Orleans and the formal guard mount which they staged for the Marquis de Casa Calvo. While in the midst of these difficulties, the Governor's family was stricken with yellow fever. On September 26 his wife and only daughter died, but he himself recovered to face his enemies once more.[10]

During all this turmoil General Wilkinson embarked for New York and reached his destination in May. On July 11 Vice-Presi-

[7] New Orleans *Louisiana Gazette*, August 7, 14, 22, 25, December 28, 1804; Carter (ed.), *Territory of Orleans*, 241–48, 261, 265–68, 304–305, 314–15.

[8] New Orleans *Louisiana Gazette*, November 2, 1804; " 'Common Sense' to the French Inhabitants of Louisiana, September 22, 1804," in Moncure D. Conway (ed.), *The Writings of Tom Paine* (New York, 1894–1896), III, 430–36.

[9] New Orleans *Louisiana Gazette*, October 12, 1804; Gayarré, *History of Louisiana*, IV, 20–21; Carter (ed.), *Territory of Orleans*, 284, 310, 317, 334–35, 344–45.

[10] New Orleans *Louisiana Gazette*, September 28, December 7, 14, 1804; Richmond *Enquirer*, November 4, 1804.

dent Burr killed Hamilton in the portentous duel at Weehawken, and three days later one John W. Burley wrote from New Orleans to Postmaster General Gideon Granger that some American adventurers had consorted with a few French inhabitants of the Creole city to cause trouble, that Livingston was the only man of talents among them, and that General Wilkinson was accused of having taken a hand in the business before his departure.

It was not until February, 1805, that Derbigny, Destréhan, and Sauvé reached Washington and presented Livingston's memorial to Congress. Wilkinson was there to meet them and introduced them to the Vice-President, saying that Burr was "the first gentleman of America" and a man of the most eminent political and military talents who, when his term of office expired, was going to Louisiana to undertake certain important projects. The general asked Derbigny to give Burr all possible information about that part of the country, which request, along with Wilkinson's line of conduct, quite mystified the gentleman from New Orleans.

Congress did not see fit to grant statehood to the Territory of Orleans, but it authorized election of a Territorial legislature and provided a regular Territorial government for the "District" of Louisiana.[11] Daniel Clark was presently elected to serve in Congress as the Territorial delegate from Orleans, and General Wilkinson was appointed governor of Louisiana Territory, with his headquarters at St. Louis. Many were astonished by this appointment of the Commanding General of the Army to a civil post. The Vice-President was presiding over the Senate, which at the moment was trying Judge Samuel Chase on impeachment charges. Jefferson was anxious for a conviction, and Burr used this temporary influence to bring about the selection of Wilkinson. At least this was the theory advanced at the time to explain why the President accepted the advice of a man whom he hated and appointed an officer who was widely and justly distrusted.[12]

But Burr's influence did not end with the appointment of Wilkinson. His stepson, John B. Prevost, was made a judge of Orleans Territory and his brother-in-law, Dr. Joseph Browne, became the Territorial secretary of Louisiana. Furthermore, James Brown,

[11] Poore (ed.), *Federal and State Constitutions*, I, 696–98.
[12] Anderson, *William Branch Giles*, 97.

brother to Senator John Brown of Kentucky, who was a close friend of Wilkinson and Burr, was appointed Federal district attorney for the Territory of Orleans. Thus were men who were closely bound by ties of family and friendship placed in the most important posts in the new Territories.

It is impossible to fix the date which marks the beginning of the Burr Conspiracy. When Hamilton was killed in the encounter at Weehawken, feeling against the Vice-President was strong and a New York warrant was sworn out for his arrest. Burr then fled to Philadelphia and took refuge with his friend Charles Biddle, also a close friend of General Wilkinson, who had married into the Biddle family. On his return from New Orleans during the previous May, Wilkinson had spent a night with Burr at his stately "Richmond Hill" estate overlooking the Hudson. Shortly afterward they met again in New York and discussed some scheme affecting relations with Spain. Biddle's home furnished them with a secure retreat, and it was during this sojourn that they evidently concocted the first definite plans for the conspiracy. Here they met an Englishman named Charles Williamson, a friend of Henry Dundas, Lord Melville, and he agreed to promote their plans. First he went to Anthony Merry, the British Minister, and reported that Burr was prepared to assist the British government in separating the Western states from the American Union. Merry recommended this proposal to his superiors and soon Williamson journeyed to London to advocate the plan.

Though under indictment in New York, Burr was still Vice-President, and when Congress assembled in the fall of 1804, he was on hand to preside over the Senate. Wilkinson also spent the winter of 1804–1805 in the national capital and the two devoted much of their time to copying maps of East and West Florida, of Orleans and Louisiana territories, as well as of Texas and Mexico. On December 10 John Adair of Kentucky wrote to Wilkinson that "Mexico glitters in our eyes . . . the word is all we wait for," and a month later the general wrote to Major James Bruff, commanding officer at St. Louis, and asked for information about Mexico, especially concerning the route to Santa Fé. Then during March, while the Louisiana delegation was in Washington, Burr had a conference with Minister Merry. He said the Louisianians were determined to secure their independence, needing only the assistance of a foreign power and the American frontiersmen. In support of this cause he wanted the British government to furnish a half million dollars and a naval force to co-operate with him at the mouth of the Mississippi and along the Gulf Coast. Merry was inclined to favor these proposals, but Williamson did not seem to be making much headway in London.

At the same time James Monroe in Madrid was making no progress in his effort to reach an agreement as to the boundaries of Louisiana, and war between the United States and Spain seemed inevitable.[13] Such a crisis would give the conspirators the opportunity they craved, and Burr was determined to be prepared. But first he needed to reconnoiter the field of operations and, accordingly, decided on a voyage down the Ohio and Mississippi rivers to New Orleans.

On March 9, 1805, Louis Marie Turreau, the French Minister in Washington, after talking with the Louisiana delegation, wrote to Talleyrand that "Louisiana thus is going to be the seat of Mr. Burr's new intrigues; he is going there under the aegis of General Wilkinson. It is even asserted that he might find the means there already prepared by a certain Livingston whom the disruption of his business has driven from New York City and who is closely associated with Burr."

His term as Vice-President having expired on March 4, Colonel Burr set out for the West on April 10, 1805. He went by way of Pittsburgh where he expected to meet General Wilkinson, who was on his way to St. Louis to assume his new duties as governor of Upper Louisiana Territory. But the brigadier did not arrive on time, and the colonel, having purchased for $133 an elegant flatboat with four glass-windowed apartments, floated effortlessly down the Ohio. One of the principal objectives of this journey was to interview certain men he hoped to enlist in his enterprise, one of whom was Harman Blennerhassett. Accordingly, he moored his boat at the island just below Marietta, Ohio, where the Irish recluse had built his luxuriously appointed home. Finding the master absent, Burr dined with the lady of the house and then proceeded downstream to Cincinnati where he was entertained

---

[13] Cresson, *James Monroe*, 211–13.

by his friend John Smith—Baptist preacher, storekeeper, land speculator, United States Senator, and commissary to Wilkinson's troops in the West. Here these two were joined by Jonathan Dayton, recently a Federalist Senator from New Jersey and an old Princeton friend of Burr.[14]

The next stop was Louisville, where the traveler left his boat and took horse for Frankfort to confer with Senator Brown, an associate of Wilkinson in the earlier Spanish intrigues. After a brief visit he pushed on to Lexington, where he tarried a few days and then set out for Nashville, arriving on May 29. In this neighborhood he spent four days at Andrew Jackson's "Hermitage" and assured his host that Henry Dearborn, Secretary of War, was secretly in league with him. Then, having been supplied by Jackson with an open boat, the colonel resumed his travels and in three days reached Fort Massac on the Ohio. Here he found General Wilkinson awaiting him, and from the sixth to the tenth of June these two were in conference. Since Burr had not previously visited the West, the general wrote several letters to introduce him. John Adair, soon to represent Kentucky in the Senate, was to have met them in Cincinnati, but since that meeting did not take place, Wilkinson wrote to him: "I was to have introduced my friend Burr to you; but in this I failed by accident. He understands your merits, and reckons on you. Prepare to visit me, and I will tell you all. We must have a peep at the unknown world beyond me." A letter of introduction addressed to Daniel Clark closed with the statement, "To him I refer you for many things improper to letter, and which he will not say to any other." Another was addressed to the Marquis de Casa Calvo, and the letter to Gilbert Leonard said that Burr "will send your Idiot black guard W. C. C. C(Claiborne) to the Devil." Also, the general addressed a mysterious letter to Major Bruff at St. Louis, advising him to cease his labors at that place!

By June 10 the colonel was ready to proceed on his journey and the general furnished him with a handsome barge, manned by ten enlisted men and a sergeant. On June 17 he reached Natchez, where he was visited by Governor Robert Williams of the Mississippi Territory, and finally on the twenty-sixth he went ashore

[14] *Dictionary of American Biography,* V, 166.

at New Orleans. Taking up residence with his friend Edward Livingston, he remained there three weeks, was cordially received by Governor Claiborne, and lavishly entertained by Daniel Clark. He paid marked attention to Morales, snubbed Casa Calvo, and made contacts with the Mexican Association, an organization of local magnates who were planning to revolutionize that Spanish colony. The Catholic Bishop of New Orleans agreed to participate in Burr's enterprise and designated three Jesuit priests to aid in the revolutionizing of Mexico. Sister Thérèse de St. Xavier Farjon, Mother Superior of the Ursuline Convent, also sympathized with the plan. A month earlier the *Orleans Gazette,* edited by James M. Bradford, proclaimed that the hour had struck for dispatching an army of liberators to give the wretched subjects of despotic Spain the blessings of American republicanism.

In New Orleans the situation was still explosive. Despite his recent personal bereavement, the young and courageous, though unsophisticated, governor was struggling as best he could against the opposition of practically the entire American contingent, led by Livingston and Clark in league with Intendant Morales, who was still in the city, and Bradford, publisher of the only English language newspaper in the Creole capital. As if this were not enough, he faced another domestic tragedy when on February 12 his brother-in-law was killed in a duel as the result of a slanderous article, involving the memory of the governor's dead wife, published in Bradford's *Gazette.*

The attack on Claiborne was only a part of an all-out attempt to discredit American rule in Louisiana. Etienne Boré, the refugee from Santo Domingo who had demonstrated the practicability of sugar production in Louisiana and who had served under Laussat as mayor of New Orleans, now headed a committee to publicize the work of the delegation sent to Congress to present the petition which Livingston had drafted. On February 26 this group gave notice in the *Louisiana Gazette* that it was planning to reprint two pamphlets which Derbigny, Destréhan, and Sauvé published in Washington, one being entitled "Reflections on the Situation of the Louisianians," and the other, "Answer to the Observations of the Committee of the Senate." On March 15 the "Reflections" were published by Editor Bradford in his *Gazette*.[15] Certainly Livingston and Clark, posing as more democratic than Thomas Paine who had denounced the scheme, knew that immediate statehood for Louisiana was not justified by the circumstances and that it would not be granted by Congress. They could have had no other object than to discredit the American administration in the eyes of the Louisianians, and this was exactly what Burr desired. During his sojourn in New Orleans he was paid marked attention by Morales, Livingston, Clark, and Jones and was obviously convinced that his plans were maturing satisfactorily.

Burr left New Orleans on July 14, giving it out that he planned to return in October. After tarrying a week in Natchez, where he spent some time with Stephen Minor, the former Spanish commandant of that place, he set out on the long 450-mile journey along the Natchez Trace to Nashville. Here he again visited Jackson and then proceeded by way of Lexington and Frankfort, Louisville and Vincennes, to St. Louis, reaching Wilkinson's headquarters on September 11. He remained there until the nineteenth, and he and Wilkinson discussed their plans with various Americans, mostly civil and military officers whom they wished to interest in their schemes. Several of these men, notably Major Bruff and Timothy Kibby, later testified as to what was said in Wilkinson's and Burr's conversations, and on the basis of their evidence it is impossible to arrive at any other conclusion than that a two-pronged invasion of Mexico, with New Orleans and St. Louis as the points of departure, was being planned, along with the revolutionizing of the Western states of the Union. To this second end Wilkinson used his position as Territorial governor to stir up strife among the people of St. Louis just as did Livingston and Clark in New Orleans.[16]

When the colonel took leave of his host, their plans seemed to be maturing as well as could have been expected, but now things

[15] New Orleans *Louisiana Gazette*, November 9, 1804, January 22, February 26, March 15, June 11, 1805; Carter (ed.), *Territory of Orleans*, 182–86, 312–13, 506–13.
[16] Clarence E. Carter, "The Burr-Wilkinson Intrigue in St. Louis," in *Bulletin of the Missouri Historical Society* (St. Louis), X (1953–1954), 447–64; Wilkinson to John Brown, January 7, 1806, in John Mason Brown Manuscripts (Yale University Library, New Haven).

began to go wrong. On August 2 an article later attributed to Spanish Minister Yrujo appeared in the *United States Gazette* of Philadelphia under the heading "Querist." It asked whether Colonel Burr planned to revolutionize Louisiana and call an immediate convention of the states bordering on the Ohio and Mississippi rivers to form a separate government, taking possession of the public lands and offering them in *bounties* to entice inhabitants from the Atlantic states; and how soon, the article queried, would the forts and magazines at New Orleans and the military posts on the Mississippi be taken by Burr's party and used for the reduction of Mexico and the appropriation of her treasures, aided by British ships and forces? Two days later Anthony Merry wrote a panicky letter to Lord Mulgrave, saying that Burr or some of his agents had talked too much, "for the object of his journey has now begun to be noticed in the public prints." [17]

News of these rumors must have reached New Orleans by early September, for on the seventh of that month Daniel Clark wrote Wilkinson: "Many absurd and wild reports are circulated here, and have reached the ears of the officers of the late Spanish government, respecting our ex-Vice-President. . . . The tale is a horrid one, if well told. Kentucky, the State of Ohio, with part of Georgia and part of Carolina are to be bribed with the plunder of the Spanish countries west of us to separate from the Union." Clark suspected that Stephen Minor was responsible for the leak, but Burr later denied that he had confided in Minor, and the story could well have come from Philadelphia.

Arriving in Washington about the middle of November, Burr hastened to find out what news Merry might have from London. There was no word from Williamson and the colonel was deeply disappointed. He told the British Minister he had found the West enthusiastic about his plans and he had agreed to return there in March. So impatient were the Louisianians under American rule, he said, that they were about to send a representation of their grievances to Paris, but he had persuaded them that independence under British protection was preferable. The people of New Or-

---

[17] Henry Adams, *History of the United States of America* (New York, 1889–1891), III, 226; Isaac J. Cox, "The Western Reaction to the Burr Conspiracy," in Illinois State Historical Society *Transactions* (Springfield, 1928), 78.

leans, according to him, were so resolved to separate themselves from the Union that he was sure the revolution there would be accomplished without the shedding of a drop of blood. All that was necessary was for William Pitt to furnish him with £110,000 and a naval force consisting of two or three ships of the line and an equal number of frigates to cruise off the mouth of the Mississippi by April 10, "and to continue there until the commanding officer should receive information from him or from Mr. Daniel Clark of the country having declared itself independent." Burr gave Merry clearly to understand that the heart of the plot was centered at New Orleans and that West Florida would be included in the plan, for overtures had been made to him by "a person of greatest influence there." But not a word was said about an invasion of Mexico. This, apparently, was primarily Wilkinson's affair.

Traveling from Washington to Philadelphia, Burr sent his good friend Dayton to see Yrujo, who was no longer accredited by the Administration. Apparently having given up all hope of British aid, Dayton suggested a plan which he said could be carried out without foreign assistance. Burr was to introduce his armed followers into Washington in a clandestine manner and carry out a *coup d'état*. They were to seize the President, Vice-President, and President of the Senate, and take possession of the Federal arsenal and the money in the Bank of the United States at Georgetown. Burr hoped then to be able to establish himself in the capital city, but in case he did not succeed in this, he planned to burn all the ships at the Navy Yard except two or three, in which he would embark his followers and his treasure for New Orleans. Once there, he would proclaim the independence of Louisiana and the Western states.[18]

This was such a fantastic proposition that one would be inclined to question either Yrujo's veracity or Burr's sanity were it not for the fact that the colonel outlined a very similar plan to "General" William Eaton, the disgruntled hero of the Tripolitan War. The truth is that the former Vice-President was desperate and was grasping at straws. In November President Jefferson had told him that there would be no war with Spain, and on December 12 Burr wrote in cipher to Wilkinson: "About the last of October

[18] Adams, *History of the United States*, III, 234–35.

our cabinet was seriously disposed to warfare with the Spanish, but more recent accounts of the increasing and alarming aggression and arrogance of the British, and some courteous words from the French have banished every such intention. In case of such warfare *Lee* would have been Commander in Chief—Truth I assure you. He must you know come from Virginia." Burr then informed Wilkinson that the most that was now intended was a sort of maritime piracy such as was carried on with the French in the previous administration. Of "a certain speculation," he said, it was unnecessary to write until the whole could be communicated; that the circumstances referred to in a letter from Ohio remained in suspense, but the auspices were favorable; and "it is believed that *Wilkinson* will give audience to a delegation composed of Adair and Dayton in February. Can 25th [?] be had in your vicinity to march at some hours notice?" [19] On April 15 Burr wrote again to the general, complaining that he had not heard from him since October and saying that his project was postponed until the following December. That October letter referred to the rumors Daniel Clark had relayed from New Orleans, and now many such tales were afloat. It seems fairly obvious that the general's wariness was due to the fact that the colonel appeared to have talked too much.

This, along with the lack of foreign aid and the failure of the United States and Spain to come to blows in the Southwest, was enough to dampen the spirits of the stoutest conspirator, but by mid-April the Western skies began to brighten. Spain, as an ally of Napoleonic France, was at war with England and on October 21, 1805, Admiral Horatio Nelson destroyed the combined fleets of the Latin allies at Trafalgar. King Charles IV and his Minister, Godoy, were therefore in no position to make a strong stand as to the boundaries of Louisiana, but with Spanish pride, they planned to do so all the same. Not only were they unable to send troops across the Atlantic where Britannia ruled the waves, they could not even depend on those already on the ground. Spanish colonial officials well knew that Napoleon was ambitious to take over control of Spain's American empire, and they were quite unenthusi-

[19] [Burr to Wilkinson], December 12, 1805 (deciphered), in Wilkinson Papers (Chicago Historical Society), II, 97.

astic about such a prospect. The only sure way to avoid it would be to achieve independence, and many neglected proconsuls and their underlings were prepared to accept such a fate. Of course Wilkinson and Burr, as well as Francisco Miranda, were familiar with this situation and based their calculations upon it.

According to her interpretation of the Treaty of San Ildefonso, Spain withheld West Florida from Napoleon but granted him Texas to the Rio Grande. As claimant under France, the United States had the right to the same boundaries, but Texas did not interest Jefferson and Spain was allowed to occupy it as far east as the Sabine River. There the President decided to make a stand, but Spain had formerly established a few small posts east of that stream and she was determined to hold all she had ever claimed. Therefore, after much hesitation, the Viceroy of New Spain (Mexico), José de Iturrigaray, on April 15—the very day on which Burr wrote Wilkinson that he was suspending operations until December—ordered Nemesio de Salcedo, Captain General of the Interior Provinces, to hold the line between Adais and Natchitoches. On May 6 Jefferson ordered Wilkinson to move his headquarters from St. Louis to New Orleans and defend the line of the Sabine. Thus it seemed that, after all, there would be a war on the Texas frontier and that Burr could proceed to carry out his plans.

But the road ahead of him was not as clear as it appeared to be. On May 12 Morales wrote from Pensacola to Iturrigaray that he had received a private letter from Gilbert Leonard, who, it will be recalled, served as intermediary in the intrigue which Wilkinson was carrying on with Casa Calvo and Folch. This message— from Baton Rouge, dated April 15—stated that there was a strong party in the United States seeking to revolutionize Mexico by means of secret agents and subversive literature. Leonard asked Morales to lose no time in notifying the Viceroy and the Court and went on to say that "a certain person has assured me that the conspirators have already suborned many employees of the government, ecclesiastics, and other persons of note, and he has promised me additional information. In New Orleans they are also recruiting partisans to infiltrate the interior provinces, which should be carefully watched, since in case of war, which I consider inevitable, it would be very easy for them to penetrate, if, as they

flatter themselves, they have already made so much progress."
Leonard said he believed this report had some foundation because
of the writer's circumstances and his connections and acquaintances
with various individuals in the North. He promised to transmit
any additional information procurable from the same source.[20]

Of course Leonard may have had other well-informed correspondents north of the border, but the finger of suspicion points
inevitably toward the American general who was at that time
drawing a Spanish pension. And there are additional reasons for
believing that Wilkinson had, by this time, decided to turn against
Burr. One of these is that, instead of taking command on the
Sabine front, as he had been ordered to do, he tarried in St. Louis
until autumn. This was a clear case of insubordination, for which
he could have been, but never was, court-martialed. The shrewd
general must have had powerful reasons for taking this risk and
only one explanation suggests itself. His orders to drive the Spaniards off the soil east of the Sabine would have made war inevitable;
if engaged in hostilities on the Texas frontier he could not have
prevented Burr from taking possession of New Orleans, and now
he was apparently determined to do just this.

Leonard's warning stirred the Mexican officials to strenuous
action. The chain of command extended from Viceroy Iturrigaray
in Mexico City, to Nemesio de Salcedo, Captain General of the
Interior Provinces, with his headquarters at Chihuahua, to Manuel
Antonio Cordero, Governor of Texas, at Bexar (San Antonio).
The King had, in 1804, given orders not to surrender any territory
claimed by Spain, but Salcedo consistently strove to avoid a clash
with the Americans. With equal consistency Cordero lost no opportunity to promote hostilities and Iturrigaray opposed any concessions.[21] Considering the limited extent and small value of the

---

[20] Juan V. Morales to José de Iturrigaray, May 12, 1806, in Archivo General de la
Nación, Mexico City, Provincias Internas, *tomo* 200, pp. 142–44; Iturrigaray to
Morales, July 10, 1806, *ibid.*, 145; Iturrigaray to Salcedo, July 18, 1806, *ibid.*, 144;
Salcedo to Iturrigaray, August 5, 1806, *ibid.*, 142.

[21] Salecedo to Manuel A. Cordero, April 8, 1805; January 17, February 23, 24,
April 4, 1806, in Nacogdoches Archives (photostats, University of Texas), X, 19–20,
58–63, 74–75, 77–81, 89–94; Iturrigaray to Salcedo, April 15, 1806, in Archivo General
de la Nación, Mexico City, Provincias Internas, *tomo* 200, p. 174; Carlos E. Castañeda, *The Mission Era: The End of the Spanish Régime, 1780–1810*, Vol. V of James
P. Gibbons (ed.), *Our Catholic Heritage in Texas, 1519–1936* (Austin, 1942), 258–60.

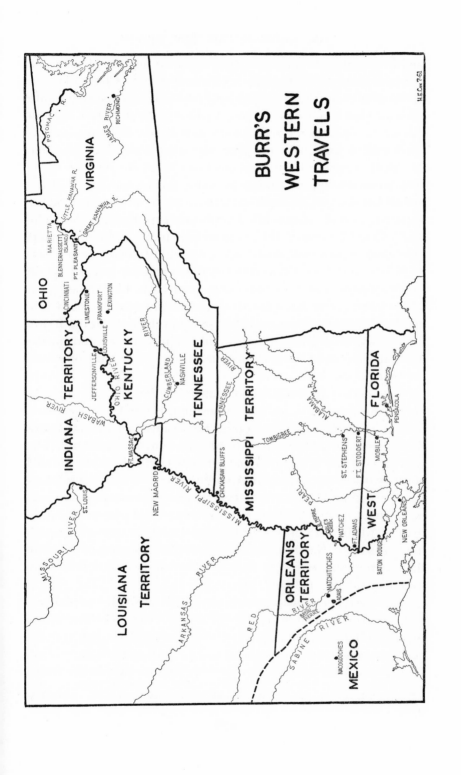

land in dispute and the inability of Spain to support Mexico in a war against the United States, the wisdom of King Charles IV and the patriotism of the Governor of Texas may well be called into question. Salcedo would appear to have been the real Spanish patriot, but Leonard's revelations played into the hands of his opponents. Accordingly, on June 12 Colonel Simón de Herrera, Governor of Nueva León, marched from Bexar for the Sabine. By June 29 he had posted his troops on the Bayou Pierre, east of the Sabine and therefore in territory claimed by the United States. Shortly thereafter an American exploring expedition under Colonel Constant Freeman, which was seeking to reach the headwaters of the Red River, was, after leaving a Caddo Indian village, overtaken near the present Texarkana by a large party under Captain Don Francisco Viana and forced to turn back. On August 5, in accordance with orders from Washington, Colonel Thomas Cushing demanded that Herrera withdraw from the post on the Bayou Pierre, which next day the Spaniard declined to do, and on the fifteenth Governor Cordero marched from Bexar with one hundred men to reinforce him.[22]

Now Colonel Cushing, who commanded the American outpost at Natchitoches, was in a difficult position. He had positive orders from the Secretary of War to push the Spanish forces back across the Sabine, but Wilkinson ordered him to avoid hostilities. The governors of the Mississippi and Orleans territories were notified of the critical situation and in August they met in Natchez to adopt a plan of action. Without hesitation they decided on offensive measures, and Colonel Cushing sent Lieutenant Thomas A. Smith to Fort Adams with orders for Colonel Jacob Kingsbury to march his garrison to Natchitoches. But Gilbert Leonard got word of these developments and notified Don Carlos de Grand Pré, Spanish commandant at Baton Rouge.

With hostilities thus threatening, Wilkinson still found it expedient to remain in St. Louis and leave to Colonel Cushing the responsibility of avoiding a clash with Colonel Herrera. But the general was not by any means idle, for on June 15 he dispatched Lieutenant Montgomery Pike on the famous expedition which

[22] Cordero to Salcedo, June 12, 29, 1806, in Nacogdoches Archives, X, 109–10, 115–20.

resulted in the discovery of Pike's Peak. This development, however, was not anticipated. In fact, the objects of the venture remain to this day shrouded in obscurity, but Wilkinson, who alone planned the enterprise, could not have done it without some compelling motive. Pike's orders were vague and Wilkinson admitted that the young officer did not himself know the object of his mission, but it was definitely planned that he should be captured and taken to Santa Fé, whence he was sent under guard to be examined by Salcedo at Chihuahua. A civilian volunteer, Dr. John Hamilton Robinson, accompanied Pike's expedition, and it was certainly he to whom Wilkinson confided his secret instructions. Though we have no information as to what they may have been, only one conclusion seems logical in the circumstances: the American general wished to notify Salcedo that he would do all in his power to avoid hostilities. But Pike's expedition was delayed in the rugged mountain terrain through which it had to pass, and the message to Salcedo arrived too late to alter the situation on the Sabine.

Burr, now encouraged by the prospect of war, was proceeding with the final implementation of his plans. New Orleans would be his principal base of operations and he thought his friends Livingston, Clark, and Bradford had so well prepared the ground that there would be no difficulty. It was there his movement would commence. Yrujo was convinced that the conspiracy would be successful and wrote to Cevallos that "Burr has opened himself to me. I consider his plans feasible with some help from us and France." [23] Accordingly, late in July the colonel sent Dr. Justus Erich Bollman down from Philadelphia to New Orleans to act as his personal representative. The doctor was well fitted for this position, for he was a German who spoke both English and French fluently, and his effort to rescue Lafayette from prison at Olmutz made him modestly famous. Bollman carried to New Orleans two letters from Burr—one, dated July 26, to Livingston, and another written three days later in cipher and addressed to General Wilkinson.

Another copy of this letter, along with others to Blennerhassett and Adair, was entrusted to two young men, Samuel Swartwout

[23] Adams, *History of the United States*, III, 247–48.

and Peter V. Ogden, son of George M. Ogden and nephew of Jonathan Dayton. This cipher letter to Wilkinson is the most significant document relating to the conspiracy, for it furnishes the most concrete evidence we have concerning Burr's plans and expectations at this time. In it he said that he had obtained funds and commenced operations. Thomas Truxton was going to Jamaica to arrange with the British admiral on that station to meet the expedition on the Mississippi, and an American naval force was ready to co-operate. Burr would start westward on August 1 and move rapidly down to the Falls of the Ohio by the middle of November, bringing the first contingent of men with him in light boats which were already being built. He expected to meet Wilkinson in Natchez by the middle of December, "there to determine whether it will be expedient in the first instance to seize on or pass by Baton Route. . . . The people of the country to which we are going are prepared to receive us; their agents, now with Burr, say that if we will protect their religion, and will not subject them to a foreign Power, that in three weeks all will be settled."

If Wilkinson were deceiving Burr as to his intentions, Burr was also trying to deceive him, for the colonel knew he would not have the support of either a British or an American naval force, and he knew that without such aid no expedition against the coast of Mexico was possible. But he did expect to revolutionize Louisiana and join Wilkinson's force in an invasion of Mexico by way of the Sabine.

During the first week in August, 1806, Burr left Philadelphia for the West, giving it out that he was never to return. He was accompanied only by Colonel Julien De Pestre, a French refugee who had served in both the French and British armies and who was now to act as "chief-of-staff," and by Charles Willie, a young German who, as Burr's personal secretary, could correspond with Dr. Bollman in his native language. This was a small retinue, but it was important that the colonel's movements should not attract undue attention.

His first business was to enlist recruits, build boats, and collect supplies in the Ohio and Cumberland valleys, and he allowed himself several months in which to make these essential preparations. Reaching Pittsburgh on August 21, he remained several days at the tavern of his friend James O'Hara and enlisted the sons of General Presley Neville, the leading Federalist of the town, and Colonel Thomas Butler, whom Wilkinson had court-martialed for refusing to crop his hair. A less distinguished but more important recruit was Comfort Tyler of Herkimer, New York. He had already been employed to do recruiting in western New York and was now engaged to deliver $40,000 worth of provisions on the Ohio during November. Also John Wilkins, a Pittsburgh merchant, agreed to deliver 20,000 barrels of flour and 5,000 barrels of pork.

While making these arrangements at Pittsburgh, Burr visited his old Princeton friend, Colonel George Morgan, who lived about fifteen miles away. During the colonial period Morgan had been deeply interested in certain land companies which secured Indian grants to huge tracts both north and south of the Ohio River. The British government failed to validate these grants, and so did the Continental Congress and the new Federal government. For years Morgan worked tirelessly to secure such validation, but his efforts were in vain, and now the prospect was hopeless. Only a separation of the West from the Union could effect a change in land policy, and Burr's purpose in visiting his old acquaintance was to suggest just such an enticing prospect. But Morgan had become reconciled to the new government and at once notified the Administration of Burr's subversive activities. This incident is significant, not only because it furnished the President with one of his earliest warnings of Burr's activities, but because it proves that the colonel was relying heavily on that numerous group of speculators, including the Yazoo men, whose claims to Western lands had been rejected by the Federal government.[24]

Leaving Pittsburgh, Burr and De Pestre journeyed by way of Marietta to Blennerhassett Island, where they arrived on August 27. From Marietta the travelers were accompanied by the son of Dudley Woodbridge, a merchant of the town with whom Blen-

---

[24] Morgan to Presley Neville, September 2, 1806 (University of Virginia Library Manuscript); Lexington *Kentucky Gazette*, quoting Frankfort *Western World*, August 5, 1806.

nerhassett had formed a business partnership. A contract was now made with the senior Woodbridge for a hundred barrels of pork, and Colonel J. Barker agreed to build fifteen boats on the Muskingum, a few miles above Marietta, and to deliver them on December 9. In addition to these commercial arrangements, Burr inspired his pliant Irish host to write a series of articles advocating the separation of the West from the Union and to publish them in the Marietta *Ohio Gazette,* beginning on September 4. Four days later Blennerhassett visited a prominent neighbor, Captain Alexander Henderson, and told him that Burr was planning to divide the Union and that the project would be carried out within nine months. Louisiana would be revolutionized; New Orleans taken; the banks and public arms and stores there seized; and if the Federal officials in Washington made trouble, they would be thrown into the Potomac.

Bidding good-by to his Irish host on August 28, Burr reached Cincinnati within a week and presented himself to his friend, Senator John Smith. At the moment, in addition to supplying Wilkinson's Western troops with provisions, Smith was building gunboats for the government and it was hinted that, if they were not promptly paid for, Burr might get them. Furthermore, Smith's two sons agreed to join the expedition. Meanwhile, the colonel and his aide having parted company at Chillicothe, De Pestre made his way to St. Louis for a visit with General Wilkinson, who later said that when the Frenchman left there in October he bore a letter from Burr to a Mr. Provenchere of Natchez assuring him that the revolution of the Western states would take place on November 15 and inviting him to take part in the affair.

From Cincinnati Burr went to Frankfort for a brief visit with Senator John Brown and then proceeded to Lexington. After several busy days there he took the road to Nashville and arrived on September 24. Riding out to the "Hermitage," he again visited General Jackson, who gave a reception for him the next evening at Talbot's Hotel in the town. Burr revealed to his host only that he was planning a campaign against Mexico, and Jackson wrote to President Jefferson and offered the services of three Tennessee militia regiments. This offer came as a complete surprise to the

President, who wrote to the Militia General requesting information as to the circumstances on which it was based. On October 27 Burr addressed Governor William Henry Harrison of Indiana Territory, sending him a copy of Jackson's order to his troops and asking him to issue a similar one.

On October 6 Burr rode back to Lexington, where he took lodgings at the tavern kept by "Judge" John Jourdan. There he was soon joined by the visionary Blennerhassett, who had accompanied Burr's daughter Theodosia and her husband Joseph Alston—said to be the wealthiest planter in the South—down from the Island. The conspirators busied themselves with preparations for their final descent of the Mississippi. While Comfort Tyler was collecting recruits and supplies in the Pittsburgh area, Davis Floyd of Jeffersonville, Indiana, was employed to carry on similar activities in central Kentucky. In addition, Burr sent Jackson $3,500 in Kentucky bank notes to pay for the construction of five large boats and for the purchase of additional supplies. The colonel was quite successful in raising money. Blennerhassett and Alston provided financial assistance, and Burr sold bills of exchange on the New York firm of Ogden and Smith amounting to $42,000. The Kentucky Insurance Company advanced $25,000.[25]

Perhaps the most significant development which took place at this time was the purchase for a down payment of only $5,000 of the Bastrop lands on the Ouachita River in eastern Louisiana. This enormous tract of about 350,000 acres was part of a grant made by Governor Carondelet to the Baron Bastrop in 1795. Subsequently it had passed through several hands, including Edward Livingston and Charles Lynch, but the terms on which the grant was originally made were never fulfilled, and it was certain that the government of the United States would never recognize the validity of Burr's claim. The colonel planned, however, to cut a road from the Mississippi to his domain—a distance of about thirty miles—and to establish a settlement there for his recruits, who would thus be well placed for reinforcing the Sabine front.

[25] William T. Barry to Dr. John Barry, January 2, 1807, in William T. Barry (typescript) Correspondence (University of Virginia Library).

All these plans were interrupted by the Federal District Attorney for Kentucky, Joseph H. Daveiss, who was a brother-in-law of Chief Justice Marshall. In connection with his legal practice, he had acquired considerable information about the earlier "Spanish Conspiracy," in which General Wilkinson; Harry Innes, now Judge of the Federal Court for the District of Kentucky; and Benjamin Sebastian, Associate Justice of the Kentucky Court of Appeals, had been key figures. When people began to talk excitedly of Burr's activities in the state, Daveiss naturally thought them a renewal of the former attempt to detach—with Spanish assistance—the West from the Union. He later decided that the Spanish connection had been abandoned and that an invasion of Mexico was planned, but the West was still to be revolutionized.

In order to avoid such a catastrophe, Daveiss twice, on November 5 and December 2, appeared before Judge Innes and brought charges against Burr. Henry Clay appeared as counsel for the accused, and since both judge and witnesses proved unco-operative, the grand jury dismissed the case. The crowds that assembled in Frankfort, thinking that Burr was interested only in fighting the hated Spaniards, were noisy in expressing their approval of the outcome of the case and the conspirators appeared to have won this round, but they also were experiencing serious difficulties. Just at this time Humphrey Marshall, former United States Senator, first cousin and brother-in-law of the Chief Justice, and Kentucky's first historian, brought charges against Judge Sebastian, alleging that he was a pensioner of the Spanish government. The legislature appointed an investigating committee which began to take evidence on November 27. Judge Innes was called on to testify, and though he did his best to exculpate his friend, he could not deny the facts. Sebastian at once resigned his seat on the bench, but the investigation continued and the House, by a unanimous vote, found him guilty.

Burr and John Adair remained in Frankfort a few days after the trial and then hurried to Nashville for another visit with General Jackson. Reaching their destination on December 13, they called at the "Hermitage," but this time the general was not at home and Rachel was distinctly cool. Alarming reports had been circulating in Tennessee as well as in Kentucky and neither the boats nor the recruits which Jackson and his friends had agreed to furnish were ready. The colonel wasted a week in a feverish effort to remedy the situation, but to no avail. Then, on December 20 he dispatched a message to Blennerhassett that he would meet him at the mouth of the Cumberland River on the twenty-eighth, and two days later he was on his way with two partially loaded flatboats, a few men, and some horses.[26]

The state of General Jackson's mind at this time is revealed by a letter which, on November 12, he wrote to General Daniel Smith stating that he believed certain parties, in concert with Spain, planned to seize New Orleans and Louisiana and attempt to divide the Union. "That some such plan is on foot, I have no doubt, and from a conversation with an entire stranger who came introduced to me by letter . . . it flashed upon my mind that plans had been named of settling new countries, of Punishing the Dons, and adding Mexico to the united states . . . were only mere coverings to the real designs." These expressions did not "amount to absolute proof, still sir the[y] are strong anough to make me believe that a plan is in operation inimical to the united states, that the Marq[u]is de *Yrujo,* is in the plan (if it does exist,) and that the army of the united states, as is hinted is to cooperate." [27]

Of course the Administration had not remained ignorant of what was going on in the West. Ever since December 1, 1805, Jefferson had been receiving messages warning him of Burr's designs, but the most persistent informant was the Kentucky District Attorney, Joseph Daveiss. His first communication was sent on January 10, 1806, and on August 10 Commodore Thomas Truxton sent the President a detailed plan for counteracting Burr's plot, but these warnings produced no effect. It was not until news came that Burr was actually in the West making preparations for his expedition that Jefferson became apprehensive, and even then he did not think he could make any direct move

---

[26] Andrew Jackson to "Dear General," January 1, 1807 (Huntington Library Manuscript).

[27] Jackson to Daniel Smith, November 12, 1806, in Bassett (ed.), *Correspondence of Andrew Jackson,* I, 153–54.

against the colonel until some illegal act should lay him liable to arrest.

The President later stated that his first definite information came in a letter, received on September 15, in which Colonel George Morgan gave an account of Burr's visit on August 22. But at about the time of this visit, John H. Nicholson of Herkimer, New York, wrote to Jefferson detailing the activities of his fellow townsman, Comfort Tyler. Jefferson asked for additional information, and on October 14 Nicholson supplied it.[28] The President was stirred to action, however, by a letter written two days later by Postmaster General Granger, in which he relayed information furnished by "General" William Eaton about Burr's conversations with him. On October 22 and 24 Cabinet meetings were accordingly held, and at the second conclave it was decided to dispatch Captains Edward Preble and Stephen Decatur to New Orleans to take command of the naval force there, which was to be strengthened if possible. Colonel Constant Freeman, who then commanded the garrison at New Orleans, and the governors of Orleans and Mississippi territories were to be notified by regular post to be on their guard. John Graham, the Secretary of Orleans Territory who happened to be in Washington at the time, was to be sent through Kentucky on Burr's trail, "with discretionary powers to consult confidentially with the Governors and to arrest Burr if he made himself liable." Graham was then to replace Wilkinson as governor of Louisiana Territory, and Dr. Joseph E. Browne, Burr's brother-in-law, was to be removed from his position as Territorial secretary, but other questions regarding the general were postponed until after Preble's departure.

Another meeting of the Cabinet was held next day, October 25, and as the previous day's mail brought no news of Burr's movements, "We therefore rescind the determination to send Preble, Decatur, the Argus or the gunboats, and instead of them to send off the marines which are here to reinforce, or take the place of the garrison at New Orleans, with a view to Spanish operations." Thus the only move which was taken against Burr was to send Graham on his track, and in spite of strong ground

[28] John Nicholson to Jefferson, October 14, 1806 (Huntington Library Manuscript).

for suspicion, General Wilkinson was left in command of the threatened frontier.[29]

Truly amazing is the fact that the failure of one day's mail to bring additional information could have resulted in this apparently reckless commitment of the safety of the whole American West to an officer who was so generally distrusted as Wilkinson. Jefferson's complacency is difficult to understand, but the wily general must have had special pleaders in high places. His closest friend in the Administration was Secretary of War Dearborn, who never failed to validate Wilkinson's most outrageous requisitions. But the Secretary was either gullible or remarkably shrewd, for there is nothing in the record to indicate that he was disloyal.[30]

Strangely enough, the very feeble action of the Cabinet in sending Graham to follow Burr and use his own discretion as to countermeasures proved to be the crucial move. Losing no time in carrying out his assignment, Graham talked with Presley Neville in Pittsburgh and reached Marietta about the middle of November. Here he was visited by Blennerhassett who, having been led to believe that Graham was a Burrite, turned out to be a valuable source of information. He said he thought the Western states would benefit by withdrawing from the Union and that Burr agreed with him, but by means of the "Querist" articles they had found that the people were not ripe for it though they thought it would come in time. Graham decided that the immediate object of the expedition, which Blennerhassett estimated at not less than 2,000 men, was an attack on New Orleans. This view was confirmed by conversations with Alexander Henderson, a neighbor with whom Blennerhassett had discussed Burr's plans.

Having obtained this information, Graham hastened to Chillicothe, where he presented himself and his evidence to Governor Edward Tiffin on December 1. The next day the governor sent a message to the legislature saying Graham had informed him that Blennerhassett had proposed to two gentlemen of great

[29] Irving Brant, *James Madison, Secretary of State, 1800–1809* (Indianapolis, 1953), 345.

[30] Wilkinson to Dearborn, June 23, 1808 (University of Virginia Library Manuscript); Adams, "Jefferson's Military Policy, with Special Reference to the Frontier," 41–119.

respectability that they join him in an enterprise conceived by Burr, the object of which was to seize New Orleans and take possession of more than $2,000,000 deposited in the bank and the treasury there, also to capture the military stores of the United States and a fine park of brass cannon belonging to the French government. This accomplished, a new government would be erected under the protection of a European power, and the rest of the Western country would then be induced or forced to throw in its lot with the government established at New Orleans, and which would control the navigation of the Mississippi River. The governor understood that a force of 1,300 men had been collected on the Ohio and that this was considered adequate to commence operations because of the disaffection of the people of Orleans Territory and because Wilkinson would have the American army concentrated on the Sabine to fight the Spanish forces there. He had also been told that a foreign gentleman was prepared to furnish Burr with ample funds for carrying out his projects.[31]

Determined to meet this crisis, Governor Tiffin at once dispatched units of the militia to Cincinnati with orders to mount one or two cannon and to stop the three hundred men whom Blennerhassett and Tyler were expected to bring with them. Another detail was sent to Marietta to take possession of Blennerhassett's boats and arrest any conspirators who might show themselves in that area. On December 9 this party accomplished its mission, intercepting ten boats which had already been launched and were headed down the river, while the rest were seized at the boatyard.

Dudley Woodbridge saw the troops leave the town and was certain of their objective. Setting out immediately for the Island to give the alarm, he met Blennerhassett, Comfort Tyler, and a group of young men who were on their way to take possession of the boats, which were due to be delivered that day. Woodbridge persuaded his friends to return immediately to the Island. Tyler, having set out from Beaver, Pennsylvania, early in December with about thirty young men, reached the Island on the seventh

[31] General Assembly of Ohio Journal, December 2, 1806 (University of Virginia Library Transcript).

and, since then, had been making preparations for an early descent of the river. Now that Blennerhassett's boats were seized and it was expected that guards would be placed at strategic points on the Ohio, it was decided to get away that night in Tyler's four boats.

The fugitives rowed all night and stopped only at daybreak, when they beached their boats and went ashore. Here Blennerhassett addressed the men, saying that Governor Tiffin had issued warrants for the arrest of himself and Tyler and that they must hurry down to the Falls. Without stopping again, they passed Cincinnati on the night of the fourteenth without challenge, and on the sixteenth they joined the boats of Davis Floyd at Jeffersonville. Blennerhassett had outrun John Graham and no official warning as to the purpose of the expedition had reached the vicinity of Louisville. Thus, before the day was over, all the boats passed over the rapids and headed for their rendezvous with Burr.

Just what the Administration knew of Burr's and Blennerhassett's movements at this time is revealed by a letter which the President wrote to Governor Claiborne on December 20 but decided not to send. A meeting of the Cabinet was held on the previous day and it appears that it was aware of the measures taken by Governor Tiffin on the second. The President now stated that Burr's object was to take possession of New Orleans and use that city as a base from which to attack Mexico. He also understood that Comfort Tyler planned to set out from Beaver, Pennsylvania, on the first or second day of December and that recruits would be collected as the expedition passed down the Ohio. But Jefferson did not know the strength of the forces which Burr was assembling nor whether the opposition which had been provided at Marietta, Cincinnati, Louisville, and Massac would be sufficient to stop them. Consequently, he stated that "it is therefore possible that he [Burr] may escape, & then his great rendezvous is to be at Natchez." [32]

At the Cabinet meeting it was decided to send new orders to the governors of Orleans and Mississippi territories warning

[32] Adams, "Jefferson's Military Policy, with Special Reference to the Frontier," 24, quoting Jefferson to Claiborne, December 20, 1806.

them of the imminent danger. Therefore on the twentieth Dearborn wrote to Governor Williams that, although measures had been taken for arresting the progress of the Burr expedition, it was "not improbable but a considerable part of their force together with larg[e] quantities of provisions and Military Stores, may elude the precaution taken for preventing their passage, and you may hourly expect their arrival at Natchez, which is understood to be intended as a general rendezvous."[33] On the same day Dearborn wrote to Governor Claiborne that he could soon "expect a visit from Col. Burr and his associates."[34] Simultaneously Secretary Robert Smith of the Navy informed Captain John Shaw, in command of the naval force in the vicinity of New Orleans, that a military expedition formed on the "Western waters" by Colonel Burr would soon descend the Mississippi and would probably be near New Orleans by the time Shaw received his letter. The young captain was instructed to aid the army and militia in suppressing Burr's enterprise by every means in his power and to station his boats in the best possible positions to intercept—and destroy if necessary—the vessels coming down the river under command of Burr.[35]

Two days later Smith informed the President: "It is probable that neither the army nor the Naval force will be able to reach N. Orleans in time to prevent the apprehended mischief; but they may be necessary to regain what may have been lost."[36] The President agreed with Secretary Smith and on December 23 wrote him that his plans were "to lay the whole matter before Congress, ask an immediate appropriation for a naval equipment, and at the same time order 20,000 militia [or volunteers] from the Western states to proceed down the river to retake N.O. [New Orleans] presuming our naval equipment would be there before them."[37]

---

[33] *Ibid.*, 24–25.     [34] *Ibid.*, 25.

[35] *Ibid.*, 26, quoting Robert Smith to John Shaw, December 20, 1806, in Letters to Officers, Ships of War, 1805–1807 (Navy Department, National Archives, Washington), VII, 274–75.

[36] Adams, "Jefferson's Military Policy, with Special Reference to the Frontier," 27–28.

[37] *Ibid.*, 29, quoting Jefferson to Robert Smith, December 23, 1806, in Jefferson Papers.

In the meantime, Blennerhassett's party proceeded down the Ohio to Shawneetown, Illinois, just below the mouth of the Wabash. Here the flotilla tarried for four or five days awaiting a message from Burr. Finally, Stockly Hays came with a message that the colonel would meet them at the mouth of the Cumberland. The flotilla now moved forward and on December 26 beached on an island opposite the mouth of the river. From there Blennerhassett wrote to his wife, who, with her two sons, had been left behind at the Island, urging her to join him at the home of Judge Peter Bryan Bruin on Bayou Pierre, about thirty miles above Natchez.

The next day Burr arrived with his two boats, and the expedition now consisted of ten craft and between sixty and a hundred men. Pushing off as soon as possible, it reached Fort Massac on the twenty-ninth. Next morning the commanding officer, Captain Daniel Bissell, came down to the boats to visit Burr and invite him to his quarters at the post. There the colonel informed his host that he had heard, presumably in Nashville, that Wilkinson had made a truce with the Spaniards on the Sabine and had occupied New Orleans. This was indeed startling news, for Wilkinson's army was supposed to have its attention concentrated on an invasion of Texas while Burr revolutionized Louisiana and Mexico. Even without this blow, the seizure of Blennerhassett's boats and the dwindling of his force to no more than one hundred men would have been enough to discourage most men, but not Colonel Burr. Even now he did not suspect Wilkinson of treachery and assumed that his action was in response to instructions from the Administration in Washington. He still counted on the general for all possible co-operation, and Bissell's helpful attitude encouraged such a view of the situation.

From Fort Massac the boats were borne downstream toward their fateful rendezvous. Stopping only at New Madrid, a primitive village they reached on New Year's Day, 1807, and the fort at Chickasaw Bluffs, Burr's small flotilla arrived at Bayou Pierre on January 10. Here the colonel's old acquaintance Judge Bruin lived, and here Burr planned to tarry several days while preparing for his next move. But he reckoned without his host. The judge showed him a copy of the *Mississippi Messenger*, a newspaper published in Natchez, dated January 6, which contained the information that Wilkinson had betrayed him, that the President had issued a proclamation condemning the expedition, and that the acting governor of the Territory had ordered his arrest. These heavy blows apparently were wholly unexpected.

Thus, in the vast forest that crowded the banks of the Lower Mississippi, the Conspiracy ran aground. To escape the clutches of the faithless Wilkinson, Burr surrendered to Cowles Mead, acting governor of Mississippi Territory. Wilkinson, nevertheless, sent an armed force to kidnap him and finally, to escape such a fate, Burr fled with a single companion toward the Spanish post at Pensacola.[38] But fate had turned against the brilliant, dapper, and plausible New Yorker.

At about eleven o'clock on the night of February 18 two strangers rode into the village of Wakefield on the Tombigbee River, county seat of Washington County, Mississippi Territory. The moon was shining brightly, but it had been raining hard and the streams were swollen. One of the men rode some thirty or forty paces in front of the other on "a small tackey of a horse"; his old saddle was covered with a bearskin, and he was disguised as a river boatman. A tattered blanket coat covered a homespun garb, a tin cup was tied over one shoulder, a butcher's knife was stuck in his belt, and a dilapidated white hat flopped over his face and partially hid it. As the wayfarers approached the only lighted cabin, Nicholas Perkins, registrar of the local land office, was standing in the doorway. The first rider passed without looking up, but the second stopped and asked the way to the cabin of Major John Hinson, whom Burr had met in Natchez and with whom he planned to spend a week. Perkins explained that swollen streams might make it impossible to reach the Hinson house and added that the major was away from home. Nevertheless, the strangers rode on in the direction indicated.

It seemed unlikely to Perkins that honest men would be prowling the woods at this hour of the night, and then an electrifying thought came to him: Could one of the men be the famous Aaron

---

[38] Lieutenant George Peter, Lieutenant C. Mulford, and Dr. Davidson's Report, New Orleans, February 16, 1807, in Wilkinson Papers (Chicago Historical Society), III, 21a. See also Abernethy, *Burr Conspiracy*, 218–19.

Burr, whom Governor Williams had, in a recent proclamation, declared to be a fugitive from justice? Acting on this hunch, Perkins notified Lieutenant Edmund Pendleton Gaines, the commandant at Fort Stoddert, and early the next morning Burr was arrested as he made his way along the road from the Hinson house toward Pensacola. Until March 5 the former Vice-President remained a prisoner at the fort, but on that day he was turned over to Major Nicholas Perkins and a guard of eight picked men who conducted him through the Creek country and then through Georgia and the Carolinas to Richmond.

After a journey of exactly three weeks, the little cavalcade passed down Main Street and put up at the Eagle Tavern, the principal hostelry in the Virginia capital, then a small city of about 6,000 inhabitants. Chief Justice Marshall presently came down to examine the prisoner, and later a grand jury held him to stand trial on a charge of treason before the United States Circuit Court, which, with Marshall presiding, convened in the hall of the House of Delegates in the capitol building which Jefferson had designed and which still serves its original purpose. While proceedings were being held up because of the failure of Wilkinson to put in an appearance, Burr arose in court on June 9 and successfully demanded the issuance of a subpoena *duces tecum,* requiring the President of the United States to appear in court and there produce certain papers. The assertion of judicial supremacy has never gone further than this, but the President, for once, won a victory over his Federalist cousin by declining to obey the summons and asserting his right to withhold confidential correspondence.

Finally, on Monday, June 15, General Wilkinson, portly, red-faced, and decked out in resplendent uniform, strode into court and, according to Washington Irving, who as a young reporter was present, "stood for a moment swelling like a turkey cock." Then, having been sworn, the general was taken before the grand jury to present his evidence against Burr. Seeing that he was wearing his sword, John Randolph, the foreman, ordered the marshal to "take that man out and disarm him. I will allow no attempt to intimidate the Jury." After this reception Wilkinson was kept on the carpet for four days and was forced to admit that he had garbled his translation of Burr's cipher letter of July 26. A motion was then made to indict the general for misprision of treason, but because of a technicality, it failed by the narrow margin of seven to nine votes. This so disgusted Randolph that he wrote: "The mammoth of iniquity escaped,—not that any man pretended to think him innocent, but upon certain wire-drawn distinctions. . . . Wilkinson is the only man that I ever saw who was from the bark to the very core a villain."

That the President entertained a different opinion is made clear by a letter which he wrote to Wilkinson on September 20. Here he averred that "the scenes which have been acted in Richmond are such as have never before been exhibited in any country where all regard to public character has not yet been thrown off. They are equivalent to a proclamation of impunity to every traitorous combination which may be formed to destroy the Union; . . . However, they will produce an amendment to the Constitution which, keeping the judges independent of the Executive, will not leave them so, of the nation." Early in September Jefferson wrote to George Hay, instructing him to see that not a single witness be paid or permitted to depart from Richmond until his testimony had been put in writing, either as delivered in court, or as taken down by Hay himself in the presence of any of Burr's counsel. "These whole proceedings will be laid before Congress," wrote the President, "that they may decide, whether the defect has been in the evidence of guilt, or in the law, or in the application of the law, and that they may provide the proper remedy for the past and the future." [39]

That the estimate of Randolph rather than that of Jefferson was the correct one is demonstrated by a letter which Hay now wrote to the President. Having pledged himself before the court to show the falsity of the charges which had been brought against Wilkinson, the District Attorney ended by admitting their truth: "The declaration which I made in court in his favor some time ago was precipitate; and though I have not retracted it, everybody sees that I have not attempted the task which I in fact

[39] Jefferson to General Wilkinson, September 7, 1807, in Lipscomb and Bergh (eds.), *Writings of Thomas Jefferson*, XI, 375; Jefferson to George Hay, September 4, 1807, *ibid.*, 360–61.

promised to perform. My confidence in him [Wilkinson] is shaken, if not destroyed. I am sorry for it, on his account, and because you have expressed opinions in his favor; but you did not know then what you will soon know, and what I did not learn until after . . . long after—my declaration above mentioned." Inexplicably, Jefferson never admitted a doubt as to Wilkinson's veracity.[40]

At last, on August 3, the trial of Aaron Burr for treason got under way as the oppressive heat of late summer settled over Richmond. It took nearly two weeks to select a jury, of which Edward Carrington, Marshall's brother-in-law, was made foreman. The prosecution called 140 witnesses to support its case, but the jurisdiction of the court was limited to Virginia, and therefore only the events which actually took place on Blennerhassett Island could be considered. George Hay, United States District Attorney for Virginia, and his colleagues knew that Burr was not there when Comfort Tyler's men joined Blennerhassett; they based their case on Marshall's recent opinion in the Bollman and Swartwout case, in which they understood him to have said that an armed force which was assembled for a treasonable purpose was guilty of an act of treason and that anyone who helped to bring about such an assemblage, whether or not he was present in person, was a party to the crime. But Hay, a son-in-law of James Monroe, was by no means certain of success. Even while the jury was being selected he wrote to Jefferson: "There is but one chance for the accused, and this is a good one because it rests with the Chief Justice. It is already hinted, but not by himself [that] the decision of the Supreme Court [in the Bollman and Swartwout case] will no[t be] deemed binding. If the assembly of men on [Blennerhassett is] land, can be pronounced 'not an overt act' [it will] be so pronounced." [41]

Hay's prediction proved to be correct. In a decision which Albert J. Beveridge declared to be "one of the longest ever rendered by him, and the only one in which an extensive examination of authorities is made," also one in which "a greater number of decisions, treatises, and histories are referred to than in all the rest

[40] Adams, *History of the United States*, III, 471.
[41] Beveridge, *John Marshall*, III, 483.

of Marshall's foremost Constitutional opinions," the Chief Justice held that the principles apparently set forth in his Bollman and Swartwout ruling did not apply in this case.[42] After that, the jury had no alternative but to bring in a verdict to the effect that "Aaron Burr is not proved to be guilty under this indictment by any evidence submitted to us. We therefore find him not guilty." Marshall permitted this equivocal verdict to stand but had the entry "not guilty" made for the record.[43] Thus ended the trial of Aaron Burr for treason, and though the case was not decided on its merits, it hardly appears that the assembling of thirty indifferently armed men on Blennerhassett Island could have amounted to levying war against the United States. On the other hand, it does not seen reasonable to doubt that Burr intended to bring about a separation of the Western states from the Union, and it is hard to believe that, after he passed Fort Massac, anyone but Wilkinson could have stopped him. His treasonable plot was thwarted before he had opportunity to commit an overt act of treason.

[42] *Ibid.*, 504.

[43] James Alston Cabell, *The Trial of Aaron Burr* (A paper read before the New York State Bar Association, January 7, 1900), reprinted from the *Proceedings of the Association* (Albany, 1900), 29.

# CHAPTER XII

# JEFFERSON AND THE SOUTH

THOMAS JEFFERSON has always been and always will be a controversial figure because of the differences of opinion among those who undertake to assess his personality and his work. Only those who knew him personally could speak with authority, and they, too, had their prejudices. Perhaps one of the most unbiased descriptions of the Master of Monticello is that given by Isaac, one of the young slaves on the place, who in the 1840's dictated his reminiscences to Charles Campbell, the Virginia historian. According to Isaac, "Mr. Jefferson was a tall strait-bodied man as ever you see, right square-shouldered; nary a man in this town walked so straight as my old master; neat a built man as ever was seen in Virginny, I reckon or any place—a straight-up-man: long face, high nose.[1] . . . was never seen to come out before breakfast—about 8 o'clock. If it was warm weather he wouldn't ride out till evening; studied upstairs till bell ring for dinner. . . . Old master had abundance of books: sometimes would have twenty of 'em down on the floor at once; read fust one then tother. Isaac has often wondered how old master came to have such a mighty head, read so many of them books: & when they go to him to ax him anything, he go right straight to the book & tell you all about it. He talked French & Italian.[2] . . . Mr. Jefferson had a clock in his kitchen at Monticello; never went into the kitchen except to wind up the clock. He never would have less than eight covers at dinner—if nobody at table but himself: had from eight to

[1] Isaac, one of Jefferson's slaves, as dictated to Charles Campbell in the 1840's, *Memoirs of a Monticello Slave* (Charlottesville, 1951), 21.
[2] *Ibid.*, 22.

thirty-two covers for dinner; planty of wine, best old Antigua rum & cider: very fond of wine & water. Isaac never heard of his being disguised in drink. He kept three fiddles; played in the afternoons & sometimes arter supper. This was in his early time: When he begin to git so old he didn't play: . . . Mr. Jefferson always singing when riding or walkin: hardly see him anywhar out doors but that he was a-singin: had a fine clear voice, sung minnits [minuets] & such: fiddled in the parlor. Old master very kind to servants." [3]

The President was seen from a very different angle by William Plumer, Federalist Senator from New Hampshire, who was not likely to be overindulgent in his estimate of the Republican Chief Executive. On November 10, 1804, he wrote in his journal: "Went in company with several of my friends, to pay a ceremonious visit to the President of the United States. Some of the Federalists think we ought not to visit him, because he acts more as the head of a faction, than that of the nation. I shall visit him, & of course intend, when invited, to dine with him. He is President, & we must acknowledge him such. These are visits & dinners of ceremony. Besides, I have a curiosity, which is gratified, by seeing & conversing with him. I gain a more thorough knowledge of his character, & of his views, & those of his party—for he is naturally communicative.

"I found the President dressed better than I ever saw him at any time when I called on a morning visit. Though his coat was old & thread bare, his scarlet vest, his corduroy small clothes, & his white cotton hose, were new & clean—but his linnen was much soiled, & his slippers old—His hair was cropt & powdered." [4]

By the middle of March, 1806, the crusty, but intellectually honest, New Englander had softened in his attitude toward the President, for then he wrote: "The more critically & impartially I examine the character & conduct of Mr. Jefferson, the more favorably I think of his integrity. I am really inclined to think I have done him injustice in not allowing him more credit for the integrity of heart that he possesses. . . . My object is truth—I write for myself—I wish not—I am determined not—to set down ought in malice, or to diminish anything from the fact." [5]

[3] *Ibid.*, 23.       [4] Brown (ed.), *William Plumer's Memorandum*, 193.
[5] *Ibid.*, 453–54.

These two descriptions are interesting because they present the impressions of men who knew Mr. Jefferson in the flesh. To the myriads of his contemporaries who did not know him personally he was the living symbol of a party and a cause, and he was all good or all evil according to the political faith of the commentator. Naturally, most Southern leaders, representing the self-sufficient small farmers as well as the owners of tobacco, sugar, and cotton plantations, were overjoyed at the election of one so well qualified to speak for them. "In no part of the Union," said the *Kentucky Gazette* on January 26, 1801, "has the success of the late Presidential election inspired more real and universal joy than in the State of Kentucky." Animated by this glorious event and the prospect of peace in Europe, the citizens of Lexington held a meeting and decided unanimously to invite their friends throughout the state to a Grand Festival at the factory of Messrs. Bastrop and Nancarrow on the twenty-second. The appointed day turned out to be clear and favorable and at one o'clock the ringing of bells and beating of drums summoned the guests to a repast. Although the notice had been short, sixty ladies and more than five hundred gentlemen attended, and, having chosen the venerable Colonel Thomas Hart to preside, the company drank toasts "to the new administration." [6] Similar meetings were held throughout the Southern states, and great was the exultation of the Republicans on their accession to the seats of power.

At noon on March 4, 1801, Thomas Jefferson left his boardinghouse and walked to the unfinished capitol in the bleak and half-cleared fields that were to become the city of Washington. Knowing that his election had been a close one, he was not in an exultant mood, and his inaugural address was brief and conciliatory. His oft-quoted statement that "we are all Republicans, we are all Federalists" has been misinterpreted, for the key words should not have been capitalized. He referred here to principles, not to parties; but his comments on the doctrine of equality and on the subject of religion can hardly be misconstrued. Concerning them he said: ". . . entertaining a due sense of our equal right to the use of our own faculties, to the acquisitions of our own industry, to honor and confidence from our fellow-citizens, resulting not from birth, but from our actions and their sense of

[6] Lexington *Kentucky Gazette*, January 26, 1801.

them; enlightened by a benign religion, professed, indeed, and
practiced in various forms, yet all of them inculcating honesty,
truth, temperance, gratitude, and the love of man; acknowledging and adoring an overruling Providence, which by all its dis-
pensations proves that it delights in the happiness of man here
and his greater happiness hereafter—with all these blessings,
what more is necessary to make us a happy and prosperous people? Still one thing more, fellow-citizens—a wise and frugal

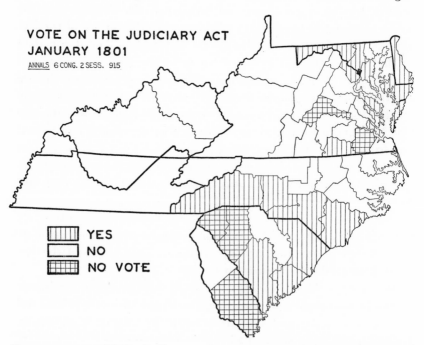

VOTE ON THE JUDICIARY ACT
JANUARY 1801
ANNALS 6 CONG. 2 SESS. 915

YES
NO
NO VOTE

Government, which shall restrain men from injuring one another, shall leave them otherwise free to regulate their own pursuits of industry and improvement, and shall not take from the
mouth of labor the bread it has earned. This is the sum of good
government, and this is necessary to close the circle of our felic-
ities." [7]

This is not the place for even a brief survey of the Jefferson
administration, but the reaction of the Southern states to the repeal of the Judiciary Act, which has been considered as second

[7] Richardson (ed.), *Messages and Papers of the Presidents,* I, 310–11.

in importance only to the Louisiana Purchase among the events of the first Republican administration, furnishes a key to the political alignments of the region south of Pennsylvania. The Judiciary Act of 1789 provided a set of district courts, and between them and the Supreme Court a series of circuit courts which were to be held by the justices of the Supreme Court, sitting with the district judges. This arrangement required extensive horseback and stagecoach travel by the aging members of

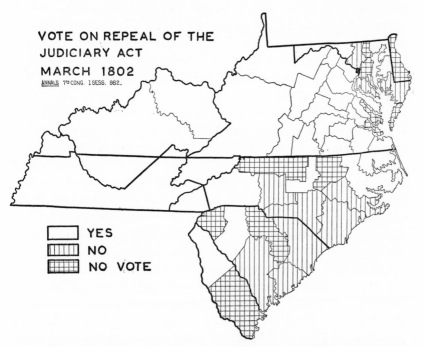

VOTE ON REPEAL OF THE
JUDICIARY ACT
MARCH 1802
ANNALS 7ᵀᴴ CONG. 1 SESS. 982.

☐ YES
▥ NO
▦ NO VOTE

the highest court in the land, but relief was provided by a bill enacted during the closing days of the Adams administration. According to its terms, sixteen new judges were appointed to preside over the circuit courts, and provision was also made for the appointment of various subordinate judicial officials. President Adams hastened to make these new appointments and thus used the last days of his administration to provide for a number of worthy Federalists.[8]

When the Republicans seized the reins of power, they felt that

[8] Channing, *History of the United States*, IV, 275–79.

they had been undercut by the grasping Federalists and were determined to rectify the situation. Accordingly, in March, 1802, they repealed the Judiciary Act and thus dispossessed the Adams appointees. This was a party measure if there ever was one, and the vote on it in the House of Representatives gives us a clear idea of the centers of Federalist strength in the Southern states. In January, 1801, the Baltimore area stood alone in Maryland as opposed to the Judiciary Act. In March, 1802, it favored repeal, but now it was joined by the Representative from western Maryland. The Virginia Representatives from the counties bordering the Chesapeake, with the exception of the one representing the Norfolk district, voted for the original act, but not a single Virginian voted against the repeal.

The alignment in North Carolina is significant because it represents a change in political sentiment. It is, in general, true that those who in 1788 voted for the adoption of the Federal Constitution now voted for the Federalists and a strong central government, but northwestern Virginia and northeastern North Carolina had now changed sides. The former area, while needing Federal aid for the improvement of transportation on the upper Ohio and Shenandoah rivers, carried on a self-sustaining economy, and was thus democratic by nature. The Albemarle-Pamlico Sound region of North Carolina apparently hoped to get assistance from the new Federal government in carrying on its trade with the West Indian islands and the Northern ports, but since its tobacco and naval stores were commonly carried overland to Petersburg or Norfolk, and Virginia welcomed this trade, there was no need for Federal support, and Jeffersonian principles now predominated. The southeastern counties, however, which divided their allegiance in 1788, now followed the lead of coastal South Carolina and voted the Federalist ticket. The Chesapeake counties of Virginia which voted for the Judiciary Act in 1801 voted with the rest of the state for its repeal in 1802. Though Georgia voted solidly for the Constitution in 1788, she followed a consistently anti-Federalist line thereafter, casting her vote against the Judiciary Act in 1801 and for its repeal in 1802. In 1801 and 1802 Kentucky and Tennessee voted the same way. These ballots indicate an extensive political realignment in the

Southern states between the adoption of the Constitution and the passage of the Judiciary Act in 1801, but they also indicate that, except in Virginia and western Maryland, there was little change in the geographical distribution of party strength as a result of the election of 1800. And in these latter cases the people appear to have been asserting themselves against the financial interests. The old alignment according to which the areas growing tobacco for the foreign market voted against a strong central government, while those which produced rice and wheat for the West Indian trade or carried on commerce across state lines were for it, was breaking down, but it still influenced the situation in Maryland and the Carolinas.[9]

In March, 1802, Congress abolished the excise taxes which, under Hamilton's influence, had been levied on distilleries and domestic distilled spirits, also on refined sugar, licenses to retailers, sales at auction, carriages for the conveyance of persons, stamped vellum, parchment, and paper. The people of Kentucky "felt indignation on the passage of the laws levying these duties—they experienced the baneful effects of their operation—particularly the excise and stamp laws"—and they rejoiced in their repeal.[10]

The Southern vote on the repeal of the Hamilton excise taxes is significant, for only the Congressmen from the Charleston district in South Carolina, the Wilmington district in North Carolina, the three districts which flanked the entrance to the Chesapeake Bay in Virginia voted with the Federalists to retain them, while all the members from Georgia, Tennessee, Kentucky, and Maryland voted for repeal.[11]

The Federalists now complained that the repeal of the internal taxes, while leaving the import duties in operation, resulted in the protection of local manufactures and thus injured the shipping interests of the Northern states. But the handicraft artisans had an entirely different point of view. Since the tariff on raw materials was practically the same as that on finished products, most craftsmen actually received little protection, and they peti-

[9] Map illustrating vote on adoption of the Constitution, in Libby, *Geographical Distribution of the Vote . . . on the Federal Constitution;* Hutton, "Southern Nationalism," charts 7, 10.

[10] Lexington *Kentucky Gazette,* July 2, 1802.

[11] Hutton, "Southern Nationalism," chart 9.

tioned Congress for relief.[12] Most of these petitions came from New York, New Jersey, Pennsylvania, and Maryland, and early in 1803 a committee of the House instructed the Secretary of the Treasury to report a plan for a system of protective tariffs.[13] President Jefferson, in his second annual message, gave his approval to such a plan, and on January 25, 1804, the committee reported resolutions favoring an increase in duties on certain

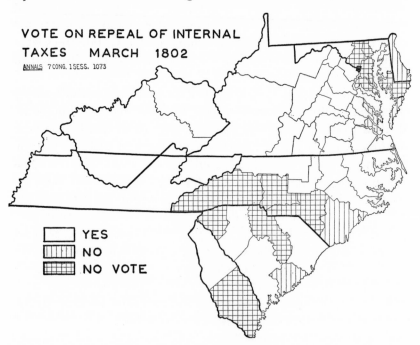

VOTE ON REPEAL OF INTERNAL
TAXES    MARCH    1802
ANNALS 7 CONG. 1 SESS. 1073

☐ YES
▥ NO
▦ NO VOTE

articles for the sake of protection.[14] Nothing decisive was done then, but it is interesting to find President Jefferson siding with the middle states in favor of protection, while the New Englanders, interested primarily in foreign trade, opposed it. This alignment was, of course, temporary.

At this time manufacturing was carried on principally by handicraftsmen who operated small shops and were by no means

[12] Richmond *Enquirer*, July 7, 1804.

[13] John P. Foley (ed.), *The Jeffersonian Cyclopedia, A Comprehensive Collection of the Views of Thomas Jefferson* (New York, 1900), 730.

[14] *American State Papers, Finance*, II, 29–36.

capitalists in the modern sense of the word. They, along with the small farmers in all sections of the country, made up the rank and file of the Jeffersonian Republican Party. The situation was entirely changed when the War of 1812 resulted in the introduction of machine manufactures on a considerable scale and thus gradually weaned capital away from its former preoccupation with foreign trade and brought it to the support of protective tariffs for the benefit of domestic manufactures. Since this policy worked to the disadvantage of the Southern states, Jefferson went back to his former advocacy of international free trade.

As already indicated, Federalist influence was rapidly waning in the South as the election of 1804 approached. In 1802 James Turner, a Jeffersonian Republican from Warren County, North Carolina, and a devotee, like Virginians, of horse racing and cockfighting, was elected governor of his state, holding that office until 1805. Though the birthday of George III was still celebrated by the predominantly Scottish elements in Fayetteville, the state sent a solidly Republican delegation to Congress in 1804. In South Carolina the Charleston district remained loyal to the Federalist faith until the autumn of 1804, when it fell into line and for the first time sent a Republican to Congress. Now all South Carolina as well as all five of the principal cities of the country were in the Jefferson camp, though most of the smaller commercial towns in the South adhered to their Federalist leanings. Continuing this trend, the Palmetto State sent another solid Republican delegation to Congress in 1806 and elected Charles Pinckney governor.[15]

In 1803 Virginia sent four Federalists to Congress in place of the single member elected two years earlier; but at the same time Anthony New, a former carriage maker, defeated the well-known John Taylor of Caroline for a seat in the Federal House of Representatives. Kentucky now elected a wholly Republican delegation to Congress and a state legislature which was unanimously of the same party. Georgia and Tennessee also remained solidly on the Republican side, and the vote of the Southern delegation in the lower house of the Federal legislature was cast all but

[15] Raleigh *Register*, November 5, 1804; Wolfe, *Jeffersonian Democracy in South Carolina*, 210–11.

unanimously in favor of the acquisition of Louisiana. In 1804 Thomas Ritchie complained in the *Enquirer* that the celebration of July Fourth was listless in Richmond and that "there is reason to believe that the fire of party spirit is expiring in Virginia." [16]

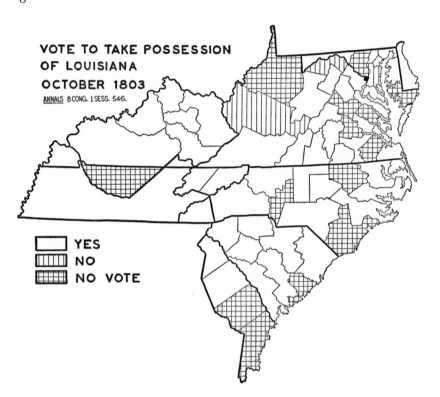

VOTE TO TAKE POSSESSION
OF LOUISIANA
OCTOBER 1803
ANNALS 8 CONG. 1 SESS. 546.

YES
NO
NO VOTE

The Northern Federalists were not slow to read the signs of the times, and realizing that their Southern counterparts would never be able to rally sufficient strength to bring them victory over the surging forces of Jeffersonian Republicanism, they decided to fall back on a policy of sectionalism. In January, 1804, Senators Timothy Pickering of Massachusetts, Uriah Tracy of Connecticut, William Plumer of New Hampshire, with Roger Griswold, Congressman from Connecticut, and perhaps others of the New England

[16] Richmond *Enquirer,* June 7, October 31, 1804; Hutton, "Southern Nationalism," chart 12.

delegation, agreed to organize a movement in their states for a dissolution of the Union. The scheme was to run Aaron Burr, still Vice-President of the United States, for the governorship of New York and to elect him by bringing the Federalist vote to his support. He was then, with the aid of Pickering and company, to replace Hamilton as leader of the New York Federalists and spearhead a movement for the secession of his own state along with New Jersey and New England.[17]

The Southern reaction to this turn of events is well illustrated by a series of articles contributed by "A Virginian" and published in the Richmond *Enquirer* during June and July, 1804. According to this account, the Northern Federalists maintained that a Southern interest had already taken control of the government and the Federalists now sought retaliation by appealing to every passion in seeking to promote hostility on the part of the Northern people toward those of the South. According to the author, the agitators wished to know whether Northern patriots "would suffer their country to remain under the dominion of the south." The Federalists, he said, attempted to excite Northern jealousy "by drawing before them the figure of a desperate rival. The manners of the southern people have been described in colours calculated to provoke their contempt." The attacks of the Federalists, the article went on, were directed particularly against the state of Virginia; they ransacked the history of American government to find proof of Virginia's "selfish spirit and grasping ambition." As proof, they gave the repeal of the internal duties since President Jefferson came to office, the impost continuing to fall only upon the Northern states. They cited the purchase of Louisiana and the Eleventh Amendment to the Constitution to prove the "Southern interest" had lost none of its force and that it now dominated the Federal government. The writer stated that such sentiments had crept into the hightoned prints of Boston, New York, Philadelphia, and other Northern towns and that they had even received the sanction of the most distinguished Federalists of Boston, who, at a recent dinner, gave as one of their set toasts: "May the dominion of Virginia be limited

[17] Adams, *History of the United States*, II, 161; Charles R. Brown, *The Northern Confederacy, According to the Plans of the "Essex Junto," 1796–1814* (Princeton, 1915), 25–45.

by the Constitution, or at least by the Delaware." In conclusion the author asked: "Who knows how far this discontent may contribute to a separation of the states, unless its progress should be arrested in time?" [18]

The author of these articles failed to penetrate to the inner workings of the Pickering-Griswold faction, but he was unduly worried. Even in the North the Federalists represented only the financial interests of the wealthier mercantile and professional classes, who candidly admitted that they were the best people, whereas the majority of the voters were small farmers, manual laborers, artisans, craftsmen, or others of similar status. Though most Federalists gave their support to Burr, Hamilton used his utmost efforts to bring about his defeat. When the election came off on April 25, 1804, New York City went for Burr by about one hundred votes, but he lost in the state by approximately 28,000 to 35,000.[19] The Burr-Hamilton duel, which took place on July 11, was an aftermath of this bitter contest.

It has often been said that sectionalism in American politics did not arise until slavery showed its ugly head as a national issue in connection with the Missouri question of 1820. Yet the situation that developed in 1804 makes it clear that a powerful Northern interest was determined to rule or ruin, and one day, with an issue that could attract popular support, it would find its opportunity. But that issue had not yet become important, for the slave trade had not yet been abolished by the Federal government, and the Republicans won an even more decisive victory in the national election then they did in New York. From the St. Marys to the Potomac and the Ohio every electoral vote went to Jefferson, while the Federalist candidate, Charles Cotesworth Pinckney of South Carolina, carried only Delaware and Connecticut and got two stray votes from Maryland, making a total of 14 to 162 for Jefferson.[20]

Naturally the results of this election did not quiet the fears of Northern Federalists; and James Elliott, member of Congress from Vermont, published a letter in the *Political Observatory* saying that his constituents believed that Virginia was using every exertion to acquire an improper control over the other states.[21]

---

[18] Richmond *Enquirer*, June 13, 1804.
[19] Adams, *History of the United States*, II, 185.     [20] *Ibid.*, 200–201.
[21] Richmond *Enquirer*, February 8, 1805.

The continued expression of opinions of this nature brought rejoinders from the South; one, published in the Richmond *Enquirer* on December 4, 1804, after saying that the North showed a hostile attitude toward Virginia and the South and apparently intended to establish its control or dissolve the Union, recommended the building of a road from Richmond to Charleston at the falls of the Great Kanawha River, thereby making connection with the waters of the Ohio.[22]

Thus was introduced a subject which, while relatively new to Southern politics, was of rapidly growing importance—so much so that in his message to Congress of December 2, 1806, Jefferson recommended the retention of the tariff duties and the adoption of an amendment to the Constitution which would provide for the construction of internal improvements.[23] During the previous March this subject had come up in connection with legislation providing for the survey of the route for the Cumberland Road. When the state of Ohio was admitted to the Union in 1803, it was provided that 2 per cent of the revenue from the sales of her public lands should be used for construction of roads giving access to the state. Now it was proposed that the route should be marked from Cumberland, Maryland, to Wheeling, Virginia, thus providing a convenient road from the Potomac to the Ohio River and the new state. This was the route which General Braddock had followed in 1755 and which in 1758 Pennsylvania succeeded in getting Forbes to abandon in favor of a new road from Harrisburg.

No route to the West could have been more favorable to Virginia, yet her Congressmen voted eleven to one against the bill providing for the survey. Strangely enough, the only affirmative vote came from Jefferson's own district; and the Clarksburg district, through which the highway was to pass, voted in the negative. Tennessee and Kentucky, showing no jealousy of the new state, voted unanimously for the measure, as did Maryland and Georgia. The opposition carried both the Carolinas, but the one South Carolina and the three North Carolina districts which gave favorable votes were in the eastern sections of these states where water transportation to the coast was available but inadequate. The Northern states could not have been expected to have much interest in this

---

[22] *Ibid.*, December 4, 1804.
[23] Richardson (ed.), *Messages and Papers of the Presidents*, I, 397.

particular road, but their votes passed the survey bill, sixty-six to fifty in the House of Representatives.[24]

It is difficult to account for the opposition of Virginia and the Carolinas to this measure authorized by an earlier Congress and approved by President Jefferson, yet John Randolph and Nathaniel Macon were already leading a movement that, anticipating the

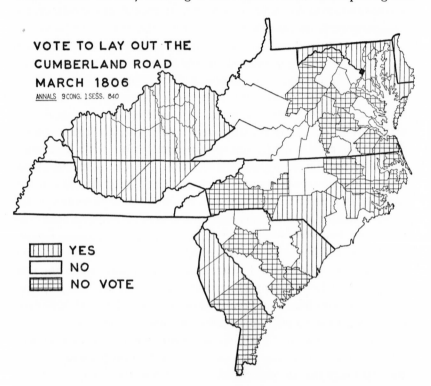

VOTE TO LAY OUT THE
CUMBERLAND ROAD
MARCH 1806
ANNALS 9 CONG. 1 SESS. 840

▭ YES
▭ NO
▭ NO VOTE

later struggle over the institution of slavery, opposed the nationalistic trend which the Administration, secure in its control of the South and the growing West, was taking. But their following was more personal than sectional, and it is difficult to believe that their influence was as impressive as this vote would indicate. Perhaps the danger of centralization of government was more widely recognized than even John Randolph realized.

However important may have been this movement to construct

[24] Hutton, "Southern Nationalism," chart 14; Payson J. Treat, *The National Land System, 1785–1820* (New York, 1910), 109.

the first Federal road, it was less so than the problem of developing adequate communications between the eastern and western sections of the several Southern states. Maryland had a peculiar situation whereby the grain of the western counties was brought to Baltimore by roads lying wholly within the state. But the Potomac also served the western area and floated its products down to Georgetown and Alexandria. Therefore, except in its vote on the Cumberland Road, which did not affect the intrastate situation, the Baltimore area consistently opposed federalization and voted the Republican ticket. The rest of the state, favoring the Potomac route, was normally on the Federalist side. In Virginia and the Carolinas the coastal regions, though outnumbered by the western counties, were overrepresented in the legislatures and thus were able to thwart the construction of roads and the improvement of river navigation which would serve their upland populations.[25]

As in the case of Maryland, Georgia's solid vote for the Cumberland Road requires some explanation. This, however, is difficult to furnish. Since the adoption of the Federal Constitution, the Georgians had been strongly anti-Federalist; why then would they now favor Federal construction of a road to which they had no possible access? The only explanation seems to be that the Piedmont Region rather than the Tidewater dominated Georgia politics and since the only important river, the Savannah, which served the settlements here, was an interstate route, Federal aid could have been used to advantage. Furthermore, it may well be that Georgians hoped that the Federal government would presently build a road through the Indian country to New Orleans, and in this they were not disappointed.

Generally speaking, the Republicans had effective control of the situation throughout the Southern states, though there were still differences of opinion on specific measures. Even in Richmond, heretofore the Federalist stronghold of Chief Justice Marshall, the Republicans elected seventeen out of twenty-four members of the Common Council in the spring of 1805.[26] Jefferson's second inauguration was celebrated here at the "Eagle" and "Washington" taverns, and Editor Ritchie touched on a highly inflammable sub-

[25] Ashe, *History of North Carolina,* II, 200–201.
[26] Richmond *Enquirer,* April 6, 1805.

ject by proposing a toast to Thomas Paine and the Rights of Man. Of course Jefferson's deism came in for bitter denunciation by the Puritan clergy of New England, and there was even some criticism in his own section, but Robert Williams, recently a member of Congress from North Carolina and now appointed governor of the Mississippi Territory, declared that the President was both moral and charitable and that he attended church services. In fact, he was a vestryman of his parish in Albemarle County, but said Congressman Williams, "We do not need his services as a preacher." [27]

The Louisiana Purchase was as popular in the Southern states as it was unpopular in New England, but there were dissenting voices. In October, 1803, Randolph wrote to Harrison Gray Otis that we needed New Orleans but nothing more. Louisiana, he said, would in time rival and oppose the Atlantic states.[28] At the time the Charleston *Courier* made no complaint, but during 1806 it several times lamented the loss of population and the lower agricultural prices which the development of the new domain would entail. Finally, on September 26 this Federalist journal declared that the unfortunate purchase was about to lead to civil war, which statement presumably referred to the Burr Conspiracy.[29]

In Virginia a blissful calm prevailed and the Fourth of July was celebrated in Richmond without fanfare in 1805 and again in 1806.[30] The announcement in the Richmond *Enquirer* on May 30, 1805, that Jefferson would not run again for the Presidency was one of the factors bringing about this peaceful scene,[31] but there was one rift in the lute, which was in the form of a "pale, meagre, ghostly man" with high-pitched voice and acid tongue—the last great scion of a great family—John Randolph of Roanoke. He had made his debut in politics when, in 1799 at Charlotte Court House, he defended the cause of Jeffersonian Republicanism against the Federalism of that patron saint of freedom, Patrick Henry. Elected to Congress at that time, he became chairman of the Committee on Ways and Means in 1801, and this position made him, at the age of twenty-eight, the floor leader of the Ad-

[27] Raleigh *Register*, March 28, 1803.

[28] Wolfe, *Jeffersonian Democracy in South Carolina*, 186–87.

[29] Richmond *Enquirer*, March 1, 1805; Charleston *Courier*, July 1, August 4, September 26, 1806.

[30] Richmond *Enquirer*, March 3, 1805; July 8, 1806.        [31] *Ibid.*, May 30, 1805.

ministration forces in the House of Representatives. Followed by one or two dogs, he would come to his seat in the House, booted and spurred, though he had the soft and beardless cheeks of a boy.[32]

Already disgruntled with the Administration over the Yazoo business and the Chase trial, Randolph definitely split with Jefferson when the President, after having taken a threatening tone toward Spain in his annual message of December 3, 1805, sent a special message to Congress three days later asking—though not in so many words—for a grant of $2,000,000 to enable him to arrange with Napoleon to induce Spain to cede West Florida and accept the Sabine River as the southwestern boundary of Louisiana. His biographer, Henry Adams, was hardly partial to John Randolph, but he said that the Virginian possessed more talent than any other member of the Republican Party then in Congress and that he was looked upon in his own state as "a sort of Virginian Saint Michael, almost terrible in his contempt for whatever seemed to him base or untrue." [33] The President's stand now infuriated his fellow Virginian. Randolph looked at it as an attempt to give the Secretary of State credit for standing up to Spain, while throwing upon Congress the ignominy of truckling to her. His attitude has been described thus: "Honestly indignant at what he considered a mean attempt to bribe one nation to join in robbing another, he thought the whole transaction only worthy of Madison's groveling character." [34] There followed a bitter debate on the $2,000,000 bill and though a majority of the Virginia members supported Randolph, Jefferson—with most of his support furnished by Northern Republicans—carried his point and the bill finally passed.

Thus began a rift in the Republican Party, which, though never really serious, was extremely annoying to the Administration. Already harboring a dislike for Madison because of his advocacy of a compromise with the Yazoo claimants, Randolph now extended his enmity to Jefferson himself. Naturally he was dropped from the chairmanship of the Ways and Means Committee, and his friend, Nathaniel Macon, could not retain the Speakership of the

[32] Dictionary of American Biography, XV, 363–67.
[33] Ibid.; Richardson (ed.), Messages and Papers of the Presidents, I, 370–73; Adams, History of the United States, III, 157.
[34] Adams, History of the United States, III, 137–39; Adams, John Randolph, 165.

House. Appearing now at the head of a small but devoted band of Southern Republicans, known to history as the *Tertium Quids*, Randolph never tired of using his brilliant oratory to nettle the Administration, though he was never able really to frustrate it.

Highly regarded as Randolph was in Virginia, his apostasy brought about serious, though largely temporary, repercussions in his home state. Republican leaders had to make up their minds as to their allegiance, and in some cases this was not an easy matter. This was true of the most important of all the local politicians, Thomas Ritchie, who after some hesitation came out on May 13, 1806, with a statement that, though he had always thought of John Randolph as a Bayard, *sans peur et sans reproche,* and though he at first thought that he might be right and the Administration wrong in the Spanish affair, he now decided that the Administration was right and Randolph wrong, and he greatly regretted this break in the Republican ranks.[35] Having thus taken his stand, the editor still had misgivings, and ten days later, stating that the power of the Executive should be reduced, he reprinted a public letter which that venerable Virginian, Edmund Pendleton, wrote on October 5, 1801, urging constitutional amendments which would bring this about.[36] Randolph was indeed a voice crying in the wilderness, but with all his eccentricity he did represent the emergence of a desire on the part of some elements in the South to return to the strict-constructionist principles of 1798.

The pinprick of *Quid* opposition was presently overshadowed by a more pressing problem confronting the Jefferson administration. With England and France at war, American ships, largely out of New England ports, were able to take over the carrying trade of the French and Spanish West Indies. This was more than usually profitable to the American merchants, and beneficial to Napoleon and his allies, but contrary to the interests of the British Empire; and British interests were further jeopardized by the desertion of English seamen in American ports. These deserters commonly took service, sometimes making use of forged naturalization papers, on American ships whose captains were frequently unaware of the real nationality of the men whom they employed. In these circumstances, fighting for her life against the Tyrant of

[35] Richmond *Enquirer,* May 13, September 2, 1806.    [36] *Ibid.,* May 23, 1806.

Europe, England resorted to a policy which the United States, under different circumstances, has not hesitated to adopt. She revived a rule which she had first applied during the Seven Years' War and declared that commerce not open to neutrals during time of peace should not be open to them during time of war. In carrying out this policy British warships intercepted American vessels on the high seas, even at the entrance to American ports, and confiscated their West Indian cargoes. Furthermore, officers scrutinized the American crews and impressed any seamen whom they took to be British citizens.

This policy of search and seizure was bitterly resented in all sections of the United States, and Jefferson authorized Monroe and William Pinkney to undertake in London a settlement of the problem, but the treaty which they negotiated was so unsatisfactory that the President refused to submit it to the Senate. The resulting impasse was too much for Editor Ritchie who, in his issue of May 12, 1807, proposed that we should cut off all trade with Great Britain, and if that power should retaliate by a declaration of war, we should "wrap ourselves in our shell, keep our navy off the seas and entrust the annoyance of Britain to private commissioned cruisers." [37]

Exactly ten days later the forty-gun frigate *Chesapeake,* a ship donated to the United States Navy by the citizens of Baltimore during our naval squabble with France, left her moorings in Hampton Roads and made for the open sea beyond the Virginia Capes, with the Mediterranean her destination. At Lynnhaven Bay, just inside the Capes, a British squadron rode at anchor. Jay's Treaty of 1794 opened American coastal waters to British warships, and this afforded them an ideal position from which to supervise our shipping. Shortly after the *Chesapeake* passed the British ships, one of them—the fifty-gun frigate *Leopard*—followed her to sea.

After both ships cleared the three-mile limit, Captain S. P. Humphreys of the *Leopard* hailed Commodore James Barron of the *Chesapeake* and demanded that he be allowed to board and search for deserters from the British navy. Commodore Barron, believing that he had no deserters on board, declined to submit to search, upon which the *Leopard* opened fire. Such an attack being wholly

[37] *Ibid.,* May 12, 1807.

unexpected, Barron had not prepared his ship for action and the decks were littered with all kinds of equipment. After receiving repeated salvos from the *Leopard,* with only one gun fired as a token of defense, Barron struck his colors and surrendered. Three men were killed, eight severely wounded, and the Commodore himself along with nine others received superficial wounds. Since the United States and Great Britain were still at peace, Captain Humphreys declined to accept Commodore Barron's surrender, but boarded the crippled ship and mustered the crew. As it turned out, there was, unknown to Barron, one actual deserter aboard, and he, without the grace of court-martial, was promptly hanged by his captors. In addition there were three other seamen, all American citizens impressed by the British but who later escaped and took service aboard the *Chesapeake.* These were forthwith reimpressed. Having thus carried out his orders, Captain Humphreys left the *Chesapeake* to limp back to port.[38]

The reaction to this event was instantaneous. Without waiting for public authorization, the citizens of Hampton destroyed two hundred casks of water belonging to one of the British warships. On June 24 the citizens of Norfolk and Portsmouth met at the Town Hall and "*Resolved unanimously* That all communication with the British ships of war, now within our waters and on our coasts, and with their agent or agents among us, be discontinued, and that we will use our best exertions to prevent all such intercourse, and that all persons guilty thereof shall be deemed infamous." [39] Two days later the Richmond troop of cavalry met at the Eagle Tavern and offered its services to the President of the United States; then the next day some seven hundred citizens met and adopted resolutions similar to the Norfolk resolves.[40] On July 2 the President issued a proclamation ordering all British warships to quit the territorial waters of the United States, "And if the said vessels . . . shall fail to depart as aforesaid, . . . I do in that case forbid all intercourse with them, their officers or crews,

[38] John C. Emmerson, *The Chesapeake Affair of 1807* (Portsmouth, Va., 1954), 13–23.

[39] *Ibid.,* 24–27; Edwin M. Gaines, "Outrageous Encounter: The *Chesapeake-Leopard* Affair of 1807" (Ph.D. dissertation, University of Virginia, 1960), *passim.*

[40] Richmond *Enquirer,* June 27, 1807.

and do prohibit all supplies and aid from being furnished to them, or any of them." [41]

Indignation meetings were held in all the South Atlantic ports from Baltimore to Savannah, and many inland towns were quick to hurl defiance at the British fleet and nation. The Savannah meeting went so far as to demand preparation for war and the State of Georgia at once purchased 10,000 stand of arms, 12 field pieces, 700 horseman's pistols, and other warlike equipment. Furthermore, one Elford was arrested in that city for trying to supply a British ship in the harbor with several casks of water, and on September 12 a "large number of republicans, headed by Governor Telfair, met to celebrate the victory of the French nation over the allies of England—events leading to peace and prosperity of the United States." Toasts were drunk to Emperor Napoleon, Thomas Jefferson, Congress, and "England, may *delenda est Britannia* be the prayer and motto of every American bosom, so long as she continues to be the implacable and insidious foe of the commerce, rights and independence of Republican America!" [42]

In Charleston a public meeting requested all citizens to wear crepe around their arms "as a respectful tribute to the memory of the seamen who were slaughtered on the Chesapeake by the British." [43] In North Carolina public meetings to express indignation over the *Chesapeake-Leopard* affair were held, not only in the coast towns but far in the interior of the state, with Federalists participating.[44] In Washington City, not only the *National Intelligencer* and the *American*, but even the *Federalist* denounced the "outrage" on the *Chesapeake*, and when Independence Day was celebrated in Baltimore, the seventeen guns which were fired from parade were answered by a salute from the French ship *L'Eole*. Following this demonstration dinner was served at the Union Tavern and toasts were drunk to the memory of the seamen killed on the *Chesapeake*.[45]

A final but futile attempt to defy the government of the United States was undertaken by Commodore J. E. Douglas of *H.M.S.*

[41] Richardson (ed.), *Messages and Papers of the Presidents*, I, 410–12.
[42] *Republican and Savannah Evening Ledger*, August 6, 20, September 15, 1807.
[43] Charleston *Courier*, July 10, 1807.
[44] Gilpatrick, *Jeffersonian Democracy in North Carolina*, 158.
[45] Annapolis *Maryland Gazette*, July 2, 9, 1807.

*Bellona,* which failed to take notice of the President's order to depart and was still anchored in Lynnhaven Bay. Referring only to the local resolution prohibiting communication between the British consul and the British warships in the bay, he pompously warned that "the British flag never has nor never will be insulted with impunity," and demanded the immediate annulment of the nonintercourse order. War, he said, would follow if his ultimatum should be ignored. To this threatening communication, the mayor of Norfolk, Richard Evans Lee, replied that the American people would not be intimidated. The question of war, he said, was for governments, not individuals, to decide, but if the commodore chose to commence hostilities, they would be resisted. This letter was delivered on board the *Bellona* by Littleton W. Tazewell, who was courteously received by Commodore Douglas and the other captains of the British squadron, with whom he talked for about an hour. Douglas now stated that he must have been misunderstood, that he had no orders to commit hostile acts and had no such intention. Tazewell then warned him against sending either officers or men ashore because the enraged populace could not be restrained from taking vengeance. And thus the parley ended.[46]

On July 30 President Jefferson issued a proclamation calling Congress into special session on October 26. His message explained the failure of our negotiations with Britain and stated that England's armed vessels were still infesting our territorial waters despite his orders. But even more damaging to our neutral rights was the recent order in council prohibiting our vessels from trading between ports not in amity with England. "Under this new law of the ocean," said the President, "our trade on the Mediterranean has been done away by seizures and condemnations, and that in the other seas is threatened with the same fate." He also informed Congress that an armed vessel had been dispatched with instructions to our ministers to demand satisfaction for the attack on the *Chesapeake*.[47]

Having failed to obtain any satisfaction from England regarding our rights on the high seas, on December 18 the President sent a special message to Congress recommending that it consider the ad-

[46] *Ibid.,* July 16, 1807.
[47] Richardson (ed.), *Messages and Papers of the Presidents,* I, 413–15.

vantages of prohibiting all our vessels from leaving ports of the
United States and of making preparations for whatever might develop out of the present crisis.[48] Believing that England would suffer at least as much as France if denied the services of the American
merchant marine, the President decided to resort to peaceful co-
ercion, but the final clause of his message shows that he realized

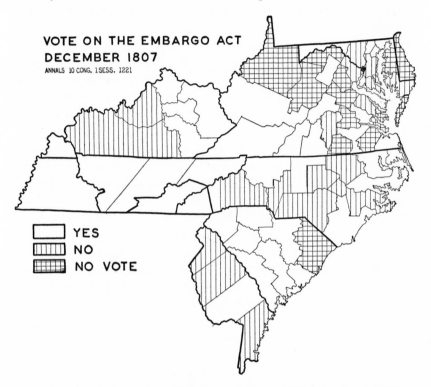

VOTE ON THE EMBARGO ACT
DECEMBER 1807
ANNALS 10 CONG. 1 SESS. 1221

YES
NO
NO VOTE

the possibility that war rather than peace might be the ultimate
outcome of this maneuver. Notwithstanding Federalist opposition, Congress was ready to try the experiment and the Embargo
Bill, supposed to have been drafted in advance by Jefferson, passed
the Senate in one day. The House debated it for three days behind
closed doors and then passed it by a vote of eighty-two to forty-six.[49]

The geographical distribution of this vote in the Southern states

[48] *Ibid.*, 421. See also Adams, "Jefferson's Military Policy, with Special Reference
to the Frontier," Chaps. III–VI.

[49] Channing, *History of the United States*, IV, 380–81.

is significant. Only in Maryland and North Carolina was the Federalist opposition considerable, and in both cases it followed the usual pattern. In the former state it had a majority of four to three, with the negative votes coming, as usual, from the districts bordering the lower Potomac River and Chesapeake Bay, while the western district and those whose trade centered in Baltimore voted for the embargo. Similarly, in North Carolina the Federalist strong-

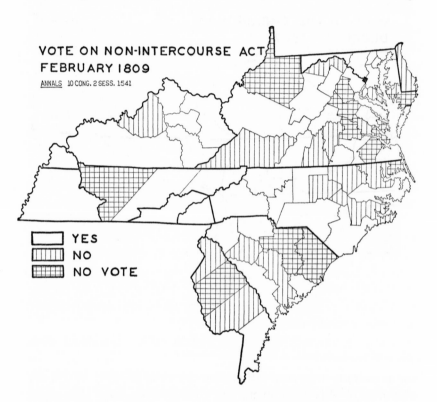

VOTE ON NON-INTERCOURSE ACT
FEBRUARY 1809
ANNALS 10 CONG. 2 SESS. 1541

☐ YES
▥ NO
▦ NO VOTE

holds in the New Bern, Fayetteville, and Salisbury districts—areas feeling the need of better transportation facilities—voted with the opposition. They were joined by the small *Quid* faction under Macon's leadership, while the northern districts which traded mostly with Virginia and the self-sufficient Wilmington district supported the Administration, giving it seven votes to six in the state.

South Carolina and Tennessee cast solid votes for the embargo,

Virginia gave it nine votes to three, and in Kentucky only the Louisville district went Federalist. But the most surprising result of all was the vote of Georgia, which gave the opposition a majority of three to one. Since the Federalists had no strength here, this can be attributed only to the friction engendered by the continuing controversy over the Yazoo claims.[50]

Naturally the sudden stoppage of foreign trade brought hardship to all classes of citizens in all sections of the country, but the merchants and the mercantile cities suffered most of all. During the first years of the embargo exports dropped from $110,000,000 to $20,000,000, yet the reaction of the people depended more on their political persuasion than on their economic interest.[51] Despite the important shipping that centered in Baltimore, Marylanders generally supported the embargo, and this included many of the dominant Federalists.[52] The Virginia legislature, in spite of opposition by Randolph and the *Quids,* approved the measure; and notwithstanding the six votes which North Carolina Congressmen cast against it, the legislature of that state passed a resolution endorsing the embargo.[53] Charleston dominated the commerce of South Carolina, and federalism had once held sway here, but now the Jeffersonian Republican, Charles Pinckney, held the line for his party. The city council offered to feed all unemployed seamen in port, and in December, 1808, the South Carolina House voted to throw its full support behind the Embargo Act. It also provided that its members should appear at the next session dressed in clothes of domestic manufacture.[54]

Georgia, apparently enjoying a considerable contraband trade with the West Indies through the Florida port of Fernandina on Amelia Island, suffered little during the early months of the embargo, but in the spring Governor Telfair convened a special session of the legislature and proposed the enactment of stay laws for

[50] Hutton, "Southern Nationalism," chart 16.

[51] Saul K. Padover, *A Jeffersonian Profile as Revealed in His Letters* (New York, 1956), 353.

[52] Andrews, *History of Maryland,* 414.

[53] Ammon, "Republican Party in Virginia," Chap. VII, 5; Richmond *Enquirer,* December 11, 1807.

[54] *Republican and Savannah Evening Ledger,* February 13, December 21, 1808; Wolfe, *Jeffersonian Democracy in South Carolina,* 220–27.

the relief of debtors suffering as a result of the stoppage of foreign trade.[55] On motion of Henry Clay, the Kentucky legislature passed a law supporting the embargo by a vote of sixty-four to one, and that of Mississippi Territory took a similar action but asked that all payments due the Federal government be postponed during the emergency. It requested also that all Territorial courts suspend for the same period the issuance of orders of execution for the payment of debts.[56]

Far different, however, was the feeling in Louisiana, where the hostilities engendered by the Burr Conspiracy were still keen, and New Orleans was naturally the focal point for opposition to the embargo. On February 5, 1808, the editor of the *Louisiana Gazette* bitterly deplored that our government, instead of calling forth all its resources to enforce our rights against foreign aggression, "had thought it more *patriotic* to declare war against our own citizens by laying a general Embargo." Surely the majority who voted for it, he added, could not realize the dreadful consequence of putting an entire stop to trade, the effects of which would fall hardest on the laboring classes, who, finding no employment, would lack the necessities of life.[57] On November 1 the same journal published a letter to the editor which stated: "I learn with great pleasure from your columns that the Embargo is becoming more unpopular every day. The Northern journals are filled with the bitterest invectives. But the embargo is the favorite measure of those who favor the views of Bonaparte." [58]

As an example of Northern sentiment the *Louisiana Gazette* published an article from the New York *Evening Post* which declared that in the present time of uncertainty, dismay, and apprehension, everyone was rushing eagerly to his neighbor for information about the embargo, which was bringing immediate bankruptcy to the merchants and loss of employment and want of bread to thousands of the laboring class. The government, said the editor, might have its reasons for keeping the people in the dark as to the

[55] *Republican and Savannah Evening Ledger*, July–August, 1808, *passim;* New Orleans *Louisiana Gazette*, June 17, 1808.

[56] Natchez *Weekly Chronicle*, September 28, 1808; *Republican and Savannah Evening Ledger*, November 17, 1808; Mayo, *Henry Clay*, 337.

[57] New Orleans *Louisiana Gazette*, February 5, 1808.

[58] *Ibid.*, November 1, 1808.

express object of the embargo, but "when we turn to the yeas and nays of Congress, and see all the talent, the patriotism and sterling integrity of the house on one side against this measure, and on the other the mere force of voting figures, we fear all is not as it should be." [59] On November 10 the *Reporter* of Lexington, Kentucky, stated: "The Federal papers in the Eastern States are openly and unblushingly advocating dissolution of the union, with a view of placing the New England States once more under the allegiance of Great Britain. If it was *treason* in Spanish Conspirators to receive Mexican dollars, we are certain there must be equal treason in British guineas." [60] This was in line with the violent partisanship of the day, but ever since the Louisiana Purchase secession talk was often heard as far south as Philadelphia.[61] On August 19 Editor Ritchie mentioned in the *Enquirer* a communication from an upper county of Virginia which condemned the Northern Federalists who assumed the name of that party only to discredit it. Ritchie commented that, though it was true that the worst examples of Federal disloyalty came from Northern papers, their Southern counterparts were not free from the same distemper.[62]

Weary of the burdens of the Presidency and anxious that there should be no mistake about his intention to follow Washington's example in the matter, Jefferson announced in December, 1807, that he would retire from office at the end of his current term. He had faced bitter opposition from many quarters, but except for Randolph's *Tertium Quids* and a few Federalists who followed the lead of John Marshall, Virginia had given him loyal support. And among Virginians, none had been more loyal or more helpful than Madison and Monroe, but now it began to look as though there would be a breach in this great triumvirate.

Having failed in London to negotiate a treaty which Jefferson felt he could present to the Senate for ratification, Monroe sailed for home and arrived at Norfolk on December 13, 1807. At once the retiring Minister wrote to Secretary of State Madison that, after a brief visit in Richmond, he would proceed to Washington to report on his mission. This simple and logical announcement

[59] *Ibid.*, March 4, 1808.        [60] Lexington *Reporter*, November 10, 1808.
[61] Andrews, *History of Maryland*, 414.
[62] Richmond *Enquirer*, August 19, 1808.

seemed to take on some significance when, on December 18, the Virginia capital turned out to welcome the unsuccessful envoy as a conquering hero. With him in the lead, the military companies marched up to the capitol and then down Main Street to the Bell Tavern where the governor and members of the General Assembly, along with loyal citizens to the number of 120, sat down to dinner in the overflowing ballroom.[63]

This was not a mere demonstration of personal admiration. Madison was the obvious heir to the Presidency, but he was opposed by John Randolph and his small following. Many Virginians felt that Napoleon was a greater menace than the British ministry, and men of this persuasion usually favored Monroe over Madison.[64] Encouraged by the demonstration at Bell Tavern, Monroe's friends talked hopefully of an endorsement for the succession by the Virginia legislature, but their leader had already departed for Washington. On the twentieth he rode into the national capital. The House of Representatives was meeting in its new chamber, resplendent with painted ceiling, sandstone columns, and crimson brocade hangings. The Embargo Bill, which was passed the next day, was the subject of debate. Monroe waited patiently to be received by the President, but no summons came. Then, sick at heart with the feeling that he had been deserted by those in whom he had put his trust, he returned to his Virginia home.[65]

But Administrative neglect did not cause him to be forgotten in his native state. Since 1800 it had been customary for the members of each party in Congress to meet and decide on their candidates for the first and second places on their tickets. Now Monroe's Virginia friends, encouraged by his triumphal reception in Richmond, were talking hopefully of an endorsement by the state legislature.[66] With the object of forestalling this move, on January 21, 1808, Madison's supporters in the legislature circulated a notice that called on "those members of the General Assembly of Virginia who are friendly to the election of James Madison . . . and they only," to meet that evening at the Bell Tavern. But the Monroe faction

[63] *Ibid.*, December 19, 1807.

[64] Irving Brant, *James Madison, The President, 1809–1812* (Indianapolis, 1956), 424.

[65] Cresson, *James Monroe,* 236.     [66] Brant, *James Madison, The President,* 424.

was not to be denied. On the same afternoon a spokesman for this group invited the entire Assembly to meet that evening at the capitol. The result was that two meetings were held by members of the Assembly on the same day; 123 of them met at the Bell Tavern and voted unanimously for Madison, while 87 met at the capitol and all but ten of them voted for Monroe.[67] Two days later 94 Republican members of Congress, out of a total of 150, met in Washington and voted 83 for Madison, 3 for George Clinton, 3 for Monroe, with 5 abstentions. Seventeen of Randolph's *Quids* protested this action.[68] Both of the Richmond meetings adopted tickets of Presidential electors and appointed committees of correspondence for each county of the state, with a central committee to serve in Richmond. Thus was party machinery organized in those days.[69]

Organizing the party machinery was only a means for winning an election, and at the time this was taken care of as follows: On August 9 the Richmond *Enquirer* printed a circular sent by the Madison committee in Richmond to the different county committees urging them, as had been done in 1804, to write out tickets equal to the whole number of voters in the county and have them distributed throughout the area previous to the day of election. This notice was signed by William Foushee, Sr., Abraham B. Venable, Peyton Randolph, Thomas Ritchie, Samuel Pleasants, and Gervas Stores—all gentlemen of eminent standing.[70]

Not quite so serious, but perhaps not entirely beside the point, was a communication from "C. Volponius to M. Callidus," also published in the *Enquirer*. Entitled "Advice on becoming a successful politician," it suggested that the candidate furnish himself with a full suit of homespun, or at least a coat, and repair to the first quarterly court held in his county. This would be his debut in politics. He should learn to be all things to all men; go to church now and then and the godly would sing his praises mightily; become a Freemason as soon as possible; and get elected into all the jockey clubs within fifty miles. "In this way," the writer continued, "you will become acquainted with some with whom you

[67] *Ibid.*, 424–25.          [68] *Ibid.*, 426; Richmond *Enquirer*, March 18, 1808.
[69] Richmond *Enquirer*, January 23, 26, 30, February 9, 11, 1808.
[70] *Ibid.*, August 9, 1808.

could not otherwise associate without some loss of character for decency and honesty." When elected to the legislature, he added, do not forget the business of hot suppers and good wine—"this much attended to in Richmond—but these often excite more ill-will in those who are not invited than good-will in those who are." The ambitious legislator was advised to mix widely with the mountain members, because they "are an honest, unsuspecting set, and very clannish. Talk about calling a convention, condemn the unequal representation in the Senate—Praise their leading men—Laugh at the sickly, sallow faces of the lowlanders, drink whiskey, and they will support you for anything." [71]

Also intended to be facetious, but in a different key, was a letter written on August 4 from a resident of Natchez to a friend in New Orleans and published in the *Louisiana Gazette*. "I hope," it said, "if we are to have a Democratic President, it may be Mr. Madison. I well know that his wife is a lady of great *spirit,* and if (as you say) she rules him, we shall have, what we have long wanted, a *spirited administration.* So, if not successfully opposed by a federal candidate, God grant him, or rather *her,* success. I like a peticoat [*sic*]—indeed I am almost in love with any thing that wears one, except a *Highlander.* So I pray for a *peticoat government,* or any other, rather than a *philosophical one.*" [72]

The fact that Madison's supporters dominated the Virginia General Assembly did not put a stop to the efforts of opposing factions. On September 17 a meeting of the freeholders of Augusta County assembled at Staunton and, with General Robert Porterfield in the Chair, framed an address to the President which condemned the embargo and accused the Administration of being too critical of England, while favoring the "oppressive and unjust conduct of Napoleon." The meeting then nominated Charles Cotesworth Pinckney and Rufus King, condemned the general ticket law applied in 1804, and formed a central corresponding committee. Generally speaking, the Valley Federalists supported the ticket of their party, whereas those in eastern Virginia decided that their best chance of defeating Madison was to support Monroe.[73]

One of Monroe's principal supporters was a scholarly Virginian,

[71] *Ibid.,* March 11, 1808.  [72] New Orleans *Louisiana Gazette,* August 9, 1808.
[73] Richmond *Enquirer,* October 4, 18, November 1, 1808; Simms, *John Taylor,* 121.

George Tucker, who was later to become a professor at the University of Virginia. Having been selected to make the July Fourth address in Danville, he said that lovers of freedom had once hailed the French Revolution but that now despotism had been re-established and Europe lay under the heel of a conqueror. He thought that many who once sided with France had changed sides and looked upon the Revolution as a calamity to the cause of freedom. John Taylor of Caroline held similar views, but with reservations, while Randolph and his followers were uninhibited in their support of them.[74]

In September Edward C. Stanard established in Richmond a newspaper which he christened *The Spirit of '76* and dedicated to the support of Monroe's candidacy. Through its columns the Monroe correspondence committee delivered an address to Virginians, advocating the claims of its candidate, because as governor he had come into office during a period of strife and succeeded in conciliating all differences and also because he was not committed to the Administration's policy of "an indefinite embargo of war" and would, therefore, have a better chance of finding a solution to our foreign problems.[75]

As the effects of the embargo began to make themselves seriously felt in the Southern states, opposition to the measure increased. Editor Ritchie gave no ground and declared that "the people of Virginia are not insensible of the pressure of the embargo, but . . . they will most cheerfully submit to any sacrifices which may preserve the rights and honor of their country." [76] This statement was followed by a series of articles in support of the editor's views on the subject. The Charleston *Courier* was less enthusiastic, and in the legislatures of both North and South Carolina antiembargo resolutions received substantial support though they did not pass, the vote in South Carolina being thirty-three to sixty-four.[77] The editor of the *Weekly Chronicle* of Natchez went considerably further and not only urged the repeal of the embargo but proposed an active war against France and her Spanish ally: "We must have

[74] Simms, *John Taylor,* 115–29; Lexington *Reporter,* May 7, 1808; Richmond *Enquirer,* July 15, 1808; *Dictionary of American Biography,* XIX, 28–30.
[75] Richmond *Enquirer,* September 30, 1808.      [76] *Ibid.,* May 21, June 3, 1808.
[77] Charleston *Courier,* January 6, 1808; Savannah *Republican,* July 5, 1808; Ashe, *History of North Carolina,* II, 206.

Cuba if we hold New Orleans. It may be necessary to occupy the whole extent of New Mexico." [78]

A drastically different idea received some support in Virginia. Monroe himself presided over a meeting in Richmond which was called to advocate the development of domestic manufactures, and a Richmond manufacturing association was organized. On June 25 a meeting was held at the courthouse of Halifax, a village just east of Danville, but there two supporters of the candidacy of Monroe urged that, even though the embargo should be permanent, it would be better for Virginia to produce provisions and raw materials and exchange them for the manufactures of the Northern states. An "Address to the People of Virginia," signed by Thomas Ritchie, William H. Cabell, William Wirt, William Foushee, and Peyton Randolph (Madison supporters), advocated a protective tariff to perpetuate the effects of the embargo and make America independent of Great Britain.[79]

Notwithstanding the efforts of Jefferson's loyal followers to make the best of it, the embargo was not a popular measure, even in the Southern states. This was demonstrated in Virginia by the movement to nominate Monroe instead of Madison and by the continued popularity of John Randolph, which was forcefully demonstrated by a meeting in Prince Edward County on September 24. This body was called by Randolph's opponents with the object of bringing about the nomination of a candidate to succeed him in Congress, but it turned out that the two or three hundred voters who attended were almost all supporters of Randolph, who continued until 1814 to be a thorn in the side of the Administration.[80]

Yet neither the *Quids* nor the Federalists were able to offer a serious threat to the hold of the Republican Party on the Southern states. This was clearly shown by the results of the election of 1808, in which Madison defeated Charles C. Pinckney by a vote of nine to two in Maryland and eleven to three in North Carolina. Virginia, South Carolina, Georgia, Tennessee, and Kentucky cast

[78] Natchez *Weekly Chronicle*, July 20, 1808.
[79] Richmond *Enquirer*, June 1, 26, 1808; Ambler, *Thomas Ritchie*, 45–46.
[80] Richmond *Enquirer*, September 27, 1808.

unanimous votes for Madison.[81] However, the opposition was stronger than this result would indicate. Maryland sent three Federalists and six Republicans to the Federal House of Representatives, and the North Carolina delegation included three Federalists and two staunch supporters of John Randolph—Macon and Richard Stanford. Furthermore, Monroe polled a substantial vote in Tidewater Virginia, and the Federalists and Republicans each elected forty members to the Maryland House of Delegates.[82]

In the nation as a whole Madison defeated Pinckney by an electoral vote of 122 to 47, George Clinton becoming Vice-President. Because of the embargo all New England except Vermont was in the Federalist column.

[81] Brant, *James Madison, Secretary of State,* 467.
[82] Richmond *Enquirer,* September 6, October 18, November 18, 1808; Ambler, *Sectionalism in Virginia,* 87–90.

# CHAPTER XIII

# THE WEST FLORIDA REBELLION

WHEN the Louisiana Purchase was consummated, the United States acquired a dispute with Spain over the eastern boundary which was not settled until we purchased Florida in 1819. This difficulty grew out of the fact that the treaty of cession contained the ambiguous statement that the territory should have the same extent "that it now has in the hands of Spain, and that it had when France possessed it." The catch was that France had originally settled Mobile when the eastern boundary of Louisiana was a small river called the Perdido, which lay between this outpost and Spanish Pensacola. But at the date of the Purchase, the Mississippi River was the boundary between West Florida and Louisiana except for the small "island" on which New Orleans stood. Napoleon had demanded that Charles IV surrender Louisiana according to its ancient limits, but the Spanish King demurred and the best that Talleyrand could get was the ambiguous phrase which was copied verbatim in our treaty of 1803. Thus France kept alive a doubtful claim to the territory between the Perdido and the Mississippi rivers.[1]

Thinking that the French government would support the claim, Livingston and Monroe advised the Administration to maintain that the Perdido was the eastern boundary of that part of Louisiana which lay below the thirty-first parallel, and neither Jefferson nor Madison hesitated to accept this advice. Accordingly, when Congress on February 24, 1804, made provision for establishing civil government in Orleans Territory and the District of Louisi-

---

[1] Brant, *James Madison, Secretary of State*, 145–50; Henry E. Chambers, *West Florida and Its Relation to the Historical Cartography of the United States* (Baltimore, 1898), 46.

ana, it also authorized the President to establish a customs district with Mobile as its port of entry. Thus it appeared that the United States was preparing to take forcible possession of the disputed territory, and Governor Folch warned Governor Claiborne that any such move would meet with armed resistance. The Spanish Minister, the Marquis de Casa Yrujo, was so outraged that on March 5 he called on Madison, used insulting language, and presently withdrew from Washington to take up residence in Philadelphia.[2] The Spanish government adopted a similarly threatening tone, and Jefferson ordered the Secretary of War to send all available troops to New Orleans. Actually, the intention of Congress and the President was to negotiate rather than to fight for Mobile, and accordingly on April 15 Madison instructed Monroe, then our Minister to Britain, to open negotiations with the Spanish authorities for the recognition of the Perdido boundary and for the purchase of all the rest of Florida.[3] Then, on May 30 the President issued a proclamation creating the customs district of Mobile, but it was to include only territory lying *within the boundaries of the United States,* and Fort Stoddert on the Mobile River just above the thirty-first parallel was to be the only port of entry.[4]

In the heat of his controversy with Madison, Yrujo sought out Anthony Merry, the British Minister, and told him that there was great dissatisfaction among the Spanish and French population of New Orleans. Spain's policy, he explained, would be to block the outlet for Georgia's produce through the Gulf ports, and thus by confining the American West to the single port of New Orleans, to deny the United States a commanding position in the West Indian trade. Yrujo thought the British government might wish to co-operate in this program, and Merry thought he saw an even more enticing possibility, for a "well-informed American" had just

[2] Arthur P. Whitaker, *The United States and the Independence of Latin America, 1800–1830* (Baltimore, 1941), 29–30; Brown (ed.), *William Plumer's Memorandum,* 190–93, 400–405; Chadwick, *Relations of the United States and Spain,* 70–71; Cox, *West Florida Controversy,* 97–99; Raleigh *Register,* July 23, 1804; Richmond *Enquirer,* July 14, 1804; Brant, *James Madison, Secretary of State,* 194, 205.

[3] Jefferson to Secretary of War, September 6, 1804, in Carter (ed.), *Territory of Orleans,* 291; Cox, *West Florida Controversy,* 100; Chadwick, *Relations of the United States and Spain,* 73–80; Brant, *James Madison, Secretary of State,* 202.

[4] Brant, *James Madison, Secretary of State,* 198; Brown (ed.), *William Plumer's Memorandum,* 190–93.

told him that the West was riper for secession than was New England. Growing enthusiastic, he reported to his government on March 13, 1804, that, by sending commercial agents to New Orleans to purchase all supplies for the West Indies, while flooding the Mississippi Valley with manufactured goods from Canada, Great Britain could build up an intimacy with the West, break its commercial ties with the East, and promote complete independence.[5] It could well be that this was the seed from which the Burr Conspiracy was developed during the following winter. If this was indeed the case, then it was the Spanish Marquis and the British Minister who furnished the original idea.[6]

Certainly neither Jefferson nor Madison could have imagined that such a development might grow out of the West Florida controversy, but there was a more immediate, though less important, conspiratorial situation which was uppermost in their minds. It will be recalled that it was the Spanish Intendant of Louisiana, Juan Ventura Morales, who, by denying our Mississippi River boatmen the right to land, store, and transship their goods in New Orleans, had lighted the fuse which led to our purchase of Louisiana. Having thus brought about the abolition of his office, he was provided with a substitute by being made Intendant of the Province of West Florida, of which Don Vizente Folch was governor. The Intendant was second in importance only to the Governor, and he had considerable authority, including disposal of the public lands, quite independent of his superior. Officially, Morales always gave the impression of being an aggressively loyal Spaniard, ever ready to defend the rights of his country against the pretensions of the United States, but actually he appears to have been adept at serving himself while seeming to serve his nation.

After having been made Intendant of West Florida, he continued to reside in New Orleans, and being a wealthy man himself, he still associated with his wealthy American friends, Edward Livingston and Daniel Clark. To these coadjutors and their associates, including General James Wilkinson, to whom Dauphin Island at the entrance to Mobile Bay had been allocated, he now made large

---

[5] Brant, *James Madison, Secretary of State*, 195–96.

[6] See also extract of a letter from Baton Rouge, dated October 16, 1804, in Richmond *Enquirer*, December 1, 1804.

grants of West Florida lands because both he and they expected that the value of this acreage would be greatly enhanced when, as was generally expected, the United States should occupy the territory as far east as the Perdido.[7] If it should become necessary for the United States to purchase this part of West Florida, then these grants would be valid, for they would have been made before the purchase. But if the Americans acquired this territory as a part of Louisiana, it would not be necessary to recognize the grants made by Morales. Therefore, in his instructions to Monroe, Madison made it clear that, though we were prepared to pay a price for the rest of Florida, the area west of the Perdido must be recognized as part of the original purchase. Furthermore, the act providing for the government of Orleans Territory invalidated all land grants made in Louisiana since Spain ceded the province to France by the Treaty of San Ildefonso, excepting only those which were for the benefit of actual settlers.[8]

In 1800, three years before the Louisiana Purchase and thus before the speculations of Morales, Senator John Smith of Cincinnati purchased 750 acres in Feliciana Parish near the village of St. Francisville, where the Bayou Sara empties into the Mississippi, not quite halfway between Baton Rouge and the southern boundary of the Mississippi Territory.[9] That part of West Florida which figures in the present discussion was bounded on the east by the Pearl River and on the west by the Mississippi. In the other direction, it extended from the southern boundary of Mississippi Territory to the Iberville and Amite rivers and the lakes which marked the actual northern boundary of Louisiana east of the Mississippi. This area was divided into four districts or parishes, with that of Baton Rouge occupying the southwestern corner and Feliciana the northwestern. Next, on the east and extending from the Amite to the Tangipahoa River, was the parish of St. Helena, and between Pearl River and the Tangipahoa was the parish later called St. Tammany.

Senator Smith, who later figured prominently in the Burr Con-

[7] Claiborne to Secretary of State, August 28, 1810, in Carter (ed.), *Territory of Orleans*, 898; Abernethy, *Burr Conspiracy*, 8, 33–34, 216.

[8] Brant, *James Madison, Secretary of State*, 202.

[9] Stanley C. Arthur, *The Story of the West Florida Rebellion* (St. Francisville, La., 1935), 20–21.

spiracy, now planned to establish a village, to be christened "New Valentia," on his Feliciana property, and for his partner and agent to carry out this project he chose a strapping Virginian, son of a fellow Baptist preacher, named Reuben Kemper, who with his brothers Nathan and Samuel had migrated to Cincinnati and had become acquainted with the Senator. But the partnership did not function smoothly and Smith entered suit to eject Kemper from the Feliciana tract. After nearly three years of litigation, Don Carlos de Grand Pré, Spanish Commandant of the District of Baton Rouge, decided the case in favor of Smith.[10]

Maintaining that their rights had been infringed, Nathan and Samuel Kemper, with four well-armed companions, proceeded to barricade themselves in a log cabin on the property, while their brother Reuben represented their interests in New Orleans. The besieged party captured the first patrol sent against it, but Grand Pré now called out the militia and prepared two gunboats for action, while sending three expresses to Casa Calvo in New Orleans for aid. But it was not necessary to wait for outside assistance. Though the settlers in the neighborhood were nearly all Americans, they held their lands under Spanish grants and were not interested in the claims of speculators. The militia therefore responded when called, and the Kempers were forced to flee across the border to their headquarters at Pinckneyville, a village near unoccupied Fort Adams.[11]

Up to this point, the incident appears to have been only a minor border dispute growing out of conflicting land claims, but there was more to it. Morales and his New Orleans associates now decided that the dispossessed Kempers would be willing tools in their hands. In St. Francisville they had an agent who kept a store and bore the distinguished name of Edward Randolph. Randolph now drew up a declaration of independence for West Florida, and on the morning of August 7 Nathan and Samuel Kemper crossed the line with this document and a force estimated by one observer at nearly three hundred men, some being American citizens and others

[10] *Ibid.*; James A. Padgett, "The West Florida Revolution of 1810," in *Louisiana Historical Quarterly*, XXI (1938), 76 ff.; *Dictionary of American Biography*, X, 323–24.
[11] Richmond *Enquirer*, August 22, 1804; Cox, *West Florida Controversy*, 152–53.

Feliciana planters. This was a nondescript party, but it marched with considerable fanfare, the men wearing deep blue and yellow cockades and carrying a banner composed of seven blue and white stripes with two white stars on a blue field. Their object was to capture Grand Pré, take the fort at Baton Rouge, and then proclaim the independence of West Florida. As soon as this should be accomplished, they said they would offer themselves and their territory "to some government accustomed to freedom." [12]

By seven o'clock on the evening of the invasion Grand Pré received news of the rebellion. He at once put his slender garrison in a state of defense and summoned the local militia. At daybreak on the following morning the fort exchanged shots with two small parties of the invaders. Later in the day John O'Connor, a Spanish alcalde who had been captured by the rebels, came to Grand Pré as a messenger from the insurgents to offer himself and his fellow captives in exchange for the prisoners held by Grand Pré. This dignitary refused to treat with the rebels who, because they had no artillery, were not strong enough to attack the fort. On the other hand, the Spanish forces did not dare venture beyond their fortifications.[13]

O'Connor reported to Grand Pré that nearly all the settlers in Feliciana were ready to revolt and that the Americans above the line were ready to assist them. But outside Feliciana the people remained loyal and willingly responded to the call for such military service as the situation demanded. In relays of a hundred each they manned the fort, kept up the patrols, garrisoned strategic points, and made their slaves available in the service of the common cause. By August 16 the commandant had organized a force of nearly 150 volunteers, largely from the vicinity of the Amite and Comite rivers, and with them he hoped to cut off the escape of the insurgents and prevent a recurrence of the revolt.[14]

While these forces were maneuvering to suppress the insurrection, Daniel Clark called on Grand Pré and presented a petition signed by Nathan Kemper and five other leaders of the revolt ask-

---

[12] Madison to Claiborne, November 10, 1804, in Carter (ed.), *Territory of Orleans*, 332–33; Raleigh *Register*, September 17, 24, 1804; Cox, *West Florida Controversy*, 155–56.

[13] Cox, *West Florida Controversy*, 156–57.     [14] *Ibid.*, 157–58.

ing for pardon and declaring that they were now ready to lay aside their arms. But Grand Pré was convinced that Clark and Randolph had incited the revolt because of their extensive property interests in Feliciana, that his own military preparations had caused them to abandon their original design and had brought Clark to ask pardon for his adherents. Consequently, the commandant was not inclined to be lenient.[15]

When Casa Calvo at New Orleans learned of the second Kemper outbreak, he reported the facts to Governor Claiborne and asked him, by notifying the neighboring officials, to prevent aid from reaching the insurgents. On September 13 he reported that the rebels had taken refuge in the Mississippi Territory and asked that they be extradited or required to move away from the border. Claiborne had no authority beyond the borders of Orleans Territory, but he promised to bring the affair to the attention of the President and the acting governor of Mississippi Territory.[16]

When Governor Folch at Pensacola first heard of the disturbances at Baton Rouge, he hesitated to advance westward until he could ascertain the position of the people in the St. Helena district. When assured of their loyalty, he sent forward a force of fifty men with artillery to construct a military road from Mobile to Baton Rouge and requested the Captain General to send him more men and vessels from Havana. As soon as he learned of the second outbreak—about three weeks after the event—he placed himself at the head of a force of two hundred men, and on August 31 left Pensacola for Baton Rouge by way of the lakes. When he reached his destination all was quiet, but he proceeded to reinforce and repair the fort and to issue orders prohibiting the sale of any more land to Americans.[17]

Finding provisions in short supply at Baton Rouge, Folch was soon ready to return to Pensacola and got permission from Governor Claiborne to pass by way of New Orleans so as to make the journey by water. Accompanied by eight or ten of his officers and a military band, he reached the city in his galley on the evening of November 1, and the next morning was greeted by a salute of guns from Fort Charles. On the following Sunday the Marquis de Casa

---

[15] *Ibid.*, 158–59.   [16] *Ibid.*, 160–61.

[17] Raleigh *Register*, December 31, 1804; Richmond *Enquirer*, December 1, 20, 1804.

Calvo entertained the American and Spanish officers at dinner, and two days later Governor Claiborne returned the compliment.[18]

Claiborne assured both Folch and Casa Calvo that neither he nor his superiors had given any assistance to the rebels, and though Folch himself blamed the uprising on the West Florida land speculations of Intendant Morales and on the 6 per cent duty that the people of that province were required to pay on exports, Yrujo and other Spanish officials were quick to place responsibility for the raid at the door of the United States government. To support their charges they pointed out that Nathan Kemper was an officer in the militia of the Mississippi Territory and that his force was made up largely of men from that jurisdiction. Though no action was taken north of the line to punish the raiders, neither had they received any official assistance. Samuel Kemper now opened a tavern at Pinckneyville and Nathan settled on a nearby plantation.[19]

For almost a year after these events the situation on this sector of the Spanish-American frontier remained relatively quiet. Then on the night of September 3, 1805, a band of masked men, both Spanish and American, Negroes and whites, raided the homes of Nathan and Samuel Kemper at Pinckneyville and captured them along with their brother Reuben, who had come up from New Orleans for a visit. As soon as the raiders had recrossed the line into Florida, they turned their prisoners over to a patrol of Spanish militia under command of an officer with the intriguing Spanish name of Solomon Alston. Conducting his prisoners to the east bank of the Mississippi, Captain Alston boarded a pirogue and headed downstream for Baton Rouge, but he passed too near the American fort at Pointe Coupee on the west bank, and the Kempers were able to inform Lieutenant Wilson, commanding the garrison there, of their distress. The lieutenant lost no time in taking possession of Captain Alston's boat and turning its occupants over to Captain Richard Sparks, who now commanded at Fort Adams. After an examination before Judge Thomas Rodney, the Spaniards

---

[18] Richmond *Enquirer*, December 18, 1804; Richmond *Virginia Gazette, and General Advertiser*, December 13, 1804.

[19] Padgett, "West Florida Revolution of 1810," *loc. cit.*, 76 ff.; Cox, *West Florida Controversy*, 162.

were released and the Kempers bound over to keep the peace.[20]

These frontier incidents were, of course, only local manifestations of an international situation. On December 1, 1804, Spain had joined France in her war against England, and though Napoleon, by the end of 1805, had succeeded in crushing his Continental enemies, on October 21 of the same year Admiral Nelson destroyed the combined fleets of France and Spain at Trafalgar. In these circumstances the Emperor-elect found himself pressed for funds and decided to provide them by inspiring his Spanish ally to sell Florida to the United States for $7,000,000. This scheme was communicated by Talleyrand to John Armstrong, our Minister in Paris, and he passed the good word on to Madison and Jefferson. The French Minister, with his usual perspicacity, suggested that we first threaten our Spanish neighbor and then offer to pay good money for the Floridas.[21]

President Jefferson, with his natural acumen, felt quite competent to handle this delicate piece of diplomacy. Accordingly, on December 3, 1805, he sent his annual message to Congress in which he stated that our negotiations with Spain had settled nothing; that our traffic on the river to Mobile continued to be hampered by "arbitrary duties [12 per cent] and vexatious searches"; that our proposals for amicably settling the boundaries of Louisiana had not been accepted by Spain; and that inroads had been made into Orleans and Mississippi territories, our citizens seized and their property plundered in the very parts of Orleans Territory which had already been formally delivered to the United States. In view of all these developments, the President said, he had found it necessary to order our troops on that frontier to stand in readiness to protect United States citizens and repel any future aggressions by force if necessary.[22]

Though there was an ulterior motive behind this message, the

[20] John Smith to Jefferson, February 2, 1807, in Carter (ed.), *Territory of Mississippi*, V, 510 and n.; Philadelphia *Aurora*, July 26, 1807; Natchez *Mississippi Messenger*, September 13, 1805; Richmond *Enquirer*, October 8, November 19, December 18, 1805; Cox, *West Florida Controversy*, 165–67.

[21] Chadwick, *Relations of the United States and Spain*, 92–94; Cox, *West Florida Controversy*, 231–32.

[22] Richardson (ed.), *Messages and Papers of the Presidents*, I, 372; Brown (ed.), *William Plumer's Memorandum*, 346–48.

forceful stand the President took was fully justified by circumstances, for in October the Spanish government announced that it would no longer abide by the terms of the treaty of 1795 which permitted American vessels to carry British goods. Henceforth Spanish privateers would help enforce the French blockade of the British West Indies, and Godoy announced to our Minister in Madrid: "You may choose either peace or war. It is all the same to me." [23]

Jefferson's communication of December 3 was followed three days later by a message declaring that the conduct of France and the part she might take in the misunderstanding between the United States and Spain were too important to go unnoticed. Since the crisis in Europe, he said, was favorable for pressing a settlement, no time should be lost in doing so. Formal war would not follow, he thought, but a show of force was necessary. He turned all pertinent documents over to Congress and left to it the measures to pursue.[24]

Yet the President was not leaving it to Congress to direct his foreign policy. He and his Cabinet had already agreed to accept in substance Napoleon's proposals. Spain was to acknowledge our claim to the Perdido boundary, but we would pay $5,000,000 for the rest of Florida and agree to accept the Colorado River of Texas instead of the Rio Grande as our southwestern boundary. None of this was explained to Congress and when John Randolph—who was chairman of the committee to which the special message was referred—called on the President to discuss the matter, he learned to his surprise that an appropriation of $2,000,000 "for diplomatic purposes" was the immediate object in view.[25]

Randolph did not approve of this proposal. He thought that Jefferson was posing before the country as a champion of American rights and putting Congress in the position of truckling to Napoleon; he did not favor anything that would hurt England while helping France; and he opposed the purchase of Florida in any case. His committee turned down Jefferson's request; but the

---

[23] Chadwick, *Relations of the United States and Spain*, 84; Cresson, *James Monroe*, 214.

[24] Richardson (ed.), *Messages and Papers of the Presidents*, I, 376–78.

[25] Chadwick, *Relations of the United States and Spain*, 92–93.

House, despite the opposition of the *Quids* and the Federalists, made the desired appropriation. The money was actually transported to Paris by Fulwar Skipwith, our consul general there.[26]

But all this effort went for naught. On March 13, 1806, Madison instructed John Armstrong and James Bowdoin in Paris to notify the Emperor that the United States was ready to carry out its part of the bargain relating to Florida. On May 1 Armstrong delivered this message to Talleyrand who, the next day, notified Napoleon. Now the Emperor handed the Minister a formal declaration from Charles IV of Spain to the effect that on no account would he alienate the Floridas.[27] One explanation which has been offered for Napoleon's sudden change of front is that Federalist Congressmen had informed Yrujo of the secret proceedings of Congress on the Florida question and that his able Minister had kept his Court posted as to what was going on behind the scenes.[28] If this interpretation of the situation is correct, it is significant in that it represents the last victory which Charles IV would win against the overweening power of Napoleon.

Realizing that, in the course of human events, Florida seemed destined to fall into the hands of the ruthless Corsican, President Jefferson wrote to Madison on September 1, 1807, to the effect that, while war with England was probable (on account of the *Chesapeake-Leopard* encounter), any move threatening hostilities with other nations should be avoided, except with Spain. "As to her," the President said, "I think it the precise moment when we should declare to the French government that we will instantly seize on the Floridas as reprisal for the spoliations denied us, and, that if by a given day they are paid to us, we will restore all east of the Perdido, and hold the rest subject to amicable discussion. Otherwise, we will hold them forever as compensation for the spoliations." [29]

[26] "Decius" [John Randolph], in Richmond *Enquirer*, reprinted in Raleigh *Register*, September 1, 8, 1806; Natchez *Mississippi Messenger*, May 6, 1806; Richmond *Enquirer*, March 12, 1805; Brown (ed.), *William Plumer's Memorandum*, 360, 366–67, 371, 414 ff.; Mayo (ed.), *Instructions to the British Ministers*, 224 n.; Garland, *John Randolph of Roanoke*, 214–18, 220.

[27] Chadwick, *Relations of the United States and Spain*, 98–99.

[28] Franklin, *Rise of the American Nation*, 159.

[29] Lipscomb and Bergh (eds.), *Writings of Thomas Jefferson*, XI, 350–51.

As critical as was the situation in West Florida, it pales into insignificance when contrasted with the events taking place in Europe. After arranging a partition of Portugal between France and Spain and stationing an army in that unfortunate country, the Corsican forced the abdication of King Charles IV and his son Ferdinand and put his own brother Joseph on the throne of Spain.[30] President Jefferson's reaction to these events was expressed in a letter to Madison on August 12 in which he said, if the present conference should end in friendship between Britain and the United States and if Napoleon should continue at war with Spain, "a moment may occur favorable, without compromitting us with either France or England, for seizing our own from the Rio Bravo to Perdido, as of right, and the residue of Florida, as a reprisal for spoliations."[31] The day after this letter was written, Sir Arthur Wellesley landed near Oporto with a British army of 12,000 men to support the people of Spain and Portugal who had risen against French tyranny.

Following these momentous events, Jefferson wrote to Governor Claiborne with the idea that his views should be relayed to the leading men in West Florida. In this letter of October 29, 1808, he said that the patriots of Spain had no warmer friend than the United States government and that, if they should succeed, the United States would be satisfied to see Cuba and Mexico remain in their possession but very unwilling to see them, either politically or commercially, in the hands of either France or England. The President's letter concluded with the statement that we considered our interests and those of Spain "as the same, and that the object of both must be to exclude all European influence from this hemisphere."[32] Here was the future Monroe Doctrine in embryo!

Adventurers like to fish in troubled waters, and by the early summer of 1810 one such person had made his presence felt on the Tombigbee. Immigrants from Georgia and Tennessee were seeking out this isolated frontier to plant that magic staple, cotton, but on the north the land of promise was cut off from civilization by the presence of the Choctaw Indians, and on the south the

[30] Charleston *Courier*, April 13, 1808; New Orleans *Louisiana Gazette*, May 24, 1808.
[31] Lipscomb and Bergh (eds.), *Writings of Thomas Jefferson*, XII, 127.
[32] *Ibid.*, 186–87.

Spaniards at Mobile, by means of their 12 per cent import and 6 per cent export duties, partially blocked the road to prosperity. Americans who depended on Mobile for their contact with the outside world were eager to take positive action. Those who came from Tennessee did not understand why they had to travel by way of New Orleans and pay duties at Mobile in order to reach their destination, and those who claimed lands under the Yazoo grants knew that their claims would be more valuable if they had free access to the Gulf.[33]

Both of these interests were represented by a typical and significant, yet usually overlooked, protagonist in the person of one Joseph Pulaski Kennedy, resident at McIntosh's Bluff on the Tombigbee and a major in the Mississippi militia. The recently promoted Colonel Richard Sparks, who still commanded at Fort Stoddert, described him as a leading young lawyer, the son-in-law of Abraham Baldwin, Sr., and brother-in-law to Joel Barlow, who had been educated in the Eastern states, was ambitious, intriguing, and popular, but without real talents. Sparks questioned "his *capacity to conduct,* yet I am well assured he is seconded by a character [Colonel James or John Caller] who has been several years a resident of this country and well calculated to meet any deficiency of the first." [34] Kennedy had formed an organization, called the Mobile Society, the object of which was to take possession of that Spanish seaport.[35] Ambiguous letters to Spanish officials in Mobile indicate that he had designs on that port which, though scotched for the moment, he continued to cherish.[36]

In the neighborhood of Baton Rouge a more portentous storm was brewing. Here there had recently been an influx of French refugees from the island of Cuba, but the newcomers were not welcomed by the Spanish officials. In 1793 these unfortunate people had been driven from their homes in Santo Domingo by the slave insurrection which had been set off as a result of the egalitarian principles of the French Revolution. They had fled to Cuba and had lived there ever since, but Napoleon's victories had aroused the patriotism of the exiles, while his occupation of Spain

---

[33] Cox, *West Florida Controversy,* 454.

[34] *Ibid.,* 445; New Orleans *Louisiana Gazette,* December 28, 1810.

[35] *American Historical Review,* II (1895–1896), 700.     [36] *Ibid.,* 700–701.

had angered the Cubans. As a result, the refugees were again driven from their homes and some of them settled in the Baton Rouge area. But here the Spanish officials were no more friendly than those in Cuba, and again many of the Frenchmen fled—this time across the line into Iberville Parish of Louisiana. Even here they were not welcomed, and a report from New Orleans stated that "the emigrants from Cuba are the worst looking creatures you ever saw, whether white or colored." It did not add to their popularity that they had imbibed the spirit of Napoleon and declared that, as soon as they could settle their families, they would return and drive the Spaniards out of West Florida.[37]

Of course President Madison was aware of the situation that was developing on the Gulf Coast east of New Orleans and thought that a movement for independence might be expected. It happened that Governor Claiborne was visiting Washington just at this time and on June 14 he was authorized by the President to write to William Wykoff, Jr., judge of the Parish of Baton Rouge, and request that he visit West Florida to promote the assembling of a popular convention which should request annexation to the United States.[38] Six days later the Secretary of State wrote to Wykoff as well as to William H. Crawford, saying to the Georgian that he was enclosing a letter which would give him a view of the President's policy regarding the Floridas and that the President wished his co-operation in selecting "gentlemen of honor & discretion qualified to execute a trust of such interest & delicacy." He added that a letter had just been sent to "respectable" gentlemen of Orleans Territory with instructions to proceed into the district of Baton Rouge and thence as far as the Perdido to ascertain the wishes of the people of the region and communicate to them the Federal government's ideas and wishes.[39] A further step was taken when General George Mathews, the Georgia governor who had signed the bill making the Yazoo grants of 1795, and Colonel John McKee, agent to the Choctaw Indians, were appointed to arrange

[37] Natchez *Weekly Chronicle*, June 18, 1810; Charleston *Courier*, August 25, 1809; Arthur, *Story of the West Florida Rebellion*, 32.

[38] *Louisiana Gazette and New Orleans Advertiser*, July 13, 1810; May 6, 1811; Arthur, *Story of the West Florida Rebellion*, 35–36; James A. Padgett, "Constitution of the West Florida Republic," in *Louisiana Historical Quarterly*, XX (1937), 881–94.

[39] Carter (ed.), *Territory of Orleans*, 883–85.

with Governor Folch for the surrender of West Florida to the United States.

But the settlers in the Feliciana and Baton Rouge districts had decided to assume control of their own political affairs. Feliciana was the richest and most populous of the West Florida districts, and most of its inhabitants were Americans who had recently moved across the line from Mississippi Territory or had come directly by way of the Mississippi River, but there were some Tories who had found refuge here during the Revolution and even a few British subjects who had moved in while their country owned West Florida before it was ceded to Spain in 1783. Among these last was a six-foot four-inch citizen by the name of John Hunter Johnson, whose father had come into the area as early as 1775, and it was he, along with his brothers Isaac, Charles, and Joseph, who initiated the movement for the independence of West Florida.[40]

Captain Carlos de Grand Pré, former commandant of the "jurisdiction" of Baton Rouge, which was made up of the western districts or parishes of West Florida, had been a popular official, but he had now been succeeded by Don Carlos de Hault de Lassus, who was neither popular nor efficient. With bribery rampant and both justice and police protection generally unavailable, the settlers decided to remedy the situation as best they could. They felt justified in doing so because the Spanish King had been deposed and popular juntas were attempting to assert the rights of the people in Spain. Furthermore, the local leaders were acting entirely on their own initiative, for Governor Claiborne's letter had not yet had time to reach Wykoff.[41]

The first meetings of the revolutionary group in Feliciana Parish, mostly wealthy planters from the United States, were held at "Troy," the plantation of John H. Johnson. Here a definite plan of action was agreed on and Fulwar Skipwith, the most distinguished of all the Baton Rouge planters, was given the task of writing the constitution for the new government.[42] It will be recalled

[40] New Orleans *Louisiana Gazette*, March 4, 1819; Arthur, *Story of the West Florida Rebellion*, 32.

[41] *Louisiana Gazette and New Orleans Advertiser*, December 18, 1810.

[42] New Orleans *Louisiana Gazette*, July 25, 27, 1810.

that this gentleman, scion of a prominent Virginia family and a son-in-law of General Nathanael Greene, had recently served as consul general in Paris. Now, with a Flemish countess as his second wife, he was growing cotton on a 1,300-acre estate at the Montesano Bluffs near Baton Rouge. Though he had only come to this area during the previous year, he already possessed a "palatial" residence, and when he drove into town he made an imposing appearance in his coach and four with outriders and lackeys.[43]

Having made its preliminary arrangements, the revolutionary group now called for a popular meeting of the citizens of Feliciana at the "Egypt" plantation about ten miles below the line of demarcation. On June 23 more than five hundred men attended, and with only eleven dissenting votes they adopted the plan which had been prepared by their leaders and was now presented by John H. Johnson. This called for the election of delegates from each of the parishes of the Baton Rouge jurisdiction, who were to meet as a convention to adopt the constitution Skipwith was drafting.[44] On July 6 the people of the parish of Baton Rouge asked de Lassus to authorize them to hold a similar assembly, and he not only permitted this but allowed the parishes of St. Helena and Tangipahoa also to hold meetings and elect delegates. However, Shepherd Brown, who had migrated from Baltimore to engage in business at New Orleans and who was now commandant of St. Helena, did not approve of these proceedings and procured the election of delegates who were expected to do his bidding and support the existing Spanish regime.[45]

The result of all this planning was that on July 25 the West Florida Convention assembled in the house of Richard Duvall at St. John's (sometimes referred to as Buhler's) Plains, some fifteen miles from Baton Rouge. There were fourteen members, with four from Feliciana, five from Baton Rouge, four from St. Helena, and one from Tangipahoa.[46] Only one of these, Manuel Lopez

[43] Padgett, "West Florida Revolution of 1810," *loc. cit.*, 76 ff.

[44] New Orleans *Louisiana Gazette*, July 25, 1810; Padgett, "Constitution of the West Florida Republic," *loc. cit.*, 881–94; Cox, *West Florida Controversy*, 340.

[45] Cox, *West Florida Controversy*, 343–45.

[46] *Ibid.*, 346; Henry L. Favrot, "Some of the Causes and Conditions That Brought About the West Florida Revolution in 1810," in Louisiana Historical Society *Publications*, I, Pt. II (1895), 37–41.

of Baton Rouge, had a Spanish name, but his unqualified support of the governor was shared at first by the whole delegation which Shepherd Brown had sent from the district of St. Helena. John W. Leonard, member of a Tory family of New Jersey, who had migrated to New Orleans in 1804 and removed to Feliciana a year or so later, was the most conspicuous member of this group, but he later changed sides.[47]

Proceeding to elect John Rhea of Feliciana as president and to declare loyalty to both Governor and King, the convention next drew up an extensive list of grievances; asserted its authority to share the responsibility of government with de Lassus; and realizing that no funds were likely to be forthcoming from Spain, expressed its willingness to defray the cost of carrying on the administration. It then fixed August 14 as the date for its next session, appointed a committee on grievances to collaborate with the governor during the interim, and adjourned on July 27.[48]

The purely tentative nature of the proceedings of this assembly is somewhat surprising. A constitution providing for a practically independent government for West Florida had been drawn up, but its existence was not even mentioned. The truth of the matter was that the leaders of the convention, looking upon the cause of Ferdinand VII as hopeless and dreading occupation by either France or England, had annexation to the United States as their real objective, but they were not sure that the Madison administration was prepared to offend either of the great European powers by taking such action. And unless prompt support were forthcoming, Governor Folch might receive sufficient reinforcements from Cuba to enable him to crush the supporters of the convention, whose members were not unaware of the necessity for extreme caution.[49]

When they reassembled at St. John's Plains, they had reason to congratulate themselves on their foresight, for their first busi-

[47] James A. Padgett, "Official Records of the West Florida Revolution and Republic," in *Louisiana Historical Quarterly*, XXI (1938), 687–709.

[48] Journal of the First West Florida Convention, July 25–27, 1810, in West Florida Papers (Library of Congress), 1–12; Carter (ed.), *Territory of Orleans*, 894–95; Cox, *West Florida Controversy*, 346–51.

[49] *Louisiana Gazette and New Orleans Advertiser*, July 25, 1810, quoting Natchez *Weekly Chronicle*, July 17, 1810.

ness concerned a message of July 30 from Governor de Lassus. He said that the movement for independence had been launched when he called out the militia to eject the French refugees who had migrated from Cuba and that he had authorized the present convention in the hope of satisfying the malcontents. But he could not agree to share his official duties with them, as he alone was responsible to Ferdinand VII, nor could he accept his salary from them. Five days later de Lassus sent a report of his proceedings to Governor Folch, but it was early September before this message reached its destination.[50] Just a few days earlier Folch had received a remittance of 50,000 pesos and he had at once sent 6,000 to de Lassus, but both Folch and Morales blamed the commandant for having permitted the convention to assemble in the first place.[51]

Undismayed by the refusal of de Lassus to recognize their authority, members of the convention proceeded to recommend in strong terms the arming of the whole body of the militia, "as we are authorized to assure you that no sentiment prevails among the inhabitants hostile to the wise laws and government under which they have lived so happily." But even more important was "an ordinance for the public security and good administration of Justice within the jurisdiction of Baton Rouge and in West Florida," which the convention proposed to put into force at its next meeting. Accordingly, de Lassus was asked to approve it without referring to any superior authority.[52]

Since de Lassus had declined to allow them any voice in the government, this was bold action on the part of the members of the convention, especially since the "ordinance" which they proposed to put into effect was the "constitution" which Skipwith had helped to frame and which would have left the commandant with very little authority.[53] One of the members of the convention wrote Thomas Bolling Robertson, Secretary of Orleans Territory—a Virginian who was later to become Skipwith's son-

[50] Journal of the First West Florida Convention, in West Florida Papers (Library of Congress), 13–16.
[51] Cox, *West Florida Controversy*, 361–62.
[52] *Ibid.*, 363; Journal of the First West Florida Convention, August 15, 1810, in West Florida Papers (Library of Congress), 14.
[53] Cox, *West Florida Controversy*, 363.

347

in-law as well as governor of Louisiana—that de Lassus would probably "accede to nothing without consulting higher authority, and his refusal might be attended with serious consequences." He thought the majority of the officeholders under the Spanish regime were English in sympathy and that this constituted the principal obstacle to independence. If the United States did not countenance their efforts, he said, they would probably send a messenger to England to propose an alliance with that government.[54]

Meanwhile, the authorities in Washington were not asleep. Robert Smith, the Secretary of State, had suggested to Governor David Holmes of the Mississippi Territory that he send a personal agent to consult with the West Florida Convention. Colonel Joshua G. Baker was chosen for this mission, and en route he called on John H. Johnson, who had been detained at his home by illness. Johnson informed his visitor that Spanish officials were enabled to "fatten on the spoils of the land" because so large a portion of the population consisted of American refugees or ignorant timeservers. These classes rendered necessary the devious methods which the convention was pursuing, but the people needed to be placed "under the conduct of a wise guardian who will transform them from slaves to men." Johnson looked upon the United States as such a potential guardian, but he confidently asserted that two-thirds of the people regarded her tardiness and neglect as worthy only of a stepmother.[55]

William G. Barrow, one of the leading members of the American party in the convention, accompanied Baker back to Mississippi. Like Robertson's correspondent, he did not expect de Lassus to approve the work of the convention, and the delegates were anxious to know whether Holmes would intervene in case they needed his aid. Through Barrow, John Rhea informed Holmes that the members of the convention were anxious for immediate annexation to the United States, and he wished to know whether their territory would be acknowledged as a sister state or attached to one of the adjoining Territories.[56]

When the convention adjourned from August 15 to 22, it was

---

[54] *Ibid.*, 363–64; Padgett, "West Florida Revolution of 1810," *loc. cit.*, 76 ff.
[55] Cox, *West Florida Controversy*, 365–66.     [56] *Ibid.*, 364.

partly to give de Lassus time to formulate his answer to its demands and partly to lay the situation before Governor Holmes, who could be relied on to relay this information to the authorities in Washington. Everything depended on the outcome of these deliberations, and it was a favorable omen that during this recess the commandant gave a dinner to members of the convention where many toasts were drunk to Ferdinand VII, with an expression of hope for his speedy restoration to the throne. The occasion closed with a salute of twenty-one guns, and the reverberations appeared to clear the atmosphere.[57]

When the convention reassembled on August 22, it met at the Government House in Baton Rouge with de Lassus present. This official now announced that he accepted the Skipwith constitution "until the pleasure of the Captain General of the Island of Cuba [the Marqués de Someruelos] . . . be made known." The convention concurred, but Manuel Lopez, the only Spanish member, registered his disapproval of these arrangements.[58] Next, the convention drew up addresses to the Captain General of Cuba and to the "Inhabitants of the Jurisdiction of Baton Rouge." It then proceeded to elect the officers who were to function under the new form of government.[59] The most important of these were the three associate judges of the Supreme Court, who would share the powers of the commandant, not only as judge, but as administrator and legislator as well. To these important posts, Robert Percy of Feliciana, Fulwar Skipwith of Baton Rouge, and Shepherd Brown of St. Helena were elected. In addition, John H. Johnson was made sheriff and Philemon Thomas, colonel commandant of the militia.[60] Having resolved to meet again on the first Monday in November at the house of Richard Duvall, St. John's Plains, the members of the convention waited on the commandant on August 29 and he approved the appointments which they had made on the twenty-fourth. A proclamation sanctioning the work of the convention was then signed by all

[57] *Ibid.*, 365, 369–70.
[58] *Ibid.*, 369; Journal of the West Florida Convention, in West Florida Papers (Library of Congress), 22.
[59] Journal of the First West Florida Convention, in West Florida Papers, 23–26.
[60] *Ibid.*, 26–27.

the members and by de Lassus, after which the convention adjourned.[61]

For the moment it looked as though a satisfactory compromise had been reached. The government in all its phases was to be in the hands of four men with equal authority; namely, de Lassus, Skipwith, Percy, and Brown, but since the last was an avowed partisan of the Spanish regime, everything would have to be settled by compromise. Yet the commandant, who represented a king without a throne, was not satisfied with this arrangement. Although he had signed the proclamation ratifying the work of the convention, he refused to abide by it and carried on the administration as though he were solely responsible for it. Furthermore, he kept up a correspondence with Governor Folch through Shepherd Brown and through this channel he urged the governor to send an armed force to his relief, meanwhile appealing to Someruelos for reinforcements.[62]

Philemon Thomas, the colonel commandant of the forces supporting the convention, knew of this correspondence, and becoming suspicious of it, he had some of the letters intercepted. When they were read to him—for he could scarcely read—he had the governor's messenger carefully guarded while he detailed a young sergeant to spy on Shepherd Brown.[63] Convinced that de Lassus could no longer be trusted, he went to Baton Rouge on the evening of September 21 and assembled a council consisting of Colonel Samuel Fulton, Fulwar Skipwith, John Rhea, Philip Hickey, Isaac Johnson, Larry Moore, and Gilbert Leonard —now civil commandment of St. Helena Parish. This group decided that, since they could no longer trust de Lassus, there was no choice but to proceed at once to take the fort at Baton Rouge and declare the independence of West Florida. Trusty messengers were quickly dispatched to notify the leaders in Feliciana and St. Helena parishes of these developments.[64]

[61] *Ibid.*

[62] *Louisiana Gazette and New Orleans Advertiser,* December 18, 1810; Favrot, "Some of the Causes and Conditions That Brought About the West Florida Revolution in 1810," *loc. cit.,* 45.

[63] Favrot, "Some of the Causes and Conditions That Brought About the West Florida Revolution in 1810," *loc. cit.,* 45–46; Cox, *West Florida Controversy,* 394.

[64] New Orleans *Louisiana Gazette,* December 18, 1810; Favrot, "Some of the Causes and Conditions That Brought About the West Florida Revolution in 1810," *loc. cit.,* 46.

By the next morning John Rhea, president of the convention, had assembled six members of that body at St. Francisville. These men doubtless thought that their lives depended on the issue, for de Lassus had declined to arm the militia for defense and was undertaking to carry on his administration in an autocratic manner.[65] Furthermore, the suave and deceitful Shepherd Brown was trying to organize St. Helena Parish to support the Spanish Commandant, while Governor Folch was believed to be on the march with troops to put down the convention.[66] Such a situation called for drastic action, and consequently three important steps were taken: de Lassus was declared deposed; Colonel Thomas was ordered to take the fort at Baton Rouge; and John Rhea wrote to Governor Holmes making application for annexation to the United States. He referred to the "unalterable determination" of the people of West Florida to assert their rights as part of the United States and said they considered its faith was pledged for their support. He hoped and expected that a declaration of independence would be adopted within a day or two and that militia and gunboats would soon be sent to support the West Florida Convention. Having made these decisive moves, the convention adjourned to meet three days later at Baton Rouge.[67]

This recess was taken, of course, to allow Colonel Thomas time to muster his forces and capture the fort at Baton Rouge, and this officer did not disappoint them. Assembling his men and marching forty miles in thirteen hours, he attacked at four o'clock on the morning of September 23, having ordered his troops not to fire until they were fired upon. De Lassus had neglected to strengthen the fortifications and they were taken without serious fighting. De Lassus was captured, and so were the 6,000 pesos which had been sent him by Governor Folch.[68]

The next day Colonel Thomas reported his success to John Rhea, and the six members of the convention who had ordered

[65] Journal of the West Florida Convention, September 22, 1810, in West Florida Papers (Library of Congress).

[66] New Orleans *Louisiana Gazette,* October 5, December 18, 1810.

[67] Journal of the West Florida Convention, September 22, 1810, in West Florida Papers (Library of Congress); Padgett, "Constitution of the West Florida Republic," *loc. cit.,* 881–94.

[68] Journal of the West Florida Convention, September 24, 1810, in West Florida Papers (Library of Congress); New Orleans *Louisiana Gazette,* September 26, 27, October 6, December 18, 1810.

the attack met again in Baton Rouge on September 25. Realizing that they had taken decisive steps on their own authority, they issued a statement as to why they had deposed de Lassus and captured the fort at Baton Rouge. Then they called on all the districts which made up the "jurisdiction of Baton Rouge" to send as many men as they liked, in addition to their delegates, to speak for them in the convention. But the next day, without awaiting the arrival of additional delegates, the convention adopted a declaration of independence and a flag with a single white star in a blue field as the standard of the "State of Florida." [69] The existing laws, as amended by the ordinance of August 22, were declared to remain in force until superseded by new legislation. Then the work of revolution was climaxed by the election of Skipwith as president.[70]

Now that the convention had set itself up as an independent government, it was forced to face the realities which that step involved. The only funds it possessed consisted of the captured 6,000 pesos, and on October 2 it decided to float a $30,000 bond issue at 10 per cent interest. Three days later it repealed the tax which, on August 22, it had levied on the importation of slaves. And if this was undemocratic, it tended to redress the balance by providing that land should be taxed, not by the acre, but according to its value. To counteract the opposition movement which Shepherd Brown had organized in St. Helena Parish, Colonel Thomas was dispatched to the disaffected area with four hundred militiamen. The opposition collapsed without the shedding of blood.[71]

In winding up its business, the convention provided for the organization of a regular force of 104 men to garrison the fort at Baton Rouge, which was now entrusted to the command of Colonel John Ballenger, an old frontier hand from Kentucky.

[69] West Florida Papers, September 25, 1810 (Library of Congress); *Republican and Savannah Evening Ledger*, November 6, 1810; Lexington *Kentucky Gazette*, October 23, 1810; *American State Papers, Foreign Relations*, III, 396.

[70] Journal of the West Florida Convention, September 25, 1810, in West Florida Papers (Library of Congress); Padgett, "Constitution of the Republic of West Florida," *loc. cit.*, 881–94.

[71] West Florida Papers, October 2, 1810 (Library of Congress); *Louisiana Gazette and New Orleans Advertiser*, October 8, 24, 1810; Cox, *West Florida Controversy*, 411–12.

Next, a committee of safety, consisting of John H. Johnson, John W. Leonard, and Edward Hawes, was appointed to carry on the administration and to draft a new constitution to be submitted to the convention at its November meeting. Before it adjourned on October 11 the convention authorized its president to transmit the declaration of independence, along with an account of all its major proceedings, to Governor Holmes, with the request that the information be forwarded to the President of the United States, and it was also sent directly to the Secretary of State.[72] Holmes responded by directing Colonel Thomas Cushing to police the West Florida line near Pinckneyville with two companies of regular troops, meanwhile reporting his policy and activities to the Administration in Washington. Three days later he received a communication from thence, dated July 21, which was entirely in line with the policy he had adopted.[73]

In his two letters Rhea made it very clear that annexation to the United States was the main object of the revolutionists, and they wished to be informed as to the policy the Administration would adopt in the matter. They would prefer, said Rhea, to be incorporated as a separate state, but if that were not allowed, they would rather be annexed to the Territory of Orleans than to the Mississippi Territory. They were anxious that the public lands should be subject to local control and requested that all refugees, political as well as military, be granted amnesty. In his letter to the Secretary of State, Rhea asked for a loan of $100,000 and declared that the revolution had been made necessary by the danger that the government of West Florida might fall into the hands of the French refugees from Cuba.[74] Realizing that they were suspect, one of these Frenchmen wrote to President Skipwith on September 27, assuring him that, though they had declared for Napoleon, they really preferred independence and would make good soldiers.[75]

[72] Gayarré, *History of Louisiana*, IV, 229.

[73] Holmes to Cushing, September 26, 28, 1810, in Carter (ed.), *Territory of Mississippi*, VI, 120, 121–22; *Republican and Savannah Evening Ledger*, December 20, 1810; Cox, *West Florida Controversy*, 407.

[74] Cox, *West Florida Controversy*, 416; John Rhea to Secretary Smith, September 26(?), 1810, in *Republican and Savannah Evening Ledger*, December 20, 1810.

[75] Rhea to Secretary Smith, September 26(?), 1810, in *Republican and Savannah*

After the convention adjourned on October 11, mutiny occurred at the Baton Rouge fort, as a consequence of which the delegates reassembled on the twenty-fourth. By this time the mutiny had been put down and the convention proceeded to adopt the constitution which had been prepared by its committee of three. This document was modeled upon the Constitution of the United States and it was to be implemented by elections to be held on November 10. After having vested full powers in a committee of five, who were to serve until the elections should be held and the government under the new constitution established, the convention adjourned again on October 28.[76]

It should be noted that this revolutionary movement in West Florida had been carried on by only four of its districts, and only Baton Rouge and Feliciana had been wholehearted in their commitment to it. The people who lived east of the Pearl River had very little communication with those west of it, but the convention had not overlooked the importance of Mobile and Pensacola, and on October 10 its committee of safety issued an address to the inhabitants of these districts. Announcing the appointment of Reuben Kemper and Joseph White to treat with them, the committee urged that they authorize the present convention to act for them or else send deputies of their own to that body.[77]

While the convention was thus planning to take over all of West Florida for the benefit of the United States, President Madison was not inclined to recognize its claims. Therefore, on October 27 he issued a proclamation annexing the region west of the Perdido to the United States as a part of the Louisiana Purchase and authorizing Governor Claiborne to occupy it. Then, in order to make assurance doubly sure, General Wade Hampton and Governor Holmes were instructed on November 2 to carry out the occupation in case Claiborne should not succeed in doing so. These instructions were reinforced in communications

---

*Evening Ledger,* December 20, 1810; *Louisiana Gazette and New Orleans Advertiser,* January 7, 1811; Audebert to Skipwith, September 27, 1810, in West Florida Papers (Library of Congress).

[76] Walter Prichard (ed.), "An Original Letter on the West Florida Revolution of 1810," in *Louisiana Historical Quarterly,* XVIII (1935), 354–62; Cox, *West Florida Controversy,* 427–28.

[77] Cox, *West Florida Controversy,* 421.

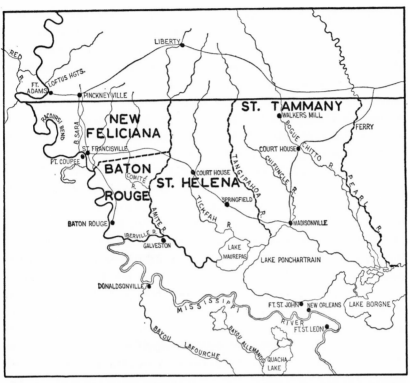

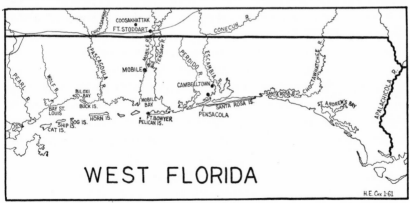

RED R.

FT. ADAMS

LOFTUS HGTS.

LIBERTY

PINCKNEYVILLE

ST. TAMMANY

WALKERS MILL

FERRY

PACOURSE BEND

B. SARA

ST. FRANCISVILLE

PT. COUPEE

NEW FELICIANA

BATON ROUGE

ST. HELENA

COURT HOUSE

BOGUE CHITTO R.

CHIFUNCLE R.

TANGIPAHOA R.

COMITÉ R.

COURT HOUSE

SPRINGFIELD

TICKFAH R.

AMITE R.

PEARL R.

BATON ROUGE

IBERVILLE R.

GALVESTON

LAKE MAUREPAS

MADISONVILLE

DONALDSONVILLE

LAKE PONCHARTRAIN

MISSISSIPPI

RIVER

FT. ST. JOHN

NEW ORLEANS

FT. ST. LEON

LAKE BORGNE

BAYOU LAFOURCHE

BAYOU ALLEMANDS

QUACHA LAKE

CHICKASAWHAY R.

COOSAKHATTAK

FT. STODDART

CONECUH R.

PASCAGOULA R.

MOBILE R.

TENSAW R.

PERDIDO R.

ESCAMBIA R.

CHOCTAWHATCHEE R.

PEARL R.

WOLF R.

MOBILE

CAMBELLTOWN

SANTA ROSA

SANTA ROSA IS.

ST. ANDREW'S BAY

APALACHICOLA R.

BAY ST. LOUIS

BILOXI BAY

BUCK IS.

MOBILE BAY

PENSACOLA

SHIP IS.

DOG IS.

HORN IS.

FT. BOWYER

PELICAN IS.

CAT IS.

WEST FLORIDA

H.E. Cox 1-61

sent by Secretary Smith to the governors on November 15.[78]

However, it was three weeks before news of the President's proclamation reached the scene of action, and in the meantime events were moving rapidly. Elections under the new constitution were held as scheduled on November 10, and on the twenty-sixth the legislature of West Florida met for the first time at St. Francisville, which was for the time being the seat of government. John W. Leonard was elected to preside over the Senate, and, by the joint vote of the two houses, Skipwith was elected governor by a unanimous vote. The inaugural ceremonies were held on November 29.[79]

Turning its attention to first things first, the West Florida legislature, on the same day that it elected Skipwith, appointed a joint committee to make arrangements for an expedition against Mobile and Pensacola. On the twenty-eighth the first contingent of the expeditionary force was enlisted with the immediate object of sending one hundred men to reinforce Kemper and Kennedy on the Mobile River. This was only the beginning. Skipwith was planning to raise a force of some six hundred men and send them forward under command of Colonel William Kirkland. Thus the West Floridians were quite serious in their ambition to conquer the whole province, and they had good reason to believe that they would have the co-operation of the people inhabiting the region.[80]

Taking into consideration the facts that the government which Governor Folch was supposed to represent no longer existed, that both France and England were anxious to take possession of the Floridas, and that the Baton Rouge government was poised for attack, Judge Harry Toulmin urged Folch to surrender the province to the United States. President Madison had a similar idea when he sent General George Mathews and Colonel John McKee to broach the subject to the Spanish governor, but for the time being no definite response was forthcoming.[81]

[78] Robert Smith to Governor Holmes, November 15, 1810, in *Republican and Savannah Evening Ledger,* December 20, 1810; Gayarré, *History of Louisiana,* IV, 236.

[79] Skipwith's inaugural speech, November 29, 1810, in West Florida Papers (Library of Congress); Prichard (ed.), "Original Letter on the West Florida Revolution," *loc. cit.,* 354–62; Cox, *West Florida Controversy,* 432.

[80] *Louisiana Gazette and New Orleans Advertiser,* December 13, 1810.

[81] Cox, *West Florida Controversy,* 458, 522.

The convention evidently believed that the Mobile garrison would surrender without serious resistance for, when Joseph White was not able to make the journey, Kemper traveled alone to Fort Stoddert, arriving there on October 24. Expressing only pacific intentions, he was at first cordially received by Judge Toulmin; Colonel Sparks, still commanding the garrison, and Captain Gaines were definitely friendly. But Kemper found even more useful friends in Colonel James Caller, who commanded the Tombigbee militia; his brother, Colonel John Caller; and Major Joseph Pulaski Kennedy, who, as previously stated, had organized the "Mobile Society." However, he discovered that the fort at Mobile had been strengthened, that several hundred Choctaw Indians had been called in to reinforce the garrison, and that, though Kennedy was prepared to furnish two companies of recruits, there was little prospect of success without reinforcements from Baton Rouge. The reason was that, though the Caller brothers were anxious to lend aid, Judge Toulmin was able to persuade most of the local people not to join in a filibustering expedition.[82]

It subsequently developed that Kemper was building his house upon the sands, but his efforts were taken quite seriously in Mobile. On November 30 the Spanish governor notified his superior officer, the Captain General of Cuba, that he would surrender his province to the United States unless he received assistance by the end of the year. On December 2 he wrote the Secretary of State, Robert Smith, to the same effect and appointed Colonel John McKee to go to Washington to make the necessary arrangements.[83]

While these events were taking place, a crisis was developing at St. Francisville and Baton Rouge. On December 1 the revolutionary government of West Florida formally authorized the expedition against Mobile and Pensacola, and it was erroneously reported that Colonel Kirkland with artillery and 1,500 troops

[82] *Ibid.*, 457; Toulmin to Innerarity, November 15, 1810, in *American Historical Review*, II (1895–1896), 701–702; Padgett, "West Florida Revolution of 1810," *loc. cit.*, 76 ff.

[83] Vizente Folch to Robert Smith and to John McKee, December 2, 1810, in Charleston *Courier*, July 3, 1811; New Orleans *Louisiana Gazette*, December 5, 1810; Cox, *West Florida Controversy*, 471, 480.

was marching to join Kemper.[84] On the fifth a small party of fifty-five men was actually sent forward, and on the same day Governor Skipwith first received notice of President Madison's proclamation of October 27, claiming West Florida to the Perdido as a part of the Louisiana Purchase. In this document the President stated that the whole area would be added to the Orleans Territory and Governor Claiborne was authorized to take possession of it.[85] Skipwith was apparently taken completely by surprise, for he had thought he stood well with the Administration and had expected his friend General John Mason of Virginia; his future son-in-law, Secretary Bolling Robertson of Orleans Territory; and John Graham, Burr's nemesis in 1807, who was now chief clerk in the Department of State, to keep him posted.[86] Nor does he seem to have taken the proclamation at its face value, for he immediately wrote to the President denying that West Florida belonged to the United States and proposing to negotiate in regard to annexation. The terms which he wished to insist upon were: (1) that the public lands remain subject to the control of the local government, (2) that all deserters from the United States Army and other refugees be granted asylum, and (3) that West Florida be erected into a separate state or annexed to Orleans Territory. Furthermore, Skipwith proposed a loan in order to finance the Mobile expedition.[87]

But Madison had not planned to negotiate nor to countenance the Mobile expedition. On December 3 Federal troops under Colonel Covington embarked at Natchez for the descent upon Baton Rouge, and Governor Claiborne had come up from New Orleans to accompany them. Before reaching their destination they expected to be joined on the river by General Wade Hampton, who was to come down the Mississippi from Tennessee and take command, but he did not reach Baton Rouge until

---

[84] Raleigh *Register*, January 3, 1811, quoting Natchez *Weekly Chronicle*, December 3, 1810.

[85] Richardson (ed.), *Messages and Papers of the Presidents*, I, 465–66.

[86] Skipwith to John Graham, December 23, 1810, in *Louisiana Historical Quarterly*, XXI (1938), 156–59; Padgett, "West Florida Revolution of 1810," *loc. cit.*, 76 ff.; Cox, *West Florida Controversy*, 417–18.

[87] Skipwith to Madison, December 5, 1810, in West Florida Papers (Library of Congress).

January 1. Meanwhile, in order to be sure that any opposition would be quickly suppressed, the militia of the two neighboring territories was to be kept in readiness.[88] Three days later the Senate of West Florida was informed that Claiborne was approaching Baton Rouge with an armed force and distributing the President's proclamation as he advanced. The Senate thereupon instructed the governor to ascertain the intentions of the invaders and then adjourned to meet again on the eighth. On the seventh Governor Claiborne, accompanied by Governor Holmes, arrived at St. Francisville and conferred with John H. Johnson, who represented Governor Skipwith.[89] We have no record of what was said, but it is certain that Johnson did not acquiesce in the highhanded manner in which he and his friends —who were also friends of the United States—were being treated. Nevertheless, Claiborne proceeded without delay to erect the Baton Rouge district into a county of Orleans Territory, thus annexing it to the United States. After this the West Florida Senate assembled according to plan and on the ninth adopted a respectful address to "Governor" Skipwith. Here the journal ends in tantalizing abruptness, with no record of adjournment. On the same day Skipwith wrote to Madison protesting Claiborne's arbitrary actions and saying that West Florida would repel the "wanton outrage." [90]

It is easy to understand Skipwith's feelings, but he was not a man to follow rash words with rash deeds. The next day he informed Claiborne that he was pleased for West Florida to be annexed to Orleans Territory, however much he regretted the circumstances under which this was accomplished. Declaring that he had not been able to make up his mind to shed American blood, he had given orders to Lieutenant Colonel John Ballenger to evacuate the Baton Rouge fort but not to lower the flag. However, Ballenger had not had time to carry out this order

[88] New Orleans *Louisiana Gazette,* January 23, 1811; Raleigh *Register,* January 3, 1811; Charleston *Courier,* December 29, 1810; Gayarré, *History of Louisiana,* IV, 238.

[89] Journal of the Senate of the "State of Florida," December 6, 1810, in West Florida Papers (Library of Congress).

[90] Skipwith to Madison, December 9, 1810, *ibid.;* Journal of the Senate of the "State of Florida," December 8–9, 1810, *ibid.*

when Colonel Covington appeared and demanded surrender.[91] There was no choice but to comply, and no terms were granted. Skipwith later commented bitterly that "our little army" had commenced its march to co-operate with the naval force under Colonel Cushing, and Mobile could have been taken within two weeks, but Claiborne would not wait. Nor did he delay in extending American jurisdiction to the Pearl River; a little later it was extended to the Pascagoula, but the Federal authorities peremptorily forbade an attack on the Spanish garrison at Mobile.[92]

News of the occupation of Baton Rouge had not had time to reach Fort Stoddert when, on December 12, Judge Toulmin wrote to President Madison that Kemper had informed Colonel Sparks that five hundred men were marching from Baton Rouge to join him in an attack on Mobile. When McKee told Kemper that he had been authorized by the President to treat with Folch for the surrender of his province, Kemper proposed to Sparks that he negotiate an amnesty with Folch on behalf of the government of West Florida. Sparks would have complied, but he was dissuaded by Toulmin because such a transaction would have amounted to an official recognition of the independent status of West Florida.[93] Yet this incident is significant in that it shows Kemper to have been a more reasonable person than he has usually been credited.

On December 13 Colonel James Caller arrived at Fort Stoddert with a copy of the President's proclamation claiming West Florida as a part of the United States. The next day Colonel Sparks sent a copy of this document to Governor Folch at Mobile, but Folch was not ready to surrender his province. Kemper looked upon this development as giving him authority to proceed with his plans for an attack, which he accordingly did. He sent messengers through the Tensaw, St. Stephens, and upper Tom-

[91] Skipwith to [John Graham], January 14, 1811, *ibid.*; Skipwith to Claiborne, December 10, 1810, *ibid.*; *Louisiana Gazette and New Orleans Advertiser*, December 11, 1810.

[92] Skipwith to Graham, December 23, 1810, in West Florida Papers (Library of Congress).

[93] Toulmin to Madison, December 12, 1810, in Carter (ed.), *Territory of Mississippi*, VI, 152–58.

bigbee settlements inviting all able-bodied men to assemble under the standard of West Florida. On December 16 he wrote to John Rhea from Fort Stoddert that a small force would leave that post the next morning and join other forces just below the line, there to await further orders. At the same time he planned to set out for the Pascagoula settlements to assist Sterling Duprée in raising and forwarding recruits. In that neighborhood he expected to meet the army advancing from Baton Rouge, and then all available forces would be concentrated near Mobile, where Major Zenon Orso was prepared to co-operate with the insurgents. These measures were apparently favored by Colonel Sparks but opposed by Judge Toulmin and his son-in-law, Captain Gaines.[94]

Colonel Sparks nevertheless feared that an attack by Kemper and his men would result in an unnecessary destruction of life and property, for he believed that Mobile would shortly surrender without a fight. Accordingly, he dispatched Captain Gaines with fifty men to take up a position close to the Spanish post and to induce Kemper and his men to return to the American side of the line, where on arrival they were immediately incorporated into the Territorial militia. This accomplished, Captain Gaines on December 22, according to instruction, sent a messenger to Captain Layetano Pérez, commandant of Fort Charlotte, and demanded the surrender of Mobile in accord with the terms of President Madison's proclamation. Pérez replied that he would have to consult Folch, who had just left for Pensacola, and a messenger was sent to overtake him. Folch's answer, as might have been expected, was that he could not surrender any part of West Florida without orders from higher authority.[95]

This was the critical state of affairs when, on January 3, Colonel Cushing arrived off Mobile Bay with his five gunboats and two companies of regulars. Judge Toulmin was already in the town collecting supplies for Cushing's force when he heard that Colonel Sparks was about to lead the militia down the river. The

---

[94] Reuben Kemper to Rhea, December 16, 1810, in West Florida Papers (Library of Congress).

[95] New Orleans *Louisiana Gazette,* December 28, 31, 1810; Cox, *West Florida Controversy,* 512–14.

President's proclamation, while authorizing the occupation of West Florida to the Perdido, specified that no Spanish post was to be attacked, but in sending instructions to Fort Stoddert, Governor Claiborne had apparently failed to make this point clear to Colonel Sparks. In this emergency Judge Toulmin decided to take matters into his own hands and called on Colonel Cushing as soon as he had established his camp. Pérez had refused to grant permission for the American flotilla to pass Fort Charlotte, but Cushing had proceeded without opposition and anchored in the bay above the fort. In this situation Toulmin succeeded in persuading him to disband the militia and thereby prevent the attack Colonel Sparks was preparing to make against Mobile with the Territorial militia under the flag of the United States. Of course, Colonel Reuben Kemper's men had to retreat with the rest, and this brought to a final conclusion the campaign which he had undertaken in the name of the revolutionary government of West Florida.[96]

Though a halt had thus been called on all local military measures, President Madison was still hopeful of acquiring all of West Florida and perhaps East Florida, too, by means of negotiation. This hope was greatly stimulated by receipt of Governor Folch's proposal of December 2, transmitted by Colonel John McKee, to surrender his province unless he should receive reinforcements by the end of the month. Folch's letter to McKee stated that since their conversation he had thought of addressing the President directly, through the Secretary of State, and propose, in more positive terms than those which he addressed to Governor Holmes, to treat for the delivery of his province to the United States, because difficulties increased every day. "From having been an eye witness," he wrote to McKee, "to all that has passed in this part of the province and the adjoining countries, you can give information respecting the alarm which reigns among its inhabitants, of the influence which the French agents in Louisiana exercise in these disturbances, and the risk which that province runs in being involved in the disorders which

[96] Cox, *West Florida Controversy*, 515–16; Governor Holmes to Secretary Smith, February 2, 1811, in Carter (ed.), *Territory of Mississippi*, VI, 173–74; *Louisiana Gazette and New Orleans Advertiser*, January 3, 14, February 6, 1811.

have had their birth in Florida, as well as the fatal consequences which may follow if the evil is not stopped in its beginning." [97]

On January 3, 1811, the President submitted to Congress Folch's communication, along with a protest from John Philip Morier, the British chargé d'affaires, against the occupation of Baton Rouge. In his message Madison suggested to Congress that he be authorized to take temporary possession of any part or parts of East Florida threatened by any foreign power or voluntarily surrendered by the Spanish authorities. Congress complied by authorizing him to use the forces of the army and navy to this end, and it also appropriated $100,000 to cover any expense that might be incurred; but any occupied territory was to remain subject to negotiation. As far as West Florida was concerned, no Congressional action was called for, and the Secretary of State authorized Mathews and McKee to negotiate with Governor Folch for the surrender of that province. [98]

On January 17 McKee wrote to Folch outlining in considerable detail terms of the proposed surrender and this letter, along with relevant documents, were entrusted to Mathews' secretary, Ralph Isaacs, for delivery to Folch in Pensacola. Isaacs reached his destination on February 25 and was surprised to find the Spanish governor and his subordinate officials obviously much impoverished, but Folch would not listen to any proposal for the surrender of West Florida to the United States. [99] As late as March 22 no report had been forthcoming from Isaacs, and on that day Mathews and McKee sent a message to Folch requesting a personal conference in order to arrange the terms of surrender. Again, the governor's reply was the same. He explained that his superior had not approved his offer to surrender the province; on the contrary, he had been ordered to hold it at all costs and had been supplied with $50,000 to enable him to do so. Even this emphatic refusal did not deter Mathews. In April, 1811, he arranged a personal interview with Folch at Pensacola,

[97] Folch to [McKee], December 2, 1810, in McKee Papers.

[98] Robert Smith to Governor Folch, January 28, 1811, in Carter (ed.), *Territory of Orleans*, 922; Charleston *Courier*, July 2, 1811; Richardson (ed.), *Messages and Papers of the Presidents*, II, 473; Cox, *West Florida Controversy*, 523.

[99] Cox, *West Florida Controversy*, 524-25; Carter (ed.), *Territory of Mississippi*, VI, 188-89.

but the Spaniard remained obdurate. Thus ended the tireless attempts of the Madison administration to acquire West Florida by negotiation.[100]

Before the revolutionary movement got under way in the Feliciana and Baton Rouge parishes, the Territory of Orleans had petitioned Congress to promote her to statehood. On March 12, 1810, Senator Giles of Virginia presented this petition, and on April 9 a bill granting the request was introduced. The Senate acted favorably on this measure, but the bill died in the House. During the following September the West Florida revolution broke out, and on October 27 President Madison issued his annexation proclamation which, however, stipulated that "in the hands of the United States it [West Florida] will not cease to be a subject of fair and friendly negotiation and adjustment." [101]

When Congress reassembled in December, 1810, George Poindexter, the delegate from Mississippi Territory, presented a bill providing that the Territory of Orleans, enlarged by the inclusion of West Florida, be admitted to statehood. Objection was made that, according to the President's proclamation, West Florida was still subject to negotiation but that, if it became part of a state, the government could no longer negotiate. Accordingly Poindexter's bill was amended so as to exclude West Florida from the new state. But the Federalists in Congress were not satisfied. They objected to the admission of any state carved from territory acquired since 1783, for they feared that New England would be swamped by an alliance between the old Southern and the new Western states. This point of view was most eloquently expressed in Congress by Josiah Quincy of Massachusetts, who on January 14, 1811, declared on the floor of the House that "if this bill [to admit Louisiana] passes, the bonds of this Union are virtually dissolved; that the states which compose it are free from their original obligations, and that, as it will be the right of all, so it will be the duty of some, definitely to prepare for a separation—amicably if they can, violently if

[100] New Orleans *Louisiana Gazette*, May 27, 1811; Cox, *West Florida Controversy*, 524–28.
[101] Richardson (ed.), *Messages and Papers of the Presidents*, I, 465–66.

they must." Poindexter called Quincy to order and demanded a ruling as to whether a member might invite any portion of the people to insurrection and a consequent dissolution of the Union. Speaker Joseph B. Varnum of Massachusetts ruled that Quincy's advocacy of secession was contrary to the order of debate. This decision was not satisfactory to many members of the House, who arose to protest against it. Representative William A. Burwell, a Republican from Virginia, said that the members of the House were responsible to the people they represented, not to the House, for any sentiments they expressed in debate. A vote was then taken on the question of upholding the Speaker's decision, and he was overruled by the narrow margin of fifty-six to fifty-three votes. Thus in later and more perilous times, Southern Congressmen had a precedent for advocating the right of secession.[102]

Despite Quincy's strenuous objection the House, with a large Republican majority, proceeded the next day to pass the Enabling Act by a vote of seventy-seven to thirty-six. When the measure came before the Senate, that body inserted the word "white" before the words "male citizens" as a qualification for electors of the constitutional convention, and the amendment passed by a vote of twenty-four to eight. Poindexter opposed this provision because he considered it unnecessary, but it received the support of most of the Northern members. Later the House struck out this provision, but the Senate insisted on it and the House acquiesced. On February 13 the bill was finally passed and was signed by the President on the twentieth.[103]

On November 22 the convention provided for in the Enabling Act met and carried out its functions. It gave the name of Louisiana to the new state and it set up a committee to draft a memorial to Congress asking that West Florida as far as the Perdido be included within its boundaries. Actually, Governor Claiborne had undertaken to claim the territory only as far east as the parishes of Biloxi and Pascagoula, the latter having been occupied and

<hr>

[102] *Annals of Congress*, 11 Cong., 3 Sess., 525; Norris W. Preyer, "The Congressional Fight Over the Admission of Kentucky, Tennessee, Louisiana, and Alabama into the Union" (M.A. thesis, University of Virginia, 1950), 57–64.

[103] Preyer, "Congressional Fight Over the Admission of Kentucky, Tennessee, Louisiana, and Alabama," 65–68.

plundered by Sterling Duprée, who acted under a commission given him by Reuben Kemper. But in these parishes it was hard to find enough literate citizens to fill the public offices, and even in St. Helena Parish there was considerable confusion.[104]

On March 4, 1812, President Madison notified Congress that Louisiana had fulfilled the conditions necessary for admission to statehood. Poindexter proposed that West Florida as far east as the Pearl River be added to the new state, and after having agreed to this measure, the House passed the Louisiana bill by seventy-nine to twenty-five votes. However, the Senate struck out the clause relating to West Florida, and the House concurred in this amendment. On April 8, 1812, President Madison signed the bill admitting Louisiana to the Union, and six days later he approved a separate bill adding West Florida as far east as the Pearl River to the new jurisdiction. Thus ended the West Florida imbroglio.[105]

[104] *Ibid.*, 71; Claiborne to Secretary of War, December 28, 1810, in Carter (ed.), *Territory of Orleans*, 907–908; Claiborne, *Mississippi, as a Province, Territory and State*, 304–307.

[105] Poore (ed.), *Federal and State Constitutions*, I, 709–11; Preyer, "Congressional Fight Over the Admission of Kentucky, Tennessee, Louisiana, and Alabama," 73–76.

# CHAPTER XIV

# THE NEW ORLEANS CAMPAIGN

BEFORE the decisive campaign for New Orleans began, Andrew Jackson broke the fighting power of the Creek Nation. Had it not been for this accomplishment, the powerful expeditionary force which the British dispatched in 1814 to attack the Southern frontier would have been able to land at any point along the Gulf Coast and, reinforced by their native allies, descend on New Orleans from above. If this had happened it is unlikely that even Jackson could have stopped them, nor is it likely that Louisiana would have remained in American hands at the end of the war.

Before the Tennessean appeared on the scene, the war on the Indian frontier went badly for Americans and natives allied with them. Tecumseh, with British support, attempted to bring the Southern Indians into an alliance with his own people to resist encroachments of the Americans. In October of 1811 he and his brother, "The Prophet," appeared with twenty-four warriors at Tuckabatchee, a Creek village on the Tallapoosa River, and delivered his war talks to 5,000 assembled Creeks. Chief Big Warrior and most of the other chiefs of the Lower Creeks stood out against the great Shawnee, but they failed to counteract his influence among the younger warriors, thereafter known as the "Red Sticks." After leaving the Creeks Tecumseh visited the Seminoles, the Cherokee, the Chocktaw, and the Chickasaw, but except among the Seminoles and the Creeks he had no great success.[1]

[1] Benjamin Hawkins to Governor David Mitchell, May 12, 1812, in Raleigh *Register*, May 29, 1812; Toulmin to Graham, March 10, 1812, in Carter (ed.), *Territory of Mississippi*, VI, 283–84; Pound, *Benjamin Hawkins*, 174; Claiborne, *Mississippi, as a Province, Territory and State*, 315; Pickett, *History of Alabama*, 510.

Creek victories at Burnt Corn and Fort Mims were followed by indecisive successes of Ferdinand L. Claiborne, brother to the governor of Louisiana and brigadier general of Mississippi Territorial militia, at the "Holy Ground" on the Alabama, and by General John Floyd of the Georgia militia at the village of Autossee on the lower Tallapoosa River. But Claiborne and Floyd succeeded only in making raids into enemy territory, and it was left for the Tennessee forces under Major General Jackson to conquer the Creeks. The Tennessee militia was organized in two divisions, with Jackson commanding the forces in the Cumberland basin and Major General John Cocke commanding in East Tennessee. The plan of campaign was for Jackson to lead his troops directly southward into the Creek country by way of Huntsville, where he would proceed to the most southern point on the river and establish a depot where supplies from East Tennessee would be received and sent to the fighting front. General Cocke would join Jackson with his contingent, and since Jackson was the senior officer, he would command the combined forces. This situation proved to be the most formidable obstacle to the success of the campaign which should not have been an unduly difficult one.

Notwithstanding failure of supplies and reinforcements from East Tennessee, Jackson led his army of about 3,000 men over a hastily constructed route across the rugged Raccoon Mountain to the Ten Islands of the Coosa River, where he erected Fort Strother.[2] Here he dispatched General John Coffee, close friend, business partner, and husband of Rachel Jackson's niece, to the nearby village of Tallushatchee which Coffee destroyed in a signal victory on November 3, 1813.[3] Shortly thereafter Jackson set out with twelve hundred infantry and eight hundred cavalry for the friendly village of Talladega, surrounded for several days by a large force of hostile Creeks. There on November 9 more than three hundred warriors were slain, while the Tennesseans lost fifteen killed and eighty-five wounded. But the desperate

[2] John S. Bassett, *The Life of Andrew Jackson* (Garden City, 1911), I, 93, 96, 97; Marquis James, *Andrew Jackson, The Border Captain* (Indianapolis, 1933), 168.
[3] Bassett, *Life of Andrew Jackson*, I, 97.

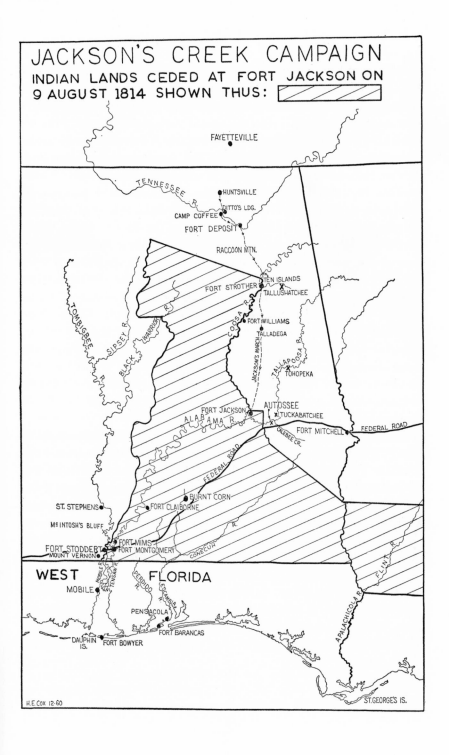

JACKSON'S CREEK CAMPAIGN

INDIAN LANDS CEDED AT FORT JACKSON ON 9 AUGUST 1814 SHOWN THUS:

FAYETTEVILLE

TENNESSEE R.

HUNTSVILLE
DITTO'S LDG.
CAMP COFFEE
FORT DEPOSIT

RACCOON MTN.

TEN ISLANDS
FORT STROTHER      TALLUSHATCHEE

COOSA R.

FORT WILLIAMS
TALLADEGA

JACKSON'S MARCH

TALLAPOOSA R.

TOHOPEKA

AUTOSSEE
FORT JACKSON      TUCKABATCHEE
ALABAMA R.
CALEBEE CR.      FORT MITCHELL      FEDERAL ROAD

TOMBIGBEE R.

SIPSEY R.

BLACK WARRIOR R.

FEDERAL ROAD

BURNT CORN

ST. STEPHENS      FORT CLAIBORNE

McINTOSH'S BLUFF      R.

FORT STODDERT      FORT MIMS
MOUNT VERNON      FORT MONTGOMERY
CONECUH

WEST      FLORIDA

MOBILE      MOBILE R.      TENSAW R.

PERDIDO R.      ESCAMBIA R.

PENSACOLA

FLINT R.

FORT BARANCAS

DAUPHIN IS.      FORT BOWYER

APALACHICOLA R.

H.E.COX 12-60      ST.GEORGE'S IS.

Creeks found a gap in the encircling Tennesseans, and several hundred escaped through it.[4]

As neither supplies nor reinforcements were arriving, Jackson was forced to retire to Fort Strother and await the new year before continuing his campaign. By the middle of January, 1814, he was ready for a blow against the Creek stronghold of Tohopeka, or the Horseshoe Bend, on the Tallapoosa, eighty miles south of Fort Strother. With nearly 3,000 newly mustered troops and with skirmishes on the way, Jackson halted on March 27 before Tohopeka, where a thousand Creek warriors under Chief Peter McQueen had for two months been preparing to make their last stand—just as William Weatherford had done at the "Holy Ground." In the gruesome battle that followed, eight hundred Creeks were slain and three hundred—all but four of them women—were captured. The Americans lost 45 killed, 145 wounded. Three of the Creek prophets whose haranguing, inspired by Tecumseh and his brother, had brought on the war were killed.[5]

The battle of Horseshoe Bend broke the power of the Creek Nation. Out of a fighting force of four or five thousand warriors they lost, from beginning to end, an estimated 2,500; another 1,000, led by Peter McQueen and Josiah Francis, now fled to safety in Florida. Jackson returned to Fort Williams on the Coosa and then moved down that stream to its junction with the Tallapoosa. On the way he was joined by a body of troops from Georgia, and Major General Thomas Pinckney, who commanded Military District No. 6, which embraced the Carolinas and Georgia, arrived on April 20. The friendly Creeks of the Lower towns on the Chattahoochee, estimated to number about 1,200, reported to Colonel Benjamin Hawkins in the expectation that the war would continue. A few of the hostile redmen, including Chief Weatherford, came to the Hickory Ground and surrendered to Jackson, but some 2,500 Florida Indians, along with the 1,000 unarmed Creek refugees who fled from their towns on the Tal-

---

[4] Jackson to Governor Blount, November 15, 1813, in Bassett (ed.), *Correspondence of Andrew Jackson*, I, 348–50; Bassett, *Life of Andrew Jackson*, I, 97–99.

[5] Jackson to Governor Blount, March 31, 1814, in Bassett (ed.), *Correspondence of Andrew Jackson*, I, 489–92; Jackson to General Thomas Pinckney, March 28, 1814, *ibid.*, 488–89.

lapoosa and Alabama rivers, were ready to renew the fight under the leadership of the English.[6]

A strong fort was built at the Hickory Ground and named Fort Jackson. The hero of the Creek War now returned to Nashville to receive the plaudits of his fellow citizens. A more tangible reward came on May 20, when Secretary of War Armstrong offered the Tennessean a Brigadier General's commission in the regular army with a brevet Major Generalship and the promise of promotion when the next vacancy occurred. Only eight days later the Secretary was enabled to carry out his promise. When General William Henry Harrison resigned his commission, it was offered to Jackson, along with command of the Seventh Military District, which included Louisiana and the Mississippi Territory. No other officer since the Revolution had risen to the highest rank in the military service quite so quickly. And now, with the new title, came orders to go back to Fort Jackson and make a treaty of peace with the Creeks.[7]

On August 1 the great council met at the fort. Most of the surviving hostile Creeks were in Florida, but the few who submitted during the preceding spring attended, along with a large number of friendly allies who expected reward for their faithfulness. Instead, they were presented with an ultimatum demanding that they surrender all their lands west of the Coosa River, plus a wide strip running along the Florida line. Such a cession would fix a barrier between the Creeks who lived within the United States and the Florida Indians, and it would open to settlement 23,000,000 acres—half the ancient Creek domain. This territory now comprises one-fifth of the state of Georgia and three-fifths of Alabama, and nearly half of it belonged to the Creeks of the Lower villages whose braves fought throughout the war under the banner of the white man. The friendly chiefs protested through their leaders, Shalokta and the Big Warrior, but Jackson replied that the interest of his country would permit no

[6] Hawkins to Governor Mitchell, Hickory Ground, April 26, 1814, in Lexington *Kentucky Gazette*, June 13, 1814; Bassett (ed.), *Correspondence of Andrew Jackson*, I, 399 n.; Jackson to Blount, April 18, 1814, *ibid.*, 503–504; Savannah *Republican*, April 19, 1814; Charleston *Courier*, May 9, 1814; Bassett, *Life of Andrew Jackson*, I, 118–19.

[7] Bassett, *Life of Andrew Jackson*, I, 119–23.

amendment of his demands. On the surface his attitude appears extremely harsh, but it should be remembered that, since the first planting of their settlements, the people of Middle Tennessee had been the victims of intermittent Creek raids, whereas the settlers committed no aggressions against these implacable foes. Now the Tennesseans had their chance for revenge, though it was largely against the wrong people. On August 9, 1814, thirty-five friendly chiefs, plus one who had been hostile, signed the Treaty of Fort Jackson. A "disagreeable business was done," the general wrote to Rachel, and "I know your humanity would feel for them." But in Georgia it was said that the treaty took from the Creeks only a small part of the territory guaranteed to the state by the Federal government in 1802.[8]

Before Jackson had settled with the Creek Nation, developments took place in Europe which concerned him quite as much as did the situation in the Mississippi Territory. At the Battle of Leipzig in October, 1813, Napoleon was defeated by the armies of England and her allies. On March 31, 1814, the Allies captured Paris and on the sixth day of the following month Napoleon abdicated his self-made throne and was presently exiled to the Island of Elba. England was now free to deal with her former colonists who had aided the enemy during her life-and-death struggle against the most powerful dictator who had appeared in Europe in modern times, and her mood was not a conciliatory one. Troops which had retrieved Spain and Portugal from the grasp of the Corsican could now be sent to the New World on a mission of vengeance, and no time was to be lost.

Up to this point the British Army had fought a defensive war on the Canadian border and the navy had blockaded the Atlantic Coast and carried out annoying raids along the shores of Chesapeake Bay with a squadron which was far too heavy for the work assigned it. But now, at last, offensive operations were to be undertaken. Officers of Wellington's army reasoned that England would now concentrate on America, "her most implacable enemy, against whom she has the justest cause of irritation; nor is it at all probable that she will let slip an opportunity so favor-

[8] James, *Border Captain*, 189–90; Lexington *Kentucky Gazette*, August 29, 1814; Bassett, *Life of Andrew Jackson*, I, 123.

able of severely chastising her, for her perfidy and ingratitude."
Accordingly, on June 2 a fleet of three ships of the line and five
frigates sailed from Bordeaux with an expeditionary force of
some 2,500 of Wellington's veterans under command of Major
General Robert Ross. At Bermuda Admiral Sir Alexander Cochrane with the eighty-gun *Tonnant* was waiting to take command
of the fleet, which now set sail for Chesapeake Bay.[9]

The fleet reached Cape Charles on August 14 and on entering
the bay was joined by the squadron of Sir George Cockburn.
This brought the number of warships up to twenty vessels, plus
some twenty transports and supply ships. Meanwhile, the land
army had been increased to about 4,000 men. The immediate
object of this impressive armament was "to effect a diversion on
the coasts of the United States of America in favor of the army
employed in the defence of Upper Canada." The point of attack
was to be decided by Vice-Admiral Cochrane, subject to the
general's approval, but the force was not intended for "any extended operation at a distance from the coast," nor was Ross to
hold permanent possession of any captured district.[10] Actually,
the Chesapeake Bay-Washington campaign was a blind to draw
attention from New Orleans, the real destination of the expedition.

These instructions show that the British government had no
intention of repeating the military mistakes which had been
made during the War for American Independence. It was not the
Atlantic Coast in which England was now interested, but the
Indian lands on the Western frontiers—the Louisiana Purchase.
The plan for 1814 was to send General Sir George Prevost down
the Lake Champlain-Hudson River route to isolate rebellious
New England from the rest of the country and to dispatch Cochrane's fleet with Ross's troops for an attack from the Gulf Coast.
This strategy was made manifest when in May Admiral Cochrane
sent Captain H. Pigot of the *Orpheus* to the Apalachicola to communicate with the refugee Creek Indians and supply them with

---

[9] [George R. Gleig], *A Narrative of the Campaigns of the British Army at Washington and New Orleans under Generals Ross, Pakenham, and Lambert in the Years
1814 and 1815; with some Account of the Countries Visited* (London, 1821), 2.

[10] *Ibid.,* 83–84; Adams, *History of the United States,* VII, 124.

arms. On May 20 Pigot received ten of the principal chiefs on board his vessel and reported on their authority that "the number of the warriors of the Creek Nation friendly to the English and ready to take up arms was about twenty-eight hundred, exclusive of one thousand unarmed warriors who had been driven by the Americans from their towns into the marshes near Pensacola, and who were expected to rejoin the main body." The Creek warriors friendly to the Americans were estimated at about twelve hundred. The fugitive "Red Sticks" were led by Chief Peter McQueen and the most fanatical followers of Tecumseh and his brother, "The Prophet." [11]

Meanwhile, Cochrane and Ross were directed to make some diversionary demonstrations in the Chesapeake Bay area, and this they accomplished in a spectacular manner by the burning of the public buildings in Washington and the unsuccessful attack on Fort McHenry which guarded the approaches to Baltimore. In regard to the former incident, Henry Adams waxes eloquent. "Ross and Cockburn," he says, "alone among military officers during more than twenty years of war, considered their duty to involve personal incendiarism. . . . They burned the Capitol, the White House," where they consumed a banquet prepared by President Madison for the defenders of the city, "and the Department buildings because they thought it proper, as they would have burned a negro kraal or a den of pirates. Apparently they assumed as a matter of course that the American government stood beyond the pale of civilization; and in truth a government which showed so little capacity to defend its capital, could hardly wonder at whatever treatment it received." (Adams probably did not think of William T. Sherman's march through Georgia when he wrote this!) Watching the public buildings of Washington going up in flames, Captain George Robert Gleig declared that he had "never witnessed a scene more sublime." [12]

[11] Adams, *History of the United States*, VII, 258–59.

[12] *Ibid.*, 146–47; [Gleig], *Narrative of the Campaigns of the British Army*, 124–26; Charleston *Courier*, September 1, 1814; "Subaltern in America," in *Blackwood's Edinburgh Magazine* (Edinburgh), XXI–XXII (1827), 427–28; Captain John Henry Cooke, Late of the 43rd Regiment of Light Infantry, *A Narrative of Events in the South of France and of the Attack on New Orleans in 1814 and 1815* (London, 1835), 157–59.

General Ross was killed in the futile attack on Fort McHenry, and the British fleet sailed from the Patapsco River on September 17, returning to anchorage off the Patuxent. But finally, cruising south, the fleet passed out of the Capes on October 18 and made for Jamaica. Before this date the Creeks made their submission by signing the Treaty of Fort Jackson on August 9 and Captain Thomas Macdonough stopped General Prevost by his naval victory at Plattsburg on September 11.[13]

When Jackson left Nashville to meet the Creek council at Fort Jackson, it was his intention to return to Tennessee and then go by water to New Orleans where he planned to set up his headquarters. But on the way to the Hickory Ground he learned that a British expedition had arrived at the mouth of the Apalachicola River, with 5,000 stand of arms for the fugitive Creeks, and also that a force of three hundred men, with a colonel and nine other officers, had landed on St. George's Island to erect fortifications.[14] Believing that this development portended a renewal of the Creek War, the general hastened to Mobile, arriving on August 22. While still on the march Jackson wrote to the governor of West Florida, complaining of the activities of the British in that area and demanding the surrender of the fugitive Creek chief, Peter McQueen, and the "prophet" Francis.[15] On August 14 Judge Toulmin, formerly so staunch in his defense of the Spaniards, wrote Governor Blount that the commandant at Pensacola took high dudgeon at Jackson's demands and declared that he would protect the Indians and furnish them with arms and ammunition. "We rejoice," wrote Toulmin, "at the expectation of seeing General Jackson in a few days. The Indians know our weakness and unless we are reinforced, we may be wiped out."[16] At the same time Jackson wrote to the Secretary of War for permission to invade Florida and promised "a speedy termination to war in the South and of British influence over the Indians forever." The Secretary of War replied, "It becomes our

[13] [Gleig], Narrative of the Campaigns of the British Army, 206; "Subaltern in America," loc. cit., XXI (1827), 539; Bassett, Life of Andrew Jackson, I, 124.
[14] Bassett, Life of Andrew Jackson, I, 127–28, Republican and Savannah Evening Ledger, July 26, 1814; Gayarré, History of Louisiana, IV, 332.
[15] Richmond Enquirer, September 17, 1814.
[16] Lexington Kentucky Gazette, September 5, 1814.

duty to carry our arms wherever we find our enemies," but he urged Jackson to use utmost caution in his movements. The letter came too late to have any bearing on the situation.[17]

On August 5 Colonel Edward Nicholls, with three ships of war and two hundred soldiers, landed at Pensacola without permission of the Spanish government. On taking possession of Fort Barrancas, he boasted that within a few days he would be followed by fourteen ships of the line accompanied by transports bringing 10,000 troops from Bermuda, that within a month Mobile and the surrounding country would be in British and Spanish hands, and that all Louisiana would be returned to Spain. It is astonishing that he had the temerity to issue a proclamation calling on the people of Louisiana and Kentucky to support him. Jackson's reply was that there would be bloody noses before Nicholls attained his objective, and on August 27 he sent a request to Governor William Blount to send him all the Tennessee militia which had been called into service, including General Coffee and his mounted command. At the same time Jackson laid an embargo on the flour trade between New Orleans and Pensacola.[18]

In 1814 Mobile was a town of 150 houses occupied by a population which, in the main, spoke either French or Spanish. It was supposed to be defended by Fort Charlotte, but this fortification, just below the town, was so placed that it had little military importance. The key to Mobile Bay was at Mobile Point, a long sandspit thrust out from the eastern mainland some thirty miles below the town and across the bay from it. Soon after his occupation of Mobile in 1813, General Wilkinson ordered the erection here of a fortification which he called Fort Bowyer. His successor, General Thomas Flournoy, thought so little of Mobile as a military post that he advised the government to withdraw the garrison. Jackson entertained different ideas and immediately after his arrival at Mobile he sent Major William Lawrence with 160 men who,

[17] Jackson to John Armstrong, June 27, 1814, in Bassett (ed.), *Correspondence of Andrew Jackson*, II, 12–13; Bassett, *Life of Andrew Jackson*, I, 127–79.

[18] Jackson to Governor Blount, Mobile, August 27, 1814, in Bassett (ed.), *Correspondence of Andrew Jackson*, II, 33–34; Richmond *Enquirer*, October 14, 1814; *Republican and Savannah Evening Ledger*, August 25, 1814; New Orleans *Louisiana Gazette*, September 3, 1814; Charleston *Courier*, January 15, 1814; Lexington *Kentucky Gazette*, September 5, 1814; Gayarré, *History of Louisiana*, IV, 337.

by working day and night for two weeks, placed the fort in a tolerable state of defense.[19]

This precaution paid off, for on September 15 Fort Bowyer was attacked by four British warships dispatched from Pensacola under Captain Percy. On September 29 the *Louisiana Gazette* published a lively description of the battle as told by "A gentleman just returned from Mobile." On the afternoon of the fifteenth Commander Percy, with two sloops of war and two brigs, attacked by water, while Colonel Nicholls led the marines, and he and a large party of Indians under the notorious Captain George Woodbine attacked the fort in the rear. The vessels received a few shots as they came up the channel and returned the fire occasionally until they came abreast of the fort where they dropped anchor and opened a broadside. The cannonading then became tremendous, with ball and grape pouring in from the fort's battery. The lead ship, the *Hermes,* became so crippled that she grounded and her deck was completely raked. While her crew was endeavoring to get her afloat, she was again raked with grape and shot from the fort. Finding she could not get free, her crew set fire and blew her up. Those in the fort cheered the firing and the sinking.

Meanwhile, Colonel Nicholls' men co-ordinated their movements with those of the fleet and took position at the rear of the fort. As soon as the fort opened fire, the Indians broke and ran. They were also demoralized by shells from the ships which passed over the fort and fell among them. Captain Woodbine did his utmost to rally them, but to no avail. The observer reported that men were seen dragged to their posts and beaten with the sword to make them stay there. The attackers, seeing there was no hope of success, finally made a precipitate withdrawal. The *Gazette* concluded: "When it is considered that Mobile Point is the key to Louisiana, every American will appreciate the conduct of Maj. Lawrence and the men who defended Fort Bowyer." [20] The public, neither then nor later, was as aware of the significance of this victory as was the editor of the *Gazette.*

Colonel Nicholls' talk of a mighty conquest was not all brag-

---

[19] Bassett, *Life of Andrew Jackson,* I, 133.

[20] *Ibid.,* 133–34; New Orleans *Louisiana Gazette,* September 29, 1814; Gayarré, *History of Louisiana,* IV, 349.

gadocio; he came nearer revealing Britain's schemes and her plan of operation than perhaps even Jackson suspected. The "Subaltern in America" reported that "the conquest of New Orleans [and of all Louisiana] was from the first the grand object, for the attainment of which our expedition had been fitted out." The Chesapeake operations "were undertaken simply as blinds, to divert the attention of the American government from the district really threatened; and so anxious were ministers to effect this, and though a general rendezvous at Jamaica of the invading army had long been planned, not a hint of the matter was dropped to the naval officer commanding there." [21] The British officer further declared that the fate of the expedition was put in danger because the admiral on the Jamaica station died, his dispatches fell into the hands of a subordinate who talked too much, and an American chartered a fast-sailing ship and carried the news of danger to Louisiana. Soon, he continued, the American governor of Florida learned from a thousand sources that he was in danger and set himself instantly to prepare his defenses.

The vessel that warned Jackson of his danger was the privateer schooner *Warren* out of New Bedford, William Gardner, captain, who put into Negril Bay, Jamaica, the latter part of November. There he saw a great armament, including men-of-war, together with a fleet of fifty transports full of troops and supplies, all ready to sail. Upon a second look Gardner stood to sea, followed all day by a frigate and a sloop of war until near the west end of Cuba. As darkness fell the little privateer beat up across the Gulf to Mobile, struggling against strong headwinds, which delayed her arrival until December 7. A courier rode day and night and delivered Gardner's information to Jackson on the morning of the ninth.[22] Jackson knew the British were planning to make Spanish Florida their base of operations and that Mobile was the logical place for their first attack against the vulnerable Gulf frontier.

For nearly three months after the victory at Fort Bowyer, the British advance expedition lay quietly at Pensacola awaiting the

[21] "Subaltern in America," *loc. cit.,* XXI (1827), 720–22.
[22] Augustus C. Buell, *History of Andrew Jackson* (New York, 1904), I, 363–65.

arrival of Cochrane's fleet from Jamaica. Cochrane was awaiting General Sir John Keane's forces from Plymouth, which were long delayed by contrary winds. This delay cost the British dearly. Had the expedition reached the Louisiana coast according to plan, it would have found the Americans woefully unprepared. But now Jackson was on the alert, and as soon as news came to Mobile that Nicholls was at Pensacola, he at once wrote urgent letters, calling out every available man for the defense of the coast. Contractors were ordered to place provisions for 3,000 men along the Coosa-Alabama line of supply, and Fort Jackson was designated as the place of rendezvous. On October 5 General Coffee rode southward with 2,000 horsemen from West Tennessee. On the journey he was joined by 500 more from East Tennessee and by some irregular companies. He arrived at the rendezvous with 2,800 enthusiastic followers.[23]

Shortly after his arrival, Judge Harry Toulmin wrote from Fort Stoddert to Governor Blount that General Jackson and suite left his house the day before for Fort Montgomery, that the Third Regiment was then on its way from Mobile to the same place, that approximately 2,000 Tennessee horsemen under General Coffee were then crossing the Tombigbee seven miles above, and that the Tennessee infantry was daily expected. He concluded by saying that "Jackson came just in time to provide for the reoccupation of the fort at Mobile point and prevent the overrunning of this whole country by the British and Indians. The first attack would have been made on Mobile as there a stranger is within our gates. The British assume all power at Pensacola, though the government is nominally Spanish. Their flag is said to fly on one side of the fort and the Spanish on the other. The British flag is also hoisted in the town and they exercise all the effective attributes of sovereignty." [24]

Jackson marched against Pensacola with about 3,000 men and on November 6 sent a flag of truce to the Spanish comman-

[23] Bassett, *Life of Andrew Jackson*, I, 136–37; Jackson to Gonzáles Manrique, commandant at Pensacola, November 9, 1814, in Bassett (ed.), *Correspondence of Andrew Jackson*, II, 95.

[24] Toulmin to Governor Blount, Fort Stoddert, October 26, 1814, in Nashville *Clarion*, November 15, 1814, reprinted in Lexington *Kentucky Gazette*, November 21, 1814, and in Richmond *Enquirer*, December 18, 1814.

dant, announcing that he came not to make war on Spain but to insist on Florida's neutrality, which should be guaranteed by the immediate delivery of Fort Barrancas and other fortifications into the hands of the American forces. Without deigning to receive Jackson's messenger, the commandant fired on the flag of truce and the next day Jackson occupied the place after a sharp skirmish in the streets.[25] A week later he sent a detailed account of this affair from Fort Montgomery to Governor Blount. He found Pensacola defended by both Spanish and British troops and immediately decided to storm the town with the regulars of the Third, Thirty-Eighth, and Forty-Fourth Infantry, a part of General Coffee's brigade, the Mississippi dragoons, and part of the West Tennessee regiment commanded by Colonel Eli Hammond, together with a detachment of Choctaw Indians. "Being encamped on the west of the Town," Jackson reported, "I calculated they would expect the assault from that quarter and be prepared to rake me from the fort and the British armed vessels, seven in number, that lay in the Bay. To cherish this idea, I sent out part of the mounted men to show themselves on the west side, whilst I passed in the rear of the fort to the east side of the town. When I appeared within a mile I was in full view." The general expressed his pride in the uniform firmness and courage with which his troops advanced and, with a strong fort ready to assail them on the right and seven armed British vessels on their left, entered the town.[26]

The Spanish commandant now hastened to surrender the place and its fortifications. It was agreed that forts, arsenals, and armaments would be given over to the Americans until a force strong enough to enforce the obligations of neutrality should arrive; but before Jackson could occupy the Barrancas, Colonel Nicholls blew it up and sailed away with Woodbine and his Indian allies. Having thus been cheated of his prey, the general evacuated Pensacola on November 9 and hastened back to Mobile. The next day John Innerarity of Panton's old firm—now known

---

[25] Toulmin to the Editor, November 26, 1814, in Raleigh *Register*, January 6, 1815; Lexington *Kentucky Gazette*, December 12, 1814; Gayarré, *History of Louisiana*, IV, 373.

[26] Raleigh *Register*, December 30, 1814.

as John Forbes and Company—wrote from Pensacola that the inhabitants were thrown into great confusion on the approach of Jackson's army. In letters intercepted by Colonel Nicholls, he said, the firm of Forbes and Company was described as the most conspicuous object on which the Americans had designs, though the colonel "had used every means to impress in the minds of the Commodore and officers of the navy that we were entirely in the American interest." All the Negroes in town, including his own, had fled to the other side of the bay. Colonel Nicholls went in a gunboat to force all the Indians to march to Appalachee and with them he drove about three hundred Negroes, impressing all available barges and canoes for the purpose. "Instead of the pillaging expected," said Innerarity, "the American army has behaved well and panic and terror gives way to favorable opinion." [27]

Before Jackson got back to Mobile, he received many letters urging him to hasten to the defense of New Orleans. He has been severely criticized for having tarried so long before complying, but he understood the situation on the Gulf Coast better than did his critics. In the spring of 1814 Admiral Cochrane had been ordered to make observations with a view to operations in Louisiana. In the summer he reported that 3,000 men, with the cooperation of the Indians and discontented natives, could take Mobile and New Orleans. His language indicated that he had in mind an expedition through Mobile, which was what Jackson expected. When Cochrane received his instructions at Jamaica, they directed him to set sail on November 20 and proceed directly to New Orleans or indirectly through Mobile, as he saw fit. Because the British authorities suspected the Louisiana Creoles of disloyalty to the United States, Cochrane was to cultivate their good will, to provide them with arms and provisions, to organize them into military bodies, and "to encourage them to commit themselves by an overt act against the United States." They were not, however, to be allowed to think that they would become permanent British subjects or to establish an independent state. On the contrary, they were to be led to believe that they would return to their former Spanish allegiance. Cochrane was also to

[27] *Florida Historical Quarterly,* IV (1930–1931), 128.

avoid exciting the slave population to rise against their masters, since the whole Creole element, many of whom were slaveholders, would be repelled if they believed that a servile insurrection was planned.

General Ross, who had originally been selected to lead the land forces against New Orleans, was ordered first to block the mouth of the Mississippi "so as to deprive the back settlements of America of their communication with the sea." His second objective was "to occupy some important and valuable possession by the restoration of which we may improve the conditions of peace or which may entitle us to exact its cession as the price of peace." The point of attack was left to Ross and Cochrane: they could attack New Orleans at once, or "move into the country of the friendly Indians." The second objective, the Ministry stated, could be obtained only with the will of the inhabitants. With their co-operation and favor, "we may expect to rescue the whole province of Louisiana from the United States." [28]

All the evidence available to Jackson at this time pointed to Mobile as the place of initial attack. Until October 30 Monroe advised that the enemy would attack through Mobile, but by late September the government was convinced that Louisiana was also in danger, and at once Monroe sent out calls for militia to the governors of Kentucky, Tennessee, and Georgia.[29] The response was generous, and in addition to the militia, the total force included 2,378 regulars. Of these Jackson left all the Georgia and East Tennessee militia, with nearly 2,000 regulars and riflemen, to protect Mobile and the surrounding country. The others he ordered to concentrate at New Orleans. A few days after he started for that city, Admiral Cochrane sailed from Jamaica for the same destination with 50 vessels and approximately 6,000 men.[30]

Entering New Orleans on December 1, Jackson first reviewed the city militia composed of the uniformed companies under Major Jean Plauché and the battalions of free men of color under

[28] Lord Bathurst to Ross, August 10, 1814, cited in Adams, *History of the United States*, VIII, 313; Bassett, *Life of Andrew Jackson*, I, 161–62.

[29] Bassett, *Life of Andrew Jackson*, I, 162–63; Monroe to Jackson, September 27, 1814, in Bassett (ed.), *Correspondence of Andrew Jackson*, II, 60–63.

[30] Bassett, *Life of Andrew Jackson*, I, 163–64.

Majors Pierre Lacoste and Louis Daquin, complimenting both on their soldierly appearance. Then he went to dinner with Edward Livingston—whom he made his military secretary—and met a group of fashionable ladies, charming them by his grave deference and natural courtesy. Two days later he began a tour of inspection, going first down the river to Fort St. Philip, where he thought the enemy, coming by that route, would receive its first check. Having spent six days examining the approaches from this direction, he next went to the Chef Menteur, a bayou connecting lakes Borgne and Pontchartrain and from which the Gentilly Road leads along a strip of dry land to the city. This seemed to be a possible route of approach, and even after he learned that Admiral Cochrane's ships were beginning to anchor off Cat and Ship islands at the entrance to Lake Borgne, he considered this a ruse to draw his attention from the river, nor had he yet given up his opinion that the enemy aimed at Mobile whence, using that as a base, he would move into the interior to cut off New Orleans by occupying a stronghold above the city.[31]

At noon on December 14 the British captured the five gunboats which constituted the only American defense on Lake Borgne, and on the afternoon of the next day this news reached New Orleans. Jackson now hastened back to the city from Chef Menteur, for he was at last fully aware of his danger, and he at once sent urgent orders to John Coffee, William Carroll, and all other commanders within reach to rush their forces to New Orleans. The general had now decided that the British would advance from the head of Lake Borgne, and he expected to meet them near the village of Gentilly, about five miles east of the city.[32]

One reason why Jackson had been so certain that the enemy would make his approach by way of Mobile was the difficulty of reaching New Orleans by water. This French-speaking city of somewhat more than 20,000 inhabitants occupied a narrow strip of dry land between the river and Lake Pontchartrain more

[31] Ibid., 166–68; Jackson to Secretary of War Monroe, December 16, 1814, in Bassett (ed.), Correspondence of Andrew Jackson, II, 115–19; James, Border Captain, 222.

[32] "Subaltern in America," loc. cit., XXI (1827), 724; Gayarré, History of Louisiana, IV, 413; Bassett, Life of Andrew Jackson, I, 169–70.

than one hundred miles from the mouths of the Mississippi. About fifteen miles below New Orleans the river makes a sharp bend known as the English Turn, and here American forts on both banks commanded the stream. A sailing vessel laboring against the current and trying to negotiate this bend would be at the mercy of the land batteries. Along both banks of the river there were strips of dry land sometimes as much as a mile wide and the small streams were similarly flanked by narrow strips, but otherwise nearly all the land about New Orleans was covered by impenetrable cypress and marsh grass swamps.

A young English officer who took part in the Battle of New Orleans, Captain George Robert Gleig, commented that "though in itself unfortified, it is difficult to conceive a place capable of presenting greater obstacles to an invader." His commanding officer certainly agreed.[33] Considering the river route impassable and the Gentilly Road too obvious, General Sir John Keane— in command after the death of Ross and before the arrival of General Edward M. Pakenham—decided, with the advice of the Baratarian smugglers and others, to approach his objective by way of Lake Borgne and the Bayou Bienvenu, thus reaching dry land along the river at the Villeré plantation about eight miles below the city. If Jackson himself had had the privilege of selecting his enemy's approach, this would have been his choice. He knew that after the British reached the river by the Bienvenu route they would, before they could advance against New Orleans, be forced to pass the narrow plain of Chalmette. This plain, flanked by the Mississippi on the right and an impenetrable cypress swamp on the left, was in effect a defile. Having no reliable topographical maps of the region and being smilingly fed misinformation of the terrain and extravagant exaggerations of Jackson's forces by the Baratarians, who hated the British with implacable Gallic hatred, General Keane was led to his destruction. It was soon discovered that the great armada, which had been destined to batter down New Orleans, would be of little use. Keane's advance troops were shifted to shallow draft boats and entered Lake Borgne on December 13. Their first concern was to destroy the five American gunboats commanded by Lieutenant Thomas

[33] [Gleig], *Narrative of the Campaigns of the British Army*, 248–49, 257–58.

Ap Catesby Jones. This accomplished, the advance brigade was ferried thirty miles in small boats to Pea Island where it remained without shelter from December 14 to 21, while the rest of the troops were similarly brought in from the fleet. One officer sarcastically commented on the fact that they were hustled into rowboats "pulled by *men-of-war's men.*" Admiral Cochrane was relentless and kept the seamen at the oars for a week, plying between ship and island. On the twenty-second General Keane again took to the boats with the advance brigade and crossed Lake Borgne to the mouth of the Bayou Bienvenu. Here he would be joined by two more brigades as soon as the boats could return for them. The next day the advance brigade reached the home of General Jacques Villeré and his sons Gabriel and Celestin. All those within were captured, but Gabriel presently made his escape and hastened to New Orleans to warn General Jackson, who had been taken completely by surprise as to the direction from which the enemy would approach.[34]

It was one-thirty in the afternoon of December 23 when Jackson received news that the foe was going into camp just eight miles south of New Orleans. Immediately the general turned to a group of officers and said, "Gentlemen, the British are below; we must fight them tonight," and before darkness fell a force of 2,131 men was assembled on the river road south of the city. In addition, Master-Commandant Daniel T. Patterson was asked to bring up the eighteen-gun schooner *Carolina* and the ship *Louisiana.*[35] Jackson also made a desperate start to fortify the line of the old Rodriguez Canal at the point where the Chalmette Plain between the river and the swamp was narrowest.

Meanwhile, the British troops went into camp on the river bank near the center of the Villeré plantation. Half a mile to the north on the river road from New Orleans they placed a strong advance guard; still farther in front a picket guard was posted near the river and a chain of pickets extended in an acute angle from the river to the main camp at the plantation. At seven o'clock the

[34] *Ibid.*, 261–63, 272, 277–78; Cooke, *Narrative of . . . the Attack on New Orleans*, 163; Charleston *Gazette*, July 17, 1815; Gayarré, *History of Louisiana*, IV, 417–36; Buell, *History of Andrew Jackson*, I, 371–73.

[35] Richmond *Enquirer*, January 28, 1815; Bassett, *Life of Andrew Jackson*, I, 176.

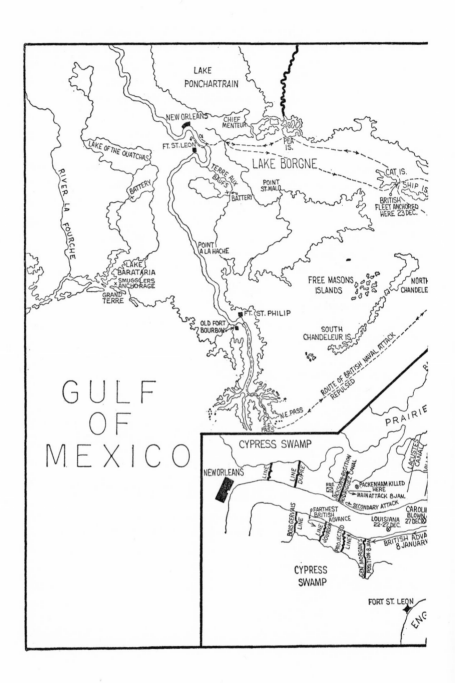

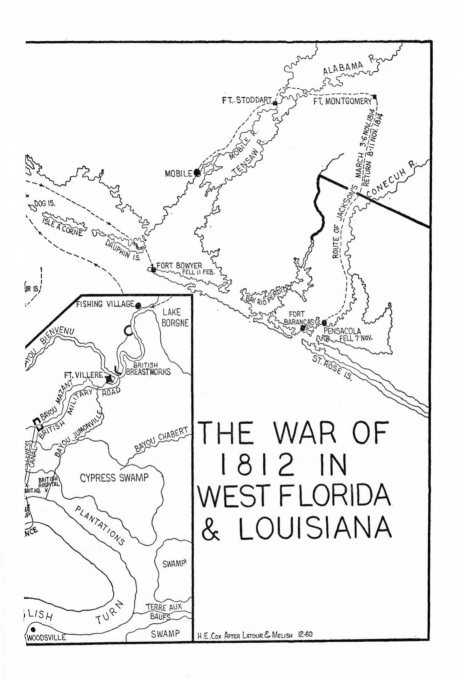

THE WAR OF
1812 IN
WEST FLORIDA
& LOUISIANA

H.E. Cox After Latour & Melish 12-60

*Carolina* came up to the brink of the batture—the dry bank of the river below the levee—where it was only three hundred yards from the front of the British camp. The invaders mistook her for a trading vessel and swarmed over the levee and down to the water's edge to see what her business was. "Their brilliant camp fires behind them made them excellent targets for the gunners, who suddenly opened fire. So great was the confusion that it was ten minutes before the British recovered themselves, seized their arms, and extinguished the fires. Then the schooner remained in her place and did so much damage during the engagement that the Redcoats were forced to keep well under the protection of the levee." [36]

About an hour later—around eight o'clock—the sound of firing from the picket line (which had remained in place) indicated a general attack was being launched from the land side. Led by Coffee, the Americans drove in the pickets and soon surrounded the advanced British brigade which the *Carolina* had forced to take refuge behind the levee. But General Keane sent reinforcements to the aid of his encircled units, and a confused, disorderly night battle raged until half-past nine. Then Coffee concluded that in the darkness it would not be safe to get between the main body and the isolated troops, and therefore did not press his advantage. Jackson also decided that the affair had yielded all the advantage possible and drew his men off to a position six hundred yards north of the enemy and across the road to New Orleans. In his preliminary engagement Jackson's forces had lost 24 killed, 115 wounded, and 74 missing, while the British reported a loss of 46 killed, 167 wounded, and 64 missing.[37] This skirmish was highly important. The fact that Jackson was strong enough to attack confirmed in General Keane's mind the accuracy of exaggerated reports of the strength of the defense and made him overly cautious, thereby giving the American time to strengthen his fortifications.

When news of the death of General Ross reached London, the

<hr/>

[36] Bassett, *Life of Andrew Jackson*, I, 176; Charleston *Gazette*, January 17, 1815.

[37] Richmond *Enquirer*, February 1, 1815; [Gleig], *Narrative of the Campaigns of the British Army*, 286–93; Bassett, *Life of Andrew Jackson*, I, 179–80.

Ministry chose Lieutenant General Edward Michael Pakenham (pronounced Pay'ken em) to replace him as commander of the expeditionary force assigned to attack the Southern coast of the United States. Pakenham, an Irishman, was born at Longford Castle, County Westmeath, and was brother-in-law to the Duke of Wellington, under whom he had fought in the Peninsula Campaign, commanding the division which captured Madrid. The assignment which now came to him was his first independent command, and he was thirty-seven years old.[38] Pakenham should have joined the New Orleans expedition at Jamaica whither reinforcements had been sent, but adverse winds delayed him. It is highly significant that the concentration of land and naval forces at Negril Bay was not ordered until after the peace commissioners had already convened at Ghent and that Pakenham's order "to proceed to Plymouth and embark there for Louisiana to assume command of the Forces operating for the reduction of that Province," was dated November 4, 1814, three months after the peace commissioners had assembled.[39] When the combined armament set sail for America three weeks after the date of Pakenham's orders, according to several British officers, there were on shipboard, besides the military personnel, "a complete civil government staff," which was to be installed as soon as General Pakenham had taken Louisiana. The customs collector of Barbadoes had resigned his post there for what he thought to be a more lucrative one—collector for the "Crown Colony of Louisiana." The civil government staff also included an attorney general, an admiralty judge, a secretary for the colony to be sent direct from England, a superintendent for Indian affairs who was to be transferred to Louisiana from Canada, and numerous others. The officers told of these plans with keen irony, for they were writing after the great debacle. It was reported that Pakenham brought in his dispatch case a commission as governor of Louisiana and the promise of an earldom. He brought also a proclamation, approved by the Colonial Office, which was to be published upon the occupation of New Orleans, declaring the sovereignty of England in behalf of

[38] *Dictionary of National Biography* (New York, London, 1950), XV, 83–84.
[39] Earl of Bathurst Papers, cited in Buell, *History of Andrew Jackson*, II, 70–71.

Spain "over all the territory fraudulently conveyed by Bonaparte to the United States." [40]

The British peace commissioners were well aware of these plans and had every reason to think they had already been carried out when they signed the peace treaty at Ghent on December 24. A stipulation of the treaty stated that it was not to go into effect until ratified by both the United States and Britain. The expedition had been planned to sail from Jamaica on November 4 and to be at New Orleans not later than the twentieth. Lord Castlereagh had delayed the peace negotiations for weeks, until he thought Keane had had ample time to wrest all Louisiana from the Americans. For England had planned well; she did not intend to fail. To effect the conquest, she had sent a huge armada—the greatest expeditionary force ever to leave her shores with the exception of the one furnished Wellington for the Peninsula Campaign. An American soldier, Captain Henry Garland, spoke truly when he said that "the peace treaty was written in the life blood of the American soldiers at New Orleans, not in the ink of Ghent." With Keane and Pakenham victorious, the treaty need never be implemented.[41]

Pakenham joined the army before New Orleans on Christmas Day only to find his brave Redcoats cowering behind the levee to protect themselves from the deadly fire of the *Carolina* and the *Louisiana*. With 5,500 troops he might have penetrated the American line, now hardly more than a skeleton, but he decided to deal first with the troublesome ships on the river. By great exertion he got batteries in place during the night of the twenty-sixth and opened on the American vessels with shell and hot shot the following morning. The *Carolina* was set afire and after being bombarded for an hour she blew up. The *Louisiana* was, with great difficulty, towed out of range and saved. These operations delayed the British advance and gave Jackson a precious opportunity to strengthen his defenses.[42]

[40] Narratives of Captain Cooke and the Subaltern, cited *ibid.*, 71–73.

[41] *Ibid.*, 70–82: Earl of Bathurst to Lord Mayor of London, December 26, 1814, in Bassett (ed.), *Correspondence of Andrew Jackson*, II, 126 and n.; James, *Border Captain*, 246.

[42] Bassett, *Life of Andrew Jackson*, I, 183–84; [Gleig], *Narrative of the Campaigns of the British Army*, 301–302; James, *Border Captain*, 249–50.

On his arrival General Pakenham declared that British troops "were never found in so strange a position," a veritable *cul de sac,* but the die having been cast, he could only make the best of it.[43] At twenty-five minutes past eight o'clock on the morning of December 28, he made his initial bid for victory. First assaulting Jackson's line with Congreve rockets and ten field guns, he sent two columns of infantry to push home the attack. The left column advanced along the line of the levee toward the positions which Jackson had assigned to his regular troops and the companies of New Orleans militia. The right column advanced against the Tennessee militia under Generals Coffee and Carroll, which held the line on the flank bordering the swamp. Here the defenses were incomplete and a determined charge might have breached the works, but the Tennesseans took good aim with their squirrel guns and the Redcoats faltered. After several refusals Jackson had finally accepted the Baratarian smugglers into his outfit, chiefly because he was in desperate need of trained artillerists and sailors. He found their leader, Jean Laffite, invaluable because of his detailed knowledge of the terrain around New Orleans. And who should know the numerous canals and the passages connecting them better than this bold buccaneer! [44] It was Laffite who recommended that the American line "be extended through the first wood to the cypress swamp and the canal Extended that Distance as they may otherwise turn our left." It was well for Jackson that he took this advice, as he was to discover a few days later. Meanwhile, the British column nearest the river was decimated by the guns of the *Louisiana* and the five field pieces which Jackson had succeeded in placing on his line. In the face of such resistance, Pakenham ordered a retreat.[45] The critical Captain John Henry Cooke said, "The affair was called, to soften it off, a reconnaissance."

On the twenty-eighth Jackson had five guns in position; on the

[43] Cooke, *Narrative of . . . the Attack on New Orleans,* 203–12.

[44] Jackson to Brigadier General David B. Morgan, January 8, 1815, in Bassett (ed.), *Correspondence of Andrew Jackson,* II, 132; Edward Livingston to Jackson, December 25, 1814, *ibid.,* 125.

[45] Jackson to Free Colored Inhabitants of New Orleans, September 21, 1814, *ibid.,* 58–59, also printed in Richmond *Enquirer,* December 3, 1814; Colonel Thomas L. Butler, aide-de-camp, to the Men of Color, New Orleans, December 21, 1814, *ibid.,* January 21, 1815; [Gleig], *Narrative of the Campaigns of the British Army,* 307–312; Gayarré, *History of Louisiana,* IV, 332.

first of January he had fifteen. Three of these were on the west bank of the river, opposite the British batteries at a distance of three-quarters of a mile. They were taken from the *Louisiana* and under Patterson's command did valuable service on January 1. During this time the British were not idle. With their fleet seventy miles away, they used small boats to bring up naval guns and gunners. Thus equipped, Pakenham prepared five batteries at a distance of seven hundred yards from Jackson's lines. The first of these, which was made up of seven light long-range guns, was brought to bear on the opposite shore where Master-Commandant Patterson erected his battery. Facing Jackson's lines were four more batteries with a total of seventeen guns, including eight eighteen-pounders, four twenty-fours, plus five howitzers. At eight o'clock on New Year's morning, just as Jackson was preparing to celebrate the day with a formal review and the issue of half a gill of whisky to the troops, these two lines of cannon began the most sustained artillery duel of the war.[46]

The British had great confidence in their artillerists, who opened vigorously but incautiously, sending their shot too high, thereby wasting much ammunition which had been brought so laboriously from the fleet. Meanwhile, Jackson's guns, handled by miscellaneous crews—one of them made up of Baratarians under Dominque You (the eldest Laffite brother who used this pseudonym)—began slowly in order to find the proper range. Once they found it, their fire grew stronger until Pakenham was forced to admit its superiority. Some of the British cannon were dismounted and by noon most of their batteries were silent. On the other side the Americans suffered little, and during the night Pakenham withdrew his remaining artillery. Realizing he could not breach Jackson's lines by means of gunfire, he decided on a different plan of attack.[47]

The grape and cannister which Patterson's battery threw across the river were a constant menace to the British. Pakenham decided to turn a liability into an asset by sending a force across to

---

[46] Bassett, *Life of Andrew Jackson*, I, 186–87.

[47] Charleston *Courier*, February 20, 1815; [Gleig], *Narrative of the Campaigns of the British Army*, 312–17; Gayarré, *History of Louisiana*, IV, 301 ff., 445–59; Bassett, *Life of Andrew Jackson*, I, 187–88.

take the guns and turn them on Jackson's lines, while the main force made a frontal assault on the barricade. These plans required time for preparation, and while making them Pakenham was also awaiting the arrival of Major General John Lambert with two additional regiments. General Sir Samuel Gibbs, who had re-marked a few days earlier that he had no patience with anyone who argued that the men who conquered Napoleon could be halted by, much less repulsed from, a "low log breastwork manned by a backwoods rabble," was not now quite so arrogant. Pakenham held a council of war on December 30, and Gibbs left it in despair, according to Captain Cooke, who heard him exclaim, "Oh, for half a day of the Old Duke!" [48] In little more than a week Gibbs, his body pierced by bullets from the "backwoods rabble," would fall lifeless before the mud and log breastworks.

While Pakenham was awaiting Lambert's troops, Jackson also was anxiously awaiting the arrival of the Kentucky militia. Fi-nally, on January 3 he received an express from Baton Rouge that the long delayed flatboat fleet was beginning to arrive there. To his dismay Jackson was also informed that many of the men were unarmed. "I don't believe it," he retorted, "I have never seen a Kentuckian without a gun and a pack of cards and a bottle of whiskey in my life!" [49] General Lambert arrived on January 6, and that night the British troops worked in relays to deepen the Villeré canal, a ditch running from the levee to the bayou, to per-mit transporting fifty boats to the river in order to move Colonel William Thornton and his command to the opposite bank to cap-ture Patterson's guns. "Never," said the subaltern, "were time and toil more thoroughly wasted." [50]

Pakenham's preparations gave Jackson additional time to strengthen his defenses, which consisted of three earthen parapets, one behind the other, and each stretching from the river to the swamp. The first was five miles from the city along the Rodriguez Canal, which was twenty-five feet wide and four or five feet deep.

[48] Cooke, *Narrative of . . . the Attack on New Orleans,* cited in Buell, *History of Andrew Jackson,* I, 413; II, 3.

[49] Buell, *History of Andrew Jackson,* I, 423; New Orleans *Louisiana Gazette,* Feb-ruary 18, 1815.

[50] Bassett, *Life of Andrew Jackson,* I, 188–89; "Subaltern in America," *loc. cit.,* XXII (1927), 324–25.

It was a dry ditch until Jackson had the levee pierced and flooded it. Thirty yards behind this ditch a palisade of logs was constructed, and earth was banked against it in the rear to a height of at least five feet and a depth sufficient to stop a cannon ball. At intervals along this line eight batteries pointed their muzzles toward the British positions down the river, and behind the earthworks Jackson placed a total of 5,172 men.[51]

Pakenham's plan was to send Colonel Thornton across the river at nightfall with 1,400 men who would surprise Patterson's artillerists and capture their guns. This done, they would await the signal for the attack on the east bank before turning the captured guns on the flank of Jackson's works across the river. Meanwhile, the main assault would be made by Major General Gibbs with 2,150 men against Jackson's left flank just before his lines entered the woods bordering the swamp. In this area they would approach within two hundred yards of battery number seven, with some protection from the trees on their right. By making the attack just at daybreak, Pakenham hoped to take the sleepless Jackson by surprise, and if everything had gone as he planned, he might have achieved a glorious victory. But the fates determined otherwise.

Unfortunately for him, the British commander chose the Forty-Fourth Regiment to lead the attack of Gibbs's column and to carry fascines and ladders to fill the ditch and scale the parapet behind which Jackson's men were posted. "The Honourable Lieutenant Colonel Mullens" who commanded the Forty-Fourth was notoriously inefficient and he lived up to his reputation by appearing at the head of the attacking column with neither scaling ladders nor fascines, made of bundles of sugar cane stalks. Three hundred men were hurried back to get them, leaving the Forty-Fourth at the head of the column with 127 men. As the minutes passed, dawn began to break, and all the advantages of a surprise attack were lost. The waiting troops became impatient and uneasy under the American cannonade which then began, and the signal was given for the attack before the formation of the Forty-Fourth could be restored. With this confusion at the head of the column, Gibbs's advance lost the precision which was necessary in the severe ordeal to which Jackson's deadly fire subjected it. The men, forgetting their duty to

[51] Bassett, *Life of Andrew Jackson*, I, 189–92; James, *Border Captain*, 262.

rush the works with the bayonet, began to fire; the detail of the luckless Forty-Fourth, rushing up with fascines and ladders, threw down their burdens and began to fire likewise. The advance then became a wavering, confused mass. The charge began at six o'clock; at half past eight the fire of the musketry ceased and at two the cannonade ended.[52]

Meanwhile, on the west bank the battle went otherwise. Colonel Thornton was supposed to embark his men at nightfall so as to capture Patterson's guns by daybreak and be ready to turn them on Jackson's lines as soon as the main attack should be launched on the opposite shore. But because of unforeseen difficulties, only a fraction of Thornton's boats were launched when, at three o'clock, he pushed off with but a third of his force. When he landed unopposed on the opposite shore, he heard the boom of the British batteries as they opened the battle. It was nearly three hours before he could come within striking distance of Patterson's guns, and by that time the fate of the British army had been settled on the eastern bank.[53]

The men behind Jackson's ramparts were a heterogeneous crowd, but the British, to their great cost, sadly underestimated Old Hickory's backwoodsmen in their nut-brown homespun, buckskin hunting shirts, and coonskin caps. Commenting on them, the Subaltern said: "We held the Americans in too much contempt to fear their attack—we never felt nor acted on the supposition that any serious danger would be incurred till we ourselves should seek it."

Most of Jackson's soldiers had handled a rifle almost as soon as they were big enough to hold one; they were conquerors of the wilderness, deer hunters and Indian fighters, and their superb self-confidence was their shield and buckler. These frontier soldiers appeared to show a reckless *sang-froid* as they awaited the soldierly red-coated British almost with nonchalance. They were high-spir-

---

[52] Alexander C. Henderson to his father, New Orleans, January 9, 1815, in Charleston *Courier*, February 10, 1815; "Subaltern in America," *loc. cit.*, XXII (1827), 326–28; [Gleig], *Narrative of the Campaigns of the British Army*, 324–30; Gayarré, *History of Louisiana*, IV, 497.

[53] Account of the battle by General Lambert, in *Republican and Savannah Evening Ledger*, May 20, 1815; Charleston *Gazette*, July 17, 1815; Gayarré, *History of Louisiana*, IV, 488–89; Buell, *History of Andrew Jackson*, II, 7 ff.; Bassett, *Life of Andrew Jackson*, I, 193–94.

ited and alert, and no doubt their morale was bolstered on the morning of January 8 by "the tune of yanky dudle . . . which was beat along the whole line." [54] A prominent military writer of France said of these victors at New Orleans that they "triumphed by total disregard of every precept taught and of every principle inculcated in European or any other civilized warfare. . . . They had little or no discipline . . . but one thing they certainly could do and they did it: they killed everybody who came within range of their rifles." [55] They were now lined up four deep, one behind the other, and as soon as the man in front fired, he moved back to reload and another stepped forward to take his place. Their tall, gaunt commander, who was ten years older than Pakenham, moved along the line, encouraging the troops, an astonishingly large number of whom he called by name.

Pakenham had already discovered that the strength of Jackson's forces had been exaggerated, and he selected his enemy's left center position for his attack because no artillery was mounted in that part of the American lines and because the canal was narrower there. Packenham was informed by spies the night before that the whole left of the American breastworks was manned by imperfectly organized militia, who "were totally unprepared with the bayonet." When the attack started, heavy fog hung low over the river, making it impossible to see one hundred feet from the breastworks; but a brisk wind arose and blew the fog away, revealing the enemy to Jackson. He ordered his soldiers to count the enemy's files down as closely as they could; then each soldier was to take care of his own file man, not to fire until told to do so, and then to aim above the Britisher's crossbelt plate. At first no sound was heard except artillery. The British advanced boldly; they were accustomed to artillery fire. Then every hunter's long rifle from the right of General Carroll's line to the edge of the swamp opened up—a new experience for British veterans. Within a few minutes the entire front formation was shaken and not a single mounted officer could be seen, most of them down and either dead or dying.

[54] Jackson to Colonel Robert Hays, February 9, 1815, in Bassett (ed.), *Correspondence of Andrew Jackson*, II, 162–63; "Subaltern in America," *loc. cit.*, XXII (1827), 75–78.
[55] Buell, *History of Andrew Jackson*, II, 42.

Each British regiment broke as it formed the advance battalion. The enemy's column lasted about fifteen minutes. Captain Cooke said that no such execution "by small arms had ever been seen or heard of." Never before had British veterans quailed, "but it would be silly to deny that they did so now. . . . I had heard and read of men being panic-stricken. This was the first time I ever witnessed it." With the first column in ruin, Pakenham in person, together with General Keane, put the second column in motion. The Sutherland Highlanders, a thousand strong and every man six feet tall, led the column, as Pakenham on his magnificent grey charger rode along its flank, calling "Come on with the tartan." Pakenham and all his staff led the color company as the kilted Highlanders advanced. His horse was killed under him, and he was slightly wounded; he mounted a second horse but soon reeled from the saddle, mortally wounded. Then the entire column wavered, with all five staff officers either killed or wounded. Gibbs had taken over, leading his regiment in person, but within minutes he fell from his horse with four bullets in him.[56] One British soldier said to another that it was not battle, but butchery. General Lambert succeeded to the command on the wounding of Keane and the death of Gibbs, but even as he took over he saw that the battle was irretrievably lost. He ordered a retreat—a retreat signalizing one of the most amazing defeats ever suffered by British arms.

When the smoke of battle cleared, a broad space before the seventh battery, placed at the edge of the cypress swamp, was red with the prostrate forms of British soldiers. Captain Cooke said the British troops had fallen "like blades of grass beneath the scythe of the mower; brigades dispersed like dust before the whirlwind." [57] It was not only the seventh battery which accounted for this carnage. General Coffee's brigade occupied the end of the line next to the swamp, and Jackson reported to the governor of Tennessee that Coffee and his troops literally lay "for the whole time in a swamp knee deep in mud and water" and that they maintained that position without a murmur. In the swamp to the extreme left of Coffee's brigade was also the half-breed Captain Pierre Jugeat—he who had proved his mettle at Horseshoe Bend—with

[57] Cooke, *Narrative of . . . the Attack on New Orleans*, 227–42.   [56] *Ibid.*, 1–31.

a detachment of Choctaw Indians. They accounted for a very large number of British casualties. Hidden by the cypress trees with their trailing strands of grey moss, their presence was undetected until the sharp crack of their rifles rang out. When Jackson inquired where the Indians were, an officer replied, "Out in the swamp, basking on logs like alligators." [58]

The British had anticipated a pleasant sojourn in New Orleans; the civil government staff was awaiting its installment in office as soon as the general became governor of the huge territory and had had an earldom conferred upon him. It was an overwhelming irony of fate that his body was delivered to his friends on shipboard in a hogshead of rum.[59] Jackson cautiously kept his men behind their ramparts of mud, and on January 9 he received a request from General Lambert for a truce so that the British might look after their dead and wounded.[60]

In his modest report of the battle to Secretary of War James Monroe the following day, Jackson stated that he acceded to the request, stipulating that, during the truce, hostilities should cease "on *this* side the river until 12 o'clock of this day, yet it was not to be understood that they should cease on the *other* side. . . . His excellency major-general Lambert begged time to consider of these propositions until 10 o'clock of today, and in the meantime re-crossed his troops. I need not tell you with how much eagreness [*sic*] I immediately regained possession of the position he had thus hastily quitted." [61] If the British had rallied, they might still have made trouble for Jackson, but through a ruse Old Hickory induced Lambert to abandon the position where the Americans were weakest. He was shrewd enough to take advantage of his enemy's every blunder.

The British soldiers would accord Americans no credit whatever for their victory but attributed it solely to mistakes on the part of their own commanders. Captain Gleig said the entire campaign was replete with errors from beginning to end, and there is

---

[58] S. G. Heiskell, *Andrew Jackson and Early Tennessee History* (Nashville, 1920), I, 537.

[59] Bassett, *Life of Andrew Jackson*, I, 196–97; Richmond *Enquirer*, February 11, 15, 1815.

[60] Lambert to Jackson, January 8, 1815, in Bassett (ed.), *Correspondence of Andrew Jackson*, II, 133.

[61] Jackson to Monroe, January 9, 1815, *ibid.*, 136–38.

much truth in his statement.[62] Every contributory part of the British plans went awry; both the rendezvous at Jamaica and the attack at Chalmette were fully a month late. The British were incredibly ignorant of their adversary and of the topography of the land over which they were to fight. They made no reconnaissance of the area, and so little did they know of it that they expected to live off the land—it was to furnish them ample provisions, shelter for the soldiers, and horses to draw the caissons. They chose the worst possible approach to New Orleans, which led them into a morass and a *cul de sac,* where their fine fleet of warships could be of no use. One of their most fatal mistakes was the indecision and delay in attacking Jackson, thereby giving him time to build up his fortifications. Despite the fact the British soldiers were hardened veterans and the Americans raw recruits and untrained militia, Jackson was the victor. But the victorious general was still wary and kept his men behind their rampart of mud until the invaders withdrew to their ships and sailed away.[63]

Thus was New Orleans and the whole Mississippi Valley saved from the invader, but historians generally treat this battle as an isolated event which, having occurred after the treaty of peace was signed, had no bearing on the outcome of the war. This amounts to a distortion, if not an actual misrepresentation, of the facts. It, therefore, requires some elucidation. Avoiding the mistakes of the last war, the British meant to invade the back country rather than the relatively well-settled Atlantic Seaboard. They planned to launch an attack in force against the vulnerable Southern frontier of the United States, where the Spaniards at Pensacola and the Creek Nation inhabiting the country just above them could afford invaluable assistance.

When Cochrane sailed from Bordeaux, he must have already heard of Jackson's victory over the Creeks at Horseshoe Bend on March 27, but there were still more than a thousand Creek warriors who were eager to fight the Americans if the British would furnish leadership and supplies.[64] The Tennessee general did not think the British would use a water route to New Orleans but

---

[62] [Gleig], *Narrative of the Campaigns of the British Army,* 334, 367–73.

[63] Jackson to Monroe, January 19, 1815, in Bassett (ed.), *Correspondence of Andrew Jackson,* II, 148–49.

[64] Adams, *History of the United States,* VII, 132; James, *Border Captain,* 195, 199–200.

would advance on the city by way of Mobile. "A real military man," said Jackson, "with full knowledge of the geography of . . . this country, would first possess himself of that point, draw to his standard the Indians, and march direct to the walnut Hills [later site of Vicksburg], . . . and being able to forage on the country, support himself, cut off all supplies from above and make this country an easy conquest." [65] As late as June 20 Cochrane still planned to make his landing at Mobile, and he thought that, with 3,000 British troops aided by all the neighboring Indians and the disaffected French and Spanish settlers on the Gulf Coast, he could easily drive the Americans from Louisiana and the Floridas. He would surely have carried out this plan had Nicholls and his Creek allies been strongly posted at Pensacola and held Fort Barrancas. [66] But without this support, which Jackson's campaign had denied him, he defeated himself by selecting an impossible approach to New Orleans along a seventy-mile stretch of shallow lakes and cypress swamps. Jackson won the battle largely because he had forced the British to fight on the cramped and almost inaccessible field of Chalmette.

The peace treaty which was signed at Ghent on December 24, fifteen days before the battle, stipulated that it was to go into effect only after ratification by both countries. These ratifications were not exchanged until February 17, 1815. Had the United States not approved the treaty, the English Ministry planned to attempt to make a separate peace with the New England states, which it thought entirely possible in view of the dissidence of the New England Federalists.

Jackson's victories had a significant bearing upon the peace negotiations which were initiated at Ghent on August 8, 1814. Until the summer of this year neither side had gained any signal military advantage over the other, but both belligerents authorized their diplomats to make excessive demands. The United States made cessation of the practice of impressment a *sine qua non* and demanded that Britain abandon all her maritime restrictions except that the Americans did not insist on the principle that free ships make free goods. The cession of both Floridas was demanded

[65] James, *Border Captain*, 207.
[66] Adams, *History of the United States*, VIII, 311.

by the United States, and all Canada was to be acquired if possible. On the other hand, the British demanded cession of the northern half of Maine and a strip of northern New York extending from Plattsburg to Sacketts Harbor. In addition, they stipulated that most of the country north of the Ohio River be constituted as an Indian reservation under British protection and that the Great Lakes be left entirely under their military control. Lord Bathurst instructed the British commissioners from the beginning of the conference to insist on the principle of *uti possidetis*—keep what you hold— and they were somewhat dismayed when the American diplomats would accept nothing but the second of the two usual bases of treaties, the *status quo ante bellum* principle. The British had to give in when Wellington advised them they had no grounds for demanding the principle of *uti possidetis*. This, however, did not affect England's designs on Louisiana inasmuch as she steadfastly refused to recognize the legality of Napoleon's sale. At Ghent her commissioners studiously avoided any mention of Louisiana. If the British campaign had been successful, it is possible that she might have turned over to Spain a part of the area; but her intention was not to augment Spain's possessions but to weaken the United States by detaching all the Louisiana Purchase and throttling the trade of the West by controlling the Mississippi River. Thus, if Pakenham instead of Jackson had been the victor at New Orleans, the United States would have been left with less than half its territory intact.[67]

Though neither side could, at the start of the negotiations, make a good case for its demands, the British had the brighter prospects because of the cessation of hostilities in Europe and the formidable expeditions sent to America under Admiral Cochrane and General Prevost. Yet the latter half of the year 1814 was a period of declining fortunes for the London government. Peace negotiations were not progressing satisfactorily at Vienna and the situation in Paris threatened a renewal of hostilities—a threat which materialized when Napoleon returned from Elba the next year.

For weeks after the commissioners had assembled at Ghent, the

[67] *Ibid.*, IX, 33–35; Frank A. Updyke, *Diplomacy of the War of 1812* (Baltimore, 1915), 198–234.

British delayed opening negotiations, hoping to hear of the success of English forces in America. On the contrary, the news was not encouraging. During July Generals Jacob Brown and Winfield Scott won victories at Chippewa and Lundy's Lane, and though General Ross may have afforded some satisfaction by the burning of Washington on August 24, he soon afterward lost his life in the unsuccessful attack on Fort McHenry. The day before this attack Commodore Macdonough halted and turned back the Prevost expedition by his brilliant victory at Plattsburg on Lake Champlain, and only four days later Major Lawrence repulsed the British attack on Fort Bowyer at the entrance to Mobile Bay. But the ministers in London were not unduly discouraged by these defeats— these minor losses which did not affect England's Grand Design.[68]

Even while she was supposedly negotiating for peace at Ghent, England dispatched the greatest overseas expedition which she had ever launched except that which she had recently sent to the Iberian Peninsula under Wellington. When Pakenham received his final orders to embark for America, the peace commissioners had been in session for three months, and England had every reason to believe that Keane was already in possession of New Orleans. When she signed the peace treaty, she was certain that Pakenham's forces controlled Louisiana and the treaty need never be implemented. When General Lambert's account of the New Orleans debacle reached England, it is safe to assume that a ministry had rarely received a report with more astonishment and consternation. Could a backwoods rabble of raw recruits under a backwoods general defeat the conquerors of Napoleon's army in Spain? Could a little band of untrained militia defeat the sailors who had made Britannia the proud mistress of the seas? Thus reasoned England, and if she had not blundered, in all probability the Mississippi River would have been the western boundary of the United States. In our history, therefore, the Battle of New Orleans is second in importance only to Washington's victory at Yorktown. Had Andrew Jackson failed to crush the Creeks, to defend Mobile Bay, and to drive the British from Pensacola, how different a turn might the course of our history have taken.

[68] Updyke, *Diplomacy of the War of 1812*, pp. 277-320.

# CHAPTER XV

# POLITICS DURING AND AFTER
# THE WAR

F OR a presumably peace-loving people, the citizens of the
United States have engaged in a surprising number of wars.
Except when they fought among themselves, they have been
rather firmly united against the enemy in all but one of their conflicts. This was the War of 1812, and scholars are still divided as
to the merits of the case. That the noncommercial states of the
South and West favored a war for the protection of our commercial rights, while commercial New England bitterly opposed it,
does not on the surface appear to make sense. Public opinion in
the Middle States was, as usual, divided between the two extremes.

The United States declared war against Great Britain on June
18, 1812, the vote in the House of Representatives being seventy-
nine to forty-nine, and in the Senate nineteen to twelve. One writer,
in giving a summary of subsequent debates behind this decision,
said that it was not the question of neutral rights alone which
caused the War of 1812. He thought that the seaboard and commercial communities preferred "wartime neutral commerce under
British arbitrary control, even with the standing insult of impressment," rather than war. But neutral rights and impressment, the
commentator stated, "served as righteous pretexts to those members of Congress who wanted war for other reasons." It is hard to
believe, but this seems to say that those who wished to defend the
national honor were hypocrites, while those Americans who were
willing to swallow national insult for the sake of profit were the
real patriots. Such reasoning is indeed confusing, but let us look
at the record.[1]

[1] Bemis, *A Diplomatic History of the United States*, 156–57.

On December 29, 1809, a resolution was introduced in the Virginia House of Delegates declaring that Congress ought to declare war on Great Britain and recall our Minister, General John Armstrong, from France.[2] But the West showed little interest in the international struggle until the *Chesapeake-Leopard* affair. Then the Kentucky legislature passed, with only one dissenting vote, resolutions which were introduced by Henry Clay in wholehearted

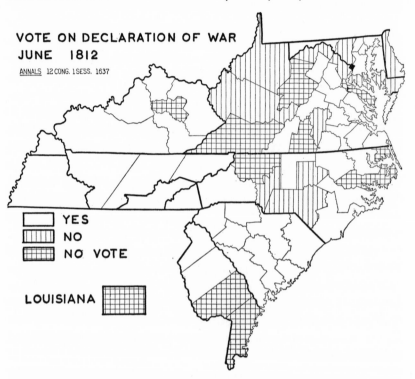

VOTE ON DECLARATION OF WAR
JUNE 1812
ANNALS 12 CONG. 1 SESS. 1637

YES
NO
NO VOTE

LOUISIANA

support of the embargo. Even after this Kentucky showed slight interest in maritime rights, but a sudden change came early in 1810 when Senator William Giles of Virginia was perhaps the first to propose the idea of protecting the frontier from Indian attacks by seizing British territory. A month later Henry Clay, now Speaker of the Federal House of Representatives, was advocating the conquest of Canada. Clay's fellow Kentucky Congressman, Richard M. Johnson, supported this idea.[3]

[2] Savannah *Republican and Evening Ledger*, January 13, 1810.
[3] Anderson, *William Branch Giles*, 154–56; Mayo, *Henry Clay*, 345.

An even stronger plea for war came in a communication to the Charleston *City Gazette* of June 25. The writer deplored the "imbecility" of the tenth and eleventh Congresses, which "yielded to the ravings of a band of New England traitors." He thought an honorable war was not then possible; yet, he said, "We must now fight like a coward driven to the wall, but fight we must." [4] Nothing appearing in the press of the Southeast at this time indicated an interest in Canada, but Kentucky was concerned over protection against the Canadian Indians, as well as the protection of Kentucky manufactures. Tennessee had visions of a trade route from the Tennessee River to the rivers flowing into Mobile Bay, and this line of development would lead to West Florida and the land of the hostile Creeks.[5]

Thus the Southwest differed from the Southeast, not only in its outlook on foreign affairs but in its attitude toward domestic problems. During 1811 Kentucky opposed the building of a strong navy and the chartering of a second bank of the United States, while strongly supporting protective tariffs and internal improvements. Andrew Jackson declared that he would fight to re-establish the national character and to thwart future aggressions by conquering the British dominions. Tennessee's economic interests were similar to those of Kentucky, but she looked southward rather than northward for both trade and enemies.[6]

War fever increased during the early months of 1812, and on January 25 the Virginia legislature again memorialized Congress in favor of hostilities, but the Valley Federalists and the eastern *Quids* were almost as strongly opposed as were the dominant Federalists of New England. The attitude of the opposition forces in the Shenandoah Valley was emphasized when, in October, the representatives of eight Valley counties met at Staunton and declared for peace.[7] The position of the *Quids* was best expressed by their leader, John Randolph, who, though opposed to the institution of slavery, pointed out that whereas there had been no threat of a slave insurrection during the Revolutionary War, the egalitarian

[4] Charleston *City Gazette*, June 25, 1810.

[5] *Ibid.*, July 4, 1810; Lexington *Kentucky Gazette*, October 2, 1810; Raleigh *Register*, September 18, 1812.

[6] Lexington *Kentucky Gazette*, June 4, October 15, 19, November 5, 1811; Mayo, *Henry Clay*, 442, 457–58.

[7] Simms, *John Taylor*, 128–31.

principles of the French Revolution and the preachments of Yankee peddlers demoralized the Negroes, as illustrated by the San Domingan butcheries and Gabriel's insurrection in Virginia. "I speak from facts," he declared, "when I say that the night-bell never tolls for fire in Richmond, that the mother does not hug the infant more closely to her bosom. I have been a witness to scenes of alarm in the capital of Virginia." [8]

Though most Southerners disliked what they looked on as the "arrogance" of the English, Randolph regarded the constitution of the mother country as the best in the world, and England was also the best customer for the Southern staples. Furthermore, while a war directed against the Canadian frontier would create a temporary market for Western produce and stimulate domestic manufactures, it would tend to promote the growth of economic nationalism and increase Federal authority. These developments, Randolph knew, would be contrary to the interests of the Southeast, but still more dangerous would be the conquest and annexation of Canada. The leader of the *Quids* looked further into the future than did most of his contemporaries, and he was in a small minority in Virginia.[9]

In the southern counties of Maryland and the western counties of Rowan, Cabarrus, and Iredell in North Carolina the Federalists had majorities, but these groups, unlike their New England counterparts, were inclined to go along with their country, right or wrong. In South Carolina the Republicans swept the election of 1812 and Joseph Alston, husband of Theodosia Burr, was elected governor. Here, as in all the Southern states, the war spelled the doom of the Federalist Party. But on January 28 it was announced that Savannah, for the first time, was to have a Federalist paper which would defend the interests of commerce against the policies of the Republicans, who favored domestic manufactures.[10]

The actual vote in the House of Representatives on the declara-

---

[8] Garland, *John Randolph of Roanoke*, 287–98.    [9] *Ibid.,* 299–313.

[10] *Republican and Savannah Evening Ledger,* January 28, 1812; Ashe, *History of North Carolina,* II, 237–38; Scharf, *History of Maryland,* III, 25; Gilpatrick, *Jeffersonian Democracy in North Carolina,* 192–99; Wagstaff, *State Rights and Political Parties in North Carolina,* 39; Wolfe, *Jeffersonian Democracy in South Carolina,* 262–63; Ravenel, *Charleston, The Place and the People,* 419.

tion of war followed partisan alignments more clearly than sectional lines. The maritime states of Delaware, New Jersey, New York, Connecticut, Rhode Island, and Massachusetts voted overwhelmingly against war, but New Hampshire, Vermont, Pennsylvania, Ohio, Kentucky, Tennessee, South Carolina, and Georgia were just as solidly in favor of the declaration. Maryland voted six to three for war; Virginia cast five and North Carolina three votes in the negative, and these all came from old Federalist strongholds lying above Tidewater but not close enough to the frontier to be much concerned about Indian hostilities. It is doubtless significant that south of Maryland not a single representative from a Tidewater constituency voted against war nor did any negative votes come from the states facing the frontier. In view of the commercial interest of Philadelphia, the unanimous vote of Pennsylvania in favor of war can be accounted for, aside from patriotic motives, by the growing interest in manufactures and the predominance of the Republican Party.[11]

On the basis of these facts, along with a considerable amount of supporting evidence, it can be stated with a fair degree of certainty that only Georgia and Tennessee were seriously interested in the conquest of Florida, that among the Southern states only Kentucky was seriously interested in the conquest of Canada, and this for the sake of protection against the Indians. Of course, it was generally realized that, since we could not compete with Britain on the high seas, the foe was vulnerable only in Canada; yet with New England offering such strenuous objections to the admission of Louisiana in 1812, one could hardly have expected the South to look upon the annexation of Canada with equanimity. John Randolph saw the danger and sounded the alarm, but only his small band of followers took him seriously. The South also stood to lose by the development of manufactures, which the war was certain to promote, but here again Randolph alone seemed to care. Only one explanation appears to account for the situation. Most historians seem to have forgotten that the South was not always a "conscious minority." To the distress of New England and her allies the South at that time had long been in control of national

[11] Bemis, *Diplomatic History of the United States,* map, 157; Hutton, "Southern Nationalism," chart 21.

affairs, and she did not yet see the handwriting on the wall. It did not seem possible, with a vast frontier still to exploit, that the commercial interest could ever gain ascendancy over the agricultural or the Federalists over the Republicans. And one important factor is generally overlooked: manufacturing was then carried on mainly by the handicraft methods of the laboring "mechanics," and the Republicans, especially in Pennsylvania and Kentucky, favored it as against the capitalistic commercial interest.

It has often been denied by those who have a different case to plead, but it is nevertheless true that the South desired war in 1812 because she felt herself in a position to speak for the nation, and her leaders believed that the national honor must be vindicated. She could not foresee that the day would come when the North alone claimed to be the Union. Southerners knew that their section stood to suffer as much as any other part of the country, but they did not realize, as did John Randolph, that they stood to be by far the greatest losers in the end.

News of the declaration of June 18 reached Baltimore in time for the *Federal Republican,* a newspaper owned by Alexander C. Hanson and Jacob Wagner—both extreme Federalists—to publish on June 20 an editorial bitterly attacking the Madison administration. Two days later a mob wrecked the printing office, destroyed the furniture and equipment, and razed the building in which the paper was published. After this holocaust the editors moved to Georgetown, where the paper was issued until July 26, when Hanson returned to Baltimore. Here he prepared to defend the freedom of the press by collecting friends and arms and distributing copies of his paper which had been printed in Georgetown. On July 27 headquarters was moved back to Baltimore and the issue published that day criticized the mayor, the governor, and the administration for acquiescing in the destruction of Hanson's plant. That night his new place was attacked by a mob which stoned the house, beat in the door, and brought up a cannon with which it was about to blow the building to pieces. The defenders then fired on the mob, killing two men and wounding others. At this critical moment a compromise was effected, according to which, in consideration of a military guard, the "garrison" surrendered to the civil authorities and its members were committed to the jail.[12]

It appeared that peace had been restored, but upon the removal of the prisoners the house was gutted by the mob, and after the militia had been withdrawn the jail was stormed. Eight of the prisoners mingled with the attackers and escaped; nine were seized, beaten, and otherwise maltreated. General James M. Lingan was killed, and General Henry Lee made a cripple for life. John Thompson, after being badly beaten, was tarred and feathered. Some of the others were hidden in hay carts and sent to friends outside the city; while those remaining, being too badly injured to be moved, were cared for at the jail hospital.[13] This disgraceful affair defeated the Maryland Republicans in the elections of 1812. Though the Senate remained Republican, the House of Delegates became strongly Federalist and the legislature proceeded to elect Levin Winder, an opponent of the war party, to the governorship. Nevertheless, Winder immediately set about making preparations against invasion and obtained appropriations sufficient to defray expenses hitherto incurred and to provide for active military operations.[14]

Strong anti-British feeling was manifested in other Southern states, as when Senator John Pope of Kentucky, who voted against the declaration of war, was burned in effigy and the editor of a Tory newspaper in Savannah was ducked at a public pump. On July 3 the Richmond *Enquirer* announced that the city would celebrate Independence Day with a "general illumination" and that the governor was issuing a proclamation affirming "America's appeal to the God of Battles." The same issue of the *Enquirer* carried an editorial entitled "Language of Treason," attacking the editor of the Boston *Repository*, which recommended to the people of Massachusetts that they resist the laws of the Union and

[12] Lexington *Kentucky Gazette*, July 7, August 11, October 20, 1812; Annapolis *Maryland Gazette*, August 6, 1812; Scharf, *History of Maryland*, III, 3–24; Andrews, *History of Maryland*, 424–25.

[13] Andrews, *History of Maryland*, 424–25; Richmond *Enquirer*, June 30, 1812; Scharf, *History of Maryland*, III, 4–24.

[14] Raleigh *Register*, July 3, 1812; Lexington *Kentucky Gazette*, July 7, 13, August 11, 1812; Richmond *Enquirer*, June 30, 1812.

rebel against constituted authority. Editor Ritchie hoped that even the Massachusetts Federalists were too deeply devoted to the Union to support such a policy.[15]

However, Ritchie's optimism was of brief duration, for on July 10 he published a proclamation by Governor Caleb Strong of Massachusetts piously appointing a day of fasting and prayer and stating that "in a war against the nation from which we are descended and which for many years has been the bulwark of the religion which we profess—the people in this commonwealth are in a peculiar manner exposed to personal suffering, and the loss of a great proportion of their substance." How things had changed in Massachusetts since 1776! On August 11 the *Enquirer* announced that both former Presidents Adams and Jefferson had made statements favoring the war and a few days later published an address from "Virginia to her Sister Massachusetts," asking why a party had sprung up there to oppose the rights of America.[16]

Questions of war and peace were naturally the principal ones agitating the people during the fall elections of this year. Federalists won a victory in Maryland, as we have seen; Delaware remained Federalist; and in Virginia Accomac on the Eastern Shore and the western counties of Botetourt, Augusta, Monroe, Hardy, and Berkeley voted for a Federalist, Rufus King, for the Presidency. A meeting of citizens at Lexington, Kentucky, on August 10 adopted resolutions (1) opposing the proposed repeal by Congress of the nonintercourse laws, (2) declaring that "our future and permanent prosperity and independence, even after the close of the war, will be best secured by the encouragement of our own manufactures," and (3) proposing a "permanent system" of protection. Yet the resolutions opposed the incorporation of a national bank as unconstitutional and pronounced anyone who advocated dismemberment of the Union to be a traitor. In the elections which followed there was a show of support for DeWitt Clinton, but Madison carried Kentucky by an overwhelming vote.[17]

Like Kentucky, Tennessee had her special interests, as demon-

---

[15] Richmond *Enquirer*, June 3, 1812; Lexington *Kentucky Gazette*, July 7, 1812.
[16] Richmond *Enquirer*, July 10, August 11, 14, 1812.
[17] Lexington *Kentucky Gazette*, August 25, October 27, November 8, 1812; Richmond *Enquirer*, November 10, 27, 1812; Raleigh *Register*, October 23, 1812.

strated by an article which the Raleigh *Register* of September 18 quoted from the Nashville *Clarion* to the effect that it would be highly desirable to take West Florida and drive the Indians across the Mississippi. "No part of the Nation," said the *Clarion*, "is so much interested in this as Tennessee." It was the old dream of using the Alabama and Tombigbee rivers for exports and imports, and though it was destined never to be realized, it had great weight in Tennessee before the advent of railroads.[18]

Not since the "revolution" of 1800 had the Federalists carried much weight in the politics of Georgia or the Carolinas, nor did they, even in Maryland, adopt the strong antiwar attitude that was so pronounced in Massachusetts. Their position is illustrated by an editorial appearing in the *Virginia Patriot*, a Federalist paper, lamenting "The disposition manifested by the people of the Eastern States (as appears from several prints) of an inclination to sever and dismember the union." But the Eastern states did not all follow the lead of Massachusetts, for the Republicans won the fall elections in Vermont, and all the leading commercial cities were said to favor the war.[19] Early in December the Republican victory was celebrated in Richmond by a dinner given at the Swan Tavern in honor of the Virginia Presidential electors. Governor James Barbour was the guest of honor and Judge Spencer Roane presided. According to the customary procedure on such occasions, eighteen set toasts (one for each state!) were proposed. Among them George Washington was not forgotten, nor was the new state of Louisiana neglected; toasts to Thomas Jefferson and to The Freedom of the Seas were tossed off; and then came one to Massachusetts with the prayer: "May the cradle of the Revolution never become the grave of our rights and liberties." [20]

As wars go, the struggle that broke out in 1812 between the United States and Great Britain was a distinctly minor affair, yet it effectually cut us off from the source of most of our needs in the way of the more advanced manufactures and thereby launched us on a career as an industrial nation. The industries which sprang

[18] Raleigh *Register*, September 18, 1812.
[19] Savannah *Republican*, August 29, October 6, November 3, 1812; Lexington *Kentucky Gazette*, September 8, 1812; Raleigh *Register*, October 16, 1812; Richmond *Enquirer*, September 18, 1812.
[20] Richmond *Enquirer*, December 5, 1812.

up to furnish the products formerly shipped from Great Britain were principally located in the urban centers of the Eastern seaboard from Baltimore to Boston, but the transmontane settlements, because of the high cost of transportation, were also developing a self-sufficient economy. Yet the Eastern cities, despite their growing manufactures which, except for a few spinning mills, were still carried on as handicraft occupations, were primarily concerned with foreign trade and the shipping which that involved.

This situation makes it possible to understand why New England, wedded to the interests of commerce as understood by the Federalist Party, overwhelmingly opposed the war, while Kentucky, with no interest in shipping but with nascent manufactures and a desire to develop a self-sufficient economy, favored anything which would decrease our dependence on imports. In this connection the partisan complexion of the Thirteenth Congress, which met in the spring of 1813, is significant. From the Southern states there were eleven Federalist members, with three out of nine from Maryland, four out of twenty-one from Virginia, and four out of eight from North Carolina. All of these came from areas dependent on interstate trade and, therefore, in need of the support of a strong central government. New England farmers, fishermen, and foresters also needed a strong government to promote their trade with the islands of the West Indies, but the handicraft manufacturer, who apparently received official support only in Kentucky, was our first isolationist. He opposed anything which would promote the interests of those capitalists who were engaged in the foreign trade.[21]

This situation is illustrated by the "embargo" problem which developed in 1813. In October, 1812, an order in council was issued to provide for supplying the British West Indies by means of special licenses, the use of which would be confined "to the ports of the Eastern States exclusively." To guard against the demoralizing and disorganizing tendencies of this system, which was intended to disrupt the Union, President Madison recommended the prohibition of any trade whatsoever, carried on under special licenses, by citizens of the United States. Also recommended was the prohibition of all exportations from the United States in ves-

[21] Lexington *Kentucky Gazette,* June 8, 1813.

sels flying foreign flags, which were almost entirely fraudulent. At first Congress took no action, but after the President on December 9, 1813, submitted a second message in which he informed the legislators that supplies of the most essential kinds were being furnished the British Army and Navy by Americans who were willing to trade with the enemy, an Embargo Act, modeled on that of 1809, was finally passed. This measure, plus the British blockade which was finally extended to most New England ports, put an effective stop to ocean-borne trade except at the two ends of the line—the easternmost ports of Maine and Spanish Amelia Island.[22]

In Kentucky and Tennessee the embargo policy was enthusiastically supported because it gave that region an opportunity to develop a self-sufficing economy, but the Tidewater regions of the South Atlantic states found it cheaper to import than to produce their own manufactures. Accordingly, South Carolina favored the unrestricted admission of imports which, however, she thought should be subjected to high duties in order to avoid the necessity of levying additional internal taxes. The leading proponent of this policy was the acidulous John Randolph of Roanoke. According to his view of the matter, the Southern states should continue to produce the staple crops and buy their manufactures from those who were better able to produce them. England and New England were the two obvious sources of such products, and the exclusion of foreign manufactures would result in the dependence of the Southern states upon Northern industry. Preferring English to Yankee civilization, Randolph saw that the war would result in the triumph of the latter, and he therefore opposed the policy of the Madison administration, for which aberration his historical reputation has suffered.[23]

The other side of the picture is presented in an article which the Raleigh *Register* of June 13, 1813, quoted from the Boston *Chronicle* to the effect that the scarcity of flour, rice, and other breadstuffs was keenly felt in Massachusetts. "Yet," said the *Chronicle*, "the 'Benevolent Sons of Washington' [Federalists], as they

[22] Channing, *History of the United States,* IV, 528–29, 535–37.

[23] Lexington *Kentucky Gazette,* September 1, 1812, August 31, September 21, 1813; Richmond *Enquirer,* July 14, 17, 1812; Garland, *John Randolph of Roanoke,* II, 20–21, 28–29; Joseph H. Parks, *Felix Grundy, Champion of Democracy* (Baton Rouge, 1940), 82.

style themselves, threaten a dissolution of the union. Suppose in return for the abuse which is daily heaped upon the Southern states, they should be roused to such a degree of resentment as to take us at our threat and *exclude us from the Union?* Suppose they should further declare that not a kernel of corn, a grain of rice, should be exported to Massachusetts. New England would starve." [24]

On August 27 Editor Ritchie expressed his views in the *Enquirer* as follows: "The enemy expects to feed her hope and ambition on the opposition in this country. Without union we should be split into small states, jealous, warring—lost. It [the Union] is the pillar of our safety. Let us swear then to preserve our Union. The surest way for England to gratify her malice and fear is to split the Union into small, independent states." Englishmen "draw this hope from the conduct of [the] opposition in the Eastern states. When they saw a representative—Mr. Quincy—from Massachusetts, declaring on the floor of Congress that certain things should be done—'Peaceably if they can, forcibly if they must'— when they saw the Legislature of the same state proposing a rebellious law in opposition to the Embargo; suggesting a Congress of the Eastern States with the view of counteracting the Congress of the Union; when they see the Federal prints of Boston teeming with inflammatory pieces and recommending disunion; declaring the Union could not continue if Mr. Madison were to be reelected; . . . when they see the Governors of Massachusetts and Connecticut flying in the face of the Constitution as expounded by Washington himself and refusing the militia of the United States to execute the will of the United States—it was then that hope brightened in England and expectation heightened that war would dissolve the Union." [25]

Reverses in 1812 got the war off to a dismal start, but the Administration hoped and believed that the situation could be reversed in 1813. A formidable force under General Henry Dearborn and Commodore Isaac Chauncy, instead of attacking Kingston, the strongest Canadian base west of Montreal, turned westward and attacked the relatively unimportant town of York, now Toronto. The British evacuated this place without making more

[24] Raleigh *Register,* June 13, 1813.      [25] Richmond *Enquirer,* August 27, 1813.

than token resistance, but in the inevitable confusion a large powder magazine exploded and killed General Zebulon M. Pike and some two hundred of his men. This disaster incited Americans to destroy the capitol of Upper Canada and other buildings. During the next year the British took revenge by burning the public buildings in our national capital.[26] Noticing comments on Canadian events, the Raleigh *Register* on June 11 quoted the Worcester *Aegis* as follows: "The manner in which Federalists have received news of our late success in Canada cannot but effect every person who has regard for our national honor.—Hearing that the valiant Pike with 200 of his men are killed, says one, 'I am glad of it'; could it answer the purpose, I myself would furnish powder to blow up the whole.' Says another, 'I wish that every man who goes to Canada may suffer the same fate.' Says another, a little more guarded, 'Well, it is a pity to lose lives, but they had no business there.' "[27]

By the fall of 1813 the tide began to turn. Oliver Hazard Perry's victory on Lake Erie and General William Henry Harrison's successes at Detroit and the Battle of the Thames led Editor Bradford of the *Kentucky Gazette* to exult on October 26: "The war in the west is closed after twenty years. The British have continually molested us from Canada—it must not be given up at the peace."[28]

As a result of the stress and strain of the war years, a significant difference of opinion was developing between Kentucky on the one hand and South Carolina on the other. Henry Clay, the young Speaker of the House of Representatives, was a faithful representative of his constituents in his wholehearted support of the struggle against England. The homespun Westerner was never inclined to look with much favor upon the aristocratic institutions of England, and when her agents sent Canadian Indians down to attack lonely frontier settlements, dislike turned into hatred. Not even the loss of Detroit dampened Kentucky's enthusiasm for the fight, and this enthusiasm was stimulated by certain economic considerations.

It was difficult and costly to transport British manufactures to

[26] Channing, *History of the United States,* IV, 496–97.

[27] Raleigh *Register,* June 11, 1813.

[28] Lexington *Kentucky Gazette,* October 26, 1813; Channing, *History of the United States,* IV, 484, 488–91.

the Mississippi Valley, and behind this natural protection, infant industries had sprung up in the Ohio Valley, especially at Pittsburgh and Lexington. Now, because of the British blockade and the American Embargo and Non-Importation acts, it was practically impossible to obtain foreign goods, and of course local manufactures profited from this situation. Leaders like Clay visualized a self-sustaining West, with the rural districts supplying the urban centers with produce and the cities and towns supplying the farmers with manufactures. Kentucky therefore favored the war for economic, as well as for military, reasons.

As the war entered its second year, it became more and more obvious to Langdon Cheves, chairman of the Ways and Means Committee, that the expense of carrying it on would have to be met by internal taxes or by opening our ports and levying high tariffs on such trade as could avoid the British blockade. As a Low Country South Carolinian, Cheves still preferred the latter alternative and in February, 1813, he proposed the repeal of the Non-Importation Act. He was supported by Calhoun but, surprisingly, a Federalist from Rhode Island opposed the measure on the ground that his constituents had invested four or five million dollars in manufactures which were protected by this legislation. And though the Federalist press had been practically unanimous in denouncing the restrictive system, it was the Federalist members of the House who defeated Cheves by a vote of seventy-nine to twenty-four! This included all the Southern Federalists in Congress except two from South Carolina. Strangely enough, with Maryland and Virginia voting solidly against repeal and with Kentucky, Tennessee, and the Carolinas taking this side by substantial majorities, Georgia cast her votes in favor of Cheves' proposal. Her Congressmen probably knew too much of the smuggling carried on at Amelia Island.[29]

When, in January of 1814, Speaker Clay was made a member of the commission to negotiate for peace, Cheves was elected over Felix Grundy of Tennessee by a vote of ninety-four to fifty as his successor. This was a signal victory for the Southeast as against the Southwest and for the interests of international trade as op-

[29] Hutton, "Southern Nationalism," 49-50, chart 23.

416

posed to the development of local manufactures.[30] If the Non-Importation Act of March 2, 1811, were repealed and British goods admitted, subject to the payment of relatively high import duties, internal taxation in support of the war might be avoided. With this idea in mind, Cheves introduced a bill on June 19, 1812, which partially suspended the restrictions. This measure had the

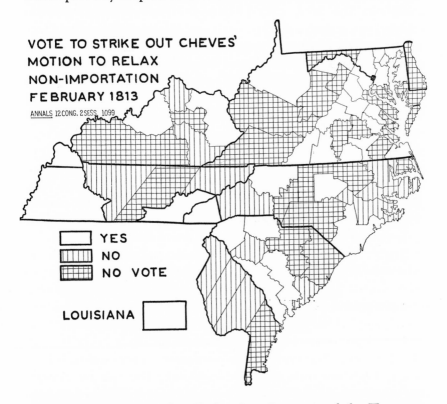

VOTE TO STRIKE OUT CHEVES'
MOTION TO RELAX
NON-IMPORTATION
FEBRUARY 1813
ANNALS 12 CONG. 2 SESS. 1099

YES
NO
NO VOTE

LOUISIANA

support of Calhoun and Gallatin, then Secretary of the Treasury, yet it failed of passage by the narrow margin of three votes. The Treasury was now compelled to recommend the levying of internal taxes in support of the war, but by a vote of seventy-two to forty-six the House decided to postpone the question until the next session. Among the Southern states Tennessee and Kentucky voted

[30] Lexington *Kentucky Gazette*, January 31, February 21, April 11, 1814; Savannah *Republican*, April 9, 21, 1814.

unanimously for postponement. About two-thirds of the vote of Virginia, the Carolinas, and Georgia favored the measure, and Maryland gave it a bare majority. The votes cast against the postponement of taxes came from the old Federalist strongholds, which would seem to indicate that the opposition party was seeking to render the war unpopular with the people.[31]

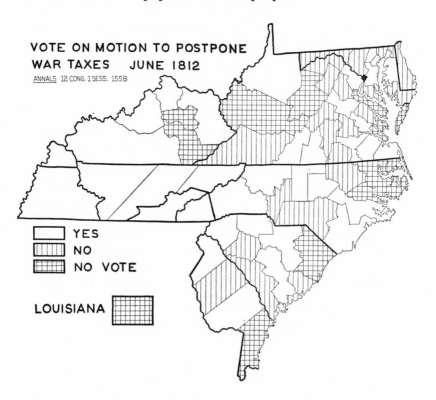

VOTE ON MOTION TO POSTPONE
WAR TAXES    JUNE 1812
ANNALS 12 CONG. 1 SESS. 1558

YES
NO
NO VOTE

LOUISIANA

By 1814 the tide was turning against the West. Peace negotiations were under way, and on March 31 the President tacitly admitted the failure of the restrictive system and recommended the repeal of the embargo and nonimportation legislation. The House received the proposal with a mixture of relief and consternation and referred it to Calhoun's Foreign Affairs Committee. Calhoun submitted his bill for repeal on April 4, but in supporting it he did not gloat over the Administration because of the victory which

[31] Hutton, "Southern Nationalism," 46–48, chart 22.

he and Cheves had won against the policy of commercial restriction. World conditions, he said, required the opening of trade routes, but manufactures, he hastened to add, would not be left unprotected. Elisha Potter of Rhode Island attacked the bill as detrimental to the industry of his section, but the House thought that manufactures were sufficiently protected and registered its approval of Calhoun's bill by a vote of 115 to 37. The Southern states approved this decision by an overwhelming majority, but Georgia's Congressmen were evenly divided on the issue, as were those of Kentucky, with the representatives of the commercial areas around Lexington and along the Ohio River taking their stand against repeal.[32]

As in 1809 the repeal of the embargo was brought about largely as a result of pressures from the New England states, Elisha Potter to the contrary notwithstanding. Of course urban craftsmen of New England did not favor repeal, for manufactures were rapidly increasing in that region.[33] As for the Southern states, Kentucky's vociferous support of the embargo must have been due, at least in part, to high hopes for her infant industries. While her sister states of the South Atlantic group did not share her views as to the embargo and approved repeal of the nonimportation laws, they nevertheless favored the development of American manufactures, and President Madison took the same stand when he advocated the continuance of wartime tariffs for two years after the end of hostilities. Both Calhoun and Cheves supported him on this proposition, but one can only surmise as to whether they hoped for the development of manufactures in South Carolina or were inclined to pacify New England by this concession.[34]

Since the Southern states were "in the saddle," they were less hostile to Federal authority than they had been in 1798, but they still opposed consolidation of authority, though by a narrow margin. The situation is clearly reflected by the vote in the House of Representatives in 1814 on a bill to recharter the Bank of the United States. This measure was defeated by the casting vote of

[32] *Ibid.*, 51–52, chart 24; *Annals of Congress*, 13 Cong., 2 Sess., 1956, 1997.

[33] Frank W. Taussig, *The Tariff History of the United States* (New York, 1914), 28–29.

[34] Lexington *Kentucky Gazette*, April 11, May 2, 16, 1814; Charleston *Courier*, April 20, 1814.

the Speaker, Langdon Cheves. In the recent elections that adamant advocate of state rights, John Randolph of Roanoke, had been defeated and the Madison-supported bill for the compensation of the Yazoo speculators was passed at this session. The principles of the Virginia and Kentucky Resolutions of 1798 appeared to have been eclipsed except in New England; but John Taylor of Caroline, who had introduced the resolutions of 1798 in Virginia's General Assembly, was still a voice crying in the wilderness. He

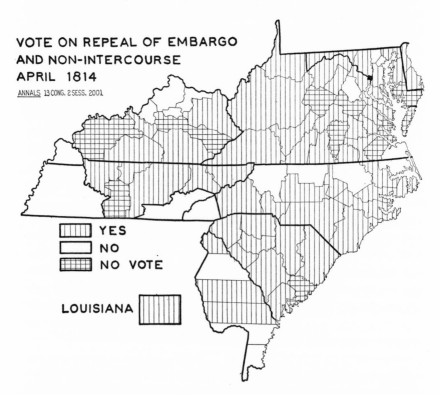

VOTE ON REPEAL OF EMBARGO
AND NON-INTERCOURSE
APRIL 1814
ANNALS 13 CONG. 2 SESS. 2001

YES
NO
NO VOTE

LOUISIANA

consistently opposed all the works of Hamilton and the Federalists —the consolidationists of an earlier period—and favored a Federal authority limited by the terms of the original compact. His views were powerfully expressed in the volume which he published in 1814, entitled *An Inquiry into the Principles and Policy of the Government of the United States.* But either he or his times were out of joint.[35]

[35] *Dictionary of American Biography,* IV, 62–64; XVIII, 331–32.

While the domestic scene seethed with intersectional bitterness, the fortunes of war did little to brighten the American skies. Kentucky still wished to obtain at least the cession of Upper Canada in order to protect her frontier, and she supported Tennessee and Georgia in their desire to acquire Pensacola and East Florida, but no progress was made in either direction. The July victories of Generals Jacob Brown and Winfield Scott were consoling to American pride, but any revival of spirits was cut short by the burning of Washington on August 24. Though the victories of Captain Thomas Macdonough on Lake Champlain and of the people of Baltimore in the defense of Fort McHenry, coming almost simultaneously on September 11 and 12, were heartening, they were both defensive actions.[36]

Nor was political rancor mollified by these events. In April the *Kentucky Gazette* stated that the New England Tories accused the Western people of having caused the war and of being responsible for its continuation. Bradford rebutted this charge and declared that the war would not have been necessary had not the New England Tories caused the shameful repeal of the first embargo.[37] The war was continued, he said, because the British had hopes of separating the East from the West, and the West preferred war to submission. He thought that commercial cupidity had caused great apathy toward the war, and on July 4 he quoted the Nashville *Whig* as saying: "The Seaman's bill, the repeal of the Embargo, the repeal of the non-intercourse [act] are all now acknowledged to be *advances made to the enemy for conciliation. But these will not avail. . . . the rulers of the nation have deserted it, and unless we awake from our stupor, all is lost.*" [38] This lugubrious note was reflected by the editor of the *Louisiana Gazette,* who on September 13 published an article headed "Desertion." It stated: "Felix Grundy and James Whitehill have resigned their seats in Congress, and Langdon Cheves, George M. Troup, Alexander McKim and Edward Crouch have declined a re-election. These were all *war* men and except one or two, the most violent of the party. The rats fly from a sinking ship." In the same issue was a statement that "by late letters from Washington we are in-

[36] Lexington *Kentucky Gazette*, May 2, 1814; Savannah *Gazette*, April 30, 1814.
[37] Savannah *Gazette*, April 30, 1814.
[38] Lexington *Kentucky Gazette*, June 6, July 4, 1814.

formed that the people there suspect General Armstrong to be hostile to that city; they think he wishes to have the seat of government removed that he may break up the Virginia combination which now stands in the way of his promotion to the presidency." [39] Indeed, the feeling against Armstrong after the burning of Washington was so strong that he resigned as Secretary of War and his duties were temporarily taken over by Secretary of State Monroe.

It was, of course, in New England that the antiwar feeling was most intense, and on November 1, 1814, Ritchie commented on that situation as follows: "There are . . . a set of dissatisfied men in the Eastern States, whom no concessions can conciliate. . . . *The Union* is in danger. Turn to the convention of Hartford, and learn to tremble at the madness of its authors. . . . No man, no association of men, no state or set of states has a right to withdraw itself from the Union of its own accord. The same power which knit us together, can only un-knit. . . . *The majority of states* which formed the Union must consent to the withdrawal of *any one branch of it.* Until *that* consent has been obtained, any attempt to dissolve the Union, or obstruct the efficiency of its constitutional laws, is *Treason.*" [40]

Though Randolph lost his seat in the House of Representatives as a result of the last elections, his voice was not silenced. On December 15 he addressed a letter "To a Gentleman in Boston" in which he said: "If you wished to separate yourselves from us, you had ample provocation in time of peace," on account of the embargo. "Then was the time to resist. (We did not desert England in a time of war). . . . Of all the Atlantic States you have the least cause to complain." He urged New England to resort to constitutional means only for redress. "When you complain of the representation of three-fifths of our slaves, I reply that is one of the articles of that compact which you submitted to us for acceptance and to which we reluctantly acceded." Such questions Randolph considered to be subjects for amicable discussion but not causes for dissolving the Union. Then he added: "And when I read and hear the vile stuff against my country [Virginia] printed

[39] New Orleans *Louisiana Gazette*, September 13, 1814.
[40] Richmond *Enquirer*, November 1, 1814; Brown, *Northern Confederacy, passim;* Lexington *Kentucky Gazette*, December 12, 1814.

and uttered on this subject, by firebrands who ought to be quenched for ever, I would remind [them] . . . that every word of these libels on the planters of Virginia is as applicable to the father of his country as to any one among us." [41] Thus New England, though thwarted for the moment in her movement toward secession, had already found the means by which she could, in the end, gain a following and conquer the Southern states.

Peace brought prosperity, and the Federalist Party, discredited by the disunionist sentiments of the Hartford Convention, ceased to function as a national organization. But this was not the only cause for the eclipse of the Federalists. They flourished during an era when the United States depended on England for its manufactured goods and shipping was their business. But the War of 1812 saw the rise of New England manufactures and created a demand for protective tariffs and other aids to the development of a self-sufficient economy, such as national banks and better facilities for transportation. But farmers greatly outnumbered manufacturers even in New England, and a more popular appeal than tariffs and banks had to be found. The slavery issue was made to order for this purpose and, since the international slave trade had been outlawed in 1808, the owners of slaves could now be attacked by New Englanders with impunity.

On May 5, 1815, the Raleigh *Register* took account of this development as follows: "The New England states have lately made a great outcry against the Southern States on account of the weight which is given them by ⅗ of their slaves being represented in the House of Representatives, but Mr. Carey has in his *Calm Address to the People of the Eastern States,* shown that in the House they are not *two per cent* below their proportion—and in the Senate are by far the most influential and powerful branch of government; that they have about 14 per cent more than they are entitled to, taking into consideration all the white population only of all the states. The same writer shows the Southern states cannot be other than friendly to *commerce* as they depend upon it for all of their produce—that at present the Manufactures of the United States are confined to the Eastern States though the South-

[41] Lexington *Kentucky Gazette,* December 31, 1814; Garland, *Life of John Randolph of Roanoke,* II, 60.

ern hold out great advantages for such institutions." [42]  Even former President Jefferson was converted to this point of view; and Madison, in his annual message of December 5, 1815, took the same stand and came out for a strong nationalist policy, including protective tariffs.[43]

This trend toward nationalism also became apparent in connection with the Federal banking policy. The chaotic state of national finances prompted President Madison to call the Thirteenth Congress into special session in September, 1814. Alexander J. Dallas, Secretary of the Treasury, described his department as suffering under every kind of embarrassment. The Treasury was, in fact, bankrupt, and in November it suspended interest payments. Jefferson thought that the proposal to enact a heavy tax program was useless for, he said, "How can a people who cannot get fifty cents a bushel for their wheat while they pay twelve dollars a bushel for their salt, pay five times the amount of taxes they ever paid before? Yet this will be the case in all the states south of the Potomac." [44] Neither taxes nor interest-bearing Treasury notes offered a satisfactory solution, and it became apparent that a national currency, issued either by the Treasury or by a national bank of some sort, was the only way out. Still the House debated, unable to come to any conclusion until Daniel Webster proposed a bank which was, on January 7, 1815, accepted in desperation by a vote of 120 to 38. Southern Congressmen voted overwhelmingly in favor of this measure, but Madison vetoed it because it offered too little relief to the Treasury.[45]

With the end of the war Southern nationalism went even beyond the support of protective tariffs and a national bank, as is plainly demonstrated by an editorial published in the Richmond *Enquirer* on September 20. Said Ritchie: "Have the Americans no water courses to clear, no canals to construct, no roads to form, no bridges to erect? Must the productions of our soil be continually subject to obstructions on the way to market? Must our want of internal communication forever remain the laughing-stock of stran-

[42] Raleigh *Register*, May 5, 1815.     [43] Padover, *Jeffersonian Profile*, 378.
[44] Jefferson to William Short, November 28, 1814, in Lipscomb and Bergh (eds.), *Writings of Thomas Jefferson*, XIV, 211–18.
[45] Hutton, "Southern Nationalism," 53–55, chart 25.

gers and the reproach of our citizens? Where are the public *schools* which we have erected, the *colleges* which Virginia has endowed? Why are our sons sent away to other states far removed from the observation of their parents, and too frequently estranged from the feelings of Virginia? Where are our public libraries, etc.? Let us seize this precious moment and devote it to *Internal Improve-*

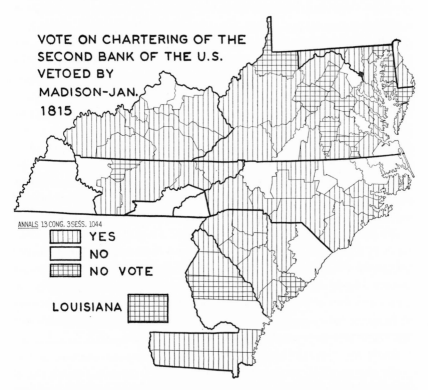

VOTE ON CHARTERING OF THE SECOND BANK OF THE U.S. VETOED BY MADISON-JAN. 1815

ANNALS 13 CONG. 3 SESS. 1044

YES
NO
NO VOTE

LOUISIANA

*ments.* Now is the time for Virginia to extend her character and preserve her influence in the union. Let us adopt some scheme of gradual improvement and go on without ceasing." [46]

Contrary to the usual impression, the Federalist Party did not, because of the war, immediately disintegrate in the Southern states. In the elections of 1815 Virginia chose six members of the opposition, including Randolph, as against seventeen Republicans; North Carolina elected three Federalists as against four in the previous

[46] Richmond *Enquirer*, September 20, 1815.

Congress; and South Carolina, which had no Federalists in its former delegation, now elected one. Maryland chose five Federalist members as against three in the previous Congress, and Delaware returned a solid Federalist delegation. No other state outside of New England, which section gave the Federalists a clean sweep, returned a majority for that party.[47] Even in New England manufactures were beginning to challenge the commercial interest, and the party of Washington and Adams was on its way out.

Though the War of 1812 can hardly be considered a great national triumph, it certainly amounted to a political victory for the Southern states. They were the principal advocates and the staunchest supporters of that struggle, both politically and militarily, and in looking back on the Battle of New Orleans, they were able to forget its darker hours. If Southern spirits were stimulated by reflections on the recent war, they were also bolstered by the fact that the Republican Party of Jefferson had been in control of the Federal government since 1801, and in view of the rapid decline of the Federalist Party as well as the prospect of support from a rapidly growing West, the end of its regime was not yet in sight.

In these circumstances it is not surprising to find Southern leaders losing some of their traditional interest in the reserved rights of the states and taking a new interest in extending the powers of the Federal government. Such an attitude would be encouraged, not only by their assurance that farmers would always dominate the Union, but by the disorganized state in which the war had left economic affairs, and by the demand for the development of a rapidly growing West.

President Madison delivered his seventh annual message on December 5, 1815, to a Congress which was again able to meet in an almost completely restored capitol building. It was natural that most of the message should be concerned with matters of national defense, but as it turned out, these were not the really important points. The significant sections of the address recommended the establishment of a national university in the District of Columbia, the creation of a system of internal improvements, the levying of a protective tariff, and the founding of a national bank to provide

[47] Charleston *Gazette*, September 13, October 13, 1815; Savannah *Republican*, May 18, 1815; Scharf, *History of Maryland*, III, 145.

a national currency. Thus Hamilton appeared to have triumphed over Jefferson, and the Republican Party to have deserted its founder.[48]

This was, indeed, the high water mark of Southern nationalism, but a closer examination of the situation discloses many crosscurrents and conflicting purposes. Jefferson's followers opposed Hamilton's Bank of the United States when it was chartered by Con-

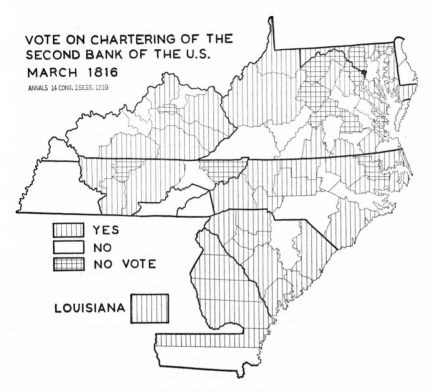

VOTE ON CHARTERING OF THE
SECOND BANK OF THE U.S.
MARCH 1816

ANNALS 14 CONG. 1 SESS. 1219

YES
NO
NO VOTE

LOUISIANA

gress in 1791, and they prevented its recharter in 1811. But the war resulted in the suspension of specie payments by practically all banks except those of much-persecuted New England, and the country was flooded with the paper currency of the insolvent institutions. In fact, since no appreciable amount of specie was available, there was no other money available for the transaction of business. A national institution which could emit a sound paper

[48] Richardson (ed.), *Messages and Papers of the Presidents*, II, 547–54.

currency and use its financial power to bring order out of the prevailing chaos appeared to be the only solution—even to men who
previously had constitutional scruples on the subject. Consequently, a bill to charter a second Bank of the United States was
introduced by Calhoun and opposed by Daniel Webster. It passed
the House by a vote of eighty to seventy-one, with the Southern
states casting over half the favorable ballots, the margin there
being about two to one. The only consolidated Southern opposition came from the Kentucky counties bordering the Ohio River
and the tobacco-producing counties of Maryland and Virginia.
These were agricultural areas which did not feel the need of Federal support for the marketing of their products.[49]

To Southerners generally the need for a protective tariff was not
obvious. As in Britain, the weaving of textiles had been carried
on in the colonies by handicraft methods until Samuel Slater established the first successful American spinning mill at Pawtucket,
Rhode Island, in 1790. During the war rapid growth of mills and
spindles continued, rendered possible by the increasing supply of
raw cotton from the South. The number of spindles was said to
be 80,000 in 1811, and 500,000 in 1815. In 1800 a total of 500
bales of cotton had been used; in 1805 the number had risen to
1,000 bales and by 1810 it was 10,000. Just five years later, nine
times this quantity of raw cotton was consumed by the industry.[50]

The machinery in these new mills was for spinning yarn only.
Weaving was still carried on in the home by means of the hand
loom; but in 1814 Francis C. Lowell built a mill at Waltham, Massachusetts, in which he introduced the power loom, and for the
first time in this country cotton was converted into cloth in one
manufacturing plant. It would be a long time, however, before
the new machinery would take the place of the handicraft worker.
The census of 1810 showed that Georgia produced more yards of
cotton cloth than did Rhode Island, the center of factory production, and the states of North and South Carolina led all others in
the number of hand looms. Furthermore, the states of Virginia,

[49] Hutton, "Southern Nationalism," 56–58, chart 26.
[50] *American State Papers,* IX, *Finance,* III, 82–83; Taussig, *Tariff History of the United States,* 28; Krout and Fox, *Completion of Independence,* 70–71.

South Carolina, and Georgia produced more homespun cotton goods than all the other states and territories combined.[51]

Given this situation, one finds it hard to see how the Southern states, which sold their cotton and tobacco in the British market and received their manufactures from that source, could have benefited by a tariff imposed for the protection of New England mills. The act of 1816 levied a duty of 25 per cent on cotton goods for three years, a duty which at that time was considered sufficiently protective.[52] The Southern members of the House of Representatives voted against this measure by a majority of thirty-four to twenty-three, with those from Kentucky, Tennessee, South Carolina, and Georgia being almost evenly divided. The two Western states had some hope of developing manufactures and the stand of their Representatives is not difficult to understand, but Georgia and South Carolina could hardly have shared their optimism. It is true that the editor of the Savannah *Republican* favored protection, but the representative of his district voted against it, as did the single voting member from Louisiana. Only one member from North Carolina and two from Maryland favored protection, but a solid block of Virginia districts backed President Madison on this issue. These were the districts which included Norfolk and the Eastern Shore, as well as the peninsula lying between the James and the Rappahannock rivers. Their trade centered in Norfolk, and they had the best water communications available anywhere. The culture of tobacco had given way to wheat in this area and its best market was in the West Indies. A strong Federal government could promote this trade. There certainly was no prospect of developing local manufactures here, but perhaps there was hope that their development in New England might loosen the hold which federalism had, until now, on that section of the country.[53]

The third program which occupied the concentrated attention

[51] Mathew B. Hammond, in *The South in the Building of the Nation* (Richmond, 1909–1913), V, 203; Victor S. Clark, *ibid.*, 310.

[52] Taussig, *Tariff History of the United States*, 29–30.

[53] Savannah *Republican*, June 20, August 22, September 13, 1816; Hutton, "Southern Nationalism," chart 27; *American State Papers*, IX, *Finance*, III, 447–48, 453, 463, 484, 533, 656–60.

of Congress during the postwar years was that relating to "internal improvements." The war had demonstrated the need for better communications between the Atlantic Coast and the Lower Mississippi Valley, and the old "War Hawks" were now the leaders in the movement toward nationalization. Indeed, there were some who believed that the East and the West would eventually separate unless the national government could develop better communications between them. Madison, in his message of December

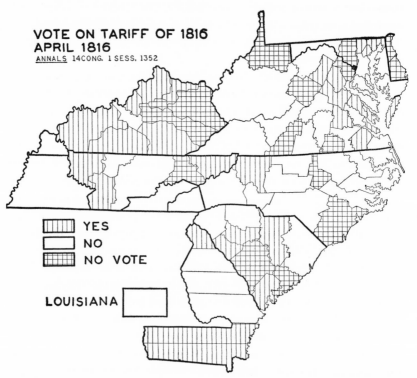

VOTE ON TARIFF OF 1816
APRIL 1816
ANNALS 14CONG. 1 SESS. 1352

YES
NO
NO VOTE

LOUISIANA

5, advocated the construction of interstate roads and canals, but being a strict constructionist on this issue, he believed that an amendment to the Constitution would be necessary to give the Federal government the authority to take such action. Jefferson took the same view of the matter, but not the former "War Hawks" who were now the "New Nationalists."

One of these, John C. Calhoun, made a motion in the House on December 16, 1816, that a committee be appointed to inquire into the expediency of setting apart the profits from the newly chartered Bank of the United States as a permanent fund for the construction of internal improvements. Calhoun became its chairman and introduced a bill on December 23, 1816, "to set apart and pledge, as a permanent fund for internal improvements," the profits received from the bank, including the $1,500,000 bonus which it was required to pay for its charter, and all profits deriving from the one-fifth interest which the government held in its capital stock. This measure was supported by Clay and the "New Nationalists" within the Republican Party. It passed the House by the narrow margin of eighty-six to eighty-four votes but was vetoed by President Madison.[54]

The stand which the Southern members of the House took on this issue affords a clue to the reaction of their section. Among the Western states, which were supposed to be the most nationalistic, Louisiana cast her single vote against the measure, Tennessee voted one to three against it, and Kentucky sided with the opposition by a vote of six to two. Georgia favored the bill by a vote of five to one and South Carolina by a margin of six to three. North Carolina was evenly divided, even as between east and west. Virginia east of the Blue Ridge was solidly against internal improvements except for the district which included Lynchburg on the upper James, but the Valley was divided and the trans-Allegheny counties voted almost unanimously in the affirmative. Maryland voted five to two against Calhoun's bill, the two favorable votes coming from the neighborhood of Baltimore. Except for these two votes, the whole Chesapeake Bay area in Virginia, Maryland, and Delaware, normally nationalistic by reason of its dependence on interstate trade, opposed the employment of Federal funds for the construction of roads and canals because its trade was largely water-borne.[55]

The Southern vote on this measure is indeed difficult to understand. Yet, taking a composite view of these three votes in the House of Representatives, certain generalizations as to the political attitude of the region at this turning point in our history may be hazarded. In the first place, it is not correct to assume that, be-

[54] Channing, *History of the United States*, V, 316–19.
[55] Hutton, "Southern Nationalism," 59–69, chart 28.

cause Clay and Calhoun were now leading the forces of nationalism, with Madison and Monroe leaning in that direction, the Southern states had gone over, lock, stock, and barrel, to the position
formerly occupied by the Federalists. The best argument for this
thesis is the wholehearted support which the Southern members
of Congress gave to the measure for rechartering the Bank of the
United States. This was a major concession on the part of a people

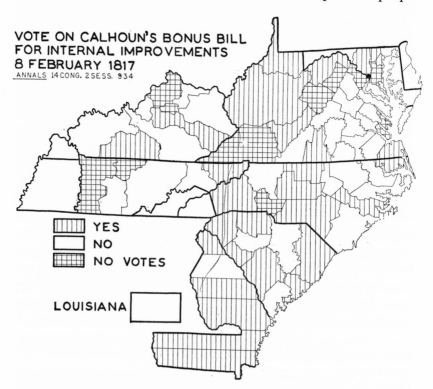

VOTE ON CALHOUN'S BONUS BILL
FOR INTERNAL IMPROVEMENTS
8 FEBRUARY 1817
ANNALS 14 CONG. 2 SESS. 934

YES
NO
NO VOTES

LOUISIANA

who were traditionally strict constructionists, and it can only be
explained by taking into account the chaotic condition which had
been brought about after the war by the unrestrained chartering
of state banks and their helter-skelter emission of paper currency
of dubious value. Their stand on this question certainly demonstrates the fact that Southerners could face realities, however contrary to their traditional views.

The vote on Calhoun's internal improvement bill is harder to understand, especially the opposition of Kentucky and Tennessee. It is less difficult to see the reason for the unfavorable stand of the whole watershed of the Chesapeake Bay, except for the Baltimore and Lynchburg districts, whose trade was fed by overland routes. Apparently the divided vote of North Carolina was influenced by the availability of facilities for transportation, and the favorable stand of South Carolina and Georgia was doubtless due to the lack of adequate water routes.

The vote on the tariff bill is perhaps the most significant of the three, for it indicated the way the political wind was blowing in the crucial year of 1816. Contrary to the situation in banking and internal improvement legislation, the Constitution clearly authorized the levying of tariff duties, and it made no distinction between tariffs for revenue and tariffs for protection. Yet it was perfectly obvious that protective tariffs had a discriminatory effect as between sections of the country and between different groups of citizens in all sections. The Federalist Party, dominated by merchants who were primarily interested in international trade, was not inclined to favor protective tariffs. These would tend to favor small-scale industries which, except in the case of the newly mechanized operations of spinning and weaving, were carried on by mere "mechanics." Jefferson had come to look on manufactures as essential to the self-sufficiency, and thus to the military security, of the country, and since the handicraft trades were not highly capitalized, his stand was not inconsistent with the popular tenets of democracy. And though there were Southern enthusiasts who hoped to see their section become a great manufacturing area, they were in a minute minority. The districts whose representatives voted for protection in 1816 were, in general, not those which had any prospects of developing manufactures. Their stand would seem to indicate that they thought the textile industry of New England, which had grown up as a result of the war, deserved to be protected for a limited time from the "dumping" of excess British goods upon the American market, thus strangling domestic industry in its infancy.[56]

[56] Norris W. Preyer, "The South's Experiment with Protective Tariffs, 1816–1820" (Ph.D. dissertation, University of Virginia, 1954), 31–41.

433

While this cautious advance toward a nationalistic policy was under way in a party and a section which had indisputable control of the machinery of government, there were already contrary forces at work. Though Jefferson and Madison had strayed from the straight and narrow path of strict construction to favor the bank act of 1816, neither Randolph nor Taylor had ever deserted the "principles of 1798." They apparently realized, along with Macon and a few other Southern leaders, that the "peculiar institution" of their section could, and probably would, in the future subject it to attack by elements whose economic and political interests could pose under the banner of moral righteousness. The bitter hostility of New England during the war and its vitriolic attack on the "Federal ratio" of the Constitution, which gave the South credit for three-fifths of the slaves in enumerating the population for purposes of representation and direct taxes, was a warning signal, as was Chief Justice John Marshall's decision in the case of Martin *v.* Hunter's Lessee in which, for the first time, the Federal Supreme Court assumed the authority to overrule decisions of the highest courts of the states.

The stepped-up reaction against the new nationalism of the Republican leaders was set in motion when in 1816 the editor of the politically powerful Richmond *Enquirer* deserted the party leadership and attacked the tariff and bank acts. In this stand Ritchie was joined by Spencer Roane, son-in-law of Patrick Henry and Chief Judge of the Virginia Supreme Court of Appeals, which tribunal held unanimously that Marshall's mandamus in the Martin and Hunter case should not be obeyed and that such appeals from the decisions of state courts to the Federal judiciary were unconstitutional. Ritchie and Roane were aided in this revival of state rights principles by a group of able young men, including Philip P. Barbour, John Tyler, and John Floyd. They were, of course, supported by Randolph and Taylor, and Jefferson soon came over to their side.[57]

Since the early days of the Jefferson administration, Roane and Ritchie had been leaders of a group of eastern Virginia politicians, known as the "Richmond Junto," which dominated the

[57] Ambler, *Thomas Ritchie*, 64, 72; Ambler, *Sectionalism in Virginia*, 100–103; Anderson, *William Branch Giles*, 207–13.

political scene in the Old Dominion. This group included Jefferson's close friend, Wilson Cary Nicholas, who stepped down from the governor's chair to become president of the Richmond branch of the Bank of the United States. The presidents of the two state banks which had their main offices in Richmond were also members of the "Junto," as were most of the members of the governor's "Council of State." The political power of this coterie stemmed from a legislative act of 1800 which provided that Virginia should elect her Presidential electors on a general ticket. This made it necessary for the legislative caucus to name the electoral slate, and the caucus consequently organized a central corresponding committee to work with the county committees in the election. The power of this central committee was great because of its control of the county committees, and it and the Richmond "Junto" were practically indistinguishable.[58]

Yet at the same time that Virginia, under the leadership of the "Junto," was reaffirming her faith in the principles of the Virginia and Kentucky Resolutions of 1798, a rift in the fabric of state solidarity appeared along the summit of the Blue Ridge Mountains. The Valley and transmontane counties had good reason to maintain that they had been slighted in the matter of road construction, banking facilities, and representation in the state legislature. The census of 1810 gave the west 312,626 white inhabitants and the east 338,827, but in the state Senate the former section had only four members to twenty for the latter, while an apportionment on the basis of the white population would have entitled the west to nine. This unequal representation resulted in successive defeats of several bills providing for the call of a constitutional convention and in repeated threats of dismemberment on the part of the western counties. Numerous mass meetings passed resolutions demanding the suffrage for all taxpayers and militiamen, and the movement finally took form in the Staunton Convention of August 19–23, 1816.[59]

This meeting was attended by sixty-five delegates representing thirty-five western counties and was presided over by the Fed-

[58] *Letters on the Richmond Party*, by a Virginian (Washington, 1823), *passim;* Ammon, "Republican Party in Virginia," Chap. VIII.

[59] Ambler, *Sectionalism in Virginia*, 93–94; Ambler, *Thomas Ritchie*, 64–68.

eralist Congressman James C. Breckinridge. It discussed the grievances of the west at great length and ended its labors by addressing a memorial to the General Assembly which advocated the
election of a constitutional convention empowered to remedy
all defects in the existing instrument of government. The eastern
leaders were disturbed by this show of western opposition and
Jefferson came forward with his famous letter of July 12, 1816, to
Samuel Kercheval, the well-known historian of the Valley of
Virginia. In this epistle the former President suggested many
changes in the fundamental law of his state, including the introduction of the New England township plan for the administration of local government, equal representation based on white
population, liberal suffrage, and the election of the governor,
judges, jurors, and sheriffs by popular vote.[60]

Ritchie supported Jefferson in his call for a convention to
revise the state constitution, but the conservatives were too strong
for them. The easterners did, however, consent to a compromise
whereby the western counties obtained representation in the
Senate based on white population alone, and the 1816 session
of the legislature established a board of public works which was
authorized to employ a civil engineer to plan a system of roads
and canals and to subscribe state funds to companies chartered
to carry out such projects. Furthermore, state banks were established at Winchester and Wheeling in 1817.[61] These concessions
quieted unrest in the western counties for a time, but partial
measures did not suffice. After a few years the trouble broke out
again and this time it led to the calling of a constitutional convention in 1829.

Much has been said of the differences between the eastern
and western sections of the South Atlantic states during this period,
but there has been much misunderstanding concerning the matter. When Jefferson spoke for the western section of Virginia, he

[60] Ambler, *Sectionalism in Virginia*, 93–96; Ambler, *Thomas Ritchie*, 64; Anderson,
*William Branch Giles*, 229; Lipscomb and Bergh (eds.), *Writings of Thomas Jefferson*, XV, 32–34.
[61] George T. Starnes, *Sixty Years of Branch Banking in Virginia* (New York, 1931),
58–62; Ambler, *Sectionalism in Virginia*, 93–94; Edward Graham Roberts, "The
Roads of Virginia, 1607–1840" (Ph.D. dissertation, University of Virginia, 1950),
68–69.

included his own Piedmont Region in it, and thus he could claim to be advocating the cause of the majority of his fellow citizens. But the Piedmont people, including the Jeffersons, had migrated up the eastward-flowing rivers as they required new lands for the cultivation of tobacco, and they brought their ideas along with their baggage. Piedmont civilization therefore differed very little from that developed from English models in the Tidewater country during the colonial period. But when one crossed the Blue Ridge, he found a different pattern of life. The people were largely of Scotch-Irish or German descent; they had few slaves and grew little tobacco, but built good barns, developed fine meadows, and sent provisions down the Shenandoah and Potomac rivers to market in Georgetown, Alexandria, Baltimore, and Philadelphia. Their customs and their economics differed markedly from those of the Tidewater and Piedmont regions, but no active hostility had ever developed. Ideological conflicts were avoided in a spirit of tolerance, and economic problems were subject to adjustment. The trans-Allegheny counties were, in many ways, similar to those of the Valley, but they were even more isolated and more "alien." They were too distant and too few to exert any great influence at this time, but later they "seceded" from the mother state and formed the state of West Virginia.

Maryland also had her sectional troubles, but they were quite different from those of Virginia. Her western counties were limited in number and extent, but they contained much good land and many good German and Scotch-Irish farmers. The produce from the region could be sent to market either down the Potomac or along the state-constructed highway to Baltimore. For this reason the Potomac counties tended to favor a strong central government which could develop the river navigation, while the counties dependent on the Baltimore market objected to such competition with their intrastate business and therefore voted the Republican ticket. There was also the rivalry between the "Eastern Shore" and the "Western Shore" of the Chesapeake, but the principal antagonism was between the rural and the urban constituencies. In this competition the Baltimore Republicans got the worst of it and had never been able to obtain representation in the legislature which was equal to that of their rural Federalist opponents.[62]

The states to the south of Virginia presented a still different sectional picture. In North Carolina only Buncombe and Ashe counties lay between the Blue Ridge and the Tennessee boundary, so that practically her whole area lay within the two regions which, in Virginia, constituted the eastern section of the state. Nevertheless, North Carolina had her east and west, and in 1816 the thirty-seven counties of the coastal region had a white population of 152,586 and 111 members in the General Assembly, while the twenty-five counties of the upper country numbered 234,090 white people who were represented by only 74 members in the Assembly. Governor A. D. Murphy recommended a reapportionment, and the question of calling a constitutional convention was submitted to the legislature, where it was defeated by a vote of eighty-four to thirty-four. Yet, as in Virginia, concessions were made, for in 1816 this body provided for making some minor improvements in river navigation and also appointed a committee to report on a plan of public education and another to consider the establishment of a state penitentiary. Public interest in such matters could not have been intense, however, for out of 60,000 eligible voters, only 9,549 actually voted in the Presidential election of this year.[63]

South Carolina extended westward only to the Blue Ridge and therefore had no "west" in the Virginia sense of the word, but her sectionalism, as between "upcountry," "middle country," and "low country" was more pronounced than in any of the other South Atlantic states. She had, however, by the end of 1816 made more political concessions than had either Virginia or North Carolina, a development doubtless facilitated by the fact that her constitution of 1790 made provision for amendment, whereas neither of her northward neighbors had done so. Under this constitution and in accord with the situa-

[62] Natchez *Mississippi Republican*, November 16, 1819; Scharf, *History of Maryland*, III, 142, 147–48; Andrews, *History of Maryland*, 445–48.

[63] Ashe, *History of North Carolina*, II, 247–48; Albert R. Newsome, *The Presidential Election of 1824 in North Carolina* (Chapel Hill, 1939), 41.

tion at the time of its adoption, the three coastal election districts or "precincts" of Beaufort, Charleston, and Georgetown, which contained all the rice plantations and most of the wealth of the state, also elected a majority of the members of the state legislature.

The introduction of the culture of upland cotton modified this situation and by 1800 the central part of the state, with Columbia as its metropolis, had adopted a slave-operated plantation economy which did not differ essentially from that existing in the coastal rice country. For this reason it was possible in 1808 for the legislature to reapportion representation so as to leave the Low Country in control of the Senate, but to give the "Middle" and "Upper Country" a majority in the House of Representatives. This reform was accomplished with great unanimity, apparently for the reason that the planter class might still hope to control both houses. Yet in 1810 the constitution was again amended so as to provide for white manhood suffrage.[64]

It is of some interest that Maryland, in the same year, amended her constitution to the same effect, and it may be possible to account for this liberalization in both states on the same grounds: both could amend their constitutions without the necessity of calling a convention, and both had, at the time of the amendments, sufficiently strong Federalist parties to create a situation of bipartisan rivalry. Meanwhile, both North Carolina and Virginia retained their freehold qualification for the suffrage, while Georgia's constitution of 1798 provided that any taxpayer could vote.[65] There had never been many Federalists in Georgia, but in 1816 and 1817 her Congressmen voted overwhelmingly in favor of the bank charter and the internal improvement bill, while they were evenly divided on the question of the tariff. Having only a small population and a southern and western frontier exposed to both the Indians and the Spaniards, she was more in need of Federal aid than any of her sister states, but she had no really serious sectional problems for the reason

[64] William A. Schaper, *Sectionalism and Representation in South Carolina* (Washington, 1901), 433–36; Poore (ed.), *Federal and State Constitutions*, II, 1634–35.

[65] Poore (ed.), *Federal and State Constitutions*, I, 394, 832.

that her cotton planters of the Piedmont Region, where Augusta was the metropolis, could easily outvote the rice planters of the coast.[66]

The progressive spirit prevailing in Georgia at this time is illustrated by the message which Governor David B. Mitchell delivered to the legislature in November of 1816. He favored protective tariffs because "much of the luxury that we ought to dread as the parent of vice must be imported from abroad." He urged larger appropriations for county academies (a state university had already been founded in 1801) and aid for private institutions of that nature. "The revision of our penal code," said the governor, "has been committed, agreeably to the wishes of the last legislature, to two gentlemen, and the result of their labours is herewith communicated. The penitentiary will be ready for occupancy before another session. The Bank of the State of Georgia, established by the last legislature, has been put into operation at Savannah and branches have been established at Milledgeville and Augusta." Finally, because "our crops are bulky and intended for export," Governor Mitchell recommended appropriations for the improvement of rivers and roads.[67]

Southern Federalists, including the strong Maryland contingent, had not looked upon the late war with favor, but they had not opposed it with the venom displayed by their New England counterparts, nor had they given aid and comfort to the enemy. Nevertheless, by 1817 this wing of the party was all but dead, not because of its past record, but because, by favoring a stronger nationalism, the Republicans had cut the ground from under them. As the Savannah *Republican* put it, "The Federalist party has no program. They would hardly repeal the United States Bank charter—our only barrier against an inundation of worthless paper, or repeal our tariff and internal taxes. They claim all the wealth, talents and honesty in the country, but can hardly show the grounds for this claim." [68]

Despite a remnant of Federalism in the North, the day of the Federalists had passed when James Monroe was inaugurated as

[66] Savannah *Republican,* September 13, 26, October 15, 1816.
[67] *Ibid.,* November 12, 1816.     [68] *Ibid.,* September 17, 1816.

the fifth President of the United States on March 4, 1817. The "Era of Good Feeling" was proclaimed in New York on August 12 of that year when Tammany Hall gave a public dinner in honor of "His Excellency," John Quincy Adams, and numerous toasts were drunk to his health.[69] Yet there was, even then, some dissent in the ranks of the Republicans. On December 25 John Hampden wrote from Washington to Thomas Ritchie concerning the report of a committee of the House of Representatives on that part of the President's message relating to roads, canals, and seminaries of learning. He strongly objected to the proposed invasion of the rights and liberties of the states: "The committee have also forgotten the existence and powers of the state governments. They do not remember that our system is only a league between the state governments on the one hand and the United States on the other. They are also not aware that it may not comport with *their* ideas of sovereignty, that the agents of one government may enter their territory and cut canals or roads at their pleasure." [70]

The question of the rights of the state as opposed to the power of the nation was to lie in abeyance for a time and so was that of the "common" man as against "his betters," yet these issues were not dead but sleeping. Charleston was the only Southern city where a class conflict came sharply into focus, and this was doubtless because Charles Pinckney, a staunch Jeffersonian in spite of his family connections, gave the democracy an able leadership while the Charleston *Gazette* furnished a voice to offset the Federalism of the Charleston *Courier*.[71] In 1818 Daniel Huger was running for Congress against Pinckney in the Charleston district. The "mechanics" strenuously supported the cause of their champion and published a "Communication to the Republican Mechanics" in the October 9 issue of the *Gazette*. Here they said they were sure that the great body of their fellows were true to republicanism and would never vote for a Federalist, least of all for Daniel Huger, who had voted against the general suffrage bill which had been introduced and carried by Pinckney and his Republican friends. Huger, they said, had also voted in

[69] Richmond *Enquirer*, August 19, 1817.    [70] *Ibid.*, December 27, 1817.
[71] *Dictionary of American Biography*, XIV, 611–14.

the legislature to tax the mechanics—a measure, the communication continued, "which Pinckney voted against and opposed. What mechanic is there among you who would vote for Huger, who tried to take from you the precious right to vote at all?" [72]

If the Southern states had their undemocratic element, the North was not without its own brand of snobbery. On July 22, 1817, Ritchie published in the *Enquirer* an editorial on President Monroe's Northern tour. He thought the attitude of the Northern press and public was unwholesome and undemocratic, which was no more than was to have been expected of Federalists, but he was shocked when the Republican Salem *Register* used such expressions as "ruler," "condescend," and "his people." The Richmond editor concluded with the exhortation, "Let us beware of those ridiculous pageantries, which are calculated to produce the spirit that inspires such a language." [73]

It may not be credited by savants unfamiliar with the *mores* of the early South, but "aristocracy" was an ugly word in the estimation of the people, both high and low. They commonly used it at this time to apply only to a despised "paper" aristocracy, by which expression they meant to designate all such as got their wealth by means of speculation in stocks, especially bank stocks. John Taylor of Caroline well expressed the attitude of his section when he denied that a landed aristocracy could exist in this country because of the extent and cheapness of the public domain. Lest the "paper aristocracy" sing too loudly the song of a landed aristocracy, Taylor compared the property created by law with that which existed naturally. All of which goes to show that, even at this early date, the differences between North and South were not confined to the single question of slavery. If that had been the only issue, it certainly could have been settled peacefully and decently. [74]

While evidences of cleavage were obvious in the East, even during the "Era of Good Feeling," the West showed a different face. As late as the 1830's Americans still thought of the West as the entire section from the Alleghenies to the Mississippi River and from the Great Lakes to the Gulf. If signs of cleavage be-

[72] Charleston *Gazette*, September 14, 26, 1816; September 29, 1818.
[73] Richmond *Enquirer*, July 22, 1817.    [74] Simms, *John Taylor*, 155.

tween the northern and southern parts of this great valley had already begun to appear, they were generally overshadowed by unifying forces.[75]

But what of Andrew Jackson during these years of partisan truce and sectional solidification? Though there were those prescient individuals who were already looking on him as Presidential timber, his political star had not yet risen above the horizon. Ritchie condemned his invasion of Florida and thereby made room for Francis Preston Blair to become the editorial spokesman of the Jackson administration. Congress absolved him of all blame in connection with this incident, but in the South Atlantic states he was looked on as merely a "border captain" who lacked every qualification for political office. The Southern movement for equal suffrage and equal representation had already got under way without his assistance.[76]

[75] Krout and Fox, *Completion of Independence*, 407.
[76] Ambler, *Thomas Ritchie*, 69; James, *Border Captain*, 322–24; Abernethy, *From Frontier to Plantation in Tennessee*, 239–40.

# CHAPTER XVI

# THE GREAT MIGRATION

O NE OF the great American migrations was the advance of the Cotton Kingdom into the region bordering the Gulf of Mexico after Andrew Jackson's campaigns, treaties, and threats not only opened large areas to settlement but made it safe to occupy them. This inevitable development had been long delayed by the Spanish occupation of the entire extent of the Gulf Coast. A brief review of the international complications resulting from this conflict of interests will clarify the situation.

When the French and Indian War broke out in 1754 as a result of the Franco-British rivalry for possession of the Ohio Valley, the French had already occupied the Gulf Coast as far east as Mobile, and the Spanish had settled as far west as Pensacola. The boundary between the two colonial establishments was the little Perdido, the river of lost souls! In 1763 the Treaty of Paris brought an end to hostilities and changed the boundary on the Gulf Coast. France now ceded Louisiana to Spain, but this province was to include only the "island" (the land south of the Iberville-Amite connection between the Mississippi and the lakes) and the city of New Orleans east of the river. Everything else between Baton Rouge and St. Augustine went to England.

Outside of New Orleans the population of this region was small at that time, but a gradual increase was assured when the new owners began to grant large tracts in the Natchez district for important civil and military services. By the early 1770's there were at least seventy-eight families raising crops along the river banks, and it was for their protection that the Royal government of the province persuaded the Indians to move out of the district. Aside from this development there was no important movement into the region before the American Revolution, but during that struggle Tories from the Atlantic states poured into Natchez and the surrounding countryside. Spain occupied the area in 1781, but England confused the issue two years later by giving the United States a claim to ownership above the thirty-first parallel at the same time that she surrendered to Spain all of Florida below that line.[1]

Spain did not accept the thirty-first parallel as the northern boundary of Florida and continued to maintain her garrison at Natchez. She also established posts at the site of the old French fort "Tombecbé" in the Chickasaw country about two hundred miles above Mobile on the Tombigbee River and at Fort St. Stephens, about halfway between this post and Mobile. On the Mississippi she maintained a post at Los Nogales, or the Walnut Hills, and in 1795, in order to check the Yazoo companies, she established Fort San Fernando de las Barrancas at the Chickasaw Bluffs. In short, she claimed all the country between the Tennessee River and the Gulf of Mexico; yet Indians, with the Creeks on the east, the Chickasaw on the northwest, and the Choctaw on the southwest, occupied practically all of this region, which included the present states of Mississippi and Alabama, along with the eastern extension of Louisiana and the western part of Florida. Outside of the Natchez region there was only one white settlement —that on the Mobile, the Tensaw, and the Tombigbee rivers, just above the thirty-first parallel.[2]

The geography here is a little complicated. About twenty-five miles below Fort St. Stephens, the Alabama and Tombigbee rivers are connected by a stream called the "Cut-off," and below this the Alabama River becomes the Tensaw, and the Tombigbee becomes the Mobile. The land between them is called "Tensaw Island," and the largest settlement of the post-Revolutionary years was established in this area. It was composed of both Whigs and Royalists, the latter having been driven from Georgia and the Carolinas. Added to these were the "Indian countrymen"—the traders, often

[1] James M. Helms, Jr., "Land Tenure in Territorial Mississippi, 1798–1809" (M.A. thesis, University of Virginia, 1955); Lawrence Kinnaird, "American Penetration into Spanish Louisiana," in *New Spain and the American West: Historical Contributions Presented to H. E. Bolton* (Los Angeles, 1932), I, 231–32.

[2] Whitaker, *Spanish-American Frontier*, 169, 214.

Scotsmen who had taken up their abode among the natives and, with Indian wives, become "assimilated." [3]

The garrison at St. Stephens was composed of only one company. The blockhouse, the home of the commandant, and the church were frame buildings, well constructed. All other houses occupied by Americans were built of small poles and covered with cypress bark. A few French farmers also lived by the river, and their houses have been described as being built almost entirely of clay. They cultivated indigo, which was worth $2.50 per pound. Another settlement located east of the Alabama River and above the "Cut-off" was made up of numerous intelligent and prosperous people whose blood was a mixture of white and Indian. This colony was formed at an early period for the benefit of the settlers' large herds of cattle which could graze on the wild grass and cane the year round. Here, besides skins of various kinds, traders bought up beeswax, hickory nut oil, and snakeroot, along with various medicinal barks and herbs. These they transported to Augusta on packhorses or to Mobile and New Orleans in large canoes. The packhorsemen drove ten small but hardy native ponies in a "lead," each animal carrying about 180 pounds. On their journey they followed old Indian trails, and from Pensacola they brought back an inferior West Indian rum called "tafia," along with powder, lead, a little iron and salt, and the few other articles required by this isolated and primitive community, which with a population of mixed blood was always on friendly terms with the neighboring Indians.[4]

Though by agreeing to Pinckney's Treaty of 1795, Spain relinquished her claim to the area north of the thirty-first parallel, she did not consent to have the boundary surveyed until 1798. Congress then, without consulting Georgia, created the Mississippi Territory to include only those lands which Spain had surrendered south of the mouth of the Yazoo River, but when Georgia, in 1802, agreed to give up her claim, the Territory was extended northward to the Tennessee boundary, with the Chattahoochee and the Mississippi rivers marking its eastern and western limits.

The act of Congress establishing the Territory provided a form of government in all respects similar to that of the Northwest Ter-

[3] Pickett, *History of Alabama*, 416–17.  [4] *Ibid.*, 417–18, 422.

ritory except that slavery was permitted and the domestic slave trade continued, but no slaves were to be introduced from "without the limits of the United States." The act also provided for sale of public lands for the benefit of the treasury of the United States, and a land system based on that of the Northwest Territory was finally adopted; yet it was not until 1803 that Congress made provision for the actual sale of lands in the Mississippi Territory. It was during this interim that Spain, by the Treaty of San Ildefonso, agreed to retrocede Louisiana to France and President Jefferson, fearing war with Napoleon on that frontier, was strengthening the forts and acquiring lands for new settlements along the Mississippi, while he sent Lewis and Clark to study the military possibilities of the vast hinterland beyond the Great River.[5]

Naturally the residents in the Natchez district wished to attract settlers from the Atlantic states to strengthen their defense in case of attack by their potential enemies, either white or red. Furthermore, there were economic reasons why they were anxious to have the public lands promptly put on the market at attractive prices. In 1795 Daniel Clark had brought the cotton gin to the lower Mississippi and by 1800 the fleecy staple had supplanted tobacco as the chief product of the region. At this time it was worth twenty-five cents per pound, and a good field hand could raise five to eight hundred pounds annually. One person in a position to know estimated that the crop of that year would yield nearly $750,000, and by 1802 the price of "Common Negro Fellows" had risen from $300 to $500. This meant wealth for those possessed of land and labor, and immigrants came in considerable numbers despite the fact that no public lands could be bought. In this situation many of the newcomers "squatted" on the public domain, and others purchased from the older inhabitants. In many cases, however, these holdings were threatened by earlier claims which were derived from grants under the British and Spanish regimes.[6]

With the Spanish authorities in Louisiana offering free lands, tax free, to bona fide settlers; with a number of the leading men in Kentucky and Tennessee suspected of favoring a separation

[5] Adams, "Jefferson's Reaction to the Treaty of San Ildefonso," Chaps. IV–V; Helms, "Land Tenure in Territorial Mississippi," 11–12.

[6] Helms, "Land Tenure in Territorial Mississippi," 14–15, 23.

from the United States and an alliance with Spain; with a Negro population nearly equal to that of the white inhabitants; with no military protection but an unorganized militia lacking adequate arms; and with potential enemies on all sides, the Mississippians were understandably resentful that the government did not make the public lands available. At this time there were over a million acres in the Territory which had been cleared of Indian claims during the British regime. This was in two tracts, one of which, with about a fourth of the acreage, extended about forty miles westward from the Tombigbee River, with Fort St. Stephens near its northern limit; the other lay along the Mississippi River from the mouth of the Yazoo to the thirty-first parallel. But the Congress was too far away to get a clear view of the problems of this exposed frontier. Moreover, there was already too much unsold land in the Northwest Territory, and new surveys would be expensive.[7] Despite its reluctance Congress did finally, on May 10, 1800, take positive action. It created a commission to investigate and report its findings and recommendations regarding all outstanding land claims within the area.[8]

Of course there was no problem as to lands already actually patented, but there were various types of doubtful claims, and there were the many families settled on public lands to which they had no legal claim but on which they had made improvements. Then there were warrants of survey issued by the British and Spanish governments, but on which they had made improvements. Of the doubtful claims those set up under the Georgia Yazoo Act of 1795 were the most extensive and the most complicated. Then there were warrants of survey issued by the British and Spanish governments but on which no patents had ever been issued. The Spanish government held these to be valid in case they were backed by three years of actual occupancy. But Spanish officials also issued warrants after the boundary treaty of 1795, taking care, however, to date them so as to make it appear that they were issued prior to the signing of the treaty. Before any new lands could

[7] Ibid., 13, 22; Bureau of American Ethnology, Eighteenth Annual Report, Pt. II, plates 1, 36.
[8] Carter (ed.), Territory of Mississippi, V, 97.

be sold, all these old claims would have to be settled and the Indian boundaries surveyed.[9]

Since prior to 1802 the State of Georgia had never relinquished the claim that her lands extended westward to the Mississippi River, the Federal commissioners attacked this problem first. On April 24, 1802, they entered into an agreement with the Georgia commissioners whereby the state, in consideration of the sum of $1,250,000, surrendered her claim to all lands lying westward of her present boundary. In addition to the monetary compensation, the United States agreed to appropriate 5,000,000 acres in the ceded territory to be applied to the liquidation of the Yazoo claims. Provision was made also for validating the British and Spanish titles of settlers resident in the Territory on October 27, 1795, and it was stipulated that a land office should be set up for the sale of the vacant lands in the Territory within a year after the ratification of this agreement.[10]

In order to carry out this provision, Madison notified Governor Claiborne on July 26 of the terms of the Georgia cession and called on him to collect all possible information on the different types of claims, as well as statistics on unclaimed public lands. Although the Indian boundaries had not yet been surveyed, it was estimated that 2,500 square miles—1,600,000 acres—were available for settlement in the Natchez district and an additional 4,600 square miles —nearly 3,000,000 acres—in Washington County on the Tombigbee. The lands on the Mississippi consisted largely of fertile, tillable soil, while more than a million acres on the Tombigbee were covered by pine forests and were useful only for grazing. In addition to the various classes of claims submitted, there were as many as 750 heads of families, with wives and children numbering possibly 2,000, who had simply settled on the public land without any semblance of a claim.[11] As to these people, Governor Claiborne said: "I do sincerely hope that these Citizens may be secured in

[9] Gray, *History of Agriculture in the Southern United States,* II, 222–23, 864–65; Savannah *Georgia Republican,* May 20, June 2, 1805, quoting Claiborne to United States commissioners, November 5, 1802.

[10] Carter (ed.), *Territory of Mississippi,* V, 142–46.

[11] Dunbar Rowland, *History of Mississippi, The Heart of the South* (Chicago, 1925), I, 390–92; Helms, "Land Tenure in Territorial Mississippi," 27–28, 32–34.

449

their improvements, and the Government will sell out the Vacant lands in this district upon moderate terms and in small tracts to actual settlers." [12]

With the Claiborne report as a core, the Federal commissioners added such information as they had been able to gather, and presently they gave their findings to the House of Representatives. In February, 1803, the House put together a bill based on the report of the commissioners and the endless string of petitions which flowed from Mississippi. The Senate passed the House measure with amendments, and the bill was approved on March 3, 1803. It adhered to the general provisions applied to the sale of lands in the Northwest Territory; authorized compliance with the terms of the Georgia Cession Agreement; and provided for the establishment of two land offices—one at Washington, the capital of the Territory, for the sale of all tracts west of the Pearl River, and one at St. Stephens to take care of sales in the area east of that stream.[13]

One of the main aims of this legislation was to validate the claims of all settlers who had established themselves in the Territory prior to October 27, 1795, the date of the Pinckney Treaty. Consequently, all holders of either British or Spanish warrants for survey who could prove that they actually inhabited and cultivated their land at that time, were confirmed in their claims just as if their titles had been completed under the former governments. Another large group of claimants was taken care of by the provision that all those who had taken up and actually occupied tracts of the public lands before the Spanish evacuation of the Territory would be granted 640 acres (one square mile or "section") free of cost. But of course an increasing number of settlers had moved in since the Spaniards moved out. To those, therefore, who arrived before the date of this act of March 3 was granted the right to purchase, when the land offices should be opened, up to 640 acres at the minimum price of $2.00 per acre and under the other conditions of sale which were in force at that time. It is

[12] Dunbar Rowland (ed.), *Official Letter Books of W. C. C. Claiborne, 1801–1816* (Jackson, 1917), I, 219–20.
[13] Carter (ed.), *Territory of Mississippi,* V, 192–205; Helms, "Land Tenure in Territorial Mississippi," 36–37.

noteworthy that this was the first general pre-emption act ever adopted by the national government.[14]

The act reserved, as had been done in the case of the Northwest Territory, the sixteenth section in each township (a unit of survey measuring six miles on each side, or thirty-six square miles or "sections") for the establishment and support of public schools. An endowment of thirty-six sections, as well as some land in Natchez, was set aside for Jefferson College, but the allotment for the common schools, amounting to 174,000 acres, and the endowment of more than 23,000 acres for Jefferson College, proved far more magnificent in the wording of the act than in the realization of the future.[15]

The Surveyor General's office for the Mississippi Territory—with rank parallel with that for the Northwest Territory—was established at the town of Washington, and Isaac Briggs, an honest and competent Maryland Quaker, was the first to fill the place. The land office for the district west of Pearl River was also set up at Washington and continued to function from July 9, 1803, until July 3, 1807. Here Edward Turner served as the first "register of claims," and Thomas Rodney, father of Caesar A. Rodney, and Robert Williams, presently to become governor of the Territory, were commissioners of claims. The office for the district east of Pearl River was established at Fort Stoddert, with Joseph Chambers as register and Ephraim Kirby and Robert C. Nicholas as commissioners. Now that lands could be purchased, new settlers trooped in to raise cotton in the limited areas that had, during the British regime, been cleared of the Indian title.[16]

But just as old claims were being settled and new lands in the Territory made available to immigrants, the United States purchased Louisiana and thus opened up a new and even more complicated series of questions concerning ownership and sale of vast tracts of unoccupied or sparsely settled lands. When war broke out between Spain and Great Britain in 1796, American settlers

[14] Claiborne, *Mississippi, as a Province, Territory and State,* 237; Carter (ed.), *Territory of Mississippi,* V, 193–95, 288–89, 292–95; Gray, *History of Agriculture in the Southern United States,* II, 663; Helms, "Land Tenure in Territorial Mississippi," 45.

[15] Rowland, *History of Mississippi, The Heart of the South,* I, 396.

[16] *Ibid.,* 395–96; Raleigh *Register,* May 23, 1803.

were welcomed in both Upper and Lower Louisiana and in West Florida. It was during this period that Moses and Stephen Austin migrated from Virginia to the future Missouri, and the large Bastrop and Maison Rouge grants on the Ouachita River were made. But after Natchez was surrendered in 1798, immigration was opposed and in the same year Juan Ventura Morales, the Intendant of Louisiana and West Florida, was put in charge of the public lands. Not only did he undertake in 1799 to carry out the new policy, but three years later the Spanish King prohibited all American immigration. Despite these restrictions, a steady stream of Americans continued to trickle into Louisiana. Most of them went to the western districts of Attakapas, Opelousas, Ouachita, and Natchitoches, where there was good grazing for cattle and where, according to the Bishop of Louisiana, Don Luis de Peñalvert y Cardenas, they employed Indians on their farms and filled Louisiana with heresy and low living.[17] Some of these heretics even penetrated into Texas, and by 1803 the peaceful occupation of the Missouri country was nearly completed, most of West Florida was occupied by Americans, and New Orleans had become an American port as far as commerce was concerned.[18]

As news of the Louisiana Purchase spread through the country, it was generally believed that West Florida, from the Mississippi to the Perdido River, was included in the bargain. Even in New Orleans Morales took this view of the matter, and while he continued to deny grants of Louisiana lands to Americans until the province was actually transferred, he now began to assign large tracts in West Florida to Daniel Clark and his New Orleans friends. These speculators expected a rise in land values when the United States should acquire jurisdiction, and Morales continued to favor his friends with grants as long as West Florida remained in Spanish hands and he remained in his official position as Intendant of West Florida.[19]

[17] Kinnaird, "American Penetration into Spanish Louisiana," *loc. cit.*, 221–25; Lexington *Kentucky Gazette*, September 9, 1799; Gayarré, *History of Louisiana*, III, 398, 408.

[18] Gray, *History of Agriculture in the Southern United States*, II, 864–65; Carter (ed.), *Territory of Orleans*, 705 n.; Kinnaird, "American Penetration into Spanish Louisiana," *loc. cit.*, 226; Charleston *Courier*, January 6, 1804.

[19] Raleigh *Register*, March 5, 1804; Carter (ed.), *Territory of Orleans*, 56, 66–67, 919–20; Gray, *History of Agriculture in the Southern United States*, II, 864–65.

In such circumstances it was natural that Americans coming down the Mississippi would settle in considerable numbers in the Baton Rouge area and that adventurers seeking fortunes would take advantage of the new opportunities which presented themselves in New Orleans. Among these there was no one who could compare in importance with Edward Livingston of New York, on whom John Randolph heaped his masterly invective: "Like a rotten mackerel in the moonlight, he shines—and stinks." Livingston and Daniel Clark were soon to become fast friends, business associates, and collaborators with Morales. While Americans were making their presence felt in these areas, they were also pushing farther afield. Some, among whom Dr. John Sibley was the most important, journeyed up the Red River to Natchitoches near the Texas border. Others settled along the Arkansas River, and still farther north the area along the Mississippi, both north and south of the mouth of the Missouri, attracted so many settlers that in 1804 it had a population of 10,000, about half of whom were French and half American. This represented a tenfold increase since 1769, but the prairie lands were still avoided by both nationalities, accustomed to living in regions where timber was plentiful and transportation by water was available.[20]

In the Mississippi Territory the act of March 3, 1803, which, for the first time, offered for sale the public lands in the limited areas that had been cleared of the Indian claim, did not solve all problems. Heads of families who had arrived before the passage of this act and settled on the public lands were entitled to purchase tracts of either 320 or 640 acres at $2.00 per acre. Though only one-fourth of the minimum sale price of $640 had to be paid in cash, there were not many squatters who could, on the spot, produce the necessary $160.[21] In view of this situation, a group of several hundred settlers drew up and sent to Congress a memorial which was presented on November 25, 1803. It is noteworthy that this petition from the frontier was expressed in excellent phraseology and couched in respectful language. Furthermore, among the numerous names attached, there was not one that was signed by the mark.

[20] Charleston *Courier*, January 6, 1804; Kinnaird, "American Penetration into Spanish Louisiana," *loc. cit.*, 221–26; Carter (ed.), *Territory of Orleans*, 878–79.

[21] Treat, *National Land System*, 111–12.

The supplicants stated: "We have to acknowledge . . . the just and liberal sanction which your honorable body have given to the titles, claims, and occupancies of lands in favor of the citizens of this territory; but we could have wished, for reasons which follow, that moderate grants had been made to actual settlers on unappropriated lands, and that similar terms of disposal had been extended to future emigrations. . . . Our territory though small, is thin of inhabitants, many of whom possessing only a pre-emption right, are unable to meet the terms of purchase. Of others who may emigrate, many will have exhausted their little resources on a long and expensive journey. These circumstances, we fear, will induce them to remove to the adjacent Spanish dominions, where both climate and soil are equally productive as our own; and where the prospect of favorable terms is a flattering incentive. . . . Your well informed body cannot but know, that we are a small community—surrounded by numerous nations whose habits, laws, principles and interests are different from our own—five hundred miles distant from the nearest settlement of our American brethren, the whole of which extent is inhabited by savages, some of whom at this time, indicate dispositions of hostilities toward us. . . . And we hope it will not be considered as assuming in us to suggest, that the defence of this country cannot be better secured, than by liberal encouragement of imigration." The petition then stated that, if instead of selling vacant lands at $2.00 per acre—which many could not afford—Congress would grant the land in small tracts to actual settlers who would continue to live on and cultivate the acreage for five successive years, this policy would secure a rapid increase in the population of the Territory. The memorialists further observed that between granting and selling it would readily appear that "if the lands are sold, they will be held in large quantities by the rich, which will render the settlement thin and exposed to invasion; whereas, if they are granted to actual settlers, they will be held in small tracts by the poor, which will render the settlement more compact and impenetrable. We would remark also, that to the former description of settlers, is generally attached a certain species of population [slaves], which would endanger the country in proportion to its increase; while the latter description generally destitute of that kind of property, would strengthen the country in the direct ratio of their numbers." Among the numerous names attached to this petition were those of a Philip Nolan, a James Robertson, and a William Blount! [22]

This petition came from the settlers in the Natchez district on the lower Mississippi River. Those in the Washington district, comprising the settlements on the Tombigbee and Alabama rivers, had even stronger reasons to desire a modification of the Land Act of March 3, for it prohibited the validation of claims to any lands lying east of the Tombigbee. Yet the "Tensaw Settlement," extending about fifty miles down the east bank of the Alabama from the "Cut-off," was the oldest and most prosperous community in the district, having come into existence shortly after the French established Mobile in 1702. Some of the land claims here went back to that era, while others dated from the British and the Spanish regimes. But a large number of those who now petitioned Congress for a validation of their claims had migrated from other parts of the United States since October, 1795, and purchased lands from the older claimants. The supplicants stated that "from any information they have had in their power to collect, from Tradition or otherwise, no Tribe of Indians, since the first settlement of this place had or pretended to have any title to the Tensaw Settlement." [23]

At about the same time that this and the previous petition were presented to Congress, the legislature of the Territory presented a plea favoring the claims of these Tensaw settlers, and simultaneously a memorial from the "Inhabitants of Washington District" urged that the Territory be divided, "and that a Separate Government be established within the now District of Washington independent of that of the Mississippi Territory." The proposal was supported by an argument that from "the late and rapid migration to this District from the State of Georgia and other parts of the United States," it was estimated that the district then contained more than 3,000 inhabitants, all of whom were subject to the laws of Mississippi Territory, which were enacted at a distance of nearly three hundred miles from Washington district, "all of which distance is a howling wilderness with its usual inhabitants

[22] Carter (ed.), *Territory of Mississippi*, V, 279–87.    [23] *Ibid.*, 293.

of Savages and beasts of prey.—That part of the Territory on the Mississippi and the settlements on the Mobile Tombecbee and Alabama rivers are composed of people different in their manners and customs, different in their interests, & nature appears never to have designed the two countries to be under the same Government." This petition was signed by 102 persons, including Nicholas Perkins, Lemuel Henry, John Pierce, John Johnston, James and John Caller, and Samuel Mims.[24]

On November 16, 1805, James Robertson and Silas Dinsmore signed a treaty between the United States and the Choctaw Indians which ceded a fifty-mile strip of land lying along the southern boundary of the Mississippi Territory and connecting the settlements on the Mississippi River with those on the Tombigbee. Yet no lands on the Alabama were included in this agreement, and President Jefferson held up ratification of the treaty until 1809. On January 7, 1806, the Cherokee ceded to the United States a triangle of land lying between the Tennessee River and the southern boundary of the State of Tennessee. In 1808 this area was organized as Madison County, with the town of Huntsville, which had grown up about the "Big Spring," as the county seat. In August, 1809, an office was opened in Nashville for the sale of these lands, and cotton planters from Georgia came in to form the nucleus of the community. No other cessions of Indian lands in the Mississippi Territory were made until, on August 9, 1814, Andrew Jackson acquired from the defeated Creeks all that area which now makes up the central and southern half of the State of Alabama.[25]

As long as the war with England continued, times were hard in this Gulf Coast region, as they were in all the Southern states. The British and their Spanish allies hampered international trade in every possible way and made it practically impossible for cotton and tobacco planters to send their produce to market. In spite of these difficulties, cotton was selling at Natchez for twelve and a half cents per pound during the summer of 1813; lands in that

[24] *Ibid.*, 288–89, 290–92.
[25] Bureau of American Ethnology, *Eighteenth Annual Report*, Pt. II, 672, 678, plates 1, 36; Abernethy, *Formative Period in Alabama*, 10; Thomas M. Owen, *History of Alabama and Dictionary of Alabama Biography* (Chicago, 1921), I, 718–19; II, 922; Carter (ed.), *Territory of Mississippi*, V, 724–25, 743.

neighborhood were worth $10.00 per acre, and the land office for the district west of Pearl River had sold acreage to the value of $58,551.12½. As the war came closer to this region, land sales dropped off and on January 19, 1815, the settlers in Marion and Lawrence counties on the Pearl River petitioned Congress to suspend payments on their lands, saying that they had "taken the field *en masse*." Three pages of signatures were attached to this document, and none of the petitioners signed by his mark.[26]

With the end of the war conditions naturally improved, and by the summer of 1815 river bottom lands in the Tombigbee Valley were worth $10.00 per acre. English mills found it impossible to obtain an adequate supply of cotton while hostilities continued, and the return of peace brought a brisk demand for the staple. The lands which were taken from the Creeks by the Treaty of Fort Jackson were perfectly adapted to the production of cotton, and planters whose lands in the Southeastern states had been depleted were keen to take advantage of this fresh opportunity. The resulting situation is well described in a letter from Mobile, dated June 6, which stated that the new tract was being settled very fast, but that it was inevitable that difficulties would exist where many strangers were trying to acquire property, and that much bad blood had been engendered by disputes over lands to which no one had a legal title. None of these new settlers was nearer to the seat of Territorial government than three hundred miles, and some were no nearer than five hundred miles; so the law had hardly begun to operate. No county had been established to embrace the new territory, the writer said, but he thought the evil caused by the distance from the seat of government would soon be remedied because the population east of Pearl River, including that of Madison County on the Tennessee, would very shortly outnumber that west of the Pearl. Then "the seat of government for Mississippi State must be established at St. Stephens, or some other site on the Tombigbee."[27]

In the hope of bringing order out of chaos, Governor Holmes proclaimed on June 29, 1815, that the lands ceded by the Creeks

[26] Carter (ed.), *Territory of Mississippi*, VI, 392–93, 494–98; Natchez *Washington Republican*, July 14, 1813.

[27] Raleigh *Register*, July 10, 1815.

at Fort Jackson would be organized as Monroe County, but this move did not end the confusion, for the Federal government had not yet authorized the sale of any lands in this area. Two months later Josiah Meigs, commissioner of the General Land Office in Washington, reported to the Secretary of the Treasury on the status of public lands in the Mississippi Territory. Three land offices were now located in this jurisdiction; in addition to those at Washington and St. Stephens there was one at Huntsville for Madison County in the bend of the Tennessee River. The report showed that all the land in Madison County, amounting to 345,000 acres, had been surveyed and 214,000 of this had been sold. In the other two districts about 7,500,000 acres had been surveyed and 361,000 acres sold, but this, of course, did not include any of the Creek lands.[28]

These figures do not indicate a great rush to buy cotton lands in the Territory. By November of 1815 desirable farms were bringing as much as $30.00 per acre, yet sales at the land offices dragged because no new tracts were put on the market, and even farms held under Spanish grants, many of which had been acquired by American settlers and speculators, were threatened by earlier grants made during the British regime. While the claims of British residents had been guaranteed according to the terms of Jay's Treaty of 1794, no provision had yet been made for those held by absentee claimants. The result of this situation was the occupation of vacant lands by hordes of squatters. Most of the intruders were honest men seeking lands on which to establish farms, but some made a business of cutting cedar timber on the public lands, and others also caused trouble with the neighboring Indians.[29]

On December 12, 1815, President Madison issued a proclamation ordering the removal of all trespassers on the public lands, and by January 12, 1816, official notice was received at St. Stephens. A few days later Judge Toulmin, always a staunch defender of law and order, wrote from Fort Stoddert to the President, asking that the deadline for removal be postponed from the tenth of March

---

[28] New Orleans *Louisiana Gazette*, July 15, 1815; Carter (ed.), *Territory of Mississippi*, VI, 538, 557–58.

[29] Carter (ed.), *Territory of Mississippi*, VI, 491–98, 534, 580–83, 605–17; Savannah *Republican*, October 31, 1815.

to the end of November. He said there were two principal settlements in the country acquired from the Creeks by General Jackson—one on the Cahaba River, a tributary of the Alabama, and the other lower down the Alabama in the neighborhood of the old Tensaw settlements, the former site of Fort Mims. Toulmin thought that several hundred families had migrated from Tennessee to the Cahaba settlement, transporting all their equipment and even all their corn a distance of 200 to 250 miles through an unbroken wilderness. Among the settlers on the lower Alabama some had come from Georgia and South Carolina, traveling at least 270 miles to reach their destination. All these people were now clearing lands and in March they would plant their crops. To remove them before they could reap the fruit of their toil would be ruinous, and the fact that lands were for sale in the old Choctaw cession of 1805 was no remedy, for the swamps and poor pine lands between the Pearl and the Tombigbee rivers would not serve their purposes. Toulmin's plea was answered when, on April 24, 1816, the President approved an act of Congress granting a stay of eviction to the settlers on the Creek lands in Mississippi Territory.[30]

In order to put this tract on the market, it was necessary first to survey it; but when this work was undertaken, it was found that all the neighboring Indian nations had claims which conflicted with those of the Creeks. Because this situation engendered hostilities it became clear that before boundaries could be established treaties would have to be made with the Choctaw, Chickasaw, and Cherokee nations. This was accomplished during 1816, with the result that, in the area that was soon to become the State of Alabama, only a small reservation along the southwestern boundary remained to the Choctaw, while larger tracts east of the Tennessee and Coosa rivers were reserved for the Cherokee and the Creeks.[31]

While the Creek and other lands recently acquired from the natives were still unavailable for purchase, the high price of cotton resulted in an increased demand for acreage in the available strip extending along the southern border of the Territory from the Mis-

[30] Carter (ed.), *Territory of Mississippi*, VI, 640–47, 667 n.

[31] *Ibid.*, 691; Bureau of American Ethnology, *Eighteenth Annual Report*, Pt. II, 682–85, plates 1, 2; Savannah *Republican*, June 18, October 31, 1816.

sissippi to the Tombigbee. On July 15, 1816, Nicholas Gray, "register" of the land office west of Pearl River, reported to Josiah Meigs that "the demand for lands since the 1st July seems as great as ever; all payments are made in the Mississippi [Yazoo] Stock— which is sold at $25 p ct discount." [32] Then, on November 10 of the same year Lewis Sewall of the office at St. Stephens for the district east of Pearl River complained of the pressure of business, saying that sometimes six or eight men from the woods entered his office at the same time. In November Commissioner Meigs reported to the Secretary of the Treasury that monies received from the sale of public lands in Mississippi Territory for the period from October 1, 1815, to September 30, 1816, amounted to $406,000, as against $1,458,000 for the rest of the country.[33]

Apparently not satisfied with this showing, Gray wrote from Natchez to Thomas O'Connor, editor of the New York *Shamrock*, that many emigrant families had lately arrived in New York from Europe and were in distress for want of employment. "Upon consulting with the Governor of this Territory," said Gray, "I am Authorized to invite to this part of the country any number of the industrious part of those emigrants who, when arrived here, will be provided with lands, rent-free for three years, with cattle and corn at the usual prices of the country, until they can pay for them, and all other things wanting for immediate use." The writer recommended to immigrants the use of the route over the mountains to Pittsburgh, and thence down the Ohio and Mississippi rivers.[34]

It is an anomalous fact that, for two years after Monroe County was created in 1815, all the residents were squatters, for none of the public lands had been put on the market by the Federal government. Since the suffrage was limited to freeholders in the Territory, the only qualified voters in the new county were such as held property elsewhere, but they elected representatives to the legislature and on September 6, 1816, Judge Toulmin held the first superior court there. A letter from Mobile which recorded these court proceedings stated that the population of the eastern

---

[32] Nicholas Gray to Josiah Meigs, July 15, 1816, in Carter (ed.), *Territory of Mississippi*, VI, 696–97.

[33] *Ibid.*, 718–19, 725.　　　　　[34] Richmond *Enquirer*, November 14, 1816.

part of the Territory had increased rapidly and that the Natchez district could no longer keep the advantage. In fact, the people of the eastern counties were said to be looking forward to admission as a state with no division of the Territory, to which end they were electing representatives to a convention that would send a delegation to Washington to advocate their views.[35]

Finally on May 24, 1817, President Monroe issued a proclamation authorizing the sale of thirty-one townships lying along the headwaters of the Alabama River in the Creek cession. The sales would be held in Milledgeville, the capital of Georgia, on the first Monday in August and were to continue for three weeks "and no longer." The prospects for a "land office business" were favorable, for population in this area had increased so fast since the end of hostilities in 1815 that already, on March 1, 1817, an act of Congress provided for the division of the Mississippi Territory, with that part west of the dividing line to constitute the new state of Mississippi. The area east of the line was incorporated as the Alabama Territory by an act approved on March 3.[36]

The office at Milledgeville opened on schedule and speculators purchased much of the land at prices averaging between forty and fifty dollars per acre. Actual settlers were generally too poor to compete at the sales, which during 1817 amounted to nearly $800,000. Additional tracts of choice river-bottom lands in the same area were sold during 1818, and this time nearly $1,000,000 was realized. The most coveted tract disposed of at these sales lay within a wide bend of the Alabama River only a few miles below the site of Fort Jackson. The land in the bend was unusually fertile and opposite it, on the south bank of the river, was a high bluff which was recognized as an excellent site for a commercial town. William Wyatt Bibb, who had been appointed governor of the Territory, and A. P. Hayne of South Carolina were anxious to acquire this tract. A land company of which Bibb was a member made the purchase and the town of Montgomery, soon to be the capital of the state, was founded on the bluff two years later. In

---

[35] Savannah *Republican*, October 31, 1816.

[36] Rowland, *History of Mississippi, The Heart of the South*, I, 482–85; Carter (ed.), *Territory of Mississippi*, VI, 791, 793; Clarence E. Carter (ed.), *The Territory of Alabama, 1817–1819* (Washington, 1952), 53–57; Richard Peters (comp.), *The Public Statutes at Large of the United States of America* (Boston, 1845–1846), III, 348–49.

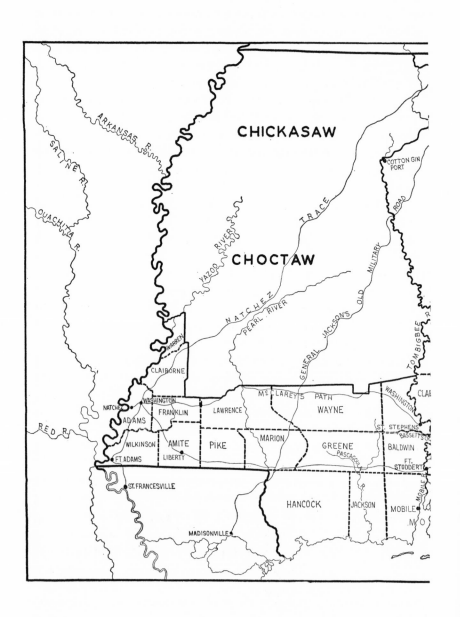

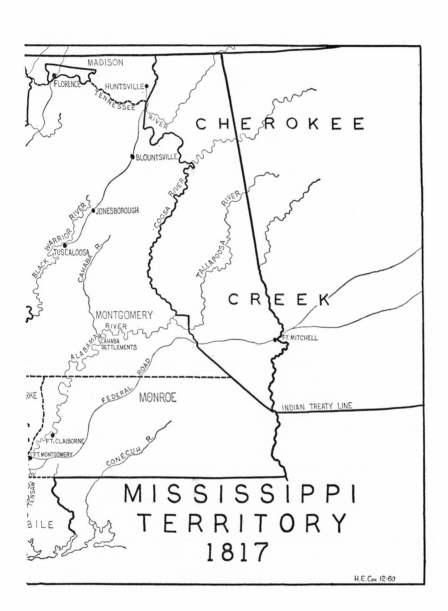

1819 large areas along the Alabama River below Montgomery were put on the market. The land office for this district was now moved from Milledgeville to Cahaba, and the sales here amounted to nearly $3,000,000 during the year.[37]

While settlers were pouring in and lands were being sold in the Alabama River Valley, the Tennessee Valley was also being exploited. The Cherokee and Chickasaw treaties of September, 1816, opened up a large area adjoining the Creek cession and taking in all the northwestern part of Alabama Territory. Between February 1 and the middle of November, 1818, all the land lying west of Madison County on both sides of the Tennessee River —about two million acres—was put on sale in Huntsville and more than half of it was either bid in at public auctions or later entered at the minimum price of $2.00 per acre. Total sales amounted to $7,000,000, one-fourth of which had to be paid in cash, and of this sum, over $1,000,000 was in Yazoo scrip.[38]

The excitement caused by these sales was nationwide. Men came from every part of the country to participate in them and speculation was rife. Sometimes human vultures would collect from squatters by threatening to bid against them at the sales; sometimes a group of speculators would combine and, by a show of force, intimidate their competitors, bid off large tracts of desirable lands at low prices, and sell out later to those who were unable to compete with them. It was stated on good authority that one such association of swindlers cleared $1,980 each on a transaction of this kind. The situation became so notorious that the government authorized its agents to bid against the combinations when they thought it advisable. Yet there were, of course, more respectable groups participating in the sales. A company was formed in Charleston to acquire acreage in Alabama, and Stephen Elliott was sent out to make the purchases. Another company composed of men from Virginia, Georgia, Kentucky, and Madison County was formed. Prominent Tennesseans bid against this com-

---

[37] Charleston *City Gazette*, August 30, 1817; Savannah *Republican*, August 19, 30, September 16, 1817; Raleigh *Register*, August 29, 1817; Richmond *Enquirer*, September 19, 1817; Abernethy, *Formative Period in Alabama*, 52–53.

[38] Bureau of American Ethnology, *Eighteenth Annual Report*, Pt. II, plate 36; *Republican and Savannah Evening Ledger*, February 21, 1817; Natchez *Mississippi Republican*, November 27, 1818.

464

bine and prices were run up to figures ranging between $50 and $100 an acre, whereas average cotton lands sold at prices of $20 to $30. By the time the credit system was abolished in 1820, Alabama had, in all, amassed a land debt of $11,000,000, or more than half the total for the entire country.[39]

Seldom in history has an area been settled so rapidly. In 1800 the Mississippi Territory had three counties, with Adams and Pickering located in the western section which would become the State of Mississippi, and Washington, including the settlements about St. Stephens and Fort Stoddert on the lower Tombigbee, forming the nucleus of the area that would become the State of Alabama. At this time the Mississippi counties had a population of 4,190, including 1,242 slaves, while Washington County numbered 1,250 persons, 494 of whom were slaves. By 1810 the western section had a population of 31,306, including 14,523 slaves, while the eastern counties—Washington, Madison, and Baldwin —had 9,046 in all, with 2,565 slaves. Ten years later the new state of Alabama had a population of 144,317, and Mississippi had 75,448. Thus, within one decade, the population of Mississippi had more than doubled, while that of Alabama had multiplied sixteen times! [40]

This flood of humanity came almost entirely from the Southern states, with the Piedmont Region apparently furnishing the majority. This was because of the run-down condition of the soil and the poor transportation facilities in the area, and also because the Virginians, the Georgians, and Carolinians were already in the cotton-raising business. They came along the road which, after passing through the capital cities of Richmond, Raleigh, Columbia, and Milledgeville, traversed the Creek country and reached the Alabama River at the site of Fort Mims, just beyond which was Fort Stoddert. Congress had first made an appropriation for a road through the Creek country in 1806 and in 1812 Colonel Hawkins reported from the Creek Agency that in the five months following October 16, 1811, 120 wagons, 80 carts, 30 chairs, 3 four-wheeled carriages, and 3,726 persons had passed that way. By

[39] Charleston *City Gazette*, April 26, 1819; Abernethy, *Formative Period in Alabama*, 52–53.
[40] Censuses of 1800, 1810, 1820.

1816 mail was delivered every Saturday at St. Stephens by post-riders who followed this route.[41] In March, 1817, the Milledge-ville *Journal* reported that a letter from Mississippi Territory said no corn could be bought after leaving Georgia until the traveler arrived at a place called Burnt Corn; that it was scarce there, selling for four or five dollars a barrel; and that none was to be had east of the Tombigbee at any price. The mail contractor assured the *Journal* it was with great difficulty that he was able to buy corn for his post horses at seven dollars a barrel, that distress on the road was very great, and that many families were starving and retracing their steps in an effort to get back to Georgia.[42]

Notwithstanding such handicaps, caravans of settlers continued to move along the Federal Road into the Alabama River basin. Most of them brought all their worldly possessions packed in wagons, while their women rode atop the baggage or in four-wheeled carriages or two-wheeled carts, depending on the economic status of the family. Cattle and hogs were driven along the road by the male members of the family or by slaves, and every night they pitched their camps near a spring or clear stream and lighted their fires for cooking and for cheer. There was something romantic in such adventure into a new world, made more so by the dark forest, the hooting of owls, the croaking of frogs, and the incessant chirping of crickets. Nor was there at this juncture any danger that Indians might disturb the travelers' repose. As for the lands they came to settle, a government surveyor reported in the summer of 1817 that those near the Alabama River were wooded, with only a little pine, and well watered. Yet the "prairie beyond," he said, "is not wooded and has little water, but it is interrupted by narrow skirts of woodland." [43]

The "prairie" referred to here is the "Black Belt" of Alabama, a crescent of black soil lying upon soft limestone, which, varying in width from about forty to fifty miles, extends across the state from the Georgia to the Mississippi line, with Montgomery as the focal point on its northern edge. Here the rich black or grey

---

[41] Abernethy, *Formative Period in Alabama*, 25; Charleston *Courier*, April 1, 1812; Raleigh *Register*, April 10, 1812; Lewis Sewall to Meigs, January 12, 1816, in Carter (ed.), *Territory of Mississippi*, VI, 641.

[42] Quoted in Raleigh *Register*, March 14, 1817.

[43] Savannah *Republican*, July 10, 1817.

soil is tenacious and difficult to traverse in wet weather. Water, when available, is impregnated with lime, and thus unsatisfactory for domestic use. For these reasons the early settlers avoided the richest cotton lands in the region and clung to the river courses, which offered fertile "bottom" lands for corn and gravelly ridge tracts which were suitable for upland cotton. Families from Georgia, being nearest at hand, arrived first on the scene, and they became the predominant element in all the southeastern Alabama counties.[44]

While settlers were reaching this part of the Territory by way of the Federal Road, others came in from the north along the road leading from the Valley of Virginia to Knoxville, and then to Nashville, where they picked up the old Indian trail leading to Natchez on the lower Mississippi. On December 20, 1801, the Choctaw made a treaty which gave the United States the right to construct a road along this route as it passed through their lands, but they reserved to themselves the right to set up taverns for the entertainment of travelers.[45] Apparently neither the natives nor the Federal government took advantage of their opportunities, for on May 25, 1804, it was reported from Natchez that a traveler with that destination in mind found no adequate road east of the Mississippi and therefore went to the Chickasaw Bluffs. There he crossed the river to the Louisiana side, whence he proceeded to Natchez by way of New Madrid.[46] During the same year Robert Tanner migrated from Beaufort, South Carolina, to the Natchez district with about one hundred dependents, white and black. Going overland by way of Augusta and Athens, he reached the Tennessee River at Ross's Landing (modern Chattanooga) and there built boats to take him to his destination.[47] It is significant that in January, 1808, Captain Edmund Pendleton Gaines reported to Henry Dearborn, Secretary of War, on a survey of the route from Athens, at the head of the Muscle Shoals, to Cotton Gin Port at the head of boat navigation on the Tombigbee River. This was the most practicable passage between the

[44] Abernethy, *Formative Period in Alabama*, 164, plate 4.
[45] Claiborne, *Mississippi, as a Province, Territory and State*, 222-23.
[46] Richmond *Enquirer*, July 11, 1804.
[47] Claiborne, *Mississippi, as a Province, Territory and State*, 242.

waters of the Tennessee River and Mobile Bay, and it was available for the transportation of produce and supplies, but by this time "passenger traffic" usually took the Nashville-Natchez Trace, which crossed the Tennessee River by way of Florence at the foot of the Shoals, and then passed southwestward through the Chickasaw and Choctaw country to Natchez.[48] In 1816 mail reached St. Stephens once a month by this route, and two years later the editor of the newspaper published at Natchez reported: "The tide of emigration from various parts of the Union is moving more rapidly to the west than ever before. From 10 to 15 families have passed Natchez in the course of one day, and their number appears to increase. The roads are crowded with travelers destined for Indiana, the Illinois and Missouri territories. Most of the other routes leading to these desirable territories are also crowded with families and others passing on to explore the country." [49] Apparently these people were coming from the Eastern seaports by water to New Orleans and then traveling overland to their destinations, but they were certainly going out of their way if they came from ports north of the Carolinas.

However this may be, the broad Tennessee Valley of northern Alabama was principally settled by families making the easy journey down from Tennessee. Nothing less than a half section of land (320 acres) could be purchased from the government, and the minimum price was $2.00 per acre. Those who could make the down payment could buy a desirable tract. Those who could not —and there were many such—moved off into the surrounding hills and valleys and carried on subsistence farming. Of course, the same thing happened as the Alabama River valley was settled, with those who could not afford the best river-bottom tracts moving off into the "wire grass" country in the southeast corner of the Territory or finding arable tracts in the hilly country north of the river. For instance, Brown's *Western Gazetteer* of 1817 stated that the "wire grass" lands along the Conecuh River were being settled rapidly, "especially by the poorer class of people and stock owners, being better calculated for men of small capital

[48] Sewall to Meigs, January 12, 1816, in Carter (ed.), *Territory of Mississippi*, VI, 641.
[49] Natchez *Mississippi Republican*, March 12, 1818.

than the Alabama [River valley]." And the *Gazetteer* went on to report that "the settlement of Madison County is probably without parallel in the history of the Union. In 1816 it had 14,200 out of a population of 33,287 for the Territory." [50]

As important as were the Georgians and Tennesseans in the settlement of the Alabama Territory, there was a third element of equal significance. Subsistence farmers and actual or prospective cotton planters coming down from Virginia and the Carolinas found the best lands already occupied in the Alabama and Tennessee river valleys and moved on into the region drained by the Tombigbee and Black Warrior rivers. This took in the western end of the Black Belt, with the town of Tuscaloosa as its metropolis. From this point a road led through Jones Valley to Huntsville and it furnished the main communication between the two contrasting parts of the Territory. In this middle area the Virginia and Carolina elements predominated, and when the prairie Black Belt was settled, they formed an important element there. Thus the central and southern sections of Alabama were influenced by Anglican and aristocratic ideals, whereas the northern Tennessee Valley was predominantly Presbyterian and democratic. Yet the Methodists and Baptists made rapid strides after the frontier revival of 1800 and the older denominations in both sections were being swamped by the more numerous evangelicals.[51]

It is important to realize, however, that this migration to the old Southwest was much more than a local affair. The origin, as well as the destination, of the population was important, and the origin extended as far east as Europe. This fact is illustrated by an article which the Savannah *Republican* reprinted in 1818 from the Edinburgh *Scotsman:* "The extraordinary emigration from all quarters of the old world to North America at this moment, is a great, perhaps a more characteristic of the moral and political European nations, than any other that could be mentioned. It is impossible to look at the vast multitudes, of all conditions and professions, who are throwing up their prospects in their native country and crowding to the land of promise, without a sensation of wonder. It is a spectacle without a parallel since the time of the crusades."

[50] Raleigh *Register*, February 7, 1817; Samuel R. Brown, *Western Gazetteer* (Auburn, N.Y., 1817), 19–20.
[51] Abernethy, *Formative Period in Alabama*, map, 164.

High wages and cheap lands, according to the author, were the inducements which attracted some refugees to America; it should be remembered, said he, that for the past twenty years Russia had promised free lands to settlers in the Crimea, but there had been practically no migration in that direction. "It is not to be denied," he concluded, "that new local arrangements and love of liberty is [sic] drawing men to America" rather than to Russia.[52]

Other forces, however, were at work. In September, 1817, a dispatch from Washington City commented on the "greatest body of immigrants," chiefly German and Irish, ever to come to America within one year. Some of these, the article went on to say, had been induced by false promises to come over so that they might be sold as indentured servants. Another account stated that about fifty Dutch redemptioners passed through Washington City on their way to Kentucky, where "they have indented themselves for three years in order to defray the expense of their transportation from Amsterdam to the United States. Three hundred are said to have arrived at Annapolis in one vessel, for which the captain gets $100 a head."[53]

On April 1, 1818, the *Black Dwarf* of London commented on the great migration as follows: "The *Courier* is alarmed at the tide of those who wish to go out of reach of the tax-gatherer—emigrants to America—and the tythe man, the usurping faction that denies them the right to be freemen. To dislike taxation and distress is no doubt foolish! The *Courier* is very angry and tells a thousand tales of distress in the wilds of America. But to no purpose; People still pack up their little, if they have anything left, and set off to America. Those who have *nothing* are still more anxious to go to the U. S., the land where the Government does not stand at the entrance to every enterprise and say 'pay me' before you go on. The *Times* is not angry, only very, very sorry that such things should be."[54] In August of the same year *Niles' Weekly Register* estimated that immigration to the United States was currently at the rate of two hundred persons per day, and

[52] Savannah *Republican*, March 8, 1818.
[53] *Ibid.*, February 25, 1817; Richmond *Enquirer*, September 23, 26, 1817.
[54] Richmond *Enquirer*, July 10, August 21, 1818.

shortly thereafter the *Mississippi Republican* of Natchez reported that five hundred families from Wales and the northern and western parts of Scotland had arrived at the port of Glasgow the preceding May on their way to America. The New York *Evening Post* ascribed this huge migration to overpopulation, but the editor of the Richmond *Enquirer* pointed out that there were many vacant areas in Europe and thought the exodus was due to lower taxes and better opportunities of every sort in America.[55]

Europe could afford to spare some of its more restless population, but the Southeastern states, hard hit by the inability to market their staple crops during the War of 1812, felt that they could not. The older tobacco-growing counties in Virginia and Maryland were especially hard hit because they had too many slaves and too much exhausted land. In November, 1815, a committee of the North Carolina legislature reported that within twenty-five years more than 200,000 people had moved to the Mississippi Valley, including thousands of the wealthier sort, and a committee of the Virginia House of Delegates made a similar complaint during the next year. Quakers and Germans from the western counties usually sought homes north of the Ohio River on account of slavery, whereas Tidewater and Piedmont families moved to the fertile cotton lands in the areas tributary to the Gulf of Mexico.[56]

Information as to the nature of this migration is furnished by an article published in the Augusta *Herald*. A man who had come directly from Alabama informed the *Herald* that on his way, as he was returning to Augusta, he met in nine days' traveling 141 wagons, 102 carts, 10 stages, 14 gigs, 2 coaches, 29 droves of cattle, 27 droves of hogs, 2 droves of sheep. These were all bound for the Alabama, most of them for the neighborhood of Fort Claiborne; and they were all met between Burnt Corn Spring and Fort Hawkins. The traveler observed that with the wagons and carts there were usually very large families. Counting these, together with those on horseback, he estimated there were probably 3,840 in-

[55] Natchez *Mississippi Republican*, September 10, 1818.
[56] Ashe, *History of North Carolina*, II, 244–45; Krout and Fox, *Completion of Independence*, 418.

dividuals. He thought the crops not equal to such an increase in population and feared the immigrants would undergo great hardships.[57]

At about the same time the Richmond *Enquirer* lamented: "At no period since the settlement of the Western Country has the tide of population set stronger . . . [that] way than at present. But a few years more and the pivot on which the union will balance will be the Allegheny Mountains, or west of them." [58] During the spring of the next year William Byrd's "Westover" was advertised for sale and Virginia and North Carolina papers commented on the large numbers of estates being sold for nonpayment of taxes. Then in August, 1817, the Charleston *Reporter* said: "We scarcely recollect a period when emigration to the Western States and Territories has been as great as in the last few months." [59] In October a traveler reported that between Fredericksburg and Richmond he was continually passing families, sometimes in large bodies, removing with their furniture and Negroes to the Alabama. At the same time someone wrote from Mobile that he dreaded the disappointment that would be suffered by people who came out because of the glowing reports being circulated, and he hoped that people who wrote to their distant friends would lower their tone a little. He said Alabama Territory contained good lands with transportation easily accessible but that twenty bushels of corn was a good yield, rather than the reported hundred bushels.[60]

The westward migration continued during 1818 and the Southeastern states, including Maryland, looked on with mounting dismay.[61] On August 25 the Richmond *Enquirer* said: "The growth of the Western Country south of Ohio is carrying off a great many slaves from this and other states. Those parts which grow the fastest take off the most. When the proprietor of a sugar or cotton

[57] Charleston *City Gazette*, December 27, 1816.

[58] Richmond *Enquirer*, November 21, 1816.

[59] *Ibid.*, January 26, May 6, 1817; Raleigh *Register*, May 16, 1817; Charleston *Reporter*, August 6, 1817.

[60] Raleigh *Register*, November 23, 1817; Savannah *Republican*, August 30, 1817; William T. Harris, *Remarks Made during a Tour through the United States of America in the years 1817, 1818, 1819* (Liverpool, 1819), 21.

[61] Scharf, *History of Maryland*, III, 143; Richmond *Enquirer*, September 11, 1818.

plantation can clear four or five hundred dollars *by the hand per year,* he is able to expand his land and his hands. The cotton lands in Alabama in this respect excite much attention. Lands have risen to an unexpected value—those which used to bring $8 or $10 an acre, now command $50 to $70." This extraordinary growth of the Western country, of course, increased the price of slaves and drained them off from the Southern Seaboard states. In Virginia slaves who formerly sold for $300 or $500 now sold for twice that much. "Could we lose the slaves and gain a corresponding number of whites, this is the very consummation Virginia has prayed for," said the *Enquirer.*[62]

During the early months of 1819 the westward movement continued unabated and in February the Mobile *Gazette* stated that "the emigration to our territory is not only immense, but very many of the emigrants are men of wealth and some noted for their political standing and intellectual powers where they came from." [63] But the end of the boom was at hand. The abnormal demand for cotton which had followed the War of 1812 had at last been satisfied, and whereas that staple was selling for more than thirty cents per pound in January, it was down to twenty cents by June, and by autumn it would bring no more than fourteen to eighteen cents. The downward trend continued until 1824, and since cotton had sparked the boom, so it spearheaded the panic, with other agricultural prices following it to lower levels. Men who had bought cotton lands at high prices found themselves unable to meet their obligations and bankruptcy blighted the face of the country.[64]

Yet the economic ups and downs which troubled the years between 1789 and 1819 resulted in a remarkable period of growth as far as the Southwest was concerned. On March 2, 1819, an act enabling the Alabama Territory to frame a constitution and apply for admission to the Union was approved.[65] The constitutional convention met at Huntsville on July 5, and the instrument of

[62] Richmond *Enquirer,* August 25, 1818.

[63] Raleigh *Register,* January 15, 1819; Savannah *Republican,* March 5, 1819.

[64] Abernethy, *Formative Period in Alabama,* chart, 172; Abernethy, *From Frontier to Plantation in Tennessee,* 225, 228; Charles S. Sydnor, *The Development of Southern Sectionalism, 1819–1848* (Baton Rouge, 1948), 104.

[65] Poore (ed.), *Federal and State Constitutions,* I, 29–32.

government which was produced provided that all white adult males who were citizens of the United States and had resided for a year in the state should be given the right to vote. Representation, both in the Senate and the House, would be apportioned according to white population, and there was no property qualification for representatives. Slaves were entitled to trial by jury when charged with offenses more serious than petty larceny, and in case of personal injury to a slave the offending party would be punished just as though the victim had been white. The legislature was given no power to emancipate slaves without the consent of their owners; but masters were authorized to provide for the emancipation of their slaves, and the legislature could prohibit the importation of such people as merchandise. This constitution was liberal, according to the standards of the time, but it went into effect without approval of the electorate, and with but three amendments, it served the state until 1865.[66]

In 1812 Congress provided that "the Territory heretofore called Louisiana shall hereafter be called Missouri," and the legislative power was vested in a General Assembly, "which shall consist of the governor, a legislative council, and a house of representatives." But the suffrage was restricted to "all free white male citizens of the United States, above the age of twenty-one years, who have resided in said Territory twelve months next preceding an election, and who shall have paid a territorial or county tax." [67] Seven years later that part of the Missouri Territory lying south of parallel 36 degrees 30 minutes was organized as the Territory of Arkansas,[68] and the Florida purchase treaty was signed during the same year. Thus, between 1789 and 1819 the South had added five states to the original five, with two additional territories (if Missouri is to be considered Southern, as it was during that period), with West Florida annexed, and East Florida bargained for but not delivered.

This represented a remarkable expansion, with the result that most of the area which then constituted "the South," so far as it was not occupied by Indians, was just emerging from the virgin

---

[66] Abernethy, *Formative Period in Alabama*, 43–46; Poore (ed.), *Federal and State Constitutions*, I, 32–48.

[67] Poore (ed.), *Federal and State Constitutions*, II, 1097–98.    [68] *Ibid.*, I, 99–101.

forest. Yet this frontier was different from the older ones which had, in Kentucky and Tennessee, produced such characters as Simon Kenton, Daniel Boone,[69] and David Crockett. No longer were the hunter and trapper in evidence, and even the subsistence farmer was relegated to a back seat—meaning back lands—in the new community. The slave-owning planter was now the pioneer, and civilization in the cotton and sugar lands developed with a rush. Within a few years log cabins gave place to weatherboarded mansions, painted white with green blinds, and the farmer-turned-planter loved the soil and the life that it afforded, as did his more aristocratic predecessors of the Atlantic Tidewater. While he did not inherit their taste for reading and contemplation, he did in some measure perpetuate their sense of responsibility for the conduct of public affairs. In any case, he and his heirs, with all their faults, furnished a better type of leadership than the market place has yet been able to provide. But it was not to last. The landowning gentry of the South had their day and ceased to be, while the market place triumphed over all America.

[69] At this time Boone was living in Missouri Territory, and the Richmond *Enquirer* of July 5, 1816, published the following interesting description of him, written by a resident of the Territory: "We have been honored by a visit from Col. D. Boone who spent two weeks with us. He has established a settlement on the Missouri about 100 miles below us. He goes a hunting twice a year to the remotest wilderness he can find and hires a man to go with him, and binds him to bring him back dead or alive. He left here for the River Platt. Col. Boone is now 85 years old, 5 ft. 7 inches, stoutly made and active for his years, is still of vigorous mind and pretty well informed. He has taken part in all the wars of America since before Braddock's defeat. He wears the dress of the roughest, poorest hunter."

# CRITICAL ESSAY ON AUTHORITIES

EXCEPT for works dealing with quite limited topics, there are no "authorities" covering the period of Southern history discussed in this volume. There are, of course, numerous monographs and articles in historical journals which throw invaluable light upon special phases of the subject and extensive use was made of them; yet the main reliance had to be on primary materials, and there was no previous pattern to follow in presenting the results. To have exhausted the possibilities of manuscript collections would have required more years than one lifetime provides. For this reason manuscripts were searched only when their use seemed essential to the author, as in the case of the Yazoo speculations and the Burr conspiracy. Contemporary publications, including pamphlet literature, accounts of travelers, and official documents were used, as were at least one complete file of newspapers for each of the Southern states.

## MANUSCRIPTS

No adequate account of the Yazoo speculations could be written without consulting the manuscript collections of the Georgia Department of Archives and History in Atlanta. These include the manuscript Journal of the Georgia House of Representatives, 1789; the letter books of Governors George Mathews and James Jackson, 1793–1798; letters relating to the Yazoo Fraud, 1796, in East and West Florida Papers, 1764–1850; Creek Indian Letters, 1782–1813; Bonds, Bills of Sale, Deeds of Gifts, Powers of Attorney, Vol. D, 1792–1813; miscellaneous Yazoo manuscripts; the unpublished letters of Timothy Bernard, edited by Louise F. Hays; and her manuscript biography of "Benjamin Hawkins, Indian Agent, 1754–1816." Also important in this connection is the De Renne Collection in the library of the University of Georgia, which contains contemporary Yazoo pamphlets. The Abraham Baldwin, Thomas Carr, and Telamon Cuyler manuscripts also are helpful, and some additional information may be gleaned from the Yazoo Papers in the Library of Congress collection.

Manuscripts were used extensively in preparing the book dealing with *The Burr Conspiracy* (New York, 1954). Since the publication of that work, the following additional manuscripts have been examined: the James Wilkinson Papers, Vols. II and III, Chicago Historical Society; an Andrew Jackson letter from the Huntington Library; the George Morgan Papers in the collections of the Illinois Historical Survey, University of Illinois; the manuscript collection of the Tennessee Historical Society, Nashville; Domestic Letters of the Department of State, XV, June 1, 1805–July 21, 1810, National Archives; Letters to Officers, Ships of War, 1805–1807, Navy Department manuscripts, National Archives; the Revolutionary War record of Major James Bruff, National Archives; Nacogdoches Archives, photostats, University of Texas; the following items from the manuscript collections of the University of Virginia Library: typescript of the family correspondence of William Taylor Barry of Lexington, Kentucky, 1798–1855, photostat of the MS. Journal of the General Assembly of Ohio, December 2, 1806, and a letter of General James Wilkinson; in addition, the correspondence of Senator John Brown of Kentucky in the John Brown Mason Collection of the Yale University Library; and documents translated from the Pontalba Collection of the Louisiana Historical Society, Filson Club, Louisville, Kentucky.

Certain other manuscript collections have been used in connection with other subjects, among which are the King's Mountain and the Tennessee manuscripts in the Lyman Draper Collection of the Wisconsin State Historical Society; the Reuben T. Durrett Collection in the University of Chicago Library; the papers of Thomas Clay, Vol. III (1796–1801), the John McKee Papers, and the West Florida Papers, 1799–1827, all in the Division of Manuscripts of the Library of Congress; the John Gray Blount Papers, 1796–1797, and the John Steele Papers, I, 1777–1802, in the collections of the North Carolina Historical Commission, Raleigh; also Series 42 of the Colonial Office Papers, Public Record Office, London; and a manuscript entitled "Restrictions on the American Trade with the West Indies, 1783–1812," by Alice B. Keith.

Last but no less important are the theses and dissertations written by graduate students at the University of Virginia. Among these the most relevant for the purposes of this study are: Mary P. Adams, "Jefferson's Reaction to the Treaty of San Ildefonso," thesis, 1952, and "Jefferson's Military Policy, with Special Reference to the Frontier, 1805–1809," dissertation, 1958; Harry Ammon, "The Republican Party in Virginia, 1789–1824," dissertation, 1948; Winston C. Babb, "French Refugees from Saint Domingue to the Southern United States, 1791–1810," dissertation, 1954; Edwin M. Gaines, "Outrageous Encounter: The Chesapeake-Leopard Affair of 1807," dissertation, 1960; James M. Helms, Jr., "Land Tenure in Territorial Mississippi, 1798–1809," thesis, 1955; George M. Herndon, "A History of Tobacco in Virginia, 1613–1860," thesis, 1956; Hamilton M. Hutton, "Southern Nationalism, 1790 to 1817: A Map Study Based upon Votes in the House of Representatives," thesis, 1940; William F. Keller, "Genêt and Jeffersonian Neutrality," thesis, 1940, and "American Politics and the Genêt Mission, 1793–1794," dissertation (University of Pittsburgh), 1951; Wesley N. Laing, "Cattle in Early Virginia," dissertation, 1952; Nicia Luz, "Spanish and French Views of the Burr Conspiracy," thesis, 1946; David K. McCarrell, "The Formation of the Jeffersonian Party in Virginia," dissertation (Duke University), 1937; Norris W. Preyer, "The Congressional Fight over the Admission of Kentucky, Tennessee, Louisiana, and Alabama into the Union," thesis, 1950, and "The South's Experiment with Protective Tariffs, 1816–1820," dissertation, 1954; Norman K. Risjord, "The Republican Quids: Political Puritans," thesis, 1957, and "The Old Republicans: Southern Conservatives in Congress, 1806–1824," dissertation, 1960; Edward Graham Roberts, "The Roads of Virginia, 1607–1840," dissertation, 1950; Elinor J. Weeder, "Wilson Cary Nicholas, Jefferson's Lieutenant," thesis, 1946; George W. Whitehurst, "The Commerce of Virginia, 1789–1815," thesis, 1951; and Albert H. Woodruff, "The Burr Conspiracy and the Press," thesis, 1949.

## OFFICIAL DOCUMENTS

Since this sectional history is not primarily concerned with either state or national affairs, official documents are of only incidental importance, yet they cannot be overlooked. Much valuable information is available in the series entitled *American State Papers: Documents, Legislative and Executive, of the Congress of the United States*, 38 vols. (Washington, 1832–1861). The series on *Public Lands* and on *Indian Affairs* were especially useful. Despite editorial shortcomings, the *Debates and Proceedings in the Congress of the United States, 1789–1824*, 42 vols. (Washington, 1834–1856), usually cited as *Annals of Congress*, is invaluable. Also essential for purposes of reference are James D. Richardson (ed.), *A Compilation of the Messages and Papers of the Presidents, 1789–1902*, 10 vols. (New York, 1903); *The Laws of the United States of America*, 3 vols. (Philadelphia, 1796); the first three volumes of *The Public Statutes at Large of the United States of America,* 17 vols. (Boston, 1845–1846); and Benjamin Perley Poore (ed.), *The Federal and State Constitutions, Colonial Charters, and Other Organic Laws of the United States,* 2 vols. (Washington, 1878). Though far from accurate, the first four censuses furnish comprehensive enumeration of the population for this period. They were published as follows: *United States Census, 1790* (Philadelphia, 1791, 1802); *Second Census of the United States: Return of the Whole Number of Persons within the Several Districts of the United States* (Washington, 1801); *Aggregate Amount of Persons within the United States in the Year 1810* (Washington, 1811); *United States Census for 1820: Fourth Census,* Bk. 1 (Washington, 1821).

The following are a few miscellaneous Federal documents which were especially useful in the preparation of this volume: James Madison, "Report to the House of Representatives on the Yazoo claimants of 1789 and 1795 as recorded in the Department of State, February 13, 1805," in *American State Papers, Public Lands,* I, 219–46; United States Congress, *Proceedings on the Impeachment of William Blount* (Philadelphia, 1799), pamphlet in McGregor Library, University of Virginia; "Despatches from the United States Consulate in New Orleans, 1801–1803," in *American Historical Review* (New York), XXXII (1926–1927), 801–24, and XXXIII (1927–1928), 331–59; *An Account of Louisiana, being an abstract of Documents in the Offices of the Department of State and of the Treasury* (Washington, 1803), Rare Book Room, Library of Congress; E. Bacon, chairman, *Report of the Committee Appointed to Inquire into the Conduct of General Wilkinson, February 26, 1811* (Washington, 1811); Levi Woodbury, *Report of the Secretary of the Treasury,* March 4, 1836 (Washington, 1836).

Of outstanding importance has been the extensive series of *Territorial Papers of the United States,* 25 vols., magnificently edited by Clarence E. Carter. The volumes herein cited are: IV—*The Territory South of the River Ohio, 1790–1796* (Washington, 1936); V, VI—*The Territory of Mississippi, 1798–1817* (Washington, 1937, 1938); IX—*The Territory of Orleans, 1803–1812* (Washington, 1940); and XVIII —*The Territory of Alabama, 1817–1819* (Washington, 1952). Also useful are *The Mississippi Territorial Archives, 1798–1803* (Nashville, 1905), and the *Official Letter Books of W. C. C. Claiborne, 1805–1816,* 6 vols. (Jackson, 1917), both edited by Dunbar Rowland; *The Virginia Report of 1799–1800 Touching the Alien and Sedition Laws; together with the Virginia Resolutions of December 21, 1798, the Debate and*

479

*Proceedings thereon in the House of Representatives, and several other Documents Illustrative of the Report and Resolutions* (Richmond, 1850); and *The Report of the Select Committee to whom was referred the Information Communicated to the House of Representatives charging Benjamin Sebastian, one of the Judges of the Court of Appeals of Kentucky, with having Received a Pension from the Spanish Government* (Frankfort, 1806), in Harry Innes Papers, XVIII, Library of Congress.

## MISCELLANEOUS DOCUMENTS

As in the case of manuscript materials, a considerable proportion of contemporary documents relates to the Yazoo speculations and to the Western intrigues of James Wilkinson and Aaron Burr. The De Renne Collection is especially rich in contemporary pamphlets relating to the Yazoo business. Among its holdings, in chronological order, are the following items: *An Extract from the Minutes of the South Carolina Yazoo Company, Containing an Account of its Views, Transactions and Present State* (The Company, 1791). No name is signed, but a note says it was drawn up by Robert Goodloe Harper. This copy is inscribed: "Will'm Gibbony, Jr. Esq. from his most ob'd't h'ble s'v't, A'x'r Moultrie Pres't B'd Prop's, S.C. Y.—Co-y." Moultrie sent a copy of this report to President Washington. Cf. Haskins, "Yazoo Land Companies," *infra;* [James Jackson], *The Letters of Sicilius to the Citizens of the State of Georgia, on the Constitutionality, the Policy, and the Legality of the Late Sales of Western Lands in the State of Georgia, considered in a series of numbers,* "By a Citizen of that State" (Augusta, 1795); *Plan of Association of the North American Land Company, Established February, 1795* (Philadelphia, 1795); *Grant to the Georgia Mississippi Company, the Constitution Thereof, and Extracts Relative to the Situation, Soil, Climate and Navigation of the Western Territory of Georgia* (August, 1795); *To the Honorable the President and the Honorable the Members of the Convention of the State of Georgia,* by the citizens of Screven County (a broadside bearing signatures, n.p., 1795); *State of Facts Showing the Right of Certain Companies to the Lands lately Purchased by them from the State of Georgia* (n.p., 1795); *Observations of the North-American Land-Company, lately instituted in Philadelphia, containing an illustration of the Object of the Company's Plan, the Articles of Association, with a Succinct Account of the States where their Lands lie* (London, 1796); *A Description of the Soil, Productions, Commercial, Agricultural and Social Advantages of the Georgia Western Territory, together with a Summary and impartial View of the Claims of Georgia and of the United States to this Territory, and of the principal Arguments adduced by the Purchasers against these Claims* (collected and stated from various authentic documents, extracted and published in this form, by permission, from Rev. Dr. Morse's *American Gazetteer,* Boston, 1797); *Articles of Association and Agreement constituting the New-England Mississippi Land Company* (n.p., *circa* 1797); *Deposition of Genl. Elijah Clarke . . . respecting a Letter from him to Don Diego Morphy, consul of His Catholic Majesty at Charleston, South Carolina* (House Document, April 27, 1798, ordered to lie on the table, Philadelphia, 1798); [Robert Goodloe Harper], *The Case of the Georgia Sales on the Mississippi, Considered with a Reference to Law Authorities and Public Acts, with an Appendix containing certain Extracts* (Philadelphia, 1799); *Report of the Committee to whom were referred, on the 24th of December, and on the 1st and 13th of January last, the several petitions of Thomas Burling and others, of John Caller and others, and of Cato West and others. April 2, 1800, Committed to a committee of the whole House on Monday next.* (Published by order of the House of Representatives, Washington, 1800); *The Tennessee Company to Messrs. Strawbridge, Jackson and Dexter.* Deed of Trust, dated June 20, 1800; "George Sibbald on the Yazoo Purchase, 1802" (printed from the original manuscript in the Ford Collection, New York Public Library), in *Bulletin of the New York Public Library* (New York, 1897——), VIII (1904), 151–54; Review in *New York Medical Repository,* V (1802), of *Notes and Observations of the Pine Lands of Georgia,* by George Sibbald (Augusta, 1801): *Memorial of the Agents of the New England Mississippi Land Company to Congress, with a Vindication of their Title at Law Annexed* (n.p., 1804); *Remarks occasioned by the View taken of the Claims of 1789 in a Memorial to Congress of the Agents of the New England Mississippi Land Company, with a Vindication of their Title at Law annexed* (Washington, 1805); *Articles of Association and Agreement constituting the New England Mississippi Land Company, as amended, March 12, 1798, February 19, 1802, and June 15, 1814* (n.p., *circa* 1814); Proof Sheets of Senate Bill 93, Report 42, 1838 (Thomas L. Winthrop and others, the New England Mississippi Land Company); "Memorial of the New England Mississippi Land Company to the President of the United States" (no names, no date. Note says the volume was purchased at the sale of General George Washington's library).

The McGregor Library of the University of Virginia has the following Yazoo items: Abraham Bishop, *The Georgia Speculation Unveiled*

(Hartford, 1797–1798); John E. Anderson and William J. Hobby, *The Contract for the purchase of Western Territory made with the Legislature of Georgia in the year 1795, considered with a Reference to the Subsequent Attempts of the State to impair its Obligation* (Augusta, 1799); William Cowan, *Memorial . . . of the Virginia Yazoo Company to the Congress of the United States* (Washington, 1803); *Sundry Papers in relation to Claims Commonly Called the Yazoo Claims* (Printed by order of the House of Representatives, Washington, 1809). The New York Public Library has: *The Claim of the Upper Mississippi Company, presented to the Commissioners of the United States in January, 1803* (n.p., n.d.); *Report of the Committee to whom was referred . . . the Memorials of Alexander Moultrie . . . and of the Virginia Yazoo Company by William Cowan, their agent* (House of Representatives, Washington, January 7, 1804). The following Yazoo items are in the Rare Book Room of the Library of Congress: *Remonstrance and Memorial of Zachariah Cox,* addressed to Congress, November 2, 1803 (Washington, 1803); *Report of the Committee appointed on the second instant to whom was referred the Remonstrance and Memorial of Zachariah Cox,* November 28, 1803 (Washington, 1803); and *The Claim of Ebenezer Oliver and others—directors of an association called the New England Mississippi Land Company* (n.p., n.d.). Two letters from Joseph Martin to Patrick Henry, dated July 23, 1789, and January 1, 1790, are published in Southern History Association *Publications* (Washington), VI (1902), 28–32; and Isaac J. Cox (ed.), "Documents Relating to Zachariah Cox," is in the *Quarterly Publications of the Historical and Philosophical Society of Ohio* (Cincinnati), VIII (1913), Nos. 2–3.

Documents dealing with the Wilkinson-Burr intrigues include: Temple Bodley (ed.), *Reprints of Littell's Political Transactions,* Filson Club, *Publications,* No. 31 (Louisville, 1926); Joseph H. Daviess, *A View of the President's Conduct Concerning the Conspiracy of 1806* (Frankfort, 1807), reprinted in *Quarterly Publications of the Historical and Philosophical Society of Ohio,* XII (1917), Nos. 2–3, ed. by Isaac J. Cox and Helen A. Swineford; *The Journal of Andrew Ellicott* (Philadelphia, 1803); Lawrence Kinnaird (ed.), *Spain in the Mississippi Valley, 1765–1794,* 3 pts., in American Historical Association, *Annual Report,* 1945, II–IV (Washington, 1946–1949); Bernard Mayo (ed.), *Instructions to the British Ministers to the United States, 1791–1812, ibid.,* 1936, III (Washington, 1941); Howard C. Rice (ed.), *Barthélemi Tardiveau, A French Trader in the West,* in *Historical Documents, Institut Français de Washington, Cahier* XI (Baltimore, 1938); William

H. Safford (ed.), *The Blennerhassett Papers* (Cincinnati, 1861); Arthur P. Whitaker (ed.), "Harry Innes and the Spanish Intrigue: 1794–95," in *Mississippi Valley Historical Review*, XV (1928–1929), 236–48; James Wilkinson, *Memoirs of My Own Times*, 3 vols. (Philadelphia, 1816); *James Wilkinson-John Randolph Correspondence* (Washington, 1807), Political Pamphlets, CV, No. 18, Rare Book Room, Library of Congress; Duvon C. and Roberta Corbitt, "Papers from the Spanish Archives Relating to Tennessee and the Old Southwest, 1783–1800," in East Tennessee Historical Society *Publications*, No. 18 (1946), 131–46, No. 19 (1947), 81–97, No. 20 (1948), 103–14. For additional references see Thomas P. Abernethy, *The Burr Conspiracy* (New York, 1954).

The best source for the Blount Conspiracy is the evidence taken by the impeachment committee and published in *Debates and Proceedings of the Congress of the United States (Annals of Congress)*, 5 Cong., 1 Sess. (1797–1798), 2245–2415. These documents, with additional material, are published in Marcus J. Wright, *Some Account of the Life and Services of William Blount* (Washington, 1884). Frederick J. Turner edited "Documents on the Blount Conspiracy, 1795–1797," published in *American Historical Review*, X (1904–1905), 574–606; and Alice B. Keith edited "Letters from Major James Cole Montflourence to Members of the Blount Family . . . January 22, 1792–July 21, 1796," in *North Carolina Historical Review*, XVI (1937), 251–87.

There is a considerable body of documentary material dealing with our multifarious relations with Spanish Florida. Included are such publications as: Duvon C. Corbitt (ed.), "Papers Relating to the Georgia-Florida Frontier, 1784–1800," in *Georgia Historical Quarterly* (Savannah, 1917———), XXI (1937), 274–93; XXII (1938), 72–76, 184–91, 286–91, 391–94; XXIII (1939), 77–79, 189–202, 300–303, 381–87; XXIV (1940), 77–83, 150–57, 257–71, 374–81; XXV (1941), 67–76, 159–71; [Captain Bryan], *Authentic Memoirs of William Augustus Bowles, Esquire, Ambassador from the United Nations of Creeks and Cherokees to the Court of London* (London, 1791), De Renne Collection, University of Georgia; Anon., *The Life of General W. A. Bowles* (London, reprinted New York, 1803), Rare Book Room, Library of Congress; Duvon C. Corbitt and John T. Lanning (eds.), "A Letter of Marque Issued by William Augustus Bowles as Director General of the State of Muscogee," in *Journal of Southern History*, XI (1945), 246–61; "Documents Concerning the West Florida Revolution in 1810," introduction and editorial notes by John S. Kendall, in *Louisi-*

*ana Historical Quarterly* (New Orleans, 1917——), XXVII (1934), 80–95, 306–14, 474–501; James A. Padgett, "The West Florida Revolution of 1810, as told in the Letters of John Rhea, Fulwar Skipwith, Reuben Kemper, and Others," *ibid.,* XXI (1938), 76–202; five letters relating to "West Florida and Its Attempt on Mobile, 1810–1811," in *American Historical Review,* II (1896–1897), 699–705; "Documents Relating to Colonel Edward Nicholls and Captain George Woodbine in Pensacola, 1814," in *Florida Historical Quarterly* (Tallahassee, 1922——), X (1931–1932), 51–54; Walter Prichard (ed.), "An Original Letter on the West Florida Revolution of 1810," in *Louisiana Historical Quarterly,* XVIII (1935), 354–62; James A. Padgett, "Constitution of the West Florida Republic," with editorial notes, *ibid.,* XX (1937), 881–94, and "Official Records of the West Florida Revolution and Republic," *ibid.,* XXI (1938), 685–805; James Cooper and Charles E. Sherman (eds.), *Secret Acts, Resolutions, and Instructions under which East Florida was invaded by the United States Troops, Naval Forces, and Volunteers in 1812 and 1813* (Washington, 1860); *The Exposition, Remonstrance and Protest of Don Vincente Pazos, Commissioner on behalf of the Republican agents established at Amelia Island, in Florida, under the Authority of and in Behalf of the Independent States of South America* (Philadelphia, 1818), Rare Book Room, Library of Congress; Arthur P. Whitaker (trans. and ed.), *Documents Relating to the Commercial Policy of Spain in the Floridas* (De Land, Fla., 1931), published as *Florida State Historical Society Publications,* No. 10.

Documents relating to the Battle of New Orleans are too numerous and too well known to require enumeration here, but a few obscure British accounts of that memorable engagement should be mentioned. They are: [George R. Gleig], *A Narrative of the Campaigns of the British Army at Washington and New Orleans under Generals Ross, Pakenham, and Lambert in the Years 1814 and 1815; with Some Account of the Countries Visited,* "By an Officer who Served in the Expedition" (London, 1821); Anon., "A Subaltern in America," in *Blackwood's Edinburgh Magazine* (Edinburgh, 1817——), XXI (1827), 243–59, 417–33, 531–49, 907–26; XXII (1827), 74–83, 316–28; Captain John H. Cooke, Late of the 43rd Regiment of Light Infantry, *A Narrative of Events in the South of France and of the Attack on New Orleans in 1814 and 1815* (London, 1835), McGregor Library, University of Virginia.

Even more than in the case of military matters, documents dealing with the political scene as it shaped up during the first thirty years of the history of the United States are innumerable and well worked, yet it is desirable to list some of the collected works of prominent public figures. Among the most important of these are: *Letters of Benjamin Hawkins, 1796–1806,* in *Collections of the Georgia Historical Society,* IX (Savannah, 1916); John S. Bassett (ed.), *Correspondence of Andrew Jackson,* 7 vols. (Washington, 1926–1935); A. A. Lipscomb and A. E. Bergh (eds.), *The Writings of Thomas Jefferson,* Memorial edition, 20 vols. (Washington, 1903–1904); Gilbert Chinard (ed.), *The Correspondence of Jefferson and du Pont de Nemours,* in Johns Hopkins University *Studies in International Thought,* 2 vols. (Baltimore, 1931); Moncure D. Conway (ed.), *The Writings of Tom Paine,* 4 vols. (New York, 1894–1896); Philip S. Foner (ed.), *The Complete Writings of Thomas Paine,* 2 vols. (New York, 1945); Stanislaus M. Hamilton (ed.), *Letters to Washington,* 5 vols. (Boston, 1898–1902). Of considerable political interest also are: Edgar S. Maclay (ed.), *The Journal of William Maclay, United States Senator from Pennsylvania, 1789–1791* (New York, 1927); Everett S. Brown (ed.), *William Plumer's Memorandum of Proceedings in the United States Senate, 1803–1807* (New York, 1923); *Letters on the Richmond Party, by a Virginian* (Washington, 1823), Rare Book Room, Library of Congress.

More difficult to classify are the following items: Churchill G. Chamberlayne (ed.), *The Vestry Book and Register of Bristol Parish, Virginia, 1720–1789* (Richmond, 1898); George D. Garrison (ed.), "'A Memorandum of M. Austin's Journey from the Lead Mines in the County of Wythe in the State of Virginia to the Lead Mines in the Province of Louisiana West of the Mississippi,' 1796–1797," in *American Historical Review,* V (1899–1900), 518–42; Daniel Smith, *Topographical Description of the Western Country of North America, Containing a Short Description of the State of Tennessee* (London, 1797), pamphlet in Rare Book Room, Library of Congress; Benjamin Hawkins, "A Sketch of the Creek Country in the Years 1798 and 1799," in *Collections of the Georgia Historical Society,* III, Pt. I (1848), 19–85; John Drayton, *A View of South Carolina as Respects her Natural and Civil Concerns* (Charleston, 1802); Rayford W. Logan (ed.), *Memoirs of a Monticello Slave, as dictated to Charles Campbell in the 1840's by Isaac, one of Thomas Jefferson's Slaves* (Charlottesville, 1951); Gertrude R. B. Richards, "Dr. David Stuart's Report to President Washington on Agricultural Conditions in Northern Virginia," in *Virginia Magazine of History and Biography* (Richmond, 1893——), LXI (1953), 283–92; Adam Seybert, *Statistical Annals . . . of the United States of America* (Philadelphia, 1818); Henry S.

485

Commager (ed.), *Documents of American History* (4th ed., New York, 1948); William MacDonald (ed.), *Documentary Source Book of American History, 1606–1898* (New York, 1908).

## TRAVEL

No attempt has been made to exhaust the travel literature of the period covered by this volume, which is so admirably assessed in Thomas D. Clark (ed.), *Travels in the Old South: A Bibliography, II, The Expanding South, 1750–1825* (Norman, Okla., 1956). Among the necessarily superficial, but sometimes enlightening, accounts of American life as viewed by British and French travelers, some of the most useful have been the following works: Anon., *Narrative of a Voyage to the Spanish Main in the Ship "Two Friends"* (London, 1819), Rare Book Room, Library of Congress; Thomas Anburey, *Travels Through the Interior Parts of America,* 2 vols. (London, 1789); Thomas Ashe, *Travels in America Performed in 1806,* 3 vols. (London, 1808); William Attmore, *Journal of a Tour to North Carolina, 1787,* in *James Sprunt Historical Publications* (Chapel Hill), XVII, No. 2 (1922); John Bernard, *Retrospections of America, 1797–1811,* edited by Mrs. Bayle Bernard (New York, 1887); Victor Collot, *A Journey in North America,* 1796 (Paris, 1826, reprinted Florence, 1924); Thomas Cooper, *Some Information Respecting America* (London, 1795); Fortescue Cuming, *Sketches of a Tour to the Western Country, 1807–1809* (Pittsburgh, 1810); John Davis, *Travels of Four Years and a Half in the United States of America; during 1798, 1799, 1800, 1801, and 1802* (London, 1803); Henry B. Fearon, *Sketches of America* (London, 1818); William T. Harris, *Remarks Made during a Tour through the United States of America in the Years 1817, 1818, 1819* (Liverpool, 1819); Charles W. Janson, *The Stranger in America, 1793–1806* (London, 1807, New York, 1935); Augustus von Kotzebue, *The Adventures of Joseph Pignata* (Petersburg, Va., 1801); Henry Ker, *Travels Through the Western Interior of the United States, 1808–1816* (Elizabethtown, N.J., 1816); Louis le Clerc de Milfort, *Memoir or a Cursory Glance at my Different Travels & my Sojourn in the Creek Nation,* translated by Geraldine de Courcy, edited by John F. McDermott (Chicago, 1956); Richard Parkinson, *A Tour of America in 1798, 1799, and 1800* (London, 1805); G. E. Pendergrast, *A Physical & Topographical Sketch of the Mississippi Territory, Lower Louisiana and a part of West Florida* (Philadelphia, 1803); Otto L. Schmidt, "The Mississippi Valley in 1816 through an Englishman's Diary," based on the diary of George Flower, in *Mississippi Valley*

*Historical Review,* XIV (1927–1928), 137–55; Major Amos Stoddard, *Sketches, Historical and Descriptive of Louisiana* (Philadelphia, 1812); Harry Toulmin, *The Western Country in 1793; Reports on Kentucky and Virginia,* edited by Marion Tinling and Godfrey Davies (San Marino, 1948); Brissot de Warville, *New Travels in the United States of America, Performed in the Year 1788,* 2 vols., translated from the French (London, 1792–1794); Winslow C. Watson (ed.), *Men and Times of the Revolution; or, Memoirs of Elkanah Watson* (New York, 1856); Isaac Weld, *Travels through the States of North America . . . during the years 1795, 1796, and 1797,* 2 vols. (London, 1807).

## NEWSPAPERS

In order to put together a well-rounded account of a little-known period of Southern history one probably can make no better approach than an extensive survey of the newspaper press. This involved, for each state and territory of the region, an attempt to cover the thirty years in its newspaper files, as far as these existed and were available. Most of the papers were small sheets appearing only once or twice a week, with Charleston having the only dailies published in the South. Local news coverage was exceedingly spotty and editorial opinion spoke with a very small voice, except in the case of a few exceptionally influential men such as Thomas Ritchie of the Richmond *Enquirer,* Joseph Gales of the Raleigh *Register,* John Bradford of the Lexington *Kentucky Gazette,* and James M. Bradford of the New Orleans *Louisiana Gazette.* Nevertheless, from these diminutive and often transitory journals one can synthesize a more vivid picture of the passing scene than can be built up from any other one source of information. The "open sesame" to all this material is Clarence S. Brigham's *History and Bibliography of American Newspapers, 1690–1820,* 2 vols. (Worcester, 1947). Here are set down in great detail the many changes in ownership and title of all the journals of the period, as far as they are known, with location of repositories and dates of extant issues.

In some instances the more important newspapers have been microfilmed or photostated, and thus made available in various repositories. The library of the University of Virginia has a microfilm copy of the Annapolis *Maryland Gazette,* and extensive use has been made of it. Much more important than this publication is the Richmond *Enquirer* (1804–1877), edited throughout the period of this study by Thomas Ritchie, spokesman for the powers that ruled Virginia in his day and one whose influence spread far beyond state boundaries. The best file of this paper is in the Virginia State Library. While Ritchie spoke for the Jeffersonians, Augustine Davis of the Richmond *Virginia Gazette, and General Advertiser* (1790–1809) represented the opposition. The Virginia State Library has a good file of this paper, and the University of Virginia Library has one of the Norfolk *Herald* (1794–1820+).

Having no large towns, North Carolina had no really important newspaper except the Raleigh *Register* (1799–1820+), edited by that staunch and able Jeffersonian, Joseph Gales. Files of several of the lesser newspapers have been photostated and are available in the library of the University of North Carolina and elsewhere. They include: the Raleigh *Minerva* (1803–1820+); the Edenton *State Gazette of North-Carolina* (1789–1799); the Edenton *Herald of Freedom* (1799); the New Bern *Gazette* (1798–1804); the New Bern *North-Carolina Gazette* (1786–1798); the Fayetteville *Gazette* (1792–1794); the Fayetteville *North-Carolina Chronicle* (1790–1791); and the Halifax *North-Carolina Journal* (1792–1814).

Charleston had three dailies, the most important of which was the Federalist mouthpiece, the Charleston *Courier* (1803–1820+). The *City Gazette, and Daily Advertiser,* title varies (1787–1820+), was the Republican organ, and the third was the *South-Carolina State-Gazette* (1794–1802). The Charleston Library Society has the most complete files of all three. Two Savannah papers give the most comprehensive view of Georgia affairs. They are the *Georgia Republican* (1802–1807) and the *Georgia Gazette* (1788–1802). The best files of these are owned by the Georgia Historical Society of Savannah.

By far the most important newspaper published in Kentucky was the Lexington *Kentucky Gazette* (1789–1820), whose editor, John Bradford, was a citizen of real consequence. The best file is in the Lexington Public Library and has now been photostated. This repository also has a good file of the Lexington *Reporter* (1808–1820+) and a few issues of the Frankfort *Palladium* (1798–1816). Unfortunately, there is no good file of the weekly Frankfort *Western World* (1806–1810). It was edited by Joseph M. Street and John Wood, spokesmen for Humphrey Marshall, United States Senator from Kentucky and first historian of that state. He was an aggressive opponent of Wilkinson and Burr and has remained a controversial character to this day. The Filson Club of Louisville has a broken file of the *Western World,* but that sheet is best known because it was so often quoted in the *Kentucky Gazette* and other contemporary newspapers. Many Tennessee prints were used in the preparation of a previous work, but the only ones pertinent to the present volume are: the Knoxville *Gazette* (1791–1798, 1799, 1801–1808), the most complete file of which is in the Lawson

McGhee Library, Knoxville; the Nashville *Whig* (1812–1820+); the Nashville *Impartial Review, and Cumberland Repository* (1805–1809), title varies; and the Nashville *Clarion, & Tennessee State Gazette* (1808–1820+), title varies.

The press in Mississippi Territory had an unusual beginning. Lieutenant Andrew Marschalk of the United States Army brought a small press with him to the Territory in 1797 and two years later he was commissioned to print the first edition of the Territorial laws. In the same year he sold his press to one Benjamin M. Stokes, who, on a sheet of foolscap paper, printed the first issue of the Natchez *Mississippi Gazette* (1799–1801). Having been discharged from the army in June, 1802, Marschalk, a Federalist, began publication of the Natchez *Mississippi Herald* (1802–1807). The American Antiquarian Society has the most complete file of this paper. Marschalk also published the Washington *Republican* (1815–1817), and in 1818 changed the name of his paper to the *Mississippi State Gazette* (1818–1820+). The *Mississippi Messenger* (1804–1808), the *Weekly Chronicle* (1808–1812), and the *Mississippi Republican* (1812–1820+), all published in Natchez, complete the list of the more important early newspapers published in the Territory. The Mississippi Department of Archives and History has the best files of them. The chief newspapers published in New Orleans were the *Louisiana Gazette* (1804–1820+), edited by the Burrite, James M. Bradford, and the *Courrier de la Louisiane* (1807–1820+), a triweekly printed in both French and English. The Louisiana State Museum and the New Orleans City Archives have broken files of these journals.

In addition to Southern newspapers, the Washington *National Intelligencer* (1800–1869?) and the Philadelphia *Aurora* (1794–1820+) have frequently been consulted.

## SECONDARY WRITINGS

Under this heading are included articles from historical journals as well as separately bound volumes. Since it would have been impossible to cover such materials on a nationwide scale, major attention has been paid to those dealing specifically with the South, yet a few works of a general nature have been indispensable. In this classified list they have been mentioned first.

## GENERAL AMERICAN HISTORY

By far the most useful general account of this period is the nine-volume *History of the United States of America* (New York, 1889–

1891) by Henry Adams. It covers only the administrations of Jefferson and Madison, and it is by no means free of error and prejudice, yet there is no other account so generally informative. The next best work, and in some ways superior, is Edward Channing's *History of the United States,* 6 vols. (New York, 1905–1925), with Volumes IV and V pertinent to the present study. Also of outstanding importance are Evarts B. Greene, *The Revolutionary Generation, 1763–1790,* and John A. Krout and Dixon R. Fox, *The Completion of Independence, 1790–1830,* which are Volumes IV (1943) and V (1944) of Arthur M. Schlesinger and Dixon R. Fox (eds.), *A History of American Life,* 13 vols. (New York, (1927–1948). In addition to the first of these volumes, there is good background material in Merrill Jensen, *The New Nation; A History of the United States During the Confederation, 1781–1789* (New York, 1950). Also useful are Claude G. Bowers, *Jefferson and Hamilton: The Struggle for Democracy in America* (Boston, 1944), and Francis Franklin, *The Rise of the American Nation, 1789–1824* (New York, 1944). Among the more pertinent works dealing with special phases of American history are: Thomas A. Bailey, *A Diplomatic History of the American People* (New York, 1950); Charles A. Beard, *An Economic Interpretation of the Constitution of the United States* (New York, 1913), and "Some Economic Origins of Jeffersonian Democracy," in *American Historical Review,* XIX (1913–1914), 282–98; Samuel F. Bemis, *A Diplomatic History of the United States* (New York, 1950), and *The Latin American Policy of the United States* (New York, 1943); Robert E. Brown, *Charles Beard and the Constitution: A Critical Analysis of "An Economic Interpretation of the Constitution"* (Princeton, 1956); French E. Chadwick, *The Relations of the United States and Spain, Diplomacy* (New York, 1909); Wesley E. Rich, *The History of the United States Post Office to the Year 1829* (Cambridge, 1924); Frank W. Taussig, *The Tariff History of the United States* (New York, 1914).

## BIOGRAPHIES

The most useful biographies have been: Henry Adams, *John Randolph* (Boston, 1910); Holmes Alexander, *Aaron Burr, The Proud Pretender* (New York, 1937); Charles H. Ambler, *Thomas Ritchie; A Study in Virginia Politics* (Richmond, 1913); Dice R. Anderson, *William Branch Giles; A Study in the Politics of Virginia and the Nation from 1790 to 1830* (Menasha, Wis., 1914); John S. Bassett, *The Life of Andrew Jackson,* 2 vols. (Garden City, 1911); Albert J. Beveridge, *The Life of John Marshall,* 4 vols. (New York, 1916–1919); Irving Brant, *James Madison, Father of the Constitution, 1787–1800, James Madison, Sec-*

*retary of State, 1800–1809,* and *James Madison, The President, 1809–1812* (Indianapolis, 1950, 1953, 1956); Augustus C. Buell, *History of Andrew Jackson,* 2 vols. (New York, 1904); Thomas U. P. Charlton, *The Life of Major General James Jackson* (Augusta, Ga., 1809); William P. Cresson, *James Monroe* (Chapel Hill, 1946); William E. Dodd, *The Life of Nathaniel Macon* (Raleigh, 1903); Hugh A. Garland, *The Life of John Randolph of Roanoke* (New York, 1866); James A. Green, *William Henry Harrison, His Life and Times* (Richmond, 1941); Thomas R. Hay and M. R. Werner, *The Admirable Trumpeter; A Biography of General James Wilkinson* (Garden City, 1941); Louise F. Hays, *Hero of Hornet's Nest, A Biography of Elijah Clarke, 1733–1799* (New York, 1946); Samuel G. Heiskell, *Andrew Jackson and Early Tennessee History,* 3 vols. (Nashville, 1920–1921); William Wirt Henry, *Patrick Henry; Life, Correspondence and Speeches,* 3 vols. (New York, 1891); James R. Jacobs, *Tarnished Warrior; Major-General James Wilkinson* (New York, 1938); James A. James, *The Life of George Rogers Clark* (Chicago, 1928); Marquis James, *Andrew Jackson, The Border Captain* (Indianapolis, 1933); William F. Keller, *The Nation's Advocate: Henry Marie Brackenridge and Young America* (Pittsburgh, 1956); Charles R. King, *The Life and Correspondence of Rufus King,* 6 vols. (New York, 1894–1900); Adrienne Koch, *Jefferson and Madison; The Great Collaboration* (New York, 1950); William Masterson, *William Blount* (Baton Rouge, 1954); Catherine Van Cortlandt Mathews, *Andrew Ellicott, His Life and Letters* (New York, 1908); Bernard Mayo, *Henry Clay* (Boston, 1937), and *Jefferson Himself* (Boston, 1942); Saul K. Padover, *A Jefferson Profile as Revealed in His Letters* (New York, 1956); Joseph H. Parks, *Felix Grundy, Champion of Democracy* (Baton Rouge, 1940); James Parton, *Life of Andrew Jackson,* 3 vols. (Boston, 1887–1888); Blackwell P. Robinson, *William R. Davie* (Chapell Hill, 1957); Manuel Serrano ỹ Sanz, *El Brigadier Jaime Wilkinson* (Madrid, 1915); J. E. D. Shipp, *Giant Days; or, The Life and Times of William H. Crawford* (Americus, Ga., 1909); Royal O. Shreve, *The Finished Scoundrel, General James Wilkinson* (Indianapolis, 1933); Henry H. Simms, *Life of John Taylor* (Richmond, 1932); Marcus J. Wright, *Some Account of the Life and Services of William Blount* (Washington, 1884).

## MONOGRAPHS

Not many adequate studies of special phases of the early history of the South have yet been made, but the following monographs, listed alphabetically, have been helpful: Thomas P. Abernethy, *The Burr*

*Conspiracy* (New York, 1954); Leland D. Baldwin, *Whiskey Rebels; The Story of a Frontier Uprising* (Pittsburgh, 1939); John D. Barnhart, *Valley of Democracy: The Frontier Versus the Plantation in the Ohio Valley, 1775–1818* (Bloomington, Ind., 1953); Henry M. Brackenridge, *History of the Western Insurrection in Western Pennsylvania, Commonly Called the Whiskey Rebellion, 1794* (Pittsburgh, 1859); Charles R. Brown, *The Northern Confederacy According to the Plans of the "Essex Junto," 1796–1814* (Princeton, 1915); John C. Emmerson, *The Chesapeake Affair of 1807* (Portsmouth, Va., 1954); Rembert W. Patrick, *Florida Fiasco; Rampant Rebels on the Georgia-Florida Border, 1810–1815* (Athens, 1954); Arthur P. Whitaker, *The Spanish-American Frontier: 1783–1795* (Boston, 1927), *The Mississippi Question, 1795–1803* (New York, 1934), and *The United States and the Independence of Latin America, 1800–1830* (Baltimore, 1941).

## POLITICS

Studies dealing specifically with political developments include: E. Merton Coulter, "The Efforts of the Democratic Societies of the West to Open the Navigation of the Mississippi," in *Mississippi Valley Historical Review* (Cedar Rapids, 1914——), XI (1924–1925), 376–89; Orin G. Libby, *The Geographical Distribution of the Vote of the Thirteen States on the Federal Constitution, 1787–8* (Madison, 1894); Eugene P. Link, *Democratic-Republican Societies, 1790–1800* (New York, 1942), and "The Democratic Societies of the Carolinas," in *North Carolina Historical Review* (Raleigh, 1924——), XVIII (1941), 259–77; Gilbert C. Lycan, "Alexander Hamilton and the North Carolina Federalists," *ibid.*, XXV (1948), 442–65; Forrest McDonald, *We the People: The Economic Origins of the Constitution* (Chicago, 1958); Albert R. Newsome, *The Presidential Election of 1824 in North Carolina* (Chapel Hill, 1939); Ulrich B. Phillips, *Georgia and State Rights* (Washington, 1902), and "The South Carolina Federalists," in *American Historical Review*, XIV (1908–1909), 529–43, 731–43; William A. Schaper, *Sectionalism and Representation in South Carolina* (Washington, 1901); Joseph I. Shulim, *The Old Dominion and Napoleon Bonaparte* (New York, 1952); Marshall Smelzer, "George Washington and the Alien and Sedition Acts," in *American Historical Review*, LIX (1953–1954), 322–34; James M. Smith, "Sedition in the Old Dominion: James T. Callender and *The Prospect Before Us*," in *Journal of Southern History*, XX (1954), 157–82; Niels H. Sonne, *Liberal Kentucky, 1780–1828* (New York, 1939), actually a history of Transylvania University; Charles S. Sydnor, *The Development of Southern Sectionalism, 1819–1848*

(Baton Rouge, 1948); Henry M. Wagstaff, *State Rights and Political Parties in North Carolina—1776–1861* (Baltimore, 1906), and *Federalism in North Carolina* (Chapel Hill, 1910); John H. Wolfe, *Jeffersonian Democracy in South Carolina* (Chapel Hill, 1940).

## THE SOUTHERN FRONTIER

In connection with this subject of primary importance, the following books and articles are most helpful: Lucas Alamán, *Historia de Méjico,* 5 vols. (Mexico City, 1942); Stanley C. Arthur, *The Story of the West Florida Rebellion* (St. Francisville, La., 1935); Henry E. Chambers, *West Florida and Its Relation to the Historical Cartography of the United States* (Baltimore, 1898); Carita D. Corse, *The Key to the Golden Islands* (Chapel Hill, 1931); E. Merton Coulter, "Elijah Clarke's Foreign Intrigues and the 'Trans-Oconee Republic,' " in Mississippi Valley Historical Association *Proceedings* (Cedar Rapids, 1909–1924), X, Pt. II (1919–1920), 260–79, and *Bulletin of the University of Georgia,* XXIII, No. 4 (Athens, 1922); Isaac J. Cox, *The Louisiana-Texas Frontier,* 2 vols. (Austin, 1906–1913), "The American Intervention in West Florida," in *American Historical Review,* XVII (1911–1912), 290–311, "The New Invasion of the Goths and Vandals," in Mississippi Valley Historical Association *Proceedings,* VIII (1914–1915), 176–200, *The West Florida Controversy, 1798–1813* (Baltimore, 1918), "The Louisiana-Texas Frontier During the Burr Conspiracy," in *Mississippi Valley Historical Review,* X (1923–1924), 274–84, and "The Border Missions of General George Mathews," *ibid.,* XII (1925–1926), 309–33; T. Frederick Davis, "MacGregor's Invasion of Florida, 1817," in *Florida Historical Quarterly* (Tallahassee, 1922———), VII (1928–1929), 3–71; Elisha P. Douglass, "The Adventurer Bowles," in *William and Mary Quarterly* (Williamsburg, 1892———), 3d Ser., VI (1949), 3–23; Henry L. Favrot, "Some of the Causes and Conditions That Brought About the West Florida Revolution in 1810," in Louisiana Historical Society *Publications* (New Orleans), I, Pt. II (1895), 37–46; Marie T. Greenslade, "William Panton," in *Florida Historical Society Quarterly,* XIV (1935–1936), 107–30; Ralph B. Guinness, "The Purpose of the Lewis and Clark Expedition," in *Mississippi Valley Historical Review,* XX (1933–1934), 90–100; Archibald Henderson, "Isaac Shelby and the Genêt Mission," *ibid.,* VI (1919–1920), 451–69; William F. Keller, "The Frontier Intrigues of Citizen Genêt," in *Americana* (New York, 1906———), XXXIV (1940), 567–95; Lawrence Kinnaird, "The Significance of William Augustus Bowles' Seizure of Panton's Apalachee Store in 1792," in the *Florida Historical Quarterly* (Tallahassee, 1922———), IX

(1931), 156–66, "American Penetration into Spanish Louisiana," in *New Spain and the Anglo-American West: Historical Contributions Presented to H. E. Bolton,* 2 vols. (Los Angeles, 1932); Lucia B. Kinnaird, "The Rock Landing Conference of 1789," in *North Carolina Historical Review,* IX (1932), 349–65; George W. Kyte, "A Spy on the Western Waters: The Military Intelligence Mission of General Collot in 1796," in *Mississippi Valley Historical Review,* XXXIV (1947–1948), 427–42; Richard Lowitt, "Activities of Citizen Genêt in Kentucky, 1793–1794," in *Filson Club History Quarterly* (Louisville, 1926———), XXII (1948), 252–66; E. Wilson Lyon (ed.), "Milfort's Plan for a Franco-Creek Alliance and the Retrocession of Louisiana," in *Journal of Southern History,* IV (1938), 72–87, and *Louisiana in French Diplomacy, 1759–1804* (Norman, Okla., 1934); Richard K. Murdoch, "Citizen Mangourit and the Projected Attack on East Florida in 1794," in *Journal of Southern History,* XIV (1948), 522–40; Frank L. Owsley, "The Pattern of Migration and Settlement on the Southern Frontier," *ibid.,* XI (1945), 147–76; James A. Padgett, "The West Florida Revolution of 1810," in *Louisiana Historical Quarterly,* XXI (1938), 76–202; Louis Pelzer, "Economic Factors in the Acquisition of Louisiana," in Mississippi Valley Historical Association *Proceedings,* VI (1912–1913), 109–28; Walter B. Posey, "The Blount Conspiracy," in *Birmingham-Southern College Bulletin* (Birmingham), XXI (1928), 11–21; Franklin L. Riley, "Spanish Policy in Mississippi after the Treaty of San Lorenzo," in American Historical Association, *Annual Report,* 1897 (Washington, 1898), 177–92, and "Transition from Spanish to American Rule in Mississippi," in Mississippi Historical Society *Publications* (Oxford, 1896–1914), III (1900), 261–311; Richard Stenberg, "The Western Boundary of Louisiana, 1762–1803," in *Southwestern Historical Quarterly,* XXXV (1931–1932), 95–108; Isabel Thompson, "The Blount Conspiracy," in East Tennessee Historical Society *Publications,* No. 2 (1930), 3–21; Frederick J. Turner, "The Origin of Genêt's Projected Attack on Louisiana and the Floridas," in *American Historical Review,* III (1897–1898), 650–71, "English Policy Toward America in 1790–1791," *ibid.,* VII (1901–1902), 706–35, VIII (1902–1903), 78–86, "The Policy of France Toward the Mississippi Valley in the Period of Washington and Adams," *ibid.,* X (1904–1905), 249–79, and "The Diplomatic Contest for the Mississippi Valley," in *Atlantic Monthly* (Boston, 1857———), XCIII (1904), 676–91, 807–17; Harris G. Warren, "Pensacola and the Filibusters, 1816–1817," in *Louisiana Historical Quarterly,* XXI (1938), 806–22; Arthur P. Whitaker, "Spain and the Cherokee Indians, 1783–98," in *North Carolina Historical Review,*

IV (1927), 252–69, and "Harry Innes and the Spanish Intrigue: 1794–1795," in *Mississippi Valley Historical Review*, XV (1928–1929), 236–48; A. Curtis Wilgus, "Spanish-American Patriot Activity along the Gulf Coast of the United States, 1811–1822," in *Louisiana Historical Quarterly*, VIII (1925), 193–215; Samuel C. Williams, "French and Other Intrigues in the Southwest Territory, 1790–1796," in East Tennessee Historical Society *Publications*, No. 13 (1941), 21–35.

## INDIANS

Except as an enemy, comparatively little attention has been paid to the American Indian as a factor in the development of our civilization. He was a powerful force on the Southern frontier, and he was more often a friend than an enemy, yet even in this volume he has hardly come under close observation except when he appeared in war paint. The following are a few studies which deal with him in a more general way and which have been found useful: Carlos E. Castañeda, *The Mission Era: The End of the Spanish Regime, 1780–1810*, Vol. V in Paul J. Folk (ed.), *Our Catholic Heritage in Texas, 1519–1936* (7 vols., Austin, 1942); John W. Caughey, *McGillivray of the Creeks* (Norman, Okla., 1938); R. S. Cotterill, "Federal Indian Management in the South, 1789–1825," in *Mississippi Valley Historical Review*, XX (1933–1934), 333–52, "A Chapter of Panton, Leslie and Company," in *Journal of Southern History*, X (1944), 274–92, and *The Southern Indians* (Norman, Okla., 1954); Randolph C. Downes, "Creek-American Relations, 1790–1795," in *Journal of Southern History*, VIII (1942), 350–73; Henry T. Malone, *Cherokees of the Old South* (Athens, 1956); Merritt B. Pound, "Colonel Benjamin Hawkins—North Carolinian—Benefactor of the Southern Indians," in *North Carolina Historical Review*, XIX (1942), 1–21, 168–86, and *Benjamin Hawkins, Indian Agent* (Athens, 1951); Charles C. Royce (comp.), *Indian Land Cessions in the United States*, in American Bureau of Ethnology, *Eighteenth Annual Report, 1896–97*, Pt. II (Washington, 1899); John R. Swanton, *Social Organization and Social Usages of the Indians of the Creek Confederacy, ibid., Forty-Second Annual Report . . . 1924–1925* (Washington, 1928); Arthur P. Whitaker, "Alexander McGillivray, 1789–1793," in *North Carolina Historical Review*, V (1928), 289–309.

## YAZOO

There have been surprisingly few studies of the great Yazoo land speculations. The following works have been helpful: Charles H. Haskins, "The Yazoo Land Companies," in American Historical Association *Papers,* V (1891), No. 4, pp. 61–103; Louise P. Kellogg, "Letter of Thomas Paine, 1793," in *American Historical Review,* XXIX (1923–1924), 501–505; M. C. Klingelsmith, "James Wilson and the So-Called Yazoo Frauds," in *University of Pennsylvania Law Review and American Law Register* (Philadelphia), LVI (1908), 1–27; Shaw Livermore, *Early American Land Companies* (New York, 1939); John C. Parish, "The Intrigues of Doctor James O'Fallon," in *Mississippi Valley Historical Review,* XVII (1930–1931), 230–63; A. M. Sakolski, *The Great American Land Bubble* (New York, 1932); Arthur P. Whitaker (ed.), "The South Carolina Yazoo Company," in *Mississippi Valley Historical Review,* XVI (1929–1930), 383–94; George White, *An Accurate Account of the Yazoo Fraud, Compiled from Official Documents* (Marietta, Ga., 1852).

## THE WILKINSON-BURR INTRIGUES

As controversial and as misrepresented as these frontier intrigues have been, the literature concerning them is not extensive. The following are the most important studies: James A. Cabell, *The Trial of Aaron Burr* (a paper read before the New York State Bar Association, January 17, 1900, and reprinted from the *Proceedings* of the Association, Albany, 1900); Clarence E. Carter, "The Burr-Wilkinson Intrigue in St. Louis," in *Bulletin of the Missouri Historical Society* (St. Louis), X (1954), 447–64; Thomas C. Cherry, "Robert Craddock and Peter Tardiveau, Two Revolutionary Soldiers of Warren County, Kentucky," in *Filson Club History Quarterly* (Louisville, 1926——), IV (1930), 78–90; Daniel Clark, *Proofs of the Corruption of Gen. James Wilkinson* (Philadelphia, 1809); Isaac J. Cox, "The Exploration of the Louisiana Frontier, 1803–1806," in American Historical Association, *Annual Report,* 1904 (Washington, 1905), 151–74, "The Significance of the Louisiana-Texas Frontier," in Mississippi Valley Historical Association *Proceedings,* III (1909–1910), 198–213, and "Western Reaction to the Burr Conspiracy," in Illinois State Historical Society *Transactions,* 1928 (Springfield, 1928), 73–87; Thomas M. Green, *The Spanish Conspiracy* (Cincinnati, 1891); Schuyler D. Haslett, "Some Notes on British Intrigue in Kentucky," in *Register of the State Historical Society of Kentucky* (Frankfort, 1903——), XXXVIII (1940), 54–56; Thomas R. Hay, "Some Reflections on the Career of General James Wilkinson," in *Mississippi Valley Historical Review,* XXI (1934–1935), 471–94, "General James Wilkinson—The Last Phase," in *Louisiana Historical Quarterly,* XIX (1936), 405–36, and "Charles Williamson and the Burr Conspiracy," in *Journal of Southern History,* II (1936), 185–210; Archibald Henderson, "The Spanish Conspiracy in Tennessee," in *Tennessee Historical Magazine* (Nashville, 1915——), III (1917), 229–43; Jennie O'K. Mitchell and Robert D. Calhoun, "The Marquis de Maison Rouge, the Baron de Bastrop, and Colonel Abraham Morehouse—Three Ouachita Valley Soldiers of Fortune," in *Louisiana Historical Quarterly*, XX (1937), 291–462; Arthur P. Whitaker, "Spanish Intrigue in the Old Southwest: An Episode, 1788–89," in *Mississippi Valley Historical Review*, XII (1925–1926), 155–76, and "James Wilkinson's First Descent to New Orleans in 1787," in *Hispanic American Historical Review* (Baltimore, Durham, 1918——), VIII (1928), 82–97.

## THE WAR OF 1812

Only Andrew Jackson's Southern campaigns have been discussed in this volume, and the following works were selected because they relate especially to this phase of the war: Dice R. Anderson, "The Insurgents of 1811," in American Historical Association, *Annual Report, 1911,* I (Washington, 1913), 167–76; Christopher B. Coleman, "The Ohio Valley in the Preliminaries of the War of 1812," in *Mississippi Valley Historical Review*, VII (1920–1921), 39–50; Warren H. Goodman, "The Origins of the War of 1812, A Survey of Changing Interpretations," *ibid.,* XXVIII (1941–1942), 171–86; Louis M. Hacker, "Western Land Hunger and the War of 1812: A Conjecture," *ibid.,* X (1923–1924), 365–95; H. S. Halbert and T. H. Ball, *The Creek War of 1813 and 1814* (Chicago and Montgomery, 1895); Major A. L. Latour, *Historical Memoir of the War in West Florida and Louisiana. With an Atlas,* translated by H. P. Nugent (Philadelphia, 1816); Julius W. Pratt, "Western Aims in the War of 1812," in *Mississippi Valley Historical Review*, XII (1925–1926), 36–50; Frank A. Updyke, *The Diplomacy of the War of 1812* (Baltimore, 1915).

## STATE AND LOCAL HISTORY

While the individual states and territories are dealt with only as parts of a section in this work, much more has been written about them than about the South as a whole. The following are the studies which have been the most valuable for the present purposes: Kathryn T. Abbey, *Florida, Land of Change* (Chapel Hill, 1941); William W. Abbot, "The Structure of Politics in Georgia: 1782–1789," in *William and Mary Quarterly,* 3d Ser., XIV (1957), 47–65; Thomas P. Abernethy, *The Formative Period in Alabama, 1815–1828* (Montgomery, 1922), *From Frontier to Plantation in Tennessee* (Chapel Hill, 1932), and *Three Virginia Frontiers* (Baton Rouge, 1940); Charles H. Ambler,

*Sectionalism in Virginia from 1776 to 1861* (Chicago, 1910); Matthew P. Andrews, *History of Maryland: Province and State* (Garden City, 1929); Samuel A. Ashe, *History of North Carolina,* 2 vols. (Greensboro, 1908–1925); John D. Barnhart, "The Tennessee Constitution of 1796: A Product of the Old West," in *Journal of Southern History,* IX (1943), 532–48; John M. Bass, "Half an Hour with some early Visitors to Tennessee," in *American Historical Magazine* (Nashville, 1896——), V (1900), 99–114; Mark F. Boyd, "The Fortifications at San Marcos de Apalachee," in *Florida Historical Quarterly,* XV (1936), 3–34; William K. Boyd, *History of North Carolina: The Federal Period, 1783–1860* (Chicago, 1919); Caroline M. Brevard, *A History of Florida from the Treaty of 1763 to our Own Times,* 2 vols., edited by James A. Robertson (De Land, Fla., 1924); Solon J. and Elizabeth H. Buck, *The Planting of Civilization in Western Pennsylvania* (Pittsburgh, 1939); Mann Butler, *A History of the Commonwealth of Kentucky* (Louisville, 1834); Absalom Harris Chappell, *Miscellanies of Georgia, Historical, Biographical, Descriptive* (Atlanta, 1874); W. Asbury Christian, *Richmond, Her Past and Present* (Richmond, 1912); J. F. H. Claiborne, *Mississippi, as a Province, Territory and State,* only Vol. I published (Jackson, 1880); Thomas D. Clark, *A History of Kentucky* (New York, 1937); Lewis Collins, *History of Kentucky,* 2 vols. (Covington, 1878); John L. Conger, "South Carolina and the Early Tariffs," in *Mississippi Valley Historical Review,* V (1918–1919), 415–33; E. Merton Coulter, *A Short History of Georgia* (Chapel Hill, 1933), and "Early Frontier Democracy in the First Kentucky Constitution," in *Political Science Quarterly* (Boston, New York, 1886——), XXXIX (1924), 665–77; Huntley Dupree, "The Political Ideas of George Nicholas," in *Register of the Kentucky State Historical Society* (Frankfort, 1903——), XXXIX (1941), 201–23; Charles Gayarré, *History of Louisiana,* 4 vols. (New Orleans, 1885); Delbert H. Gilpatrick, *Jeffersonian Democracy in North Carolina, 1789–1816* (New York, 1931); Josephus C. Guild, *Old Times in Tennessee* (Nashville, 1878); John Haywood, *The Civil and Political History of the State of Tennessee* (Nashville, 1915); Hugh T. Lefler and Albert R. Newsome, *North Carolina: The History of a Southern State* (Chapel Hill, 1954); John P. Little, *History of Richmond* (Richmond, 1933); Humphrey Marshall, *The History of Kentucky,* 2 vols. (Frankfort, 1824); Samuel Mordecai, *Richmond in By-gone Days* (Richmond, 1946); Thomas M. Owen, *History of Alabama and Dictionary of Alabama Biography,* 4 vols. (Chicago, 1921); Hamilton Owens, *Baltimore on the Chesapeake* (Garden City, 1941); Albert J. Pickett, *History of Alabama* (Birmingham, 1900); J. G. M. Ramsey, *The Annals* of *Tennessee* (Kingsport, 1926); Mrs. St. Julien Ravenel, *Charleston, The Place and The People* (New York, 1925); Mary U. Rothrock (ed.), *The French Broad-Holston Country: A History of Knox County, Tennessee* (Knoxville, 1946); Dunbar Rowland, *Mississippi,* 3 vols. (Atlanta, 1907), and *History of Mississippi; The Heart of the South,* 2 vols. (Chicago, Jackson, 1925); John T. Scharf, *The Chronicles of Baltimore* (Baltimore, 1874), and *History of Maryland, from the Earliest Period to the Present Day,* 3 vols. (Baltimore, 1879); Zachariah F. Smith, *The History of Kentucky* (Louisville, 1901); Mary N. Stanard, *Richmond, Its People and Its Story* (Philadelphia, 1923); William B. Stevens, *History of Georgia,* 2 vols. (New York, 1847, Philadelphia, 1859); Lyon G. Tyler, *History of Virginia,* II, *The Federal Period, 1763–1861* (Chicago, 1924); David D. Wallace, *The History of South Carolina,* 4 vols. (New York, 1934); Thomas J. Wertenbaker, *Norfolk, Historic Southern Port* (Durham, 1931); George White, *Historical Collections of Georgia* (New York, 1854); Rosa F. Yancey, *Lynchburg and Its Neighbors* (Richmond, 1935).

# INDEX

Adair, Senator John, on Alien and Sedition acts, 234; letter to Wilkinson, quoted, 267; in Burr Conspiracy, 279–80, 284

Adams, Abigail, 187

Adams, Henry, 313; quoted, 374

Adams, John, President, 39; appoints governor of Mississippi Territory, 158; appoints commission to inquire into land claims, 161; reports to Congress on Blount's conspiracy, 187; lukewarm on Alien and Sedition acts, 229; favors war with England, 410

Adams, John Quincy, represents appellants in Fletcher v. Peck, 166

Adet, M. Pierre, French Minister to United States, sends Collot on reconnaissance of West, 173

Agriculture, description of, 4; markets for, 16; in South Carolina, 28; system of, 41

Alabama, Indians in, 3; created a Territory, 461; Bibb appointed governor of, 461; land office in, and immigrants to, 464; settlers of, 465–66, 469; "Black Belt" in, 466–67; admitted to statehood, 473; provisions of her constitution, 474

Albemarle-Pamlico Sound Region, 26, 27

Alexandria, Va., center for Potomac trade, 25

Alien and Sedition acts, Congress passes, 229; violent reaction to, 230

Alston, Joseph, finances Burr's Conspiracy, 283; elected governor of South Carolina, 406

Alston, Solomon, 337

American Philosophical Society, supports Genêt, 107; Ellicott a member of, 210

Amis des Noirs, effect of, on Southerners, 127, 128

Anderson, Joseph, 189

Annapolis Convention of 1786, p. 22

Antifederalism, 24, 25

Armesto, Don Andrés, secretary to Carondelet, reports on the West, 212–13

Armstrong, General John, Minister to France, reports on plan to sell Florida, 338, 404; Secretary of War, 376; hostility against, causes resignation, 422

Ashe, John B., 41

Assumption Bill, 96; opposition to, 36; Jefferson lines up votes to pass, 37

Atlantic Seaboard, 43

Augusta Herald, describes travels of immigrants, 471–72

Aurora of Philadelphia, publishes text of Jay's Treaty, 131; quoted in Kentucky Gazette, 228

Austin, Moses, 452

Austin, Stephen, 452

Baker, Colonel Joshua S., and West Florida, 348

Baldwin, Abraham, 41; investigates land claims, 162

Balize, 256

Ballenger, John, 66; commands fort at Baton Rouge, 352; surrenders fort, 359

Ballew, Bennett, agent of Sevier, 59; holds conference with Indians, 85–86, 90

Baltimore, population of, 13; opposes Judiciary Act, 302; riots in, 408–409; a center of trade, 437–38

Bank of the United States, Hamilton's plan for, opposed, 37–38; second, 405, 419; Madison recommends founding

Holder, Captain John, agent for South Carolina Yazoo Company, 76; failure of, 79

Holmes, David, governor of Mississippi Territory, approached concerning annexation of West Florida, 351; proclamation of, 457–58

Holston, settlements of, attack Cherokee, 200

Holston Treaty, 183–84

Horseshoe Bend, Battle of, 300

Houston County, 85

Howard, Colonel, Spanish commander protests American expedition, 121

Huger, Benjamin, 240

Huger, Daniel, Charleston mechanics oppose, 441–42

Huger, Isaac, partner in South Carolina Yazoo Company, 76

Huguenots, French, small admixture of, in Southern population, 4; welcome Genêt, 104

Humphreys, David, 93

Humphreys, Captain S. P., 315–16

Husband, Hermon, 223

Hutchins, Anthony, 176; offers help to Ellicott, 211

Imlay, Captain Gilbert, urges France to take possession of Louisiana, 104

Impeachment, of Blount, 188; Senators not subject to, 190

Impressment, 314–15, 400, 403, 421

Indians (See also Cherokee, Chickasaw, Chickamauga, Choctaw, Creek, Seminole), in Southern population, 3; controlled by Spain, 43; Washington condemns settlement on lands reserved to, 82; governors of Upper Canada cultivate, 173, 196; in Blount Conspiracy, 182; their attacks on frontier, 404; their removal across Mississippi threatened, 411

Ingersoll, Jared, land speculator, 141; employed to defend Ross, 188

Innerarity, John, merchant, quoted on American victory at Pensacola, 380–81

Innes, Harry, favors Spanish alliance, 53; made Federal judge, 72; charged with

holding Spanish commission, 83; follows activities of Democratic Society, 112–13; member of "Secret Committee of Correspondence of the West," 195; Gayoso's letter to, quoted, 196; his letter to Wilkinson, quoted, 202; opposes separation of Kentucky after navigation of Mississippi secured, 215; in Spanish Conspiracy, 284

Innes, James, brother to Harry, and Attorney General of Virginia, 201, 202

*Inquiry into the Principles and Policy of the Government of the United States*, by John Taylor of Caroline, 420

Internal Improvements, 309–11, 430–33; vote on Bonus Bill for, 432; reasons for Southern vote on, 433; Monroe recommends, 441

Iredell, James, Supreme Court Justice, 224

Iroquois, in Blount Conspiracy, 182

Irvin, General Jared, 121

Irving, Washington, reporter at Burr's trial, 293

Isaac, Jefferson's slave, characterizes his master, 297–98

Iturrigaray, José de, Viceroy of Mexico, 275, 276

Jackson, Andrew, receives protest of Democratic Society, 115; helps draft Tennessee constitution, 170; elected to Congress, 171; recommended for Congress, 183; works for rehabilitation of Blount and elected Senator, 189; Burr calls on, 269, 282, 284; offers services of Tennessee militia to Jefferson, 282–83; letter to Daniel Smith quoted, 285; breaks power of the Creeks, 367–77; commissioned general in United States Army, 371; asks permission to invade Florida, 375–76; begins War of 1812 campaign, 378; victory at Pensacola, 379–90; enters New Orleans, 382–83; engages enemy in first skirmish, 387–88; in engagement of December 28, p. 391; in engagement of January 1, p. 392; in final battle of January 8, pp.

| DATE DUE | |
|---|---|
|  |  |
|  |  |
|  |  |
|  |  |
|  |  |
|  |  |
|  |  |
|  |  |
|  |  |
|  |  |
|  |  |
|  |  |
|  |  |
|  |  |
|  |  |

GAYLORD                                    PRINTED IN U.S.A.